This

EALI

2196

PICTURES
WILL TALK

PICTURES
WILL TALK

The Life and Films of Joseph L. Mankiewicz

BY KENNETH L. GEIST

Charles Scribner's Sons • New York

Material on pages 258 and 259 is excerpted from the book *Bud: The Brando I Knew* by Carlo Fiore. Copyright © 1974 by Carlo Fiore. Reprinted by permission of Delacorte Press.

Material on pages 273–274 is reprinted by permission from TIME, The Weekly Newsmagazine; Copyright Time Inc., 1957.

Material on page 118 is reprinted from *I Remember It Well* by Vincente Minnelli, with Hector Arce, by permission of Doubleday & Company. Copyright © 1974 Vincente Minnelli.

Copyright © 1978 Kenneth L. Geist
Introduction copyright © 1978 Richard Burton

Library of Congress Cataloging in Publication Data
Geist, Kenneth L
    Pictures will talk.
    "The films of Joseph L. Mankiewicz": p. 401
    Includes index.
    1. Mankiewicz, Joseph L. 2. Moving-picture producers and directors—
United States—Biography. I. Title.
PN1998.A3M3198 791.43'023'0924 [B] 78-1104 ISBN 0-684-15500-1

To Chauncey Howell, who first encouraged me to write my criticism of films.

To John L. Hochmann, the first editor who asked me to write a book and then championed this one.

To all my friends and acquaintances who sustained me by their assurance that this long labor was worthwhile.

Contents

ACKNOWLEDGMENTS

MY QUALIFIED GRATITUDE TO JOSEPH L. MANKIEWICZ, WHO GRANTED me eleven interviews and a helpful letter of authorization and loaned me many of his scripts and a few of his prints and papers.

My unqualified gratitude to Christopher Mankiewicz, who, unlike his father, has made the many hours in his company constantly pleasurable. His information and suggested revisions of the manuscript have been invaluable, and I cherish his friendship and bountiful kindness.

My thanks to the following people who granted me interviews; their recollections, combined or contrasted with Mankiewicz's, are the major substance of this book: Lucinda Ballard, Anne Baxter, Robert Benton, Philip Berg, Abraham Bienstock, Richard Brooks, Anthony Burgess, Michael Caine, James B. Clark, Shirley Potash Clurman, Joseph J. Cohn, Joan Crawford, Hume Cronyn, Peggy Cummins Dunnett, Claude Dauphin, Johanna Mankiewicz Davis, Ossie Davis, John De Cuir, Howard Dietz, Kirk Douglas, Philip Dunne, William Eckhardt, C. O. Erickson, Chester Erskine, Henry Fonda, Dr. Saul Fox, Martin Gang, Sidney Ganis, Sir John Gielgud, Marius Goring, Cary Grant, Edith Mayer Goetz, John Green, Nancy Green, Nancy Guild, Alice Guinzburg, Mel Gussow, Dr. Frederick J. Hacker, Rex Harrison, Jack Hildyard, Celeste Holm, William Hornbeck, Mr. and Mrs. Arthur Hornblow, Jr., John Houseman, Kenneth Hyman, Mr. and Mrs. Sam Jaffe, Nunnally Johnson, Alfred Katz, Danny Kaye, Elia Kazan, Milton Krasner, Fritz Lang, Martin Landau, Robert Lantz, Joseph Losey, Mary Anita Loos, Ranald Mac-Dougall, Roddy McDowall, Barbara McLean, John Lee Mahin, Frank Mankiewicz, Mrs. Sara Mankiewicz, Tom Mankiewicz, Samuel Marx, "Doc"

Merman, Gary Merrill, Lewis Milestone, Mike Mindlin, Oswald Morris, Henry Myers, David Newman, Edmond O'Brien, George Oppenheimer, Vincent Price, Sidney Poitier, H. C. Potter, Otto Preminger, Dr. and Mrs. Marcus H. Rabwin, Sir Michael Redgrave, Walter Reisch, Cliff Robertson, Edward G. Robinson, Joseph Ruttenberg, Richard Sale, Dore Schary, Stanley Scheuer, Joseph Schoenfeld, George Seaton, Peter Sellers, Irene Mayer Selznick, Sol C. Siegel, Jean Simmons, Walter Slezak, Erna Mankiewicz Stenbuck, George Stevens, Donald Ogden Stewart, Howard Strickling, Jessica Tandy, Norman Taurog, Benjamin Thau, Regis Toomey, Adelaide Thorp Wallace, J. Watson Webb, Lyle Wheeler, Billy Wilder, William Wright, and Frederick Young.

My thanks for telephone conversations with Richard Conte, Jackie Cooper, Richard Diggs, Gene Kelly, Myrna Loy, Vincente Minnelli, Allen Rivkin, Sigrid Schultz, and William Wyler, and for letters from Pandro S. Berman, Richard Burton (the introduction to this book), Elizabeth Young Darbee, Dr. Frederick J. Hacker, Samuel Marx, Henry Myers, H. C. Potter, Thomas Pryor, Mrs. Marcus Rabwin, Doris Vidor, Michael Wilson, and Joseph Youngerman.

My appreciation to Daniel Melnick, Peter Nelson, and the story department of MGM for making scripts, prints, screening room, and office space available to me and to Edith Tolkin of the legal department for the list of dates of Mankiewicz's Metro productions.

Similar thanks to George D. Stephenson of Twentieth Century–Fox for the loan of scripts and for dates of production, and to various executives of Universal Pictures for allowing me to read the scripts of Mankiewicz's Paramount films.

My deep gratitude to Robert Epstein of the UCLA film archives for arranging screening facilities and prints of all of Mankiewicz's Paramount films and several of his Fox pictures.

My thanks for the helpfulness of the staffs of the research library of the British Film Institute, the Library of the Performing Arts at Lincoln Center, the library of the Academy of Motion Picture Arts and Sciences in Hollywood, Charles Silver of the film department of the Museum of Modern Art, Charles Champlin for granting me access to the clipping file of the *Los Angeles Times,* Mary Meerson of the Cinémathèque Française for privately screening two obscure Fox films, and Columbia University's Oral History collection.

For the book's photographs I am indebted to Carol Carey and Mary Corliss of the stills collection of the Museum of Modern Art, Howard Mandelbaum of Movie Star News, Cinemabilia, the Memory Shop, and donations from the private collections of Adelaide Wallace, Christopher Mankiewicz, Sara Mankiewicz, and Peggy Cummins Dunnett.

My thanks to Kip Gowans and Anthony Shaffer for their transportation to Pinewood Studios during the filming of *Sleuth,* and to Richard Meryman, Peter Davis, and Daniel Selznick for their information and encouragement.

My gratitude to my film scholar friends Donald Chase, René Jordan, Ron Mandelbaum, and John Springer for correcting factual errors in my text, and to Adelaide and Alfred Wallace and Christopher Mankiewicz for their revisions.

I would never have persevered in writing this book had it not been for the steadfastness of my attorney, Barry Lee Cohen, the support of editor Lawrence Ashmead, and the reassuring praise of film scholar and publicist John Springer.

The book would never have attained its polished form if I had lacked the assistance of a succession of talented editors—John Hochmann and Gladys Topkis, formerly of Praeger, Patricia Cristol (who took on the book and made the major cuts) and Dorothy Coover of Scribners, copy editor Ginny Croft, and, most especially, my skillful and demanding friends Jon Arlow and Donald Chase.

Introduction

*J*OE MANKIEWICZ IS A MAN I HAVE GREATLY ADMIRED FOR MANY years, and for whom I retain a great affection. A gifted writer and director of films, he has nevertheless always seemed to me to be an Oxford don *manqué*. This might surprise those who expect directors to act with a certain Hollywood ostentation, but one has only to experience his ever-present pipe, his way of making considered statements with his twinkling eyes peering through a miasma of tobacco smoke, his philological digressions, and his skill as a raconteur to understand what I mean. Unlike the more flamboyant among us, such as Ustinov, Sellers, and Welles, he tells stories quietly; his stories are unacted, but delivered with many pauses for which they are all the more effective. Above all, he is witty. Witty with the kind of wit that makes people laugh and retell his tales, not merely smile and admire. His mind has an elaborate, paradoxically practical capacity for fantasy. For instance, some notable figure in our mad business had committed suicide by taking an overdose of sleeping pills—perhaps it was Monroe, I can't remember—whereupon Joe mused that if some sort of pill were invented, a sleeping pill, I mean, that could only be taken rectally, a great many of these beautiful would-be suicides would find it not only boring but supremely undignified to stuff twenty or thirty suppositories up his or her beautiful ass. That was, of course, only the bare bones of his tale. He elaborated and wove around each pill a world of increasing tedium on the part of the pill taker until the beautiful one by, shall we say, pill six, said, "Oh, to hell with it, I'll go and get me an enema." The image he created in my mind—the bending over, missing the entrance, dropping the thing on the floor and carefully washing it before trying again, for the beauty must be hygienic even in death— reduced me to hysteria.

It is unfortunate that the only time that Joe Mankiewicz and I worked together was on the notorious *Cleopatra.* I doubt whether in the eleven or twelve months that we worked on that infinitely forgetta- ble film Joe had more than two or three hours of sleep a night. He wrote by night to keep ahead of the studio's executive hounds baying behind him. He was dealing with three actors of massive temperament, all charming (especially this shrinking violet) but murderously intent on hacking their way through the film and to hell with everybody else, and he had to direct them all day long. His physical constitution, to say nothing of his muscular intelligence, must have been remarkably strong. A weaker man would have gone mad. Humor, of course, must have saved him too. Brother of the gifted and acerbic Herman and son of a distinguished academician, he couldn't possibly have looked on the Hollywood scene without a permanent belly laugh lurking in him. I still think that if Joe could wade knee-deep through the million feet or so of cutting-room-floor *Cleopatra,* he would find a fine film there some- where. But it was taken away from him by Sad Zanuck, and that was that.

As a director, for me he was well-nigh perfect. He let me have my head and curbed me very gently and subtly when I threatened to tear a passion to tatters, which I am prone to do. In *Cleopatra,* Joe gave me a great many beautiful lines to say, most of them, alas, on the cutting room floor, so I'm told. I have never seen the film. It was also a rare experience to work with a "Hollywood" director who was not only widely read but in some areas deeply read. Run down all the directors you can find and ask them, for instance, where Descartes asserted the seat of man's animal spirits resides in the human body. If more than two in a hundred know the answer—the pineal gland—I'll drown my books. Joe knew.

Richard Burton

Preface

"**Y**OU HAVEN'T GOT THE INFORMATION TO WRITE A BOOK ABOUT my life. Nobody ever will, except me. I can promise you!" So raged the celebrated screenwriter-director Joseph L. Mankiewicz, smoke billowing from his ever-lit pipe filled with a mixture called Barking Dog, his swatter poised to exterminate an elusive fly. The fly's buzzing disturbed the prevailing silence of the great barn on Mankiewicz's estate in Bedford, New York, which has been converted into the imposing office-library where he now spends his working days. The swatter deals with intrusive insects; Joe's often charming, now scathing tongue is a handy dispatcher of a meddlesome biographer.

"Herman [Joe's elder brother, the author of *Citizen Kane*] was a public character. He enjoyed being a great public wit. . . . I wasn't a mingler. Herman was a very external guy. I'm a very, very internal guy. . . . I don't think I've ever told the truth or confided in anyone the way external people do."

Although Mankiewicz is known for his superhuman poise as a director and, according to several observers, exploded only once during all the vexations of making *Cleopatra*, I had anticipated this blowup. In fact, it had been forecast in October 1972, precisely a year before it occurred, by a member of Mankiewicz's family.

This relative could not understand why Mankiewicz, even grudgingly, was making himself available to me, when he is generally leery about publicity and almost "never grants interviews to anybody." The same intimate warned me that unless I intended to submit my manuscript for Mankiewicz's approval and consequent revision, I would be obliged to face an intimidating tongue-lashing. "Only two men, to my knowledge, have ever stood up to [him]—Louis B. Mayer and Darryl Zanuck—and they both fired him."

My confidant was equally baffled about the letter of authorization that Mankiewicz had given me in order to gather the recollections of his colleagues and acquaintances. "When in top form, he tells great stories, but he claims *his* versions are the only accurate ones," said Mankiewicz's relative, "though practically not a single story involves him. . . . Joe is brilliant at analyzing the foibles of others, but he has one blind spot—he can't laugh at or tell a joke about himself."

I explained that had it not been for Mankiewicz's hurling a copy of Peter Bogdanovich's *Fritz Lang in America* at me in the course of an early interview, I might never have been granted a letter of authorization. That day Mankiewicz was outraged that Lang had made no mention of his contribution to the German director's first American film, *Fury*, which Joe produced (see Chapter 4). He demanded to know if I, like Bogdanovich, intended to make an "instant book" by merely editing our interviews and adding pictures. I retorted that I would attempt to interview all his past associates who were still alive, if he would provide me with a letter of introduction.

Mankiewicz's relative assured me that my endeavor would be worthwhile if I could withstand the chiding of "one of the most cruel wits in Hollywood . . . as when he dies, the greatest movie tales will go with him." I should be forewarned, however, that "he can be just like Addison De Witt [the venomous drama critic played by George Sanders in *All About Eve*] in spades. No one in Hollywood . . . could take people apart the way he could." While cautioning me that "everybody is a liar in the picture business," in that "by retelling anything often enough it changes from the truth," the source asserted that Mankiewicz possessed not only "the greatest catalog of Hollywood stories [but maintained] the most vivid memories. Though, when he's not in the mood, it's difficult to get them out of him, as he doesn't volunteer them . . . except at dinner parties, and then only when he has everyone's undivided attention."

My informant was understandably curious about what had motivated me to attempt to pry these tales from the usually unwilling subject who, since the critical savaging of *Cleopatra* in 1963, has become a crotchety country squire like Evelyn Waugh in his later years. I explained that my fascination with the subject dated back over twenty years, to the time when I was a teen-age theater and film buff and Joe Mankiewicz had emerged as one of the most prestigious screenwriter-directors in America. In rapid succession, the scintillating wit of *A Letter to Three Wives* (1949), *All About Eve* (1950), and *Five Fingers* (1951), three studies of social and sexual duplicity, had made me a youthful devotee of Mankiewicz's work.

As a fan I was curious to know more about the creator of these brilliant films. At sixteen I had an opportunity to question the famed baritone Robert Merrill, who had just been directed by Mankiewicz in a production of *La Bohème* at the Metropolitan Opera, which remains Mankiewicz's only stint in the theater. I asked Merrill what it was like to be directed by Joe and he replied that although he had played countless Marcellos, none of his previous *Bohème* directors was as articulate and stimulating as Mankiewicz.

In my seventeenth year my mother brought home a tidbit of gossip about Mankiewicz that she had gleaned at the party of a prominent figure in the movie business who was holding forth on the maladies and strange peccadilloes nurtured by Hollywood's hothouse atmosphere. He maintained that more peculiar than Spencer Tracy's bouts of alcoholism or Judy Garland's drug-taking and suicide attempts were the "sinister *Gaslight* tactics" of Joe Mankiewicz. He claimed that Mankiewicz's kick was to persuade women who had fallen helplessly in love with him that they were in serious need of psychiatric care, if not institutionalization. (Such calumnies are the price paid by a discreet but highly active ladies' man dwelling in a community that thrives on gossip, especially gossip about the bedmates of its female stars.) Needless to say, I was fascinated by Mankiewicz's Svengali-like powers on and off the sound stage.

Six and a half years later, in 1959, while I was a theater student in London, an influential film attorney asked whether I would be interested in watching a day's filming of *Suddenly, Last Summer.* I said I would be fascinated to watch Mankiewicz direct such fabled stars as Elizabeth Taylor, Montgomery Clift, and Katharine Hepburn, but that the drama school frowned on my cutting classes. The next morning, however, when I found a Daimler limousine waiting to drive me to Shepperton Studios, I decided to play hooky.

Being allowed to pass through the immense sound stage's vault-thick doors marked "Closed set. No visitors allowed" gave me a sense of rare privilege. It was quickly dispelled. When Kate Hepburn imperiously demanded to know "Who is that young man?" I hastily hid among the exotic flora that Oliver Messel had collected for the cultivated jungle that dominated the sound stage. While a team of workmen moved strands of Spanish moss and Messel and his aides made a ceremony of feeding the Venus Flytrap, a shattered Montgomery Clift arrived on the set.

It was a considerable shock to see this sensitive actor's deplorable condition. Although three years had passed since Clift's serious auto accident and subsequent plastic surgery, he was now a mass of tics and spasms, constantly snorting from an ever-handy inhaler.

The scene to be shot required that Clift conduct a deferential yet probing interview with Hepburn as they sat on the rim of a conch shell fountain that could not be made to gush water on cue. My curiosity about how Clift could be photographed in this condition, let alone act, was soon satisfied.

The famed director appeared, a stocky figure oddly wearing white film editor's gloves. (Mankiewicz suffered from a dermatological ailment that caused his fingertips to split open; it frequently afflicts him under situations of extreme pressure, like filming.) Mankiewicz grasped Clift by the shoulders and began to impart his directorial suggestions. While riveting Clift's attention with a piercing gaze, Mankiewicz surreptitiously started to massage Clift's neck and shoulders. The result was astonishing. Clift's tremors subsided and despite the annoyance of the malfunctioning fountain, he maintained his composure through a series of repeated takes.

Eleven years later, on an interview assignment for a magazine, I sat staring into those same mesmeric eyes that had calmed Clift, as well as so many other temperamental movie stars.

Joe's blue eyes are the most arresting feature of a long-youthful face that now bespeaks much pain and care. As characteristic as his constant pipe-smoking are the fixating moments when Mankiewicz's eyes open wide in animation, in a manner similar to, though far more electrifying than, William Buckley's parodied eye-poppings. These oeillades punctuate his commandingly articulate speech as frequently as the expletives that enliven it.

In a series of interviews between 1970 and 1974, I became acquainted with Mankiewicz's eye-widening and, occasionally, bore the brunt of his scathing tongue.

Mankiewicz has written "that the offstage or offscreen moral and/or political propensities of creative talent should not be applicable to a judgment of their work," and cited as an example Pope Julius II's commissioning Michelangelo to paint the ceiling of the Sistine Chapel despite the artist's known homosexuality.[1] Commenting on this assertion, I argued that while the Pope had wisely chosen the greatest painter of his time, Michelangelo's adoration of the male body is evident in both the figures of his Sistine Chapel painting and his heroic sculpture of David. Despite Mankiewicz's protestations to the contrary, I believe the conflicts and obsessions of his off-screen life are also embodied in his films, and I offer this study as evidence.

Kenneth Geist

[1]*More About All About Eve,* Random House, 1972, p. 51.

"The oldest whore on the beat" 1

"I am never quite sure whether I am one of the cinema's elder statesman, or just the oldest whore on the beat."

> *(Joseph L. Mankiewicz to Derek Malcolm in the* MANCHESTER GUARDIAN, *August 11, 1970)*

"Never is an artist more self-enhancingly self-deprecating than when fashioning himself as a whore."

> *(James Wolcott on Truman Capote's surrogate artist in* ANSWERED PRAYERS, VILLAGE VOICE, *September 6, 1976)*

*I*N THE FIFTIES THE SOURCE OF JOSEPH L. MANKIEWICZ'S CELEBrity was that he had scored the yet unequaled coup of winning Academy Awards for both writing and directing, in two successive years, *A Letter to Three Wives* (1949) and the internationally acclaimed *All About Eve* (1950).

These were not discreditable Oscars like many voted for the sake of sentiment or because the industry's voters capitulated to a heavy publicity campaign or the great box-office popularity of a film. In the campaign for the awards of 1949, the odds were stacked heavily against Mankiewicz's winning. Joe's boss at Twentieth Century–Fox, production chief Darryl F. Zanuck, had mobilized the studio's publicity department to push his personal production, *12 O'Clock High*, rather than *A Letter to Three Wives*. Moreover, the year's Best Picture Award went to the more weighty political drama *All the King's Men*, admirably written and directed by Robert Rossen, so Mankiewicz's dual awards for a comedy could hardly have been expected by the forecasters or their recipient.

The following year Mankiewicz was backstage at the awards ceremony clutching his solo screenwriting Oscar for *All About Eve* and assuring his chum Billy Wilder, who had been obliged to share his writing award with his two collaborators, that Wilder would undoubtedly win the directing award for *Sunset Boulevard*. In mid-deprecation

Mankiewicz's name was called again, and Wilder was abruptly abandoned as Joe raced back to the podium.[1]

Suddenly Joe Mankiewicz, who had been working in Hollywood as a screenwriter since 1929 and spent a decade as a writer-producer at MGM before moving to Fox in 1943, had become a major movie celebrity, receiving lengthy profiles in such mass periodicals as *Life* and *Collier's*.

The 1951 *Life* article by Robert Coughlan was a compendium of comments by Mankiewicz and his intimates titled "15 Authors in Search of a Character Named Joseph L. Mankiewicz," which the subject still regards as the best study of him to date. It grappled with but failed to arrive at a convincing solution to the puzzle of how Hollywood, a great importer of literary talent, had itself spawned a forty-two-year-old master.

In the late summer of 1951, Mankiewicz roundly denounced the film enclave as an "ivory ghetto" and Los Angeles as "a cultural desert" and moved with his family to New York City. His announced intention was to devote himself to writing and directing for the theater and to make only one film a year. It was a decision that bespoke an awareness that the theater was a more congenial medium to a writer given to eloquent loquacity.

Today Mankiewicz views himself as a figure in a geographical limbo. In New York critical circles[2] he believes he is regarded as an old-hat Hollywood writer-director. In Los Angeles he thinks he is considered either an eastern-based deserter by the old-timers who remained, like Billy Wilder, or a legendary, enigmatic figure by the new breed of studio moguls, whom Mankiewicz denigrates as "the Carpetbaggers."

Mankiewicz's status as "the thinking man's Hollywood director" of the fifties has been downgraded by those critical charters of cinematic divinity, Andrew Sarris and Richard Corliss, who have relegated him to a rear sanctuary of their temples of American directors and screenwriters.[3]

---

[1]Mankiewicz denies this incident, maintaining it is a fabrication by Wilder.

[2]With the exception of Judith Crist (who has become an idolator since her pan of *Cleopatra* in the *New York Herald Tribune*), Vincent Canby, Richard Schickel, and Hollis Alpert, who venerate many of the noncult figures among the Old Guard of Hollywood directors.

[3]Sarris places Mankiewicz well outside his pantheon of directors in the category

Notwithstanding the erosion of the American film critics' esteem and his celebrity, what is genuinely remarkable about Mankiewicz's development is that he learned his craft exclusively in Hollywood and that his elegant literary style was chiefly honed by writing what were termed "family-type" pictures at Paramount and writing and producing generally glossy trifles at Metro. Granted the opportunity to direct his own scripts at Fox, Mankiewicz emerged as a unique talent. His rare skill as a writer was best described by the critic Richard Schickel, who termed him "one of the tiny handful of epigrammists that have written for the screen."[4]

Mankiewicz's favorite, recurring self-characterization as "the oldest whore on the beat" has multiple, allusive meanings. Factually, the adjective *oldest* can be dismissed as hyperbolic when directors such as George Cukor and Alfred Hitchcock, who are ten years Mankiewicz's senior, are still active. The curious word is *whore,* for ever since resettling in New York in late 1951, Mankiewicz has remained a fiercely independent operative whose fastidiousness in choosing film projects is a rare luxury in the increasingly diminishing movie business. Unlike the majority of directors who are often obliged to take on unworthy ventures in order to pay their bills, to keep their names in print, or out of sheer restlessness, Mankiewicz has almost never bowed to these pressures.

Mankiewicz is one of the few directors with the temerity to resist the Mediterranean-yacht-cruise blandishments of the fabled producer Sam Spiegel, for whom he directed *Suddenly, Last Summer* (1959), who offered him such big-budget productions as *The Chase* and *Nicholas and Alexandra.* Likewise, his friend Paul Newman unsuccessfully implored him to direct a number of his defective vehicles, which Mankiewicz turned down and John Huston eventually took on.

In 1975 Newman sent Robert Redford to see Mankiewicz about directing Redford's production of *All the President's Men.* Despite

labeled "Less Than Meets the Eye" (*The American Cinema,* E. P. Dutton, 1968), in the estimable company of Kazan, Lean, Wilder, Wyler, and Zinnemann. Corliss ranks Mankiewicz in the third level of his Acropolis of American screenwriters (*Film Comment,* Winter 1970–71), alongside John Huston, Nunnally Johnson, and Dudley Nichols.

[4]*Life,* July 14, 1967, p. 12. Mankiewicz asserts, "I am essentially a writer who directs," and admits his yearning to direct stemmed largely from his desire to protect his screenplays from butchery by others.

Redford's persistent visits to Joe's picture-book estate in Bedford, New York, the potent combination of Redford and Dustin Hoffman as drawing cards, and Joe's intimate knowledge of Watergate from his politically active nephew Frank, Mankiewicz balked at William Goldman's wisecracking script and stalled Redford by pleading his commitment to complete his adaptation of Dee Wells's novel *Jane.* On the brink of putting aside the script of *Jane,* which he was having great difficulty completing,[5] Mankiewicz learned from his screenwriter son, Tom, in Los Angeles, that Redford had engaged Alan Pakula as his director, and so the decision was no longer Joe's to make.

In light of the daily revision of Goldman's script during the filming of *All the President's Men,* Mankiewicz's unfavorable judgment of the original screenplay was most likely sound. In view of the picture's enormous success, the potential of the property and its stars, and Mankiewicz's capability of rewriting, his inability to accept Redford's offer may prove to be the final miscalculation of his career.

Just as Redford has attempted, subsequently, to interest Mankiewicz in other properties of his, so did Mike Frankovich earlier in the seventies, when he was Columbia Pictures' most active producer. Frankovich first tried to get Mankiewicz to do his trashy murder mystery–soap opera *Doctors' Wives* (1971) and later, heedless of Joe's taste, pitched him an equally unworthy project.

As Mankiewicz tells it, he knew the *shmeer* was on when Frankovich invited him to lunch at the Brown Derby and began the meal by ordering caviar and champagne. According to Joe, the following exchange took place:

> FRANKOVICH: I've got a property that, in your hands, could be the definitive exposé of American television.
> MANKIEWICZ: I'm fascinated. What is it?
> FRANKOVICH: Now, don't jump to conclusions when you hear the title. It cost me a mint, but with your screenplay and direction it could make us both a bundle.

---

[5]Long past his deadline and unable to complete his typically overlong, two-hundred-page screenplay of *Jane,* Mankiewicz was obliged to return $50,000 of his advance to Columbia Pictures. Ironically, Mankiewicz was succeeded on the project by Mart Crowley, whose most famous play, *The Boys in the Band,* has bits of dialogue from Mankiewicz's *All About Eve.* Neither Crowley's completed version of Mankiewicz's script nor the subsequent one he wrote from scratch has ever gone into production.

MANKIEWICZ: I'm sufficiently tempted. What's the title?

FRANKOVICH: Jacqueline Susann's *Love Machine.*

MANKIEWICZ: I'm still game, but in this instance, I'd like to make a step deal [a contract with a series of provisional "steps," whereby the producer has the right to terminate the contract at specified steps, such as the treatment or the first draft].

FRANKOVICH: Come off it, Joe. You haven't made a step deal in thirty years.

MANKIEWICZ: Well, in this case, I'd like to.

FRANKOVICH: Good enough. What's the first step?

MANKIEWICZ: The first step is how much you'll pay me just to *read* that piece of crap![6]

Frankovich swiftly terminated the meeting by snapping his fingers for the waiter.

Whorish directors rarely risk antagonizing such influential and formidable egos as Frankovich, and with the single, glaring exception of *Cleopatra,* which proved to be a bitter lesson, the evidence is that Mankiewicz cannot be bought. In recent years he has spent most of his time reading and rejecting countless submissions of novels and screenplays, and the infrequency of his films since *Cleopatra* (three in fifteen years) attests to his selectivity.

While Mankiewicz applies *whore* appreciatively in speaking of his screenwriting mentor, Grover Jones, as a pragmatist like himself, the term takes on a debunking connotation when he describes various people's false sincerity as "about as convincing as a whore's moan." Joe also acknowledges his adoption of the pejorative label as a self-deprecating ploy, saying, "To a certain extent, I've called myself 'the oldest whore' because I want to hear, 'No, no you're not!' But I don't hear it."

Mankiewicz concedes the truth of Elia Kazan's observation that he was "too easily seduceable" when the lure of movie money continually drew him away from his gifts as a playwright and stage director.

"Gadge [Kazan, who shuttled successfully between plays and films, as Mankiewicz yearned to do] played a very important part in my whole attitude toward the theater," says Joe. "He would also stir up my guilt at my very real fear of working in the theater, where I've always

---

[6]Mankiewicz knew precisely how dreadful *The Love Machine* was, as he had skimmed it prior to the luncheon meeting with Frankovich.

known I belonged, more than I do in films. It's almost like a man's concept of whom you sleep with and whom you don't, or whom you marry. . . . It's as if the theater were the one woman I wanted to go to bed with, and she's gonna turn me down. Gadge recognized this very early on. . . . I've got a fat notebook full of play ideas, and Gadge has known of it for many years.[7] . . . I don't nearly miss the films I didn't direct as much as the [plays and books] I haven't written. In that sense, I suppose, I have been a whore. . . .

"I had or have more talent than I've played fair with. I've pissed away a lot of talent . . . and when I call myself a whore, it has to do with a kind of displeasure with myself I have at this time."

Joe's chronic depression over the "deeply neurotic block" that inhibits his writing stage plays is aggravated by frequent bouts of insomnia, which account, in part, for his often querulous and prickly personality. Ill-tempered weariness now often blocks access to his fabled charm. His time is precious and grudgingly dispensed. When he uses the phrase "as I approach the end of my career and my dotage," it becomes apparent that time has become as great an obsession to Mankiewicz as to Cecil Fox, the mouthpiece-protagonist of his last screenplay, *The Honey Pot* (1967).

Mankiewicz's contemporary Billy Wilder, who has experienced a similar fall from the critics' grace in recent years and whose mordant wit resembles Joe's, empathizes with Mankiewicz's dilemma. Wilder says, "I imagine he's just as tortured and tormented as I am about what to do next. Most of the time we make the wrong decision. Sometimes we decide to do a film to honor an obligation or because it's good for our financial future. But too often we guess wrong, and a year and a half has gone down the drain. When you're a young man, it's of small importance, but now that there are so few bullets left in our elderly pistols, we had better be careful as to the next targets we choose."[8]

The difference between the two men is that Wilder, despite his reverses, begins collaboration on his next screenplay soon after he has completed directing a picture, whereas Mankiewicz continues to reject,

---

[7]Kazan, who codirected the Lincoln Center Repertory Company in the early sixties, earnestly tried to commission for it the social comedy Mankiewicz is so richly capable of writing. Mankiewicz declined, however, and Kazan was obliged to settle for the last, nonvintage work of S. N. Behrman, *But for Whom Charlie.*

[8]Mankiewicz was originally announced as the director of the unsuccessful remake of *The Front Page* (1974), which Wilder took on.

brood, and complain about what is or is not offered to him. Six years have elapsed, and he has yet to make a film since *Sleuth*, for which he was nominated for an Academy Award as Best Director.

Mankiewicz now speaks of devoting himself to a book on the subject of his longtime fascination, the history of actresses. In October 1975, at a retrospective of his films at the San Francisco Film Festival, shortly after Mart Crowley was assigned to take over the scripting of *Jane*, Mankiewicz declared that he had "no firm 'next' project," and "I don't know how to write films today" *(Variety*, October 29, 1975).

"Let's say I'm a choosy whore," says Mankiewicz by way of qualification. "I've been around the 'brothels' (the studios) for as long as anybody. I know the 'madams' (agents). I know the 'cops' (censors). I know the tricks. I also know the 'whores' that masquerade as 'non-whores.' "⁹

---

⁹Joe, like his brother Herman, whose cruelest wit was displayed in baiting phonies, has pet hates, such as the director Michelangelo Antonioni, whose films he deems fraudulently cryptic. "He [Antonioni] wants to make a buck and would prefer a box-office smash to an artistic success," Mankiewicz maintains. He savages Antonioni's artistic and financial triumph, *Blow-Up*, by branding its final mimed tennis match as "the ultimate cheat." He cites Antonioni's subsequent film, *Zabriskie Point*, as further evidence of the phony intellectuality of this director who abandoned Europe to follow the American radical left, fashionable in the sixties, and wound up making a trashy inanity.

"Horses eaten by wolves. Gold safe, however"

*A*LMOST EVERY ONE OF THE TWENTY FILMS THAT JOE MANKIE-
wicz has directed contains a centrally enshrined icon that stands in
mute reproof of its possessor's achievements. The motif is nearly constant from the portrait of the great grandmother, the siren of doom in
Dragonwyck (1946), the first film he directed, to the diminutive man-
telpiece bust of Edgar Allan Poe in his most recent picture, *Sleuth*
(1972).

In Mankiewicz's own study, above the fireplace mantel laden with
four Oscars and every existing award for screenwriting and direction,
there is a portrait of his revered and intimidating father. Professor
Frank Mankiewicz died in December 1941, the year of Herman's
triumph, *Citizen Kane*, but seven years before *A Letter to Three Wives*
inaugurated his younger son's international fame and the consequent
trophy collection. "When Father died, a great influence went out of
my brothers' lives," says Joe's sister, Erna. "Joe regretted terribly that
Father hadn't lived to see him win his Oscars."

The handsome portrait of "Pop" Mankiewicz by Leo Mielziner,
which radiates the pedagogue's keen, skeptical intelligence, was commissioned by Joe's older brother, Herman, in honor of his father's
sixtieth birthday. It hung in Herman's home in Los Angeles until his
death in 1953, and though he wished to bequeath it to his second son,
whom he namesaked Frank, Joe's insistence on possessing the painting

was so great that Sara, Herman's widow, could not deny the priority of his claim to it.

Of its subject Herman said, "Pop was a tremendously industrious, brilliant, and vital man. A father like that could make you very ambitious or very despairing. You could end up by saying, 'Stick it, I'll never live up to that. I'm not going to try.' That's what happened to me. Joe [however] was fiercely ambitious as a kid."[1]

Joseph Leo Mankiewicz was born on February 11, 1909, in Wilkes-Barre, Pennsylvania. He was the third and youngest of the Mankiewicz offspring, after Erna, born in 1901, and Herman, born in 1897. His parents, Frank Mankiewicz and Johanna Blumenau, were both German immigrants who met and married in New York. German rather than Jewish culture permeated the Mankiewicz household, abetted by a number of trips during Joe's childhood to visit relatives and family friends in his father's "home town," Berlin.[2]

Pop Mankiewicz is described by his like-minded younger son as a "rip-snorting atheist." His daughter recalls that his last, placating gestures toward Wilkes-Barre's Jewish community were to have a bar mitzvah for Herman and to send Herman and Erna to the Reform Jewish Sunday School. However, the congregation's rabbi took exception to the Mankiewicz family's refusal to relinquish such German traditions as Christmas trees and Easter eggs, and Herman and Erna, much to their relief, were dismissed from the class.

Since Joe was only four years old when the Mankiewicz family departed Wilkes-Barre for New York City, he never received this smattering of religious education and consequently lacked a real awareness of himself as a Jew. Despite the fist fights initiated by Irish

---

[1]Robert Coughlan, "15 Authors in Search of a Character Named Joseph L. Mankiewicz," *Life*, March 12, 1951. In this article Herman Mankiewicz quoted his father's credo: "To brag about being smart is like bragging about having blue eyes. It is just a characteristic. It's what you do with it that matters." To illustrate Pop's philosophy, Herman told the tale of Joe, as a schoolboy, proudly telling his father he had received a grade of 97 on an exam, the highest in his class. "What about the missing 3 percent?" asked the professor. "But no one else got more than 90," Joe protested. "Maybe it was harder for him to score 90 than for you to get 97," remarked Pop. "It's not good unless it's *your* best."

[2]The Mankiewicz family's Polish name derives from their origin in Poznan, a disputed city in West Poland, near the German border, known as Posen when under German rule. The Blumenaus lived in Latvia before being driven to Germany by a pogrom.

and Italian boys, Joe occasionally maintained that the Polish Man-kiewiczes were Catholic in origin. (Possibly he adopted this view in later years in order to disassociate himself from the predominantly Jewish executives who ran the motion picture industry, most of whom he despised.) In any case, Mankiewicz's disbelief in all forms of organized religion made him tolerantly indifferent to the baptism of his offspring sought by his three gentile wives in their respective faiths. In fact, his present wife, Rosemary Matthews, is the daughter of an Anglican archdeacon.

Mankiewicz enjoys telling of the conflict of national loyalties experienced by his father and fellow German émigrés when the United States entered World War I. He remembers, as a boy, the wave of Germanophobia that precipitated the following ludicrous acts: "Among the first things renamed, [the public] called sauerkraut 'liberty cabbage.' Dachshunds were being attacked in the street. My father was ordered to shave off his moustache because it looked too much like von Hindenburg's. Then they made a rule they were going to stop teaching German in the schools forever. In the midst of these idiotic reprisals, my father, along with many other Germans, was very torn. They loved America and they were loyal Americans, but they used to sit around and say, 'The Boche must be driven back from the gates of Paris,' and 'The Huns must be defeated.' Then one would say, 'Yeah, but it will take a hell of a long time.' "

As Billy Wilder observes, Mankiewicz's personal crisis of di-vided national loyalties came with the second German-American conflict: "Joe, as a Germanophile, was not totally opposed to a *Pax Germanicus* taking over the world, were it not for that nasty little slip—anti-Semitism. . . . He's also Jewish, so there's nothing pro-Hitlerian or pro-Nazi about him." In his favorite company of the German Jewish artists and intelligentsia who fled the holocaust and quartered in Los Angeles, Mankiewicz was obliged to discover his true ethnic identity and primary allegiance, though some contend that he never looked upon these refugees as Jewish, but simply as gifted people.

The twofold reason for the Mankiewicz family's return to New York in 1913 was academic. New York's public high school system offered the opportunity of better-paying teaching jobs for Pop, nar-rowly affording him the income to pay for fifteen-year-old Herman's tuition as a freshman at Columbia University. Herman had actually passed the Columbia entrance exam at thirteen, but the headmaster of Harry Hillman Academy, his private school, advised holding him back a year. Frank Mankiewicz had been the editor of a German American newspaper in Wilkes-Barre. The headmaster, who became a close friend of Pop's, was instrumental in persuading him to change his vocation from journalism to teaching by giving him his first opportunity to teach foreign languages at Hillman Academy.

Although the New York school system offered rapid opportunities for advancement to the energetic or outstanding teacher, Pop Mankiewicz had to start at the bottom as a high school substitute. To supplement his earnings in order to provide for his family of five, Pop was obliged to fill every free hour with private tutoring. That he managed to find the time to earn a master's and a Ph.D. in education at New York University on top of his teaching load was an incredible feat. Herman described his father's prodigious industry as that of "an earth-moving machine," teaching "night school, summer school, student tours, home courses . . . when he wasn't studying, he was working."[3]

Since Pop had little time to spend with his children, Joe's rearing was left largely to his mother, although he frequently depended on his older brother's intercession in getting out of numerous scrapes. Erna recalls, "We were living in a walk-up in Harlem, then a lovely neighborhood, on Seventh Avenue above 110th Street, while Herman was at Columbia. When Joe would discover he was late in returning home, he would ring the bell and ask, 'Is Herman home yet?' If he wasn't, Joe would wait outside until Herman got back in order to escape a scolding. Herman could always be depended upon to intercede by alternately claiming, 'He's too young,' 'He can't tell time,' or simply, 'Leave him alone!' "

Herman's special pleading to allay parental punishment foreshadowed his even more vehement partisanship toward Joe as a fledgling screenwriter in Hollywood. With his corrosive tongue, big brother could always be counted on to browbeat and cajole studio chiefs, producers, and story department heads into pay hikes and writing assignments.

Joe's first and best audience was his mother, a jolly woman whose abundant flesh would shake with unrestrained laughter at his favorite

---

[3]All subsequent quotes from Herman are drawn from the Coughlan article.

routine. "Joe would appear with his bathrobe⁴ draped over one shoulder like a cape," Erna remembers. "He would fling himself at Mother's feet, gaze soulfully at her, and then beseech, in a simulated Spanish accent, 'Madonna, I love you. Flee with me to my hacienda. I will learn you to make love.'⁵ This happened thirty times or more, and each time Mother would howl. Then Joe would start laughing hysterically, while lamenting, 'You don't take me seriously.' " In Joe's salad days in Hollywood, this technique of comic lovemaking endeared him to the mothers of young actresses he courted. "Joe romanced the mother and the daughter," Erna recalls. "Elderly ladies adored him. No woman is immune to compliments and flowers, and when he would tell them how much nicer they were than their daughters or how he only wished they were twenty years younger, they really ate it up."

Herman recalled that "by necessity, Joe spent most of his time with our mother. She was a round little woman who was uneducated in four languages. She spoke mangled German, mangled Russian, mangled Yiddish, and mangled English. She raised Joe—Pop had no time for him." Erna says, "Mother was very bright. Not an intellectual like Father, as she hadn't a formal education, but she was a great newspaper reader and would talk back, aloud, to the editorials. . . . She was very philanthropic and socially minded, which was not a standard practice fifty years ago. She was most interested in crippled children, and the standing gag in the family was that Mom took care of crippled bodies, while Pop took care of the crippled minds."

Mankiewicz says, "I grew up an only child in the sense that my brother and sister were a generation older than I was, and I was a very tiny little fellow among screaming, articulate giants." (A relation sug-

---

⁴Erna tells how Joe adored this "filthy old bathrobe. He's never loved any article of clothing as much before or since, and it's odd because Joe likes to be well dressed. Mother gave it away once while Joe was away one weekend. When he returned, he insisted she get it back, and she was obliged to buy it back from the charitable organization to which she had donated it." Erna's great friend Judy ("a very brilliant, witty, but inhibited and conventional girl") would frequently visit the Mankiewiczes while Joe was attending Columbia and the family was living on 124th Street. "Joe would insist on taking Judy home in the car, wearing the bathrobe," says Erna. "When they arrived at her elegant apartment, he would insist on taking her past the doorman to her door. He knew it annoyed and bothered her conventional sense, and he always tried to take a lick at conventionality."

⁵A more sober version of this routine turns up as one of the soap opera satires in *A Letter to Three Wives.*

gests that his parents' fights were particularly unbearable to young Joe, and the defensive wall he created to shut out these unpleasant episodes developed into a layer of protective callousness that has grown "more and more impenetrable as he formed associations that became painful.")

"I have literally no childhood friends, because I literally didn't grow up with anybody but myself," says Mankiewicz. "The fact that I had close relations with people for a while and then moved or grew away from them is something that I was accustomed to doing since I was a child." (This pattern of dropping intimate friends and becoming more and more reclusive has persisted to the present day.) "We moved as many as six times a year, and I found new friends every three months. I can't remember all the different places we lived in New York City. I know we lived in Bensonhurst, Sheepshead Bay, three or four locations on the Lower East Side, Harlem, and Madison Avenue. We were moving all the time."[6]

"There were always new neighborhoods, new gangs of kids, new adjustments. I became skillful at taking on the color of my environment without absorbing it, at participating in almost everything without becoming part of anything. I acquired an awareness of people the way an animal knows the woods in which he lives. I escaped into fantasies —thousands of fantasies. It isn't surprising that I ended up as a writer and in show business."[7]

When Joe, aged eight, contracted influenza in the epidemic of 1917, the infection spiraled into a near-fatal case of double pneumonia and pleurisy for which he was bedded down in a semipublic ward of Lenox Hill Hospital. "I was saved from death by a very famous doctor, Willie Meyer," Mankiewicz recalls, "who, on his rounds one day, happened to be caught by my grin or something. He came over and talked to me and took me in hand by operating to remove a piece of my rib, which fixed me up."[8]

---

[6]Erna explains that these frequent moves were related to Pop's various teaching assignments as well as to the need to find larger apartments at lower rents so that he might have his own study.

[7]This paragraph is from Robert Coughlan's article in *Life*.

[8]Erna contends that her little brother was very proud of the fact that he had a silver rib inserted to replace the one removed. Mankiewicz denies that he has one, saying that if he did, "I'd have had a mortgage on it long ago, I'm sure." The missing rib seems appropriate to the creator of Eve, among other famous female characters.

This illness kept Joe out of school for a year, but he still graduated from P.S. 64 (junior high school) at the precocious age of eleven. The following year his mother took Joe to Berlin for a taste of German *kultur*, to spend time with Herman (then a correspondent for the *Chicago Tribune*), and to delay Joe's entering Stuyvesant High School, where Pop taught French and German, until the age of twelve.

Like his brother and sister before him, Joe zipped through high school in three years, which enabled him to enter Columbia University at the age of fifteen. In later years he enjoyed telling that of the five hundred questions on the special entrance exam, he missed only one —the definition of the word *hernia*, which he assumed, from its suffix, to be a flower.

Joe, like his older brother, majored in English and wound up in the honors program tutored by Professor John Erskine, the author of such popular twenties historical novels as *The Private Life of Helen of Troy*. Without mentioning the considerable amount of time he spent in playing team sports, Joe summarized his extracurricular activities at college by stating that his "four years were devoted to establishing an all-time attendance record at the Nemo movie theater and an all-time nonattendance record at a course in neoclassicism."[9]

At the Phi Sigma Delta house where Joe lived, he became fast friends with a lodger named Chester Eckstein on the basis of their mutual passion for the theater. Eckstein was a member of the Union College chapter of the fraternity and was taking advantage of the Columbia house's economical rate for boarders while attempting to forge a career in the Broadway theater. Since he was totally unsuccessful in gaining employment as an actor, his board fees were continually in arrears, and he was relegated to sleeping on a cot between the beds of two paid-up boarders.

When the situation of the nonpaying boarder became chronic enough to warrant a fraternity meeting on the subject, Joe decided to

---

The operation doubtless influenced the invention of Margaret Sullavan's unusual, sacrificial suicide in Mankiewicz's production of *Three Comrades*. Unlike the ending of the Remarque novel, in which the heroine finally succumbs to tuberculosis, the Mankiewicz revision, which caused Scott Fitzgerald such distress, has Sullavan rise from her bed, after a rib removal operation requiring total immobility for recovery, to wave farewell to Robert Taylor, thus ridding him of an intolerable emotional and financial burden.

[9] *The Deltan* (Phi Sigma Delta), December 1936.

introduce his friend to Herman, who, as an assistant drama editor for the *New York Times* under George S. Kaufman, had numerous theatrical connections. Joe remembers that "Herman looked at [Chester] and said, 'I think the first thing we have to do is change your name. You're not going to get Eckstein in lights very easily.' " Herman renamed him Chester Erskine, after Professor John, and then delivered one of his typical telephone tirades to secure an interview for him with Lee Shubert's grudging casting director. A few years later the Mankiewicz brothers could look back in satisfaction at their agentry for having helped launch the meteoric Broadway career of one of the prominent director-producers of the thirties.

Erskine retains fond memories of the days when he and Joe were still show-biz outsiders, saying, "Joe and I used to share gossip about the theater because you feel you're in it if you talk about it." Both young men were aspiring humorists as well as men of the theater. They would try out on each other the twenty-five- to fifty-word squibs they would regularly concoct and send—Joe to the humor magazines *Life* and *Judge,* along with regular contributions to Columbia's *Jester,* and Chester to F. P. Adams's column. "One day Joe came tearing upstairs to the second floor of the house," says Erskine, "and announced with great excitement, 'They've bought it!'—a paragraph purchased by the old *Life* magazine for $6[10]—and we immediately went out to celebrate the beginning of Joe's professional career." "I wrote it under the name of Joe Mason," says Mankiewicz, "as I didn't want to use my brother's name—the name of Mankiewicz, at that time, belonging to him in the world of art and letters and to my father in the world of pedagogy."

Joe was dabbling in both of these worlds to earn his pocket money. During the school year he taught English to foreigners at a night school. For teaching three evenings a week he earned $150 per semester. During the summers he served as the dramatics and baseball counselor at Camp Kiwana, in then less celebrated Woodstock, New York. He got the job through Herman's friend Groucho Marx, since the camp was owned largely by the Marx Brothers. "That was his beginning in show business," said Groucho. "They used to present little shows at the camp. Joe used to teach the kids to perform so their parents could see them."[11]

---

[10]Mankiewicz believes it was bought by *Judge* magazine for $17.
[11]Groucho Marx and Richard J. Anobile, *The Marx Bros. Scrapbook,* Grosset & Dunlap, 1974, p. 148.

"That's where I had a fist fight with Zeppo," Mankiewicz recalls of his summer camp antagonist, "when he wanted to play first base on the camp team. I was the coach, and the kids were supposed to play first base, not one of the owners of the camp. After all, the kids' parents had paid a lot of money for these activities. I told him to get off the field, and one word led to another."

"It was very important to my father that I follow his footsteps in the pedagogic world," and Joe consequently determined to pursue his graduate studies on the European trip Pop Mankiewicz provided all his children to complete their education. Joe's announced plan was to enroll at the University of Berlin, then go on to the Sorbonne, and finish at Oxford, to read English.

Joe's tutor, John Erskine, encouraged an academic career by offering a tangible incentive. "On graduation day, after the ceremony," Mankiewicz relates, "Erskine sent for me, and we had a talk. He told me of his fear that I was going to follow the easy road and succumb to the blandishments of Hollywood, which I swore to him I wouldn't. He nurtured great hope that I would come back to Columbia [as an instructor in the English Department] and by teaching, writing, and taking it more slowly, perhaps develop into a good writer. He thought I might possibly write some plays and some books, and he was probably goddamned right."

Upon arriving in Berlin in September 1928, Mankiewicz quickly abandoned the path of pedagogy in order to follow in his brother's footsteps. At the cramped office of the *Chicago Tribune* in the posh Hotel Adalon at 1 Unter den Linden, he applied to Sigrid Schultz, Herman's successor as chief correspondent for central Europe, and landed his first job as one of her cub reporters. He promptly adopted the title of "assistant correspondent" and was sent by Miss Schultz to the port city of Stettin to interview the explorer Umberto Nobile on his return from his polar expedition, cut short by the wreck of his dirigible.

Herman, who had gone to Hollywood in 1926 to write for Paramount Pictures, had become the head of Paramount's scenario department by the end of 1927. Since Paramount was the American distributor for Germany's largest film company, UFA, and Erich Pommer, the distinguished producer of *Caligari* and *Metropolis,* was a good friend of Herman's, Joe had little difficulty in lining up a second job translating intertitles from German to English for foreign release. Ever ambitious, Mankiewicz landed yet a third job as the Berlin stringer for

Variety. In his own words, "I was earning about $100 a week and living like a king. I learned more about everything in those four months in Berlin than I think I've learned in the rest of my life, and I got to know everybody."

Whether it was his adoration of the English revue dancer Pat Kendall,[12] "one of the most beautiful women I've ever seen on a stage, with whom I fell madly in love," or his general enthrallment with the wonders of Berlin, which he describes as an "absolute intoxication of theater, excitement, glamour, and sex," is indeterminable, but in four months Mankiewicz managed to live a bit above his "kingly" means. While admitting he "got run out of town" and had to retreat to Paris, Mankiewicz contends that the sum he owed was paltry. "I was overdrawn about $75 on my account at the bank, the manager of which was my uncle. The cashier called me and said that my uncle, being the Prussian s.o.b. he was, was not going to make good my $75 check, but rather he was going to send it to the police, which is what he typically did. I said, 'Well, fuck it,' and went off to Paris. As soon as I got to Hollywood, I sent my uncle the $75 check." (Mankiewicz denies another debt of 420 marks [approximately $105], which he owed the *Chicago Tribune,* but Sigrid Schultz remembered it and insisted the office treasurer present the debt for collection when Joe returned to Berlin for a visit in 1931.)[13]

Mankiewicz describes his indigent stay in Paris (December 1928– March 1929) as "the three most miserable months of my life. Hardly speaking to a soul and broke, I developed a loathing for the French as a people that I don't think I've completely overcome yet, even though they have been terribly kind to me as a film director."[14]

---

[12]The partner in a dance act with her brother, Terry, the father of comedienne Kay Kendall. Mankiewicz told his frequent leading man Rex Harrison, Kay Kendall's husband until her death, that he might well have been his "uncle-in-law" if he had married Pat.

[13]Mankiewicz did acknowledge in a 1936 article that in the course of a subsequent European vacation one of his duties was "to pay off a great number of debts I had incurred there, which is more than Europe has done for us" (*The Deltan,* December 1936).

[14]Mankiewicz is proud of the laudatory appraisals of his work by the first corps of *Cahiers du Cinéma* critics in the early fifties, many of whom, like Godard, Truffaut, and Rohmer, have gone on to become distinguished directors themselves. He was also greatly flattered by the retrospective of his films made by the Cinémathèque Française in 1967.

In response to a very depressed letter mailed from Joe's Parisian exile, Herman once again came to his younger brother's rescue. "For Christ's sake, come out to Hollywood!" was Herman's exuberant reply, and he arranged a job for Joe at Paramount as a junior writer at a starting salary of $60 a week.[15] At the outset, Herman, according to his widow, paid this salary out of his own pocket to get Joe started. For one of Hollywood's biggest spenders, the gesture was not prodigal; in the year the Great Depression was to strike America, Herman Mankiewicz was earning a colossal $1,250 a week. At the time, this tiny gesture of fraternal benevolence in an industry rife with nepotism was hardly cause for comment. The irony is that of all the distinguished New York literary talent that Herman lured with whopping salaries to Hollywood, his $60-a-week investment was to prove his greatest screenwriting discovery besides his great friend Ben Hecht.

"I went from New York to California on a system of trains that nobody else had ever taken," Mankiewicz recounts. "My father arranged it for me. I went out in an upper berth and didn't change stations in Chicago, although everybody else had to. . . . I arrived nineteen hours late, on a train called the Apache on the Rock Island Line. [From it,] I sent a famous telegram to Herman, which he showed to everyone—HORSES EATEN BY WOLVES. GOLD SAFE, HOWEVER. JOE.

"The night I arrived in Hollywood, Herman took me to my first Hollywood party. I remember vividly I borrowed a tuxedo of his. I only had one pair of brown shoes, but with black shoe polish I made them black. I went to Jesse Lasky's [the head of Paramount] beach house. It was the first time I ever gave my hat to a butler in my whole life, and it's also, I think, the last time in my life I ever wore a hat. I then wandered around, and the spectacle left me gaping. My God, I could see Kay Francis, Clara Bow, Olga Baclanova, Gary Cooper. It was the most incredible sight to suddenly hit the eyes of a twenty-year-old.

"And then I saw this very large back that I thought I recognized. While I was trying to figure out who it was, the back turned around, and it was John Erskine, whom I hadn't seen since graduation day when I swore I would never go to Hollywood. Erskine looked at me, and I looked at him. He said, 'Joe, what are you doing here?' I said, 'Professor Erskine, what are you doing here?' He said, 'I'm working at Warner

---

[15]In another version Mankiewicz says, "He [Herman] got me a job because I went back to New York and couldn't find anything."

Brothers. Where are you working?' At that moment, an illusion shattered that I don't think I've ever recovered from. He had just sold *The Private Life of Helen of Troy* to Warners and was out there working on the screenplay. It skipped his mind completely that he'd delivered that impassioned speech about not going Hollywood, and he talked to me exactly like one Hollywood pro to another."

Before Mankiewicz could begin working at Paramount, he was obliged to undergo a legal formality. Joe says, "I think I'm probably the only writer in the history of film who went down with the Wampas baby stars [promising starlets annually designated by W.A.M.P.A.S., a group of publicists] to have his contract approved by a Los Angeles judge, which was required, under California law, for anyone under the legal age of twenty-one. The judge thought it was a little odd my being in the company of thirteen babes, all of them luscious, so he asked me if I was an actor. I replied, 'No sir, I'm a writer!' " The legend of Joe Mankiewicz, the celebrated Hollywood ladies' man, began simultaneously with his career in the movies.

"If it's a Paramount picture, you don't have to stand in line" 3

"*W*ITH TALK CAME THE JEW" IS JOE MANKIEWICZ'S CAPSULE DE-scription of the encroachment on the preserve of the predominantly gentile writers of the silent film era. The advent of talkies created a need for writers who were capable of creating speakable dialogue rather than written titles.

New York's heavily Jewish theater and literary circles offered the obvious talent pool to tap, so screenwriting became, by necessity, the first of the Hollywood crafts to lift the exclusionism that was countenanced by the odd sense of inferiority of the industry's mainly Jewish executives. American Jewish directors and actors, with such notable exceptions as Mervyn LeRoy or Edward G. Robinson, were to remain as anomalous in Hollywood in the thirties and forties as the token or "house goys" were in the studio executive buildings.

While Herman Mankiewicz was snaring such big fish from his New York circle as Robert Benchley and Ben Hecht with the lure of Hollywood lucre, the studios were eager to spawn their own pool of writers. To this end the studios set up junior writers programs in which bright young aspirants could apprentice under the tutelage of experienced screenwriters.

At Paramount the program was instituted and administered by the youthful Walter Wanger, assistant to studio chief Jesse Lasky. Although Wanger was fifteen years Joe's senior, as pipe-smoking, Ivy

League graduates with cultivated literary tastes they were similarly distinctive figures in the film colony.[1] Wanger had logically plucked a major portion of his junior writers from the graduates of the esteemed George Pierce Baker's playwriting workshop at Yale.

Unfettered by Professor Baker's dicta, Joe was free to absorb and appreciate the lore and techniques of the professorial Percy Heath and the madcap but savvy Grover Jones and Bill McNutt—the three old pros to whom he was assigned. "They were awful hacks, in a literary sense," Mankiewicz says; "they couldn't have written a decent letter in words, but they were real writers nevertheless in their own medium."[2]

Jones and McNutt taught their young apprentice the tricks of the trade, and their lessons were so graphic that Mankiewicz remembers them to this day. For example, to establish the element of jeopardy that would "carry the furniture of the film," Grover would say, "You're always going to fade in on a long shot. Now be sure, when you fade in, you've got a sign down in front which reads 'DANGER—EXPLOSIVES' because that's where the chase is going to go through in the eighth reel."

Jones and McNutt also inculcated the strategic importance of the "what the audience (or the protagonist) doesn't know" precept of dramatic irony as a plot device. "For example, Claudette Colbert is a society girl. She's fed up with life, and she's walking along the street, and she sees a fellow working underneath a car. So she says to herself, 'Now that's the kind of man I want, a guy who works with his hands. Look, he's covered with grease!' Of course, it's Richard Arlen, and 'what she doesn't know' is he owns all the five-and-ten-cent stores in Australia and is richer than she is. Then you've got yourself a movie." If this example, and the countless variations on it spun by McNutt and Jones, seems crude, Mankiewicz points out that the device is fundamental and that the whole framework of *All About Eve* is predicated on a "what-they-don't-know" device.

The apprentice would also accompany his mentors to story confer-

---

[1]Fittingly, Mankiewicz and Wanger were reunited on the last two films Wanger produced in his long movie career—*I Want to Live!* (1958), directed by Robert Wise for Figaro, Inc., Mankiewicz's production company, and *Cleopatra* (1963). The acrimony surrounding the latter film served to cancel their anticipated collaboration, as producer and director, respectively, on Lawrence Durrell's *Alexandria Quartet*, the project with which they planned to crown their careers.

[2]Robert Coughlan, "15 Authors in Search of a Character named Joseph L. Mankiewicz," *Life*, March 12, 1951.

ences, where he would watch them demonstrate their fabled extemporized "cigar" routine, in which "you kept going as long as you could, and the moment you put down your cigar, the other fellow would jump in."[3]

"They didn't do an awful lot of work in their office," Mankiewicz explains, "so when the secretary would announce, 'Mr. Fineman wants to see you in his office about the new George Bancroft picture,' they'd break off their backgammon game, or whatever they were playing, and would each light a cigar. Then they would go down and burst into Bernie Fineman's office and say, 'We're so glad you called us, because we were just about to call you.' 'Now, we've got this story for George,' Grover would start. 'This man is the wolf of Wall Street, a man who bankrupted millions, destroyed families, and ruined friends. He had no time for his wife or children, who grew up rebellious.' At about this point, Grover would put down his cigar, and Bill McNutt would jump up and say, 'What Grover forgot is that the son is really a radical and is behind a plot to destroy his old man's combine.' Bill would then put down his cigar, and Grover would continue, 'But the daughter, in the meantime, has fallen in love with the general manager of her father's combine, and the big tension is whether she is going to betray her own brother's plot.' This left Bernie Fineman oohing and aahing, though it bore no relationship to what Jones and McNutt ultimately wrote.

"That's where I learned to 'wing it,' " claims Mankiewicz. "You can give me an original story idea, and I can wing three or four separate versions of it, but you'd better have somebody to take them down, because I won't remember any of them."

Mankiewicz's obstacle in distinguishing himself from the other junior writers was the anonymity of his job, writing titles for the silent versions of Paramount films shown in theaters that had not yet converted to sound projection. His UFA training in Germany enabled him to title a record number of six films in eight weeks. (These included *The Dummy*, written by his brother; Wellman's *Man I Love;* and von Sternberg's *Thunderbolt.*) The feat garnered him his first publicity in the trade papers as the youngest member, at twenty, of Paramount's writing staff, but his achievement only served to label him as an invaluable titlist in the studio's estimation.

"I determined to write my way out of the junior writers group,"

---

[3]The improvised plot line at story conferences was a widespread Hollywood practice.

says Mankiewicz, and he seized upon the title of an announced Clara Bow vehicle, *The Saturday Night Kid*,[4] and concocted six different stories in one week to fit this title. "I got a memo back from B. P. Schulberg [Paramount's general manager] saying that he'd read all my six stories and found them all pretty dreadful, but he did like my dialogue."

So did David O. Selznick, Schulberg's young assistant in charge of hiring and assigning writers. Selznick proposed that Mankiewicz write the dialogue for *Elmer the Great*, the Ring Lardner and George M. Cohan play about an egotistical, lame-brained baseball star. Retitled *Fast Company*, this movie established the former vaudevillian and chorus boy Jack Oakie and his sidekick-mentor Skeets Gallagher as a phenomenally popular team.[5] The script led to Mankiewicz's being cited in the *Los Angeles Record*'s list of the ten best dialogue writers of 1929, in the estimable company of George Abbott, Edmund Goulding, and Frank Capra. It also earned him the assignment of writing malapropisms for Oakie in six subsequent films.[6]

The timing was fortuitous. According to William Wright, Mankiewicz's close friend of the period, "The junior writers project didn't last long. Joe was one of the few to make it out of that group. None of the Yalies made it."

At the outset, Mankiewicz was so naïve he was literally obliged to devise the comedy team's formula on the set. He explains, "I wrote what I thought were the dramatic necessities, but when I got to a scene between Oakie and Gallagher, I wrote quite simply, 'And now follows a comedy sequence between the two comics, at the pleasure of the comedians,' since I figured they scripted that dialogue themselves. I didn't think anyone ever *wrote* that nonsense.[7]

---

[4]Mankiewicz ultimately wrote the titles for the silent version of *The Saturday Night Kid* (1929). The dialogue for the sound version was written by Lloyd Corrigan and Edward E. Paramore, a writer whom Mankiewicz was later to employ on two of his productions at MGM.

[5]*Elmer the Great* was more successfully remade in 1933 under its original title. The title role was played by Joe E. Brown, who had starred in the Broadway play, and the film was directed by Mervyn LeRoy.

[6]Mankiewicz denies participation in the Oakie films *Sap from Syracuse, Dude Ranch,* and *Touchdown,* listed in the various filmographies of his work, and points out his lack of screen credit for any of these films, all of which are inferior to his own scripts for Oakie.

[7]It was a common practice in Broadway musical librettos merely to indicate that a spot would be filled with a specialty turn by an established vaudevillian such as W. C. Fields or Wheeler and Woolsey.

"In those days we used to start shooting at Paramount after five in the afternoon, and we'd shoot until five in the morning, because we were using the old silent stages, with enormous carpets and tapestries hung down the walls for soundproofing. The reason we'd start at five was because that's when the traffic got quieter, so that the mikes wouldn't pick up the traffic noise.

"My vivid memory is that very early on in the shooting of *Fast Company,* I had taken Mary Brian [a star ingenue at Paramount] to the theater, the Biltmore, in downtown Los Angeles. Halfway through the first act, I felt a tap on my shoulder. I looked up and there was Charlie Barton, Eddie Sutherland's [*Fast Company*'s noted comedy director] first assistant. Charlie just crooked a finger at me, indicating I was wanted in the lobby, so I ducked out of the theater. Charlie said, 'You'd better get your ass out to the studio, 'cause Sutherland wants you right now.' I said, 'What for?' and Charlie simply said, 'They're waiting for you, so get your ass in a cab, and I'll bring Mary.'

"Out I went, like Dr. Kildare on an emergency call. I thought, 'What the hell is going on?' and I found them sitting around the set, absolutely furious. That was the first time I learned that 'Yeah?' / 'Oh yeah' / 'Is that so?' / 'Yeah' type of dialogue was actually written. I didn't know they wrote that kind of crap. I always thought, as many people think, that comics like the Marx Brothers made up their lines —which they didn't. So I was put to work at a typewriter on the set to turn out the missing lines."

Mankiewicz summarizes the Oakie formula that lasted through a thirty-five-year movie career during which he slid from top to second banana. "He was the sap who spoke in malapropisms, the ingenuous country bumpkin always taken for a ride by the society girl. He found out just in time that she was wrong for him [*The Social Lion, June Moon*] and wound up with the more plain and virtuous girl—Mary Brian or the equivalent."[8]

Mankiewicz's own social progress in the film colony was considera-

---

[8]Richard Watts, Jr., writing in the *New York Herald Tribune* on *The Social Lion,* more precisely describes the Oakie character as a variant of Ring Lardner's "most famous character, the Busher, [who] is both comic and pathetic in his ignorance and his arrogance, but there is no escaping that he is an entirely contemptible person. Jack Oakie plays the same character, with even a touch of the unbearable William Haines hero thrown in, but he manages to inject into his role a certain note of embarrassment, a touch of gentleness and even a stray bit of wistfulness. The result is hilarity combined with an honest strain of sympathy; the sure sign of a first rate comedian."

bly more adroit. His youth, looks, wit, and charm, combined with his perpetual high spirits, swiftly made him a social catch.

Metro mogul Louis B. Mayer's palatial beach house in Santa Monica was a Sunday port of call, since Joe was a frequent guest of Mayer's daughters, Irene and Edith. When Irene married David O. Selznick, Joe became the Selznicks' weekend "mascot," accompanying them in the rumble seat of their roadster to tennis and picnic outings.

One evening Joe was a guest at a little dinner party for a school-mate of Irene's, along with his friends Bill Wright and Regis Toomey, a contract player at Paramount. Selznick joked that the assemblage was "a junior group," inferior to his more important social gatherings. Having chastened his guests with their lowliness, Selznick announced that as an after-dinner treat he was taking them to meet the celebrated playwriting team of Ben Hecht and Charles MacArthur, newly arrived in L.A. and suitably ensconced in a huge, Spanish-style hacienda in Culver City near the Metro lot.

When MacArthur, described by Bill Wright as "saturnine and intense," opted for sleep and left his more affable partner, Hecht, to show their guests around the elaborate residence, the evening promised to be singularly dull, until Selznick's brother, Myron, the noted agent, arrived, typically soused, to liven up the proceedings. Myron shouted that MacArthur's retiring to bed was a personal insult and insisted on waking him up. The result was a furious, twenty-minute donnybrook, with the Selznick brothers wrestling MacArthur to the floor in the space between the twin beds, while Mankiewicz and Wright looked on from a good vantage point atop a dresser and Irene Selznick vainly pounded on the door. Mankiewicz says, "Irene was very upset by the fight and sent me in to stop it, but I couldn't stop laughing at the spectacle of those three men, because David was swinging and flailing away, while MacArthur was biting Myron and David, and there wasn't a blow being landed. I was hysterical, but Ben Hecht was standing by the fireplace smoking a cigar and watching it all very calmly."

The following morning at Paramount, David Selznick asked Bill Wright to accompany him on a drive to his doctor's office, on the pretext of working on some titles en route. In the car he revealed the souvenirs MacArthur had inflicted the previous evening—tooth-bite lacerations all over his body. "What if a gun had dropped out of the night table?" Wright inquired. "I'd have used it," Selznick replied.

The battling Selznick brothers were an exception to the generally decorous social circuit Mankiewicz traveled. The "in crowd" favored more professional prize fights on Fridays, danced at the Coconut Grove, and dined at the large restaurants on Sunset Boulevard—a ramshackle street of clapboard houses in the era before it became the Sunset Strip.

Mankiewicz met with his peers at the "Yale Bowl," a bungalow on Alta Loma Terrace near the Hollywood Bowl. Bill Wright shared the dwelling with two of Mankiewicz's fellow junior writers from Yale, William Robson ("the Genius") and Richard Diggs. For social gatherings the bootlegger would deliver two bottles of Gordon's gin for $5, lending the place the nostalgic, boozy aura of a frat house.

At the Malibu home of Sam Jaffe, Paramount's production manager, Joe, dressed in his usual Ivy League clothing (tweed jacket, gray flannel trousers, and a bow tie) and puffing on his ever-present pipe, would perform his deft imitations of such Paramount stars as Jack Oakie, for whom he wrote, and Bing Crosby, whom he idolized.

At the Pasadena mansion of Tom Geraghty (a then famous name from silent film days, when he had written many of Douglas Fairbanks's films), Joe became fast friends with Geraghty's children. The beautiful Geraghty daughters, Carmelita and Sheila, both became actresses, and the son, Gerald, became a member of Joe's social clique, along with Bill Wright, Richard Diggs, and the young leading man Phillips Holmes, who had an apartment in the opposite wing of the building on Havenhurst Drive where Joe lived.

Like Mankiewicz, except for Joe's Berlin baptism, Holmes had come directly from college to Hollywood at the age of twenty. Mankiewicz describes him as "the most exquisitely handsome young man I've ever seen in my life. As a matter of fact, I first saw Phil when the Columbia University Players traveled to Princeton to see the Princeton Triangle Club show called *Napoleon Passes,* in which Phil played Josephine so exquisitely. I turned to Ben Hubbard, our director, and said, 'What the hell, Princeton is using girls,' [an illusion dispelled when] I went backstage and met him. . . . He was a crazy, marvelous guy who drank a good deal too much and came to a tragic end—killed in training practice as a volunteer in the Canadian Air Force [in 1942]."

In 1930, the year after Joe's arrival in Hollywood, the Mankiewicz brothers placed a full-page ad in the trade papers reading, "Herman & Joseph Mankiewicz, writers at Paramount. How about Erna?" This come-on was devised as a means of prompting the studios to send for their sister, Erna, then working as a schoolteacher in New York. Herman followed up the ad by placing one of his insistent phone calls to his close friend Sam Jaffe; in a matter of weeks there were three Mankiewiczes on the Paramount lot. Erna's two-year career proved she was the one Mankiewicz sibling not adept at screenwriting.

Regis Toomey, who lunched with Joe and his regular tablemates at Paramount (writers Jones and McNutt, brother Herman, and actor Paul Lukas), remembers that "the dialogue around that table was out of this world." Toomey and his wife, Kathleen, referred to Joe, Erna, and Phillips Holmes, who were alone on the Christmas holidays, as "the Orphans," and they would always invite the waifs to their home for festive dinners.

Joe's lunchmate Paul Lukas, though a versatile theater star for Max Reinhardt in Berlin and in his native Budapest, was early typed by his Hungarian accent as an elegant villain. He played this typical supporting role in *Slightly Scarlet,* a formula romantic melodrama that provided Mankiewicz's second dialogue credit. In it Mankiewicz has some fun at the expense of an American nouveau riche family summering in a villa on the Riviera. The exasperated head of this household, played by the hefty Eugene Pallette, is chiefly homesick for a T-bone steak and moans, "For months I've been eating French words, and everything turned out to be cauliflower."

This falsely genteel family is socially snubbed until they are taken up by a pair of aristocratic impostors (Clive Brook and Evelyn Brent) who have designs on an expensive pearl and ruby necklace belonging to Pallette's snooty wife. The thieves forego the jewels in favor of each other.

> BROOK: Why don't we quit together?
> BRENT: That would be more thrilling than any adventure I've ever known.

This specimen of Mankiewicz's jejune dialogue may suggest why *Slightly Scarlet* never comes close to the level of Lubitsch's similarly plotted *Trouble in Paradise,* made just two years later on the same Paramount lot.

Slightly Scarlet's most memorable scene is of Lukas, the chief of a European crime ring, blithely turning to play the organ as one of his disobedient operatives is dragged off pleading for his life. Lukas's glacial put-down ("To me you are merely number 14") of his agent, Evelyn Brent, a striking brunette, is a high spot of the scene. Mankiewicz, equally uninterested, had eyes for the film's blonde ingenue, Virginia Bruce.

The static camera work of *Slightly Scarlet* is indicative of the restrictions imposed on the early talkies by the need to muffle the noise of the camera by enclosing it in a soundproofed booth. The stagey tableaus and theatrical delivery of dialogue are attributable to the collaboration of a theater director (Edwin Knopf) with a silent film director (Louis Gasnier). These odd collaborations were devised by the front office to help the actors accommodate themselves to spoken dialogue and at the same time to school theater directors in film technique.

In the Writers' Building, similar alliances were forged between the established silent film writers, who would turn out the "Continuity" (stage directions and plot line) on the left-hand side of the page, and novices like Mankiewicz, who would fashion the complementary "Dialogue" typed on the right side of the script.

Seated across a desk from young Mankiewicz on his next Oakie-Gallagher comedy, *The Social Lion,* was a formidable woman, Agnes Brand Leahy, whom Mankiewicz terms "one of the great continuity writers of silent films." The work they fashioned, though adapted from a story, *Marco Himself,* by Octavius Roy Cohen, closely follows the *Fast Company* formula. This time Oakie is a swelled-headed but credulous ex–prize fighter who works as a garage mechanic. He is adopted by the local polo club set for his prowess as a polo player but is mocked for his social gaucherie.

The film contains a replica of the central humiliation scene in *Fast Company,* in which Oakie, on the eve of the World Series, is inveigled into giving an impassioned speech to a national radio audience, but, in fact, the fake microphone apparatus he speaks into is merely suspended from the ceiling by a rope and filled with liquor bottles. ("Millions are waiting to *drink up* every word you utter" is the prankster's put-on.) In *The Social Lion,* on the eve of the big polo match, Oakie is led on by Olive Borden, the snobbish society vamp he has fallen for, to sing her his doggerel marriage proposal to a hidden audience of her mocking friends. This mortifying treachery convinces him to return to his own social class and his wholesome, faithful girlfriend (Mary Brian), who works as a coat-check girl at the polo club. Oakie scores a dual triumph in first winning the big polo match and telling off his club tormentors and then taking the middleweight boxing crown by pulling the "your shoelace is untied" routine on his opponent.

Richard Watts, in the *New York Herald Tribune,* called Mankiewicz's dialogue "genuinely fresh and lively," and on April 12, 1930, the studio head, B. P. Schulberg, sent him an interoffice memo of commendation terming his writing "really first class." "Young Writer Rewarded for Clever Dialogue" was the headline of an item in a Los Angeles paper on May 10, announcing the new contract Paramount had awarded Mankiewicz, but without disclosing the minimal amount of his salary increase.

Mankiewicz's success in writing for Oakie led to his assignment to write dialogue for Leon Errol, an older comic on the lot. Errol's appeal seems mystifying today; his specialties appear to have been rubber-legged pratfalls and a minimal gift for double talk. He was given ample opportunity to display these skills and generally hog the proceedings in Mankiewicz's first opus for him, *Only Saps Work* (1930), derived from a stage farce by Owen Davis. The origins of Mankiewicz's funny bird epithets for W. C. Fields in the subsequent *If I Had a Million* may be found in the similes he wrote for Errol to apply to his irate landlady, named Mrs. Partridge. ("She has the eyes of a dove and the nose of a Bavarian bluebird.")

Errol's big set piece is a rhymed nonsense lyric with orchestral accompaniment ("You ride upon a bagel until you get to hunting the wild Cadduchas [a Japanese bird]" is a typical line) leading to his devastation of a resort hotel's kitchen by incorporating every comestible ingredient at hand into an improvised "Jappalappa waffle." This wearisome jape is intended as a delaying action so that heiress Mary Brian will not discover that Richard Arlen is working as a busboy at the resort rather than managing it, as he had told her in order to give himself some status. The situation inspired a rueful depression-era line from Mankiewicz: "One thing a college education does for you—you can get a job in a pantry with practically no experience."

Scenarists Sam Mintz and Percy Heath recycled the formula that while Mary Brian is the daughter of "an oil king," "what she doesn't know" is that Richard Arlen will gain a vast inheritance from his father in only two months' time. The love interest "meets cute" (a prime objective in romantic comedies of the period) as Arlen aids Brian out of a stalled elevator, injuring his thumb. Brian bandages it by tearing a strip from her slip, and the repetition of this bandaging bit throughout the film substitutes for more intimate physical contact.

According to Regis Toomey, Joe was quite taken with Mary Brian, who was "already something of a star at Paramount when he arrived and one of the sweetest people in the business." Like Richard Arlen on the screen, "Joe looked at her sort of moon-eyed," says Toomey, "though I don't think he was in love with her—just fascinated."

His new contract enabled Mankiewicz to purchase a Buick convertible (termed a "roadster" in 1930) and move from his apartment to a house he aptly christened "Option Downs." He was also moved to demand a printed retraction from the *Los Angeles Record* for stating that Herman, not he, wrote the dialogue for *The Social Lion*, a confusion that has plagued him to the present day on his classic comedy, *Million Dollar Legs*.

Being mistakenly called by his better-known brother's first name, even around the studio, became an increasing irritant. At one point Joe quipped, "I know now what they will put on my tombstone: 'Here lies Herm—I mean Joe—Mankiewicz.' "[9]

His next Jack Oakie picture, *The Gang Buster*, was a spoof of gangster melodrama, with Oakie as a foolhardy insurance salesman invading the lair of a villainous thug (William Boyd) to rescue single-handedly his kidnapped sweetheart (Jean Arthur). One exchange between the gangsters while Oakie noisily plays hide and seek in their mansion hideout—"It must have been mice." / "Mice don't knock on wood"—is probably drawn from an incident that took place on the antic fourth floor of the Writers' Building at Paramount.

The story, which Mankiewicz cherishes, concerns the successful playwright Zoë Akins, then a prominent Paramount screenwriter, who, though she came from Kansas City, says Mankiewicz, "wrote all those terribly elegant imitation Maugham plays and had adopted the most

---

[9]Even in the fifties, when Mankiewicz had become an important director and MCA was a top talent agency, the problem continued to plague Joe. The courtship of Mankiewicz by MCA's chief executives, Lew Wasserman and Jules Stein, was assiduous. "I was in New York," says Mankiewicz, "and Jules Stein used to have me to lunch in his beautifully paneled private dining room. He also kept inviting me to parties and screenings. After three or four months of wooing, I ran into Lew Wasserman in Hollywood. Lew said, 'Why don't you level with me? I know that Jules has been talking to you in New York, trying to get you as a client. Now, why won't you come with us?' I said, 'Well, frankly, Lew, I don't think I should be represented by an agent who calls me Herman!' "

incredible English accent that ever existed. . . . Zoë had the corner office, mine was next to hers, and Jim [James M.] Cain was right across the hall. . . . There was a tremendous crap game that went on in my office every afternoon,[10] and being writers, there was no rolling on the carpet—you had to hit the wall with the dice. Zoë used to have tea every afternoon for some of her friends like Ethel Barrymore, Ruth Chatterton, or George Cukor. . . . One afternoon Bill McNutt or somebody was trying to make a hard ten, banging away at the wall while Zoë was having tea, and she called the writers' supervisor, Mr. Hurley.[11]

> AKINS: (*imperiously*) Mr. Hurley, you had better come to my office at once. I do believe there are *mace* in the walls.
> HURLEY: There can't be any mice in the walls, Miss Akins. For Christ's sake, the building was just built.
> AKINS: Oh no, no. I do hear *mace,* and if you will come up, you will hear them too.

So Hurley went up to her office, and, sure enough, he heard this scurrying and crackling against the baseboard. Wondering if I had heard it too, he came into my office . . . and stayed long enough to drop a couple of hundred dollars. Then he went back to Zoë's office and, in her doorway, announced, 'Not *mace,* Miss Akins, *dace!*'

"One day she stuck her head into the office where I was working with Grover and Bill on something and inquired, with that affected accent, 'Do pardon me for interrupting you, but could you tell me what exactly is the *shedule* on *Tom Sawyer?*' Grover looked up and simply said, 'Oh skit!' "

In September 1930 the *Hollywood Reporter* printed the item, "Two plums have just been handed the younger element at Paramount. Joe Mankiewicz has been assigned to do the dialogue for 'Skippy' and 'Mr. and Mrs. Haddock Abroad' [the film was eventually titled *Finn and Hattie*] from the novel by Donald Ogden Stewart. Norman Taurog will direct both productions."

Taurog, a director whose career spans the silent era to films with

---

[10]Henry Myers, Mankiewicz's collaborator on *Million Dollar Legs,* says there was a perpetual poker game in the office of a writer named Brian Marlowe, and occasionally this was varied with a crap game.

[11]"Harold Hurley, though listed as a producer, was the executive whose job it was to see that the writers were happy and functioning, but we called him 'the House Dick,' " says Henry Myers.

Elvis Presley, still remembers his first meeting with Mankiewicz. "He was very young and almost handsome looking, and he projected assurance and a sense of security. The way he talked, you felt you could trust him with anything. When I proposed Norman McLeod [Taurog's codirector on *Finn and Hattie*] to collaborate with him on *Skippy*, he admitted that at that time dialogue was his forte and that he would like someone to work with who would provide the construction. I was strongly impressed by his not trying to bluff me that he could do everything."

Taurog related that Leon Errol was imposed on him by the studio to play Haddock on a "take it or leave it basis," and though the results "were a bit on the broad side, Joe did retain a lot of the original book."

Donald Ogden Stewart, the distinguished author and scenarist, calls the casting of Errol "an unbelievable thing." He describes his novel as a satire "in the Lardner vein . . . designed to expose the soul of Columbus, Ohio," through the behavior of the provincial Haddocks touring Europe with their daughter for the first time. Stewart says, "It would have been [funny] played straight, but as they tried to make it funny, the whole book, which Joe respected, was betrayed." Stewart remembers that Joe came "very apologetically to inform me he had just written the screenplay from my book, and forewarned me, 'Don't go to see it.' . . . I've always liked him since then for that voluntary apology."

Mankiewicz's only serviceable inventions in this forgettable farce are the running gags devised to exploit Errol's comic pratfalls—a "sure-fire" wrestling hold that always lands Errol on his back—and the inauguration of a comic feud between the child stars, Jackie Searl, the snot, and Mitzi Green, his precocious tormentor, which Mankiewicz continued in two other films for Taurog, *Skippy* and *Forbidden Adventure*.

Finn and Hattie also contains an "in joke" about Mankiewicz's sex appeal, for Taurog surreptitiously used a photograph of him for a magazine ad illustrating the "It" pose, which Errol, the would-be lady killer, attempts to emulate. The ad's copy inquires, "Do women thrill at your approach? Have you got 'it'?" This photo represents the only time Mankiewicz's face has appeared in a film, except for a bit part as a newspaper reporter in William Wellman's forgotten *Woman Trap* (1929). He must have photographed well, because Mankiewicz says Wellman urged him "to give up this crap about writing" and offered to put him under personal contract as an actor. Though flattered, Mankiewicz sensibly declined.

Mankiewicz's next Oakie vehicle, *June Moon*, could not have required a great deal of effort on his part. Except for adding a few typical malapropisms for his star (for example, "I'm not a confederate [for *inveterate*] smoker" or "I want a chance to defray my talents"), he hewed closely to the script of the Broadway comedy hit by Ring Lardner and George S. Kaufman about a talentless simpleton from Schenectady who comes to New York with dreams of success as a hit-song lyricist.

This time the faithful brunette who rescues him from a mis-alliance with a sluttish blonde gold digger was a new Paramount discovery, Frances Dee, a winsome graduate of Northwestern who had just scored a success opposite Maurice Chevalier in *Playboy of Paris*. She was destined to play a more pivotal role in Mankiewicz's life than in *June Moon*.

The *Variety* review of the play asserts that *June Moon* was "a riotous . . . smash that provoked not only laughs but howls." The only genuine howl in the film was surely inadvertent—the sight of palm trees in the rear projected landscape outside the railway window in the opening train ride from nontropical Schenectady to New York.

Variety termed Mankiewicz's next effort, *Skippy*, "the most effective juvenile attraction among full-length films made in years." This praise was generally echoed by the public, the Motion Picture Academy, and the press, with the exception of Phillip Scheuer in the *Los Angeles Times*, who termed it an enjoyable picture only if one were a boy or a dog. Director Taurog promptly chastised him by inquiring, "Since you are neither one, how could you review it?" The picture was based on the character of the lovable little scamp Skippy, "famed for his bright and cute sayings"[12] in Percy Crosby's comic strip, and it made a star of ten-year-old Jackie Cooper, whose chief previous experience had been playing minor parts in a few *Our Gang* comedies.

Mankiewicz and McLeod skillfully fabricated a mixture of pathos and humor out of well-to-do Skippy's friendship with a younger boy named Sooky (five-year-old Bobby Coogan), who lives with his widowed mother and a beloved mongrel dog in Shantytown, a slum village across the tracks. The plot revolves around the confiscation of Sooky's

[12] *Variety*, April 15, 1931.

unlicensed dog, the boys' futile efforts to raise the money to reclaim it, and the reconciliation of Skippy and his father, a physician and civic leader whom Skippy convinces to reconsider his plan to level the slum as "a dangerous sociological juxtaposition to our own homes."

The film's charm lies in the natural performances Taurog managed to elicit from blond, doleful-eyed Cooper and the appealing, gap-toothed, squeaky-voiced Coogan. Taurog insists, "Joe and I never talked down to their level," but they were canny enough to institute a daily monetary incentive by way of a competition among the children, including Skippy's haughty neighboring peers, played by Mitzi Green and Jackie Searl. "Whoever did best got 20¢," says Taurog, "and they worked harder for it than the $500 a week some of them were actually making, which they never saw."

Taurog says that Mankiewicz's best humor arose not from one-liners but from the situations he and McLeod created and the supreme naturalness of the characters' speech. Taurog speculates that "Joe must have played the parts to himself," as, in fact, he did. His happiest inventions are Skippy's rationalizations to achieve his ends without literally disobeying his mother's orders. Since she has prohibited Skippy from crossing over the tracks to Shantytown, he determines crossing *under* them is as permissible as wetting his toothbrush rather than actually brushing his teeth.

Taurog particularly adores the sequence in which Skippy and his father explain the protective warmth of a maternal kangaroo's pouch to the incredulous Sooky, who exclaims, "I sure wish my mother was a kangaroo last winter." He also recalls how useful Joe was on the set in improvising gags. In one sequence Skippy and Sooky stage a theatrical to raise funds for the dog license. Taurog planned to have Sooky, acting as M.C., outsmart the audience of kids pelting him with tomatoes by shielding himself with a garbage can lid and making it safely offstage. After watching a take, Joe advised, "Let him take the lid down to say, 'You missed me,' and then get it straight in the puss." He then added the charming line "Who fling that?" to cap the bit.

"Ah," sighed Taurog, "Joe Mankiewicz ruins you for anyone else. He never let me down in all the pictures we made together. When he didn't think it was working, he'd ask for more time to change and polish it. When I ran into a problem on other pictures, I could always reach Joe on the phone, and he'd come over. He'd say, 'Give me twenty or thirty minutes—I know how to fix it,' and he would, with a few words or a piece of business. He was a great fixer, especially of his own material."

Taurog is understandably fond of Mankiewicz and *Skippy* (although he admits, "I wouldn't dare do it today") since they helped earn him his sole Academy Award for direction in his long career. Jackie Cooper was also nominated for Best Actor but lost out to Lionel Barrymore, and Joe, aged twenty-two, received his first nomination for screenwriting.

Mankiewicz explains the mortifying presentation of the 1930–31 awards: "In those days they used to have a banquet at the Biltmore Hotel. All the nominees sat on a raised, two-tier dais around the room so that all the diners could look up at them. This was the awards ceremony, by the way, when Hoover's vice-president, Curtis, spoke for over two hours, while on the dais Jackie Cooper fell asleep in Marie Dressler's lap. Just to explain to you what kind of ceremony it was in those days, the president of the Academy was M. C. ("Mike") Levy, an executive at Paramount, and it was his wedding anniversary, so everybody had to get up and drink a champagne toast to him and his wife.

"The ballots were not counted by Price, Waterhouse but by representatives from every studio in a Biltmore bedroom upstairs. Those were the days of block voting, so if you were a member of the Academy and worked at Warners, you signed your ballot in Jack Warner's office, and David O. Selznick, who was the head of RKO, carried a pack of votes in his back pocket like all the rest of the studio heads.

"Two-thirds of the way through the banquet, Bud Lighton, the producer of *Skippy*, came down and whispered to me, 'Start making up your speech, kid, because you are way ahead [in the voting].' I said to myself, 'You're very young. Don't get cocky; don't get snotty; be humble.' I was about to fall into the cliché, the protocol, and started to make up the traditional big speech about how unworthy I was of this great honor, et cetera.

"While I was composing and rewriting this speech of mine, the director's award was given to Taurog for *Skippy*, which led me to think mine was in the bag. Then an old-time, famous screenwriter, Waldemar Young, got up to make the writing awards. As he opened the slip of paper, he smiled a little in my direction and said that the choice was particularly pleasing to him because it was a friend of his—which I was, a young friend—but also because the subject matter was so American and so fresh within the memory of some of us, and went on describing *Skippy*. Then he announced, 'Ladies and gentlemen, the Best in Screenplay Award goes to . . .' and I stood up, 'Howard Estabrook for *Cimarron,*' and there I was, standing with egg dripping off my face. Fortunately, God put Howard Estabrook right in front of me on the next level down, so I did the big ham bit of reaching over and shaking his hand, when I actually hated the son of a bitch. That was my most embarrassing moment—standing up just before my name was not called."

While Mankiewicz admits "the Academy Award nomination meant nothing to anyone in those days," his protective brother Herman felt it merited at least a raise in Joe's salary from a paltry $65 a week. When his fulminations failed to secure this objective, Herman, always the extravagant gambler, risked his own paycheck by tendering his resignation from Paramount. To win him back, B. P. Schulberg offered Joe a new seven-year contract at a small increase in salary ("somewhere between $75 and $100, with $50 raises every year, so at the end I'd be getting something like $600 a week if the options were all picked up"). Mankiewicz also earned the lasting admiration of the kindly producer of many of his subsequent films, Louis D. ("Bud") Lighton, himself a former writer who was very well regarded at Paramount. Mankiewicz fondly recalls Lighton as "a great influence on me. He took me under his wing . . . and showed me a lot of the ropes. He was a really marvelous man."

Mankiewicz's next picture for Taurog was coauthored with Edward ("Ted") Paramore and originally released as *Newly Rich*, later less aptly titled *Forbidden Adventure*. It was based on a short story by Sinclair Lewis, "Let's Play King," which Taurog recalls as "simply awful material, with a stupid mystery running through it."

As adapted by Agnes Brand Leahy and written by Mankiewicz and Paramore, the picture starts very well as a combat between two splendid character actresses, Louise Fazenda and Edna May Oliver. Fazenda returns in chauffeur-driven triumph to the gas station run by her former friend and neighbor, Oliver. The source of her new affluence is her son's (Jackie Searl) rise to fame as a child film star, Tiny Tim Tiffany. While Fazenda lords it over Oliver with a lorgnette and talk of her new mansion ("one of the show places of Beverly Hills, with twelve master bedrooms and thirteen baths"), Oliver's mischievous daughter, Daisy (Mitzi Green), is destroying Tiny Tim's getup for a personal appearance by cutting the curls off his Little Lord Fauntleroy wig with garden shears and reapplying the shorn hairpiece with rubber cement.

Edna May Oliver determines that the only way to compete with the haughty Fazenda is to make her daughter a child star equal to or greater than Tiny Tim. Daisy's rapid rise from extra to juvenile lead at the Hi-Art Studio (an "in joke" on Paramount) is accomplished by her crashing into Tiny Tim's set on a runaway dolly and being deemed the perfect replacement for Tim's costar, who has been felled by whooping cough.

Mankiewicz and Paramore had a good time satirizing studio types like the director and his supervisor[13] feuding over who discovered Daisy and depicting the privations of a child star's daily regimentation while the luxurious lifestyle her income provides is enjoyed only by her authoritarian guardians.

The picture starts to run downhill when the action shifts to London, where the mothers compete for the social triumph of acquaintance with the visiting young king of Slovaria, who is their children's contemporary in age. The child stars and royalty share a common yen to run away from their official obligations and play with kids their own age. The "forbidden adventure" is their escape for a day, in the course of which they befriend a gang of street urchins, are kidnapped by thugs, and are rescued. Only the film's concluding shot of this conventional series of episodes is memorable—a close-up of a wart on the young king's thumb, a status symbol among the urchins that it has been his supreme ambition to attain.[14]

Like so many sequels, *Sooky*, Mankiewicz's fifth film to be released in 1931, was an unsuccessful attempt to replicate *Skippy* as a heartwarming tearjerker. The only moderately clever escapade in *Sooky* is the boys' method of collecting coal from a freight train by pelting the motormen with tomatoes and receiving a return hail of salable fuel. The climax of the film, the death of Sooky's ailing mother, is intolerably

---

[13] *Supervisor* was the original designation for a film's producer, a term that Mankiewicz believes accurately describes his function as a studio overseer and that should have been retained.

[14] When Mankiewicz viewed the first dailies of the wooden actor playing the boy king, he asked Taurog, "Where does this kid come from?" "From England," Taurog replied. Joe queried, "Can we send him back?"

protracted; earlier, events had crawled to a dead halt because of an expository speech by Sooky to Skippy's parents.

A writer named Sam Mintz drew the top writing credit on *Sooky* over Mankiewicz and McLeod, and the film's tedium might be credited to him were redundancy not a characteristic of Mankiewicz's later films. As Mankiewicz's former production manager in the sixties, Doc Erickson, describes it, "Joe has a terrible habit of telling you the same thing in the first, fifth, and ninth reel, in case you weren't listening. His excuse is that if he wants to cut the picture [as he is frequently obliged to], he may lose important story points without this reiteration. . . . He's a better writer and picture maker than that, particularly in this day and age." Erickson believes this later tendency is a "hangover" from Mankiewicz's days at Metro, a studio that favored the preview and retake system of tinkering with films, which "imbued in him the philosophy 'we can always fix it if there is enough stuff in the cutting room!' " This characteristic may also be allied to what one of Mankiewicz's sons describes as his "pogrom complex," manifested in his habit of traveling with a large cache of contingency funds. (This custom proved costly in April 1963, when a robber made off with $7,050 in cash from his suitcase, left in a cottage adjoining the La Quinta Hotel in California.)

Mankiewicz's first two scripts of 1932 continued his string of flops after the success of *Skippy*. While only the name of the director, Frank Tuttle, appears in the credits as the adapter of the first of these, *This Reckless Age*, Mankiewicz is the author of the screenplay. According to a trade journal of the period, the film was "recklessly adapted" from a play, *The Goose Hangs High*, by Louis Beach. The trade paper summarized the moral of this hokey domestic drama of self-sacrificing parents and their thoughtless collegiate offspring as "intending to show, with a wealth of platitude and an unlikely climax, that ill-conducted adolescents are capable of acting generously in an emergency." The picture represented Buddy Rogers's last film as a contract star at Paramount and featured Mankiewicz's romantic interest, Frances Dee, as the spoiled daughter who makes amends for her selfishness at the end of the movie by marrying her long-suffering, indulgent, affluent godfather (played by the invariably endearing Charlie Ruggles), although he is more than twice her age.

The next clinker, *Sky Bride*, was scripted by the prestigious trio of Mankiewicz, Grover Jones, and Agnes Brand Leahy from a story by

Waldemar Young, the presenter at the Academy Awards banquet. The story is about a daredevil aviator (Richard Arlen) who loses his nerve after accidentally killing his buddy-rival in an aerial circus act and regains it in the final reel when he is obliged to fly once more in order to rescue his dead comrade's little brother (Bobby Coogan).

Sky Bride may well have been the picture on which Pop Jones, Grover's salty father, who was employed on the Paramount lot as an electrician but whose instincts were so well respected that directors like William Wellman would look up to him on the catwalk for his approval of a given take, delivered himself of a typically down-to-earth opinion. Strolling over from the side of the commissary where he ate with his fellow crew members to his son's table in the writers' section, he said, "Well, son, I read your script last night." "What did you think of it, Pop?" Grover dutifully inquired. "That I could tie a pencil to a cow's tit and she'd walk a better one!"

Mankiewicz's pet story of the period stemmed from his attendance at the 1928 Olympic Games in Amsterdam. It was the tale of a pathetic Albanian pole vaulter, and fellow sports buff Regis Toomey recalls that Joe's account of it first drew him to Mankiewicz as a friend. This anecdote and the wild events of the 1928 games provided a source of inspiration for Mankiewicz's most cherished film at Paramount, the antic *Million Dollar Legs.*

"That was the greatest shambles of any Olympic Games in history," Mankiewicz recalls. "The American team was quartered on the S.S. *Roosevelt,* with General Douglas MacArthur in charge. Half the squad was pissed, and we only won one race. It was absolutely insane. For example, we had no water polo team, so a makeshift one was devised with Johnny Weismuller suddenly deciding to play. Needless to say, it was a shambles.

"But I'll never forget the poor Albanian pole vaulter who trotted out with all the other vaulters wearing a pair of goatskin shorts. He held the Albanian vaulting record of ten feet, eight inches, and when he heard the qualifying jump was going to be eleven feet, six inches, he simply roared with laughter, as he assumed they were simply playing a great joke on him. He used to train like mad, this poor bastard, running around the track every day, and his interpreter couldn't make him understand the officials were serious about the qualifying height. Finally, a vaulter from Yale, Sabin Carr, tapped him on the shoulder and mimed, 'Watch me.' Carr took off in his sweat suit and went over the bar at twelve feet while the little Albanian just looked at him in dismay. Then his whole body just sagged, and he trudged off the field dragging his pole."

The opportunity to translate some of these memories into a film came when Paramount studio chief B. P. Schulberg sent out a staff memo saying that since the 1932 Olympics were to be held in Los Angeles, he urgently wanted a story idea built around the event. "As a junior writer," Mankiewicz relates, "I answered every one of those memos, including one for Rin Tin Tin, titled 'The Idiot Rin Tin Tin,' about a dog that hates its master, which never got made. I went to Schulberg, or wrote him a memo, arguing that if you wrote a straight story about the Olympics, the finish could only be Buddy Rogers and Dick Arlen competing in the big race so the winner can wind up with Mary Brian—or Buddy Rogers deliberately losing the race, knowing that Mary Brian really loves Dick Arlen. Rather than do a nonsensical film of that sort, I said I wanted to do a great satire on the Olympics and make it a real goofy comedy. So I wrote a story, *On Your Mark*, which they bought for $2,500. Herman was assigned to supervise it, and he assigned a writer named Henry Myers to write it with me. . . . Henry was considerably older than I—in those days everybody was older than I was—and a wonderful character, a marvelously daffy and very funny man."

Henry Myers recalls how he and Joe leaped their first hurdle. "The first thing Herman wanted us to do was overcome an objection of B. P. Schulberg's to the story's satiric treatment of royalty, for the main character, as conceived by Joe, was the king of a mythical kingdom, and B. P. felt that this would rub imperial theatergoers the wrong way, notably those of England. 'You see how Mr. Schulberg's mind operates,' said Herman sarcastically. So Joe and I went into conference and came up with the not too difficult solution of making the king a president and the mythical kingdom a mythical republic, which we named Klopstokia.[15] Then the three of us went to Mr. Schulberg's office to tell him the story in its new setting. Joe was a good talker, a

---

[15]Myers only perceived the comic sound of the name, which is a German literary "in joke" devised by Mankiewicz for the delectation of his father. Klopstock, an early German romantic poet, was one of the idols of the young Goethe, and in the famous love scene of Goethe's novel *The Sorrows of Werther,* the lovers, Werther and Charlotte, manifest their "elective affinity" by simultaneously uttering "Klopstock," whom they both revere.

very important asset for a writer, and we had him do the talking. This consisted of his telling the story in detail, which was unchanged except for king and kingdom now being president and republic and the latter having a name. (I still don't see why it had to be done like that—just describing the change would seem enough—but that's how things were done then in Hollywood.) B. P. listened attentively, and Joe told it glibly, although he stumbled a couple of times, saying, 'The king—I mean the president,' and Herman commented to B. P., 'You see the ingenious device the boys have invented to solve our problem!' Anyway, we got an O.K. and were told to go ahead and write it."

In Schulberg's solicitude for English sensibilities, he evidently overlooked the irony that Klopstokia is bankrupt and the president's cabinet busies itself devising comically nefarious means of overthrowing him. The satiric parallel to President Hoover in 1932 in the depths of the depression and to Schulberg himself, who was to be ousted shortly when Paramount went into bankruptcy, should have been obvious.

How the mischievous Myers and Mankiewicz failed to get the boot is equally surprising. James M. Cain recalls, "B. P. Schulberg shouted at the Paramount writers that they were all disloyal to the studio: so Henry Myers went down to his office and composed an honest-to-god Gregorian chant that concluded, 'Let us all give our loyalty and best co-operation / To Paramount Pictures. A Delaware Corporation.' Joe Mankiewicz dashed into the hall to announce that he had a new slogan: 'If it's a Paramount Picture, you don't have to stand in line.' "[16]

Million Dollar Legs is the predictably anarchic product of these pranksters—a sixty-four-minute blitz of outrageous sight gags, wild verbal jokes, and zany performances from a host of old-time comics, comprising what a recent *New Yorker* squib terms "one of the silliest and funniest pictures ever made."[17]

In his Paramount feature film debut, W. C. Fields is in top pugnacious form[18] as Klopstokia's literal "strong-man" president, who

---

[16]John Carmody, "James M. Cain at Twilight," *Potomac Magazine* section of the *Washington Post,* June 19, 1969.

[17]*New Yorker,* April 22, 1974, p. 24.

[18]Sample dialogue of Fields to his daughter over her suitor, Oakie:

ANGELA: But Father, isn't he handsome?
PRESIDENT: Yeah, but I'll fix that.

ANGELA: Father, they won't hurt him, will they?
PRESIDENT: Only for about two hours. Then they'll shoot him.

is obliged at each cabinet meeting to best his secretary of the treasury and chief rival (Hugh Herbert) at Indian wrestling in order to remain in office. From his first entrance in a ceremonial coach, doing a classic vaudeville balancing act with his top hat and cane, to his final contemptuous gag line about Los Angeles but alluding to booze[19] ("It's the climate. I've been drinking too much orange juice"), Fields is a belligerent delight.

The tenuous plot into which Mankiewicz and Myers crammed all their lunatic whimsies concerns the scheme of an American brush salesman, Tweeny (Jack Oakie, once again as the genial boob), to win the president's daughter (Susan Fleming) and save his own neck. His bright idea is to exploit the extraordinary Klopstokian athletic abilities to win the Olympics and pay off their $8 million national debt by his brush company's commercial sponsorship.

The cabinet's counterplot is to utilize the wiles of "the greatest woman spy of all time—the woman no man can resist," Mata Machree (Lyda Roberti), to demoralize the team. "I want to see this woman no man can resist," says one member of the cabinet's delegation paying court to Mata. "Sorry," Mata's butler replies, "Madame is only resisted from two to four in the afternoon." This is a sample of the writing team's best repartee. Even when the banter nosedives, it descends, for instance, to what critic Richard Watts described as "the best bad pun of the season," when Fields is informed by an aide that eight bogeymen are waiting for him outside. "Fine," Fields responds, "I'll take them for a bogey ride."

The conventionality of the Oakie-Fleming "love interest" is constantly undercut by such absurdist echoes of Dorothy Parker and Lewis Carroll as:

FLEMING: If you laid all the athletes in this country end to end, they'd stretch 484 miles.
OAKIE: How do you know?
FLEMING: We did it once.

---

[19]Fields's thirst for spirits was well known. According to Henry Myers, "Among the terms of Fields's agreement [with Paramount] was a promise by him to lay off liquor. He vowed that during the three or four weeks before shooting began he would spend every morning playing golf, and he did. A couple of Paramount executives saw him playing his daily eighteen holes. What they did not see . . . was that his golf bag was filled, not with golf clubs, but with beer."

FLEMING: All the girls in this country are called Angela and all the men are named George.

OAKIE: Why?

FLEMING: Why not?

One of Henry Myers's send-ups of movie romance was to write gibberish lyrics to the title song sung by Maurice Chevalier in Paramount's *One Hour with You*. In this nonsensical form, it is presented as Klopstokia's ancient national anthem, and performing it becomes Oakie's tongue-twisting test to win Fleming's hand.

Mankiewicz makes exaggerated use of the pathetic events of the 1928 games. The Klopstokian team engages in a wild nightclub brawl over the favors of Mata Machree and parades in for the opening-day ceremonies bandaged and on crutches. The Albanian pole vaulter's goatskin uniform inspired Mankiewicz to make the goat Klopstokia's national emblem, source of food, and chief commodity. At the games Klopstokia's pole vault entrant protests at the height of the bar: "I'll never make it. It's already three feet higher than I've ever jumped!" An arrow shot into his butt successfully propels him over the bar.

The controversy that still surrounds the authorship of *Million Dollar Legs* is attributable to the fact that Herman Mankiewicz, the film's uncredited producer, contributed to two previous Marx Brothers films at Paramount, *Monkey Business* and *Horse Feathers*, and the film's potpourri of satire, farce, and slapstick is reminiscent of the Marx Brothers' vehicles. The contention of Herman's authorship, as put forward by Pauline Kael in *The Citizen Kane Book*, is probably based on Herman's widow Sara's recollection of a script of *Million Dollar Legs* with Herman's penciled revisions.

Joe's memory is that "both Herman and Sara dismissed the picture by kidding about it at the preview, and I don't think Herman, throughout his entire life, mentioned *Million Dollar Legs* as something he'd been connected with."[20] Henry Myers, who also wrote for the

---

[20]Sara Mankiewicz offers this strong rebuttal: "Herman always boasted about *Million Dollar Legs* and regarded it as one of his happiest and most delightful pictures. He had a great deal to do with its writing and casting [Henry Myers claims Herman lured W. C. Fields away from MGM] and contributed enormously to its success. I had frankly forgotten Joe was connected with it, as I don't recall his being in on any of the story conferences, but he was certainly carrying out all of Herman's ideas of

Marx Brothers, stoutly maintains that "nobody but Joe Mankiewicz and I wrote a syllable of that script or created one of its ideas," although he surmises that after the film's first preview to a bewildered audience Herman composed the opening title for comic orientation:

> Klopstokia, a far-away country.
> Chief exports: goats and nuts.
> Chief imports: goats and nuts.
> Chief inhabitants: goats and nuts.

Myers appropriates a somewhat larger share of the credit by his contention that "stories can be worked out in conference, but actual writing went best as a solo job. So it was arranged that I was to do the first draft alone, turning it in to Herman a piece at a time so that he and Joe could work on that. And that's how it was done, except that I got into a very fruitful vein, and nothing had to be changed." To substantiate this claim, he recalls that "I had just written the opening shot . . . left it in my typewriter, and was on my way out to lunch when I heard Joe, in my office, roaring with laughter and calling to another writer, Gertrude Purcell, 'Hey, Gertie! Listen to Henry's fade-in!' and then reading it to her."

Mankiewicz calls this claim "absolutely absurd," insisting that he wrote together with Myers in the same office, "and, as a matter of fact, I was the one with a secretary, a Miss Strock, who was sixty years old. I called her Miss Strock, and she called me Joe. It's probably the only time in the history of filmmaking where a writer's secretary called him by his first name and he by her last name."

Despite the fact that the film received marvelous notices in New York and the Paramount Theatre was so jammed that Henry Myers was unable to get in on his first few attempts, the picture was not a national success and, according to Mankiewicz, was not even shown in many towns. Although Paramount was so enthusiastic about the script initially that they imposed the unusual stricture on the director, Edward Cline, of not making a single alteration, they evidently thought so little of the finished product that they used the same title, *Million Dollar Legs*, for a subsequent obscure Betty Grable musical

---

humor." It is unlikely that Sara Mankiewicz had any firsthand knowledge of the story conferences on *Million Dollar Legs*, but it is evident that she is Pauline Kael's source in perpetuating the myth of Herman's authorship of the film in *The Citizen Kane Book* (Atlantic–Little, Brown, 1971).

(1939), for which it was doubtless more appropriate.

"I don't think *Million Dollar Legs* would ever have come to public notice and acquired its status as a classic today," says Mankiewicz, "had it not been for the championship of Man Ray, the famous photographer, in Paris. His Surrealist group discovered it, and it became the terribly 'in' thing at a theater on the Left Bank where it ran for two or three years."[21]

In a slightly facetious autobiographical article, contributed in 1936 to his college fraternity's publication, *The Deltan*, Mankiewicz makes the casual reference that following *Million Dollar Legs*, "I spent a short time in a sanitarium, and returned to write *If I Had a Million.*"

This oblique reference is explained by William Wright, Joe's friend and fellow worker at Paramount, with whom, in 1932, he rented a small house on Palm Drive in Beverly Hills, maintained by a devoted German housekeeper. Both young men were involved in serious courtships—Wright with his future German wife, Greta, with whom he had fallen in love during the Olympics, and Joe with the captivating Paramount starlet Frances Dee. Wright describes the idyllic weekends the couples spent in Laguna Beach before the area was developed and the strand packed with bathers. Wright speaks of their avid rock climbing in deserted Three Arch Bay, where they discovered a pool in a cave with octopuses and sea anemones. Driving along the highway in the open roadster with Bill and Greta in the rumble seat, Joe would make jokes with Greta in German between the unison songfests of the joyous quartet.

While Mankiewicz provided a great Prohibition-era liquor shower for Wright and served as best man at his friend's wedding, he was planning his own honeymoon with Frances—a 1933 summer tour of New England that they carefully mapped out from tour guides and brochures. The culmination of this six-month courtship was that about a week before they were to be married, Mankiewicz was shocked to learn that Frances Dee had eloped with Joel McCrea, her handsome but placid costar during her loan-out to MGM, and that they had

---

[21]In his study *The Art of W. C. Fields* (Allen & Unwin Ltd., 1968), the noted film scholar William K. Everson acknowledges that "the film was short enough and sufficiently zany and unpredictable to be constantly entertaining." However, he rejects such terms for it as "a comic masterpiece" and "a piece of 'American dadaism,' " which strike him as "a perfect example of how a reputation can be inflated."

embarked on the very itinerary that she and Joe had so minutely planned.

"Joe suffered an illness shortly after she broke up with him," Wright recalls. "He began to run a fever and went to the hospital, where they indicated he was close to a partial nervous breakdown." On his return to the social swim, Joe made light of his private grief. He regaled friends by spreading David O. Selznick's story that Frances Dee had confided that she had chosen McCrea when she came to the realization that her attraction to Mankiewicz was purely physical, while McCrea appealed to her intellectually.

Some time later Mankiewicz confessed to an intimate that Frances Dee "was the great love of his life" and that there had been a romantic epilogue to their split-up. "He said he was driving through Coldwater Canyon when a car suddenly zoomed past him and the girl who was driving waved to him and pulled up at the side of the road. He pulled up behind her car, walked up, and discovered it was Frances Dee. They looked at each other for a moment, and she suddenly reached out and embraced him passionately, kissed him, and then threw her car into gear and zoomed away. . . . Joe was a master at telling stories in which he usually emerged rather triumphant, so sometimes you had to try to separate reality from his fertile imagination, but I believed that one, though Joel [McCrea] may not.[22] . . . It [Dee's treatment of him] also seemed to me, at times, to account for Joe's dealings with women, which I often considered somewhat unscrupulous."

Other acquaintances have speculated that the event forged Mankiewicz's private resolve that he would never again be abandoned by a woman. In the future he would be the first one to break off, even when the woman was still enamored, which appears to have been the pattern of his many subsequent romances.

If Frances Dee's rejection was a depressing turnabout, the en-

---

[22]Mankiewicz says the story of McCrea and Dee using the exact itinerary of the New England honeymoon he had plotted with her "may have been apocryphal. I may have made that up. It may be true. The Selznick story *is* true." As to his original story of their subsequent embrace in Coldwater Canyon, Mankiewicz maintains it never occurred, terming the tale "ridiculous." "Frances would have been incapable of that," he asserts. "The only time I ever saw Frances Dee after she married Joel McCrea was when I ran into them on a train going across the country, and they were both very friendly."

trance of the redoubtable W. C. Fields into Mankiewicz's office, carrying six illustrated volumes of Audubon's *Birds of America* under his
arm and extending a $50 bill, was a pleasant, though unexpected,
surprise. Mankiewicz explains his amazement at the parsimonious
Fields forcing money on him by stating that Fields "was a horror
. . . in some ways, one of the meanest human beings who ever lived.
. . . Bill Fields and Wallace Beery were probably the only two major
stars who were never known to leave a tip at the Paramount commissary
and who never contributed to the Motion Picture Relief Fund or any
other charity. Their attitude was 'Fuck 'em. Let them make it on their
own.' Bill came up the hard way, and it made him bitter. Other people
come up the hard way, and when they get an enormous amount of
success and money, they suddenly expand and become generous.

"Don't forget, show business doesn't breed only hearts of gold. It
breeds hearts of shit too. For example, in a famous episode, Greg La
Cava [a famed director in the thirties], who also drank a lot, ran into
Bill one night at a café and said, 'Congratulate me. I've just signed a
new five-year deal at RKO.' And Fields said, "Why, you can't go to
work for RKO. The goddamned place is run by Jews!' To which La
Cava remonstrated, 'What are you talking about? George Schaefer is
the head of RKO and he's a Catholic!' To which Fields replied, 'Catholics are the worst kind of Jews!'[23] So you see, it wasn't that he hated
Jews, he just *hated.*

"Yet he had this incredible punctiliousness about material that is
one of the great attributes of the old-time vaudevillian. . . . Material
to the vaudevillian was his bread and butter. Because when he went out
on the road for a year and a half to play the Pantages circuit or the great
Keith Orpheum circuit, he showed up in some town, and he had his
jokes. So if some fella had been in town three days before him doing
the same jokes, he was out of work, he was dead. And so jokes or
'material' was never stolen, and you didn't louse up another man's act.

"Fields was absolutely fanatic on this subject, and this was after
I'd written an episode ["Rollo and the Roadhogs"] especially for him
and Alison Skipworth in *If I Had a Million.* So he breezes in and says
to me, 'Say, Joe, I'd like to buy that material.' I said, 'What material,

[23]In Howard Dietz's memoir, *Dancing in the Dark* (Quadrangle / New York
Times, 1974), he attributes the story to Fields's warning his Follies assistant, Shorty,
of the perils of RKO.

Bill?' And he says, 'That "My little magpie, my little chickadee, my little tomtit" that you wrote for Skipworth and me.' I replied, 'Well, Bill, you don't have to buy that because that belongs to Paramount.' And he said, 'I know that 'cause my lawyer says I don't have to buy it from you, but I'd feel better if I did, because then I'd know it was mine.' "[24]

The diminutive bird endearments are addressed by Fields to the distinctly nondiminutive Skipworth. They play two retired vaudevillians (he had a juggling act, as did Fields, while she had a bird act) who eke out a living by running a Los Angeles tea shop.[25] Although Mankiewicz's name is buried in the list of eighteen writers credited to the multi-episode, all-star production, "Roadhogs" is a solo effort, in contrast to his collaboration on the less successful final sketch, "The Three Marines." In the latter episode Jack Oakie and Gary Cooper as marines barter their million-dollar check for $10 to the owner of a hamburger stand, losing in one stroke their fortune and the blonde they desire.

In collaboration with his mentors, Jones and McNutt, Mankiewicz devised *If I Had a Million*'s motivating, central framing story of a dying millionaire (Richard Bennett) so infuriated by the patent avarice of his predatory heirs that he capriciously decides to bequeath million-dollar legacies to eight strangers selected at random from the telephone directory with the use of a dropper from one of his medicine bottles. How each of the recipients makes use of the unexpected legacy creates the eight sober or funny, ironic vignettes.

Mankiewicz also wrote the story for the delectable episode "The China Shop," with henpecked Charlie Ruggles turning into a literal bull in a china shop; as well as "The Streetwalker," in which Wynne Gibson uses her newfound wealth for the novelty of sleeping in a first-class hotel bed alone; and "The Forger," starring George Raft as a criminal on the lam, unable to cash his check. The creation of this

---

[24]As usual, Fields got his money's worth, because he used the salutations as part of his repertoire and as the title of his 1939 Western spoof for Universal, *My Little Chickadee*, playing opposite another former Paramount star, Mae West.

[25]One of Mankiewicz's favorite weekend diversions was to drive over to the then sparsely populated San Fernando Valley, across the Hollywood Hills, where many vaudeville families had quartered in the hope of breaking into the entertainment medium that had supplanted theirs. In order to maintain their acts in the event of a vaudeville revival, and to pass on their craft to their children, they devoted their weekends to practicing in their backyards. The vista of swarms of jugglers, acrobats, and the like was a spectacle that appealed to Mankiewicz's delight in the theatrical.

last vignette was the occasion for Joe's first association with Oliver H. P. Garrett, with whom he was teamed two years later to write the film that launched Mankiewicz at MGM, *Manhattan Melodrama.*

In both "The China Shop" and "Rollo and the Roadhogs" our pleasure at the outbreak of comic violence is based on the sure-fire appeal of watching the worm turn and injustice to an underdog rectified on a grand scale. In "Rollo" Fields and Skipworth are victimized when the brand-new roadster they have scrimped and saved for is demolished by a reckless driver. With their million-dollar check the couple is able to mount a massive vendetta against reckless drivers by hiring a motorized armada of jalopy drivers to wreck any vehicular offender.

William K. Everson's assessment that Norman Taurog's direction of the successive auto wrecks was too repetitive and gentle to give the episode "the vicious bite it needs" may be just. Nevertheless, he calls the sketch "famous" and concedes the "delightful, demoniacal inspiration of the sequence."[26]

Except for Fields's $50 gratuity and the enthusiastic recognition of Bud Lighton, Mankiewicz felt that his contribution to *If I Had a Million* was lost in a sea of names. The omnibus film was eventually released by Paramount as a second feature in many cities, indicative of the studio's low estimate of its commercial potential.

Mankiewicz is vague about the circumstances that led to the dismissal of his bosses, B. P. Schulberg and Jesse Lasky, but it is likely that their departure coincided with Paramount's 1932 bankruptcy. Mankiewicz had, however, facetiously forecast their downfall in a parody lyric to the Southern Cal rallying song, "Fight on for USC," written for the amusement of his office mates.

> Fight on for old B. P.
> And Zukor, too,
> And Wrig-a-lee.[27]

---

[26]Everson, *The Art of W. C. Fields,* p. 75.
[27]The Wrigley family held a considerable block of Paramount stock at the time. It was selling for $3 a share.

Old Paramount
Is down to three
Or maybe two
Or maybe one
Or maybe none.
Fight on!

How Mankiewicz came to be "loaned out" to RKO to write his next two films is recalled differently by the principals concerned. Henry Myers contends that he and Joe were both back in New York with Myers resuming his playwriting career and Joe hankering to get back into pictures.[28] Myers says that Joe phoned to say that Adeline Schulberg, the wife-turned-agent of Paramount's dethroned production chief, had told him she could sell Mankiewicz and Myers as a team because of the success of their collaboration on *Million Dollar Legs* and that she could get them the writing assignment for a new film at RKO for the comedy team of Wheeler and Woolsey.

Sam Jaffe, who had shifted to RKO as production manager under David O. Selznick and was assigned to produce the Wheeler and Woolsey vehicle, believes that he had first signed Henry Myers to write the project and only took on Joe after a typically hectoring phone call from Herman, who "in language profane and obscene" insisted that Myers alone was worthless and that Joe's talents were essential.

Mankiewicz says the situation was precisely the reverse. As with *Million Dollar Legs,* he was the one commissioned (for $2,000) to write an original story, *In the Red,* on which *Diplomaniacs* (the eventual title of the Wheeler-Woolsey musical comedy) is based, and that he requested Henry Myers as his collaborator on the screenplay.

Mankiewicz's documents substantiate his claim. They also reveal that while in June 1932 RKO offered a handsome year's contract of $500 a week from July 1932 to July 1933, it was not until November 1932 that Paramount agreed to the loan-out. The studio's groundless concern was that Mankiewicz might in some way have plagiarized his story from a contemplated Marx Brothers script, *Cracked Ice.* "I had

---

[28]Chester Erskine, then a leading figure in the Broadway theater as a director, playwright, and head of the prestigious Frohman Company, recalls that on a visit to New York, Mankiewicz approached him about work in the theater, and Erskine discouraged him and advised him to return to the movies.

a big fight with Paramount and quit," says Mankiewicz. "They demanded I show them my treatment or tell them what my story was. I called a lawyer immediately and outlined my original story, *In the Red.*" In December 1932 the studio was mollifed but still suspicious, writing that although "Paramount does not consider it an infringement on *Cracked Ice,* we still want to make a comparison of *In the Red* when the script is completed, so that any incidental similarity between the two may be avoided."

Paramount need not have been overly concerned. Bert Wheeler and Robert Woolsey, RKO's resident comedy team whose fourteenth movie this was, were not in the same zany league with the Marx Brothers, and *Diplomaniacs* shows only sporadic flashes of the inspired lunacy Mankiewicz and Myers brought to *Million Dollar Legs.*

Just as their earlier work had as its topical pretext and culmination the 1932 Olympic Games in Los Angeles, *Diplomaniacs* makes mockery of the peacekeeping efforts of the League of Nations. Once again a title card to the conference segment clues us in. It reads: "Geneva —where the nations of the world fight over peace." The Peace Conference in Geneva, to which the useless barbers, Wheeler and Woolsey, are sent as delegates of the disenfranchised American Indians, is depicted as a slapstick chaos of paper-throwing, with one delegate sharpening his sword while the presiding officer wields a machine gun from the rostrum.

A group of nefarious munitions makers, led by Louis Calhern, have pursued the incompetent diplomats, Wheeler and Woolsey, to the conference, intending to steal their documents and funds. Their more massive sabotage scheme is seemingly thwarted when the bomb they detonate converts the soot-stained conference delegates into a unified, blackface minstrel chorus singing, "Are You Ready for Judgment Day?" The conspirators are themselves blown to kingdom come by their own new weapon, an exploding bullet. However, the jubilation is short-lived. Wheeler and Woolsey, returning in anticipated triumph to the Indian reservation, are preceded by a headline proclaiming "WAR DECLARED" and, upon arrival, are inducted, handed rifles, and trooped off to serve.

Aside from such novelties as a conventional shipboard love duet turned into a wrestling match between Wheeler and the ingenue, and the expansion, by means of bread spitballs, of Wheeler's familiar vaudeville *lazzo* of wiping his eyes with a sandwich and eating his handkerchief, the only unforgettable bits are the cellophane-wrapped cuties extruded from a pneumatic tube in the ship's kitchen. "One vamp on rye," orders the chef, and a girl drops out of the chute. "See," he boasts, "untouched by human hands," which is as felicitous as a steward's compliment to Calhern on his apt attire: "In that suit you can conspire freely."

The film's femme fatale, Fifi (Phyllis Barry), queen bee of a Parisian apache club, the Dead Rat, alluringly invites, "Kiss me, fool," before emitting a smoke screen from her fiery lungs, but she is not a worthy successor to Lyda Roberti's spectacular Mata Machree in *Million Dollar Legs*.

Wheeler often commented that his films with Woolsey "were pretty bad, but they all made money."[29] Mankiewicz was less philosophical. According to his sister-in-law, on the return ferry ride to San Diego after a disastrous preview of the film in Coronado, he cried, "I'm ruined. This is the end of me," and made a determined attempt to jump overboard until he was restrained.[30]

Diplomaniacs' producer, Sam Jaffe, while admitting the film was "no great success" and that Wheeler and Woolsey were "mediocre talents," thought the team had written "a good script" and that it was "a funny picture, but ahead of its time."[31] Jaffe was evidently satisfied enough with Joe's writing talent to assign him as sole author of his next film, *Emergency Call*, an ambulance vehicle for the often teamed William Boyd (the young doctor) and William Gargan (his buddy, the ambulance driver).

The RKO publicity blurb terms *Emergency Call* an exposé of "America's latest racket—organized 'accident' graft," but the plot summary suggests a rather old-hat round of retaliatory homicides enliv-

---

[29]Leonard Maltin, *Movie Comedy Teams*, Signet Books/New American Library, 1970, p. 86.
[30]Mankiewicz denies the incident, claiming the account is a fabrication of Sara's.
[31]Leonard Maltin radically revised his view of *Diplomaniacs*. Writing in 1970, in *Movie Comedy Teams*, he refers to the film's "story by a decidedly pre–*All About Eve* Joseph L. Mankiewicz." In his program notes for the comprehensive American Film Comedy series, which he assembled for the Museum of Modern Art in 1976, Maltin writes of "a superb script by Joseph L. Mankiewicz and Henry Myers. . . . It is certainly eclipsed by [their] more famous screenplay for *Million Dollar Legs* (1932), but it ranks as an equally worthy comic achievement. . . . *Diplomaniacs* is one of the 1930s' most endearing—yet forgotten—excursions into the realm of comic lunacy."

ened by Mankiewicz's humorous touches. These felicities by Mankiewicz must be taken on faith because the film has vanished, although as a run-of-the-mill genre picture its loss is less than calamitous.

Following his two-picture stint at RKO, Mankiewicz returned to Paramount, under a new administration (although in receivership), to write what proved to be his last two films for his Hollywood alma mater. The first, *Too Much Harmony,* was a meandering and dreary musical for Bing Crosby, the crooner he idolized and mimicked. While *The Times* (London) noted that the picture broke the film musical convention of relegating the supporting cast (Oakie, Gallagher, Lilyan Tashman, and Harry Green) to a "respectful chorus" for the leading man and woman by giving the featured players more prominence, *Variety* termed *Too Much Harmony* "a backstage story without even the suggestion of a new idea." The shift in emphasis from the romantic leads to the supporting comics may have been due, in part, to the negligible talents of the leading lady, Judith Allen, about whom the *Variety* critic wrote "[she was] picked for looks only and that's all she delivers."

Mankiewicz told an interviewer[32] that on the morning the film was to begin shooting, he, director Eddie Sutherland, and producer William LeBaron were summoned to the office of Emanuel Cohen, Paramount's new production chief, to be informed that while the script was "wonderful," its filming would have to be halted. When Mankiewicz asked why, Cohen replied, "You have made one terrible mistake. You have Crosby falling in love with the girl. The public will never accept that. You must make the girl fall in love with him!" The solution was to have Jack Oakie, Judith Allen's swain, impersonate a gullible tycoon to lure away Lilyan Tashman, Crosby's gold-digging fiancée. Thus the engaged crooner is freed for a final domestic duet with his badly dubbed costar, his manly virtue intact for not having made the first advances. The picture's dialogue is attributed to Harry Ruskin, with Mankiewicz getting the major "scenario" credit. However, such lines as the characterization of Oakie ("If naïveté were sex appeal, he'd be Mae West") or a drunken blonde at a party incongruously inquiring of amorous couples, "Would you like to play a little bridge?" sound unmistakably like Mankiewicz's.

In sum, Mankiewicz's first foray into the comedy of backstage mores, prior to *All About Eve,* is derived strictly from movie formulas.

---

[32]Thomas M. Pryor, *New York Times,* May 24, 1950.

Today the film is chiefly notable for its vulgar production numbers, which include a line of chorus girls transformed by lighting to black women in "Black Moonlight," a song that features some wonderfully fatuous lyrics by Sam Coslow, such as "Just like me, you're faded, jaded, and degraded too," and "Madly I await you / Even though I hate you." For the finale, "Buckin' the Wind," the lovelies have their tops, skirts, and panties blown off by the gale, only to be prudishly covered by a banner titled "Censored."

Mankiewicz recalls he lent an uncredited hand to his writer friend Claude Binyon on another Crosby musical of 1933, *College Humor*, but his major task for Paramount was an all-star production of *Alice in Wonderland*, written, or rather edited, in story-board collaboration with the noted scenic designer William Cameron Menzies. (The two-volume mimeographed script, illustrated in its left margin with Menzies's line drawings of every cut, is a great and rare collectors' item, and Mankiewicz cherishes his bound copy.)

The film itself is a generally tedious illustration of the classic Carroll tales, unredeemed by the fidelity to the Carroll text, lavish physical production, or novel special effects. Most of the film's plodding, episodic quality stems from cramming selections from both *Alice in Wonderland* and *Through the Looking Glass* into one film.

It appears as though Paramount wanted to include nearly all of the eccentric characters Alice encounters in both novels to provide roles for a constellation of stars and its entire roster of fine character actors. The irony is that the encasing character masks and costumes designed by Menzies almost totally disguise the famous faces, so all we are left with, by and large, are a couple of distinctive voices, like Cary Grant's emanating from his Mock Turtle casing.

The truth is that the unwieldy number of scenes and characters stems from the studio head's ignorance of the source material. Mankiewicz recalls asking at the outset, "Mr. Cohen, which do you want to do—*Alice in Wonderland* or *Through the Looking Glass?* Because you can't do them both in one film." Cohen responded, "We own them both. We're going to do them both."

"The result was a disaster, but a well-intentioned disaster," is Mankiewicz's judgment of the film. "The costumes and the headpieces were so heavy that the actors couldn't carry them, so they had doubles walking through all the master or long shots. But it had a fantastic cast —just everybody: Cary Grant, Gary Cooper as the White Knight,

Richard Arlen as the Cheshire Cat, W. C. Fields as Humpty Dumpty, Jack Oakie as Tweedledum, Alison Skipworth as the Duchess, and Edna May Oliver as the Red Queen, and many others. A girl named Charlotte Henry played Alice, but I remember it as the first time I met Ida Lupino. She was a little girl of sixteen who had just come over from England to Hollywood." (Mankiewicz had developed a prescient eye for screen talent. Paramount did sign Lupino, but found her "too sexy for Alice.")[33]

The discontinuity of *Alice*'s narrative and the bewildering number of characters introduced and then dropped, until they are granted a brief reprise at the banquet finale, become progressively tedious, with only the guessing game of who's who left to sustain interest. Only two performances remain in the memory—W. C. Fields relishing the absurdist dialogue of his turn in a gigantic eggshell head as Humpty Dumpty and Gary Cooper, a stalwart in Westerns, cast against type as the bald and moustached White Knight, a dotard who keeps falling off his horse.

Toward the end of Mankiewicz's Paramount tenure, his skills as a story sleuth and script doctor were pressed into service by an anxious management. This time he was sent for by Emanuel Cohen, the new studio head, and Merritt Hulburd, a former editor of the *Saturday Evening Post,* who was in charge of the studio's writers. As Mankiewicz relates it, they said, " 'Joe, you gotta help us.' They were in total panic. Their story was that this absolute mad man, [Josef] von Sternberg, had just put out the script for his latest Dietrich vehicle, *The Scarlet Empress,* with no punctuation marks or capital letters, so there was no way of telling where one sentence ended and another began. I asked, 'Why does he do that?' and Merritt replied, 'Nobody knows why; this is the way he wanted the script, and all the departments are going crazy, as no one can read it. Now, we know that you know Joe and that you're friendly with him.' (Which I was. I knew him slightly, and he rather liked me.) 'As we are executives, naturally we can't approach him. Would you, as a favor to us, go to von Sternberg and get his permission to punctuate one copy of the script so we can know what the hell the picture is about?' I said, 'All right. Of course.' So they gave me a copy of the script. It was utter gibberish, like e. e. cummings, only it was an entire motion picture script. . . .

[33]David Shipman, *The Great Movie Stars: The Golden Years,* Hamlyn, 1970.

"I went to von Sternberg's office. In the outer office he had a big blackboard where he had chalked, 'Opus # 1 *(The Salvation Hunters),*' 'Opus # 2 (*The Exquisite Sinner*—Sabotaged by Thalberg),' and so on. The man regarded himself as a legend in his own time. . . . He greeted me affably, and I frankly told him why I had been sent to him. I told him I had tried to read the script, and that although I was very good at puzzles, it was impossible. I remonstrated that the property men, wardrobe people, and cutters had to read this, and they were used to reading English.

"He shook his head, saying, 'That is utter nonsense. No one should have to be able to read this script. Tell me, when you look at an artist's palette, do you see the finished painting? He tapped the script, and said, 'These are my paints and with these paints I will paint the picture upon the screen.' (That was the way he talked.) I placated him by saying, 'You're probably absolutely right, but as a favor to the more illiterate people on the lot, would you let me punctuate the script? I think I can figure it out.' He said, 'Certainly, my boy. Go ahead, if they feel they need such a thing.' I asked, 'What about the actors?' He replied, 'Ah, the actors. It is most important for them that there's no punctuation. I don't want any actor to come on stage with a preconceived notion of how to read the lines. I want them to learn the words. I will tell them how to say them.' (Which, indeed, he used to do. Over and over and over—with Marlene particularly. He'd have her stress every word in a sentence and have her do it fifty times so he would have every conceivable reading.)

"As I started out of the office, he said, 'By the way, Joe, if you should feel so inclined, some of the speeches need a little polishing, and I would appreciate you polishing them. Mind you, I don't want the speeches lengthened or shortened. I want you to lift the speeches, polish them, and put them back in.' So I went down to my office and punctuated the bloody script, which took me three hours. Then I started to put in little phrases here and there. For example, I changed 'This Russia' to 'This imperishable Russia' for a little irony. [*The Scarlet Empress* concerned the reign of Catherine the Great.] Around lunch time, I said, 'What the hell am I doing this for? I'm not being paid to work on Josef von Sternberg's script.' So I sent the punctuated script, with a few changes, down to Merritt Hulburd's office.

"That night, at dinner, I got a phone call from von Sternberg. He said, 'I have been reading over the changes that you've made in some of the scenes, and I must say that while they told me you were a talented young man, I had no idea you were *that* talented. As a matter of fact, your work is so good, I intend to use several words of it,' and he's written that in his book [*Fun in a Chinese Laundry*]."[34]

William Wright, Joe's housemate at the time, suggests that Mankiewicz's labors occupied considerably more than one day's effort. Rather, Wright recalls, "It was Joe's biggest assignment to date. I remember he was delighted with it and spent a lot of time boning up on the history of the period. When von Sternberg said he was quite pleased with it and was going to use a few words of it, Joe was devastated, but he soon turned it to humorous account. He knew von Sternberg was an idiosyncratic man."

Turning painful experiences "to humorous account" is Mankiewicz's creatively productive defense. Wright, however, found some tangible consolation for Joe. "I saw a beautiful girl at the Pacific Southwest Tennis Tournament at the L.A. Tennis Club. So when I came back home, I said to Joe, 'You're looking for a gal. Well, I saw a beauty today—a New York stage actress named Elizabeth Young.' "

---

[34]Von Sternberg implies that what Mankiewicz took to be a high-handed put-down was intended as a compliment. He refers to Mankiewicz's revisions as work he "had been commissioned to do for me" and sarcastically notes, "That was, of course, before the complaining writer became a director who would not tolerate any interference" (*Fun in a Chinese Laundry*, Macmillan, 1965, p. 220).

"Ars gratia artis, my arse"
(Joe Mankiewicz, among others)

*E*LIZABETH YOUNG WAS NOT ONLY A FETCHINGLY PRETTY BRU-
nette in the Frances Dee mold but a breed apart from the average
starlet. (She had just completed a small but notable role as the secretly
affianced, giggling confidante to Greta Garbo in *Queen Christina*
[1933].) Elizabeth Young was an authentic New York socialite. Her
mother was a von Schermerhorn from Pottsville, Pennsylvania, and her
father was a prominent New York judge.

Although Bill Wright's commendation was a spur, it was inevitable that Elizabeth and Joe would make each other's acquaintance since
they were both members of the film colony's young smart set. This
crowd gathered for the high-toned parties of the week and intermingled
during weekends of racing, casino gambling, and nightclubbing at the
resort town of Agua Caliente, near the Mexican border.

Even among these social nobs, Elizabeth was a classy standout.
Winning her hand was something of a social conquest for a "Jewish
boy" with a Polish name. Not that Elizabeth was bigoted, for, according to Mankiewicz, "her social register background affected her not at
all," but her von Schermerhorn mother was sternly opposed.

Mankiewicz's confidence may have been bolstered by the hefty
salary ($750 a week) he was drawing under his new affiliation as a writer
at the town's most prestigious film factory, MGM. An assignment from
his early Paramount patron, David O. Selznick, to collaborate with

Oliver H. P. Garrett on writing *Manhattan Melodrama* came as a distinct reprieve, for Joe, on previous occasions in 1933, had managed to make himself *persona non grata* on the Metro lot.

The chain of misfortune began with a move designed to increase Mankiewicz's price as a screenwriter. Myron Selznick, Joe's agent, had arranged a loan-out from Paramount on a ten-week guarantee deal with Sam Marx, the head of MGM's story department. Mankiewicz arrived at the Culver City lot on a Saturday, the end of the six-day work week then in force, and Marx dispatched him to producer Harry Rapf, "a tremendous power on the lot," telling Joe how lucky he was to start with such a terrific assignment. Rapf was celebrated both for his discovery of Joan Crawford in a Broadway chorus line and for a nose so huge it was said to keep his lower parts dry while he was showering. He told Mankiewicz that he was going to do a great revue called *The Hollywood Party* and that his director, the esteemed Edmund Goulding, would outline the story they wanted Joe to script. "Goulding was a tremendous ham," says Mankiewicz, "and he started by telling me, 'We fade in on the earth, and we pull back and it's spinning on Karl Dane's finger, which leads into a sketch between Dane and his partner. Then Joan Crawford sings "Blue Diamond" and Jean Harlow croaks "Make Me a Star." ' All of this was gibberish to me, and as I sat there listening, I thought, 'They're kidding me. This is a put-on.' When Goulding finished, I laughed and said, 'O.K., fellows, you've had your fun. Now tell me what the story is.' Rapf, who was a very explosive man, got up and screamed at me, 'Get out, you fake. They told me you were a good writer. Get out, you don't know your business,' as he drove me from his office. I went back to Sam Marx and told him what had happened. He said, 'Oh boy, this is terrible. You'd better go have lunch.' "

Lunch proved equally disastrous, thanks to the costly custom at the Metro writers' table of rolling three caged dice for the check, with the man rolling the lowest obliged to pick up the tab for the entire table. To add to his morning's misery, Joe rolled a four and got stuck for his colleagues' lunches, a hefty bill that he could ill afford.

Mankiewicz trudged back to Sam Marx's office to find that Harry Rapf had gone for the day and that he was to report again for assignment on Monday morning. On Monday Marx announced, "You're the luckiest guy who ever lived because David Selznick wants you!" Joe's luck was not in evidence at lunch when he rolled low again and had to pay an even larger check for the jammed Monday table. The Selznick project turned out to be a vehicle, titled *Meet the Baron,* "for the greatest radio entertainer in America, Jack Pearl." When Selznick finished outlining Norman Krasna's original story, Joe simply declared, "David, I don't want to do it."[1]

When Mankiewicz returned to the story department, Sam Marx regretfully informed him that Harry Rapf was adamant about not giving him a second chance and, since RKO wanted him for a second picture, Metro was going to recoup its ten-week option by loaning him out to do *Emergency Call.*

Having completed this programmer (the trade term for a routine feature of only moderate appeal, likely to form the second half of a double bill), Mankiewicz once more reported to Marx, who exclaimed, "I don't know what star you live under, but Harry Rapf has forgiven you, and if you go up to his office, he's got another story for you." After losing for the third time running with the writers' table dice, Joe must have had a premonition of what was to follow. When Rapf, after sarcastically remarking, "I hope this story will satisfy you," opened with Selznick's exact phrase, "I've hired the greatest radio entertainer in America," to describe Ed Wynn, Mankiewicz's heart sank. Rapf asked his director, Charles ("Chuck") Riesner, to outline the story of *The Chief.* The wretched story was scarcely aided by the teller, for Riesner had a severe asthmatic condition from being gassed in World War I and emitted an odd noise every time he began to speak, continually causing Mankiewicz to jump.

"Rapf, Riesner, and I went across the bridge [connecting the producers' offices to screening rooms] to see an early film Wynn had made in Astoria [an early sound stage facility in New York City], and

---

[1]Mankiewicz has truncated the story of his involvement with *Meet the Baron.* George Seaton *(Miracle on 34th Street)* says that when he was a fledgling of twenty-one, his first writing opportunity came about as a result of the scripting crisis on *Meet the Baron.* In August 1933 young Seaton was summoned to Selznick's office to confront the imposing writing pool of Herman and Joe Mankiewicz, Norman Krasna, Allen Rivkin, P. J. Wolfson, Jack Pearl with his gag writers, and the film's director, Walter Lang. This team had been stymied for two weeks trying to motivate the character of Baron Munchausen (Jack Pearl), and Seaton turned up the next day with two possible approaches. Herman Mankiewicz approved these, and Seaton was put to work with Krasna rewriting the story. Joe said to Seaton after the meeting, "The only reason you solved the problem was that you didn't know how difficult it was." Seaton says that it has taken him the forty intervening years to realize just how wise Joe's perception was.

I simply couldn't stand Ed Wynn," says Mankiewicz. "He had no shape and looked rather like a bowl of Jell-O that had gone mad. I just left the dark projection room, walked off the lot, and went to Europe. When I came back, that's when David Selznick, the only man at MGM, besides Thalberg, powerful enough to hire me in spite of Rapf's hostility, asked me to do *Manhattan Melodrama.*"[2]

On his return, Joe was to discover that his judgment had been borne out. The three assignments he had turned down proved to be "three of the biggest flops MGM ever made."[3] Instead of starting behind the eight ball by writing a certain flop, Mankiewicz was canny enough to hold out for a feature that promised and later proved to be a commercial success. This prescient selectivity should be taken into account with Mankiewicz's statement that he was simply luckier than Herman in having hits at the opportune moments of contract expirations.

By odd coincidence, the plot of *Manhattan Melodrama,* derived from a story by Arthur Caesar titled "Three Men," when divorced of its crime and punishment trappings, can be read as a parable of the two Mankiewicz brothers—one sibling a reckless gambler who destroys himself but paves the path for the other's conscientious climb to professional eminence and power.[4]

Joe had already had a foretaste of his brother's profligacy. In 1932 Joe had prudently put aside $5,000 in convertible annuity bonds, telling his housemate, William Wright, "If I had a few more of these, no matter what happened to me out here I could go back to Germany and live like a king." When, some years later, Wright asked what had happened to these bonds, Joe replied, "Hell, Herman got those before the year was out." At Metro, where Herman was working in an office

---

[2]Mankiewicz neglects to mention that between this abortive stint at MGM and *Manhattan Melodrama* he returned to Paramount to complete his contract by writing *Too Much Harmony* and *Alice in Wonderland.*

[3]Mankiewicz reports that *Hollywood Party* was one of the few MGM feature films ever cut up and released as a series of shorts. According to Mankiewicz, this measure was adopted after producer Rapf had taken the full-length film for a preview in San Bernardino, only to have the theater manager angrily admonish him after the screening, "Don't you ever bring your rushes up here again."

[4]In the original ending of the script, the governor's (William Powell) resignation is so vehemently protested that he is obliged by the clamor of the populace to return to office. In the film Powell terminates his political career by departing the capital, reunited with Loy.

far more handsome than Joe's—on the days when he made it to the studio—Joe was obliged to witness the pathetic weekly spectacle of Herman being accompanied on Wednesdays to the bank by a contingent of creditors to whom he owed gambling debts that devoured at least half of his paycheck.

With the passage of forty years and scores of intervening imitations, *Manhattan Melodrama* now seems as blatantly contrived as its title—a fusion of the familiar triangular romance, though without jealousy between the male suitors, and "a favorite Depression plot"[5] of two ghetto children whose paths divide in adulthood between lives of vice and virtue. As predictable as the plot is from the first reel, Garrett and Mankiewicz took pains to achieve novelty in the form of the unlikely obeisance made by the renegade to authority figures and morality. Thus young Blackie's (Mickey Rooney) vengeful threat, "Someday I'll get even with dirty, rotten cops," is belied by the behavior of the mature Blackie (Clark Gable), who lends unstinting encouragement to the racket-busting campaign for district attorney of his boyhood chum and coadopted orphan, Jim Wade (William Powell).

This esteem for the law enforcer by the law breaker is taken to the ludicrous extreme of abnegation when Blackie not only consents to his mistress's (Myrna Loy) becoming Wade's respectable wife but submits to Wade's successful prosecution of him for a murder he committed on the D.A.'s behalf to silence an informant threatening to Wade's campaign for governor of New York. The exchange of personal notes between the adversaries after the trial—"Sorry, Blackie, but I had to do it." "O.K., kid, I can take it, and you sure can dish it out"—might seem simply indicative of Blackie's masochism were it not for his exclamations of inferiority, telling his mistress, "Jim's out of your class or mine," and his trial lawyer, "You've been licked by the best. . . . Class, it's written all over him." This obsequiousness reaches absurd proportions in a final, death-cell reunion of these friends with their boyhood priest (Leo Carrillo)[6] that for sentimentality and stereotypes exceeds even Lenny Bruce's prison picture parodies. As governor, Powell has refused all appeals for clemency for Gable, including Loy's. She abandons Powell for his obduracy. During the death-cell meeting Powell has a last-minute change of heart. He offers to commute the death

[5]René Jordan, *Clark Gable*, Pyramid Publications, 1973, p. 60.
[6]The priest is doubtless the "third man" of Arthur Caesar's story.

sentence, but Gable compels his own execution. In a parallel display of unlikely nobility, Powell resigns his office because of this thwarted moment of injudicious compassion and regains the companionship of Loy for having proved he could judge himself as harshly as Gable.[7]

The appeal of Gable's looks and brutish charm and the fact that both his murder victims are conniving creeps tend to undermine Powell's contention that the public's lionizing of criminals was fostered by the odiousness of Prohibition. His speech is characteristic of the dubious pieties that dot the film, including Loy's defense of "marriage, home, and babies" in the face of "fashionable callousness or cynicism" or the ecumenical "Catholic, Protestant, or Jew—what does it matter now?" uttered by the elderly Jew who adopts the orphaned gentile boys after their parents perish in the film's opening scene. These instances, however, may be rationalized as sops to the brand of Andy Hardy sentiment that Mayer liked interjected into all Metro films.

There is an appealing light comic scene between Myrna Loy and William Powell, featuring Powell's line, "I was born at home, as I wanted to be near my mother at the time." The blitheness of this line's delivery augurs the happy chemistry between Powell and Loy that *Manhattan Melodrama*'s director, W. S. ("Woody") Van Dyke,[8] would utilize in *The Thin Man* (1934) and its sequels.

When Gable, on death row, orders a black negligee for the blonde bimbo he has left behind, he utters the film's most comic line: "Black for me; the negligee for the next guy." Such cracks and the refreshing Powell-Loy interlude are overshadowed by the puerile antics of Blackie's cretinous but loyal bodyguard (Nat Pendleton) and his dumb blonde girlfriend (Muriel Evans), which provide the film's major comic relief.

The chief importance of *Manhattan Melodrama* to Mankiewicz's career is that its commercial success, hypoed by the publicity it received as the film that lured Dillinger to his death, earned Joe a favorable

---

[7]Loy's eleventh-hour change of heart, as the "lady with a past" who is on the threshold of deserting the man she has married out of a need for respectability and security but has come to love, was to become a plot staple of such subsequent Mankiewicz productions as *Mannequin* and *The Shining Hour.*

[8]Mankiewicz says Van Dyke, who is credited, directed only the first half of *Manhattan Melodrama* and that it was completed by Jack Conway. The use of more than one director on a picture was typical of Selznick, who, says Mankiewicz, "was trying to destroy the power and concept of the director as the one who makes the film."

reputation at MGM, where he was to spend the next decade. It also earned him his second Academy Award nomination, and although Arthur Caesar won an Oscar for Best Original Story for *Manhattan Melodrama,* Mankiewicz and Garrett lost out to Robert Riskin for his screenplay of a rival Gable hit, *It Happened One Night.*

Despite the acclaim of his epics for Metro, *The Big Parade* (1925) and *Hallelujah!* (1929), King Vidor could not interest Irving Thalberg in his "back to the land" project titled *Our Daily Bread.* According to Vidor, the idea for this film came from an article in *Reader's Digest* by a college professor who "proposed the organization of co-operatives as a solution to the unemployment problem . . . [and the] possibilities of operating a farm on a co-operative basis."[9]

Vidor was obliged to mortgage all of his property in order to raise the film's shoestring ($125,000) production costs because the banks were opposed to being portrayed in the film as unfeeling. Only through Charlie Chaplin's guarantee of distribution by his independent company, United Artists, was the picture released, since the studio thinking was that the public wanted escapist entertainment rather than sociological education. The box-office returns on *Our Daily Bread* confirmed this assessment.[10]

The idea of contributing to a renegade production likely appealed to Mankiewicz's maverick streak, as did the film's social idealism and Vidor's prestige as a director; the paltry $3,000 Vidor offered him as "script, continuity, and dialogue writer" could not have been the sole inducement. As it turned out, Vidor and his wife usurped the major writing credits for the sentimental and melodramatic screenplay. Mankiewicz received credit for only the film's dialogue, which is banal and synthetic, lacking a Steinbeck's ear and feeling for the poetic commonplaces uttered by laborers of multiple nationalities.

The film's one great sequence, which occupies its last twelve minutes and has given the picture its status as a classic, has only an orchestral score and the minimal sounds of the commands and noises of the men at work. In depicting the desperate, thirty-six-hour struggle

---

[9]King Vidor, *A Tree Is a Tree,* Harcourt, Brace & Co., 1953, p. 220. Vidor's autobiography, in the chapter on *Our Daily Bread,* neglects to mention Mankiewicz's contribution to the film.

[10]Vidor, however, maintains in *A Tree Is a Tree* that "the film was well received by the critics . . . nor did it do badly at the box office. Nobody lost any money on the venture; we were well compensated for our efforts."

to dig a two-mile irrigation ditch from a river to the parched corn fields before the crop dies,[11] Vidor achieves a high level of cinematic poetry, notably absent in the previous hour. The sequence is modeled on the work of masters of the Russian silent cinema, just as the concept of the collective farm is derived from the Bolshevik agrarian model.

On the romantic front, Joe ultimately prevailed over the opposition of Elizabeth Young's family. Cloyingly termed "one of the sweetest romances that has ever blossomed in the much marrying Hollywood colony,"[12] the Young-Mankiewicz nuptials of May 20, 1934, were characterized by Louella Parsons as "a Hollywood marriage that is 'different.'" The Sunday noon ceremony was held in the garden of the Herman Mankiewicz home on Tower Road, with Herman serving as Joe's best man.

From his nuptials Mankiewicz turned to adapting a play about a bride being jilted at the altar, *Forsaking All Others*, which Tallulah Bankhead had tried to keep afloat during the bank holidays of the 1933 Broadway season.

Mankiewicz's frothy screenplay so delighted Metro producer Bernie Hyman that he asked Joe to wait in his office while he went to discuss it with Louis Mayer. As Hyman exited, he exclaimed, "By God, if David can do it, so can I," referring to the all-star cast Selznick had assembled for *Dinner at Eight* in the manner of Thalberg's *Grand Hotel*, even though the rule at Metro was to use no more than two stars in a picture. When Hyman returned two hours later, he announced, "My boy, instead of Loretta Young, you've got Joan Crawford. Instead of George Brent, you've got Clark Gable, and instead of Joel McCrea, you've got Robert Montgomery"—in short, the three biggest stars on the MGM lot.

Hyman's one criticism of Mankiewicz's script was that it so briefly posited Gable's unavowed love for Crawford since childhood that their final union seemed unmotivated. The dispute was taken to Metro's "Court of Last Resort," the imperial office of L. B. Mayer. When

---

[11]Raymond Durgnat (*Film Comment*, July 1973, p. 32), in discussing *Our Daily Bread*'s unrealistic sense of economics, cites the astute observation of an unnamed "French interviewer" that the film's "dramatic structure hinges on the co-operative producing an abundant corn crop during the Depression, a period of catastrophic under-demand during which farmers were notoriously burning the very crop which Vidor's co-operative was laboring so heroically to produce."

[12]Louella Parsons's column, *Los Angeles Times*, May 21, 1934.

Mayer sided with Hyman, as he always did with his producers, Mankiewicz advanced a more pragmatic argument. "Mr. Mayer, if I faded in on New Year's Eve at midnight with a million of New York's citizenry congregated in Times Square and then cut to Thirty-ninth Street and Broadway, where Joan is going [screen] right to left, and then I cut to the corner of Fiftieth and Broadway, where Clark is moving left to right, it wouldn't be a question of *why* they would meet but *how,* because outside on the marquee it says 'Joan Crawford and Clark Gable *in,*' and that's the motivation." Having lost the argument, Mankiewicz dutifully added more clarifying exposition, and the prop department contributed a childhood photo of the trio with their famous adult faces incongruously pasted onto children's bodies.

The director of *Forsaking All Others,* "Woody" Van Dyke, was a celebrated character on the Metro lot, famed equally for his unusual capacity for liquor (he would start mixing gin with his orange juice at nine in the morning) and his propensity for shooting scenes in one take. This rapid-fire technique was as speedy as the pace of his films and the tempo of his overlapping dialogue. It left stars like Garbo, at whom he would bark, "Don't just stand there kiddo, let's go," helpless with laughter, and it usually required countless retakes by other directors to patch up.

Van Dyke's furious personality is best illustrated in one of Mankiewicz's tales of the great Hollywood "meanies." Woody's longtime assistant, Red, whom he constantly bullied, habitually dined at Barney's Beanery and devoured his steak in three huge slices. One night he choked to death when one of these pieces lodged in his windpipe. The next morning on the set there was much trepidation about breaking the news to Van Dyke, since the presumption was that despite his gruffness, he was deeply fond of Red. Finally, a crew member broached the subject, and the following dialogue ensued:

CREW MEMBER: Did you hear about Red?
VAN DYKE: No. Where is the son of a bitch?
CREW MEMBER: He's dead.
VAN DYKE: What?
CREW MEMBER: He choked on a piece of meat.
VAN DYKE: That cocksucker. I told him to stop cutting such big pieces.

Van Dyke immediately plunged into the day's work as though nothing untoward had occurred.

Van Dyke starts *Forsaking All Others* at such a clip and maintains such an exhilarating pace throughout that he generally keeps the rather conventional predicaments of this romantic comedy from growing wearisome. Gable's line, "I pumped up the tires on the bicycle, but Dill [Montgomery] did all the riding," best summarizes the antic plot in which Crawford is deserted by Montgomery at the altar, only to resume an illicit courtship with him while Gable, on the sidelines, is obliged to disguise his yearning for Crawford as mere companionship.

The film is peppered with wisecracks by Charles Butterworth, Gable's wry sidekick, and a newcomer to films, Rosalind Russell, in one of her familiar aggressive spinster parts. When Roz laments, "I wish somebody'd marry me so I could wear a decent hat," Butterworth is on hand to supply the retort, "That's the best reason for getting married I've ever heard."

The film's best sequence is the slapstick misadventures of accident-prone Montgomery taking Crawford for a tryst in the country. After being muddied in bicycle, car, and pedestrian crashes, Montgomery winds up in drag (a negligee being the only available change of clothing) at the country hideaway originally intended for his honeymoon. In attempting to light the fire that ultimately incapacitates him for any hanky-panky with Crawford, he delivers the now classic Mankiewicz line, "I don't need matches. I can make a fire by rubbing two Boy Scouts together."

Mankiewicz had discovered that three stars plus a smattering of sparkling banter was his own best formula for a raging commercial success. In this movie, "what Crawford doesn't know" is that it's Gable, rather than Montgomery, who has been sending her profusions of her favorite blossoms, aptly, cornflowers. When she discovers her true benefactor, she sails off with Gable and turns the tables by leaving Montgomery at the altar.

Joan Crawford's off-screen comment was that *Forsaking All Others* "was not much more than a fashion layout."[13] When she got to know the author personally as her regular producer, she realized that well-tailored scripts were as invaluable as Adrian's extravagant wardrobes and that script conferences could be far more stimulating than being pricked at fittings.

---

[13]Joan Crawford, *A Portrait of Joan* (originally published by Doubleday & Co., 1962), Paperback Library, 1964, p. 77.

Another significant woman in Mankiewicz's life was introduced to him as a child in the following year, 1935. This was Frances (renamed Judy) Garland, the twelve-year-old daughter of a vaudeville couple from Minnesota, the Gumms, whom Marc Rabwin, a surgeon friend of Joe's, had persuaded to follow his lead and migrate to California. Mankiewicz first heard Frances sing at a house party given by Dr. Rabwin and his wife, Marcella. The Rabwins next persuaded Joe to hear the astonishing girl solo, as the youngest member of the Garland Sisters act, in a concert at the Wilshire Ebell Theatre.

Joe was so taken with the child's performance that he made a great pitch for her to Ida Koverman, Mayer's trusted executive secretary-confidante. Nothing came of this recommendation, but it paved the way later that year, when an agent brought the girl to audition for Mrs. Koverman, who got her boss to hear and sign Garland.

Forsaking All Others was such a success that producer Hyman prevailed on Mankiewicz to turn out another Crawford formula picture —rich bitch tamed by penniless but handsome intellectual (Brian Aherne) indifferent to wealth—titled *I Live My Life*. Even the ebullient Van Dyke failed to extract much brio from this one, but as *The Observer* critic conceded, "It has everything that's needed for a popular success—romance, luxury, tantrums, uplift, cave-man tactics, smart lines, smart (and hideous) clothes, a wedding, two comic butlers [Eric Blore and Arthur Treacher], bigger and better eyelashes [batted by Crawford], and Brian Aherne."[14]

"It was at this time that dysentery was very prevalent throughout the eastern part of the U.S. and whimsy spread through Hollywood in even greater proportions," wrote Mankiewicz. "I was badly taken with it and in rapid succession wrote *Forsaking All Others* and *I Live My Life*."[15]

In the autumn of 1935, having reached a salary of $1,250 a week after scripting three hits in a row and with the inducement of impending fatherhood the following summer, Mankiewicz petitioned Mayer for an opportunity to direct his next picture. "You have to learn to crawl before you can walk," pontificated Mayer, meaning that Joe would have to serve his directorial apprenticeship as a producer. Mankiewicz calls this the best description of a producer's posture he has ever

---

[14] *The Observer*, February 2, 1936.
[15] *The Deltan* (Phi Sigma Delta), December 1936.

heard. It was the one he was to assume for the next eight years. Mayer did not think of the position as an indignity; Metro was known as a "producers studio," and the salary and status that went with such an office made it among the most coveted in the industry. In truth, Mayer had a genuine admiration of Mankiewicz's powerful ambition and intellect. With a constant need of men who could find and develop film properties to fulfill the studio's annual quota of fifty-two or more features, and with an eye for Mankiewicz's potential as an executive, Mayer hoped that the producer's role would shift Joe's interest away from the directorial province best left to the rough-and-tumble, hard-drinking, *goyim* pros.

Mayer had faith in the value of surrounding himself with ambitious executives pitted against one other. He viewed Ben Schulberg's downfall at Paramount as the result of his failure to ally himself with strong men, and he intrepidly engaged Sam Katz, one of the men most responsible for Schulberg's overthrow. Katz was a mogul in his own right as cofounder of the mighty Balaban & Katz theater chain based in Chicago. When Balaban and Katz allied their firm with Publix (the theater arm of Paramount that superseded Famous Players–Lasky), Katz installed himself on the Paramount lot to pursue his own producing ambitions.

At Metro, Mayer ("the Pope") pitted Katz against the equally aggressive head of sales, Al Lichtman, in the inner-circle executive committee known as the "College of Cardinals." "Both men wanted Mayer's job," says Mankiewicz, "and Mayer knew it, but that's the kind of men he wanted." At what point Mayer learned that both these aides were conspiring against him with New York chief Nick Schenck is a matter of conjecture. Apparently he tolerated or was oblivious to it for the better part of a decade.

Like the other top MGM producers, Irving Thalberg, David Selznick, Bernie Hyman, and Hunt Stromberg, each of whom was in charge of a group of lesser producers, Katz had his own unit. Mankiewicz and Katz had struck up a friendship while they were both at Paramount, and although Katz's producing unit at Metro was devoted chiefly to fashioning musicals under the aegis of Jack Cummings and, later, Arthur Freed, Katz prevailed on Mayer to assign him Mankiewicz as the one nonmusical producer in his division.

Not that Joe wasn't eager to attempt a musical. Shortly after he had been made a producer, he found a sophisticated German musical, *Drei Waltzer,* that spanned three generations of scandalous love matches (from the socially frowned-on union of a nobleman and a flower girl to the misalliance of a Hollywood sex goddess and a baron working as a movie extra). But Joe's enthusiasm for the property blinded him to the industry's fixation on replicating current hits, and the prevailing standard of that period was Warner Brothers' *42nd Street.* After patiently listening to Mankiewicz outline the story, Mayer said, "So you think that's a very clever idea for a musical?" To which Joe replied, "Yes, L. B., I think it's new, different, enchanting." "New, different, enchanting," mocked Mayer, rising from his desk. "Young man, let me tell you what I want from you. I want *43rd Street, 44th Street, 45th Street."* As Mayer came barreling toward him, Mankiewicz fled the office, only to be pursued down the hall by the agitated studio chief yelling, "Don't come to me with anything new. Give me *46th Street, 47th Street . . . !"*

For his debut as a producer of supposedly low-budget B pictures, Mankiewicz was saddled with refurbishing a fourth film version of *Three Godfathers,*[16] a biblical-parable Western about three outlaws rescuing a baby in the Mojave Desert. The Western was a neglected genre at Metro and the material was an unlikely choice for Mankiewicz, but the result bespeaks his diligence. The script by Manuel Seff and Edward Paramore, Jr., closely supervised by Mankiewicz, may be faulted for the excessive number of literary quotations from Schopenhauer and Shakespeare spouted by Lewis Stone as the intellectual bandit who carries a portable library. Equally, the well-drawn characters of the other two bandits, the redeemed blackguard (Chester Morris) and the endearing fool (Walter Brennan), mitigate the sentimentality of the tale.

Mankiewicz, conscious of his status as an A picture writer, had deliberately upgraded the material beyond the B picture norm. The location shooting in Joshua Tree Desert nearly doubled the $250,000 budget,[17] which made *Three Godfathers* as expensive as the average A picture. "I knew enough then, as a very young whore," says Mankiewicz, "to know that the one thing in the world they were looking for was someone who could produce good B pictures, so I wasn't about to

---

[16]The only previous sound version was *Hell's Heroes* (1930), directed by William Wyler. John Ford directed the second silent version, *Marked Men,* in 1919.

[17]Metro's ledger lists the cost of *Three Godfathers* as only $251,000.

produce a good B picture, though there are some very nice things in
Three Godfathers."[18] The results certainly worried the Metro brass,
who huddled on the sidewalk outside Grauman's Chinese Theatre after
the bewildered audience response to the first preview. ("It was so bad,"
Mankiewicz once quipped, "the footprints walked out of the cement
in the forecourt.")[19] Mankiewicz emerged with a broad grin and
blithely announced to the startled group, "Well, fellas, that just goes
to show I can't make B pictures."[20]

According to Sam Marx, Mayer was not only amused by Joe's
chutzpah but thought he possessed genuine talents worth the gamble
of entrusting him with a big-picture budget. However, both Sam Katz
and Mayer loathed the lynch-mob story that Mankiewicz proposed as
his first major feature. The idea for this film had come from Norman
Krasna two years earlier, prior to his departure for New York to do his
play *Small Miracle* (1934). Krasna told Mankiewicz in a single sentence
of a play he hoped to write, based on the actual lynching of two kidnap
suspects in California in the early thirties. The premise was that when
an innocent man is lynched, a photographer takes a picture of the lynch
mob. The notion fascinated Joe, who, in toying with the idea, invented
the key plot development. The innocent victim, presumed dead from
incineration in a jailhouse fire set by the mob, surreptitiously returns
to wreak vengeance on his would-be murderers. Rather than a photographer, a newsreel team would film the event, which would later incrim-
inate the participants.

Mankiewicz had sold the idea of playing the victim turned persecutor to a new Metro contractee, Spencer Tracy. Tracy had made two
inauspicious films for the studio after being fired from Twentieth,
despite his acknowledged talent, for his drunken binges. "Tracy was
crazy about it," says Mankiewicz, "but Mayer said, 'I think it stinks,' and
we had a big fight about whether it should be made. Mayer then said,
'Look, I'm going to do something right away, at the beginning of your
career. I'm going to let you make this film, young man, and I'm going to

[18]Mankiewicz, deferring to a director he reveres, says that his production of
Three Godfathers was "nowhere near as good as John Ford's later version [1948], as
it was rather intellectual and had far less action."

[19]Frank S. Nugent, "All About Joe," *Collier's*, March 24, 1951.

[20]In the *Collier's* article, Mankiewicz delivered this retort the next morning at
Metro, beating the reproachful-looking L. B. Mayer and his aide Eddie Mannix to the
punch.

spend as much money advertising this picture as Irving Thalberg spends on *Romeo and Juliet.* Otherwise, if it fails, you'll always say we didn't get behind it properly. This way, I'm going to prove to you that this picture won't make a nickel. Now, go make it!' "

According to Mankiewicz and Marx, Norman Krasna, when contacted in New York, had no recollection of the story idea that Mankiewicz had related. Joe was therefore obliged to write a ten-page outline of Krasna's nonexistent story, "Mob Rule." The tale earned Krasna an easy $25,000 for the screen rights and, subsequently, an Academy Award for Best Original Story for what became the acclaimed film *Fury.*

In 1934 David Selznick had brought to MGM Fritz Lang, the noted German director of *Metropolis, Die Niebelungen,* and *M.* Lang was in flight from the Nazis, who had asked him to run the German film industry. Lang claims his acquaintance with the Mankiewicz brothers was purely social; he played poker at Joe's bachelor digs, where they would tease him about his fractured English. "I have an ass," Lang said at one game, using the German for *ace.*

Mankiewicz says he "was assigned to Fritz to work on a story he was doing about a crooked D.A., possibly an adaptation of one of his German films," but for some reason the project was tabled, and Joe was elevated from screenwriter to producer. "Then I heard that Fritz was going to be let out without having done a film, because the film with David [Selznick] collapsed." Mankiewicz pleaded with the front office that Lang be retained to do *Fury.* [21]

---

[21]Fritz Lang says that at the point of being dropped by MGM, after the cancellation of several projects, he pleaded with general manager Eddie Mannix, "You can't do this to me. I am the first director of Europe." When Mannix asked him what he wanted to do, Lang says he proffered a four-page outline he had found in the story department "which contained the seed of *Fury.*" In Peter Bogdanovich's *Fritz Lang in America* (Praeger, 1967, p. 16), Lang says, "Eddie Mannix gave me another chance, and he handed me a four page outline [called "Mob Rule"] written by Norman Krasna. MGM assigned a man named Bartlett Cormack to me, and together we started to write the script."

Lang maintains that if Mankiewicz was involved at this early stage, Joe, rather than the story editor, would have recommended that Tracy's character be made a John Doe figure, to secure the audience's empathy, instead of the articulate lawyer that Lang and Cormack had written in their first draft. "In my opinion," says Lang, "Mankiewicz came in when the script was finished, and he said he would rewrite something in the ending, which he never did, not a word."

Mankiewicz says, "I hired Bart Cormack, and between us we worked out the

"Joe was much impressed by the Great German Director and his monocle, long cigarette holder, etc.," writes the former Elizabeth Young, but the cast and crew of *Fury* were incensed at his autocratic demands and grew mutinous at his regular disregard of their lunch break. Lang, who would become fanatically immersed in his labors, contends, "In Europe I was used to working on a scene until it was finished. I didn't know that in the U.S. there's a law you have to feed people after five hours. Nobody told me. It was one of the mistakes that I made." "It's very possible he knew nothing of American production methods," says Mankiewicz, "that is, if German production methods meant that you never called 'lunch' and that you had your secretary bring you a pill and a glass of brandy on the set."

After several days of working past the midday meal break and with the crew miming its hunger, Spencer Tracy took matters into his own hands. "What about some lunch?" he inquired of Lang. "It is I who will decide when lunch is called, Mr. Tracy," the director replied. "Oh," said Tracy, smearing his makeup by rubbing his hand across his face and yelling, "Lunch!" "As Tracy walked off the set, all the crew followed him, and after that, lunch was called at a fairly reasonable hour," says Mankiewicz.[22]

The *Fury* company's hostility to Lang turned murderous in the week of night shooting required to film the famous sequence of the mob storming the jail where the innocent suspect (Tracy) is held

screenplay, and by then Lang was available. He had nothing to do with the story of *Fury*, and I don't know why he gets co-screenwriting credit with Bart Cormack."

In *The Lion's Share* (E. P. Dutton, 1957, p. 221), Bosley Crowther supports Mankiewicz's version of *Fury*'s origin, but with a slight difference, possibly furnished by Krasna. Crowther writes, "He [Krasna] had to call Mankiewicz from New York and get him to refresh his memory so he could put it down on paper when the story editor, Sam Marx, offered him $25,000 for it."

According to Sam Marx, "Norman told it, though he never put a word down on paper. I think we paid him $11,000, which wasn't bad pay for a story that wasn't written, but Norman Krasna was a great opportunist, and between telling me and Joe the story, he got us to get the studio to buy it, and that became Joe's first big picture."

[22]Lang's speculative interpretation of Tracy's further retaliation is as follows: "Spencer Tracy had a contract with Metro—because he drank like a fish—that if he had so much as a glass of beer they could throw him out. My friend Peter Lorre, a former drug addict, explained to me that when people are deprived of a craving, they turn to something else—Lorre to drink, Tracy to whorehouses. I assume that's where he'd disappear after lunch, since he didn't come back till four o'clock. I'd be sitting there with the whole crew, wanting to work, when he'd arrive and say, 'Fritz, I want to invite the crew to have coffee.'"

captive. Mankiewicz was awakened one morning at 4 A.M. by his assistant, Bill Levanway, who begged him to come immediately to the set to intercede. The electricians were so incensed they had rigged a lamp and were planning to drop it on Lang at the first opportune moment.

A series of events had precipitated this insurrection. The kindly and gifted cameraman Joseph Ruttenberg, who describes Lang as "mean, ornery, German arrogant, and domineering," had been trying to set his lamps for the opening scene in which Sylvia Sidney takes poignant leave of her fiancé, Tracy. The script called for the scene to be shot in the rain, but the actual rain that spattered the back lot caused problems in covering the lights. The first time Lang stood in front of the light source and informed the cinematographer, "I've got to stand here," Ruttenberg obligingly moved his instruments to the other side. The second time it happened, Ruttenberg remonstrated, "Just tell me where you want to stand, and I'll light around it." The less accommodating Tracy, getting progressively drenched in the rain, hissed at Ruttenberg, "You son of a bitch, if you don't kick him in the balls, I'll kill you."

The murderous light-rigging scheme occurred on the night they were filming the fire-bombing of the jail. Over the protests of the experienced special effects man, Lang insisted on personally throwing the smoke pots, one of which hit Bruce Cabot, playing the mob's ringleader, in the head and opened a cut above his eye. Bloodied and nearly blinded, Cabot screamed, "I've had it," and rushed to assault Lang, but the crew interceded by informing Cabot that while they all wanted to take on Lang, the "accident" they were about to stage would absolve them of individual guilt. Mankiewicz's intercession curbed hostilities for the evening, and the crew's retaliation was confined to irritating acts of benign sabotage, such as striking the furniture Lang had approved one day so that he walked onto an empty set the next, or providing him with a four-seater when he had specified a two-seat roadster.

Lang received his come-uppance only after *Fury* was completed. While today only one blemish in the masterful film is remarked upon —the courtroom reunion embrace between the contrite Tracy and the devoted Sidney, which served as a sop to the censorious Hays Office —*Fury* originally contained another ludicrous episode. As Mankiewicz explains, "We had a first preview at which the film was literally laughed off the screen because Lang had a sequence in which ghosts chased Spencer Tracy through the streets. He turned around and the ghosts would disappear behind trees à la Walt Disney. Obviously that sequence had to be cut out of the film, but Fritz refused to cut anything. It was Eddie Mannix [Metro's general manager] who fired Fritz off the lot and told me to cut the film. The subsequent preview was a smashing success, after that one deletion, and the reviews were rapturous.

"After the opening I went up to Fritz, who was sitting at the Beverly Hills Brown Derby with Marlene Dietrich. I'll never forget it. I went up and held out my hand and said, 'Well, Fritz, we wind up with a good picture anyway.' He refused it, saying, 'You have ruined my picture.' I looked away and thought, 'Screw you.' " Lang contends that he resented overhearing Mankiewicz asking reporters, "Do you really think it's such a good film?" but regrets refusing to shake hands to this day, saying, "I was absolutely wrong. I should have let bygones be bygones."

Although Lang's conduct served to bar him from the MGM lot for the next twenty years, *Fury,* which is possibly his finest American film, established him as an important director in Hollywood, just as it created Mankiewicz's cachet as a gifted producer. Lang, however, proceeded to build on his reputation as a director of socially significant films by making *You Only Live Once* and *You and Me,* while Mankiewicz, having successfully broken the skein of Metro's escapist entertainments, returned to fashioning a series of trivial, glossy vehicles for Joan Crawford. The front office evidently persuaded Mankiewicz that *Fury* was noncommercial, because he wrote later in the year (1936), "My first major production, intended to revolutionize the entire industry, was *Fury.* It was received enthusiastically by the press; exploited magnificently by the MGM organization; and with a great deal of luck and a good wind behind it, the organization may finally succeed in getting its money back."[23]

In fact the film eventually showed a respectable $248,000 profit on its $604,000 cost, but "Louis B. Mayer . . . was furious about Fritz Lang's *Fury* because it didn't *look* like a Metro film. (Even the titles used different lettering.)"[24] Ever timorous about antagonizing officialdom, Mayer may have been fearful of a film that voiced misgivings about justice in America, displayed barbaric acts as not uncommon in

[23] *The Deltan,* December 1936.
[24] Peter Bogdanovich, "Hollywood" column in *Esquire,* April 1973, p. 42.

civilized society, and depicted a Midwestern governor's complicity in the deed for political motives. *Fury* drew heavily on newspaper accounts of an actual lynching in San Jose a few years earlier. In that case the mob had broken down the jail doors and hanged the inmates, inspiring the benediction of California's governor, who lauded the crime as "a shining example of how law and order flourished in the State of California."[25] In the future, films of social criticism would be left to Warner Brothers and, later, Twentieth Century–Fox. Not until *Intruder in the Dust* (1949), under Dore Schary, would Metro depart from its escapist entertainment to tackle controversial subject matter.

On July 1, 1936, the month of *Fury*'s premiere, Elizabeth Young gave birth at Cedars of Lebanon Hospital to a son she and Joe named Eric. The mortifying comment of Elizabeth's mother on her first visit from New York to see her grandson was, "Isn't it a shame he looks so Jewish?" Unfortunately, Joe happened to be standing in the nursery doorway at that moment.

A more rapturous response to the infant was made by Mankiewicz's new leading lady. As recalled by writer John Lee Mahin, the coauthor of *Love on the Run*, a Mankiewicz production for Crawford later in the year, "I was a guest at a dinner party at the Mankiewiczes' home to which Joan Crawford came unescorted. In the course of the evening, she and Joe very obviously disappeared, and I went to find him because Elizabeth was getting very teary. I discovered them in the nursery, with Joan kneeling before the child's crib, saying, 'This should have been mine.' "

Mankiewicz describes Crawford as "the prototype movie star—there will never be another like her. I think Joan Crawford has received as much fan mail as any two stars put together, and I'm willing to bet she answered in her own handwriting all she has received that she knew about. [The studio held back stacks of it because of her propensity.] Three times a week she'd sit down at a desk just to answer the fans' letters. As the consummate movie star, she dressed the part, played it off screen and on, and adored every moment of it. Her [protean] characterizations were something I adored about her that the executives never understood."

Crawford's off-screen role-playing often took place in Mankiewicz's informal office (Joe had removed the barrier of his desk, which was unusual for a Metro producer). If an advance call from the gate describing the automobile (sports car, sedan, or limousine) Crawford was riding in that day did not provide the clue to Mankiewicz, her outfit was a sure tip-off. "You'd have to watch the way she came in," Mankiewicz relates. "If Joan was wearing a pair of slacks, that meant you'd go over and slap her right on the ass and say, 'Hiya kid. You getting much?' In turn, she'd be as raucous as Billie Cassin[26] from Texas at that moment, and you'd have an absolute ball. She could come back the next day wearing black sables and incredible sapphires, and, by Jesus, you'd better be on your feet and click your heels, kiss her hand, and talk with the best British accent you had, but never in any way indicate she was different in any respect from the way she was yesterday, because the following day she'd come in in a dirndl or a pinafore and you'd be on the floor playing jacks with her. I loved it. You had to be an actor and be adaptive to what she was playing, though the moment she left my office, I went back to what I was before she came in." Crawford explained, "I was trying to find myself. . . . I didn't know what I was or who I was. He knew that. That's why we got along together so well. He picked up on my moods. At the time I didn't realize it."[27]

What Crawford couldn't fail to appreciate was Mankiewicz's flattering cultivation of her intellect and ambitions by allowing her to participate in the scripting of her productions. "He knew I had a greed for learning. I think that's the only thing in life I'm greedy about, really," said Crawford. "Joe was the first producer to let me come into his office, sit in a corner, and listen to the director's idea of my character. I never uttered a word but just sat and knitted or made notes."

Mankiewicz would also go over the role with her, planning character development and "business," which served as valuable orientation

---

[26]Although Crawford's real name was Lucille Le Sueur, she adopted her stepfather's last name, Cassin, during her early years in vaudeville.
[27]Crawford and Mankiewicz also communicated by a secret code. Mankiewicz had a private phone installed in his office that was not connected to the studio switchboard. He instructed his secretary, Adelaide Thorp (later Wallace), that if the phone rang while he was out, she was never to answer it but only to make note of the number of rings. One day when Mankiewicz was out of the office, the phone began to ring persistently. Despite the annoyance, Addie restrained herself and kept careful count. But when the phone began to ring again for a considerable period, she answered it and found that the caller was Crawford. The next day the telephone was removed.

since most scenes would be shot out of sequence. Inviting Crawford's participation not only served to disarm her criticism but engendered her admiration of Mankiewicz's skills as a revisionist. As she wrote in her autobiography, "Joe has a genius for extracting the suds from soap opera,"[28] and in conversation added, "You should have seen those scripts before Joe got hold of them. Oh Jesus, he was a fantastic writer, and he loved my enthusiasm or concern for a part even before it was finally scripted."

Knowing Crawford's desire to break away from formula roles and undertake more prestigious dramatic parts like Norma Shearer's, Mankiewicz proposed the role of the innkeeper's daughter, Peggy O'Neal, who becomes the maligned confidante of President Jackson in Samuel Hopkins Adams's novel *The Gorgeous Hussy.* David O. Selznick asserted that the public identified Crawford with contemporary roles and would not find her convincing in a costume picture. Selznick's view gave Crawford a strong incentive to disprove him. Mankiewicz's giving her such a part was for her a vote of confidence and "proof that Joe didn't take David's word as gospel."

Despite the illustrious cast of Lionel Barrymore as Andrew Jackson and Melvyn Douglas, James Stewart, Robert Taylor, and Franchot Tone as "the Hussy's" suitors[29] and a lavish production costing $1.1 million, *The Gorgeous Hussy* managed to convert a mildly scandalous historical saga into a decorous and pedestrian Metro romance.

More dramatic than the content of the film were the tensions on the set between Crawford and her husband, Franchot Tone. The wealthy and cultivated Tone had abandoned a promising career on Broadway, where he had been acclaimed as Curly in *Green Grow the Lilacs,* the source of *Oklahoma!* In Hollywood he was typecast as the stuffed-shirt second fiddle who usually lost Crawford to Gable. Although he was to win Crawford on screen at the end of *The Gorgeous Hussy,* his recalcitrance in making the film helped break up his marriage to her. Miss Crawford explains that L. B. Mayer had personally asked Tone to accept the minor role because it was imperative that she

---

[28]Crawford, *A Portrait of Joan,* p. 85.

[29]Among these more famous names, the character actress Beaulah Bondi provides the film's most moving performance as Andrew Jackson's (Barrymore) wise, pipe-smoking, reproving wife. Bondi's performance earned her an Academy Award nomination for Best Supporting Actress of 1936.

go off into Spanish exile with a handsome leading man. Tone consented for the sake of his wife but was so hurt by the humiliating casting and what it augured for his future movie career that he would frequently keep the esteemed director, Clarence Brown (who was only twenty minutes late the morning he broke his arm in three places), and the distinguished cast waiting for his arrival. On the day Tone arrived an hour and a half late, Crawford greeted him with a tongue-lashing: "Goddamnit, you're not going to keep this entire cast waiting," which earned her a round of applause from the company and served to terminate her marriage. "That was the finish of it," said Crawford. "Nothing interferes with my work on the set. He's an actor and I'm an actress, and his behavior was unprofessional and intolerable."

Unfortunately, Mankiewicz had prepared another madcap triangular romance for Crawford, Tone, and Gable, titled *Love on the Run*, to begin filming four days after *The Gorgeous Hussy* was completed. "I had a personal problem on that one, as we were breaking up," Crawford related, "but we got through it somehow. If I'd been doing a heavy drama, I just couldn't have made it."[30] *Love on the Run* was nothing more than a mediocre retread of *It Happened One Night*[31] set in Europe with a spy spoof subplot tacked on.

Mankiewicz, now espousing the doctrine of success measured by profit, the industry's criterion, wrote of his new outlook following *Fury:* "Then I produced *The Gorgeous Hussy*, into which I put a little less artistic impulse and a little more showmanship, with the result that it is making a lot of money. I followed this with *Love on the Run*, which everyone will agree possesses not so much as an artistic [moment], but which will make an enormous amount of money. I expect someday to produce a picture which will cause every literate acquaintance of mine to snub me on the streets—and this picture, I expect, will have the highest gross in the history of the cinema."[32]

Crawford's marriage to Tone had lasted just under a year, although they were not officially divorced until 1939. Mankiewicz managed two and a half years before he announced to the press, on

---

[30]Crawford generously declared, "Franchot walked off with the picture" (*A Portrait of Joan*, p. 82), which is manifestly untrue.

[31]Whereas the heiress (Crawford) runs away with the headline-seeking journalist (Gable) near the start of *Love on the Run*, Claudette Colbert runs off with Gable at the *end* of *It Happened One Night*, after their combative road trip.

[32]*The Deltan*, December 1936.

November 24, 1936, that he and Elizabeth Young "were just unable to make a go of it." He moved out of his home in Beverly Hills to the Beverly Wilshire Hotel, issuing a formula statement of incompatibility, irreconcilable differences, and parting on friendly terms. At the court hearing of February 14, 1937, Mankiewicz's attorney, Martin Gang, filed a motion denying Elizabeth's charges that Mankiewicz treated her cruelly by being overcritical of her household management and telling her he no longer loved her. The divorce action itself was not contested, although Gang cautioned Mankiewicz, in a letter, that he would regret his generous settlement of $50,000—$1,000 a month for fifty months to Elizabeth in alimony until she remarried, plus $500 a month for his son's maintenance.

The divorce suit was dropped when the couple resumed living together, but the reconciliation was short-lived. On April 30 they parted, and on May 5 Elizabeth filed again. This time she charged that Mankiewicz had left home for extended periods of time without explanation other than he was bored and that, following his advice, she went to visit her family in New York, only to be told on her return that she should have remained there. Further, she contended that her husband addressed her in harsh language and belittled her in front of their friends.

One close friend, Sam Marx, tried to intervene. After the second separation Elizabeth, "in a terrible state, terribly broken up," had gone to stay with Marx and his wife. When Mankiewicz explained to Marx in a "highly rational" manner that Elizabeth could not accept the fact that he had fallen out of love and no longer found her sexually desirable, Marx therefore terminated his efforts to bring the couple back together. Back in a courtroom on May 20, 1937, Elizabeth Young bowed her head and weepingly declared, "He wouldn't speak to me for days. He made me desperately unhappy."[33] On the third anniversary of their marriage, the Mankiewiczes were granted a divorce.

The untimely death of Irving Thalberg at age thirty-seven, in September 1936, resulted in the division of the producer-in-chief's domain among Mayer's executive producers, with Sam Katz rising in power. Elated by Katz's proclaiming him "the next Thalberg" and lauding his genius, Mankiewicz was now committed to making sure-fire

[33]*Los Angeles Times,* May 21, 1937.

successes to sustain Mayer's belief in his boss and himself. One means he found was to make near replicas of the hits its stars had made at other studios in an attempt to strike pay dirt twice. Mankiewicz had emulated Gable's smash for Columbia, *It Happened One Night*, with *Love on the Run.* Now he proceeded to "knock off" William Powell's highly successful *My Man Godfrey* (1936) for Universal by creating a similar screwball comedy about a redeemed vagrant, *Double Wedding*, for the illustrious team of Powell and Loy, featuring a slapstick finale reminiscent of the Marx Brothers' jammed stateroom sequence in Metro's *Night at the Opera* (1935).

Next, Mankiewicz dusted off a long-shelved Metro property, *The Girl from Trieste*, a play by Ferenc Molnár. Although the picture was originally planned to star Luise Rainer,[34] Mankiewicz revamped it as his next vehicle for Joan Crawford. He provocatively retitled it *The Bride Wore Red*, which, as it turned out, is the only aspect of the film in which Mankiewicz takes pride. It was shot simultaneously with *Double Wedding*, which by coincidence was also derived from a Molnár play, *Great Love*.

Although *Double Wedding* proved a solid hit, *The Bride Wore Red*, despite a witty opening scene, became one of Mankiewicz and Crawford's most humiliating flops. In concept, this rueful Cinderella story of a squalid nightclub singer's near conquest of a wealthy blade during an all-expense-paid, two-week vacation at a fashionable hotel in the Tyrol must have seemed a natural. It provided all of Crawford's favorite costume changes, from tawdry décolletage to Adrian formals to peasant blouse and dirndl, climaxed by the crimson creation of the title, the emblem of the impostor's social defiance. It offered Crawford a typical romantic conflict between two handsome leading men— Robert Young as the upper-crust playboy and the equally bland Franchot Tone as the nonmaterialist, nature-loving postman who exposes

---

[34]Dorothy Arzner, the only noted female director of her era in Hollywood, told a *New York Times* interviewer in 1976 that although she knew Mayer had signed her to an MGM contract in 1937 in order for her to give Joan Crawford a new image, "I thought I was going to direct Luise Rainer in *The Girl from Trieste*, Molnár's intimate case history of a young girl who is forced to take to the streets. I was out scouting locations when I got the news that Miss Rainer had been suspended for marrying a Communist and that Joan would replace her in the movie, which was now being called *The Bride Wore Red*. Right away, I knew that it would be synthetic, but Mayer knelt down, with those phony tears in his eyes, and said, 'We'll be eternally grateful to the woman who brings Crawford back.' "

her and drives off with her in his pony cart. The film also offered Crawford a sympathetic guide in the gifted director Dorothy Arzner, but its disastrous box-office reception led to Crawford's being listed in a notorious exhibitors' poll as "box-office poison."[35]

Spencer Tracy, Joe's pal from *Fury*, whose critical judgment he most esteemed, silently left the preview of *The Bride Wore Red* with only an ambiguous pat on the shoulder, causing Mankiewicz to search and phone all night to determine his reaction. When Mankiewicz finally reached him at 3 A.M., Tracy laughed a lot, but the shoulder clasp bespoke condolence rather than praise. David O. Selznick was less circumspect, and whenever he wanted to get a rise out of Joe, he would teasingly broach the title of this famous fiasco.

Less than a month after *The Bride Wore Red* completed shooting, filming began on Mankiewicz's production of *Mannequin*, which paired his intimates, Tracy and Crawford, for the first time. While this picture was little more than a reversion for Crawford from playing wealthy clothes-horse parts to the "shop girl's delight"—the working-class heroine enterprisingly fighting her way up the social ladder to affluent romance despite the vicissitudes of marriage to an exploitative swindler—the effect of playing opposite Tracy was salutary. Tracy's masterful technique of underplaying was an unfailing corrective to the excesses of his costars. While Crawford's earnestness and intensity were still in evidence, new notes of appealing simplicity and "subdued poignance"[36] were introduced, and many critics termed it her best performance in years. (Crawford, predictably, manifested no trace of her character's Lower East Side origins, unlike her mischievous younger brother in the film, Leo Gorcey, who is a standout in a bit part.)

The only elements mitigating the 100 percent purity of *Mannequin*'s soap opera formula are Tracy's adulterous courtship heedless of the married Crawford's peerless virtue, and the divorcée Crawford's consent to marry him even though she feels no reciprocal passion. A scene documenting the couple's subsequent married bliss in a fraudulently overdecorated Irish cottage is the quintessence of offensive Metro schmaltz, redeemed only by Tracy's delightful set piece on the arduous task of smoking Irish clay pipes. (This activity was probably

---

[35]Metro was not deterred by the failure of *The Bride Wore Red* and gave Crawford a new $1.5 million, five-year contract.
[36]Stephen Harvey, *Joan Crawford*, Pyramid Publications, 1974, p. 76.

written in by Mankiewicz, an inveterate pipe smoker.)

Mankiewicz had a rare opportunity to witness Tracy's well-concealed but arduous preparation of such "business" at first hand, because during this period Tracy would stay for a week at a time at Mankiewicz's small beach house in Santa Monica. While Tracy was shooting *Test Pilot* (1938), his film after *Mannequin,* Mankiewicz says, "I remember him working out this business of nut cracking, to be performed all during Gable's big scene, which he worked out very carefully all night long. Christ, he used up five pounds of nuts, and then he pretended on the set it had just occurred to him. It was perfectly timed so he would never crack a nut on Clark's line, but you would always have to cut to him."

While *Mannequin* was before the camera, an Edward G. Robinson film, *The Last Gangster,* was winding up filming on the Metro lot. In her American film debut as Robinson's imported Slavic wife (a device to account for her Austrian accent) was Rosa Stradner, a beautiful, statuesque blonde star of Reinhardt's Josefstadt Theatre in Vienna. She had been signed by Benjamin Thau, head of Metro's talent department, on a 1937 European talent hunt with L. B. Mayer that landed such foreign beauties as Greer Garson, Hedy Lamarr, and Ilona Massey to swell Metro's fabled roster of "more stars than there are in the heavens." Since one of Stradner's major tasks in Culver City was to perfect her English, it was natural she would be introduced to Mankiewicz, as he was the most able German-speaking figure on the lot.

Socializing with Rosa Stradner was a far happier assignment than Mayer's previous imposition of the famed German director Leopold Jessner, one of the growing number of German theater artists colonizing in Hollywood after fleeing the Nazi takeover. When Mayer blithely announced he was making this fifty-eight-year-old theatrical eminence the assistant to Mankiewicz, aged twenty-seven, Joe protested, "Mr. Mayer, you can't do that. . . . This is too absurd for words, this is beyond belief!" "Look, you want this guy to have a job or not?" Mayer countered. "That's the only slot we can find for him because he speaks very little English. You're going to teach him how to be a producer." "That's like teaching Einstein to add," said Mankiewicz resignedly. Dreading the impending meeting with one of his idols from Berlin, where Jessner's theater rivaled Reinhardt's and Piscator's, Mankiewicz hit upon the idea of offering Jessner the production of an updated version of Andreyev's classic play, *He Who Gets Slapped,* which was MGM's first production and one of its most celebrated silent films.

Mankiewicz deferentially told Jessner that by rights he should be working for him and inquired, "Of course you know the play, *He Who Gets Slapped?*" "Young man, I knew Andreyev," was Jessner's terse rebuff, prompting Mankiewicz to table the notion by privately concluding, "What's the use? He probably worked with Andreyev on the play and told him what was wrong with the second act."

Serving as the studio's liaison with German-speaking arrivals was only one of Mankiewicz's minor services. Of more major value was that his youth, charm, intellect, and ease with women stars made him the ideal soother of such volatile and outspoken temperaments as Margaret Sullavan's, Myrna Loy's, and especially Joan Crawford's. "They were delighted with the fact that I sort of 'took over' Crawford, made most of her films, and could 'handle' Joan," says Mankiewicz. "In other words, I knew Joan and I knew how to get her to do things. She trusted me . . . and we made some very successful pictures together." Crawford declared, "I was madly in love with him and it was lovely. I don't know of any woman who knew him at all who wasn't in love with him. At one time or another, all the ladies at MGM were in love with him, I'm sure. He had a crooked little smile that was absolutely irresistible to any woman. . . . He gave me such a feeling of security I felt I could do anything in the world once I got on that stage. . . . At that time, I didn't have much sense of humor about myself. . . . I was still struggling, trying to get there, learning. He relaxed me, teaching me to have fun in my work. I'd had joy, not fun. He brought that out of me, frothy or not."

To reward him for his invaluable services and proven skills as a producer-writer, Mayer brought Mankiewicz into his inner circle by appointing him to Metro's executive committee. In addition to an increased workload (Mankiewicz in 1938 personally produced five features of the ten he had under development), Mankiewicz was put in charge of a junior writers program.

As a graduate of a similar program at Paramount, Mankiewicz was aware of the ambitions of such young talents as Waldo Salt, Hugo Butler, Lawrence Hazard, and David Hertz. He decided to give them immediate, practical experience, under his supervision, by assigning them to write or revise the screenplays of many of his own productions. Several of these writers were thus employed, without screen credit, to deal with a script crisis on Mankiewicz's first film of 1938, an adaptation of Erich Maria Remarque's international best seller *Three Comrades.*

Mankiewicz once wryly commented, "If I go down at all in literary history, in a footnote, it will be as the swine who rewrote F. Scott Fitzgerald."[37] He refers to the now famous, bitter letter that Fitzgerald wrote Mankiewicz in January 1938, condemning the revisions made in his script of *Three Comrades.*

When Mankiewicz engaged Fitzgerald, believing that he could best capture the aura of Germany's postwar lost generation and the character of the ethereal, tubercular heroine, Fitzgerald was an alcoholic has-been struggling to remain on the Metro payroll. The irony, as Mankiewicz points out, is that he was the only producer to use a substantial portion (approximately one-third) of a Fitzgerald script, and *Three Comrades* represents the only screen credit Fitzgerald received from the many pictures he worked on. Moreover, despite Fitzgerald's gloomy prediction, the film's enthusiastic critical reception (which noted the chivalrous and elegaic qualities characteristic of Fitzgerald's doomed romances) earned him a year's extension of his Metro contract and a raise in his weekly salary from $1,000 to $1,250.

Mankiewicz pinpoints Fitzgerald's screenwriting problem, common to other novelists like Sinclair Lewis and Hemingway, by stating that the craft of writing dialogue for the eye on the printed page is quite distinct from the dramatist's gift of writing speech that sounds natural to the ear.[38] Margaret Sullavan, the star of *Three Comrades*, complained to Mankiewicz that many of her speeches were unspeakable. It was Sullavan's protests, says Mankiewicz, that led him and his staff[39] to rewrite Fitzgerald's dialogue, though Scott blamed Joe entirely.

---

[37]"People Will Talk," *The Movies*, BBC-TV, March 13, 1967.

[38]This charge is borne out by Fitzgerald's failed play, *The Vegetable*, and by the unsuccessful films of his novels, *Tender Is the Night* (1962) and *The Great Gatsby* (1974), which made extensive use of Fitzgerald's original dialogue.

[39]Mankiewicz believes that both Waldo Salt and Lawrence Hazzard had a hand in rewriting *Three Comrades.* He specifically recalls that Margaret Sullavan's most touching speech, which begins, "Is that the road home? . . ." was written by David Hertz, "a brilliant, young, sensitive American poet who wrote a great deal of *Three Comrades.*"

Aaron Latham's assertion in *Crazy Sundays* (Viking Press, 1971) that Margaret Sullavan suspended filming until revisions were made to her satisfaction is inconsistent with the date of Fitzgerald's letter of complaint (January 20, 1938), which suggests that the rush job was undertaken before shooting began on February 4.

Fitzgerald's objection in his letter to Mankiewicz's bosses, Mannix and Katz, that the intention of his ending had been distorted *("The march of four people, living and dead, heroic and unconquerable, side by side back into the fight")* is contradicted by the film's upbeat, final tableau of the superimposed ghosts of Pat and Gottfried linking arms with the living Erich and Otto, which precisely conveys Fitzgerald's intention.

Over and above Fitzgerald's limitations as a writer of spoken dialogue was his difficulty in abandoning fidelity to the source material of the Remarque novel. His successive drafts reveal that having reluctantly conceded the propriety of a marriage to sanctify the cohabiting of Erich (Robert Taylor), the garage mechanic, and Pat (Margaret Sullavan), his tubercular, formerly rich girl, Fitzgerald was unwilling to relinquish the amiable whores, the futilely patriotic German Jews, and the vicious proto-Nazis that populate Remarque's depression-era Berlin. Mankiewicz was mindful that whores, Jews, and Nazis were taboo to the front office. Because of Metro's preference for wholesomeness, Joe was aware that much of the novel's seamy milieu would have to be jettisoned and the identity of the political factions concealed in order to get the film made, no less released.

When Fitzgerald, taking a leaf from his novel *The Beautiful and Damned,* inserted a fantasy sequence of an angel and Saint Peter as heavenly telephone operators connecting Erich's first call to Pat, Mankiewicz had a likely pretext to call in Ted Paramore *(Three Godfathers)* to collaborate on the script. The subsequent jockeying for control between Fitzgerald and Paramore led to acrimonious rivalry rather than harmonious reconstruction. Mankiewicz's precaution in obscuring the political affiliation of the film's violent insurrectionists similarly failed to avert the application of outside pressure tactics.

L. B. Mayer, though Jewish, was not eager to lose Metro's lucrative German market.[40] To placate the Fascist regime, he invited a representative of the German consulate in Los Angeles to a private screening of *Three Comrades* to gain approval of its content. When Mankiewicz spurned the German's suggested changes, the industry censor, Joseph Breen, stepped in and recommended that if the rioters were clearly designated Communists, the Germans would be placated and the film's export assured. Mankiewicz felt that the political realities of the period had already been too thoroughly cosmeticized, though Pat's suitor, Breuer (Lionel Atwill), is recognizably a Nazi recruiter. Joe threatened to resign and give the story to the *New York Times* if

---

[40]Mankiewicz says that because of its policy of appeasement, MGM was able to distribute its films in Germany long after the other majors had boycotted Germany or been barred. "Warner Brothers had guts," says Mankiewicz. "They hated the Nazis more than they cared for the German grosses. MGM did not. It kept on releasing its films in Nazi Germany until Hitler finally threw them out. In fact, one producer was in charge of taking anyone's name off a picture's credits if it sounded Jewish."

Breen's compromise was implemented. For this courageous act of defiance, Fitzgerald clasped Mankiewicz in a warm, public embrace and kissed him when he entered the Metro commissary.

While Fitzgerald's gesture contradicts the impression of irreparable grievance created by his three published letters concerning *Three Comrades*, two of Fitzgerald's criticisms have merit and significance. His charge that the revised *Three Comrades* script "is as groggy with sentimentality as *The Bride Wore Red*" is a low blow but more accurate than his earlier contention, in the same letter, that Mankiewicz had converted a piece of quality material into "a flop . . . as thoroughly naïve as *The Bride Wore Red.*"[41] In fact, both films were calculated rather than naïve. Mankiewicz was giving Metro, Margaret Sullavan, and Frank Borzage, a director who doted on syrupy sentimentality, precisely what they wanted—tearjerking arias for Sullavan as a latter-day Camille. They are perfectly suited to what was then termed "a woman's picture," of which Mankiewicz, through his work for Crawford, had become a high-class practitioner. In fact, Crawford was scheduled to play the role of Pat but declined it in the belief the picture would be dominated by the male stars. This was a stroke of luck because Margaret Sullavan had the ideal wispy glamour and fragility for the part and gave a memorable performance. Her wistful aura largely redeems the maudlin speechmaking, though the quaint back-lot sets lend an air of fraudulence to the film and the all-American trio of Robert Taylor, Franchot Tone, and Robert Young is the most unlikely group of German comrades imaginable.

The altercation with Fitzgerald also reveals how large a part Mankiewicz typically played in the revision of the scripts of the films he produced. Under the studio's agreement with the Screen Writers Guild (of which Mankiewicz was a founding member),[42] a producer could not take credit for his contributions to a script. Mankiewicz

---

[41]Andrew Turnbull, ed., *The Letters of F. Scott Fitzgerald*, Charles Scribner's Sons, 1963, pp. 563–64.

[42]The Screen Writers Guild, founded in 1933, was bitterly opposed by Irving Thalberg, abetted by Louis Mayer and Darryl Zanuck. These studio chiefs sided with the conservative "company union," the Screen Playwrights, and viewed the SWG as a leftist menace. Although Thalberg threatened to shut down Metro in opposition to the Guild, he came to realize that he was being used as a pawn by the reactionary Screen Playwrights, who were opposed to collective bargaining, among other union rights. When Thalberg withdrew his support, the Screen Playwrights faded into oblivion and the Screen Writers Guild prevailed.

always thought of himself as a writer equal or superior to any he engaged, and he begrudged the ruling that made his literary contributions anonymous.

At the end of March, two days before *Three Comrades* completed shooting, Mankiewicz put his next film into production. *The Shopworn Angel* was a remake of an early, partial-sound film that Mankiewicz doubtless remembered as one of the great successes of 1929, the year he came to the Paramount lot: it was the film that established Gary Cooper and Joe's friend Paul Lukas as stars of the "talkies." The melodrama concerned Lukas's jealousy over his kept woman (Nancy Carroll) becoming infatuated with a younger man (Cooper), an ingenuous soldier.

In keeping with Metro's preference for wholesome romances and the period's strict censorship, which had barred the studio from producing Fitzgerald's *Infidelity* on the basis of its title, Joe instructed Waldo Salt, his young screenwriting protégé (now famed for his script of *Midnight Cowboy*), to temper the sexual rivalries of the original *Shopworn Angel*. In the revised version it is the soldier's adoration of the selfish show girl ("the shopworn angel") that reawakens her affection for her longtime "fiancé" and patron and prompts her sacrificial gesture of marrying the doughboy before he goes off to the front, where he is killed. These alterations served to maintain the chastity of all three figures in the triangle.

When Joan Crawford once again turned down a film announced for her, Mankiewicz logically turned once more to Margaret Sullavan to play the world-weary "angel." He also had the notion of pairing her with Jimmy Stewart, a fellow member of the University Players, the stock company founded by Joshua Logan that served to launch their theatrical careers. The appeal of this teaming, under the able direction of another theater recruit, H. C. Potter, almost transcends the triteness of the material, and their affecting quality subsequently inspired Lubitsch to cast Sullavan and Stewart as the lovers in his classic comedy, *The Shop Around the Corner* (1940).

One problem posed by the script of *The Shopworn Angel* was whether Margaret Sullavan, as a Broadway musical star, could perform two versions of "Pack Up Your Troubles"—first as a rouser at an army camp benefit and then through her tears at the end, when she receives word of Stewart's death. Mankiewicz had his friend and most frequent composer, Franz Waxman, on hand when Miss Sullavan came to his office for a meeting. As Mankiewicz relates it, the following dialogue ensued:

> MANKIEWICZ: Can you sing?
> SULLAVAN: You're goddamned right I can. Of course I can sing.
> MANKIEWICZ: Well, that's marvelous.
> SULLAVAN: Don't you want to hear me?
> MANKIEWICZ: Well, of course, we'd love to.
> SULLAVAN: Well, let's go.

"Maggie, Franz, and I then went down to a stage where there was a piano. Franz got behind the keyboard and asked what she wanted him to play. She requested a popular song of the day, 'I'm Putting All My Eggs in One Basket.' Franz played it, and Maggie opened her mouth, and out came the goddamnedest caterwauling you've ever heard in your life. There was nothing approaching a note that was anywhere near true, and Franz and I just stared at her incredulously."

Margaret Sullavan stopped and explained that she had found that giving these appalling demonstrations was the only way she could convince producers and directors that she really couldn't sing. When she had proclaimed her inability in the past, her employers always thought she was being shy and spent hours trying to reassure her. "That's the day I realized," says Mankiewicz, "that this marvelous, offbeat delivery that Maggie had was because she was utterly tone deaf and couldn't hear herself talking." (Margaret Sullavan's nearly total deafness was suggested in some obituaries as the cause of her presumed suicide during a Broadway try-out in 1960.)

H. C. Potter picks up the story of the singer engaged to dub Sullavan's numbers. "I never met the girl who was selected until the moment when I walked onto the recording stage to find it set up with a full orchestra, ready to record. Nobody had thought to tell the girl (an unknown who had been singing around with 'big bands') anything about the story—or to give me a session to get her ready for this difficult assignment. And Joe wasn't there to keep the MGM staff (*very* cost conscious) off my back. So in ten minutes the poor girl had to absorb not only the whole story line but also *how* the song should be sung, where she should choke up, falter, convey the 'show must go on' spirit, *move* an audience with her bravery, et cetera. After only one rehearsal with the orchestra, she did it magnificently, and we printed the first take. I was wild about the girl and tried to get MGM to sign her. But all hands declared she was just a singer and would never amount to anything. Her name was Mary Martin." (Later in the year, 1938, Miss Martin created a sensation on Broadway singing Cole Porter's "My Heart Belongs to Daddy.")

Having bypassed two hits, Joan Crawford came up with her own project by persuading the studio to buy a Broadway play she had admired, Keith Winter's *The Shining Hour.* Mankiewicz engaged the whimsical poet Ogden Nash to work with Jane Murfin on transposing the play's locale from Yorkshire to Wisconsin; Frank Borzage, who had guided Crawford in *Mannequin* and triumphed with *Three Comrades,* to direct; and Melvyn Douglas, Robert Young, Margaret Sullavan, and Fay Bainter to costar. Even with this collection of talent the film was nothing more than a stodgy soap opera.

The Shining Hour proved dismal at the box office, as did Mankiewicz's subsequent picture, a scrupulous adaptation of Dickens's *Christmas Carol,* done in the Selznick style of treating literary classics. Reginald Owen, the veteran English character actor who had contributed amusing bits to *Love on the Run* and *The Bride Wore Red,* capitalized on the part of Scrooge when Lionel Barrymore, long identified with the part on radio, was forced to drop out because of illness. *A Christmas Carol* was completed in early November and rushed into release as the holiday attraction at New York's Radio City Music Hall. "It did over $200,000 Christmas week at the Music Hall," says Mankiewicz, "which was a huge gross in those days, but I don't think it played another theater in the U.S. after that." The film is still shown annually on television, a revival as frequent as his later *Julius Caesar* at Shakespeare film festivals, causing Mankiewicz to pine, "I only wish I had a piece of the *Christmas Carol* and *Julius Caesar* residuals."

Significantly missing from Mankiewicz's list of favorite literary classics he has filmed is his production of *The Adventures of Huckleberry Finn,* with Mickey Rooney in the title role, which was Mankiewicz's final production of 1938. Either awed by the task of carrying the film in his first solo starring role or under injunction from Mankiewicz to suppress his usual outrageous mugging, Mickey Rooney gives a generally sober and restrained performance as Huck, to the detriment of a film in need of all his spontaneity and exuberance.

Although Mankiewicz was pulling down a substantial salary of

$3,000 a week,[43] he had begun to emulate his brother Herman by dropping heavy sums at the town's big poker games[44] and at the crap tables of the Sunset Strip gambling houses like the Clover Club or the ship *Rex,* anchored three miles off Long Beach. Besides his costly gambling, Mankiewicz acquired a passion for boats, graduating from "stink pots" (motorboats), in the early thirties, to extravagant sailing vessels later in the decade. The first of these he bought from Jascha Heifetz and the second, a magnificent eighty-seven-foot schooner, "The Sartartia," he purchased from the Western star Buck Jones, until he found himself the indebted possessor of one motorboat and two yachts.

These drains on his earnings in no way curbed his pursuit of desirable actresses. During this period Mankiewicz was romantically involved with Loretta Young, but the relationship had no future. "She wanted to get married," says Mankiewicz, "but I was a divorced man and she was a rabid, Paulist Catholic, which is the worst kind in the world. It would have meant getting a dispensation from the Pope, and you can just see me, as anticlerical as I am, trying to get that."[45]

---

[43]On January 25, 1938, the *Philadelphia Bulletin* inaccurately reported that "the 28-year-old producer isn't a bad catch at $5000 a week, 52 weeks a year." Even by his own computation, Mankiewicz was earning only $156,000 a year. He minimizes this salary by saying that with ten pictures in work, as in 1938, his producer's fee amounted to a trifling $15,600 per picture. However, Mankiewicz produced only one film in 1939 and two annually between 1940 and 1942.

[44]Among his opponents in these days were Sid Grauman (the theater owner), Jack Conway (a Metro director), Eddie Mannix (Metro's general manager), and the big winners, MGM's Bennie Thau and Twentieth Century–Fox mogul Joe Schenck, termed by Mankiewicz "one of the great poker players of all time."

[45]Loretta Young's ardent Catholicism led her to adopt a system of fines, whereby anyone who used a swear word in her presence would be obliged to pay a quarter or more, depending on how offensive she deemed the oath, with the proceeds donated to charity.

In 1949, when Mankiewicz was working at Twentieth Century–Fox, where Miss Young was playing a nun in *Come to the Stable,* she happened to overhear Joe utter a profanity while conversing over lunch in the Fox commissary. The following dialogue ensued:

LORETTA: *(extending her collection box)* That will be fifty cents.
JOE: What will cost me fifty cents?
LORETTA: You took the name of the Lord in vain.
   Mankiewicz drops the change in her canister, but as Young walks away, he calls after her, with perfect timing—
JOE: Oh, Loretta, how much would it cost me to tell you to go fuck yourself?

At the studio another Catholic actress, Rosa Stradner, had fewer religious scruples. Stradner had become a fixture at the table of Joe and his crew of writers. The contingent was christened "Snow White and the Seven Dwarfs" by a publicist who learned that Rosa had written to Joe of attending her first baseball game in New York "between the Giants and the Dwarfs," and Mankiewicz was presented with the statuette of Sleepy.

Joe's helping Rosa perfect her English, the pretext for her dining with his group, in time gave way to his consoling her over her stalled career. Despite her fine reviews for *The Last Gangster*, there was no further assignment from the studio. After a year's inactivity (which was a grievous slight for the actress whom Metro's two-time Academy Award winner, Luise Rainer, had understudied at Vienna's Volks Theatre), Stradner was finally loaned to Columbia to do a sixth-billed supporting part in an inauspicious Chester Morris film, *Blind Alley* (1939). Mankiewicz professes puzzlement over why Stradner, "a brilliant actress," did not catch on, though he concedes she lacked "the obvious glamour of Hedy Lamarr" and the endearing quality of her compatriots Luise Rainer and Lili Palmer, whom he describes as conscious "audience wooers."[46]

Walter Reisch, Rosa's friend and fellow emigrant from Vienna who had written her first German film, describes Stradner as "beautiful beyond description. . . . Not a sweet ingenue, but the Viennese equivalent of Ava Gardner, a femme fatale or dangerous woman with syndromes, which were part of the chemistry of her own life." Stradner's most famous part was her creation of the title role in a dramatization of Schnitzler's story *Fräulein Else*. Mankiewicz describes the work as the tragedy of an introspective, narcissistic beauty with social pretensions who kills herself after being forced to disrobe by a vulgar, wealthy, older man she has importuned for a loan to her financially pressed father.

For Mankiewicz, whose greatest fascinations were celebrated actresses, distinguished theater, and the society of German artists, Rosa Stradner's allure was obvious. He moved into the house she

---

[46]Dr. Frederick Hacker says that Rosa was "extremely arrogant, choosy, and elitist—everything that one shouldn't be at that time, even in Hollywood, if one wanted to get a job." Hacker says that only stardom like Garbo's or Bergman's would have pleased her, and this unrealistic ambition caused her continual misery.

had rented on Alpine Drive in Beverly Hills and was soon confronted by the turbulence and threats that were to mark their relationship. Marcella Rabwin, Selznick's secretary and the wife of Mankiewicz's surgeon friend, says that Rosa's intimidation of Joe and her incipient madness were manifest at this early stage, for "when Joe wouldn't marry her, she tried to kill herself." Dr. Rabwin amplifies this allegation by saying, "Joe's life with Rosa was never a happy life, right from the beginning. She made his life miserable for years. He was actually physically afraid of Rosa, as she could be violent. Joe is a very forceful person and can be pretty dominating. But where Rosa was involved, he would accede to anything she wanted, just to keep peace."

On July 28, 1939, Rosa and Joe were married in New York before a municipal court judge in the home of Joe's sister, Erna, and her physician husband—an event termed "a surprise marriage" in the *Los Angeles Times*. On the couple's return to Los Angeles on July 31, they were accorded a tumultuous reception at the railway station by a contingent of producers and writers from Metro who had engaged an eighteen-piece orchestra for the occasion.

The atmosphere in the top-floor executive suites of the new, white, monumental Irving Thalberg Building was distinctly cooler. The freeze was occasioned the previous winter when the executive committee assembled to pacify "the General" of Metro's parent company, Loew's, Inc., Nick Schenck, who had journeyed from New York when the cost of Mervyn LeRoy's production *The Wizard of Oz* had reached $2 million, with no end in sight. The explanations provided by each of the executives Mayer called on did not fool Schenck, who thundered, "I am not getting any answers. I want to know what the hell is going on with Merv's picture!"

"My mind was wandering," says Mankiewicz. "I was thinking of entirely different things, like 'How in hell do I get out of here?' Suddenly I heard Mayer saying, 'Nick, we've got a young man on the committee who's been a writer. He knows scripts, and he knows all the writers, actors, and producers. In other words, he is a creative-type fella, Nick, and he knows where the money goes, because he knows how creative people operate. So if anyone can tell you why this picture is costing so much, Joe Mankiewicz can.' Suddenly I saw everybody on the executive committee staring at me, 'cause nobody knew, and Schenck says, 'Well, suppose you tell me, young man.' I blurted out, 'I suppose LeRoy *s'amuse.*'[47] Schenck said, 'What?' so I repeated it. Larry Weingarten, from down at the end of the table, said, 'That's French.' Schenck asked testily, 'Why are you talking French to me, and what did you say about LeRoy?' All I could think of was 'Why am I here? I didn't mean it about Mervyn. It was just a marvelous crack, but why didn't I save it for the writers' table?' In order to extricate myself, I found myself going into a long explanation of Louis XIV [*sic*] and the meaning of the phrase *"Le Roi s'amuse,"* though they still didn't know what I was talking about. In the middle of this lecture, Schenck looked at Mayer as if to say, 'Louie, you've hired a lunatic,' and Mayer agreed. I don't think Mayer ever trusted me after that day. That was the end of my executive career."

Mankiewicz's standing as a producer was still substantial enough to garner the studio's top stars, Gable and Crawford, fresh from their respective performances in *Gone with the Wind* and *The Women.* The picture was titled *Strange Cargo,* and it was to be the eighth, last, and best pairing of this lustrous duo. Crawford improves on her Sadie Thompson performance as a hardened "dance hostess" on the tawdry tropical circuit, and Gable is a tough, fearless convict, escaping with a band of inmates and Crawford in tow from an island prison camp in French Guiana.

"It was almost a good film," says Mankiewicz. "I wish it could have been made later. It was tough doing any kind of a film that even approached reality in any way." Despite Mankiewicz's scrupulous precautions ("Christ, you couldn't even indicate that Clark Gable screwed Joan Crawford in their trek through the jungle on the way to the beach"), the picture ran afoul of the Legion of Decency. To win the approval of the Catholic censors, the virtuous Christian of Richard Sale's novel, *Not Too Narrow, Not Too Deep,* had been made into a Christlike figure, Cambreau (Ian Hunter), who redeems all but one of *Strange Cargo*'s impious escapees. The Legion found this blasphemous and took the unusual step of condemning the film in its entirety. The

---

[47]Mankiewicz was playing on the title of Victor Hugo's play *Le Roi s'amuse,* the source of Verdi's *Rigoletto,* loosely based on the escapades of the libertine French King François I. Schenck's literacy was so meager that Mankiewicz says the publicity department was obliged to change the original copy puffing Metro as having "more stars than there are in the firmament" to "in the heavens" because Schenck thought *firmament* was either a laxative or a fixative for false teeth.

film therefore was banned in Boston, and major cuts had to be made in order to open it in cities such as Detroit and Providence. In consequence, *Strange Cargo* grossed poorly.

When Philip Barry's *Philadelphia Story* became the biggest hit of the Broadway season in the spring of 1939, the movie studios promptly forgot that its star, Katharine Hepburn, had been driven from Hollywood when she was declared "box-office poison" by a group of theater owners. Miss Hepburn, a canny careerist, remembered and had the foresight to acquire the film rights to the play. Playwright Barry had tailored to her the role of Tracy Lord, "a priggish, wisecracking patrician"[48] humbled and humanized by an amorous peccadillo on the eve of her second marriage to an upwardly mobile prig. Hepburn's motive in acquiring the film rights was not only to guarantee that she would re-create her role in the film version but to make sure, as the film's packager, she retained control over the selection of every creative figure who would contribute to the picture.

As stipulated by Hepburn's "protector" at the time, Howard Hughes, who is reputed to have staked Hepburn to her 25 percent interest in the play's production, any studio's acquisition of the rights to make the film was contingent on a guarantee of two top male stars to appear opposite Hepburn in a move to strengthen her weak box-office draw. The catch was that there was only one part in the play, the antagonistic reporter who falls for the spoiled heiress, large enough to attract a name.

"L. B. Mayer wanted that property as much as I did," says Mankiewicz, and the studio chief dispatched Joe to New York to see the play and solve the casting problem with the short admonition, "Lick it!" The logical solution Mankiewicz devised, in the treatment that won the property for Metro, was to combine two parts in order to enlarge the role of the socialite bride's former husband who takes her back. (The husband takes over the brother's role as the aegis for the reporter and photographer from *Spy* Magazine [*Destiny* in the play] to infiltrate the household.)

As a sideliner for most of the film, C. K. Dexter Haven remained a secondary part, yet Hepburn (and top billing) succeeded in luring Cary Grant,[49] whose magnetism and aplomb enliven the role Mankie-

[48]From an uncredited capsule review in the *New Yorker*.
[49]In *On Cukor* (G. P. Putnam's Sons, 1972, p. 124), Cukor says, "We tried to

wicz invented. The casting of Grant and the engagement of Donald Ogden Stewart to script and George Cukor to direct, at Hepburn's behest, made *The Philadelphia Story* a reunion of the key creative figures from *Holiday* (1938), an earlier social comedy by Barry that Hepburn had masterminded before she departed Hollywood in failure.

With James Stewart in the role of the reporter (which earned him an Academy Award) and an accomplished supporting cast, *The Philadelphia Story* gave Mankiewicz his first smash hit as a producer, earning the studio a prodigious $1.3 million in profits. Mankiewicz was aware that the film's quality was vastly superior to that of his recent productions, as he sarcastically remarked in the commissary, "I'm going to be fired. I've made a good picture."

Mankiewicz claims credit for the film's prologue, which he outlined in his lengthy screenplay treatment. In the prologue the quarrelsome, broken marriage between Grant and Hepburn is synopsized in a silent sequence. As Grant strides out of the house carrying his bags, Hepburn follows after with his pipe rack and golf bag, which she dumps at his feet. To add to this gesture, she removes one of the golf clubs and breaks it over her knee. Grant is about to retaliate by slugging her but settles for a more comic shove that lands her backward through the front door.[50]

Mankiewicz's script suggestions proved considerably more useful to screenwriter Donald Ogden Stewart than the recording Mankiewicz had made of the stage performance so that Stewart could note and preserve all the audience laughs. Stewart found this imposition "a little irritating," though he terms his association with Mankiewicz "very friendly and helpful." Mankiewicz recognized that the laugh track was

---

get this and that star, but they weren't available, and we finally chose Cary Grant and James Stewart, neither of whom was considered absolutely top-notch at the time—and they were perfect." Considering Grant's top billing and his succession of *Topper, The Awful Truth, Bringing Up Baby, Holiday* (these last two with Hepburn), *Gunga Din, Only Angels Have Wings,* and *His Girl Friday* prior to *The Philadelphia Story,* Cukor's assertion seems inaccurate. Stewart had won the New York Critics Award the previous year for *Mr. Smith Goes to Washington,* which was followed by *Destry Rides Again* and *The Shop Around the Corner.*

[50]Mankiewicz also takes credit for the brief epilogue, which consists of a riffling through of the wedding photos of Grant and Hepburn surreptitiously snapped by the editor of *Spy,* the exposé magazine whose team Hepburn has disarmed. This series of stop-action shots ends with a freeze frame of the couple's startled embrace, which Mankiewicz claims anticipated the vogue started by the ending of Truffaut's *400 Blows* by twenty years.

useless because films cannot be timed to accommodate anticipated laughs, but the idea suggests the fidelity to the text of established plays he has always observed.

Although Donald Stewart modestly dismisses the Academy Award he won for his adaptation[51] as "the easiest Oscar anyone ever got . . . all you had to do was get out of the way of Barry's dialogue," his skill is remarkable in expanding the play's two sets to a wide variety of apt locations and writing a number of scenes indistinguishable in style and quality from Barry's. Despite its one boring passage, the sluggish, "morning after" talk fest, *The Philadelphia Story* ranks as the most elegant American comedy of manners on film previous to Mankiewicz's own *Letter to Three Wives* and *All About Eve*.

On October 8, 1940, a month and a half after the completion of filming *The Philadelphia Story*, Rosa gave birth prematurely to a son the Mankiewiczes named Christopher. As godparents for the Catholic baptism, Rosa selected writer Walter Reisch's wife, Lisl, and Mankiewicz picked his friend Spencer Tracy. The day before the baptism, Metro's casting director, Billy Grady, approached Tracy in the commissary and said, "I hope you've studied the Apostles' Creed." "You Mick son of a bitch," Tracy replied to his compatriot, "I happen to be not only the world's greatest actor, but a very devout Catholic. There'll be no problem with me. I'll be 'all right on the night.'" (Mankiewicz says that Tracy was always letter perfect on scripts. "He would frequently stay up all night studying his lines, but he loved to come on a set, walk up to the continuity girl, and say, 'What are we shooting today?' preferably with the director standing nearby. The director would curse when the continuity girl, who had turned white, repeated his question, and word would quickly get to the other actors, so that everyone on the set would be nervous except Tracy.") The baptism turned into a calamitous farce. Lisl Reisch only knew the Apostles' Creed in German, so her prompting was of little use to Tracy, who couldn't remember a word and had to be cued by the officiating Monsignor.

For his next production Mankiewicz unearthed a comedy written by his brother and Marc Connelly, *The Wild Man of Borneo*, which had flopped on Broadway in 1927. Of this project Mankiewicz says, "I made it because it meant a sale to Herman and Marc of the dramatic

---

[51]Waldo Salt contributed a number of revisions to Stewart's screenplay, as noted in Metro's copy of the shooting script.

rights, which was very little but something. [At $298,000 it was Man-kiewicz's smallest budgeted production at Metro other than *A Christ-mas Carol,* which cost $9,000 less.] I liked the play. I thought it was an amusing idea for a small comedy, and it made an amusing small comedy. Frank Morgan was very funny in the part. [Morgan plays a former patent-medicine pitchman obliged to sustain the fiction of his wealth and theatrical eminence for his daughter and the boarders of a theatrical rooming house by secretly selling homemade soap on street corners and appearing in the freak show of a dime arcade as the "wild man" of the title.] I can't take an oath that I would have produced the picture if my brother hadn't written the play, but I don't feel guilty. I didn't take a bad property and make it into a film." Metro quietly buried this picture by delaying its press screening for four months while dispatching the film around the country as a programmer for the second halves of double bills.

Mankiewicz followed *The Wild Man of Borneo* with a negligi-ble comic trifle, *The Feminine Touch,* about a college professor (Don Ameche) who has written a book on his thesis that jealousy has no place in a modern, civilized society. He clings to this belief until the end of the film, when he assaults his womanizing pub-lisher (Van Heflin) under the mistaken impression that the wolf has been consorting with his wife (Rosalind Russell). The authors of the script were George Oppenheimer, Edmund L. Hartmann, and Ogden Nash. When the ailing Nash, who had been growing feverish in the late afternoons, returned to the East, Oppenheimer took over and finished the script. "Joe liked it enormously," says Oppenheimer, "but said he wanted to do a bit of rewriting. I said, 'If you like it so much, why don't you let it alone?'" To pacify him, Mankiewicz said they would exchange roles, and after Oppen-heimer came back from a two-week vacation, he was to evaluate Mankiewicz's rewrite as though he were the producer.

A memo to this effect was attached to the revised script that awaited Oppenheimer on his return. Oppenheimer "was furious" at Mankiewicz's changes, especially the loss of what he considered Ogden Nash's funniest scene between the psychology professor (Ameche) and a cretinous football star. (Since there exists a still from this scene, it was most likely filmed and later cut.) Oppenheimer claims he was so in-censed by this and other changes he considered inferior that he exer-cised his "producer's" prerogative and ordered the front office, by phone, to fire Mankiewicz. "All hell broke loose," says Oppenheimer, "but I knew I was safe because I had a contract, so I wasn't being very brave. Sam Katz, the goddamnedest hypocrite that ever lived, called me up to his office and said, 'How can you do this to your friend?' I replied, 'Because I think it's high time he let writers do their writing.' We had a big fight, and I was in bad odor for a long time. I don't think Joe cared about it nearly as much as Katz, who hated any breach of duty or respect. It was clearly a joke, but I really meant it."

Mankiewicz dismisses the tale as "an utter fabrication," the sour grapes invention of "an untalented writer whose dialogue required improvement. . . . I would never have made an agreement like that with Oppenheimer," Mankiewicz asserts. "I didn't know him well enough and I didn't like him well enough.[52] Believe me, I rewrote very little of Ogden Nash," Mankiewicz avers, and he cites as evidence the rather favorable *New York Times* review of *The Feminine Touch* ("Oppenheimer, Hart, and Nash have dropped some chortling repartee . . . the film has too many lines, but they do have a sort of dizzy spin to them")[53] and Nash's flattering inscription to him, at the time, in his collection *The Face Is Familiar* (1940), which reads:

> For Joe Mankiewicz—
> Always at my back I hear,
> Winged release dates hurrying near.
> I'm glad my producer's literate,
> Gentle, kindly, and considerate.

[52]George Oppenheimer, who was noted at MGM for his sophisticated dialogue and skill in polishing scripts, offers detailed corroboration of this incident. Moreover, Sam Marx writes, in a letter of December 17, 1973, "As to the Oppenheimer story, I think it could have happened. The reason I say this is that Joe once told me, with great relish, that when he was at Paramount, one of their many temporary studio heads, Manny Cohen, refused him a raise but said, 'Joe, you sit in my chair and I'll be you, and I'll ask you for a raise and you can see that it should be refused.' So Joe sat in the boss's chair, and when Cohen said he was Mankiewicz and wanted a raise, Joe said, "You deserve it, and I'm going to give it to you.'"
In the version of this tale that Mankiewicz told Frank Nugent (*Collier's*, March 24, 1951), he was asking Cohen for a raise of $25 after his Academy Award nomination for writing *Skippy*. Cohen remonstrated that Paramount was in receivership, but when they exchanged seats, Joe, playing Cohen, snapped, " 'I'm a busy man, Mankiewicz! You ought to know better than to bother me about a lousy $25 raise. You have it. Now, get out!'"
[53]Theodore Strauss, *New York Times*, December 12, 1941.

> We are the boys of the Thalberg Building,
> Hard at work at lily gilding;
> Southern wits and Yankee wits—
> For Thalberg and for Mankiewicz.

Having completed a national stage tour of *The Philadelphia Story*, Katharine Hepburn was peddling Metro a ninety-page story treatment titled *Woman of the Year* that she wanted to make as her next film. L. B. Mayer was somewhat nonplussed that she had placed the same $100,000 price tag on the unaccredited script as she had on her own services, so he relayed it to Mankiewicz for an opinion. Joe was enthusiastic and assumed, from the price and from the newspaper setting of the bumpy romance between a highbrow foreign affairs columnist, like Dorothy Thompson, and a down-to-earth sports columnist, that it was doubtless the handiwork of the former journalists Ben Hecht and Charles MacArthur, "doing it anonymously because they had a commitment somewhere else."[54] Actually, the script was the work of the then unknown team of Ring Lardner, Jr., and Michael Kanin—Hepburn had shrewdly gauged that she could get them a top price only if the studio believed their work was that of "name" writers.

Since Cukor was directing Garbo in *Two-Faced Woman*, Hepburn insisted on Metro's importing from Columbia another of her favorite directors, George Stevens. Her first choice for the sports writer, Spencer Tracy, was also unavailable, but the cancellation of *The Yearling* freed him for what proved to be the most auspicious pairing in films since William Powell had been linked to Myrna Loy.

The teaming seemed less than promising at the outset. Mankiewicz and Tracy were leaving the Thalberg Building on their way to lunch, when Hepburn walked in, an imposing figure in her upswept hairdo and platform shoes. After Joe introduced his costars, who had never met before, Hepburn gave Tracy the once-over and commented, "Mr. Tracy, I think you're a little short for me." "Don't worry," said Mankiewicz. "He'll cut you down to size." If Hepburn was skeptical about Tracy's height, Tracy had misgivings about how he would fare at the hands of Hepburn's director. George Stevens persuaded him that the film required a woman's director, but Tracy still kept referring to Hepburn as "that woman." This situation prevailed until they each

---

[54]Ring Lardner, Jr., quoted in "The Films of Ring Lardner, Jr.," by Kenneth Geist, *Film Comment*, Winter 1970–71, p. 46.

started requesting Stevens to favor the other in his setups. Then everyone on the set knew why their love scenes seemed so genuine—they were no longer acting.

George Stevens was, in fact, very much his own man, and in order to get his way on the unorthodox lighting of a scene and a set he demanded, he twice walked off the picture. Sam Marx says that on one of these occasions, Joe Cohn, the studio's production manager, prevailed on Mankiewicz to take over the direction of a scene between Tracy and Hepburn that Stevens had already rehearsed. When it was completed, Mankiewicz came up to Marx, who had been watching in back, and announced, "I have just become a director." "Why do you say that?" Marx inquired. Mankiewicz explained, "Did you see what happened when I wanted to sit down? A man put a chair under me. I put my pipe in my mouth and a guy rushes over with a match. Everyone is standing still till I say, 'Action,' and then they're all waiting till I say, 'Cut.' This is for me. I want to have that job."

Mankiewicz says, "Sam's wrong. I never directed Tracy and Hepburn in my life. The only direction I ever did at MGM was the screen test of Lena Horne for *Cabin in the Sky* (1943), which I directed with Frank Davis, a writer who had some directing or editing experience. I also did the test of Luise Rainer for her first film, *Escapade* (1935), in which she replaced Myrna Loy."

Mankiewicz's incontestable contribution to *Woman of the Year* is the final scene he devised with John Lee Mahin of the comic holocaust Hepburn makes of Tracy's kitchen. Mankiewicz explains that unlike *The Philadelphia Story* ("the best Hepburn vehicle ever written"), "*Woman of the Year* cleverly dramatized the incredible superiority that Hepburn exuded over other women" without giving her "the come-uppance always essential to making her palatable to the average American audience."

"The average American housewife, seated next to her husband, staring for two hours at this paragon of beauty, intelligence, wit, accomplishment, and everything else, cannot help but wonder if her husband isn't comparing her very unfavorably with this goddess he sees on the screen. . . . John and I came up with the idea of having the Woman of the Year try to fix a very simple breakfast [in order to win back Tracy through her supplicating domesticity] and completely fuck it up."

The enthusiastic audience at the first preview had been distinctly cool to the Lardner-Kanin ending, which saw Tracy and Hepburn reconciled at a prizefight after she had written an uncharacteristic sentimental piece under his byline to regain his affection. Although Miss Hepburn termed the new breakfast scene ending "the worst bunch of shit I've ever read," according to Mahin, "the women absolutely shrieked at it," says Mankiewicz, "not only with admiration, but relief. Now they could turn to their *schmuck* husbands and say, 'She may know Battista, but she can't even make a cup of coffee, you silly bastard.' " Even the Academy Award for Best Original Screenplay failed to kindle the gratitude of Lardner and Kanin, who remained miffed at what they considered a vulgarization of their script. As they passed Mankiewicz's table at the awards banquet, Joe rose to shake their hands, and they pointedly snubbed him.

As a result of his ill health, "Pop" Mankiewicz had taken a leave of absence from the City College of New York to spend the winter in Beverly Hills recuperating near his sons. On December 2, 1941, less than two weeks after his arrival and just two days after celebrating his sixty-ninth birthday, the professor died of a cerebral hemorrhage. His death was a source of bereavement not only to Joe but to numerous friends of Joe's who had been captivated by his father on the professor's summer visits to Los Angeles to teach at UCLA. Joe loves to tell the story of how James Cagney, at the height of his thirties stardom, had stopped by their table at the Brown Derby one evening to pay his respects to his former Stuyvesant High School teacher. Pop's dedication to his academic pursuits had left him little time for seeing movies other than those made by his sons. In response to Cagney's query about whether the professor remembered him, Pop replied, "Yes indeed, Mr. Cagney. Tell me, what are you doing now?"

Pearl Harbor was bombed five days after Pop's death. The approach of Mankiewicz's thirty-third birthday and the fact that his wife was expecting a second child disqualified him for the draft. Also, the circle of those dependent on his Metro salary was multiplying with the appeals of European relatives and friends to underwrite their emigration and serve as their American guarantor.

One of these relatives for whom Mankiewicz had signed an affidavit was a short, bald man who had changed his name to Ernst Manville and who possessed very little English and even less cash. He was having difficulty opening a restaurant on the Sunset Strip. "One day he came to me in tremendous distress," says Mankiewicz. "He needed $200 immediately or the sheriff was going to take away his tables and chairs, and he was planning to open the next night. I remember writing out the check, and as I was writing, it occurred to me, because Herman and I would often discuss it, that these people, without exception, had all given up the name of Mankiewicz and adopted various Anglo-Saxon names. I said to him, very innocently, 'Tell me, Ernst, why is it that the first thing you and Kurt and all the other Mankiewiczes did when you got to this country was to change your name?' As I was affixing my signature to this check, he looked at me and said, 'I figured, "Where could I get in America with a name like Mankiewicz?"' The enormity of his reply didn't hit me until about a half hour later, but I tore out the check and said, 'Here, I guess that's a pretty good answer.' "

As his contribution to the war effort, Mankiewicz served as an airplane spotter, fire watcher, and nighttime member of the patrol guarding the small, undefended stretch of coastline near his home in the Pacific Palisades against the threat of Japanese assault teams. In response to Joe's appeal that his patrol was shorthanded, his superior, writer John Larkin, informed him that two of his neighbors had volunteered and would attend the next secret meeting that evening. The volunteers lent literary distinction to the gathering, though their physical infirmities precluded any truly practical aid. As Mankiewicz stood outside his house waiting to greet them, he discerned two figures making very slow progress down Amalfi Drive. The one leaning on a cane proved to be Thomas Mann, who was leading the practically blind Aldous Huxley.

At Metro, Mankiewicz was supervising construction of two "bombs" thinly justified as patriotic morale builders. The first was a spy spoof musical, *Cairo,* starring Jeanette MacDonald in her shrill coloratura swan song at the studio, opposite Robert Young. *Cairo* made scant use of the available talent of such eminences of the American musical theater as E. Y. Harburg, Arthur Schwartz, and Harold Arlen[55] and relied on dreary repertoire arias for MacDonald. The result was so

[55]The only memorable song in *Cairo* is the distinctively Arlen-Harburg, "Buds Won't Bud," recycled from Metro's *Andy Hardy Meets Debutante* (1940), which they had originally written and dropped from their 1937 Broadway musical *Hooray for What.* In *Cairo* it is performed by the great Ethel Waters, first as a solo and then as a duet with her black supporting "soul mate," Dooley Wilson *(Casablanca),* in a sequence that could be easily cropped for southern theaters. The most egregious music in the film is a sentimental medley of nostalgic American songs ("The most beautiful songs of all," intros MacDonald), concluding with a cornball wartime original by Arthur Schwartz, "Keep the Lights Burning Bright in the Harbor," which is reprised by all hands at the end of the picture. It is, in fact, the MacDonald showpieces, like

dismaying that Mankiewicz had his name removed from the picture's credits. The second dud, *Reunion in France*, was Joe's ninth and last picture with Joan Crawford, whose lengthy career at MGM was also terminated after one more film. In *Reunion in France*, Crawford, despite the confiscation of her Paris home and possessions under the German occupation, is spectacularly gowned and jeweled as a selfish rich bitch turned Resistance fighter. Defiantly, she hides and helps in the escape of an American flier played by John Wayne.

Crawford disowns this ludicrous romantic melodrama as "undiluted hokum," but it later served to keep Mankiewicz one up on his precocious sons. One of the boys' favorite bedtime games was to mock their father in a routine called "The World's Leading Authority," whose refrain was "But I'm an expert on that . . . ," delivered in a tone of injured protest. Their mother caught them in a variant of this mockery, satirizing their father's constant use of nicknames to indicate his intimacy with the famous people whose names he dropped. Rosa was helpless with laughter when one boy said, "Gee, Dad, what about John Wayne?" and the other replied, "Duke? Well, Duke. . . ." Rosa got the point but was obliged to tell them that, unlikely as it seemed, their father had indeed worked with Wayne. Years later, when the younger son, Tom, criticized his father's ignorance of the new generation of brilliant film directors, Joe challenged him to name one of these paragons with whom he was unfamiliar. Tom cited the new French director of *Rififi*, Jules Dassin (French pronunciation). "You mean Julie Dassin," Mankiewicz corrected, "who did one of his first pictures for me." This early and dubious credit was *Reunion in France*.

Mankiewicz was growing increasingly restive and miserable at the direction his career was taking. While listening to the broadcast on which his brother won the 1941 Academy Award for his screenplay of *Citizen Kane*, he lamented to his wife, "I don't think I'll ever win an Oscar," and he remembers his feeling of pride and elation soured by the envious thought, "He's got the Oscar and I'm a producer at Metro, goddamn it!"

L. B. Mayer evidently detected this distress and was eager to find a means both of cheering and of retaining hold of the services of the

this medley, that really stop this feeble comedy cold, and their inclusion allegedly required numerous cuts in the continuity to reduce the film to its sluggish 101-minute running time.

man who had delivered the two big Hepburn winners. He picked the inappropriate occasion of Bernie Hyman's funeral in September 1942 to suggest the enticing prospect of becoming Thalberg's successor as Metro's top producer.[56] Nodding at Hyman's casket, Mayer decreed, "He was weak. You are strong."

In June of 1942 Rosa had given birth to their second son, Thomas. Eddie Mannix, Mayer's gruff, gravel-voiced aide, who began with the Schencks as a bouncer at Palisades Amusement Park and who was admired by Mankiewicz as one of the few "honest and decent" movie executives, was nominated as godfather this time.

In October, while the Mankiewiczes were vacationing at Arrowhead Springs with their close friends, the Franz Waxmans, Rosa fell into a catatonic state, was brought home by ambulance, and was dispatched to the Menninger Clinic in Topeka, Kansas, where she remained for nine months of treatment.

During this period of separation, Mankiewicz found companionship with another troubled actress who was also temporarily unattached. Judy Garland, aged twenty, was making the difficult transition from child to adult star and was newly separated from her musician husband, David Rose, after only a year and a half of marriage. Gossip attributed the split to the pressures exerted by Judy's domineering mother and by the studio on Rose, an MGM staff composer, whose union with their star chattel they had bitterly opposed. Two intimates report that Garland was actually having an affair with Tyrone Power, which shattered his marriage to Annabella and was terminated only by Power's enlistment in the Marine Corps at the end of 1942.

Power's close friend J. Watson Webb describes Garland during that period as enjoying "the reputation of being Hollywood's wittiest woman. A highly strung creature of immense vitality, intensely gay, and with a rare quality of warmth poised on the brink of sadness." Mankiewicz says, "I just thought she was enchanting. In many ways I've never met anyone like Judy at that time. I'm not talking about her talent. She was just the most remarkably bright, gay, happy, helpless, and engaging girl I've ever met."

---

[56]Hyman was the Thalberg protégé who took over several of his unfinished films *(The Good Earth, Camille)* after Thalberg's death in 1936 and became one of the studio's key executive producers in the subsequent realignment. Both Thalberg and Hyman died prematurely, Thalberg at thirty-seven, Hyman at forty-seven.

Garland and Mankiewicz shared a common love of intrigue and indulged it in keeping their affair an ill-kept secret from the columnists[57] and studio heads by surreptitiously checking out restaurants for familiar faces and arranging meetings through the studio switchboard under Garland's alias, Miss Sherwood. "She would lie in wait for Joe to call at the Beverly Wilshire Hotel, where Joe sneaked in and out," an intimate reveals. "This made her feel all the sorrier for herself, but when Joe arrived, it made it all the more passionate and great."

To an analysand like Mankiewicz, avid for collecting women's psychiatric histories, the tales of Judy's "Draconian mother," who would lock her in a closet to compel obedience, were of particular fascination. "By and large, the women I knew, or had relationships with, were as neurotic as I was," says Mankiewicz. "It was not unknown to find neurotic women and men in show business. One thing a neurotic, male or female, dearly loves is to have his neuroses discussed, preferably by another neurotic." Concerning his perceptions about Garland, Mankiewicz says, "I knew that her behavior patterns revealed she was in trouble. . . . She was full of unconscious hostility toward the parent, represented by the studio, which she manifested by not showing up on time. They told her she was a hunchback. Christ almighty, the girl reacted to the slightest bit of kindness as if it were a drug. . . . We think of Judy now as a really big star [Garland's name appeared above the title for the first time in *For Me and My Gal* (1942)], but she was really pushed around. She was treated by most people, including her mother, as a *thing*, not as a human being."

From his visits to Topeka, Mankiewicz had become friendly with Karl Menninger and began an intimate correspondence with him. While Menninger, on a visit to Los Angeles, was staying at the Beverly Hills Hotel, Mankiewicz arranged for Garland to meet with him. "Menninger said that she needed help," Mankiewicz relates, "and that it was urgent that not too much time be allowed to go by before treatment was begun. . . . He recognized her unconscious motivations and felt that as she was only twenty, they were still fairly easy to get at, bring out into the open, and possible to get her to recognize and be able to handle." Since the year's stay at his clinic in Kansas that

---

[57]Mankiewicz says, "I'm sure Hedda and Louella knew of my relations with Garland, but they were discreet about it because I was married at the time." Composer Johnny Green, a mutual friend to Garland and Mankiewicz, says, "They were a *scandale* in this 'free-thinking' community."

Menninger recommended was made impracticable by Garland's studio commitments, the doctor, with Mankiewicz's delighted concurrence, sent her to the noted German psychiatrist Dr. Ernest Simmel, who had analyzed Joe's brother. Judy began intensive therapy with a regimen of five sessions a week.

As a vehicle for Garland, Mankiewicz began adapting S. N. Behrman's farce *The Pirate*, in which the Lunts had just made a great hit on Broadway.[58] Behrman, working on the Metro lot, was delighted with the first forty or fifty pages Mankiewicz submitted to him, writing, "This is delicious stuff. You have, I am happy to see, struck your own vein on it. As a result, what comes off your pen is felicitous and very funny." To placate his Metro producer, Sam Katz, who was impatient that the work was progressing so slowly, Mankiewicz sent him two contradictory memos. The first one was sent by Joe Mankiewicz, the producer, with a copy to Joe Mankiewicz, the writer. In it he complained that he "could never get the s.o.b. on the phone, as he was always out screwing, gambling, or playing tennis at the Beverly Hills Tennis Club. Any help that Katz could give him to help control this writer would be greatly appreciated." The second was a responding memo from Mankiewicz, the writer, to Katz, saying, "I am in receipt of a memo from the producer Joseph L. Mankiewicz. Let me tell you that Mr. Mankiewicz doesn't read what I give him, and when he does, he fails to comprehend it. He is just this side of an illiterate, and I'm writing my ass off, et cetera."

The Pirate adaptation never was completed. Mankiewicz was returning on the Super Chief from a visit to Rosa in Topeka and, as was his custom on trains, had changed into pajamas and robe and settled down with his puzzles and books. To his surprise, Metro's head publicist, Howard Strickling, appeared at his compartment to inform him that Mr. Mayer was on the train and wanted to see him at once.

"I went to see Mayer in my slippers and bathrobe," says Mankiewicz, "and a screaming fight ensued. First he accused me of wanting to have an affair with Judy and just making believe I was her friend.

---

[58]In 1947 Garland appeared opposite Gene Kelly in a musical version of *The Pirate*, written by Frances Goodrich and Albert Hackett and directed by Garland's husband, Vincente Minnelli. In his autobiography, *I Remember It Well* (Doubleday, 1974, p. 164), Minnelli takes credit for suggesting the play to Garland; evidently he was unaware of Mankiewicz's previous effort.

Then he accused me of fucking around with Judy. He was absolutely uncontrollable in his rage and said something to the effect of 'I won't have it.' Then, at the end, in the typical L. B. Mayer fashion, he said, 'You have to understand. I have the welfare of all my players at heart,[59] and I'm talking to you like a father.' I said, 'No, you're not. You're talking like a jealous old man,' and walked out of the compartment. That's what really generated L. B.'s hatred, I think."

When Mankiewicz returned to the studio, he stormed into Eddie Mannix's office, related what had transpired on the train, and said, "I don't feel I deserve that kind of abuse, and I expect Mr. Mayer to apologize." "What if he won't?" Mannix inquired. "Then I quit, I'm out, that's it," Mankiewicz replied. Mannix said that this was a matter only Mayer and Mankiewicz could resolve between themselves and suggested that Joe take it up with Mayer, who was in his office. Mannix tipped off Mayer, via the office intercom, that Mankiewicz was on his way in and that he would have to apologize if he wanted to retain him.[60]

Before Mankiewicz could deliver his ultimatum, Mayer began berating him for meddling with Garland's mental health by suggesting she needed psychiatric care when the studio and her mother knew what was best for her. Mayer revealed that Mrs. Gumm, Judy's mother, had called on him to protest that the meeting with Menninger and the visits to Simmel, which Mankiewicz had arranged, were twisting her daughter's mind and alienating her affections. "Mayer was a great executive and could have run General Motors as successfully as MGM," says Mankiewicz, "but he had a superstitious terror of psychiatry, as many men had at that time. Though his own wife was constantly being treated for psychosomatic ailments, a medical doctor isn't going to help you face the fact that you hate your mother or that your mother is your enemy." Taking Mrs. Gumm's side, Mayer went into his favor-

---

[59]Mankiewicz scoffs at the description by several Garland biographers and intimates that Mayer's feelings toward Judy were paternal. "That's like Joan Crawford or Maggie Sullavan telling me that Louis B. Mayer would frequently refer to her as one of his daughters, and, for some reason or other, on the word *daughter*, his hand would always clasp one of her tits." However, Mayer's elder daughter, Edith Goetz, told a friend of Judy's that her father had footed all of Garland's medical bills when she was hospitalized in Boston in the fifties.

[60]This account of the exchange between Mankiewicz and Mannix was furnished by Sam Marx, who had it from Mannix.

ite tirade "about the holiness and divinity of mothers."

Thoroughly fed up with what he considered a "damagingly destructive meeting," Mankiewicz abruptly terminated it by announcing, "Obviously, Mr. Mayer, this studio isn't big enough for both of us," an audacity at which Eddie Mannix, who had joined the meeting, "fell out of his chair laughing." The upshot was that Mankiewicz left the studio and Garland ceased her visits to the psychiatrist, both moves that Metro would, in time, regret.

"I had a year or two to go on a five-year, noncancellable contract with Metro," says Mankiewicz, "so they had the right to assign my contract, and I was very much afraid they were going to send me to Warner Brothers, where I didn't particularly want to go. However, my agent, Bert Allenberg, fixed it for my contract to be assigned to Twentieth Century–Fox."

"Running Twentieth at that time [August 1943] was Joe Schenck, who was as honest and gentlemanly as his brother [Nick of MGM] was devious and dishonest. Darryl [Zanuck] was away liberating South Africa, and Billy Goetz was sort of keeping an eye on production, but Joe Schenck was the boss."

"Allenberg set up a meeting with Joe Schenck the next day. Schenck said, 'I know you and Louie had this fight. . . . I don't want to know any of the details, but how do you feel about having your contract assigned here?' I said, 'Well, Mr. Schenck, there are two things I want. One is a raise in salary, because I don't want anyone to think I've been fired by Mayer and that I have to move on to an inferior spot. Second, I want the right to direct if we can agree on the subject matter.' He gave me a contract that I haven't had the equal of since. Besides a token raise of $500 a week, I had the right to stipulate on every property I undertook whether I wrote and/or directed and/or produced. I could do all or just one, at my choice, which was an unheard-of deal at the time."

The psychological boost of no longer being forced to beg for an opportunity to direct proved immense. Mankiewicz's crawling days, the era he looks back on as his "black period," were at an end.

"You've earned your wings.
You can come down now"   5

AT THE COMMENCEMENT OF HIS HIGH-SALARIED, FIVE-YEAR CON-
tract, Mankiewicz was installed in one of Fox's most spacious bungalow
offices, along with Adelaide Thorp, his devoted secretary from Metro.

As his first production for the studio, Mankiewicz chose A. J.
Cronin's inspirational novel, *The Keys of the Kingdom,* a 1941 best
seller about a Scots Catholic priest, Francis Chisholm, whose humble
sanctity triumphs over all manner of adversity in his thirty-five years
as a missionary to a remote Chinese village. While the subject seems
unlikely for a man like Mankiewicz, who thinks "all religion is utter
nonsense," the priest's admiration for the Confucian's superior sense
of humor, his respect for his atheist doctor friend's virtue, and his
friendship for a couple of rival Methodist missionaries, which lands him
in trouble with his superior, possibly appealed to Mankiewicz.[1]

The studio was eager to repeat the success of *The Song of Ber-
nadette* (1943), their previous religious epic, and hoped that Gregory
Peck, their new, gravely sincere, and handsome leading man, might, as
Chisholm, score as great a personal triumph as Jennifer Jones, another

---

[1]A critic for *Catholic World* (August 1941), Joseph McSorley, wrote, "The book
may be described as a thesis on the futility of organized religion." Both the book and
the film vaunt the good works of an individual over and above the Catholic Church
as an institution.

find of David O. Selznick's, had as Bernadette. (Their thinking was not
far off the mark, since the year's hit film, *Going My Way*, concerned
the comic conflict of two contemporary Catholic priests.)

Fox's ace screenwriter, Nunnally Johnson *(Grapes of Wrath)*, had
already completed a screenplay when Mankiewicz took over the project. Mankiewicz, as usual, rewrote it and claimed sole screenplay
credit. The issue was settled by the arbitration committee of the Screen
Writers Guild, who ruled it a cocredit, with Mankiewicz billed before
Johnson.

Even with substantial cuts,[2] the film runs "two hours and seventeen minutes of high thinking in low lighting,"[3] and Mankiewicz admits it contains "long, talky stretches." The film is curiously dull for
being based on a novel praised as "an adventure and travel story packed
with melodramatic action."[4] In fact, the picture's only genuine action
sequence comes when the priest, in defense of his mission-hospital,
blows up the cannon of the vicious Imperial army, killing numerous
soldiers. The script is devoid of humor except for an occasional salty
line from the down-to-earth doctor (Thomas Mitchell), and most of the
emotional climaxes are marred by sentimentality and stilted writing.

Evidently, Mankiewicz was eager to establish the priest's virtue
and the worthiness of his endeavors in the face of his self-doubt and
the prejudices the film's principal characters hold against him. To
this end, Mankiewicz interspersed the film's episodes with a literary
framing device taken from the novel—readings from Father Francis's
autobiographical journal by a representative of the bishop who has
come to demand his retirement. Just as this cleric (Cedric Hard-
wicke), at the end of the film, is converted by this journal to a perception of Father Francis's saintliness, so, in the course of the action,
are most of the missionary's antagonists.

In the body of the film, the missionary's example significantly
alters four lives. Two of these people are from Francis's own social class
and home town. The devotion of Francis's doctor friend (Mitchell)

---

[2]Three principal sequences from the early part of the film were eliminated, along
with a lot of scene endings of young Francis gazing reverently toward church spires.
These cut sequences are: the Dickensian maltreatment of Francis as an orphaned boy,
forced by his grandparents to work in a shipyard; the suicide of Francis's childhood
sweetheart, à la Anna Karenina; and Francis's flight from his Spanish seminary and
innocent night with a "fallen woman."
[3]C. A. Lejeune, *The Observer*, March 4, 1945.
[4]*New Republic*, July 28, 1941.

leads him to follow Francis to China and meet his death healing the wounded in the Sun Yat-sen–era battle between Republican and Imperial forces. Conversely, Francis's fellow seminarian, Mealy (Vincent Price), who has rapidly risen in the church hierarchy, is contemptuous and patronizing when he comes to inspect Francis's mission, only to find it in ruins after the military combat. (Mealy is the bishop who demands the aged Francis's retirement from their home-town parish.) Two aristocrats are humbled by Francis's sanctity—the skeptical village mandarin (Leonard Strong), who becomes the mission's patron, and the haughty mother superior (Rosa Stradner), who eventually bows to Francis's innate humility, which she secretly envies.

While these characters serve to authenticate Father Francis's goodness, only one encounter is genuinely affecting. This is the poignant leave-taking scene between the priest and the mother superior, which by its understatement achieves the pathos that the tear-jerking death-bed scene of the expiring doctor and the anguished priest does not. C. A. Lejeune describes Rosa Stradner in the former scene as "an actress who apparently knows how to make her hands speak. It is largely due to the beautiful timing and precision of her silent playing—the hands knitting busily, then more slowly, then laying down their work in a tiny gesture of grief and resignation as her companion's [Peck] voice speaks of departure—that the farewell scenes are so touching."[5]

Mankiewicz was aware of how much Rosa's status as Mrs. Mankiewicz, the wife of a successful producer, housewife and mother, rather than as an important actress, had contributed to her psychological miseries. The role of the imperious mother superior was tailor-made for Stradner's Austrian accent and a facet of her personality,[6] and while

---

[5]Lejeune, *The Observer.*

[6]The mother superior in Cronin's novel is a German descendant of Bavarian nobility. Rosa Stradner was educated at the Sacred Heart Convent in Vienna, and Mankiewicz made the character's nationality Austrian, like hers. He did retain a line of the mother superior's from the novel: "For centuries the men in my family have been soldiers." Sam Marx relates, apropos of this assertion, "In the early days of the war, my wife remembers going to a charity affair and sitting at the same table with Rosa and Greer Garson. The talk turned to the war in Europe, and Greer mentioned that she had a brother in the artillery, and Rosa said, 'So do I.' They got talking very animatedly until they discovered Greer's was in the British artillery and Rosa's was in the German. My wife said that ended the chat right there."

Joe and Rosa's elder son, Christopher, claims to recognize his mother less in the part of the severe nun than in the flamboyant actress played by Bette Davis in *All About Eve,* which he found much closer to his mother's personality.

she demonstrated her claim to the part in a successful screen test, she came close to losing it.

At the start of shooting, Ingrid Bergman, the studio's first choice for the role, became available. Zanuck pointed out to Mankiewicz that despite the publicity ballyhoo, *Keys'* star, Gregory Peck, had made only one previous, unreleased film, *Days of Glory,* and in view of the public's unfamiliarity with Peck's name, Bergman's was an essential box-office lure. Zanuck guaranteed that Rosa would be given a two-picture contract by way of compensation.

It is likely that the prospect of a largely unsympathetic supporting role deterred Bergman from agreeing to do the film. However, Nunnally Johnson says that he "heard that Joe practically got down on his knees to get her [Stradner] into *The Keys of the Kingdom,* with the appeal 'this will save or doom my marriage.' [Mankiewicz denies ever having made such an appeal.] The studio wanted Ingrid Bergman, but Stradner was accepted mainly for Joe's sake and because they knew she wouldn't harm the picture."

Beyond thinking of the therapeutic value of Rosa Stradner's return to acting, Joe may well have been feeling guilty about the resumption of his affair with Judy Garland. While Mankiewicz contends that this relationship ended after Garland fell for Vincente Minnelli while he was directing her in *Meet Me in St. Louis* (1944), Minnelli gives a different account: "She'd been seeing another man before we started going together. He was tortured and complicated, and very much the intellectual. She simply gravitated back to him just as she had toward me at the start of our affair. I theorized that Judy must have been flattered by the attentions of such a brilliant man, and intrigued by the fact he was in analysis. It didn't alleviate my pain."[7]

Mankiewicz and Garland's friends, Dr. and Mrs. Marcus Rabwin, were deeply distressed. At the height of their previous courtship, Judy and Joe had told the Rabwins they wanted to get married. Subsequently, Dr. Rabwin says, while riding east on the Super Chief, he "wrote Joe a long, disapproving letter," which he never sent, articulating his apprehensions about the relationship, "because she was mad about him, and I knew it wasn't going to come to anything. It had to terminate, and she was going to get hurt."

---

[7]Vincente Minnelli, with Hector Arce, *I Remember It Well,* Doubleday, 1974, p. 142.

Gerold Frank reveals that Judy precipitated the inevitable breakup by using the desperate ploy (but fervent wish) of announcing to Joe that she was pregnant. Mankiewicz allayed her fears of news leaking to the Hollywood press corps by arranging to be with her in New York to await the results of a medical examination. When the test proved negative and they returned to California, Joe stopped returning Judy's phone calls.[8]

Mrs. Rabwin's view that "Judy's downfall began with Joe; she was so depressed after the breakup she began taking pills very heavily," is widely and perhaps unfairly held by many people in the film community who knew Mankiewicz and Garland. This belief is doubtless colored by the hurt resulting from Mankiewicz's dropping the Rabwins and other formerly intimate friends, which was his social pattern. Garland never stopped singing "Happiness Is Just a Thing Called Joe." She named her son, by Sid Luft, Joseph and in later years would periodically phone Mankiewicz in late-night moments of distress.

After Garland persuaded Minnelli to take over the direction of *The Clock* in September 1944, their romance bloomed again, and they were married in June 1945, once her divorce from David Rose had become final. Perhaps Mankiewicz planned a different resolution, for on November 3, 1944, the *Los Angeles Times* announced the Mankiewiczes' separation, stating that Joe had moved out of their Pacific Palisades home and taken an apartment in Beverly Hills. The article concluded that the separation was mutually agreed upon and that the couple was not contemplating legal action. The separation proved short-lived, though as Mankiewicz says of his marriage to Rosa, "I know that I acted contrary to what any analyst would have told me, which was to get out of the situation, but I didn't, I wouldn't, mostly because of Chris and Tom [their sons]."

However, as one intimate notes, "I'm not sure there wasn't a need for a lot of drama, not unlike the problem of another of Joe's great romances, Judy Garland. They [Rosa and Joe] wouldn't have lasted if there wasn't some need. He's not a nice enough man to have stayed with her that long."

---

[8]Gerold Frank, *Judy,* Harper & Row, 1975, pp. 191–93. In relation to this episode, Garland said of Mankiewicz, "He was probably the great love of my life. I almost had his child, except I wasn't pregnant by him" (Lloyd Shearer, "Judy Garland: The Child Who Never Grew Up," *Parade,* April 13, 1975, p. 6).

Friends of the Mankiewiczes were frequently subjected to ugly scenes—Rosa would get tight on two drinks at parties and either hold forth in her most abusive fashion or arbitrarily accuse men of molesting her. Friends invited to the Mankiewicz home might arrive to witness domestic havoc. The producer-agent Sam Jaffe reports, "We were invited for dinner. Rosa was sick. Joe looked terrible. He had a dazed look, petrified and despairing. He'd called the analyst, as she was shrieking upstairs." Composer Johnny Green recalls, "We spent a couple of agonizing evenings when there was real trouble with Joe and Rose, who was a highly neurotic woman. The thrust of those evenings was to 'catharsize' their marital difficulties with a couple of close friends. Rose would sit there sobbing while Joe walked out of the room, losing his temper [and raging], 'You see. How can a man live like this?' Their friends were impotent. There was nothing to do except bleed for them both. It was 'some unhappy.' "

Although *The Keys of the Kingdom* reputedly earned back its cost, it received as disappointing a critical reception as did Darryl Zanuck's similarly ambitious effort *Wilson* (1944), which shared a number of actors from the supporting cast of *The Keys of the Kingdom* (Thomas Mitchell, Vincent Price, Ruth Ford, and Ruth Nelson). Its unpopularity in comparison to the novel and the studio's expectations served to obliterate Rosa Stradner's fine performance. She received no subsequent offers, whereas Gregory Peck was deluged with them.

In looking for his next project, Mankiewicz busied himself writing critical evaluations of the numerous submissions he received for Zanuck and the Fox executives. He had written the following appraisal of *Dragonwyck,* a best-selling gothic novel by Anya Seton, on November 3, 1943, three months before *The Keys of the Kingdom* began filming: "I think careful consideration of this [novel] will reveal less to this than meets the eye. The love story is apt to be very unsatisfying in its conclusion. The young doctor cannot be half so glamorous or exciting as his murderous heel/rival. I can imagine no woman preferring the hero to the villain, in this case, for either bed or breakfast. The melodrama must inevitably conflict and suffer in comparison with *Rebecca* and *Suspicion*. The political and economic applications are naïve, oversimple, and made unexciting by the times in which we live. The background is new. The opportunities for production values are exciting and the cost will be overwhelming!"

Despite this negative appraisal, Fox purchased *Dragonwyck* and assigned it to Mankiewicz's idol, Ernst Lubitsch, who had also joined the studio as a producer-director in 1943. Late in 1944 Lubitsch suffered a heart attack while directing *A Royal Scandal* and was obliged to withdraw. Otto Preminger completed the picture, robbing it of humor.

Knowing of Mankiewicz's eagerness to direct his first film after anguishing over John Stahl's handling of *The Keys of the Kingdom,* Lubitsch, while recuperating, assigned Joe to write and direct *Dragonwyck* under his supervision. Despite his reservations about the material, Mankiewicz felt that Lubitsch's guidance would be invaluable in making his directorial debut. He welcomed the chance to resume his lessons with the master that had begun during his apprentice years at Paramount, when Lubitsch had lunched regularly with the young, German-speaking writer.

The ultimate working relationship, however, proved to be far less gratifying.[9] Mankiewicz describes Lubitsch as "stubborn and touchy" because of his anxiety about the heart condition that was to prove fatal two years later (1947). "We differed about some of the direction," Mankiewicz recalls, "mostly about where I put the camera.[10] I felt a little more inclined, since I was to be a director, to feel my oats a bit. I had Arthur Miller [*The Ox-Bow Incident, How Green Was My Valley*] as my cameraman, who is just the best. Artie was very kind to me and sided with me very often."[11]

---

[9]Mankiewicz does concede that on at least one occasion he found Lubitsch's criticism just. When Lubitsch, after viewing the "dailies," said, "My dear boy, when this man comes into his wife's bedroom, throws her down on the bed, and upbraids her, he should close the door behind him," Joe replied, "Oh my God, you're absolutely right."

[10]Lubitsch was in the habit of dictating to directors whose films he supervised. Lewis Milestone says that Frank Borzage "submitted absolutely to Lubitsch's direction of him during the Dietrich picture [*Desire* (1936)]," on which Borzage was the titular director.

[11]Mankiewicz said, "One of the greatest cameramen who ever lived, Mr. Arthur Miller, who photographed *A Letter to Three Wives* and *Dragonwyck,* told me, 'Relax about the camera. Set it up the way you would in the theater. Set it up the way you see the scene played, and then call the cameraman over and say, "How do you see it?" Now if he comes up with something you would never have thought of, you can always say, "Gee, that's precisely what I had in mind." And if he comes up with something you don't like, you can always throw it out. But you're taking advantage of the vast experience of the cameraman.'" (From an unpublished interview between Mankiewicz and Gary Carey that served as the basis for *More About All About Eve.*) Arthur Miller recalled, "In *Letter to Three Wives,* I again had a director who knew nothing of camera technique: Mankiewicz (for whom I had worked on *Dragonwyck*)" (Charles Higham, *Hollywood Cameramen,* Indiana University Press, 1970, p. 153).

Fox's art director Lyle Wheeler maintains that "the conflicts with Lubitsch were so great that it got to the point where Mankiewicz called Zanuck to have Lubitsch barred from the stage. Lubitsch would sneak in the side door and stand in the dark until Joe was tipped off." Mankiewicz says "nothing of the kind" occurred, but the fact remains that Lubitsch withdrew his name from the film, and no producer's name appears in the title credits. Mary Loos adds, "He [Lubitsch] and Joe didn't talk for a long time [after *Dragonwyck*]. All their friends tried to bring them together. They finally made up."

Dragonwyck is as handsome a production as Mankiewicz forecast and looks as polished and workmanlike as a typical offering by such veteran Fox directors as Henry King or, later, Henry Koster. Also just as Mankiewicz predicted, the young doctor (Glenn Langan) is a dullard as the romantic rival to the suave, despotic patroon, Nicholas Van Ryn (Vincent Price, in his first starring role in films). Price recalls that "Joe made me lose a lot of weight for the part" and had him corseted to achieve the "perfectly erect" posture that Mankiewicz thought essential to the haughty character. For the pivotal scene of Van Ryn's marriage proposal to Miranda, Mankiewicz had instructed the crew that absolute silence was crucial. In the ensuing stillness, Joe's concise, last-minute instruction, "All right now, Vincent. Nice erection!" was highly audible. Rather than the quiet Mankiewicz had demanded, this direction produced a pandemonium of laughter and terminated work for the day.

"He [Mankiewicz] felt he got more out of his female stars if they were in love with him," says Lyle Wheeler. But the mad crush of *Dragonwyck*'s leading lady, Gene Tierney, on her director failed to vary greatly her breathy, monotonous delivery, though Mankiewicz briefly reciprocated her romantic interest. Despite her frequent use of the expletive *golly*, which Mankiewicz had written in to suggest the heroine's provincial ingenuousness, Tierney seems inappropriately sophisticated as Miranda, a poor farmer's daughter, snubbed at the ball by the bitchy socialites for not having a *Van* to her name. (This social ostracism scene gave Mankiewicz an opportunity to take a dig at his former mother-in-law. As Miranda departs the snooty circle, she retorts, "And what's more, I never even *heard* of Victoria Schermerhorn!")

Dragonwyck's derivation from *Jane Eyre* and *Rebecca* is apparent, but Mankiewicz is unable to make anything very chilling from the gothic paraphernalia of a stormy night, murder, madness, drug addiction, and the curse of an ancestral ghost that plays the harpsichord in moments of doom for the Van Ryns.

At one point Mankiewicz fills the screen with a close-up of an oleander plant to tip us off to Van Ryn's means of murdering his gluttonous first wife. But when the doctor finally reveals that the plant is a toxic glucoside and recalls, "Your wife had a bad cold. She couldn't possibly have tasted anything in the cake, it was soaked with rum anyway," it is still somewhat unclear why the plant's presence in the room is essential or how Nicholas poisons the cake with it. (The novel details that the oleander leaves were grated by the victim herself in the silver nutmeg mill she used to season her cake.) Zanuck demanded the deletion of the scene in which Price explained the oleander's poisonous potential, and Price maintains that this excision prompted Lubitsch to take his name off the picture.

Mankiewicz was probably equally incensed by the upbeat ending the studio made him tack on between Tierney and her persistent suitor Langan. Joe had devised an ingenious final scene, quite different from Nicholas's demise in Seton's novel. When the crazed Nicholas is shot, holding forth in his tithe-collecting patroon's chair, he smugly acknowledges the deference of the posse of tenant farmers by commenting, "That's right. Take off your hats in the presence of the patroon."

The small but memorable part of Miranda's Irish personal maid, a cripple, was played by the gifted English actress Jessica Tandy. Mankiewicz had been impressed with her performance in a Los Angeles production of Tennessee Williams's one-act play *Portrait of a Madonna,* directed by her actor husband, Hume Cronyn. To no avail, Mankiewicz wrote a laudatory memo to Zanuck, exhorting him to take advantage of Tandy's presence on the Fox lot, but Tandy and Cronyn did become part of the Mankiewiczes' social circle, and the friendship has endured for the subsequent thirty years.

When Rosa was not indisposed, the Mankiewiczes were great hosts, noted for the fine cuisine they served and the sparkling conversation of the friends they entertained. The setting for their parties was their comfortable hillside home on North Mapleton Drive in Beverly Hills, to which they had moved in the forties to conserve on rationed gas and provide more romping space for their growing sons. The colonial-style house, equipped with a swimming pool and tennis court on its spacious grounds, contained a good-sized living room, although it was not so huge as to warrant Herman's crack, "I always expect two men to come in lugging a bloody deer."

Mankiewicz, who would not pay court at the weekend gatherings of his bosses, Mayer and Zanuck, did participate in such special events as an all-star Yiddish *Mikado*[12] performed at his friend Danny Kaye's house in 1943. Joe played with relish the woman's role of Yum-Yum opposite Kaye's Ko-Ko. Their supporting cast included James Cagney, John Garfield, Judy Garland, Gene Kelly, and Mervyn LeRoy, in an ecumenical performance.

The real party craze of the period was not theatricals but parlor games like "Sardines" and "Guggenheim" or "Categories," in which the erudite Mankiewicz ran a close second to the champion player, composer Jerome Kern. The rage was "The Game," a form of charades, with captains assigning quotations to be acted out by their teams. The Mankiewiczes were occasionally thwarted by Rosa's language limitations. One evening Joe gave his wife "Procrastination is the thief of time," and she burst into tears, confusing the quotation's subject with "prostitution," but she soon became an expert partner. The acknowledged masters of "The Game" were Gene Kelly and his wife, Betsy Blair, who were therefore never permitted on the same team with the nearly-as-proficient Joe and Rosa. The Cronyns recall these evenings as "marvelous, silly, and wild," despite the earnestness of the rotund Fox character actor Laird Creger, "who was very good, and had absolutely no sense of humor. If anyone muffed it, he'd sulk all around." No doubt the antics of such regulars as Danny Kaye, Nancy Walker, and Phil Silvers provided contrasting hilarity.

Mankiewicz was equally competitive on the softball diamond, where he played second base on the Fox team, as he had at Metro, with such wits as George Seaton and George Jessel. For "upsmanship" in a game with Metro, they razzed Dore Schary by wearing T-shirts lettered "Hughes Tool Company," because Howard Hughes had been Schary's domineering boss at RKO before he left to head production at MGM. On a previous occasion at Metro, Mankiewicz declared that, in circling the bases, Ed Sullivan (then a visiting columnist) had failed to touch second, and so Mankiewicz tagged him out. "What started as a ribbing turned into a real argument," says Dore Schary. "Sullivan

---

[12]This adaptation was originally done as a summer entertainment by Kaye's wife and frequent lyricist, Sylvia Fine, for Max Liebman ("Show of Shows"), when he was in charge of entertainment at Tamiment in the Poconos.

was furious and wanted to punch Joe in the mouth. They didn't speak for a long time, and Sullivan still remembers 'that s.o.b. Mankiewicz trying to cheat me out of a home run.' "[13]

For his next directorial effort at Fox, Mankiewicz was eager to be free of an assertive producer's interference. As he puts it, "I really don't mind who is my producer as long as he doesn't get in the way."

Anderson Lawler had appeared as the playboy rival to Richard Arlen for Mary Brian in *Only Saps Work* (1930), for which Mankiewicz wrote the dialogue. Mankiewicz describes him as "one of the early southern boys. He was a great friend of Tallulah Bankhead and was considered 'very safe' to go out with producers' wives. He therefore escorted Virginia Zanuck a great deal." Mankiewicz liked "Andy" and agreed to do a mystery, titled *Somewhere in the Night*, that Lawler was trying to produce from a script by Howard Dimsdale, which Joe, of course, revised. Although it was an unlikely subject for him ("I certainly wouldn't have gone looking for it, and it wouldn't have come looking for me"), Mankiewicz was eager to master his new craft, and an intricately plotted thriller presented a challenge.

Nancy Guild, the Fox discovery who debuted in *Somewhere*, has a set of snapshots of the film's editor, James Clark, showing Mankiewicz the cuts he needed to build a suspenseful night-and-fog sequence in the pilings underneath a pier. "Joe was smart enough to know that he didn't know enough about editing," says Guild. "He had Clark on the set every day to pick his [Clark's] brain, and he really listened. . . . As he was doing, he was learning."

Somewhere in the Night is a forties *film noir*, derivative of the Raymond Chandler "private eye" hunts featuring encounters with eccentric Angelenos in seedy locales. The plot concerns the quest of an amnesiac war veteran, George Taylor (John Hodiak), for the one link to his past, a hated detective named Larry Cravat, whom he discovers was involved in a 1942 murder over $2 million in Nazi funds bootlegged to Los Angeles. Taylor's intuitive skill as a sleuth is eventually justified by the revelation that he is actually Cravat, the missing "private eye."[14] Otherwise, this twist is unsubstantiated and Cravat's

---

[13]Schary's remarks were made prior to Ed Sullivan's death in 1974.
[14]Both the $2 million hoard and the detective have vanished. The haberdashery link between Cravat and Taylor is made by the revelation of a jacket label found in the suitcase with the stash, reading, "This suit was made for Larry Cravat by W. George—Tailor."

odious reputation is absolved only to the extent that he is not the murderer. The explanation for no one recognizing Taylor as Cravat— because of facial plastic surgery for his war wounds—is tossed in as part of the film's implausible denouement. Similarly, Cravat/Taylor's pre-war attempt at heisting the $2 million in tainted loot and his perfidy in jilting his former fiancée at the altar, which leads to her despondency and death, are never rationalized.

Our acceptance of the ending requires the amnesiac's forgetfulness, which appears also to blind the memory of the sleuth's nightclub singer sweetheart (Nancy Guild) to the fact that his deserted fiancée was her best friend. To her, Taylor/Cravat's moral nature remains constant ("You could never have killed a man"), while his reformation is patly explained by her contradictory contention, "Three years of war can change a man." Mankiewicz attempts to distract us from this illogical, dissatisfying resolution with a conventional unmasking of and last-minute rescue from the real villain, the solicitous nightclub owner (Richard Conte).

Mankiewicz's detached view of the disparity or the congruence of film conventions to reality is evidenced by a two-part, joking observation in the film. The joke has been set up, midway in the picture, when a plain-clothes police lieutenant, Kendall (Lloyd Nolan), comments, "It's almost impossible to make a pinch without your hat on; they just don't believe you. That's the movies. If they'd only make pictures where detectives take their hats off indoors like everybody else." Yet, after Kendall has shot his friend (Conte) in order to save the lovers and wind up the case, we get the following payoff:

> KENDALL: Moscowitz, have you ever wondered why a detective keeps his
> hat on all the time? . . . I found out why tonight. You see, when you
> have to shoot a man, you don't want to be holding your hat in your
> hand. It turns out, Moscowitz, that the movies are right.

Mankiewicz's problem in harmonizing the dissonant talents and techniques of his cast proved as insuperable as accounting for the mystery's implausibilities. Mankiewicz's fondness for great German actors likely prompted him to write Fritz Kortner a great set piece and allowed Kortner to make a tour de force of his role as Anzelmo, a vicious but unsuccessful criminal forced to eke out a living as a boardwalk fortune teller.[15] Kortner's grandiose performance all but overwhelms the lower-keyed contributions of the other supporting players, such as the charmingly droll policeman of Lloyd Nolan and Josephine Hutchinson's pathetic spinster.

The gripping momentum of the film's opening is lost with the introduction of a love interest between the grim and bewildered protagonist (Hodiak) and the sympathetic thrush (Guild) who befriends him. Nancy Guild ("rhymes with wild" was the Fox publicity slogan) was an eighteen-year-old student at the University of Arizona with no previous acting experience when Darryl Zanuck saw her photo on the cover of *Life,* and her beauty, reminiscent of Gene Tierney's, prompted him to sign her.

In the course of lunching with Guild every day for three months, Mankiewicz extracted every pertinent detail of her life story. This gave him salient material to draw upon in preparing her for difficult scenes. "He would sit with me for half an hour reminding me of things I'd told him about myself," says Guild. "I never would have stayed in the picture if it hadn't been for Joe, because he really fed me every line."

While this dedicated coaching largely succeeded in concealing Guild's amateurishness, it failed to develop the much-needed Bogart-Bacall type of chemistry between Guild and the sullen Hodiak. "John was a very sweet man, but very cold," says Guild. "He had a terrible chip on his shoulder. I remember when we were playing the scene in the derelicts' mission house, I made the cavalier statement, 'Gee, everyone really looks very poor and like a bum.' Hodiak misinterpreted this as a cruel remark and snarled, 'That's what I come from.' "

---

[15]The chart of fees outside Anzelmo's pier-side fortune-telling parlor is significant for the joke about Anzelmo's last and highest-priced technique. It reads:

> THE FUTURE ??
> THE PAST ??
> THE PRESENT ??
> Bring your problems to Dr. Oracle !!
> By the Stars $3.00
> By the Palm $5.00
> Psychoanalysis $10.00

William Wright recalls that one evening in the early forties he and the Mankiewiczes visited a pier-side fortune teller in the company of their Viennese psychoanalyst friend, Dr. Frederick Hacker. Although Rosa was never a patient of Dr. Hacker's, he had met her while interning at Menninger's and subsequently began a successful practice in Los Angeles. Wright says that Hacker, aware of Rosa's fragile psychological state, raced in ahead of them, undoubtedly to brief the fortune teller on what subjects were to be avoided in dealing with Rosa.

Mankiewicz spent so much time with Guild that word got to Zanuck he was making advances, for which Zanuck called him on the carpet. The reprimand was groundless. "He kissed me once," says Guild, "but there was nothing sexual about our relationship. I only went out with him once in the evening. He did ask a number of times. I didn't say, 'You're too old for me,' but I did say, 'What about your wife?' Joe replied, 'She doesn't understand me.' I only wish I had it to do over, that I was older, and that I knew what I know now, because I've always had a wild, mad crush on him."

"Nancy and I were the two last virgins at the studio," says the former Shirley Potash (now Mrs. Richard Clurman), who at seventeen began her career as an apprentice publicist on *Somewhere in the Night.* The former Miss Potash describes herself at that time as possessing "an epic case of acne," weighing 174 pounds, and being so "abysmally in love with Joe Mankiewicz" that every time she approached him she would begin to "giggle with nervous laughter. . . . Joe really changed my life in enormous ways," says Shirley Clurman. "One day he came up and said, 'We're going to have to work together, and you can't come on the set and just giggle. You have such beautiful eyes, I can't understand why someone like you doesn't lose a little weight.'[16] That night, I was at the 'fat' doctor, and I lost forty-five pounds."

Mankiewicz also skillfully advised the young publicist on the strategy for declining the proposition of a Fox executive without injuring his ego or losing her job.[17] He recommended she read Karl Menninger's works, *Man Against Himself* and *Love Against Hate,* which made her think, "My God, I'm so neurotic, I have all of these symptoms." He also astonished her with his intuitions about unhappy young women by

---

[16]Dr. Rabwin relates that "Joe was a tremendous eater, especially as a kid. When he was eleven or twelve, on one of the transatlantic boat trips his parents made to Europe each summer, his father got into an argument about how much his son could eat. He bet a man that Joe could eat his way through the entire menu. Joe was delighted to win the bet for his father, and as he left the dining room [as a parting gesture], he picked up a banana. In his early days [in Hollywood] he used to have to fight his weight. He would frequently call me from a projection room to send him a diet by Red Arrow messenger, saying he was going to start it immediately. These resolutions were generally short-lived."

[17]Mankiewicz advised her to meet the Fox executive and tell him, "I like you very much, but I cannot mix my personal and professional lives. I would have an affair with you, but I can't afford to quit my job. If that is the relationship we're going to have, I will be obliged to leave the studio." "I said just that and it worked," says Shirley Clurman.

conjecturing, "I bet you like to get into your car and drive up the coast while you listen to music." Like many women before and after, she exclaimed, "How did you know that?"

Guild and Potash, along with Dorothy Miles (an older publicist), Susan Hammerstein (Oscar Hammerstein's stepdaughter, later married to Henry Fonda), and Barbara Ford (director John Ford's daughter and a junior film editor at Fox), formed a very exclusive Joe Mankiewicz fan club. Two of Mankiewicz's leading ladies, Gene Tierney *(Dragonwyck, The Ghost and Mrs. Muir)* and Peggy Cummins *(The Late George Apley, Escape)*, wanted to join but were denied membership. "Otto Preminger was very jealous," says Nancy Guild. "He came up to me with a hurt expression and said, 'Vy don't you haf a fan club for me?'"

"We existed only to buy him presents and to entertain him," says Shirley Clurman, "though he gave us very thoughtful gifts to fulfill our fantasies of ourselves, like a gold cigarette holder for Nancy and a cashmere sweater for me." "We had pictures and signs made, and he loved it," Nancy Guild recalls. "Once a week we had lunch with him. I was the link because I was working with him, but I had more 'friends' coming around to see me because everyone had a crush on him."

"Joe was one of the most pursued men of all time out there," says Shirley Clurman. "He had a drawer full of gold pencils, mostly from actresses." (His father had a drawer full of wallets from grateful students.)

"He treated me like an intelligent woman instead of someone who was predominantly attractive," says Guild. "I think maybe he required that attention from a younger woman with whom he could be professorial and pedantic. . . . Psychiatry can be a substitute for religion, and it probably was his at the time," Guild relates. "He was psychoanalyzing me all through the picture, breaking down my inhibitions,[18] by playing 'doctor and patient.' . . . I think he brought up emotional material that was too overwhelming for Gene Tierney and Judy Garland to handle, who were about the same age I was. . . . He was devoted to sending people to psychiatrists,[19] and he talked me into going to my

---

[18]The inscription to Nancy Guild on her autographed photo of Mankiewicz reads, "Sometimes it gets so quiet you can hear an inhibition drop."

[19]"I don't make it a rule to go around recommending therapy to people," says Mankiewicz. "I probably told some neurotic people if that's really a problem that you want to kill yourself, I think you ought to go see somebody. I was a nut about the

first psychiatrist. I went to his friend, Dr. Frederick Hacker.... Hacker was very impressed with names, which I don't like in a doctor, and I only went four times.

"Joe's interest in you is astounding," Guild recalls. "He soon knew everything about me. Ten years after *Somewhere,* we met again at a dinner at Cole Porter's. [Nancy Guild married Ernest Martin, the coproducer of the Porter musicals *Can-Can* and *Silk Stockings.*] I made a seating list with Joe next to me, because I've always been kind of in love with him. When I first knew him, I had a cyst under my arm. The first things he said to me [at the party] were all very personal. He asked, 'How are your cysts? Is your brother out of the hospital? I heard your father killed himself.' All of a sudden I felt like a little girl again. He always made me feel like a little girl."

Mankiewicz describes his three films subsequent to *Somewhere in the Night*—namely, *The Late George Apley* (1946), *The Ghost and Mrs. Muir* (1947), and *Escape* (1948)—as three pictures "done in rapid succession, not of my own writing, in which I concentrated upon learning the technique and craft of directing—indeed, upon disassociating myself as far as possible from the writer's approach."

The congenial author of these three films was the urbane man of letters Philip Dunne, who had established himself at Fox by his script of *How Green Was My Valley* (1941). As a native Bostonian and Harvard graduate, Dunne was an appropriate choice for adapting John P. Marquand's study of the rigidities of a Boston patrician, *The Late George Apley.* In 1944 Marquand had collaborated with the theatrical ace George S. Kaufman in fashioning a successful dramatization from his novel written in the form of a diary, and Fox had paid a handsome $275,000 for the screen rights.

Dunne says he "felt Kaufman had conned Marquand into destroying the book, to some extent, by making Apley into a clown figure, while in the book he is a very sympathetic figure trying to break out of the bonds of the society in which he is trapped." Dunne tried to emphasize the latter theme by "straddling the novel and the play" and

potential value of psychotherapy and the study of the human psyche. I still am. I don't think we've even begun to uncover the tip of the psychotherapeutic iceberg. It's only a split second of time that man has known anything about himself or the way he works."

shifting the clown's role to Horatio, the meddling gossip, prissily played by Richard Haydn, to fine effect.

Many critics noted that the sting of the play's social satire had been taken out by transforming the work into a family comedy and making Apley sympathetically genial. "In the play and the novel, Apley stuck firmly to his guns, a snob and deadening conformist right to the bitter end, and shaped his poor son in his own image, which was the irony of the whole thing," wrote Bosley Crowther in the *New York Times*.[20]

Philip Dunne regrets, in retrospect, that he provided the happy ending "everybody was looking for"—a joyful double wedding of Apley's children—instead of the play's wry epilogue that takes place after Apley's death (justifying the title). This epilogue reveals that Apley's daughter eloped without his permission, but in the film Apley benignly consents and provides the passage for a European honeymoon, and the ugly-duckling relation he insists his son marry blooms into the lovely Vanessa Brown. Dunne also agrees with Marquand that there were two "serious mistakes in casting"—the too polished and assured Ronald Colman as Apley (though the film required a star as a box-office lure and Colman is delightful in the role) and another Britisher, Peggy Cummins, as his daughter. The pert, blonde Cummins had earlier been imported and miscast as the eponymous siren in *Forever Amber* (1947), only to be replaced by Linda Darnell. Dunne says that the role of Apley's daughter "should have been played by one of those angular Boston girls, like a young Kate Hepburn, who looked like she had gone to Miss Winsor's," but that Darryl Zanuck crassly declared, "People will think she's Bostonian because she's got an English accent." Cummins, while trying to regain her self-esteem after the *Amber* fiasco, was aware that the glamour treatment accorded her in *Apley* "gave the film a few false notes."

By and large, however, Mankiewicz obtained subtle performances and a genuine sense of ensemble from his cast of estimable character actors. All of them were new to the material, with the exception of Percy Waram, who repeated his Broadway role as Apley's wise and cynical brother-in-law. ("Waram steals the picture," says Philip Dunne, "and he should. It's the best part.") The scene in which Waram defrosts Colman by reminiscing about Apley's own thwarted, youthful love for a socially unacceptable girl is among the best in a picture filled with memorable encounters.

An English reviewer asserted that the film "negates the natural laws of the cinema by being closed and static to the point of inviting claustrophobia." He would have been amused to learn of the furor at Fox created by Mankiewicz's radical use of a 360-degree panning shot to convey the torpor and the humor of the protracted silence of the Apley clan resuming their drawing-room seats after the traditional Thanksgiving dinner. Philip Dunne recalls the extreme intricacy of maneuvering the camera so that the lighting equipment and other impedimenta would not appear in the shot. Dunne says he told Mankiewicz at the time, "It's beautiful, but no one's going to appreciate it but other directors. For Christ's sake, make some close-ups, because that's the way it's going to be in the picture." Mankiewicz refused, but Dunne observed him making those close-ups the following day after an edict from Zanuck, who viewed the rushes of every Fox picture each evening.

Zanuck had previously inhibited his new director's propensity for crane shots ("I was boom crazy," says Mankiewicz) by sending him a brief memo reading, "You've earned your wings. You can come down now." Mankiewicz suggests that his crane shots were confined less by Zanuck's memo than by the fact that Fox possessed only one big crane (or "boom," as Mankiewicz refers to it). Because of the number of times he was compelled to relinquish this boom to the studio's senior directors, Mankiewicz says he was told by Fox's production manager, Ray Klune, "One of the things we love about you is that you are cooperative." Mankiewicz proceeds to dispel this image by commenting, "Everybody knows Henry King *(Song of Bernadette)* is a crotchety, old, *noncooperative* director. Everybody knows Joe Mankiewicz is a young, *cooperative* director. They both want the boom. Who's going to get it? Henry King, because if he doesn't, he's going to raise hell. Whereas Joe Mankiewicz will figure out another way of doing it. The man who is noncooperative always gets what he's after. The bigger the shit-heel you are, by and large, the more you get from the company. The cooperative fellow wound up earning less money and getting the inferior equipment."

Mankiewicz's next Dunne-scripted picture, *The Ghost and Mrs. Muir,* which began filming in late 1946, is another quietly charming achievement, even superior to *Apley.* While neither film made a great noise at the box office, they established Mankiewicz as an accomplished director in Zanuck's estimate, and *The Ghost and Mrs. Muir* subsequently contributed to the studio's coffers as the source of a late sixties television series that ran for several years. (The impossibility of consummating the sexual attraction between the vital widow, Mrs. Muir, and the lusty but incorporeal sea captain made the romantic comedy ideal material for the prevailing television code, which parallels the film censorship of the late forties.)

The Ghost and Mrs. Muir provided Mankiewicz with an introduction to Rex Harrison, the gifted English film star whom Fox had imported to make his debut in *Anna and the King of Siam* (1946). *Ghost* was his second film for Fox and the first of four he was to make with Mankiewicz, who considers him his "Stradivarius," a virtuoso of high comedy style and the ideal interpreter of his elegant dialogue.

As *Ghost*'s scripter, Philip Dunne, explains, "The basic trouble in the script is that once the ghost [Harrison] drops out of the story, it tends to sag, and we had to go through a series of big time lapses to get him in again at the end.[21] That was the weakness inherent in the book [a novel by R. A. Dick], and there was really no way to solve it."

Another problem, created by the era's strict censorship, was how to convey the salty language that spices the Captain's speech and the sensational autobiography, *Blood and Swash*, he literally ghostwrites to provide the penniless widow, Mrs. Muir, with an annuity. The oath "Blast" became Dunne's euphemism to suggest the Captain's swearing, and he borrowed an anecdote about Hemingway in having the widow reluctantly peck out a forbidden four-letter word on the typewriter.[22]

---

[21]Mankiewicz acknowledges his enormous debt to Bernard Herrmann's appropriately haunting score, as Herrmann should to Ravel's *Daphnis and Chloe*, Suite No. 2. Herrmann's surging sea music not only invigorates the more sluggish passage-of-time sequences in the last part of the film but breaks with tradition by supplanting the heraldic brass theme behind the opening Twentieth Century–Fox logo, the equivalent of cutting Leo the Lion's roar in an MGM movie. The score's grandeur is such that Herrmann saw fit to recycle it by incorporating large passages of it into his opera, *Wuthering Heights.*

[22]Dunne relates that Maxwell Perkins, the famous Scribners editor, could not bring himself to utter the offending word in a line from Hemingway's novel *To Have and Have Not:* "A man alone hasn't got a fucking chance." Hemingway asked what word was causing him such distress, and the editor wrote "fucking" on his appointment calendar. Hemingway then inquired, "What do you use when you want to convey that meaning?" and the editor replied, "I don't use any." (Dunne gave Hemingway's question to the ghost and the editor's reply to Mrs. Muir.) When Hemingway and the

Dunne permitted Mankiewicz to enliven the dialogue of the lecherous literary cad, Miles Fairley (George Sanders), who pursues Mrs. Muir (Gene Tierney). "Joe wrote some excellent lines for Sanders," says Dunne, who quotes his favorite, delivered by Fairley during a typical London downpour: "It's easy to understand why the most beautiful poems about England in the spring were written by poets living in Italy at the time."

The *Time* magazine critic's assessment that Gene Tierney's acting as Mrs. Muir "is neither better nor worse than usual" is supported only by her unvarying upward inflections and her approximation of an English accent. But the *Hollywood Reporter* critic[23] described Mrs. Muir as "Tierney's most engaging screen effort," and Edwin Shallert[24] wrote, "Tierney enacts her role with studious care and is remarkably effective." Tierney's performance is even more charming than the one Lubitsch obtained from her in *Heaven Can Wait* (1943) and Mankiewicz, by skillful modulation, gives the illusion that this rather inept beauty actually possessed range and technique.

Philip Dunne, who later had the misfortune of watching Michael Curtiz's nondirection of Tierney in his screenplay of *The Egyptian* (1954), explains that Tierney had the surprising "tendency to go way overboard and ham it up, and you have to hold her down." Dunne was appalled to find, in the first day's rushes of *Ghost*, that Tierney "was playing her kooky. When she came into the house [the nautical seaside cottage designed and haunted by the ghost], she was tiptoeing around and making funny little grimaces or monkey faces. . . . I rushed up to Joe and said, 'This is all wrong. The character should be an absolutely straightforward, practical woman who takes no nonsense from the ghost.' He didn't agree, so we went to Zanuck, who sided with me, and we redid the first two days and got her on the right track. I think it was her idea in the first place, rather than Joe's, as we had been all through the script together, but Joe let her do it."

Countering the often accurate rumor that his female stars give Mankiewicz their best performance only when they are in love with

editor returned from lunch, publisher Charles Scribner came into the office, saw the notation on the editor's calendar, and said, "I had something for you to do this afternoon, but I won't bother you as I see you are otherwise employed." Hemingway's offending line was amended to "A man alone ain't got no chance."

[23]May 16, 1947.
[24]*Los Angeles Times,* July 4, 1947.

him, Mankiewicz maintains that though he and Tierney "were kind of
'stuck' on each other for a very short time" (presumably during the
making of *Dragonwyck*), "there was no involvement of any kind on
The Ghost and Mrs. Muir, just work."

The last of the trio of Mankiewicz-directed films scripted by
Philip Dunne was an updated version of the 1926 John Galsworthy
play, *Escape.* Rex Harrison fondly recalled a 1930 film version of
Escape, starring Sir Gerald Du Maurier as the hunted gentleman
convict, and prevailed on Zanuck to purchase the rights to the property
as a vehicle for him. Harrison is sympathetic in the uncharacteristic role
of the convict who cannot escape his own decency, which Pauline Kael
termed his "best 'serious' performance,"[25] but the film is trivialized by
the escapee's soppy romance with a loyal debutante (Peggy Cummins)
and its conventional chase scenes.

Rather than using the California locations that had approximated
the English coastline in *The Ghost and Mrs. Muir,* Twentieth Century–Fox determined to film *Escape* in England, with exteriors shot in
the village and heaths near Dartmoor Prison, from which the convict
escapes.

Escape was the first American postwar production in Great Britain under a special tax-settlement agreement. The production introduced Mankiewicz to the privations of the battered nation's austerity
(he first met his friend and future agent, Robert Lantz, while sharing
a then luxurious meal of Spam and fresh eggs) and the infuriating
perquisites of English film crews. "The lower and laboring classes of
England, having finished the war, had their revolution," says Mankiewicz. "They threw out Mr. Churchill, and the unions flexed their
muscles, they kicked people around. This is when the motion picture
unions, in particular, did their best to destroy motion picture production. Right up through *Suddenly, Last Summer* (1959), the British
unions were the world's toughest, most erratic, unpredictable, and

[25]Pauline Kael, *Kiss Kiss Bang Bang* (originally published by Little, Brown &
Co.), Bantam Books, 1969, p. 459. Kael also claimed that the film was unjustly
"neglected"; however, *Escape*'s ultimate inconsequence is more astutely analyzed by
the English critic who observed, "The film (as the play) sidetracks the problem it poses
by fortuitousness of plot: the moral that justice even when unjust is all for the best loses
its point through the undeviating gentlemanliness of the escaped convict . . . and the
tidy romantic solution [in the film] that lets out his resentment" (*News Chronicle,*
March 29, 1948).

irritating to work with. On *Escape* they had just come into power and they were enjoying it. All the unions were doing this in England at that time. They were paying back for a hundred years' humiliation of their fathers and their grandfathers. It's practically over now except for isolated unions."

Added to the arduous problems of shooting on location in the autumn mud, fog, and rain of the Devonshire moors near Dartmoor Prison was the crew's alarming penchant for going on strike. They demanded a tent be erected for their lunch breaks on location, with no preference on the chow line accorded the stars or the director, and "the electricians on high received lime juice every afternoon at four-thirty," says Mankiewicz, "and if the mixture of lime juice and water was not exactly right, they would strike. We'd have these sudden rainstorms in Devonshire, and electrical equipment was expensive and scarce just after the war. In one squall I grabbed a lamp to get it under cover, and the crew struck because I was not a member of the electrical union. When we were using fog machines for some interior, they struck again. They wanted 'fog money,' an extra one-sixth for working in artificial fog."

"I suppose this will be the last film I shall ever direct unless I've written it myself," Mankiewicz remarked to Harrison during the filming of *Escape*. His resolve led to the enormous fame and success he was to enjoy in his next four years at Fox.

"If he gets a hit with this, he'll be unlivable!"   6

*T*HAT MANKIEWICZ HAD THE OPPORTUNITY TO WRITE AND DIRECT his breakthrough picture, *A Letter to Three Wives*, was due, principally, to the faith of its producer, Sol C. Siegel. Mankiewicz had had first crack at the source material, a *Cosmopolitan* short story, "One of Our Hearts," by John Klempner, which was later expanded by the author into a rather dull and repetitious novel, *A Letter to Five Wives*, which Zanuck purchased on the basis of a synopsis. The property passed in turn from Mankiewicz to Ernst Lubitsch to producer Sam Engel, none of whom came up with a persuasive screenplay treatment. When producer Siegel selected it as his favorite among the properties that Zanuck offered him, he engaged the writer Vera Caspary *(Laura)* to do a treatment. The novel takes place at a meeting of a suburban war-effort club composed of five wives and its missing sixth member, the town's femme fatale divorcée, Addie. The truant sends word that her absence is occasioned by having run off with one of the wives' husbands, which catalyzes each wife's reflective terror that it is most likely hers.

Siegel found the setting "too confining," since any of the women could "go to the ladies room and make a phone call to her husband's office" (which, in the novel, most of them do, only to find their husbands away from their offices). Siegel sought "a gimmick" to cut off communications so that the wives would have to wait until the end of the day to discover which of their husbands is missing. He and Caspary reduced the number of wives to four, invented the device of the wives' obligation to take a group of orphans on an all-day outing up the Hudson River, and Siegel determined that the nefarious Addie would never actually appear in the film, relegating her presence to a voice-over narration.

Zanuck loved the treatment but protested Siegel's choice of Mankiewicz as the writer-director, saying, "For Crissake, that arrogant bastard. I can't get along with him now, after four flops. If he gets a hit with this, he'll be unlivable!" Siegel replied, "I'll take my chances," though he knew that he would be obliged to wait five or six months until Mankiewicz returned from making *Escape* in England.

Mankiewicz departed with the assurance to Siegel, "If you wait for me, I'll make a hell of a picture," but Zanuck kept badgering Siegel to assign the film to Lubitsch. Siegel felt that while Lubitsch was "very smart and able, he was already over the hill," and the succession of heart attacks he had suffered made him a health risk. Zanuck pleaded, "You'd be taking me out of a hell of a spot. Lubitsch is going to make *Lady in Ermine* with Betty Grable. We've gotta take a beating with Betty Grable, and that picture is going to cost us two to three million." Siegel therefore felt obliged to show the treatment to Lubitsch, who was annoyed at his having changed the setting from the club meeting at the garishly appointed home of the wealthiest wife to the Hudson ferry ride. "You do it your way," said Lubitsch, which got Siegel off the hook. After eight days of shooting *That Lady in Ermine*, Lubitsch suffered his sixth heart attack and was replaced by Otto Preminger. After a period of convalescence, Lubitsch had seemingly recovered, but was stricken again and died on November 30, 1947, while Mankiewicz was still in England filming *Escape*.

Mankiewicz's original script of *A Letter to Four Wives* was overlong. He broached the problem to Zanuck, who shrewdly advised, "You've got one wife too many."[1] Although Mankiewicz concedes that Zanuck had brilliant first instincts as an editor of both texts and footage, the elimination of one of the wives is the only cut or suggestion of Zanuck's for which he admits his appreciation. Mankiewicz says that

---

[1]This is Mankiewicz's summary of the detailed memo that Zanuck sent him, excerpts of which are printed in Mel Gussow's biography of Zanuck, *Don't Say Yes Until I Finish Talking*, Doubleday, 1972, p. 157.

the longer Zanuck had to analyze a film, the greater his tendency to cut from peak to peak of action, dropping crucial motivation and nuance en route. For example, in *Escape* Zanuck cut the key "thesis" scene between the convict (Harrison) and a kindly judge (Felix Aylmer) who lets him go.

In this instance, Mankiewicz gratefully lopped the role of Martha, portrayed in the novel as a mother obsessed with the rearing of her son, and in Mankiewicz's script as "an upper-middle-class matron with attendant problems," according to the recollection of Anne Baxter, who had been cast for the part.[2] With the excision of Martha and her spouse, Mankiewicz was able to concentrate on his three other couples, the examination of whose marital disharmonies provided him with the three "acts" of his satiric comedy.

The first couple is the Bishops—Brad (Jeffrey Lynn), formerly the town's most eligible and wealthy catch, and Deborah (Jeanne Crain), the farm girl he fell in love with while they were both in the service. Deborah's flashback reflection on why her husband might be the one to have run off with Addie concerns her humiliating local debut at a country club dance three years earlier.[3] As an outsider anxious about how she will be received in her husband's circle (the two other couples) and mortified by her antiquated, mail-order gown, she keeps downing martinis and gets crocked.

Mankiewicz thinks the problem that Deborah reveals in her autobiographical speeches is genuine and compelling—the plight of the provincial girl who feels deglamorized upon shedding the uniform that made her equal and attractive to her husband. She feels she has reverted to "a caterpillar while her husband remains a butterfly," according to Mankiewicz. However, he blames the weakness of this segment of the film on the performance of the two Fox contract actors foisted on him for the parts, neither of whom he admired. He describes Jeffrey Lynn as "a leaner" (an actor who requires the physical support of

---

[2]Mankiewicz told the critic Philip K. Scheuer, "There was a fourth wife—a woman married to a guy whose grandfather had been Governor of the State and who couldn't forget it . . ." (*Los Angeles Times*, February 13, 1949).

[3]The day on which the film takes place is also the first Saturday in May, the annual occasion of the first country club dance. Mankiewicz formally emphasizes the connection by having Deborah (Jeanne Crain) and Porter (Paul Douglas) seated miserably "alone together" at the group's table at the beginning of both dance sequences.

mantelpieces and furniture) and Jeanne Crain as a nonactress who always seemed to him out of place at the studio.

The second couple, George (Kirk Douglas) and Rita (Ann Sothern) Phipps, are upwardly mobile childhood sweethearts whose connubial bliss is being jeopardized by her new career as a writer of trashy radio soap opera scripts. Her week's salary, of "one hundred pieces of . . . the most restful shade of green in the world," permits them to live more graciously than they could on George's pitiful salary as a high school teacher, but the tyranny of Rita's sponsor-minded radio producer is taking its toll. This growing hostility is aggravated when George is forced to accept the fact that not only is his wife the bigger breadwinner (a role reversal underlined by her having bought him his tuxedo for the black-tie dance rather than his having purchased her gown), but she earns her money from a medium he loathes.

The occasion Rita remembers in her flashback is the awful evening she attempted to entertain her producer, the castrating Mrs. Manleigh (Florence Bates), and her milquetoast husband at an elegant, home-cooked dinner prepared by her sassy, no-nonsense domestic, Sadie (Thelma Ritter, inimitable in her first major screen role). This dinner party was an opportunity for Mankiewicz to take some potshots at targets he detests, like soap opera ("the literature of the masses"), tasteless and meddling producers, and advertising. It also allowed him to enunciate the plight of the despised and underpaid schoolteacher. The sequence is dotted with autobiographical allusions. George (a sardonic, pipe-smoking intellectual) is as pedantic in reproving his guests' incorrect English usage as Mankiewicz is to his family and friends.

GEORGE: I wish you wouldn't say it in radio English. *That,* not *those kind.*
RITA: There are men who say *those kind* who earn $100,000 a year.
GEORGE: There are men who say, "Stick 'em up," who earn even more. I don't expect to do either.

MR. MANLEIGH: *Tempo fugit.* Right, professor?
GEORGE: Almost.

MRS. MANLEIGH: *(consoling Rita over George's losing a script editor's position by his denunciation of soap opera)* Don't feel badly.
GEORGE: *Bad,* not *badly.* You feel badly this way [*waggling his hands above his ears in a batty gesture (in the film), which is less clear than Mankiewicz's original stage direction to pantomime vomiting*].

In one scene Mrs. Manleigh patronizingly translates for a dinner guest, Lora May (Linda Darnell), a common foreign word used in a soap opera that the party endures as part of the evening's obligatory radio listening.

> LATIN SEÑOR: *(on radio) Gracias.*
> MRS. MANLEIGH: *(to Lora May)* That means "thank you."
> LORA MAY: *Gracias.*

The exchange is reminiscent of an episode from Mankiewicz's salad days. When Joe was in Berlin in 1928, he persuaded his sister's friend Judy to come with him and Erna to the theater, though she protested she knew no German. Mankiewicz promised he would provide her with a running translation but remained silent throughout the first act, saying only that nothing of consequence had occurred. In the second and final act, one English phrase, "The Star Spangled Banner," was uttered. At this, Joe turned to Judy and helpfully whispered, "That's the American national anthem," which proved to be the only translation he offered all evening.

The usually astute critic Richard Corliss is inaccurate in putting down Mankiewicz for attacking an easy target in mocking advertising that exploits human fears. The following is part of the excoriating speech that Corliss describes as "a pat diatribe against the vacuity of radio advertising . . . the manifesto has no bite, and the moral victory that follows gives little satisfaction":[4]

> GEORGE: The purpose of radio writing, as far as I can see, is to prove to the masses that a deodorant can bring happiness, a mouthwash guarantee success, and a laxative attract romance. . . . *Don't think,* says the radio, and we'll pay you for it! Can't spell *cat?* Too bad—buy a yacht and a million dollars to the gentleman for being in our audience tonight! *Worry,* says the radio! Will your friends not tell you? Will you lose your teeth? Will your body function after you're thirty-five? Use our product or you'll lose your husband, your job, and die! Use our product and we'll make you rich, we'll make you famous!

Even today, the speech has too much bite for a considerable number of television stations, which, according to Mankiewicz, regularly delete it from their screenings of *Letter* for fear of offending their sponsors that still conduct similar ad campaigns. What makes

---

[4]Richard Corliss, *Talking Pictures,* Overlook Press, 1974, p. 240.

the satire still pertinent is that television, like radio programming, chiefly offers "precisely timed driblets of distraction between advertisements,"[5] in Mankiewicz's phrase.

Besides the radio satire, the sequence is rich in comic moments related to the charade of "putting on the dog" for the benefit of the unappreciative Manleighs. For the occasion Sadie (Ritter) has been coached to announce, "Dinner is served," instead of, "Soup's on," and outfitted with a maid's uniform and cap, which she despises. ("The cap's out. It makes me look like a lamb chop with pants on.") These proprieties set up the grand moment when Sadie fights a losing battle with the folding screen shielding the resplendent table and, with cap askew, bedraggledly announces, "Soup's on."

Less broad is Mankiewicz's directorial touch of having the boorish appliance-store magnate, Porter Hollingsway (Paul Douglas), thrust rather than drape a fur stole on his taunting wife, Lora May (Darnell), when they depart the nonfestive dinner party.

The courtship of the Hollingsways provides not only the "third act" but the comic peak of *A Letter to Three Wives*. Mankiewicz pits the luscious Lora May against her brutish employer, Porter, in as funny a battle of the sexes as there is in American film. The running gag used throughout this segment is the rattling clatter created by the passage of a train just outside the railroad flat of Lora May's family, which she facetiously terms "the Finney Mansion on the other side of the tracks." The origin of this sight and sound gag was the shattering roar of the Third Avenue El just outside one of the Mankiewicz family's grubbier New York apartments during Joe's youth. Mankiewicz recalls, "My father would pause right in the midst of a sentence [till the train had passed] and then continue *his* blast."

The conflict between Lora May and Porter is that she keeps him hot and bothered but will only give herself for a wedding ring, while he, soured on marriage since his divorce, wants her sexual compliance for gifts or a promotion, but without the snare of a marriage license.

> PORTER: It's an old act and you're good at it, but you don't fool me. The come-on, give a little, promise a lot, just so far, no further. There's all kinds of names for that act of yours.
> LORA MAY: And what do you call your office routine? There's a brand new act for you, it's got a beard a mile long!

[5]Joseph L. Mankiewicz, *More About All About Eve*, Random House, 1972, p. 64.

Lora May's "taming of the crude" is brilliantly synopsized in a cut between the leave-takings of their first two dates. On the first, Lora May insists on the etiquette of Porter getting out and opening the car door for her. While he is performing this uncharacteristically gallant service, she craftily rips her stocking both to display her shapely leg and to obligate him to buy her a new pair of nylons. After evading his good-night kiss at her front door, she quickly shuts it to reveal the wartime charitable placard reading, "We Gave," in the door frame. By cutting to the same angle of the couple in Porter's car (after a quick establishing shot of the car pulling up sharply in front of Lora May's house), Mankiewicz immediately conveys that Porter has been frustrated a second time. This sight gag is topped when Lora May, having been obliged to exit the car herself, makes Porter screech to a halt again by calling after that she has left her gift nylons in the back seat. Displaying her rump as she reaches in to collect them, Lora May then imparts an impassioned "farewell" kiss that so mesmerizes Porter that, after lighting a cigarette to gain composure, he dazedly shakes out his dashboard lighter and tosses it out the car window like an extinguished match. (Judy Garland told her musician friend John Meyer that she was the actual source of this visual joke, as she had once absentmindedly thrown out Joe's car lighter in the days of their courtship. Mankiewicz disclaims any recollection of such an incident.)

Porter's capitulation, after a few months' split-up ("You win. I'll marry you"), is accepted by Lora May as she responds, "Thanks for nothing," in a great directorial moment, as Darnell, back to the camera, turns to reveal her tear-filled eyes. This rueful scene is climaxed by a howling finish as the couple announce their marriage plans to Lora May's mother, in the middle of her informing them of her plans for the evening.

MA FINNEY: I'll be at the Callahans playing—
LORA MAY: Happy New Year, Ma. We're gonna be married.
MA FINNEY: Bingo!

As Ma Finney collapses in a faint, the train passes for the fourth and last time, while Lora May and Porter enjoy a rattling embrace.

As an apostle of social Darwinism, a social climber, and a business tycoon progressively enlarging his chain of department stores, Porter's not-so-secret ambition was to wed Addie Ross, a wealthy divorcée and the paragon of "class," beside whom the husbands measure their wives. Prior to his marriage to Lora May, Porter kept Addie's picture in a silver frame on his piano. This icon becomes the focus of Lora May's jealousy when she visits his home during their courtship. It becomes her professed ambition to be valued enough by a man to keep her photo "in a silver frame on a piano."

To elicit the proper expression of distaste from Linda Darnell when she sets eyes on the photo, Mankiewicz substituted a studio photo of Otto Preminger in a Nazi uniform. Darnell despised Preminger because of his treatment of her in *Fallen Angel* (1945) and the disastrous *Forever Amber,* which she had made the year before *Letter.* Almost equally effective was having Kirk Douglas, during rehearsal, help Ann Sothern achieve the proper level of delighted surprise at finding him safe at home by stripping to his undershorts and jumping up from behind a sofa.

To provide the mocking, provocative voice of Addie Ross (the film's bitchy, omniscient narrator whom we never see but who is constantly discussed). Mankiewicz prevailed upon Celeste Holm, the gifted actress who had temporarily abandoned a brilliant career in the theater to do such *shlock* at Fox as *Carnival in Costa Rica* and *Three Little Girls in Blue,* although she had won an Oscar for her supporting role in *Gentleman's Agreement* (1947). Mankiewicz phoned Holm and pitched, "How would you like to be a character that is never seen in a movie?" Thinking it was a put-on, Holm replied, à la Sarah Bernhardt, "Oh my, that's wonderful. My wooden leg won't have to show." Mankiewicz pressured, "You know Joan Crawford wants to do it." "Oh really? Good," Holm replied, "but you're asking me, aren't you?" Holm, of course, consented, furnishing the perfect, insinuating voice for the acid-tongued commentary that weaves through the film.

Mankiewicz's favorite formal device is the flashback, predicated on his belief that "there is a tremendous amount of the past in all our presents." For *Letter* he and the Fox audio technicians developed an ingenious "flashback sound" device similar to the familiar Alka Seltzer filtered-mike commercials of the period. For Deborah the phrase, "Is it Brad?" is combined with the diesel engine noise of the ferry, as she drifts into her reverie of her drunk and frumpy embarrassment at her first country club dance. For Rita the troubling question, "Why didn't George go fishing?" is cleverly mixed with an inane singing commercial emanating from Sadie's persistent radio to foreshadow the satire on radio programming to follow. For Lora May the sound of a dripping pipe in a locker room combined with Rita's provocative question,

"Have you really got all you want?" leads her back, with the aid of a match cut, to the dripping sink pipe in the Finney railroad flat.

Mankiewicz's ending is so clever it is misconstrued by many viewers, and he admits, in retrospect, it was "a boo-boo" on his part. As it is set up, we anticipate, as do the wives, that the suspenseful question of which of their husbands has run off with Addie will be answered as soon as they return home. When Deborah (Crain) is given a written message by her butler, "Your husband will not be home tonight," read for us on the sound track by Addie, we are certain that Addie has made off with Brad as her "souvenir." When Mankiewicz pulls his twist by having Porter (P. Douglas) confess to the group at the country club dance that he was the actual fugitive but thought better of his flight, it is easy to mistake this gesture as a generous white lie told to assuage Deborah's distress. This mistaken impression is abetted by the admiring comments of the Phippses—

> GEORGE: *(to Porter)* You're quite a guy.
> RITA: She'd have known in the morning anyway.

—which can ambiguously support their expression of esteem for Porter's compromising himself to spare Deborah, as well as a confession to Lora May before witnesses, giving her grounds for a richly alimonied divorce, which Mankiewicz intended. (One prominent viewer, General Douglas MacArthur, then serving in Tokyo as chief of the Far East occupation forces, was so perplexed that he had his aide write Mankiewicz inquiring with whom, in fact, Addie had run off.)

A Letter to Three Wives advanced the reputations of many of its players as well as its author-director, and Mankiewicz received his first two Oscars for both of these functions in the spring of 1950. (The film was not released until January 1949 although filming was completed early in August 1948. It received kudos on its premiere at the then prestigious Radio City Music Hall rather than Fox's regular New York premiere site, the Roxy.)[6]

Kirk Douglas had had a rather checkered career since he came to Hollywood in 1946, indentured as a contractee to Paramount producer

---

[6]According to producer Sol C. Siegel, after *Letter*'s triumphant opening, Zanuck fired off a memo to Fox's head of publicity, Harry Brand, stating, "It's an outrage that all they can talk about is Mankiewicz on this picture. Mankiewicz had a crack at this material and couldn't lick it. He gave it back to me after ten weeks. It wasn't till Siegel and Caspary came along that it came to life."

Hal Wallis. He had subsequently bounced from RKO to Fox and "was on his way to becoming an intellectual leading man," says Mankiewicz, "and you could starve on that in Hollywood." Mankiewicz describes the part of George, his schoolteacher mouthpiece, as Douglas's "last, shall we say, placid role, or one in which he tried to work anything out in his mind." (He forgets Douglas's 1957 role in Kubrick's *Paths of Glory.*) During the filming of *Letter,* Douglas showed Mankiewicz the script of *Champion,* about the rise and fall of an unscrupulous boxer, which producer Stanley Kramer had offered him. "He was very concerned about whether or not he could play the part," Mankiewicz recalls, but his performance in *Champion* served to make him Hollywood's biggest new male star of 1949–50.

The roles in *Letter* in which Paul Douglas and Thelma Ritter made their film debuts[7] not only launched two notable movie careers but pretty much defined the type of tough-mouthed, soft-hearted characters they would be given to play time and again. Equally surprising were the performances Mankiewicz elicited from two veteran female stars, Ann Sothern and Linda Darnell. Sothern, at this point in her career, had become so identified as the B series' character Maisie or the conventional musical comediennes she was called upon to play that her sagacious warmth and wit in *Letter,* under a great director of women, came as a refreshing rediscovery. Linda Darnell, Fox's dark beauty, had graduated from virgins to sluts (Zanuck's two categories of women's roles), but no one really thought of her as an actress until her performance as Lora May.

Once again Darnell's Pygmalion fell in love with his idolatrous creation, and an affair ensued throughout the remainder of Mankiewicz's tenure at Fox. Like Garland, Darnell was mother-ridden and psychologically troubled. She had been married to Peverell Marley, a Fox cameraman twenty-two years her senior, since 1943,[8] and although

---

[7]Thelma Ritter's brief but distinctive cameo appearance as a Macy's shopper in Fox's *Miracle on 34th Street* (1947), which she did for a lark as a favor to her friend, writer-director George Seaton, brought her to Mankiewicz's attention. Paul Douglas had originated the role of the brutal wheeler-dealer Harry Brock in the 1946 stage version of *Born Yesterday,* opposite Judy Holliday.

[8]"Then she married Pat Marley, and that was the end of it," says Mankiewicz of his relationship with Darnell. Actually, Darnell had been married to Marley for five years prior to *A Letter to Three Wives* and did not remarry until 1954. Mankiewicz's memory about the termination of his affair with Darnell is likely as inaccurate as his recollection that his liaison with Judy Garland ended with her meeting Vincente Minnelli while making *Meet Me in St. Louis.*

they had adopted a daughter in 1948, the gossip columns announced one of their many "trial separations" that very year. Mankiewicz became the man in her life until her divorce from Marley in 1951, the year that Fox dropped her contract, after twelve years of yeoman service since the age of sixteen, along with Anne Baxter, another star of the forties and leading lady for Mankiewicz. (Two years later Jeanne Crain got her pink slip, as all the studios began to drop their contractees in panic at television's overwhelming competition for the mass American viewing audience.)

While Mankiewicz's romance with Darnell was scarcely a secret on the Fox lot, where their private lunches in her dressing room did not escape notice, the affair was news to another woman, a Broadway producer Joe had met on his return voyage on the *Queen Elizabeth* after completing *Escape*. This woman was also married but believed that she was Mankiewicz's only extramarital involvement. When Mankiewicz's longtime friend Mark Hanna, a celebrated New York press agent, casually asked her, in the course of a lunch, whether she had heard of "Joe's latest 'thing' with Linda Darnell," unaware that her relationship with Mankiewicz was romantic, she says, "My stomach fell to my feet. . . . Though I was young and terribly embarrassed about saying it, the next time I saw Joe, after Hanna's revelation, I said, 'I hear you're having a "thing" with Linda Darnell.' He replied, 'I don't have *"things." '* " About all Mankiewicz will say of Darnell is that he "adored" her and that "she was a marvelous girl with very terrifying personal problems."

Out of friendship for Mankiewicz, Mark Hanna became Rosa Stradner's companion and guide to New York when she came east in the summer of 1948 to resume her stage career by costarring opposite Oscar Homolka in *Bravo!*, a play by Edna Ferber and George S. Kaufman. (*"Bravo!* is the story of a refugee European playwright, said to be patterned after Ferenc Molnár, and his mistress, a faded European star, who live in a shabby boarding house with assorted refugees like themselves. They manage a bare subsistence working in a restaurant and doing other odd jobs.")[9]

Mankiewicz says that he flew to New Haven for Rosa's opening night and left "thoroughly happy . . . as she was in the highest good humor. . . . She got all the notices, the only ones, and was replaced in Boston in a particularly cruel and unexpected way. [Stradner was re-

[9]Scott Meredith, *George S. Kaufman and His Friends,* Doubleday, 1974, p. 506.

placed by Lili Darvas, the actress wife of the playwright Molnár.] It came as a total shock to her, and I remember flying back to Boston when I heard this."

Sam Marx's recollection differs somewhat about the time and place of the firing. Marx got his New Haven first-night seats from George S. Kaufman and was invited by Kaufman to attend a party after the opening. As Joe had flown in to surprise Rosa, Marx assumed that Kaufman and Ferber were unaware that he was in New Haven, so Marx brought Joe and Rosa to the party along with his wife. On their arrival they received the most "astonished looks," but "they didn't dare tell us why they were so disconcerted, so we had a very gloomy and perplexing evening," says Marx. "Kaufman and Max Gordon [the play's producer] were interrogating Eddie Chodorov [a playwright] about the revisions they were contemplating, and they were totally ignoring Joe. Joe was incensed at this neglect, and, in fact, we didn't stay at the party very long. The news next morning explained the mysterious evening. Though Rose was not bad in the show, in fact she was quite good, they had already decided to replace her. Under the circumstances, they were embarrassed about asking Joe about changes in the play."

Mankiewicz says his wife was very bitter about the dismissal. "As you know, it can never be the play at fault. The director has to be replaced or the actors." (*Bravo!* lasted only forty-four performances on Broadway after its opening in November 1948.) "I don't think she ever recovered from that," says Mankiewicz. "She was just on her way back up and that really was a tremendous blow to her. . . . There was occasional talk of this or that play, but she never auditioned or appeared again."[10]

For his next film after *A Letter to Three Wives,* producer Sol C. Siegel had engaged writer Philip Yordan to develop the character of a shady, Lower East Side lawyer, Max Monetti, "who figures in only ten pages" of a Jerome Weidman novel, *I'll Never Go There Any More.*[11] While Siegel concedes that Yordan "did help develop the

---

[10]Christopher Mankiewicz remembers his mother's performance as Madame DuBarry in a fifties television play and recalls the tremendous solicitude of his father, who insisted that the boys make a great fuss out of flattering her.

[11]Siegel refers to "Max," a thirty-eight-page chapter in the Weidman novel, which charts the riches-to-rags saga of Beniamino (Max) Maggio, a celebrated criminal lawyer who, to spare his ailing father's health and the surely fatal trauma of a court appearance, alters the father's finance company ledgers to make himself appear the

characters in 'spitballing' [verbally improvising] the original outline,"
after reading the first seventy-five pages of the first draft, Siegel determined that "it was not coming off" and fired Yordan. "Zanuck was
desperate for material," says Siegel, "so he read Yordan's script, even
though it lacked a third act, while weekending at his home in Palm
Springs. Since Joe was between assignments, he took it [the screenplay]
from the three-quarters mark, along with the treatment. Joe's screenplay, compared with Yordan's, made the difference between night and
day," since he scrapped all of Yordan's dialogue and substituted his
own.[12] However, the Screen Writers Guild decreed that the screen
credit should read, "Original Story by Philip Yordan; Screenplay by
Philip Yordan and Joseph L. Mankiewicz." "Joe hit the ceiling and
refused to split the credit," says Siegel, "and so got none." Siegel feels
that the Guild's verdict was in retaliation for Mankiewicz's successfully
contesting their decision that he share screen credit with Vera Caspary
on *A Letter to Three Wives* (Caspary received the lesser credit of
"Screen Adaptation by"), which Siegel says Joe had completely forgotten by the time of the dispute over *House of Strangers,* as the film from
the Weidman story was ultimately titled.

Siegel's belief in the plot of *House of Strangers* was not dimin-
ished by the film's commercial failure. (It is, essentially, the biblical
story of the favorite son, Joseph, and his jealous brothers, with a
greater emphasis on the role of Jacob, the father.) Five years later
Siegel produced a Western with the same plot, *Broken Lance* (1954),
starring Spencer Tracy as the tyrannical father, and Philip Yordan
was voted an Academy Award for Best Original Story. "Yordan took
out a two-page ad in the trades, saying, 'Thank you, Sol Siegel,' for
something he had nothing to do with," says Siegel. "Phil Yordan
made a career out of that screenplay," Mankiewicz says derisively.

---

usurer, sacrificing his own reputation to save his father's, when his three corporation
lawyer brothers refuse to volunteer. Siegel says that originally Jerome Weidman had
written of a Lower East Side Jewish family, but since "he had been pilloried by the
irate Jewish community and critics over his treatment of Jewish garment district types
in *I Can Get It for You Wholesale,*" he converted the family to the Italian-American
Maggios (the Monettis, in the film).

[12]Typical of Mankiewicz's construction, the body of the film is a long flashback,
starting and ending with Max (Conte) contemplating his father's imperious portrait
on the day he has gotten out of prison. It recounts the events leading up to his
disbarment and subsequent seven-year imprisonment, and his justified vendetta against
his brothers.

The role of Gino Monetti, the barber turned usurious banker[13] for Lower East Side emigrants seeking loans without collateral, lured Edward G. Robinson from a European vacation. Appreciative of Robinson's background as a distinguished stage actor and anticipating the problem of directing this exacting perfectionist on the set, "Mankiewicz invited Robinson to his office every day for two or three weeks prior to the start of filming, to go over such matters as props and 'business,'" recalls the film's assistant director, William Eckhardt.

Many of the film's English critics were puzzled by the father's alternative benevolence, bullying, and final vindictiveness. However, if one can accept the artificiality of Robinson's theatrical Italian accent, his performance as Gino Monetti is one of his most robust and memorable. It earned him the Best Actor award at the Cannes Film Festival. Robinson has said of *House of Strangers* in his autobiography, "I loved it," and "Joe Mankiewicz can direct me anytime he wants to, *if* he wants to."[14]

Robinson's chief objection to the script of *House of Strangers* was that the love affair between his favorite son, Max (Richard Conte), the lawyer, and his wealthy, spoiled, and demanding client, Irene (Susan Hayward), was not only "a brittle, shallow story" but "so over-elaborated that it unbalanced the film." Moreover, the transformation of both the Conte and Hayward characters from scrappers[15] to pacifists in order to accommodate the contrived, upbeat ending is equally objectionable.

The initial protest over *House of Strangers* came from the Giannini family, founders of the Bank of America, the American film industry's first and biggest bankroller. The Gianninis' distress over the film's invasion of privacy was well founded in terms of its unflattering portrait of the senior Monetti's slipshod banking practices, which lead to the government's foreclosure and demand for his bank's reorganization in 1932.

---

[13]Mankiewicz inventively has the opera-loving Gino (Robinson) loudly play, on his huge phonograph, the barber Figaro's aria *"Largo al factotum,"* bragging of his civic importance, as mounting accompaniment to a feuding dinner table scene.

[14]Edward G. Robinson, with Leonard Spigelgass, *All My Yesterdays,* Hawthorn Books, 1973, p. 254.

[15]The *Manchester Guardian* critic wrote that Susan Hayward's "love duet with Richard Conte has at least the distinction of being one of the most acid tongued to be heard in an American film" (August 27, 1949).

Lyle Wheeler, Fox's head of art direction, had been asked to duplicate exactly the original Giannini bank in San Francisco, though it was transplanted to New York's Lower East Side in the film. According to Wheeler, there were many resemblances in the script to actual infighting in the Giannini clan, as it was "Zanuck's idea to make the parallel as close as possible," a predilection for making films from factual newspaper accounts he had cultivated since his days at Warner Brothers.

Although Zanuck overrode the objection of the Gianninis, he capitulated to the protests from Spyros Skouras, Fox's president in New York, who found that the story's domineering patriarch and his sons bore too close a resemblance to his own family and maintained that the Italian nationality of the Monettis was only a disguise for mocking his thick Greek accent and heritage. "You're making fun of me, so don't tell me you're not," Skouras howled, and Zanuck yielded over producer Siegel's wail. *House of Strangers,* "which had opened very big at Grauman's Chinese Theatre [in Hollywood], was yanked out after only two weeks," Siegel bitterly recalls, and Mankiewicz says it received very limited national distribution, maintaining that it played in only seven theaters across the country, which is doubtless an exaggeration.[16]

Coincidentally, around the time of the film's release (July 1949), Mankiewicz had delivered, in a *Life* Magazine "Movie Round Table" (June 27, 1949), his famous crack about movie exhibitors who fraudulently termed themselves "showmen" when they were totally dependent on a flow of Hollywood product and "whose chief concern should be taking gum off carpets and checking adolescent love-making in the balcony." Reporters speculated that the exhibitors had boycotted *House of Strangers* in retaliation for these remarks, but Mankiewicz dismissed that theory, saying the picture had failed commercially "because it was a bad film." His current view, however, is that "it was a good film."

One souvenir of *House of Strangers* is that Siegel subsequently nicknamed the unflappable Mankiewicz "Max," from the legal fixer's characteristic expression, "There's nothing to it. [Finger snap] Period." It was also the second film in a row on which Zanuck had permitted

---

[16]Since Mankiewicz also says that *No Way Out* played nationally in only seven theaters, it is likely a hyperbolic figure of speech meaning that Fox restricted these pictures to their major urban showcases.

Mankiewicz to go to New York to shoot his exterior locations, a rare privilege in an era of movie making when the economic practice was to use either stock footage or a small second unit crew for establishing shots of authentic backgrounds. (For *A Letter to Three Wives*, Mankiewicz maintained that he wanted to capture the "different tonality of the sun [on the East Coast] for the boat and picnic exteriors." When he encountered nine straight days of rain on the Hudson River, Zanuck thundered, "Jesus, we'll get killed," and the Fox production office recommended that the sequence be shot on the sunny Sacramento River in California. Mankiewicz, doubtless mindful of the critics' calling attention to the substitution of the Sacramento for the Mississippi in his *Huckleberry Finn*, was not about to give up. Siegel phoned him from California and kiddingly suggested, "Why don't you just change the weather?" while mollifying Zanuck by reminding him that since most of the cast were under contract to Fox, they couldn't actually be losing very much money. Mankiewicz admits that, as much as he wanted the different quality of sunlight in New York, "I was well into my loathing for California" and was yearning to transplant himself. "Though he is not what you would call a quickie director," says Siegel, "he subsequently made up a good deal of the lost time" and brought in the picture for $1.6 million, which Siegel terms a considerable achievement.)

Darryl Zanuck, a liberal not unmindful that controversial subjects were frequently big at the box office, had pioneered a series of personally produced films on prejudice in America, starting with *Gentleman's Agreement* (1947) on the taboo subject of anti-Semitism. This was followed by a study of anti-Negro bigotry, *Pinky* (1949), about a mulatto woman who has passed for white in the North but who comes to accept her identity as a black in the South for the sake of social responsibility and personal integrity and at the cost of marriage to her white fiancé.

Pinky, like *Lost Boundaries*, released the same year and also dealing with the problem of "passing," was compromised by the Hollywood convention of having the mulatto protagonist played by a white actor (Jeanne Crain as the medical nurse, Pinky; Mel Ferrer as the doctor in *Lost Boundaries*). This substitution placated southern theater owners and drew the empathy of white audiences toward one of their own for the intolerance displayed to the persecuted "mulatto."

For the next in this series of Fox films on American social prejudice, the writer Lesser Samuels, who ten years earlier had contributed
additional dialogue to Mankiewicz's 1939 production of *Strange Cargo*,
turned his screenplay on racial problems to more virulent forms of
prejudice. His script was pessimistically titled *No Way Out*, and it
concerned the vicissitudes of a black intern in the municipal hospital
of an unidentified American city.

Zanuck, who described *Pinky* as "tea" and *No Way Out* as "dinner," forecast that the latter would "be as real as sweat . . . deal[ing]
with the absolute blood and guts . . . of Negro hating," and offered the
script to Mankiewicz to rewrite and direct. Mankiewicz, who has always had strong sympathies for the plight of blacks in America,[17] had
an additional incentive in tackling the project. Elia Kazan, whose status
as the American theater's most eminent director Mankiewicz envied,[18]
had directed the rather genteel and bland scripts of *Gentleman's Agreement* and *Pinky*, and *No Way Out* provided an opportunity to top him
by writing scorching dialogue and shocking situations.

The source of *No Way Out*'s most vicious verbal and physical
attacks on the black intern is the small-time hoodlum and psychopathic
racist played by Richard Widmark. This performance is the apotheosis
of the psychotic criminal roles Widmark had perfected in a series of
gangster films for Fox, starting with the giggling villain in his first film,
Kiss of Death (1947). The persona had brought Widmark instant
fame, but he was fearful of permanent typecasting, and his role in *No
Way Out* "determined him not to play any more such parts—and he
was sufficiently strong at the box office for 20th to give way."[19] This
decision, unfortunate in view of his great talent for portraying eccentric

---

[17]As early as 1938, in his production of *The Adventures of Huckleberry Finn*,
Mankiewicz had his screenwriter, Hugo Butler, transform Huck into an unequivocal
abolitionist at the end of the film, proclaiming of the slave, Jim, "No human being
has a right to own another human being." Subsequent to *No Way Out*, the usually
undemonstrative Mankiewicz marched with Marlon Brando and Paul Newman in the
1968 rally led by Martin Luther King, Jr., at the Washington Monument. He later
contributed his directorial services to a commemorative documentary of Dr. King
produced by Ely Landau.

[18]Kazan had firmly established his place in the theater through his acclaimed
productions of *A Streetcar Named Desire*, late in 1947, and *Death of a Salesman*, early
in 1949.

[19]David Shipman, *The Great Movie Stars: The International Years*, St. Martin's
Press, 1972, p. 539.

villains, was consistent with the actor's nonflamboyant off-screen personality, described by his costar, Sidney Poitier, as "so retiring, shy, and gentle . . . in fact, he's one of the shiest men I've ever met."

If *No Way Out* marked the end of Widmark's vicious hoods, for Poitier it launched his "model of black respectability" persona that was to make him "the most important black actor in the history of American motion pictures"[20] and Mankiewicz's most notable acting discovery. "He [Mankiewicz] is totally responsible for all the success that's come to me in the motion picture business," says Poitier. Mankiewicz not only selected Poitier for *No Way Out* on the basis of the most negligible experience (two years touring as the general understudy of the road company *Anna Lucasta* and one Army Signal Corps short) but got him his second film role by recommending him to Zoltan Korda for Korda's screen version of *Cry, the Beloved Country* (1952). "Every job subsequent to that was the result of those two pictures," says Poitier.

As it happened, Poitier's unusual sense of loyalty very nearly obliged him to turn down Mankiewicz's offer, though he wanted the part so badly that he boosted his real age of twenty-two to twenty-six (the age of an intern) and, consequently, has had to put up with some film guides listing the year of his birth as 1924 rather than the actual 1927. Mankiewicz had flown to New York to direct his personal choices from the eight to twelve black actors winnowed out by a casting director for screen tests. During Poitier's test, Mankiewicz had a chance to chat with the novice, who says, "I shall be forever grateful for what he did. I suspect he saw the desperation in my eyes." According to Poitier, they exchanged the following dialogue:

MANKIEWICZ: What's your name again?
POITIER: Sidney Poitier.
MANKIEWICZ: I see you like this part.
POITIER: Very much.
MANKIEWICZ: You want to do it?
POITIER: I'd love to.
MANKIEWICZ: You've got it.
POITIER: I'm not sure I can take it. I have a verbal commitment elsewhere
    [to director Rouben Mamoulian to play the nonsinging, juvenile lead

[20]Donald Bogle, *Toms, Coons, Mulattoes, Mammies, & Bucks* (originally published by Viking Press), Bantam Books, 1974, p. 254.

in the Maxwell Anderson–Kurt Weill musical, *Lost in the Stars*]. The question is whether you are going to go before or after the start of rehearsals.

There was a definite conflict, as *No Way Out* began filming on October 28, 1949, two days before *Lost in the Stars* opened on Broadway.

When Poitier's agent called Victor Samrock, the Playwrights' Company's general manager, to confirm Poitier's contract for *Lost in the Stars*, Samrock thought the Hollywood offer was merely a ploy to increase his salary and offered a meager $150 a week. Poitier urged his agent to contact Mamoulian directly, but he couldn't reach the director, and as Samrock would not budge, Poitier felt free to accept the film for the stingy fee of $7,500. ("Mankiewicz was shocked that my agent had sold me so cheap," says Poitier.)[21]

No Way Out also marked the Hollywood debut of two other black actors who went on to illustrious careers—Ossie Davis and Ruby Dee. Davis, now a film director himself, recalls that although Mankiewicz manifested "an aura of authority and artistic competence," he did not attempt "to intimidate or overawe" the black newcomers. Rather, says Davis, "Joe put you at ease by telling stories," several of which Davis remembers to this day.

— Carole Lombard flabbergasting a self-important director, who constantly demanded silence, by telling him, "I know precisely what's on your mind." "Oh really," the director asked. "What?" "Not a goddamned thing," Lombard shot back.
— Lombard deftly extricating her costar, John Barrymore, from a brothel and returning him to the set.
— Tyrone Power, after a bad night, answering a Fox publicist who inquired, "How do you begin a typical day?" with "Well, first I take a crap . . ."

"He had enormous skill in making an actor 'unact,' or do the most natural thing," says Sidney Poitier. "He kept asking me to feel what *Sidney,* not the character, would feel under the circumstances. I was a very alert kid and wanted more than anything to develop skills. Anything he asked me to do, I would and could do. I wasn't afraid.

---

[21]Moreover, though he played the film's protagonist, Poitier received only ordinary, featured billing after the three bold-lettered "stars," Widmark, Darnell, and McNally.

. . . I felt safe in his hands, knowing that if I went overboard, he would turn down the volume and protect me. Under his gentle handling, I knew that if I made a fool of myself, he wouldn't hold it against me."

Mankiewicz also transformed Linda Darnell, in the role of the slatternly former sister-in-law and former mistress of the fanatic racist, who discovers her conscience in overcoming her own prejudice toward blacks. The treatment was the deglamorization that Mankiewicz had authorized for Joan Crawford in *Strange Cargo*—no makeup and the cheapest of dresses.[22]

The film's melodramatic finale features an ingenious escape by Darnell, who outwits her deaf-mute captor (Harry Bellaver) by turning up the volume of her radio to draw her tenement neighbors to the rescue. The sequence concludes with a great theatrical tableau of Poitier making a tourniquet for Widmark's injured leg from Darnell's scarf and Widmark's pistol, which has wounded the intern in a blackout melee. As Poitier tends his persecutor's injury, he bitterly admonishes the whimpering Widmark, "Don't cry, white boy. You're gonna live."

The chief ironic emblem of the racial conflict throughout the film is the dark black Poitier[23] in gleaming hospital whites. Mankiewicz was not above more subtle sarcasms, such as having the tune "Don't Get Around Much Anymore" accompany Widmark hobbling on his crutch in the picture's final scenes.

Mankiewicz has said of *No Way Out* that it was "the first time racial violence was shown on screen—except for *Birth of a Nation*—in modern times."[24] In fact, the big race-riot scene in which the blacks of "Niggertown" anticipate the attack of their white tormentors from Beaver Canal and ambush them by flare light at a junkyard was reduced to a long shot of the hostilities, although the original scene required

---

[22]This approach had been wittily forecast in an exchange in *A Letter to Three Wives*. Thelma Ritter says to Darnell, "If I was you, I'd show more of what I got. Maybe something with beads." This fashion pointer earns Darnell's rejoinder, "What I got don't need beads."

[23]Cameraman Milton Krasner recalls that in a scrapped version of the ending, in which Widmark forced a dark-suited Poitier to dig his own grave in a coal bin while calling him "Sambo," "You could only distinguish his [Poitier's] white cuffs and collar. He was literally as black as coal, as Negroes hate 'shine' put on their faces to take the light."

[24]Gussow, *Don't Say Yes Until I Finish Talking*, p. 158.

three nights' filming.[25] The film's chief violence, however, is verbal, with the employment of every imaginable racial epithet from *dinge* to *coon* to *boogie.*

Nevertheless, the censors in Chicago, where several race riots had occurred in the late forties, demanded that Fox delete the charged scenes showing the blacks (with clubs) and the whites (with chains and broken bottles) preparing for the combat. The film met similar opposition from censorship boards in Pennsylvania, Virginia, and Ohio, and Mankiewicz was prompted to remark, "I find it highly commendable for the city fathers to be keeping Chicago, with its high cultural standards, isolated from any violence."[26] Calling their insistence on cuts "absurd," Mankiewicz justified the film's bleak portent by saying, "Even Hollywood does not have the right to offer a solution to a problem which has baffled this country for 175 years."[27]

Despite a sensational ad campaign and generally excellent reviews from the New York critics, the film received limited exhibition, after protests were lodged by censorship boards in several states, and negligible public interest.

While Mankiewicz's Fox films are continually revived on television, *No Way Out*'s inflammatory dialogue is still anathema to station managers fearful of offending any minority. This notable picture, therefore, remains as unknown to American viewers as the negligible *Escape.*

---

[25] Assistant director William Eckhardt reports that the first night's shooting was cancelled because of a strike of the black extras, who had been committing such "malicious acts" as "messing up the dressing rooms . . . and stuffing hand towels down the toilets." The strike was settled the next day by the Screen Extras Guild for certain unspecified concessions.

[26] Attributed in *Variety,* August 30, 1950, to a statement given to *Life* Magazine.

[27] *Variety,* August 30, 1950.

And Joe created Eve   7

"Bette forgot to tell you that on the Seventh Day, I rested."

On the occasion of Davis's award from the New York Film Critics Circle

*T*HE MAJOR THEME OF *ALL ABOUT EVE*—THE RIVALRY BETWEEN the ambitious young ingenue (Eve) and the tempestuous aging star (Margo) whom she supplants—recurs in different forms in such later Mankiewicz films as *The Quiet American* (in which a cynical aging writer vies with a young do-gooder for the affections of a beautiful Vietnamese girl) and *Cleopatra* (in which Antony is haunted by the awesome shadow of Caesar, whom he has succeeded as ruler, general, and lover of Cleopatra).

These analogies seem to parallel the presumed sibling rivalry between the ambitious Joe[1] and his celebrated older brother, Herman. "Herman started at the top, while Joe had to work his way up," says their sister, Erna. "Joe was bucking for recognition of his name as Herman wasn't," says screenwriter-director Richard Sale. The result was that "Herman's kid brother" ultimately became the high-salaried, witty, and well-known Mankiewicz in Hollywood, and, as Pauline Kael

---

[1]Michael Wood, in *America in the Movies* (Basic Books, 1975, p. 78), observes that, despite Mankiewicz's contention in *More About All About Eve* that he detests Eve as a "competitive" and "predatory" creature, his description "reveals a thoroughgoing fascination" with her. On page 80 Wood says Mankiewicz's statement that Eve "wants nothing less than all of whatever there is to be had" is a perfect definition of "ambition in America." "You gather I don't like Eve?" Mankiewicz says to his interviewer Gary Carey. "You're right, I've been there" (*More About All About Eve*, Random House, 1972, p. 29).

has commented, "there wasn't room for two Mankiewiczes in movie history, Herman became a parenthesis in the listings for Joe."[2]

Mankiewicz declines comment on such statements as that of his unnamed friend in the 1951 *Life* Magazine study of him[3] who said, "But someplace along the way, you see, the two brothers passed each other, one going up, the other going down. What that may have done to Joe's heart—and his ego—is something to think about." Similarly, Andrew Sarris, writing of Joe's following in his brother's footsteps, recalls James Mason's telling him "that Joe Mankiewicz had been profoundly, perhaps traumatically, influenced by his older brother."[4]

"Joe subconsciously patterned his life on Herman's," says Sara Mankiewicz, Herman's widow, "and Herman exerted a very powerful influence on Joe's formative years." Sara says that even in later years, when the brothers' paths diverged and they grew apart, Joe's compulsive gambling and psychoanalysis were in imitation of Herman. Alternatively, Herman described himself in the *Life* article as "a good bad example" to Joe, and Joe's son Christopher says, "So many of my father's attitudes and much of his behavior seem to be in reaction to what he regarded as Herman's bad traits, which made him determined to do the opposite."

Eve's (Anne Baxter) patterning her behavior on her idol, Margo (Bette Davis), is viewed with suspicion by the perceptive Birdie, the star's loyal dresser and confidante:

MARGO: She only thinks of me, doesn't she?
BIRDIE: Well . . . let's say she thinks only *about* you, anyway . . .
MARGO: How do you mean that?
BIRDIE: I'll tell you how. Like—let's see—like she was studyin' you, like you were a play or a book or a set of blueprints. How you walk, talk, think, eat, sleep—

"The meek-looking young woman [Eve] is as closed as the older one [Margo] is open, and working diabolically to get on, has at least as much talent," wrote the *New Statesman* critic William Whitebait.

---

[2]Pauline Kael, *The Citizen Kane Book*, Atlantic–Little, Brown, 1971, p. 83. Joe's son Christopher relates that the fraternal rivalry has been passed on to the brothers' children. He says all of them "would race to check the index of the latest film history or biography to see which Mankiewicz was listed. Herman's children would be particularly delighted if their father was listed and Joe was not."

[3]Robert Coughlan, "15 Authors in Search of a Character Named Joseph L. Mankiewicz," *Life*, March 12, 1951.

[4]Andrew Sarris, "Mankiewicz of the Movies," *Show*, March 1970, p. 27.

"Herman was expansive natured," said his daughter, Johanna, "while Joe's nature is close guarded and calculated." "Joe built up his defenses so as not to be hurt," says Sara, "while Herman was very vulnerable. As he was so frequently hurt, he had great empathy for all unhappy human beings." "Margo has been temperamental and bitchy, to be sure," writes Molly Haskell, "but [she is] kind and loyal . . . and gloriously intelligent. Her one lapse—her trust in Eve—is a function of her generosity."[5]

Herman was a convivial lush, dispensing his wit and wisdom from a barstool at the Brown Derby or Romanoff's to his many adoring cronies. "Here in Hollywood, the life of most people is built around the frantic avoidance of being alone, because this requires one to think, even to think about oneself," said an unnamed psychiatrist in the 1951 *Life* article by Robert Coughlan, "but Joe is essentially a solitary man. He has a natural introspective interest in himself."

Joe Mankiewicz says, "Herman did a great deal to help me at the start of my career, and I did what I could to help him when his career wasn't going too well.[6] . . . As a kid, I absolutely adored Herman as only an eight-year-old can adore a twenty-year-old. . . . I didn't really know Herman until I came to Hollywood, and then I suddenly had to [construct] a relationship with him. After all, you don't really know people until you too are a grownup. . . . We never grew up as brothers in that sense. If anything, he was a father figure to me. We led completely different lives and had completely different interests. We both gambled, we had that in common, except [that] I gambled in a different way. [More successfully?] He drank and I didn't drink, and I stopped my neurotic gambling.

"But it's very difficult for me to talk about Herman because I loved him. I'm sure he hurt me at times and that I hurt him . . . but when the chips were down, Herman would have stuck with me and I certainly would have stuck with Herman, and I think I did and he did. . . .

"For a man of his considerable talents to face the fact that I was, in Hollywood terms, successful and that he was not [was understand-

---

[5] *Village Voice*, April 28, 1975, p. 77.
[6] Although some of Herman's friends dispute this claim, Joe has shown me one memo, which he says was typical, recommending Herman to Darryl Zanuck as the ideal author of a film biography of W. C. Fields that Fox was contemplating. In many instances, Mankiewicz says, Herman had antagonized so many studio heads that Joe's agentry was futile.

ably difficult]. He felt very keenly about his position. He was a great oral wit. As a speaker, I don't know of a greater wit. Like many great oral wits, he couldn't put as much of it on paper as he would have liked. His personal problems, more than anything, destroyed his career. He was very quick tempered and frequently quarreled with producers [like Margo in *Eve*] and studio heads. He would inevitably tell anyone he was working with, be it Harry Cohn or Jack Warner, to 'go screw!' ''

Pauline Kael contends in *The Citizen Kane Book* that Herman could be "capable of some very small gestures" and "as soon as Joe had some success, began behaving atrociously, referring to him as 'my idiot brother.' ''[7] Mankiewicz says that, to his knowledge, "My brother never referred to me as his 'idiot brother Joe.' . . . That crack made Herman out to be a very mean person, which he wasn't. He was a very disillusioned person, but his bitterness was directed mainly against himself. . . . I had nothing to do with *Kane* and Herman had nothing to do with *Eve.* "

Citizen Kane and *All About Eve,* the supreme achievements of Herman and Joe Mankiewicz, have more in common than the biographical quests of their plots and the reliance on flashbacks to uncover their subjects' pasts.

Joe Mankiewicz describes *Citizen Kane* as "an absolutely perfect marriage of writer and material, as it combined the political and the sociological aspects that Herman knew better than almost anybody I know." Like Kane, Herman loved newspapers. Prior to his involvement in the movie business, he had written for the *Chicago Tribune* and the *New York Times.* Although he abandoned journalism for the more lucrative salaries to be earned as a film producer and screenwriter, Herman remained an avid scholar of American history and, in the opinion of many of his intimates, could and should have become America's greatest political commentator—on a par with, but wittier than, Walter Lippman. *Citizen Kane* is fired with Herman Mankiewicz's fascination, scorn, and pity for the newspaper magnates Hearst and Pulitzer, but it is just as clearly fueled by Herman's personal longing for his true métier in journalism.

Analogously, Joe's great passion has been the study of the theater. As an unnamed film critic in the *Life* article said, "If you ask me, he's stage-struck. *Eve* showed that—it was full of surface cynicism about

---

[7]Kael, *The Citizen Kane Book,* p. 33.

the Theatre, but fundamentally it was a poem to Thespis. That's one reason it was good: he was absolutely fascinated by his subject matter."

Erna Mankiewicz Stenbuck says that Herman's self-hatred (and, by inference, his drinking) stemmed from his "not having the guts to break away from the movies' money trap, which forbade his going back to journalism." Erna says that both her brothers planned to return to New York by the age of forty to work at their true vocations, and although Joe realized the first part of this ambition, only two years off schedule, he never succeeded in abandoning the movies to devote himself exclusively to the theater.

Screenwriter Frank S. Nugent, the author of many of John Ford's finest films, wrote that in *"All About Eve"* he [Mankiewicz] took a psychiatrist's view of the theater, introducing the audience to the Freudian compulsions of its characters."[8] (The frequent use of the word *paranoiac* to describe Margo's outbursts was likely a novelty to many filmgoers. Mankiewicz's inspired directorial invention of Margo suppressing and then succumbing to her urge to eat a candy from a series of filled party bowls, while having a jealous quarrel with her lover [Gary Merrill], is an amusing and concise illustration of compensatory behavior.)[9]

One of *Eve*'s stars, Celeste Holm (Karen), characterizes *All About Eve* as "the exploration of a neurosis. The compulsion that people have toward the theater, in the neurotic sense of something you keep doing that causes you pain. . . . I don't believe I have known a good actress who was as competitive as Eve, because if the theater were that competitive, we'd never get a show on. But Joe was in love with the concept of the theater as a wolverine's lair of skullduggery and bitchcraft. . . . Being enraptured with theater for the wrong reasons, he thought it [was something] that it isn't, something that we want in ourselves that we can't have but are forever craving. . . . The grass is always greener for a neurotic person. . . . The theater to Joe was a neurosis that he himself had tried to lick. I think Joe is as batty about the theater as kids [who want to make a career in it]. I think his making of *All About Eve* was an attempt to handle his own compulsion toward the theater."

---

[8]Frank S. Nugent, "All About Joe," *Collier's*, March 24, 1951.
[9]The candy-eating business does not appear in the published screenplay of *All About Eve*. Since Mankiewicz prides himself on prior scripting of all such activities, the likelihood is that it was invented on the set.

At the time of *Eve*'s creation, Mankiewicz issued various disclaimers concerning his favoring the theater over movies. In the *Life* interview he maintained that there were just as many notable American films produced each year as there were distinguished plays or novels.[10] In *Eve*, Mankiewicz has one of his mouthpieces, the director Bill Sampson (Gary Merrill), disparage the notion of any innate superiority among the myriad forms of theater. Sampson, like Elia Kazan in 1944, is preparing to depart Broadway to direct a film in Hollywood for none other than Darryl Zanuck, Kazan's and Mankiewicz's boss and *Eve*'s titular producer.[11] When Eve asks why he *has* "to go out there" and temporarily abandon the theater, Sampson/Mankiewicz delivers an eloquent tirade on the theater's multifarious forms ("Wherever there's magic and make-believe and an audience—there's Theatre. . . . It may not be your Theatre, but it's Theatre for somebody, somewhere.")[12] This egalitarian defense of all forms of popular entertainment fails to square with Mankiewicz's own elitist taste. Although Mankiewicz, in *Eve*, stigmatized Broadway as the "ivory green room," just as he had labeled Hollywood "the ivory ghetto" in the *Life* article, it is clear that he shared the view of Eve and the venomous critic, Addison (George Sanders), Mankiewicz's more snobbish mouthpiece in the film,[13] who denigrate the film capital's creations.

Despite the comparable mediocrity of much of the New York theater's offerings to those of Hollywood, Broadway's aspirations

---

[10]Coughlan, "15 Authors in Search of a Character Named Joseph L. Mankiewicz."

[11]Producer Sol C. Siegel says that Mankiewicz had first given him the script of *All About Eve* because of their amiable working relationship on *A Letter to Three Wives* and *House of Strangers*. However, Bert Allenberg, Mankiewicz's agent at the time, appeared in Joe's stead at a meeting with Siegel to inform him that Zanuck "had gotten hold of a copy of the script and wants it as his picture of the year. Joe feels very bad, and that's why he ducked this meeting with you."

Mankiewicz says, "*Eve* started out as a picture to be written, directed, and produced by Joseph L. Mankiewicz. It was not until the complete screenplay treatment or the first draft of the screenplay was sent to the production department [for budgeting] and thence to Mr. Zanuck in Sun Valley that I received word back that Mr. Zanuck was to be the producer of *All About Eve*. That is, he didn't become the producer until he read the screenplay. I didn't want a producer."

[12]This speech was plagiarized by a correspondent to *Theatre Arts* magazine and printed alongside the earlier speech from *Eve* in an "Unusual Coincidence" squib in the *New Yorker*. Brother Herman teased, "Oh, she stole it from you. I was afraid it was the other way around."

[13]"To a certain extent, in some of his externals—his asides, as it were—Addison is me," says Mankiewicz (*More About All About Eve*, p. 44).

were usually higher, and the theater depended on critics' approval in a way that movies did not. At the time of *Eve,* strictures against language and sexual reference were minimal for Broadway compared to those for film; the Broadway audience was more sophisticated and theater was not a mass entertainment. It was not until the sixties that films in America gained precedence over the theater as a more prestigious medium for both critics and directors. This phenomenon coincides with television supplanting movies as the visual mass medium.

But in 1950, the year of *Eve*'s creation, the film companies still chose to view television, as they had radio, as a crude though annoying competitor for the mass audience's leisure-time entertainment. Witness Mankiewicz's own justifiable contempt for TV in *Eve:*

> MISS CASWELL: Tell me this. Do they have auditions for television?
> ADDISON: That's all television is, my dear. Nothing but auditions.

Just as an English critic's commendation of *All About Eve* as "the greatest woman's picture of all time" traces the film's evolution from the genre that Mankiewicz began to specialize in at Metro, so *Eve*'s epigrammatic wit is the ultimate refinement of the distinctive wisecracking style evidenced even in Mankiewicz's earlier Paramount comedies.

In fact, what keeps *All About Eve* evergreen is the quality of its writing. Like Wilde's *Importance of Being Earnest,* the felicity of its epigrammatic style is such that it can still be relished even when the surprise of its repartee has been lost through familiarity.

Although Pauline Kael acknowledges that *All About Eve* is "one of the most enjoyable movies ever made," she goes on to denigrate it as "ersatz art," contending that "the dialogue and atmosphere are so peculiarly remote from life that they have sometimes been mistaken for art."[14] But, of course, "the dialogue and atmosphere" of a comedy of manners have always been artificial, and the pleasure derived from the dialogue of the best of them is chiefly a result of the author's deliberate heightening of mundane conversation.

Mankiewicz does concede that some of his characters in *Eve* are "perhaps a little overwritten, but bear in mind that these were all new

---

[14]Pauline Kael, *Kiss Kiss Bang Bang* (originally published by Little, Brown & Co.), Bantam Books, 1969, p. 283.

characters then, and I had to make sure people caught on."[15] Mankiewicz elaborates on this point in relating a dinner-table argument he once had with Humphrey Bogart, accompanied by his friend William Faulkner, while they were filming *The Barefoot Contessa* in Rome. Opposing Bogie's theories about using actual conversation as the basis for screenplay writing, Mankiewicz remonstrated, "There is no such thing as realistic dialogue! If you [simply recorded] the real conversation of any people and then played it back from the stage, it would be impossible to listen to. It would be redundant. . . . The good dialogue writer is the one who can give you the *impression* of real speech. You people [the critics] have only listened to the 'wonderfully articulate' characters I've been writing in recent years. But I wrote for Bill Fields, Harry Green, a Jewish comedian, and Jack Oakie. I've written cab drivers as far back as *Mannequin* [1937]. I can write a cab driver just as well as I write a playwright. [In *All About Eve*] Thelma Ritter spoke like a vaudevillian; she didn't speak like Bette Davis. For example, she says things like 'There's some loose characters dressed like maids and butlers. Who'd you call—the William Morris Agency?' or 'I'll say she's loyal. Like an agent with one client.' That is a vaudeville metaphor. She wouldn't say, 'She's as loyal as an empress with one foot soldier.' I can write the inarticulate, but even inarticulateness has to be very, very carefully constructed so that the audience can understand it's inarticulate and not just boring."

Film historian Gary Carey was commissioned to interview Mankiewicz for a paperback reissue of the script of *All About Eve*.[16] In the resulting volume, *More About All About Eve* (Random House, 1972), Mankiewicz and Carey only touch on the difference between

---

[15]Mankiewicz speaking at the Tarrytown Conference Center (November 23–25, 1973). Hollis Alpert (*Saturday Review*, October 21, 1950) described Eve's dramatis personae as "some fairly familiar theatre types . . . [who] have almost reached the stage of being stock types by now." Richard Winnington (*Sight & Sound*, January 1951, p. 374) describes the critic played by George Sanders as "a favorite Hollywood stereotype."

[16]Mankiewicz exercised his prerogative to approve the interview by rewriting it as an essay-introduction to the screenplay, with the small typeface credit, "a colloquy by Gary Carey with Joseph L. Mankiewicz" (printed in bolder type, four times larger than Carey's name). Carey is understandably incensed, and while the essay is polished and witty, it lacks the spontaneity and bite of the interview, not to mention many typically nasty things Mankiewicz said about a number of prominent movie names such as Marlene Dietrich, whom Zanuck wanted to play Margo Channing.

All About Eve and its source, Mary Orr's 1946 *Cosmopolitan* short story, "The Wisdom of Eve," which is dismissed as "little more than an anecdote,"[17] the "McGuffin" or story peg on which Mankiewicz could hang his themes. By emphasizing all the new characters that Mankiewicz invented and their significance, Mankiewicz and Carey fail to note how cleverly Mankiewicz not only utilized but transformed almost every detail of Orr's story and the changes in plot that make Mankiewicz's so much more effective.

Orr's Eve, at the end of the story, heads off to Hollywood with a fat contract and a playwright she has lured from his wife. Mankiewicz's Eve is foiled in her attempt to snare the playwright (Hugh Marlowe) by the satanic critic (Sanders), who makes her his unwilling slave. Desolate on her award-winning night of triumph, Eve returns to her apartment to resume packing for her trip to the movie capital. She finds that a young fan, Phoebe (Barbara Bates), has gained access to her living room, and although Phoebe pledges devotion, she is clearly going to use Eve in the same fashion as Eve has used Margo.

Mankiewicz ends the film with a dazzling image of Phoebe queenly posing in Eve's three-way mirror, with Eve's award as orb and her richly embroidered cloak as raiment. This final image, with its mutiple reflections, not only recalls Eve's posing with Margo's stage costume before a backstage cheval glass but also implies the existence of the Eve type as "a recurring evil."[18]

Several critics have condemned this last scene and shot of *All About Eve*. Richard Corliss has written that "Mankiewicz then proceeds to turn a rather trite punchline into a tedious, totally redundant coda, which not only blunts his modestly ironic point but also reaffirms the filmmaker's failings. In screenwriting, the excessive destroys the incisive; the profuse negates the profound; the filibuster ruins the film."[19] While this criticism can be justly applied to many of Mankiewicz's films, it is not germane to the conclusion of *All About Eve*.

What critics have failed to note are the hints of lesbianism that Mankiewicz dotted through the film to justify Eve's falling for her own tactics, which are employed by Phoebe, and her rapid switch from

---

[17]Mankiewicz, *More About All About Eve*, p. 18.

[18]Mankiewicz at Tarrytown.

[19]Richard Corliss, *Talking Pictures*, Overlook Press, 1974, p. 243. Another possible reason for the critics' dissatisfaction with the ending of *All About Eve* is that Bette Davis, who plays the film's most dynamic character, drops out of the picture.

antagonism to attraction toward the intruder.[20]

Besides introducing Eve's successor, the film's ending is chiefly concerned with the disillusionment and despair that often afflict the award winner. During the writing of *All About Eve*, Mankiewicz was already experiencing the "strangely unenduring gratification" of the Screen Directors Guild's annual achievement award conferred on him in May 1949 for *A Letter to Three Wives*.[21]

Mankiewicz says that his dedication of the published screenplay of *All About Eve*, "To Rosa—the critic on my hearth," was only a pun on *"cricket* on the hearth." He maintains, "There was no appreciable difference in my work between the time I met Rosa and afterwards," a highly debatable contention. He insists that she was "very circumspect" in criticizing his writing, but allows that "she was very tough on my films. I mean she wouldn't say she liked something when she didn't."

The agent Robert Lantz, who became an intimate of Joe and Rosa's in New York, says that Rosa's policy was one of "total honesty in artistic matters where Joe was concerned. All *total* honesty is, of course, part cruelty and self-indulgence. Of all the people [close to Joe] in all their years together, Rosa was always the person who saw all of his work first, and she knew a lot about theater and acting. [After she had delivered her criticism,] there came a minimum of three days when they wouldn't speak. Often, murderous fights would ensue, but after Joe went into a rage, he would then do the work," that is, revising parts that Rosa said required it.

Significantly, Mankiewicz required total isolation from his family to write the first draft of *All About Eve*. To accomplish this task, he holed up for six weeks at the San Ysidro Guest Ranch near Santa Barbara, just as for *A Letter to Three Wives* he had immured himself behind a set of folding screens in the living room of a rented twelve-room house in Malibu.

In view of Mankiewicz's fascination with women, his statement

---

[20]Mankiewicz says that only within the past five years (1968–73) has his mail reflected viewers' comprehending the significance of Eve and her roommate, in night clothes, linking arms as they ascend the staircase. By revealing Eve's mannishly cropped hair after she removes her curled stage wig, and by having Eve suggest that Phoebe stay the night rather than make a long subway trip home, Mankiewicz subtly suggests Eve's Sapphic nature.

[21]In *More About All About Eve* Mankiewicz describes this phenomenon as "a sort of reverse alchemy: the gold, as you hold it, turns into shit."

that he "is not as interested in Adam as in Eve"[22] is not surprising. It is curious, however, that a man as complex as Joe would say that male behavior is so elementary that *"All About Adam* could be done as a short."[23]

While the title *All About Eve* would suggest that the film is principally about one woman or the predatory female type, Celeste Holm holds the view that her outsider's role as the playwright's wife (the nonprofessional "Wife to ———," in Mankiewicz's generic categorization of the film's "three distinctive types of women"[24] is not the third part in the film but "the third part of one person. To me," Holm says, *"All About Eve* was not all about the character of Eve, but it was 'All About Women.' [Joe] meant that there are aspects of each other in Eve, Margo, and Karen.

"[Karen] is a gentle woman. She's not passive or without guts. She simply finds that she can accomplish her purposes in life without acting like a Boadicean chariot with knives on the wheels, like that little ferret Eve on one side, or that constant Catherine wheel, Margo, on the other. I said, 'It's going to be very interesting to see if I can make this woman strong enough to be worthy of the situation,' that is, as one-third of a whole, total character." Although virtuous wives in modern drama have a tendency to be pallid and wearisome, like Mary in *The Women,* Holm triumphs in the part, and Mankiewicz asserts that "in conception, Karen is the film's most original character."[25]

All About Eve began filming, out of sequence, in April 1950, on location at San Francisco's Curran Theatre, which doubled as a Broadway house. Holm recalls her flight to San Francisco, aboard Darryl Zanuck's pontooned private plane, in the company of her costars Hugh Marlowe and Gary Merrill, both Fox contract players. The conversation turned to the newly signed Bette Davis, who was a last-minute replacement for the injured Claudette Colbert, as the virago star, Margo Channing. Shouting to make herself heard above the plane's propellers, Holm inquired, "I wonder what it's going to be like working with the queen bee from Warners?" "I can tell you one thing," Gary Merrill replied, "it's all going to be over in eight weeks." As it turned

---

[22]Mankiewicz at Tarrytown.
[23]*Ibid.*
[24]*Ibid.*
[25]Mankiewicz, *More About All About Eve,* p. 40.

out, life imitated art, and the romance of the screen lovers, Merrill and Davis, during the making of *All About Eve* culminated in a marriage that lasted ten years, which was a longer duration than any of Davis's three previous unions.

While Davis and Merrill's growing attraction provided "good chemistry" for the picture, the alliance tended to exclude the other members of the company. Holm says, "They [formed] a kind of cabal, like two kids who had learned to spell a dirty word. It was not a very pretty relationship, as they laughed at other people together.[26] They were obviously the kind of people who felt they were two rebels against the world. [This gave them an] aggressive kind of challenging attitude . . . [as if to say,] 'I'm stepping on your foot. What are you going to do about it?' [but] we still worked well together."[27]

Mankiewicz was evidently on to the burgeoning romance. Holm recalls that he broke up an overly fervent embrace between Merrill and Davis—in the scene in which Bill returns to comfort Margo over Addison's venomous column—by joshing, "Cut. Cut. This is not swing and sway with Sammy Kaye."

Davis's aggressive behavior toward Holm was manifested at the end of filming the Stork Club celebration scene, which concludes with Karen breaking into hysterically relieved laughter at Margo's declining the role in her husband's new play, which Eve has just threatened her with blackmail in order to get. After Holm had emitted peals of her inimitable, bubbling laughter and Mankiewicz had called, "Cut," Davis said, "*I* can't do that. How do you do that?" "Easy," Celeste replied. "Well, *I* can't do it," Bette declared. Mankiewicz, who, according to Holm, "enjoyed showing [Davis] that there were other actors in the picture, in case she hadn't noticed, said [to Holm], 'Would you like to do it again?' So we did another five minutes of giggling,"

---

[26]Gary Merrill recalls that Celeste Holm had a compulsion about washing her hair, and he and some other cast members had her roaming all over Los Angeles looking for a new, miraculous shampoo they recommended, called F.A.G.

[27]Holm, who makes clear that she is sure Bette Davis has mellowed with age and many forms of adversity, was one of the speakers who paid tribute to Davis at the American Film Institute's banquet on March 1, 1977, conferring a Life Achievement Award on the actress. Bette Davis, however, is unforgiving. At the party after the banquet, commenting on Mankiewicz's laudatory speech to the AFI's director, George Stevens, Jr., Davis loudly proclaimed, "Joe did give me a second career. But he was slightly in error describing 'the wonderful cast of *Eve*.' They were wonderful, but there was one bitch—Celeste Holm!"

says Holm, until Joe halted her with an evidently pleased "O.K."

Earlier in the production, Davis had quashed Holm's usual cheery "Good morning" by snapping, "Oh, these terrible good manners." "I never spoke to Bette after that," says Holm.

"George Sanders never spoke to anyone," Holm relates. "He was a brilliant actor, but he wasn't much fun." Anne Baxter says that while she was always keyed up with opening-night tension, Sanders's "energy was nil," as he would usually appear on the set having just waked from a nap in his dressing room. "Joe just pushed and prodded him into the part for which he earned the Academy Award for Best Supporting Actor," says Baxter, "but it usually took seven takes to do it, so Joe would just tell me to cool it after the third take." Gary Merrill relates that when Sanders's wife, Zsa Zsa Gabor, wandered onto the set beseeching that she "must haff George to go shopping," Mankiewicz politely informed her, "We're making a fucking picture, honey."

Another cast member who required an extraordinary number of takes was the then comparatively unknown Marilyn Monroe. Although she was involved only in two scenes, the shorter one (with George Sanders in the lobby of a theater) required twenty-five takes, according to Gary Merrill. Celeste Holm remembers that on Monroe's first day on the set for the party scene, which involved the entire company, she arrived an hour late. Gregory Ratoff, who played the producer, prophesied in his Russian brogue, "That girl ees going to be a beeg star!" "Why," Holm snapped back, "because she's kept us all waiting an hour? I think it takes more than that. Besides, she's dressed ridiculously in that *tit*ular number. It's a cocktail party. No one else is in an evening gown." Recalling Monroe, Holm says, "I confess I saw nothing special about her Betty Boop quality. I thought she was quite sweet and terribly dumb, and my natural reaction was, 'Whose girl is that?'[28] It was the performance of a chorus girl [typecasting, as Addison describes her as 'a graduate of the Copacabana School of Dramatic Arts']. She was terribly shy. In fact, she was scared to death, because she was playing in a pretty big league, you know, but Joe relaxed her into it."

The text of *All About Eve* is strewn with sarcastic references to

---

[28]Mankiewicz relates that Monroe got the part through the persistence of her devoted and influential agent, Johnny Hyde. (See *More About All About Eve*, p. 77.)

stars eclipsing the limelight of their more deserving writers and directors. For example:

> ADDISON'S VOICE: . . . Minor awards are for such as the writer and director
> —since their function is merely to construct a tower so that the world
> can applaud a light which flashes on top of it.

or

> LLOYD: I shall never understand the weird process by which a body with
> a voice suddenly fancies itself as a mind! Just when exactly does an
> actress decide they're *her* words she's saying and *her* thoughts she's
> expressing? . . . It's about time the piano realized it has not written
> the concerto!

These speeches accurately reflect Mankiewicz's own feeling toward actors. Although actors fascinate him and he takes pleasure in speaking of his intimate acquaintance with most of the great stage and screen stars of his time, his constant reference to actors as "displaced personalities"—people who have to *impersonate* someone else, as they have no significance or character aside from their impostures—reveals his essential contempt for most of them.

The cast of *All About Eve,* however, were deferential to their leader. To commemorate Mankiewicz's newly won Oscars for *A Letter to Three Wives* shortly after filming of *Eve* began, they presented their director with two Kewpie dolls, which remained perched on the lectern where he kept his annotated shooting script for the rest of the production.

Anne Baxter says that the filming was "like a delightful group-therapy session, and Mankiewicz was the psychiatrist. . . . Joe knows more about women than any man I've ever met. We're all just glass to him, and he sees everything that makes us tick."

The irony of *Eve*'s expression of resentment toward actors gaining more recognition than writers and directors is that Mankiewicz, rather than his cast, proved to be the big winner in the 1950 Oscar derby by winning two awards for his screenplay and direction. While *All About Eve* was named the year's Best Picture and received fourteen nominations for awards, Bette Davis and Anne Baxter divided the vote for Best Actress[29] (the award went to Judy Holliday for *Born Yesterday*), as did

---

[29]Bette Davis did win the prestigious New York Critics Circle Award and the award for best female performance of 1951 at the Cannes Film Festival. Since her studio, Warner Brothers, had dropped her, Davis confided to Anne Baxter, shortly after

Celeste Holm and Thelma Ritter for Best Supporting Actress (won by Josephine Hull of *Harvey*).

Mankiewicz has said that an even greater satisfaction than getting unanimously favorable reviews is to get one isolated pan from a subsequently mortified critic. *All About Eve* garnered its one notable American put-down[30] from the *Life* reviewer, who found it "bears little relation to the facts of life" in the theater and its veteran female stars, and that it "[tossed] around epigrams with the profusion but hardly the polish of Oscar Wilde."[31]

Most would concur with the the contrary judgment of the estimable David Shipman, who proclaims that *Eve* "has the highest quotient of (verbal) wit of any film made before or since."[32]

Eve began filming, that "she thought her career was finished." Her triumph in *All About Eve* restored her status as a film star.

[30]Richard Winnington harshly denigrated *All About Eve* in the British publication *Sight & Sound*, January 1951, pp. 373–74.

[31]*Life*, October 30, 1950, p. 79.

[32]David Shipman, *The Great Movie Stars: The Golden Years*, Hamlyn, 1970, pp. 149–50.

Paramount's youngest writer in a romantically blurred studio shot.

Joe savoring the air of untour-
isted Laguna Beach in the early
thirties. *Courtesy William Wright*

A costume party of Paramount employees in the early thirties. LEFT TO
RIGHT: William Wright (Joe's housemate), Mary Brian (the leading lady in
several early Mankiewicz-scripted films), Joe, and his fiancée, Frances Dee (a
promising ingenue on her way to stardom who never made it to the altar with
Joe). *Courtesy William Wright*

Joe and his first wife, Elizabeth Young, a New York socialite and Universal Pictures contractee. Mankiewicz shortly stayed from the hearth in thrall of Joan Crawford.
Courtesy the Museum of Modern Art/Film Stills Archive

A wedding-day photograph in Herman Mankiewicz's garden, May 20, 1934. On Joe's left, his close friend actor Phillips Holmes. To the right of Elizabeth Young, her close friend actress Gail Patrick.
Courtesy the Museum of Modern Art/Film Stills Archive

The principals of *Forsaking All Others* (1934), Mankiewicz's first script for Crawford and first solo-credit comedy hit at MGM. LEFT TO RIGHT: Clark Gable, Joan Crawford, Robert Montgomery, Billie Burke, and their speedy director, W. S. ("Woody") Van Dyke.
Courtesy the Museum of Modern Art/Film Stills Archive

The tweedy Man-
kiewicz brothers, Her-
man and Joe, circa 1936.
Courtesy Mrs. Sara Mankiewicz

The Mankiewicz
family, circa 1936. TOP
ROW, LEFT TO RIGHT:
Herman, Erna, and Joe.
BOTTOM ROW, LEFT TO
RIGHT: Father Frank
and Mother Johanna.
Courtesy Mrs. Sara Mankiewicz

Joe dancing with
the rarely photographed
Louise Tracy, wife of
his pal Spencer Tracy,
circa 1937–38.

Outside Joan Crawford's dressing room during the filming of *The Bride Wore Red* (1937): mannishly garbed director Dorothy Arzner, Crawford, turbaned and shoulder padded by Adrian, and Mankiewicz, the young producer with two pipes.

Courtesy Larry Edmund's Book Store

Joe chuckling with the irrepressible Mickey Rooney, the star of Mankiewicz's production of *The Adventures of Huckleberry Finn* (1938).

The next Young (Loretta) among Joe's numerous romances with movie stars, circa 1938.

Rosa Stradner and Joe in love in the year of their marriage, 1939.

Courtesy Christopher Mankiewicz

The fiercely handsome Rosa Stradner. The sea was calm, her psyche ever turbulent.

Courtesy Christopher Mankiewicz

Christopher Mankiewicz's baptism, December 21, 1940 (the day that Spencer Tracy, who never blew a line, forgot the Apostles' Creed). LEFT TO RIGHT: Lisl Reisch (godmother), proud Joe, beaming Rosa, pensive Chris, and doting Tracy (godfather).   *Courtesy Christopher Mankiewicz*

Papa Joe dotes on his son Christopher at his first birthday party (1941). The onlooking blonde girl, on the right, is Herman Mankiewicz's daughter, Johanna.

Courtesy Christopher Mankiewicz

Professor Frank Mankiewicz, shortly before his death in December 1941. Scholar, indefatigable worker, and the perfectionist authority figure in Joe's life.   *Courtesy Mrs. Sara Mankiewicz*

Rosa Stradner, Mankiewicz's second wife, displaying a radiant off-screen smile between takes as the stern mother superior in *The Keys of the Kingdom* (1944).
Courtesy the Museum of Modern Art/Film Stills Archive

Rosa and her sons, Tom Mankiewicz (LEFT), the future screenwriter, and Christopher Mankiewicz, future studio executive and film producer. The family spaniel is not really biting the diamonded hand that fed (1944).
Courtesy the Museum of Modern Art/Film Stills Archive

Joe with his sons in 1944. Chris (RIGHT) is staring intently at his cradled brother, Tom, two years his junior. *Courtesy Christopher Mankiewicz*

Mankiewicz directing his first film, *Dragonwyck*, in 1945. Here he coaches Gene Tierney for her mortification during the ballroom scene. (The actress on the right, in sausage curls similar to Tierney's, is Ruth Ford.)

Joe directing three principals in his third film, *The Late George Apley*, during the summer of 1946. LEFT TO RIGHT: Charles Russell, Peggy Cummins, and the star, Ronald Colman.

Trench-coated Mankiewicz directing Peggy Cummins and Rex Harrison in *Escape*, on location near Dartmoor Heath in the autumn of 1947. *Courtesy Peggy Cummins Dunnett*

Joe instructing Jill Esmond (LEFT, Laurence Olivier's first wife) and Peggy Cummins in *Escape*. *Courtesy Peggy Cummins Dunnett*

On location in New York along the Hudson River for *A Letter to Three Wives*, during the summer of 1948. LEFT TO RIGHT: Linda Darnell, Ann Sothern, cinematographer Arthur Miller (seated), and Mankiewicz. *Courtesy the Museum of Modern Art/Film Stills Archive*

Joe gazes at his boss, Darryl F. Zanuck, at what appears to be a Screen Directors Guild awards ceremony for *All About Eve.* Zanuck took credit as *Eve*'s producer but was unhappy that Joe got all the publicity.

Courtesy the Museum of Modern Art/Film Stills Archive

Happy winners after *All About Eve*'s triumph at the 1950 Academy Awards ceremony. Mankiewicz holds his Oscars for Best Screenplay and Direction, producer Darryl Zanuck clutches the one for Best Picture and his Irving Thalberg Award, and George Sanders grasps his award for Best Supporting Actor.

Courtesy Christopher Mankiewicz

"The night they drove old C. B. down" 8

"Probably never in history has there been a series of occurrences affecting so many prominent men in the motion picture industry."

> *Joseph L. Mankiewicz in the* LOS ANGELES TIMES, *October 29, 1950*

*N*INETEEN FIFTY WAS A TRIUMPHANT YEAR FOR JOE MANKIE-wicz, although toward the end of it there occurred an incident that nearly finished his career. In February he completed the shooting script of his masterpiece, *All About Eve.* On March 29 he won his first two Academy Awards, for writing and directing *A Letter to Three Wives.* On May 31, a week before shooting was completed on *Eve,* Mankiewicz's peers elected him president of the Screen Directors Guild (SDG), succeeding George Marshall. He had been nominated for this office by the Guild's longtime kingmaker, Cecil B. DeMille.

DeMille had gradually gained control of the Guild through seniority and cliquishness with a faction of like-minded elders he had helped install. Grateful presidents were expected to preside over meetings and follow his dictates. DeMille was as much a believer in the virulent threat of Communists infiltrating the film industry as he was in the morality of his opulently vulgar, hugely profitable screen epics. ("DeMille had his finger up the pulse of America," quips Mankiewicz.) As a self-appointed watchdog, he had set up the DeMille Foundation for Americanism to compile dossiers on all screen directors' "Leftist" affiliations.[1] The Foundation's dossiers acquired spurious legitimacy when

---

[1]The Foundation was run by Tom Gerdler, former president of Republic Steel and a figure notorious for his strike-busting in the thirties and, according to Mankie-

leaked to legislative committees like California State Senator Jack Tenney's, which would, in turn, feed them to the House Un-American Activities Committee (HUAC).

With the jailing, in 1950, of the "Unfriendly Ten,"[2] Hollywood's first sacrifices to the rapacious HUAC, open season for witch hunters commenced. Fed by the tension of the Korean conflict, launched in 1950, and Senator Joseph McCarthy's demagogic ravings, the interrogation of Hollywood "names" became a prime method of headline making for HUAC. Denouncing coworkers conferred automatic patriotism on the film capital's more self-righteous bigots and chauvinists; naming names became the refuge of those threatened by disclosure of their past or present associations with the burgeoning list of organizations designated as "Red Front" or Leftist.

Although he has subsequently been a supporter of liberal Democrats,[3] Mankiewicz had shown, in the course of twenty years in Hollywood, a sweeping aversion to the host of political and charitable causes that regularly besieged affluent figures in the film community.

"I am the least politically minded person in the world," Joe declares. "My brother, Herman, and I shared this. Herman was as politically knowledgeable as I was politically illiterate, and it was Herman, more than anyone else, who kept me from ever joining any organizations." When the United Jewish Appeal instituted the coercive practice of reading off salaries at their film industry "fund raisers," the Mankiewicz brothers made a noted exit to express their disapproval.

It was Herman's skeptical view of idealistic causes as either futile or endangered by cooption that made him an early, savage denigrator of Hollywood converts to Leftist and anti-Fascist causes. One such convert, the elegant writer of comedy-of-manners screenplays, Donald

---

wicz, for his involvement in the Republic strike of 1937, in which twelve workers were shot.

[2]Alvah Bessie, Herbert Biberman, Lester Cole, Edward Dmytryk, Ring Lardner, Jr., John Howard Lawson, Albert Maltz, Sam Ornitz, Adrian Scott, and Dalton Trumbo were the celebrated band of writers, producers, and directors who in 1947 refused to tell HUAC whether or not they were members of the Communist party. In 1950, after the defeat of their legal appeal protesting the Committee's right to question their political affiliations, they all served short jail sentences and were subsequently blacklisted by the motion picture industry.

[3]Although not a speechwriter or active campaign worker, he was an ardent supporter of the presidential candidacies of Adlai Stevenson, Robert Kennedy, and George McGovern, the latter two through his fondness for his nephew, Frank Mankiewicz, the candidates' prominent aide.

Ogden Stewart *(Philadelphia Story)*, recalls Herman's mocking characterization of him as a naïve novice in the ranks Herman had long before abandoned.

Mankiewicz's support of Wendell Willkie in the 1940 presidential campaign identified him as a Republican and made him persona non grata at a dinner party for the distinguished publisher Alfred Knopf, a Roosevelt loyalist, who demanded Joe leave his brother Edwin's house.[4]

Joe's only publicized charitable endeavor was his leadership of the Finnish Relief Fund for the film industry in 1936 at the behest of Herbert Hoover, a deed that served at the time to ameliorate the attacks on his production *Fury* as "Communist" and "anti-American" for its depiction of lynch mob violence. Curiously, Mankiewicz's writing the dialogue for King Vidor's *Our Daily Bread* (1934), a now quaint, "back to the land" fantasy of the depression that advocated collectivist communes, never became the subject of retrospective political condemnation.

In fact, the only Red Front organization Mankiewicz could be linked with was the Actors' Lab, where he taught a course in ancient Greek drama in the early forties. The Lab was tainted, for the Red hunters, by the presence of some militant Communists and numerous refugees from New York's Group Theatre. (The Group Theatre was founded in the depth of the depression and was committed to performing plays of social protest and reform. This ambiance led many of its members to join the Communist party.) The Actors' Lab was an essentially nonpolitical workshop in theater craft, and every studio was solicited for contributions and interested instructors like Mankiewicz. Joe's affiliation with the Lab was clearly insufficient evidence for the zealous Red hunter DeMille.

Mankiewicz's first knowledge that DeMille was trying to make him appear politically suspect came in early October, less than six

---

[4]Edwin Knopf was, at the time, the head of the story department at MGM, a post that Mankiewicz says he procured for him despite Knopf's snub in his early days at Paramount. While Joe was lunching one day with Ernst Lubitsch, Knopf inquired if Lubitsch would attend a star-studded dinner party at his home that weekend and explained to Joe, "If I invited you at this stage in your career, what would there be left for you to look forward to?" Knopf codirected two of Mankiewicz's early screenplays at Paramount (*Slightly Scarlet* and *Only Saps Work*). According to Joe, Knopf was a theater snob because he had previously directed his own company in Baltimore, which had featured such luminaries as the Barrymores and the Lunts.

months after DeMille had touted Mankiewicz as president of the
Screen Directors Guild, from Joe's writer-director friend George Seaton. Seaton was sitting in Paramount production chief Y. Frank Freeman's office when DeMille popped in through the back door. De-
Mille's first statement breached the confidential deliberations of a
Guild board meeting. "Mr. Mankiewicz was very eloquent last night,
and I was very eloquent in return," he said. DeMille than announced
to Freeman, the president of the Producers Association, "I think I'll
straighten out our young president. He's a good boy, so I think he'll
see the error of his ways. He's just feeling his oats a bit."

Freeman countered, in his slow Georgia drawl, "Look, C. B., I
know Joe Mankiewicz. He used to work here. He's no more a Communist than you are."

DeMille politely demurred. "Frank, I know he's not a Communist. But I know that his father, a professor, campaigned for Morris
Hilquit, a Socialist, in the New York mayoralty campaign of 1914, and
those tendencies are very often inherited."

At this point Seaton excused himself by saying he had to go to the
men's room and used the pretext to phone Mankiewicz at Fox. Seaton
confided, "You are not going to believe what I have just heard," and
relayed DeMille's suspicion of inherited political taint.

"Shit, they've got me!" Joe kidded.

"Then you won't mind if I never speak to you again," Seaton
facetiously concluded.

The prelude to DeMille's guilt-by-association smear tactic began
in the summer of 1950. DeMille and his rubber-stamp cronies on the
board, Albert S. Rogell and George Marshall, had well-founded misgivings that Mankiewicz would not enthusiastically endorse their patriotic
plan to have the Guild become the first Hollywood craft union to adopt
a membership loyalty oath identical to the one the Taft-Hartley law
demanded of all union officers. The time to railroad it through was
before Mankiewicz returned from a two-month European trip that he
embarked upon in July, after completing post-production work on *Eve.*

Mankiewicz agreed to remain in New York on his return from this
trip for interviews with the press on Guild business, providing, as he
expressly requested of the Guild secretary, in a letter from Paris on
August 3, that he "first . . . be brought up to date on Guild affairs and
briefed on controversial points." Significantly, there was no reply, for
on August 18, the day after Mankiewicz had sailed from Le Havre,

when telephone communication was impracticable, DeMille convened a special emergency meeting of the board to draft a bylaw making a non-Communist oath compulsory for its present membership and those seeking admission to the SDG.

To create a show of endorsement for their action and to expose any dissidents, the board "courteously" mailed out numbered open ballots with boxes to be checked "Yes" or "No" underneath the oath. The results (547 "Yes" and 14 "No" on the 618 ballots mailed)[5] might have seemed to indicate widespread support for the oath were it not for the unpublicized fact that the balloting was open.

Not many directors were willing to risk the prospect of identifying themselves in opposition to a loyalty oath when the daily threat of blacklisting hung over them. In the words of Richard Sale, a colleague of Joe's at Fox, "You couldn't go to the studio without the fear that any day you might turn up on the '10 Most Wanted' list." In fact, Sale's name did come up before the California legislature, as did the name of almost every director who had contributed even token sums to the numerous liberal organizations newly labeled "Red Front."

A considerable number of directors privately made known to Joe their opposition to being bullied into signing an oath to a nongovernmental authority without a membership meeting to explain the reasons for the bylaw. (Jules Dassin, who subsequent to *Reunion in France* had become a very successful director with such films as *Brute Force* [1947] and *The Naked City* [1948], implored Mankiewicz over a private lunch at "21" that Joe must take action, since Dassin's budding career and those of others like him were in jeopardy. Dassin had cause for alarm as he was eventually blacklisted and his reputation was restored only through successes in his European exile such as *Rififi* [1954] and *Never on Sunday* [1960].)

Many telegraphed protests awaited Mankiewicz when he arrived in New York on August 23, as well as a flock of reporters that swarmed around him at the pier, hurling questions about his reaction to the oath and the "emergency" that occasioned its lightning adoption and approval. Mankiewicz was scarcely in a position to comment since his only previous warning of the impending press interrogation was a shipboard cable the previous day from Carl Post, the Guild's public

---

[5]Only 561 ballots were returned. The 57 abstentions represented directors working in foreign or out-of-state locations.

relations man, warning, "PRESS MEETING YOU RE TWO OVERNIGHT, CONTROVERSIAL QUESTIONS. STALL THEM UNTIL PRESS CONFERENCE. WILL EXPLAIN. COVER UP WITH ANY KIND OF STATEMENT ON EUROPEAN SITUATION, ETC."

Despite this instruction, Mankiewicz knew that he could not evade the question of the oath's implications before reporters like Thomas Pryor of the *New York Times,* Jack Harrison of the *Hollywood Reporter,* or Dorothy Manners (for Louella Parsons of the Hearst Syndicate) without their drawing inferences one way or the other. To placate them, he drafted a statement that was studiously noncommittal: "I had no knowledge of the action taken by the SDGA until my return last night from Europe. As President of the Guild, I was not consulted nor was I informed of the action. I will have a statement to make when I arrive in Hollywood next week, at which time I will ascertain what prompted the move and I'll have a complete picture."

Mankiewicz diplomatically relayed the statement to Carl Post for him to issue only after requesting the board's consent, which was quickly granted. Despite the subsequent allegation of his opponents that "on Aug. 24, in N.Y., he [Mankiewicz] issued a press statement criticizing the action of the Board of Directors and the membership without first consulting them,"[6] this was the only statement Mankiewicz issued in New York on the loyalty oath balloting.

The only addenda to his formal press release were those he offered in response to a phone call from Dorothy Manners. As he recalls, "I was in bed, and it is very tough to get a press counselor in between you and the phone when you are in bed and when he is in another hotel. Dorothy Manners said, 'We have read the story. What is it you are going to want to find out?' I said, 'Dorothy, all I know is what I read in telegrams, and people want to know. Some of the questions that have been put to me by members and by the press are, "Why the emergency?" and "Why the open ballot?" and "Why no open discussion?" ' She ran that in her column."[7]

This disclosure also served to forewarn the board members of the questions Mankiewicz would bring to the meeting he convened immediately on his return to Los Angeles on September 5. At this

---

[6]Extract from the recall committee telegram of October 14, 1950.
[7]From the minutes of Mankiewicz's report to the membership, October 22, 1950.

session Joe was briefed on the pretexts for the emergency action. He was told that all the guilds and unions in Hollywood were going to adopt a mandatory oath for their memberships (only the Producers Guild actually did), and the board wanted the Directors Guild to lead the way.

Moreover, a large number (thirty-four, by DeMille's fabrication) of New York directors wanted to secede from their union and join the SDG but were afraid that without the oath they would be followed "by a pro-Communist group of which they wanted to be rid. [The] oath was to be their assurance, since, as everyone knows, Communists will not sign a non-Communist oath," Joe ironically related.[8]

As indicative of the falsehood of this "emergency" as these fictitious applicants was the fact that five weeks had elapsed since the oath's "ratification" without the affidavits being mailed to the membership. Mankiewicz pointed out this suspicious delay to the board at the meeting of October 9. He repeatedly urged that either a meeting be held or a written explanation be given to inform the membership that by noncompliance with the bylaw they could be expelled from the Guild or refused permission to work, but his efforts were rebuffed by the board.

Although Mankiewicz carefully stipulated that there was no point in debating the bylaw, since it had been passed by the board and voted on by the membership, he questioned its legality under the Taft-Hartley Act, which required only officers of unions, like himself, not members, to sign a loyalty oath. "According to the Taft-Hartley Act, we have not the right to deny a man the right to work because he won't sign an affidavit," Joe pointed out. The members of the board, however, refused to acknowledge this legal objection to their action, despite their attorney's support of Mankiewicz's contention.

The manner in which the oath was imposed on SDG members and its utility for blacklisting became heated issues on which Mankiewicz would not relent. "Russia is the only place I know where the populace is not entitled to a secret ballot," he contended, to which a board member replied, "Maybe we should use some of those tactics here!"[9]

---

[8]*Ibid.* (There were no actual applications from individual New York directors at the time, according to Mankiewicz, and it was six years before the New York branch merged with the SDG.)

[9]This exchange echoes an earlier one at a board meeting when George Stevens's tale of liberating a death camp in Germany (Dachau) when he was an army officer was

Since the board intended to inform only producers, rather than the directors, of the bylaw's implications, a new bylaw was proposed. In it the producers, who formerly received only a list of members in good standing, would be sent two additional lists: one, of those directors in bad standing for nonpayment of dues, and another, of those directors ineligible for employment by not having signed the oath.

The board made only one concession. They withheld forwarding a list of those members who were behind in paying their dues. The board was thus lenient only because one of the board members argued that "if a man can qualify to get a job on his merits, then he can arrange to pay up his dues—but if you call attention to his dues in arrears, it makes it hard." Evidently penury was forgivable, whereas nonconformist political or moral convictions were not. "To my knowledge," Mankiewicz later said, "no other guild, union, or group of professional and creative men had ever issued such a list of their members to prospective employers."

On September 14 Mankiewicz went to New York to accept a B'nai Brith award as "the one who did the most in the field of art during the preceding year to further the American democratic ideal." (His screenplay and direction of *No Way Out,* a study of anti-Negro prejudice, had earned him the honor.) At the ceremony he made a passionate indictment of the witch hunt climate and called for the preservation of American liberals as the "new minority," a minority "as much as the Negro and the Jew . . . being slandered, libeled, persecuted and threatened with extinction."

Addressing himself both to the legislative investigative committees and to the board of the SDG, he said the American liberal "does not recognize the right of individuals or groups of individuals to set themselves up in such a manner as to usurp the power and jurisdiction of legally appointed courts of law—thereby depriving their fellow Americans of protection under law for their good names and perhaps even their livelihood."

Back in Los Angeles, DeMille began mobilizing his forces after privately screening all of Mankiewicz's films and finding them devoid of Communist propaganda.[10] His faction's first public move, on Sep-

---

greeted by another rabid board member who suggested, "We should leave some of those concentration camps for our Commies!"
  [10]Robert Parrish, *Growing Up in Hollywood,* Harcourt Brace Jovanovich, 1976, p. 205.

tember 26, was to have Albert S. Rogell, a vice-president of the Guild known to be DeMille's "factotum and hatchet man,"[11] accuse *Daily Variety,* the leading trade paper, of being Leftist for printing statements made by Mankiewicz criticizing the Guild's loyalty oath when he returned from Europe the previous month. In a signed editorial rebuttal, *Daily Variety*'s editor, Joe Schoenfeld, cited Mankiewicz's actual discussion of European versus Hollywood filmmaking; Mankiewicz had made no allusion to the oath other than his subsequent Guild-approved statement. "The absurdity that the suppression of news is patriotic speaks for itself" was Schoenfeld's terse rebuttal.[12]

While condemning Mankiewicz and *Variety* for disparaging the Guild in print in order to fan the controversy, the DeMille faction leaked a fragment from the minutes of the subsequent board meeting on October 9, although all such closed deliberations were, by rule, strictly confidential.[13] The *Daily Variety* headline of October 11 read, "MANKIEWICZ WILL NOT SIGN OATH." The text that followed stated that Joe was leading a revolt within the SDG over a blacklist and an open ballot; that he had "won the support of Board members Frank Capra, Mark Robson, Clarence Brown and John Ford against the blacklist"; and that one of these figureheads had made the plea that the SDG "get out of politics and back to directing pictures."

In fact, Mankiewicz had won over neither Capra nor Brown, and his refusal to sign the loyalty oath as a Guild member (which he had thrice signed as an officer under federal law) was a tactic adopted to quash the proposed new "penalty" bylaw, by which a list specifying those directors who had protested the oath was to be sent to producers. Mankiewicz had boldly branded this a "blacklist," despite the protest of the term by some of the board members,[14] and the board eventually adopted a compromise measure of sending out only a list of members not in good standing. The reason for their lack of good standing was

---

[11]Quotation from H. C. Potter in an interview with the author. Rogell was a former cameraman and a director of second features from silent film days. His films of the period include *Heaven Only Knows* (1947), *Northwest Stampede* (1948), and *The Admiral Was a Lady* (1950).

[12]Rogell's attempt at intimidation resulted in making Schoenfeld an invaluable behind-the-scenes aide to the Mankiewicz forces as the conflict increased.

[13]Mankiewicz later termed it "a shocking violation of confidence and [reported] in a distorted manner" (report to the membership, October 22, 1950).

[14]One board member said, "I do not know it is a blacklist. That we are assuming. I wish to place an objection to that. I think it is a fine, patriotic thing to do" (quoted in Mankiewicz's report to the membership).

to be furnished to the producer upon inquiry.[15] Mankiewicz and one board member[16] who refused to sign the oath, *as Guild members,* were assured that the oath would not be submitted to them because they were already in compliance under the Taft-Hartley Act.[17]

Rather than "leading a revolt," Mankiewicz was only urging the board to call a meeting of the full membership "to dispel the [present] dissension and undercurrent of feeling." To bolster this appeal, he said, "I do not know how much longer we can keep this business of a tight little Board of Directors sitting on a membership who have a lot of questions to ask, as it has already taken [during the interim between the two board meetings] all the persuasion at my command to convince a group of members to refrain from calling a General Membership meeting for the sole purpose of openly debating the entire situation."[18] Mankiewicz went so far as to suggest deferentially that the consensus of such a meeting might prove that he could better serve the membership by stepping down as president, in view of his rift with the board, which "separated [us] definitely on some very important things."

When the board met, its members once more dissuaded Mankiewicz from this action "by their determination to avoid open disunity at any cost," Mankiewicz recalled, "and particularly by their reassuring attitude toward my voiced doubts as to whether or not the membership would want me to continue as president." The following day, October 10, Mankiewicz reiterated his promise not to call a general meeting to a friend on the board "whose admonitions against calling the meeting had had the strongest effect on me."

His reward for not calling the meeting was the October 11 *Variety*

---

[15]DeMille's follow-up proposal at a board meeting, says Mankiewicz, was that "every director, at the conclusion of a film, file a report on all the actors he has used in that film, in terms of their Americanism, loyalty, and patriotic attitudes. These reports were to be kept in a dossier in the SDG files, and the producers were to have access to them, in order to know whether they were hiring good Americans."

[16]Presumably, Merian C. Cooper, whose service as a brigadier general in the Asian Theater made his loyalty indisputable. According to Mankiewicz, Cooper told his friend and colleague John Ford that even if DeMille put a pistol to his head, he would not sign a loyalty oath that was not required by the government.

[17]Mankiewicz pointed out that it would create considerable embarrassment if the name of the nonconsenting board member appeared on this proscribed list. As "everyone was in agreement that no Communist would hesitate to sign that affidavit," there were not likely to be any actual Communists on the list of dissidents.

[18]From the minutes of Mankiewicz's report to the SDG membership, October 22, 1950, as are the subsequent quotations.

headline, "MANKIEWICZ WILL NOT SIGN OATH." He quickly comprehended that this misrepresentation implied "a seemingly independent avowal of purpose," rather than his actual "calculated threat made in order to win a point," and that it "could not only bring discredit upon the Guild, but upon my own good name and character."

In his own words, "I think that during the day and night of Wednesday, October 11, I considered every possible result and ramification that might eventuate from that story in the trade paper, except that it should be assumed by anyone in [his] right mind that I could have given the story to the paper. It could never conceivably have occurred to me that men whom I have known and with whom I have worked for as long as twenty years and that many members of a Guild to which I have given so much of my time and my energy would have simply assumed my guilt."

He might have anticipated the vindictive use Louella Parsons (a vengeful enemy of the Mankiewiczes since the time Herman modeled *Citizen Kane* on her employer, Hearst) would make of it in her syndicated column and network radio show. Louella's verbal and printed gush reached even the grade-school level, so that Joe's sons, aged eight and ten, felt obliged to ask their father why he had not signed a loyalty oath.

It served to stiffen the spine of Joe's wife, Rosa, a woman passionately concerned with American historical precedent because of her citizenship studies and possessed of *zivilcourage* (personal bravery in quixotically defying governmental tyranny),[19] which she had evidenced in rejecting the blandishments of Nazi leaders by leaving Austria in 1936.

The DeMille faction next called a secret meeting of selected members of the board and other sympathetic director members for 6 P.M. on the eleventh. Known Mankiewicz partisans were deliberately excluded. For instance, the telegram inviting board member and former SDG president George Stevens arrived at his Paramount office at 6:30 P.M., even though DeMille worked at the same studio.

The outcome of the meeting was a decision to recall Mankiewicz as president of the Guild by means of a ballot on anonymous stationery. The entire text was as follows: "This is a ballot to recall Joe Mankiewicz. Sign here ☐ Yes." The ballot was enclosed in a return enve-

---

[19]The term and characterization are by Robert Lantz, a dear friend and Austrian compatriot of Rosa Stradner.

lope addressed to the SDG. No reasons for requesting the ouster were included.

As Mankiewicz subsequently pointed out, "The recall 'ballot' is a refinement over the open ballot which the membership was forced to use in voting on the non-Communist oath. That ballot permitted members to vote either 'Yes' or 'No.' The recall ballot permits the choice of either voting 'Yes' or not at all."[20] Once again each member's vote would be known and recorded.

It took the next working day (Thursday, October 12) plus overtime for DeMille's former assistant director, Vernon Keays,[21] the executive secretary of the Guild and totally DeMille's creature, to mobilize the entire staff of the Guild's office to mimeograph the ballot and address all the designated envelopes.

The most time-consuming chore for Keays, in concert with De-Mille, was to weed out from the roster of 278 senior directors those potentially loyal to Mankiewicz. The fear was that any loyalist might tip him off to the action and thereby impede the coup. Sixty percent (167 votes) of the Guild's membership was needed to recall their president. DeMille's committee hoped to oust Mankiewicz within thirty-six hours after the recall resolution was instituted so that Mankiewicz and his partisans would have no time to rally forces in his defense.

Fifty-five names were scratched from the list, and in a move reminiscent of the sequence from Capra's *Meet John Doe* (1941) in which the corrupt reactionary played by Edward Arnold sends out uniformed cyclists to stave off the ideological threat of Gary Cooper, motorcycle messengers were dispatched into the night to hand-deliver the ballots. (Ironically, Capra was among the members of the recall committee.)[22]

While the Rapid Messengers, frustrated by the number of wrong addresses, were obliged to carry out their deliveries until 3 A.M. (a late hour for a town that retires early), a supplementary telephone campaign was under way. Recall committee members took on the task of phoning directors of their acquaintance to gain a sympathetic response prior to

---

[20]A portion of an advertisement in the *Hollywood Reporter,* October 16, 1950.

[21]Keays's credits as an assistant director or, more often, a unit production manager date back to 1918. Working in this latter capacity on *Our Daily Bread,* he impressed King Vidor favorably.

[22]Prophetically, the Arnold villain, Norton, is known by his initials, D. B., just as DeMille was called C. B.

the receipt of the ballot. Delmer Daves *(Destination Tokyo, Dark Passage)* remembered asking his caller, "Why not call a membership meeting? . . . Maybe Joe has talked himself out on a limb, [but] let's hear what he has to say." H. C. Potter *(The Story of Vernon and Irene Castle, Mr. Blandings Builds His Dream House)* received his call from Andrew Stone, who made the "impassioned plea [that] he had a son in Korea with the army, and we all feel that Joe Mankiewicz is not only destroying the Guild but sticking a knife in the backs of all our boys who are over there fighting for us in Korea."[23]

Joe had been tipped off only that evening by a phone call from his brother, who located him in a screening room at Fox. In his typically profane fashion, masking his concern, Herman inquired, "Did you know, for Christ's sake, there's a fucking recall action on against you? Johnny Farrow said some guy just drove up on a motorcycle to his house to get him to sign the petition."

Mankiewicz received his own recall ballot at breakfast. "At that very moment," he noted, "I was reading in the newspapers of the only other place in the world, I imagine, where exactly the same kind of ballot was being used on the same day. I was reading of the Communist election in East Germany."[24]

The trade papers of Friday the thirteenth carried a well-calculated ad proclaiming, "The Screen Directors Guild takes pride in announcing the tabulation of the membership ballot on the Guild by-law requiring the non-Communist oath . . ."

That evening, while *All About Eve* was premiering to critical huzzahs at the Roxy in New York, Mankiewicz and his key supporters launched their counterattack. They hastily organized a dinner, in the back room of Chasen's restaurant, which was attended by many of the industry's leading directors, including the four Oscar winners before Mankiewicz (Billy Wilder, William Wyler, Elia Kazan, and John Huston), as well as George Seaton, Don Hartman, King Vidor, Richard Brooks, John Farrow, and H. C. Potter.

Martin Gang, Mankiewicz's attorney and one of the most prominent legal figures in the film business,[25] emphasized the gravity of the

---

[23]From an interview with H. C. Potter.

[24]Minutes of the SDG membership meeting, October 22, 1950.

[25]Director Joseph Losey, later blacklisted, maintains that Martin Gang was "pretty well known" for his influence with the HUAC and could get clients off "if you named names, which were subsequently leaked."

recall action by saying that its passage would most likely terminate Joe's career as a filmmaker. Gang advocated a twofold measure to counter the recall: a legal injunction to halt the circulation and counting of the ballots, and a petition for a general meeting of the membership to inform them of Mankiewicz's side of the events.

John Huston volunteered the use of his name for the injunction, but a petition for a membership meeting required the signatures of twenty-five members. The ensuing hunt for additional signatories occupied the remainder of the evening. After canvassing the main dining room at Chasen's for directors, phone-call solicitations were made all over town and even to New York.

Although the act of a member's petitioning for a meeting was clearly sanctioned by a Guild bylaw, in this instance it meant risking DeMille's wrath. One of the signers, Richard Brooks, remembers that agents were taking their director clients aside to warn them of the possible consequences, especially to immigrants whose final citizenship papers had not come through. A couple of pledged signatories got convenient "headaches," and it was not until 2 A.M. that William Wyler thought of calling the screenwriter Walter Reisch, who, though inactive as a director, had maintained his membership by paying his dues to the Guild. A limousine was dispatched, and Reisch added the twenty-fifth signature[26] to what Mankiewicz termed "our declaration of independence," of which he later sent framed copies to the signers as a memento of their courage.

On Saturday at 9 A.M. jubilation turned to cold shock when a delegation went to file the petition and found that the Guild office was closed, although it was regularly open on Saturdays. The group realized

---

[26]The petitioners signed in the following order: John Huston, H. C. Potter, Peter Ballbusch, Michael Gordon, Andrew Marton, George Seaton, Maxwell Shane, Mark Robson, Richard Brooks, John Sturges, Felix Feist, Robert Wise, Robert Parrish, Otto Lang, Richard Fleischer, Fred Zinnemann, Joseph Losey, William Wyler, Jean Negulesco, Nicholas Ray, Billy Wilder, Don Hartmann, Charles Vidor, John Farrow, Walter Reisch.

Joseph Losey says that he and fellow signatory Nicholas Ray were incensed at the handwritten clause, inserted in the petition for the membership meeting, which read: "Each of us hereby swears for himself alone that I am not a member of the Communist Party or affiliated with such party and I do not believe in, and I am not a member of nor do I support any organization that believes in or teaches the overthrow of the US Government by force or by any illegal or unconstitutional methods." Losey says he and Ray protested that by signing this added clause they were, in effect, advocating "exactly what we were opposing." Losey contends that Martin Gang quieted them by maintaining that even if they were Communists, "it's not perjury. There are no witnesses!"

they were still forty-eight hours from stopping the recall, as now the petition, like the injunction, could not be filed until Monday. Any further move was impeded because neither Mankiewicz nor Robert Aldrich, representing a group of assistant directors, could procure a membership list from secretary Vernon Keays, whose wife contended he had left town before breakfast.

While Mankiewicz's forces feverishly conducted a phone campaign throughout the weekend to locate directors and urge them not to sign the recall ballot,[27] the recall committee issued its final, deceptive bid, in the form of a telegram, to legitimize their action and induce the quota of votes required. The four-page, 709-word wire sent to all 278 senior members listed fourteen specific charges against Mankiewicz that the committee had somehow neglected to include on the recall ballot. The telegram contained twelve citations that mentioned the board of directors. To further the illusion that the telegram was issued by the *entire* fifteen-member board, four other directors' names were inserted among the eleven board member signatories.[28]

The *Daily Variety* headline of Monday, October 16, read, "MANKIEWICZ RECALL TO FAIL." Its text included the information that Mankiewicz had "taken the wind out of the recall petition's sails" by signing the member's loyalty oath he had previously refused. (Actually, Mankiewicz had never received the famed "open ballot" and was obliged to use George Seaton's. All twenty-five signers of the petition, including the shortly-to-be-blacklisted Joseph Losey, scrupulously signed the loyalty oath in order to be in full compliance with the Guild bylaw.)

The article did not mention that *Daily Variety*'s editor, Joe Schoenfeld, had personally emended, in longhand, the typed petition at Chasen's. In print Schoenfeld proceeded to clobber Albert

---

[27]They succeeded in persuading 106, only 4 short of the 110 needed to block the recall.

[28]The eleven board members of the recall committee were Clarence Brown, David Butler, Frank Capra, Cecil B. DeMille, Tay Garnett, George Marshall, Frank McDonald, Albert S. Rogell, William A. Seiter (alternate), Richard Wallace, and John Waters. The four unofficial director signatories were Henry King, Leo McCarey, Lesley Selander, and Andrew Stone. The abstaining board members were George Stevens, John Ford, Claude Binyon, Merian C. Cooper, Walter Lang, Frank Borzage, George Sidney, and Mark Robson (alternate). This makes the actual total of the board of directors seventeen members and two alternates, but, presumably, fifteen board members usually sat at board meetings, as the fifteen-member figure is frequently cited in the minutes of the October 22 meeting.

Rogell by charging that "Rogell, on Thursday evening, had deliberately misinformed *Daily Variety* by saying he had no part of, nor any knowledge of any movement or petition to oust Mankiewicz from the Presidency." He followed up by exposing Rogell's fabrication "that the Mankiewicz recall movement was started by the rank and file members, particularly the assistant directors, and was well along before being presented to the Guild Board."

In a paid ad in both trade papers that morning, signed by thirty-eight directors including the twenty-five petitioners, Mankiewicz reiterated his patriotic bona fides as head of the industry's Finnish Relief Fund and his supervisory direction of memorial services for the American Legion on October 8.[29] He alluded to the previous board meeting of October 9 by stating, "The Board severally and collectively would not hear of my stepping down as President. Mr. DeMille, for example, expressed no dissatisfaction with me except that I was stubborn."

He concluded that "as long as I am president of the Screen Directors Guild of America, I will continue to fight for the right of every member to an open discussion and a closed ballot. As an American, I will fight as long as I live to maintain that distinction . . . between properly constituted governmental authority and the attempt of any individual or group of individuals to usurp that authority."[30]

Although unavailable to the Mankiewicz contingent all weekend, Vernon Keays had been making furtive trips to the Guild at odd hours on Saturday and Sunday. Keays had the office open early on Monday, October 16, to greet a bristling Joe Mankiewicz, George Seaton, Fred Zinnemann, Mark Robson, and Martin Gang. They served their petition, scheduled the membership meeting for the following Sunday, October 22, and received, in turn, the complete membership list they had sought, along with a number of proxy blanks for the use of members who would be unable to attend the climactic assembly.

---

[29]Not only did the American Legion form a powerful reactionary lobby against films that displeased them, but a special Legion committee served as a means for numerous Hollywood figures to clear themselves of blacklisting. Director H. C. Potter tells of Fred Zinnemann's agonizing decision to appear before it to clear himself, after being blacklisted for nearly two years for innocently giving a lecture on "The Film Director" to a group at UCLA that, without authorization, added his name to their letterhead and was subsequently named a Red Front organization.

[30]In the *Los Angeles Times* of October 15, Mankiewicz more precisely stated his intention "to conduct a fight to return the Guild to the hands of the members and get it out of the hands of a small clique within the Board of Directors."

Keays, pleading the advice of the Guild's legal counsel, Mabel Walker Willebrandt, refused to divulge the extent of his participation in preparing the recall ballot and the reasons for his unavailability over the weekend.

Martin Gang countered by showing Keays the complaint for an injunction he had filed in Superior Court, which stated that "the whole Mankiewicz recall procedure was unauthorized and not done in accordance with the union's law. Further, the move of the pro-Mankiewicz Guild members to get a membership meeting was thwarted by assertedly questionable means." Gang concluded by bluntly telling Keays he would secure a court order to compel his deposition prior to the Sunday meeting.

While Keays succeeded in delaying his personal testimony, he could not stop Martin Gang and George Stevens from questioning the staff of the Guild's office. The staff members were convened on Friday, October 20, and their testimony supplied Stevens with enough details of Keays's malfeasance to cram his red loose-leaf binder. In Stevens's estimation, he had gathered enough evidence "to blow DeMille right out of the water."[31]

On Wednesday evening, October 18, the board of directors called a special meeting ostensibly to determine the form of proxy to be used at the membership meeting. The real intent was to defuse the growing controversy between the factions.

The session began with an airing of the charges in the recall committee's telegram, reiterated in Albert Rogell's affidavit in response to the court injunction. Mankiewicz proceeded to demolish the allegations relating to his "press release" of September 24 and the "press leak" of October 11 and strengthened his position with a letter from Joe Schoenfeld testifying that Mankiewicz had refused to issue a statement regarding the board's deliberations.

"Almost to a man," Mankiewicz recalled,[32] "the Board members admitted to me openly and privately that they had never known the true facts and that they were shocked at the falseness of both accusations."

---

[31]Quotation from an interview with George Stevens. Gang donated his high-priced legal services and Stevens initiated and financed the investigation of the Guild staff.

[32]From the minutes of the SDG membership meeting, October 22, 1950.

Disregarding the telegram's charge that Mankiewicz had "pitted himself against the legal governing body of the Guild, its board of directors," and used "his office as president in such a dictatorial manner as to render the democratic procedure of the board of directors impossible," the board swiftly adopted Frank Capra's motion to give Mankiewicz a unanimous vote of confidence. As a further conciliatory gesture to their president, the board unanimously "approved in principle" a revision of the bylaws calling for the use of a closed ballot.

The previous Sunday Mankiewicz had told a group of assistant directors that the recall action was deliberately timed to keep him from attending a Wednesday night meeting of the Motion Picture Industry Council.

Thursday morning's *Daily Variety* noted that Mankiewicz and his arch enemies, DeMille and Rogell, had "beelined over to the MPIC conclave, and made smiling entrances." "The SDG announcement [of the vote of confidence] came with startling suddenness and surprise," *Daily Variety* concluded, "and completely vitiated the expected excitement of the general membership meeting of the SDG on Sunday."[33]

That prediction proved as accurate as the *Chicago Tribune* headline of Dewey's victory over Truman. "What *Daily Variety* didn't know" was that Mankiewicz was holding daily strategy sessions at Fox with directors John Huston, George Stevens, H. C. Potter, and occasionally William Wyler, in anticipation of the Sunday meeting, since the recall committee had not formally withdrawn its action.

The reason DeMille refused to quash the recall was that in a private tête-à-tête in his office, Mankiewicz had refused to express contrition and thereby save face for DeMille, Rogell, and Marshall, the key triumvirate of the recall committee. When Frank Capra learned of their refusal to desist, despite the vote of confidence, he resigned in disgust not only from the committee but from the Guild's board of directors.[34]

Two incidents, one sad, the other comic, highlight the preliminaries to what Walter Reisch terms "the most tumultuous evening in

---

[33] *Daily Variety*, October 23, 1950.
[34] George Stevens reveals that he and Capra, "a great friend of mine, fell totally apart on this [blacklisting]." " 'They've got the goods on some of these guys,' " Capra told Stevens, "and he mentioned a director's name that happens to be the same last name [spelled differently] as Paul Robeson's" (i.e., Mark Robson).

Hollywood" and Mankiewicz calls "the most dramatic evening in my life"—the gathering of nearly 500 directors[35] on Sunday, October 22, at 7:30 P.M. to attend the emergency membership meeting of the SDG in the Crystal Room of the Beverly Hills Hotel.

The first incident occurred in Mankiewicz's car as it pulled up to the hotel. Joe had brought with him for moral support his friend and colleague at Fox, Elia Kazan. At the time, Kazan was the foremost director in the American theater and was rapidly extending his preeminence to film.

Kazan informed Mankiewicz he could not go in with him. Joe desperately pleaded, "I need you. I need every vote. My career's on the line." Kazan explained that DeMille knew of his Communist party membership, and his presence at the meeting as a Mankiewicz partisan could only damage Joe's cause.[36] Mankiewicz, severely shaken by the episode, went up to the suite in the hotel where his colleagues John Huston and H. C. Potter were fine-combing his opening address.

They were presently joined by William Wyler, bristling for the fight, who fortified their morale by relating how he had just intimidated Albert Rogell in the crowded lobby downstairs. A month earlier the government had invited Wyler to make a documentary of the Korean conflict from the front lines, but because he was in the midst of a production (*A Place in the Sun*), he was obliged to decline. "With malice aforethought," he transferred the invitation to Rogell, saying, "this is a great opportunity to go out and make a documentary under fire."[37] Rogell stammered his apologies at declining the great honor, begging off because of the press of his current affairs.

When Wyler caught sight of Rogell among his peers in the hotel lobby, and knowing that Rogell would take some part in the accusations against Mankiewicz, he positioned himself about ten feet away from Rogell:

---

[35]Only 240 senior directors or their proxies had voting privileges, but assistant and television directors were permitted to attend.

[36]Kazan was reported, by *Variety*, to have attended the Chasen's dinner, but, significantly, his name does not appear on the petition for the membership meeting. Kazan appeared before the HUAC in January and April 1952 and was pressured by the committee into naming the members of his Communist cell group from his days in the Group Theatre.

[37]Related by H. C. Potter. Wyler had made a noted wartime documentary, *Memphis Belle* (1944), about the final run of a B-17 bomber and its crew in combat over Germany. He lost most of his hearing in a subsequent bombing run over Italy.

WYLER: *(bellowing)* Al. Al Rogell.

ROGELL: *(turning and giving a wave of recognition)* Hi, Willy.

WYLER: Whatever happened to the government's asking you to go to Korea to shoot combat footage?

ROGELL: *(stuttering)* I told you about that, Willy. It's very unfortunate I couldn't . . .

WYLER: *(cupping his hand to his deaf ear)* Louder, I can't hear you.

ROGELL: *(shouting his previous lines)* I told you about that, Willy. It's very unfortunate . . .

WYLER: What? You mean you didn't go? What's the matter, were you afraid?

ROGELL: No, no.

WYLER: *(crossing to Rogell and whispering)* Al, when you're sitting at that table on the dais, I'll be sitting up front, right below you. And if you so much as open your mouth with accusations about Joe Mankiewicz, I'm going to get up *(delivered in a tone of withering contempt)* and disclose the whole, sordid story.

During the seven-and-a-half-hour meeting that ensued, each time Rogell got up to speak he glanced down nervously at Wyler, fearing he would carry out his threat.

Wyler's tale momentarily broke the tension and bolstered spirits, but Mankiewicz was pacing back and forth, glancing over Potter and Huston's expert editing. Potter recalls that "when Joe would come over and say, 'Listen, I'm the guy who's making the speech, and I've got to deliver it in a couple of minutes,' we'd say, 'Go away.'"

The speech, an hour's report to the membership, lucidly and dispassionately outlined the chronology of events leading up to the meeting and implicitly refuted every allegation of the recall committee. Walter Reisch says that the address's great "cleverness" lay in its device of never using the first person "I," but always using the impersonal "Mankiewicz."

Only in his reference, near the end, to the "Politburo quality" of the recall's instigation as "so foreign to everything I have ever known or learned or thought as an American" did the dispassionate tenor of his remarks waver. His discretion in never referring to opposing board members by name was absolute (except for one necessary allusion to an exchange with DeMille), and he added an element of suspense in tactfully sidestepping his knowledge of the recall conspiracy by saying, "I prefer not to include in this report any of the details of which I have since become aware."

The ovation accorded the report was indicative of how completely Mankiewicz had won over his audience. It so nonplussed the recall faction of the board, seated on a raised dais, that it took a perceptible nod from DeMille to Rogell to indicate that Rogell should assume the ungrateful task of following a star turn with a response.

Rogell's fumbling effort mainly consisted of reading portions of his already refuted affidavit. The Mankiewicz faction had determined to hold its fire, however, until DeMille or one of his cohorts said something characteristically scurrilous.

At his own direction DeMille was cosmeticized by the special baby-pink spotlight he favored to bathe his bald dome. In a variation of Antony's funeral oration, he said, "I have come before you neither to praise Caesar nor to bury him." His equivalent for the "Brutus is an honorable man" refrain was, at first, to characterize the "minority" who refused to sign the loyalty oath as "twenty-five or thirty sensitive, honorable, good Americans"[38] and later as "good American men . . . who are tough fighters, and believe me, Mr. Mankiewicz is a tough fighter." The latter encomium received a round of applause, as did DeMille's later statement, "No one has accused Mr. Mankiewicz of being a Communist. When I nominated him for president of this Guild, I thought he was a good American, and I still think he is a good American."

DeMille artfully played a series of sentimental riffs on his impartiality ("There is nothing I want from the Guild. There is nothing the Guild can give me"); his venerable age, sixty-nine (". . . my race is nearing its end. It is the last lap . . ."); the Korean casualties ("You all read this morning about the American boys who were prisoners, who were taken out, promised food, and then were machine-gunned with their hands tied behind their backs").

DeMille concluded by citing the board's beneficence in giving every member an opportunity to vote on the oath, even though the board was not required to submit new bylaws to the membership. "Throughout this whole business, the board has acted democratically and with every regard for the individual rights of its membership. That statement cannot be challenged."

"I challenge it," said one voice from the floor.

That taunt provoked DeMille's fatal blunder. In a move to dis-

---

[38]Actually only fourteen had voted "No." DeMille was confusing the figure with the twenty-five petitioners for the meeting.

credit the chief Mankiewicz partisans, he read off a list of the Red Front organizations with which some of the twenty-five petitioners had been affiliated. The list had been drawn, he contended, from the reports of the 1947–49 Un-American Activities Committee of the California legislature.

"Troubled waters attract strange specimens sometimes," DeMille said ambiguously. When he contended, "I am making no accusations against anybody, least of all Mr. Mankiewicz," an audible hissing and booing began in the hall, and a challenger from the floor inquired, "What are they [then]?"

DeMille blithely explained, "I am simply bringing to light the coincidence that the group opposed to the recall happened to be so heavily loaded with the elements that have been repudiated by this Guild in election after election and vote after vote." (The "tainted" twenty-five actually comprised most of the leading figures in the "New Guard" of American directors—Mark Robson, Robert Wise, John Sturges, Richard Fleisher, Fred Zinnemann, Nicholas Ray, and Billy Wilder, in addition to those already mentioned—and a few old-timers like Charles Vidor and John Farrow. The conflict can be viewed as one between competing generations as much as between liberals and conservatives.)

In rhetorically questioning the motive of these petitioners ("Is it to protect Mr. Mankiewicz from injury?"), DeMille direly speculated that the *Daily Worker* and *Pravda* would "gloat over the spectacle" of the publicized rift between the president and the board of directors, leading "members of the board [to] resign and leave the door open for these repudiated elements." After invoking the menace of a Red cabal, DeMille berated Mankiewicz for refusing to sign the joint statement of recantation drafted by the recall committee, "which could have avoided this laundering of rather soiled linen tonight."

Following his convoluted disclaimer, "I recognize that Mr. Mankiewicz has now signed the oath which he didn't have to sign because he had already signed it," DeMille made a non-sequitur resolution that the recall balloting be closed, with no count or record made, and that the ballots be destroyed—in sum, the precise terms sought by the Huston-Gang injunction, except for the crucial withdrawal of the initial recall action.

While declining to comment on the major portion of DeMille's tirade, Mankiewicz explained his refusal to sign the recall committee

disclaimer by saying, "I would have signed . . . only over my dead body
. . . a statement saying that I signed the oath to put myself back into
a compliance from which I was never out."

The venerable John Cromwell, a prominent victim of legislative
committees for his alleged Leftist affiliations and one of the "repudiated elements" DeMille had alluded to, rose to launch the counterattack. He tersely pinpointed DeMille's hypocrisy in pleading for unity
in the Guild while making "acrimonious" and "unfounded accusations" about its members.

Don Hartman,[39] one of the petitioners, followed by boldly admitting he had signed, not "in defense of Mr. Mankiewicz," but in opposition to the "insinuations" put forth by DeMille. "I resent paper-hat
patriots who stand up and holler, 'I am an American' and contend that
no one else is." He justified his membership in several of the subsequently tainted organizations during the war "when Russia was our
ally," saying "it is a very sad commentary on our times that it is
necessary today for decent people, because the house across the street
is robbed, to sign a paper with the man next door saying, 'I am not a
burglar.' "

Referring to the open ballot, Hartman said, "I think there is no
possibility of honesty when you ask people to vote and tell them they
are likely to lose their jobs unless they vote the way you want them to
vote," admitting that this fear had compelled him to sign the oath.

George Seaton, another petitioner, frankly identified himself as a
member of some of the organizations cited by DeMille and felt obliged
to exonerate himself, in the manner that was to become the evening's
ritual for disparaged Mankiewicz spokesmen, by stating he had left
these groups when he became aware of Communist infiltration. Seaton
cited his security clearance for a trip to blockaded Berlin, conferred
only after rigorous State Department investigation. He quoted Occupation General Lucius Clay's rationale for releasing the known war criminal Ilse Koch for lack of evidence (". . . if I resort to totalitarianism
to defeat totalitarianism, we have lost our democratic soul by doing it")
as a contrast to DeMille's star-chamber indictment of Mankiewicz.

As rebuttal to DeMille's false claim that Mankiewicz had leaked

---

[39]Hartman was nearly as influential a figure as DeMille at Paramount because
he was the writer-director of many of the immensely successful Crosby and Hope
"Road" pictures. Hartman became an executive producer at Paramount in 1951.

stories about board meeting deliberations to the press, Seaton revealed that it was DeMille who was guilty of divulging board meeting secrets to Paramount's production chief Y. Frank Freeman, the scene Seaton had witnessed. At one of the Mankiewicz group's strategy sessions, Seaton had said, "Wouldn't it be perfect if, at some point, Bill Wellman got up and delivered a typical 'This is the goddamnedest thing I've ever seen in my life!' " Just as conjectured, William Wellman took the floor after Seaton and delivered the exact line, which convulsed the audience and brought doubly rich laughs to the Mankiewicz strategists.

Wellman identified himself as one of the two members cited by DeMille as saying, "We need this Guild as much as we need a hole in the head" but emphasized the misconstruction of his actual statement, which decried the Guild as it *is*, not as it could and should be.

Wellman lamented that "... [Frank Capra] a guy I am very proud of and very fond of has resigned because he can't stand it any longer." Wellman said that if he were a Guild officer, he would have acted similarly and that it was "impolite" to take action against a president "without [his] knowing about it." Characterizing himself as "a simple guy" dismayed by this "very intricate, involved, and horrible puzzle," Wellman wished "we could forget this whole mess" and urged that Mankiewicz ("a good guy" and "very capable") remain as president and strive for a reconciliation with DeMille "for the sake of the Guild." (Wellman's remarks give credence to Mankiewicz's observation that the simplistic good guy/bad guy and white hat/black hat conflicts of the traditional Western and crime films permeated most of Hollywood's political perceptions. Also symptomatic of the small-town, frontierlike social structure of the film colony were the continual allusions by speakers to having "been to someone's house" as a badge of friendship or intimacy.)

Michael Gordon, the next signatory to speak, offered a succinct rebuttal to DeMille. "I wish to say that I deeply resent a meeting that was called for the purpose of preserving the president in office being called a meeting to disrupt the Guild" (as DeMille had charged). "If there has been any disruption of the Guild . . . in my opinion, that disruption was initiated by the recall committee, which attempted to effect the recall of our president," said Gordon to a burst of applause.

Herbert Leeds, with credentials as an investigator of Communists abroad for the Office of Strategic Services, volunteered that "probably everyone or almost everyone who has any prominence at all, by giving

$5 to a worthy charity has had his name on a Communist front organization. In the state of California, there are three hundred Jewish Communist front organizations, so it is almost impossible for anyone to stay off of one." Leeds said his informants ("a few nasty people I happen to know who infiltrate Communist organizations") reported, " 'We checked Mankiewicz for you and he is pretty clean,' " their only reservation being Joe's tutelage at the Actors' Lab.

Mankiewicz humorously responded, "I don't think that [the Actors' Lab affiliation] was why my recall was called. I am grateful for any shred of cleanliness I can pick up here or there. It only makes me feel cleaner."

John Huston, his lips trembling with anger, read a *New York Times* article completely corroborating Mankiewicz's report and then inquired of DeMille, "In your tabulation of the twenty-five at the restaurant the other night, how many men were in uniform? How many were in uniform when you were wrapping yourself in the flag?"[40]

Next, Delmer Daves recalled DeMille's previously expressed contempt for the membership ("You are all fools!") when a vote on the bylaws went against him by a count of 200 to 2, saying that he resented "beyond belief" DeMille's "disgraceful" characterization of the twenty-five petitioners, and that the recall committee's actions were "indecent" and an "abuse of the privileges of the Guild."

Mankiewicz interjected that he was "mad enough to be sick" at the information that a member was leaking a running account of their closed deliberations to a newsman outside the hall. "Let's not spread this malicious talk," he admonished, "because everything that you say will be distorted into a 'hot' story." He cited his own recent radio tarring by Louella Parsons as an example.

The subject of the Guild's unprecedented Saturday shuttering, which prohibited filing the petition for the meeting, cued what Man-

---

[40]Huston's wartime documentaries of fighting in the Aleutians and the grim *Battle of San Pietro* attest to his valor under fire. George Stevens, who served with a tank brigade that drove through Germany, had similarly enraged DeMille at a board meeting by his response to C. B.'s query, "While I was risking my job [Lux Radio Theatre] being shut out by the union, what were you doing?" Replied Stevens, "I was snowed in at Bastogne while you were piling up your bloody capital gains." (DeMille, an unswerving ideologue, forfeited his role as host of his highly rated radio show in 1945 rather than pay the dollar his union, AFRA, required to oppose an election proposition abolishing "closed shop" unions like AFRA.)

kiewicz termed the evening's coup de grace, delivered by George Stevens.

The eminent director, uncomfortably seated on the dais next to his fellow board members, whom he had grown to despise for their accumulated wealth and consequent indifference to the welfare of nonaffluent members, had been taking ominous glances throughout the evening at his red ring binder whenever DeMille or one of his faction rose to speak. It was now the appropriate moment for Stevens to open it and release the story of the machinations behind the recall ballot's preparation at the Guild, which Mankiewicz had tactically withheld.

With the dramatic announcement that as soon as he finished his report he intended to add his resignation from the board to Capra's, Stevens summed up the recall committee's action, saying, "It was rigged, and it was organized, and it was supposed to work. And gentlemen, it hasn't. . . . If there hadn't been a slip-up somewhere, or if the integrity of the membership of this Guild . . . hadn't frustrated that recall, Mr. Mankiewicz would have been out, and nobody would have had to clear him and say he was a good American. He would just have been smeared and out . . . quick, overnight, or in thirty-six hours, if you please. . . . As the subject of Communism is often the theme, brother, if they can do it better, they are pretty good."

Stevens went on to detail the damaging facts, provided by the intimidated Guild staff, of Vernon Keays's running the recall operation between the Guild and DeMille's office at Paramount. He told of the Guild being closed on the previous Saturday and the membership lists locked in the office's vault to impede the petitioners for a meeting from gaining access to them. He mentioned the incriminating list, with fifty-five names of possible Mankiewicz supporters crossed off, which Keays had confiscated. He condemned Keays for suborning the Guild staff by giving them false cover stories and instructions to make themselves unavailable over the critical weekend, while Keays himself conducted secret meetings at the office at odd hours.

Stevens concluded by saying that the recall conspiracy was merely a symptom of the board's basic orientation. ("I think that this board at no time works for the director as a director. . . . I think this Guild is interested in nothing besides the fight against Communism.") He echoed John Ford's statement at a recent board meeting that there were proper government organizations constituted for this pursuit and cited his previous resignation from the Guild's presidency in 1942 to join the military, "because I don't think you can win wars of the United States here."

DeMille rose to protest the "conspiracy" charge, citing the eminent names of those on the recall committee, and stating, "that is not a committee that would be guilty of a conspiracy in anything but the interests of this Guild." Stevens rebutted by pointing to the recent resignations of Clarence Brown and Frank Capra from the recall committee after they had learned of the conspiratorial tactics of DeMille and Keays.

Then a debate arose over the parliamentary propriety of the long-delayed DeMille resolution abrogating the recall vote. As Mankiewicz commented, "It seems to me that if the fifteen members of the recall committee wish to recall my recall, they should do it. I don't see that they should ask the membership to stop something they started. . . . The point is the board of directors has by the unanimous vote of confidence instructed it [the recall committee], but the recall hasn't been stopped. This thing has been done in a slightly crazy continuity," he quipped in film terminology, and declared the DeMille resolution out of order.

To conform with this ruling, John Huston revised the motion so that the "membership *endow*[41] the board with the power and authority to destroy the recall ballots," and he was seconded by DeMille.

In response to Fritz Lang's concern that Guild funds had been illegally appropriated to pay for the recall telegrams, Leo McCarey confessed that he had personally put up $5,000 to underwrite the expenses. (George Marshall volunteered that he had contributed an equal amount so no Guild funds had been appropriated.)

McCarey rationalized the committee's intemperate haste by saying that "everybody was moving pretty fast, and it was a fire, and maybe we used the wrong nozzle." Mankiewicz replied, "As far as using the wrong nozzle is concerned, I am the only one that got wet."

A member asked for Joe's response to DeMille's contention that Mankiewicz had "implied that the majority of the membership did not have the courage of their convictions and did not honestly sign the statement of their opinion about whether there should be a loyalty oath in the Guild."

---

[41]This wording was amended to *instruct,* as George Stevens pointed out the board already possessed the "power and authority."

Mankiewicz responded that the crux of his opposition lay in the qualifying word *mandatory* in "mandatory loyalty oath." While not implying that the Guild would necessarily have defeated the mandatory oath on a closed ballot, "I still say that I do not think and I cannot be made to think that the result of any election on an open ballot is an honest reflection of the people participating in that election." Then, by a standing vote, the entire membership rose to its feet to approve the Huston motion to instruct the board to destroy the recall ballots. Mankiewicz expressed his gratitude, but pointed out that the recall committee had still not independently withdrawn its action.

Next, the esteemed, Russian-born theater and film director Rouben Mamoulian rose to make what Richard Brooks recalls as the most "heart-wrenching" address of the evening. Mamoulian attributed his nervousness to his accent, saying that the only previous foreign accent he had heard that evening was Fritz Lang's. In deploring the necessity of members having to trace their genealogy by way of proving their Americanism, he asserted that though not American by birth, he had chosen his citizenship. "The work I have done in this country [for example, the stage production of *Oklahoma!* and the film *Summer Holiday*] glorifies the country and shows my love for it better than any words can do."

Mamoulian recalled that he was one of the fifteen founders of the SDG, who were branded "red, left, revolutionaries" at the time (1937), and rebuked DeMille for sowing seeds of suspicion by anonymous and unsubstantiated accusations against the twenty-five petitioning directors. He concluded with a moving appeal for the "high and mighty" DeMille to proclaim his faith in these members and the Guild itself, saying, "We all need it [the Guild] morally, and in practical terms we may all need it tomorrow."

Vernon Keays, the executive secretary under fire, followed with a rambling apology for his actions. He confessed he had only taken the job out of penury. He claimed he had capitulated to the demands of the recall committee because it comprised eleven, or a "quorum," of the board of directors. Finally, he admitted instructing the Guild receptionist to say he was not in because of the endless importunities of the press.

"Is that why your wife told me you were out of town on Saturday, because of the press?" snapped Mankiewicz, who then hastily apologized for his intemperate interjection.

A motion requesting George Stevens and Frank Capra to reconsider their resignations, which Mamoulian had urged, was unanimously approved.

Then Don Hartman asked DeMille to withdraw his charges made "by insinuation and association, which is the method of rabble rousers. I don't mean to imply he is one," said Hartman, parodying the DeMille technique. "I mean this is the method used by them."

DeMille remained adamant, allowing only "that there were many fine Americans" among the twenty-five, but "I have only heard those who apparently belong to some of those organizations complain about my suggestion."

"Mr. DeMille, I don't belong to any of them. I signed it," Peter Ballbusch[42] protested. ". . . By association and insinuation, you have accused everyone!"

"I am a little astounded that the attack has turned so completely against me," DeMille loftily replied, "but I have taken attacks before, and I will have to take this one, I presume. I cannot retract it, because my statement is fact."

Don Hartman delivered the haymaker. "Mr. DeMille, I have charges against you, and I would like to put them before the meeting. You now go further. You say if anyone speaks in his defense it is proof of his guilt. When you speak in your defense that is not proof of your guilt. . . . I accuse you of misconduct in the Guild, and I ask for your resignation." This audacity was received with tumultuous applause.

Hartman's motion was seconded by the angered John Cromwell, a former Guild president who had been exonerated by the Guild of Red affiliation charges before the HUAC, only to have his accuser named to the Guild's board of directors. An additional second came from Ralph Seiden, a former second-unit director for DeMille who had long nurtured his grievances against the tyrant infamous for his abuse of subordinates.

The Mankiewicz faction had anticipated this contingency and were fearful that they might possibly be accused of having engineered DeMille's deposition and that an industry-wide backlash would ensue from having humbled such a revered figure in the movie business.

George Seaton tried to divert the mounting wave of hostility

---

[42]A protégé of Josef von Sternberg, Ballbusch was the Swiss sculptor of the memorable gargoyles that dominate the décor of von Sternberg's *Scarlet Empress.*

toward DeMille by championing a proposal of William Keighley (De-Mille's successor as director-host of the Lux Radio Theatre) to launch a full investigation of the board's dealings, as recommended by George Stevens's report.

But William Wyler, furious over DeMille's smearing of him as a petitioner, roared that "this has been going on for years. I am sick and tired of having people question my loyalty to my country. The next time I hear somebody do it, I am going to kick hell out of him. I don't care how old he is or how big."

To bursts of applause he concluded, in support of the motion to depose, "Gentlemen, it is not going to work when the Guild is being run from Mr. DeMille's office. Mr. DeMille said he didn't need the Guild. Well, I think he ought to give it back to the membership."

When George Seaton attempted to quash the issue of DeMille's malfeasance in making disclosures about a board meeting to Frank Freeman, which Seaton himself had earlier raised, by saying they related only to a statement about Mankiewicz, Joe at last unburdened himself on the subject of being smeared.

"It seems that everybody has said an awful lot of things about Joe Mankiewicz, including Louella Parsons, who said from coast to coast that I had [not] recanted and I had not signed, but that after I said I would not sign a loyalty oath—which was a lie—I had now turned around and signed one, which made me a good American and a god-damned fool in the eyes of millions of Americans. I would also appreciate knowing the source of Miss Parsons's information, which she repeated to me over the telephone, to see to it that perhaps Miss Parsons could be disabused of some of the things that were said about Joe Mankiewicz."

Don Hartman offered to withdraw his motion in favor of Seaton's proposed investigative committee if it would also "look into the right of a board member to get up at an open meeting and vilify other members without . . . foundation."

At this point, the dean of American directors rose from the dais and identified himself. "I am a director of Westerns," said John Ford, his self-deprecation convulsing the audience. "I am one of the founders of this Guild . . . [and in defense of the board] I would like to state that I have been on Mr. Mankiewicz's side of the fight all through it. I have not read one item of print in the newspaper or trade papers. I have not read one telegram or one ballot or one recall notification. I have been sick and tired and ashamed of the whole goddamned thing. I don't care which side it is. If they intend to break up the Guild, goddamn it, they have pretty well done it tonight."

Playing the role of conciliator, Ford chronicled his opposition to the blacklist. "We organized this Guild to protect ourselves against producers. . . . Now somebody wants to throw ourselves into a news service and an intelligence service and give out to producers what looks to me like a blacklist. I don't think we should . . . put ourselves in a position of putting out derogatory information about a director, whether he is a Communist, beats his mother-in-law, or beats dogs.

"I don't agree with C. B. DeMille. I admire him," said Ford. "I don't like him, but I admire him . . . [and] if Mr. DeMille is recalled, your Guild is busted up." To Ford, the spectacle of "the two blackest Republicans I know, Joseph Mankiewicz and C. B. DeMille . . . [fighting] over Communism . . . is getting laughable to me."

In a tone of bonhomie, Ford concluded, "Everybody has apologized. Everybody has said their say, and Joe has been vindicated. What we need is a motion to adjourn."

Mankiewicz would only concede he was a "Pennsylvania Republican"[43] but maintained that the recall committee had not been heard from and that "as long as this oath is mandatory, there is no way of avoiding sending out [to the producers] a list of members who are not in good standing for any reason except they have refused to sign the affidavit."

Mankiewicz then asked Ralph Seiden if he would withdraw his second if Don Hartman withdrew his motion asking for DeMille's resignation. Seiden, fortified by grievance and drink, truculently persisted, "I still maintain the motion for the good of the Guild." Lacking a second to Seiden, however, the motion was dropped.

The discussion returned to the formation of an investigative committee, but in the midst of the formulation of a resolution to define its goals, John Ford rose again to provide the evening's thunderbolt.

---

[43]Although born in Wilkes-Barre, Mankiewicz spent only his early childhood years in Pennsylvania. His use of "Pennsylvania Republican" was to differentiate himself from Ford's self-characterization as "a State of Maine Republican." Joe says that socially Ford would call him a "Pennsylvania Polack" (the lowest of the low among Polish-Americans), and he would familiarly refer to Ford as a "Mick" or "Harp." He explains that these ethnic epithets served as jocularities rather than slurs in their day —an age of ethnic levity whose departure Mankiewicz regrets.

"I believe there is only one alternative, and that is for the board of directors to resign and elect a new board of directors," Ford proclaimed to thunderous assent. "They are under enough fire tonight. It appears they haven't got the support of the men that elected them. . . . I would like to hear a discussion on that."

Procedure required that the complex matter of effectively empowering an investigative committee continue. However, the contentions (later withdrawn) of George Stevens and Leo McCarey that, without the auspices of a new board, its findings would only lead to a rehash of the evening's allegations proved persuasive in tabling the issue in order to act on Ford's motion for the board's resignation.

Despite warnings by John Farrow and King Vidor that the resignation of the board would give the unfavorable impression of a victory for the Mankiewicz forces rather than a show of restored unity in the Guild, John Ford was adamant in drawing the issue to a vote. This key motion, containing an amendment by Mankiewicz that the past presidents of the SDG form an executive committee to run the Guild's affairs until a new board was elected, was voted on by ballot. The announcement of its passage, by Mankiewicz, received the evening's final ovation from an emotionally spent membership.

Each of the board members rose in turn to offer his resignation. The sight of DeMille regally descending from the podium to the floor and retreating to the back of the hall past rows of heads averted from his defiant gaze is an indelible memory for many of the evening's chief participants, who mourned the titan's fall as deeply as they despised his tactics.

Mankiewicz, in command to the very end, summarily dismissed John Huston's suggested conciliatory "expression of gratitude" from the membership to the board as "a little superfluous." He then deleted the "editorializing" of H. C. Potter's revised motion for the formation of a five-man investigative committee by striking out the phrase "that such a situation can never again occur in the Guild." While Mankiewicz maintained his authority as president to appoint the five investigators, he removed himself from consideration, in the event the committee should "uncover something which would embarrass me in some way."

After a swift, unanimous vote of confidence for the maligned twenty-five petitioners and a similarly unanimous vote, at Mankiewicz's urging, to retain counsel Willebrandt for an impending "cat fight" with the National Labor Relations Board, the marathon session ended at 2:20 A.M.

As the packed Crystal Room emptied, only the chief antagonists remained. A small congratulatory band surrounded Mankiewicz on the podium, while, standing below them, DeMille and Keays filled De-Mille's briefcase with the explosive files that had backfired on detonation. (The image of the vanquished persecutor shuffling off into the night carrying a briefcase of nonincriminating documents is the penultimate shot in Mankiewicz's subsequent film, *People Will Talk.* In this scene the vindictive, defeated Elwell [Hume Cronyn] trudges through the university's deserted corridor as the exonerated Dr. Praetorius [Cary Grant] conducts a triumphal overture.)

The Guild ruckus subsided rather timorously.

In an open letter to the membership that appeared in the trade papers of Friday, October 27, Mankiewicz issued the following surprise entreaty:

> Some of us have always known and all of us know now, that the late and lamentable rift within our ranks had nothing whatsoever to do with the pros or cons of a loyalty oath. As I told you the other night, no member has ever voiced to me his opposition to one. Certainly I have never opposed one.
>
> And most certainly it has occurred to you that throughout the seven hours of our meeting, the loyalty oath was at no time a subject of discussion. And yet there exists a wicked and widespread misconception to the contrary—both within our industry and without. A misconception that continues to vilify and smear both our person and our Guild. It is essential that you help to remove that misconception.
>
> My signing [the Guild's own oath] was a voluntary act since the Guild considered me already in compliance and had not submitted its oath to me.
>
> I ask you to do no less. I ask you, as a voluntary act in affirmation of the confidence in your Guild you so vigorously professed last Sunday night, to set aside whatever reservations you may have concerning any aspect of the oath or its method of adoption, and sign it now.

Mankiewicz's present justifications for this seeming repudiation of his views are various and sometimes inconsistent.[44] "If I got the direc-

---

[44]As the dominant factor, he cites the climate of the time ("New York State had just passed a loyalty oath for its teachers and the country was berserk") and "the context

tors to vote for a closed ballot [in the revised bylaws], that would be
almost the equivalent of their saying 'we would have voted differently,' " though "at the meeting, there was no doubt in the minds of
the majority that they thought the loyalty oath stank."

Mankiewicz contends his personal view was "we've got the loyalty
oath, let's forget the goddamned thing. Everybody had signed it anyway." (The question then is why there was a need to exhort publicly
the recalcitrant to sign, except to demonstrate to the public the Guild's
willingness to comply.) Mankiewicz contends that the oath "couldn't
have been properly enforced, because I know of any number of men
who wouldn't have signed the oath, and the Guild took them in
anyway."[45]

If politically prudent, the open letter seems compromising in the
light of Mankiewicz's honesty in handling the conflict. Perhaps the key
to this capitulation lies in his private resolution. "I'd also made up my
mind I was getting the hell out of Hollywood anyway." Three weeks
after the imbroglio, he announced his intention to divide his future
time between films and the Broadway theater.[46]

---

of what Hollywood was like under the shadow of the Hollywood Ten, McCarthy, and
Jack Tenney. . . . Even the *New York Times* was not editorially in favor of us, not to
mention Louella and Hedda."

[45]Although "the boys in the East always felt I was their champion," says Mankiewicz, "some of the more vehement [eastern members] not only would not sign it,
but wanted to test it in court." Fifteen years later, in 1965, a group of six New York
directors petitioned to have the Court of Appeals rescind the restrictive clause and
ultimately gained a favorable ruling from the Supreme Court in 1967. Mankiewicz
claims he was "proved right" by this decision, in that his "big fight with Mabel Walker
Willebrandt [the Guild's counsel]" was always that the oath was in violation of the
Taft-Hartley Act."

[46]*Los Angeles Times*, November 12, 1950. Having cleansed the Guild of the Old
Guard (Vernon Keays was fired and replaced by Joe Youngerman as executive secretary), Mankiewicz decided to relinquish his office when his year's term ended the
following May. However, in the remaining six months of his term, in consort with a
newly appointed board of directors, he instituted a new constitution and bylaws that
gave power in the Guild back to its members and prohibited a recurrence of the
attempted recall or blacklisting.

Parting shots 9

JOE MANKIEWICZ HAS ALWAYS BEEN A MEDICAL BUFF. IN PREPA-ration for a career as a psychiatrist, he had begun a program of premed studies at Columbia. However, his horror and nausea at dissecting frogs in biology and his unparalleled grade of F— in physics were sufficient to dissuade him from majoring in the sciences.

If Mankiewicz has not gone quite as far as his friend Danny Kaye, whom Joe claims once aided the famed heart surgeon Michael De-Bakey in the operating theater, Joe was fond of going to watch his friend Dr. Marcus Rabwin operate at Los Angeles County Hospital.

Because Joe's descriptions of his reactions to drugs were so precise, Rabwin gave him a pill designed to treat asthma without the side effects of adrenalin, which was then generally employed. "Joe gave a wonderfully detailed report on Benzedrine," says Rabwin, "describing how it curbed his appetite, made him very talkative, kept him awake, but left a peculiar taste and dryness in his mouth." Mankiewicz requested a vast quantity of the drug that was to become the rage in Hollywood as a diet and pep pill in the days before its harmful side effects were known. "Joe used to take it before he went into a story conference," Rabwin recalls.

Agent Robert Lantz remembers spending late nights at Reuben's with Joe, after Mankiewicz moved to New York, "arguing about theater, while Joe described his 'totally new' sleeping pill that had second and third time phases, so that if taken at twelve, it would go off again at three-thirty and five in the morning."

Lantz recalls that during the time he was an executive at Figaro, Mankiewicz's independent company, an hour of Joe's services every other Thursday morning would be lost when the magazine *M.D.* would arrive. "He was much too eager to be kept from it," says Lantz, "and so he would closet himself with it, in the men's room, until he had read it through."

On Lantz's last day at Figaro, he says that Joe was thoughtful enough to come to his office and spend the end of the afternoon with him. Lantz was suffering from stomach spasms at the time, for which he was taking Donnatal. Noticing the bottle of pills, Mankiewicz could not curb his fascination. "What are you taking?" he asked Lantz. After being informed, Joe inquired, "May I try one?"

Mankiewicz keeps up-to-date in pharmacology with supplements to his copy of the *Physician's Desk Reference.* "If you develop any kind of misery, Joe wants to know what the prescription is," says his friend Hume Cronyn. "He then looks it up and tells you whether or not he approves."

Given his choice of any property that took his fancy, after the worldwide success of *All About Eve,* Mankiewicz decided to adapt a popular German play about a miraculous physician, *Dr. Praetorius.* [1]

Mankiewicz's doctor is a brilliant and unconventional gynecologist who maintains his own lavish clinic and teaches at a university medical school. He is also an outspoken crusader who rails at stodgy teaching and inhumane hospital practices. That the character is Mankiewicz's self-idealization is suggested by his description of the film's "main theme" to a *Newsweek* interviewer: ". . . psychiatry [is] as necessary to the doctor as anatomy itself, and that medicine should be more than pills, serums, and knives."[2]

Who better to play Mankiewicz's paragon, Noah Praetorius, than Cary Grant, the debonair star whom both Cole Porter and John

---

[1] Curt Goetz, the author of *Dr. Praetorius,* also wrote, directed, and starred in a German film of his play. Although this screenplay is credited in the titles of *People Will Talk,* Mankiewicz says that he never saw the picture. Mankiewicz says, "*People Will Talk* departs rather broadly from its source, *Dr. Praetorius,* which is full of jokes about the fact that the girl speaks with a Saxon accent. Praetorius's clinic and his comments on the treatment of patients, doctors, and schoolteachers are all mine. The Shunderson mystery is in the original [play]."

[2] *Newsweek,* August 27, 1951.

Kennedy wanted to impersonate them on film. Grant found the role a change from the knock-about farce figures he was usually called upon to play in this period, such as the title role in *I Was a Male War Bride* (1949).

Mankiewicz named the film *Doctor's Diary,* but its producer, Darryl Zanuck, retitled it *People Will Talk.* Several critics have observed that this latter title aptly describes the loquacity of Mankiewicz's screenwriting, but Zanuck hoped to suggest that the daring content of the film was likely to set tongues wagging. "One of the most startling things about *People Will Talk,*" says Mankiewicz, "is that I think it's the first time in American films, since the start of the Hays Office, that a girl [Jeanne Crain] who is pregnant by one man and marries another [Grant] is not punished. Whether they didn't get it or just let it slip by . . . I don't know to this day. . . . I was really terrified they were going to throw the whole thing out, and I didn't know what to use in its place."

Most probably to avert censorship, the script has Deborah (Crain)[3] mortify herself in undergoing a pregnancy test by Dr. Praetorius; reveal that she had similarly steeled herself to sleep with her Medicorps beau before he left for the Korean War and met his death; and attempt suicide with a pistol rather than have her father (Sidney Blackmer) learn of her condition.

The censors may have felt the screenplay to be so high-toned that there was no reason to fear for the morals of impressionable women. Their confidence was borne out by the film's disappointing box-office gross. In fact, Cary Grant contends it is one of only three films[4] he made as a free-lance actor that failed to turn a profit, although his delight in negotiating the sweet and sour shifts in the role of Praetorius is evident.

People Will Talk is one of Mankiewicz's personal favorites among his films, for it contains his humanist views on a host of topics, including the idiocies of medical practice, witch hunts, unfair income-tax exemptions, and modern food processing.

The patchwork plot of *People Will Talk* is often sustained only

[3]Ironically, Anne Baxter's pregnancy prevented her from playing the role, which was inherited by Jeanne Crain, the vapid Fox star for whom Mankiewicz had a distinct antipathy. As to the coincidence of Crain's playing a character named Deborah in both *A Letter to Three Wives* and *People Will Talk,* Mankiewicz says, "I don't like the name Deborah and I don't like Jeanne Crain."

[4]Along with *None but the Lonely Heart* (1944) and *The Bishop's Wife* (1948).

by a brilliant supporting cast, which includes the fine character actors Hume Cronyn, Walter Slezak, Sidney Blackmer, and Finlay Currie (seventy-three years old at the time of the filming).[5]

Cronyn's malevolent Professor Elwell ("ill will") represents the petty intriguers of the McCarthy era, pervasive in universities as well as the movie industry, who tried to destroy the reputations of those they envied by digging up skeletons from their pasts. Appropriately, Elwell, who teaches anatomy, uses the skull on his desk as a pencil holder. The first time we see Shunderson (Currie), Dr. Praetorius's mysterious companion whom Elwell is having investigated, he is posed opposite a human skeleton in a closet of Elwell's anatomy classroom.

In the memorable monologue Mankiewicz wrote for Shunderson to deliver at Dr. Praetorius's academic trial, Shunderson finally reveals his long-past justifiable homicide and his revival, after being hanged for his deed, by his subsequent guardian (Praetorius). Blackmer is given a similar showpiece, in which he reveals a stoic benevolence while recounting his professional failures. Walter Slezak provides amiable comic relief as an atomic-scientist crony of Praetorius who bumblingly plays a bass fiddle in the doctor's student orchestra and enjoys Noah's toy train set and knackwurst.

The script of *People Will Talk* is as dotted with allusions to Mankiewicz's private life as it is filled with his observations on the quality of American life circa 1950. Praetorius's mention of his "usual twilight sadness" is reminiscent of Mankiewicz's frequent reference to "the most terrifying period of time" in conjugal life, the interval between the evening meal and bedtime, and his belief that theater originated at the cavemen's evening campfire to dispel this mournful lull. Praetorius's speech beginning, "I nearly died once as a kid. The doctors gave me up for lost," refers specifically to Mankiewicz's near-fatal case of pneumonia as a child. Deborah's momentary reproof of Praetorius, "Stop being such a pompous know-it-all," is an echo of Rosa's and Judy Garland's impatience with Mankiewicz for his occasional pedantry. More characteristic of Mankiewicz, the ladies' man, is the following exchange between the soon-to-be lovers:

DEBORAH: You know all about women, don't you?
PRAETORIUS: Not nearly enough . . .

---

[5]The remarkable Scots actor who made an astonishing impression as the convict Magwitch in David Lean's *Great Expectations* (1946).

DEBORAH: Are all your patients women?
PRAETORIUS: Practically.
DEBORAH: I guess they all fall in love with you.
PRAETORIUS: Not all of them.
DEBORAH: Just most.

People Will Talk was the third and last film of Mankiewicz's on which studio chief Zanuck took credit as the producer. According to Joe, Zanuck withdrew his prestigious patronage in a memo charging that Mankiewicz's dual credit as writer-director reduced him to the intolerable position of playing "second fiddle":

December 20, 1950
PERSONAL AND CONFIDENTIAL

Dear Joe:
    This is a confidential note. Regardless of who finally plays the role in DR. PRAETORIUS, I want you to know that I am not going to take any screen credit as producer. I will of course function in exactly the same way that I functioned on NO WAY OUT and ALL ABOUT EVE and give you as much of my time, energy and attention as I have given you in the past.
    My reasons for avoiding screen credit on your assignments are purely personal and selfish reasons.
    When you are both the writer and director on a film the producer is inevitably subjected to a forgotten or completely secondary role. I am experiencing this now on ALL ABOUT EVE and it is the first time I have ever experienced it. Usually I give a director a finished script to work with. That script is the result of my collaboration with the writers. It is *my* job. PINKY was handed to Kazan when the script was completed. The same was true of GENTLEMAN'S AGREEMENT. I worked it out with Moss [Hart] and then we called in Gadg [Kazan]. As a matter of fact, it has always been true, including TWELVE O'CLOCK HIGH, HOW GREEN WAS MY VALLEY, GRAPES OF WRATH, etc. I gave the script to Henry King on DAVID AND BATHSHEBA after the entire script had been completed to the last detail, sets designed and the picture cast.
    I am saying this to you because I don't want you to feel that later on I am ducking out. You completely deserve all of the credit you are getting on ALL ABOUT EVE. By the same token, when I put my name on a picture as the producer I have my own conscience as well as my own reputation to consider. In DR. PRAETORIUS you will again make the major contribution and if the picture is a hit you will get the major share of the credit since you will serve in two capacities.
    On DAVID AND BATHSHEBA Phil Dunne is the writer, Henry King

is the director and D.F.Z. is the producer. Both my conscience and my reputation will survive or fall on the result of my work and good or bad, I will not be lost in the shuffle.

(The role of Dr. Praetorius was played by Cary Grant, the title of the film was changed to *People Will Talk*, and Darryl F. Zanuck did take producer's credit on the film. Both it and *David and Bathsheba* were failures, although *People Will Talk* received some favorable reviews.)

While the industry and the press believed that Zanuck would agree to any terms demanded to keep Mankiewicz at Fox, Joe had no intention of renewing his $4,000-a-week contract when it expired in August 1951. In order to complete it, he latched on to Michael Wilson's *(A Place in the Sun)* fictionalized adaptation of *Operation Cicero*, a factual exposé by L. C. Moyzisch (a wartime attaché to the German embassy in Ankara) of how the valet to the British ambassador to Turkey had surreptitiously photographed and sold to the Germans all of the Allies' top-secret documents from October 1943 to April 1944. These included the minutes of the Teheran Conference and the plan for the Normandy invasion ("Operation Overlord"), all of which the German command chose to disregard, despite confirmations of their authenticity, because of their unshakable belief that their spy, code-named "Cicero," was an agent planted by the British.

On May 12, 1951, one week after production was completed on *People Will Talk*, Mankiewicz sent Zanuck the following memo:

Dear Darryl:
    In line with our talk the other day, I have found a script I am most enthusiastic about. It has more than just potentialities—it is *on the verge* of being superb. OPERATION CICERO.

I know you don't underestimate it; properties this good do not come along very often. Structurally, it is fine—at most, it would need some tightening and a little more ingenuity here and there. The story of CICERO and the COUNTESS is just delightful. A wonderful, fresh, exciting pair of lovers, antagonists, people with plenty of sex and skullduggery . . . and a last act as good as any I know.

The dialogue needs help. It needs humor, sex and excitement. I think I could supply it in a very short time. The background is altogether one I revel in, and the characters delight me. They're not the dreary soap-opera or caricature cut-outs we usually run across—they're off-center, provocative people.

Casting is a problem, but surely not an insurmountable one. It should, above all, be exquisitely *acted*. In this case, the whole venture—not the starring personalities—is what smells of box-office to me.

Here's one I'd be very happy to do a polish job on—and direct. And with the short time left on my contract, I don't think my cost would be prohibitive.

What do you think?

J.L.M.

Zanuck agreed, provided Mankiewicz would take no credit as a writer for his revision (see Appendix on page 219 for comparison of Mankiewicz's and Wilson's dialogue) and would accept Zanuck's nominal producer, Otto Lang, a former Sun Valley ski instructor whom Zanuck had befriended and brought to the studio for producing lessons, in return for those he had received on the slopes.

In June Mankiewicz hastily prepared a trip to Ankara and Istanbul to film authentic locations to conform with the mode of the studio's Louis De Rochemont–style semi-documentaries of the period, which were directed by Henry Hathaway.[6] Like Fox's successful *House on 92nd Street* (1945), *13 Rue Madeleine* (1946), and *Call Northside 777* (1948, produced by Otto Lang), the film featured a sonorous narrator and had a number in its title. "The meaningless title, *Five Fingers*, comes from Darryl F. Zanuck," says Mankiewicz, "who decreed that unless it had a numerical title it was a sure flop." (Several critics of the period wrote that Zanuck had removed *Cicero* from the title for fear the public would associate it with the race riots that had taken place in Cicero, Illinois. Fox's publicists promulgated the notion that the title was supposed to suggest "the clutching hand of greed.")

While Mankiewicz was in Turkey shooting 33,000 feet of film in seven weeks (chiefly, several chase sequences through Istanbul's mosques and bazaars, with doubles for the actual cast members), he got to meet the real valet-spy, Eliaza Bazna. His meetings with this sinister-looking figure[7] were as clandestine as those between "Cicero" and his Nazi employers, as Bazna was persona non grata with the Turkish secret police. The former spy was desperate for money, "since the Turks had screwed him out of his small investment in a shipping concern, just as he'd been screwed by the Germans, who paid for his

---

[6]Hathaway was to be the director of *Operation Cicero* before Zanuck reassigned it to Mankiewicz.

[7]Mankiewicz describes Bazna as "the most obvious-looking villain I've ever met. He was almost bald, with wisps of hair across his head, gold teeth, and two different-color eyes."

photographs with counterfeit money," Mankiewicz relates. Bazna therefore suggested the "little café of a hotel garden" for their rendezvous. Since Mankiewicz, on principle, refused to pay him for his recollections, Bazna gave Joe nothing specific he could use.[8] However, Mankiewicz took a leaf from the spy's book by stationing his unit's still photographer first in a tree and then in an upstairs hotel bedroom during these secret meetings. The hidden camera shots he produced gave *Five Fingers* a unique publicity break when they became the basis for an article in *Life* magazine.[9]

While *Five Fingers* proclaims itself a factual study by opening with a scene in Britain's House of Commons depicting the hue and cry that attended the publication of *Operation Cicero,* many of the best things in it are fictional inventions.

Michael Wilson invented the glamorous Countess Staviski to supply the film's romantic interest. Idolized by Diello/"Cicero" from the time he had been valet to her late husband during his years as the Polish ambassador to Great Britain, the countess provides the perfect foil for the spy.

Mankiewicz not only changed her name to the feminine Staviska (possibly to avoid confusion with the celebrated French swindler of the thirties), but revised the dialogue of her scenes with Diello (the film's substitute name for Eliaza), making them a superb distillation of sexual combat and role reversal between master and servant.

The relationship neatly develops from their first encounter in the countess's (Danielle Darrieux) tawdry apartment, where Diello (James Mason) servilely picks up her strewn clothing until she orders him not to behave like a valet with her. He then gives her £5,000 from his first sale of secrets, to redeem her pawned jewelry, and says he will underwrite her move to a fashionable house if she will set aside quarters for him to transact his private business and safeguard the proceeds of it. When she asks for a brandy, he pours two glasses, and she reproves him for his presumption by saying, "I shall only drink out of one glass, thank

---

[8]What Mankiewicz did learn from Turkish sources about Cicero's real *modus operandi* did not appear in either *Operation Cicero* or in *Five Fingers.* The gossip in Ankara was that Bazna responded to the aging British ambassador's homosexual needs. After evenings at the Turkish broadcasting station's excellent grand piano, on which the ambassador liked to accompany his valet's singing, the servant would knock out the diplomat with sleeping pills in order to photograph his secret documents.

[9]*Life,* April 7, 1952.

you." She baits Diello for agreeing with her that because of his new-found wealth they are "now, at last . . . equals," by slapping him across the face. She later explains that this brutal reproof was occasioned not because he addressed her as an equal, but "because—in the manner of an inferior—you tried to buy something you didn't think you merited on your own." As proof of this acknowledged equality and with a hint of sexual promise, she insists he call her Anna rather than Madame. Their next meeting, in Diello's room at the posh villa he has provided the countess, concludes with Diello certifying his new status by ordering the countess to get him a drink.

Their final rendezvous takes place back at the countess's earlier hovel. Diello is terminating his "business affairs" in Ankara because British Intelligence has become aware of the security leak. In turn, the countess has agreed to flee with her provider to Rio, where they will live as husband and wife under the forged Argentine identity papers that she has procured at his instruction. Diello now asserts his bread-winner's authority over his mistress by thus rebuking her:

CICERO: *We?* We have more than enough?
(She looks at him, startled, apprehensive. Cicero smiles.)
CICERO: My dear Señora Antonini [the name on their forged passports], where I come from, a man's money is his own. And if his wife is a good wife, he gives her some from time to time.
(Anna gives a nervous little laugh of relief.)

The scene concludes with the couple's embrace, the first in the film,[10] but the over-the-shoulder shot of the countess reveals a discon-certing detachment on her part. Her "strange and mystifying smile" is Mankiewicz's means of foreshadowing the countess's betrayal; she absconds to Switzerland with all of Diello's loot.

"Cicero" is thus obliged to recoup his fortunes by photographing the plans for "Operation Overlord" (the Normandy invasion), which his paymasters have specifically requested. His obstacle is that the British Intelligence officer (Michael Rennie), sent to Ankara to plug the embassy's security leak, has installed an alarm system on the safe

---

[10]While Mankiewicz, in a memo to Zanuck, forecast the wave of sex and violence to come in American movies, there is little of either in his own films. Although pistols are frequently drawn in *Five Fingers*, not a shot is fired. The repeated slapping scene in *The Barefoot Contessa* or Margo's tantrums in *All About Eve* are especially shocking because they violate the typical decorum of Mankiewicz's films.

in which the documents are stored. The alarm is set to go off if the dial of the safe's combination lock is turned. The sequence in which "Cicero" attempts to pull off this final job (he removes an electric fuse, thereby shutting off the alarm, but an industrious cleaning woman replaces it without his knowledge) is at once the film's suspenseful highlight and a paradigm of one of its major themes: the defeat of expectation through double-cross.

Five Fingers is cleverly structured at every turn. In the latter part of the film, Mankiewicz and Wilson use a thrice-repeated action— throwing away formerly prized paper—to interconnect the chain of ironies. While escaping by railway to Istanbul, Diello reads the countess's letter betraying him to the English ambassador as a German spy. On finishing the letter, Diello rips it up furiously and tosses the scraps out the train window. Next, at the German consulate in Istanbul, the Gestapo agent's suspicion that "Cicero" is a British plant is falsely corroborated by the news that the countess has denounced "Cicero" as such to the German ambassador. The agent (Herbert Berghof) consequently tears up the photos of the Allied invasion plans and throws them out the window. (The window fronts on the harbor where Diello's ship is embarking for Rio de Janeiro, Diello's fancied haven.)

In the film's final scene, Diello seems to have realized his dream of becoming a gentleman of leisure, but is rudely awakened by his Brazilian bank manager, who informs him that his £100,000 deposit (from the sale of the Overlord plan) was in forged notes from Germany. The only consolation, which causes Diello to break into gales of laughter, is that similar bills have shown up in Switzerland. The nest egg that the countess stole was also composed of forged notes. As the camera cranes up and away, Diello tosses his now worthless cash to the wind.

The countess's presence in Diello's memory, during the railroad and Rio scenes, is indicated by two worn recordings played on the soundtrack. They are two haunting songs sung by a French chanteuse (possibly Darrieux); Anna has played them before as a nostalgic accompaniment to her scenes with the valet. Alternating with the evocation of Turkey in the exotic instrumentation of Bernard Herrmann's score, these scratchy disks lend a paradoxical poignancy to the schemers' futile plotting.

Their suave behavior and outspoken contempt for the Nazis make "Cicero" and the countess the audience's "rooting interest," and Mason and Darrieux perform with consummate elegance. Mankiewicz has softened the couple's amorality and emphasized their grace by making the Gestapo agent arrogant and overbearing, the British Intelligence officer slow-witted (he's always a step or two behind "Cicero"), and the German attaché Moyzisch (Oscar Karlweis) foolishly nervous.

There is nothing nervous in the deportment of the prescient German ambassador, von Papen (John Wengraf), who is being supplanted by more aggressive boors, and his English opposite number, the aged, gentlemanly Sir Frederic (Walter Hampden), whose authority is being undermined. Their presence serves as internal commentary in *Five Fingers*, making the film something of an elegy for refined deportment and stylish screenwriting.

Although the English critic Fred Magdalany scants the suspenseful elements in *Five Fingers*, the conclusion of his review pinpoints the film's essential quality very well. Magdalany writes, "On [a] core of irony, Wilson and Mankiewicz have constructed a light comedy which in its cynical zest reminds one of the vintage Lubitsch pictures during the '30s."[11] Such comparison with his master would undoubtedly have delighted Mankiewicz, had he seen this review. No amount of critical praise, however, can persuade him to retract his opinion that Zanuck edited "the last two reels of the film with his polo mallet."[12]

In his biography of Zanuck, Mel Gussow writes that after the favorable reviews of *Five Fingers* appeared in the New York papers in early March of 1952, Joe phoned Herman to intercept the furious night letter he had sent Zanuck protesting the cuts.[13] Gussow says that "Zanuck remained one up on Mankiewicz," since by the time Herman got to Zanuck's secretary in order to retract the telegram, she was able to inform him that the message had already been delivered. Joe says that anyone who knew Herman would know that he would never have undertaken such a mission, "nor was I about to ask Herman to do so." Mankiewicz adds that in response to his indignant wire he received an

---

[11]The *Daily Mail*, April 4, 1952.

[12]Mankiewicz is probably alluding to cuts in the more extensive chase scene detailed in *Five Fingers'* shooting script. "Cicero" eludes Travers (Rennie) in a rug shop and a mosque and beats him in a rowboat race to his Argentine escape ship. Zanuck may well have wanted to minimize the artificial matching of the long-shot location work done with doubles to the close-ups of Mason and Rennie taken on studio sets or against rear-screen-projected landscapes, and he probably wanted to keep the film moving quickly toward the ironic twist of the final sequence.

[13]Mel Gussow, *Don't Say Yes Until I Finish Talking*, Doubleday, 1971, p. 159.

equally "angry letter" from Zanuck. (Ten years later an argument between Zanuck and Mankiewicz over cuts in *Cleopatra* was to culminate in widely reported name-calling, followed by a temporary dismissal of Mankiewicz from the editing of the film.)

The official announcement of the termination of Mankiewicz's unproductive contract talks with Fox on September 27, 1951, the day he was to complete shooting of *Five Fingers,* came as no surprise to industry insiders. Mankiewicz's saying "that he did not wish to tie himself down for seven years to any particular company and had decided to operate in the open market"[14] was a discreet way of indicating that, as the most celebrated American screenwriter-director of the period, he was no longer obliged to submit to the strictures of any intellectually inferior studio head.[15]

Having denounced Los Angeles as "an intellectual fog belt,"[16] which venerated a football coach rather than an intellectual,[17] Mankiewicz had prepared for his exodus to New York. His expectation was that Broadway would provide employment for his and Rosa's theatrical talents and that eastern prep schools would supply a proper education for their sons.

Unfortunately, in liberating himself from Zanuck's authority, Mankiewicz rid himself of precisely the kind of intuitive film sense necessary to restrain his preference for static speeches over visual ac-

---

[14]Thomas M. Pryor, *New York Times,* September 28, 1951.

[15]Mankiewicz says, "The reason I didn't sign my new contract with Fox is that I wanted a clause stipulating that if I didn't produce my own films, Zanuck had to produce them." Mankiewicz was undoubtedly eager for the studio's best promotional efforts, which Zanuck's personal productions received. Since it was highly unlikely that Zanuck would back down from his position that he no longer wished to take a producer's credit on films written and directed by Mankiewicz, Joe must have known that his demand was futile.

[16]Hume Cronyn recalls that while flying with Mankiewicz into Los Angeles on a clear night, they tried to orient themselves by identifying some landmark. As they flew over a dark rectangle in a brilliant patch of lights, Cronyn supposed it to be a park. "Nonsense," said Joe, "it's the public library."

[17]In a straw poll conducted by the *Mirror* to determine Los Angeles's most distinguished citizen of 1950, the public gave first place to the football coach of UCLA. Mankiewicz is himself a great sports fan who on the sound stage has listened to ballgame broadcasts through an earphone and has watched televised games during story conferences. Joe's father once took him to meet his friend Albert Einstein and his Princeton circle. Instead of engaging him in heady intellectual talk as Joe had anticipated, the pedagogues bombarded him with questions about the private lives of movie stars.

tion. As James Mason said, in a statement made prior to the success of Mankiewicz's ingenious *Sleuth* (1972), "I thought that the last good film that he made was *Five Fingers,* because I personally have not seen a Mankiewicz film that appeared to be well directed since then."[18]

A more balanced assessment of Mankiewicz's subsequent work might be that he abandoned his forte, satirical social comedies, to establish himself as a director of prestigious pictures in any genre. Without a tough producer or studio head to discipline him, he indulged his writer's gifts to the fullest in longer and talkier scripts.

APPENDIX

Michael Wilson vehemently contended, in a 1972 letter, that no more than twenty-five to thirty lines in *Five Fingers* were written by Mankiewicz. The charred copy of Wilson's mimeographed script in Mankiewicz's files, which shows Joe's penciled revisions, proves precisely the opposite of this contention. Almost none of Wilson's dialogue was used, though the scene-by-scene continuity of his screenplay was largely retained. The following example illustrates the difference in style between Wilson's original and Mankiewicz's complete rewrite:

Wilson Version
CICERO: Which reminds me. I am forced to increase the price of future documents.
VON RICHTER: Your price is already outrageous.
CICERO: Let me explain. If the truth be known, I am not a very brave man. The idea of facing a firing squad does not appeal to me. The more frustrated I become, the more money I want. It's the only motive force to keep me at work.
VON RICHTER: *(sourly)* How much more?
CICERO: *(musing)* Oh—£25,000 per roll.
VON RICHTER: Preposterous. There's a limit to what my government will pay.
CICERO: Do you think so? When every roll of film I sell is worth more than a division of Gestapo agents. How pennywise can they be?
VON RICHTER: But we don't have an inexhaustible supply of English currency. Perhaps—if you would accept payment in Reichmarks . . .
CICERO: I have no confidence in the stability of German currency. No, we will stick with English pounds till the well runs dry.

Mankiewicz version
VON RICHTER: Then at least satisfy my personal curiosity on one point. *Why* are you selling us information.
(Cicero finishes counting the money, puts it aside in a neat stack. He hands von Richter the roll of film.)
CICERO: I thought that was self-evident—for money.
VON RICHTER: But you must have some other motive. Perhaps you share our

---

[18]Rui Nogueira, *Focus on Film,* March–April 1970, p. 25.

disgust with British decadence—or our faith in the future of Germany . . .

CICERO: Colonel von Richter, if I have a disgust for anything, it is poverty. And if I have faith in the future of anything—it is in the future of money.

VON RICHTER: Then I cannot understand why, on the one hand, you sell us information which will help us to win the war—and on the other hand, you insist upon being paid in money with a very dubious future—British pounds . . .

CICERO: *(smiles)* What makes you think I think Germany will win the war?

VON RICHTER: Apart from all other considerations, apparently you attach little importance to these documents . . .

CICERO: In the first place, I cannot sell you the ability to make proper use of the information I get for you. In the second place, by informing a man about to be hanged of the exact size, location, and strength of the rope, you do not remove either the hangman or the certainty of his being hanged. *(He crosses.)*

And now I am sure you will want to rejoin your friends. One week from tonight I shall have more film for you. *(He opens the door.)*

Good night.

VON RICHTER: Good night. *(He goes out.)*

"I'm a bit concerned that the playwright is such a novice at writing pictures"   10

THE MANKIEWICZES TOOK A LARGE CORNER APARTMENT AT 730 Park Avenue, and Rosa set about furnishing the huge rooms in a comfortable, elegant style. Not only was her husband the newest and most important film celebrity in Manhattan, which would mean reciprocating many social invitations and entertaining new friends, but their neighbors were highly prosperous and distinguished in New York society. Directly above them lived the Wall Street tycoon John Loeb, who became a friend, and below them lived the reigning monarch of the musical theater, composer Richard Rodgers, who did not. (The Mankiewicz sons' bedroom was directly above Rodgers's study, and he pleaded through a mutual friend that the crash of billiard balls from the boys' miniature pool table was driving him to distraction. Chris and Tom were suitably admonished.)

Although Mankiewicz had his own study in the apartment, from which he monitored the household's comings and goings, he was soon able to get away from the domestic bustle by receiving an MGM office in the parent company's Loew's Building on Broadway in the heart of the theater district.

During the second week in December, Mankiewicz was back in Los Angeles for a series of secret meetings with Dore Schary, the screenwriter Herman had first brought to Hollywood who had become the production head of MGM, succeeding L. B. Mayer. On December

16 Joe returned to New York after concluding an unusual deal for three pictures in five years, as producer, writer, and director, which would accommodate his New York residence and prospective theater work by requiring his presence in Culver City for only fourteen weeks a year. Mankiewicz undoubtedly thought he was "one up" on both his former bosses, Zanuck and Mayer.

When Mayer was ousted from Metro in the autumn of 1951, about the time Mankiewicz terminated his contract with Fox, "the first person he tried to make a deal with [for three pictures] was me," says Joe. Mankiewicz was summoned to Mayer's house in Beverly Hills. "I was amused by the idea of the meeting, as I couldn't believe he would send for me," says Mankiewicz. "I went there almost in terms of research. He fabricated a whole situation in which we were both the victims of these conspirators at MGM, conveniently forgetting all that had gone before. I said, 'I'll have to think about it, L. B.,' and walked away. Then I let Bert Allenberg [Joe's agent] handle it" (that is, decline the offer).

On March 25, 1952, the first of these "three hat" projects for Metro was announced—Mankiewicz's adaptation of Carl Jonas's novel *Jefferson Selleck. Jefferson Selleck* is a compassionate *Babbitt,* chronicling the first four decades of the twentieth century and limning the sadness of the American success myth through the life of an ordinary midwestern businessman who has suffered what Mankiewicz terms "the all-American heart attack."

Metro saw it as a vehicle for their star Spencer Tracy, and Mankiewicz looked forward to directing his longtime friend. Joe expected to return to California by mid-June with the completed screenplay, but another project intervened.

Jefferson Selleck had also been coveted by the eminent MGM producer John Houseman, but Houseman had put in his bid to produce *Julius Caesar,* which had been previously announced by the studio and then delayed until David O. Selznick's preemption of the title had expired. Since he had produced Orson Welles's celebrated Mercury Theatre version of *Caesar* in 1937, Houseman's qualifications to do the film should have been incontestable, but he forced the issue with Schary by threatening to leave the studio if it was not assigned to him.

This ultimatum left Schary free to let Mankiewicz have *Jefferson Selleck* and may also have prompted Houseman's selection of Mankiewicz as the director of *Julius Caesar.* Houseman simply recalls that

"Joe was one of the first people I thought of. He is so literate and such a good dialogue director, I knew he'd be interested." Although Houseman knew Joe Mankiewicz only casually, from the time he had nursed Herman through the completion of his screenplay for *Citizen Kane,* his intuition was perfect.

Joe was exuberant at the prospect of making a film in the town that had declared Shakespeare's plays unfilmable after the disaster of Max Reinhardt's stagy *Midsummer Night's Dream* in 1935, and at the very studio that had produced the dull Thalberg-Cukor *Romeo and Juliet* in 1936. Moreover, this would be the most prestigious possible type of film to mark his return to the lot from which he had been banished in 1943.

Evidently, John Houseman's view of *Julius Caesar* was still colored by the memory of the famous Orson Welles modern-dress version of the play. Welles's interpretation, which was directly influenced by the then contemporary rise of Mussolini's regime in Italy, presented Caesar as the repressive tyrant of his day and Antony as the consolidator of his dictatorship. Houseman says that the film's cinematography and use of black and white stock were meant to evoke newsreel coverage of the Fascist dictators' balcony harangues and pact signings.[1]

Mankiewicz gives little credence to the play's many references to the crime of regicide and the justice of retribution meted out to its perpetrators. He scoffs at Shakespeare's moral in the play, "Striving to better, oft we mar what's well," by maintaining that the antiregicide theme was obligatory for an Elizabethan dramatist, and compares Shakespeare's censorship problems to his own in stating that "Elizabeth was a very tough queen, and she served as a form of one-woman Breen Office. You couldn't kill a monarch, what with Essex, Southampton, and all the boys waiting to knock off Elizabeth. Mr. Shakespeare was not about to write [a play sympathetic to the assassins' cause], and they were not about to put that on the stage of the Globe [without some form of admonition]."

Mankiewicz does perceive that *"Julius Caesar* should really be

---

[1]One shot early in *Julius Caesar* does evoke memories of Riefenstahl's great Nazi propaganda film, *Triumph of the Will.* From a high angle, the camera takes in the verticals of the ceremonial standards held aloft by the imperial guards in the procession of Caesar accompanying Antony to his unshown race at the Colosseum. None of the rest of the film reflects the style of a documentary or newsreel.

titled *Brutus*. It is his conflict as a man of tremendous ambivalence that Cassius could play upon," and, finally, it is his undoing. However, the closest political analogue Mankiewicz could think of was the impending defeat, in the presidential election of 1952, of the high-minded liberal Adlai Stevenson by the overwhelming popularity of the nonintellectual General Dwight Eisenhower.

In line with Houseman's description of the play as "a very sober and very intimate political thriller," Mankiewicz had some notion of depicting Caesar as "a Tammany boss," Casca as "a ward heeler," and Antony as "a political opportunist," but their togas tend to cloak this interpretation.

Although Mankiewicz maintains that a good director always should have a strong concept for a production, he actually had little more than a half-baked or sketchy one, as his film would reveal. Little or no thought, it appears, was given to what aspects of the play might be of particular visual interest, unlike Orson Welles's *Othello*, which won the Grand Prix of the 1952 Cannes Film Festival for its cinematic virtuosity, despite its being shot on a shoestring budget with an undistinguished supporting cast.[2]

John Houseman says that "had Mankiewicz suggested imaginary or transition scenes, I would have allowed him to take liberties, but he stuck rigidly to the text," and "as our work progressed, it was Joseph Mankiewicz, the movie maker, who proved to be the most conservative among us."[3]

What Houseman and Mankiewicz were immediately concerned with was putting together a more exciting cast than the list of names, including the competent but dull Leo Genn, that Metro had proposed to them. Working from his office at MGM in Culver City, Houseman selected Louis Calhern, whom he had directed as King Lear on Broadway, for the role of Caesar, and Edmond O'Brien, who had toured with the Mercury *Caesar*, for Casca. To achieve the optimum box-office magnetism of an all-star cast, MGM contractees Deborah Kerr (a demure Portia) and Greer Garson (a florid Calpurnia) agreed to lend

---

[2]The French, of course, had the perfect rationale for the profound difference between the directors' styles in their approach to Shakespeare. *Cahiers du Cinéma* diplomatically avoids the issue by distinguishing between *"le sage classicisme de Mankiewicz contre le baroque de Welles."*

[3]The second quote from John Houseman is from his article "Filming Julius Caesar," *Sight & Sound*, July–September 1953, p. 25.

their names, playing the rather minor roles (one scene apiece) of the wives to Brutus and Caesar.

From New York, Mankiewicz concurred on the nomination of his *Five Fingers* star James Mason for Brutus and journeyed to London to convince John Gielgud to overcome his long-standing refusal to appear on screen by offering him Cassius, a role in which Gielgud had triumphed in a 1950 Stratford production. Mankiewicz was so elated by Gielgud's acceptance that he jokingly told his sister, "The cast we've lined up is so remarkable, I'm a bit concerned that the playwright is such a novice at writing pictures."

According to Gielgud, Paul Scofield,[4] who was first considered for Brutus and would have been ideal in the role, had just been wigged and togaed to test for Antony when word came down to the sound stage that the MGM management had approved the most surprising piece of casting suggested by Mankiewicz and Houseman—Marlon Brando as Mark Antony. Mankiewicz recalls that when he had first suggested the part to Brando in New York, the famed mumbler and paragon of the Actors' Studio naturalistic style responded, "Oh, my God!" and made no further comment for a month.

Brando finally invited Mankiewicz to his apartment ("a filthy pad on Fifty-seventh Street that bore the remnants of many broads," Mankiewicz recalls) to play him the tape-recorded results of a month's intensive study of every recorded Shakespearean actor from Barrymore to Olivier. "You sound exactly like June Allyson," was Mankiewicz's dismaying verdict. Brando's reading obviously improved, because when Mankiewicz played a tape of the funeral oration for Dore Schary, the studio head was at first convinced it was a hoax and exclaimed, "I love Brando, but I can't believe it's him." The columnists were equally skeptical, and nightclub comics made the prospect of a loutish Stanley Kowalski reading of "Friends, Romans, countrymen" a staple of their routines.

The skeptics were in for a surprise, because, as Mankiewicz attests, "Marlon worked his ass off, and it's a very talented ass." So were his

---

[4]Paul Scofield was a star of the English theater. In fact, he was playing opposite John Gielgud in a West End production of *Much Ado About Nothing* when Mankiewicz came to London to meet with Gielgud. Scofield was little known to American audiences prior to the film *A Man for All Seasons* (1966), in which his performance as Sir Thomas More suggests what an ideal Brutus he could have been.

fellow cast members, many of whom worked for a fourth of their usual salaries in order to play Shakespeare in this prestigious but low-budget ($2,070,000) production. (Mankiewicz says that Metro's executives had no confidence in the commercial prospects of *Julius Caesar* and therefore confined him to an inadequate budget and the use of only one principal sound stage.)

At the first reading during the preliminary three-week rehearsal period in early August, Brando delivered his lines sotto voce, while Gielgud gave a full, performance-level reading. Mankiewicz managed to tone down Gielgud somewhat for the camera, although his musical style of speaking verse is so distinctive that it could never have truly harmonized with the more natural, conversational style of speech that Mankiewicz sought from his cast.

Brando was just holding back during rehearsal. Ultimately, the power of his funeral oration moved the crowd of extras[5] to wild cheering, though he repeatedly lost his already strained voice by shouting during the numerous extra takes he requested.[6] Brando's mushy diction, a result of the orthodontia he had undergone in his youth, is transcended by the electrifying spontaneity of his readings. If his voice lacks melodious range and color, his impassioned and sullen Antony is fascinating, and his hair style and glowering, heavy-lidded eyes give him, more than any other member of the cast, the look of a heroic Roman bust come to life.

Gielgud's nervous energy is nearly palpable, and the keen intellect of Cassius, the intriguer, is magnified by the grandeur of Gielgud's speech and manner. Compared with these two principal connivers,

---

[5]Estimated by producer Houseman as numbering between 900 and 1,000, though the *New Yorker* critic commented that "the crowd in the Forum wouldn't overtax the facilities of a supermarket."

[6]John Gielgud's dissenting view is that Mankiewicz "covered the emotional peaks missed or undiscovered by Brando with cutaways to crowd reaction shots." Gielgud feels that he "could have helped Brando build the Forum speech from a climax to an anticlimax" and back again. (Mankiewicz is especially proud of what he deems the innovative, angry approach he had Brando give to "Friends, Romans, countrymen, lend me your ears"; Antony, in this version, has lost his temper after the mob's commotion has drowned out his first two attempts to start the speech.)

At Brando's request, Gielgud had recorded Antony's speeches and given him a half hour of notes on the only scene they had together, after Caesar's murder, when Antony makes an interim truce with the conspirators. "The next day he incorporated every single thing I suggested with a marvelous coloring of words and phrasing," says Gielgud, who desisted from further coaching for fear of becoming "unpopular" with the company by "interfering" with the director's prerogative.

James Mason's Brutus, the central character of the drama, seems distinctly colorless. In fact, the casting of Brando, the male sex symbol, antihero of his day who had succeeded in making even the brutal Stanley Kowalski sympathetic, prejudiced the audience to side with Antony and commiserate little with the tragedy of Brutus. (It is a rare *Julius Caesar* in which Antony bests Brutus at funeral oratory through flamboyance rather than cleverness.)

The director's task in any production of *Julius Caesar* is to delineate Brutus's position in the center of Shakespeare's triptych of male portraits. He must make us empathize with Brutus as he arrives at the difficult decision to commit his knife and tongue to the assassination conspiracy and face the dire consequences.

As Gielgud, a Shakespearean scholar as well as actor, points out, "Brutus is the most difficult part in the play. He is Shakespeare's first sketch for Hamlet and Macbeth, and he should be fascinating. The problem is that Brutus is almost always overshadowed [in performance] by the effectiveness of the parts of Cassius and Antony."

James Mason as Brutus compounds the problem because his personality is not inherently good-natured, and his bitter, unsympathetic quality, though muted, continually works against the domestic pathos of his scenes with his wife (Deborah Kerr) and his surrogate son, Lucius, his boy attendant and minstrel. The qualities that made Mason a star in the forties—the arrogance and coldness that made him "the man you love to hate"—are wrong for Brutus, and Mason rightly suppresses them. But the result is a performance restrained to the point of self-effacement.

Mankiewicz's miscalculation of Mason's aptitude for Brutus may have been influenced both by the actor's splendid performance in *Five Fingers* and by Joe's closeness to Mason and his wife, Pamela, with whom Joe frequently socialized during this period. The Masons and Mankiewicz were seen together so often that they became a gossip column item and the subject of malicious conjecture in the Hollywood colony.

John Gielgud says of Mason, "There is something a bit murderous about him, and [Brutus] should be the last one you'd think [to be a murderer]." Gielgud recalls that Mason, in his years at the Old Vic usually playing opposite Charles Laughton, was "a very good Shakespearean actor in rather an understated way. He had great intelligence, but he hadn't really big guns."

Muting Gielgud's volleys posed a different problem. According to

Edmond O'Brien, "Mankiewicz got Gielgud from stage to camera level by explaining the relative distance of figures in the shot," and enjoining him to "just *say* it." Mason and O'Brien privately suggested he "just *think* it and do nothing, or at least at the lowest level possible, using his eyes rather than his voice." "John had a tendency to freeze if the camera was too close to him," says O'Brien, "so Mankiewicz shot his close-ups from a good distance, as though he were playing the scene on stage."

Gielgud, in turn, expresses his gratitude to Mason for teaching him how to underplay, though John Houseman says that it was Gielgud's energy that enlivened his scenes with Mason, whose low level "became one of Joe's big problems." This is most evident in the famous "tent scene" of quarrel and reconciliation between Cassius and Brutus, which Gielgud takes at a furious clip, making it the only scene in which Mason truly rises to the occasion. The late critic and screenwriter Paul Dehn summed up the problem by writing that he "would have been led to conclude, solely on the basis of the film, that the character of Brutus is a bore."[7]

As Casca, Edmond O'Brien offers a malicious account of Caesar refusing the crown Antony offers him and Caesar's subsequent epileptic fit that is devastating fun. Spencer Tracy, an astute judge of acting and a close friend of Mankiewicz's, confided to O'Brien that his Casca was "the best thing in the picture," but threatened to deny it if O'Brien publicly quoted him.

Despite Louis Calhern's imposing stature and his movie persona as a suave criminal ringleader (capped by his performance in *The Asphalt Jungle* [1950]), as "imperious Caesar" he appears to be no more than a querulous dotard in a toga. John Houseman's facetious description of Caesar and his wife (Garson) as "a nice, middle-aged, neurotic couple" is accurate but damaging to the credibility of Caesar's image as an awesome and threatening dictator.

While casting *Cleopatra* nine years later, Mankiewicz commented to actor Martin Landau that he didn't want to make the mistake he had in *Julius Caesar* of mixing English and American accents. In *Caesar* it tends to convey that the vitality of American political gangsterism is bound to triumph over the effeteness of English intellectuality.

---

[7] *Sunday Chronicle,* November 8, 1953.

Mankiewicz views Antony's final tribute to "the noblest Roman of them all" as a piece of public relations rhetoric, masking the victor's contempt for the virtue of his vanquished foe. If this veiled contempt is indiscernible in Brando's performance in the final scene, we are meant to remember the three previous revelations of Antony's private as opposed to public character. Two of these are snide smiles of private satisfaction at having roused the rabble with his funeral oration, and a third occurs later, when a tight grin appears on Antony's face after viewing the Philippi rout and massacre.

In addition to these smiles, there is a brief but significant scene of Mankiewicz's own invention. This scene follows the division of spoils at Caesar's hilltop villa, which Antony has commandeered after the assassination. Once Octavius has departed, Antony wrenches a bust of Caesar, which overlooks the city, from its pedestal on the balcony and turns it to face himself, after which he sits in Caesar's eagle-backed consular chair.[8] This act symbolizes the succession of tyranny and resolves Shakespeare's deliberate ambiguity toward Antony's character in favor of villainy.

Mankiewicz begins the film with a citation from Plutarch that "Caesar had grown odious to moderate men through the extravagance of the titles and honors heaped upon him." The first scene of the tribunes, Marullus and Flavius, chastising the commoners for hanging garlands on a bust of Caesar is used to establish the prevalence of the Roman "police state," as Marullus is taken into custody by a Roman guard for his seditious outburst. However, as the *New Statesman* critic remarked, after this opening orientation the film "then relies on the overtones of dictatorship to do the rest."[9]

Many critics find the film anticlimactic after the peak reached by the funeral orations, where the division of the picture is marked by another expository quote from Plutarch on the impending showdown between the rival factions, but they attribute their dissatisfaction to what they perceive as Shakespeare's lame ending. In fact, the letdown is as much attributable to the cuts, movie clichés, and ludicrous sets that Mankiewicz sanctioned as well as to the ill com-

---

[8]This interpolation by Mankiewicz contains the seed of motivation that was to germinate in *Cleopatra*, in which Antony vainly attempts to transcend Caesar's overshadowing accomplishments.

[9]W. W. Whitebait, *New Statesman*, November 14, 1953.

parison of the sluggish second half with the hurtling pace with which he imbued the conspiratorial events leading up to the assassination.

Mankiewicz's resort to the time-worn device of superimposing the figure of Caesar, in the scene in which Caesar's ghost appears in Brutus's tent on the eve of the battle, seems a concession to the text and fails to terrify. This movie cliché is surpassed by Mankiewicz's use of the Western's traditional Indian ambush to summarize the victory of Mark Antony's legions at Philippi. The sequence is particularly unfortunate because the film cries out for the visual relief of a great action sequence.

The producer's and director's excuse for resorting to this ludicrous chestnut of a battle scene was the film's "starvation budget," which prohibited location shooting and obliged them to employ a familiar Western location, Bronson Canyon, a granite quarry near the Hollywood Bowl, for a single day at the end of the shooting schedule. The canyon's topography—a clear contradiction of "the *plains* of Philippi" —is additionally piquant. The penury excuse won't fully wash, considering what Orson Welles managed to do with the battle scene in his *Chimes at Midnight* (1965–66) with far more limited resources, though without the encumbrance of a large Metro crew and studio overhead.

Mankiewicz was certainly not economizing in order to save sufficient money from the film's budget to afford the battle scene. For example, Edmond O'Brien relates that prior to Brando's entrance for his "Cry havoc" speech, the studio's general manager, Eddie Mannix, burst onto the set protesting the cost of Joe's having moved a portion of the Senate's antechamber wall in and out fifteen times. "It's costing a fucking fortune every time you do that," croaked Mannix. Mankiewicz blithely replied, "I'm sorry. If you don't like it, that's tough, but I'm shooting in continuity. That's the only way I can go. If you don't like it, get yourself another fella!"

Mankiewicz denies the episode; yet the fact is that he has an innate distaste for battle scenes and spectacle and views them as a sop to popular taste. They are not the sort of thing he does easily or well, as he was to discover in undertaking *Cleopatra*. Joe claims that a revealing exchange between characters supplies greater thrills for him than the most exciting *Bullitt*-type chase scene.

The subsequent suicides of Cassius and Brutus are undermined by the textual omissions that precipitate these deaths,[10] our lack of sympathy for the victims and their histrionics, and the pathetically fake hilltop sets where they take place, which are meant to re-create "exterior" locations.

MGM's senior cameraman, Joseph Ruttenberg, who shot Mankiewicz's first two productions at the studio *(Three Godfathers* and *Fury),* especially requested assignment on *Julius Caesar* "for sentimental reasons." By placing the majority of his lights on a scaffolding above the sets and using only "fill" lights below, Ruttenberg creates such a credible sense of outdoor sunlight that the artificiality of the sets becomes blatant.

Although the art directors for the film, Cedric Gibbons and Edward Carfagno, won Oscars for their sets and decoration, the phoniness of the mocked-up exteriors throughout the picture makes the film look quaint and impoverished. One visitor during the filming, the distinguished Italian director Vittorio De Sica, dismissed the sets by exclaiming, "Ah, what realism! It looks exactly like modern-day Ferrara!"[11] Mankiewicz defends the unworn steps of the Senate, which figure so prominently in the funeral orations and look more like plywood than stone, by saying that, historically, the Forum was undergoing a period of reconstruction. The archeological accuracy of this renovation has been questioned by at least one critic,[12] and John Gielgud contends that the dates carved on most of the film's numerous commemorative

---

[10]One can only speculate about why Mankiewicz chose not to extend the logic of the characters' situation by showing vignettes, suggested by the text, illustrating the irony that Brutus, the hapless intellectual strategist, has a measure of military success against Octavius, while Cassius, his superior in combat experience, has none against Antony and, ignorant of Brutus's victory, takes his life with characteristic impetuosity. Not to mention the dramatic irony of Brutus's men looting while Cassius is being overrun, after Brutus had accused Cassius of "an itching palm" in the tent scene.

In Cassius's death scene, as in the denouement of a subsequent film, *The Quiet American,* Mankiewicz fails to take advantage of a situation that lends itself to showing two different aspects of the same event by reprising the scene and filming it from a different angle. As a hypothetical instance of how this might have been achieved in *Caesar,* from a distance (long shot) it appears to Cassius that his emissary, Titinius, has been surrounded by hostile forces. In a medium close-up Titinius could be shown actually being greeted by his comrades with the news of Brutus's victory over Octavius. Instead, the scene is filmed by Mankiewicz as in the theater, with lookouts reporting on the events offstage.

[11]Gary Carey, *Brando!,* Pocket Books, 1973, p. 99.

[12]Campbell Dixon in the *Daily Telegraph,* November 7, 1953, wrote, "It was Augustus, not Julius, who found Rome of brick and left it of marble."

statues were incorrect. However, the scaffolding opposite the Senate gave Mankiewicz the opportunity to make clever cutaways from the funeral orations by shooting through the spectators' dangling legs.

The designers' assertion that the columns of that era were flat rather than curved effected a considerable budgetary economy, according to Mankiewicz, as did the recycling of one of the principal sets from MGM's *Quo Vadis?*, which was flown to Culver City from Rome and superficially modified.

Distressed by the abundance of bric-a-brac in Caesar's villa,[13] John Gielgud recalls that he "kept hissing in Joe's ear, 'Much too much stuff in this scene. It looks like a palm court,' " and he remembers "Joe sending back mountains of props that came onto the set."

Heroic busts and statues figure prominently throughout *Julius Caesar*, notably in the foyer niches of the Colosseum, where Cassius ensnares Brutus in the conspiracy. Like the recurrent shot of the graveyard statue of the barefoot contessa, in Mankiewicz's next film, these marble myths of former mortals endure as reproving testimonials to human fallibility.

Concerning the choice of black and white film stock, Mankiewicz made a typically dogmatic, though conjectural, assertion at the time he was making *Caesar*. Unlike Housemen, he was not thinking of allusions to newsreels. He stated, "It's not in color because I've never seen a good, serious, dramatic movie in color, except maybe *Gone with the Wind.* . . . You can't get drama and make people real in color. This is a picture of mood, of violence, of real people—their ambitions, their dreams. People dream in black and white. They don't dream in Technicolor."[14]

Today Mankiewicz contends that he rejected MGM's offer of Technicolor because its tomato red would have made the assassination scene hideously gory. In fact, the decorous patches of blood on the assassins' togas are the one ludicrous element in a scene whose power and terror derive chiefly from the facial reactions of the attackers and their victim.

Of the film's plethora of close shots, Bosley Crowther wrote that Mankiewicz "has brought us so close to them [the characters] that the

---

[13]Caesar's villa is most likely the redressed *Quo Vadis?* set and is certainly the most glamorous one in *Julius Caesar.*
[14]Sidney Skolsky's syndicated column, September 17, 1952.

very warmth of their body heat and the intensity of their passions in thoughtful or violent moods seem to come right out of the picture and create the dynamic of the film."[15] Crowther might be somewhat abashed to learn that Mankiewicz's shots were not so carefully thought out. As Joe no longer carries a finder, after having looked through the wrong end of one on his first film, *Dragonwyck,* he relies heavily on the judgment of his experienced cinematographers. In *Julius Caesar* his terse instruction to Joseph Ruttenberg for the conspirators' plotting scene was, "Give me a whole lot of goddamned heads."

The studio's notion of enhancing the cultural aura of *Julius Caesar*'s world premiere in New York was to precede the feature with a short from its "good music" series, "MGM Concert Hall," with Joe's friend and head of Metro's music department, Johnny Green, conducting a symphony orchestra. The unfortunate selection was Tchaikovsky's "Capriccio Italien," and the implied connection between this nineteenth-century Romantic tone poem and the Elizabethan view of Rome in 44 B.C. exasperated Mankiewicz and Houseman and mortified Green.[16]

---

[15]*New York Times,* June 14, 1953.

[16]Both Houseman and Mankiewicz had enjoyed highly successful collaborations with Bernard Herrmann (the composer of the scores for *The Ghost and Mrs. Muir* and *Five Fingers*) and wanted him to write the music for *Julius Caesar.* The debonair, always impeccably attired Johnny Green, who was both the administrative and artistic head of Metro's music department, tried to sell them on the idea of using Miklós Rózsa, who was available and contracted to Metro for $1,500 a week. "Joe was adamant," according to Green, "saying there was no comparison between the talents of Herrmann and Rózsa, and that he did not want a neo-Kodály sound."

Consequently, Green phoned every studio in an attempt to loan out Rózsa, but he was unsuccessful. He was obliged to tell Houseman and Mankiewicz that he could not sanction paying Herrmann's salary on top of Rózsa's, but because they were vehement, he invited them to take the matter up with Dore Schary. Schary sided with the producer and director until Green produced his ledgers to show how much the huge added cost of engaging Herrmann would be. Schary therefore ruled that they would have to use Rózsa. Houseman indignantly left the office and never spoke to Green thereafter, although, according to Green, "He bad-mouthed me all over town as an illiterate and fixed me for life with Benny Herrmann." Mankiewicz, ever the conciliator, threw his arm around his pal Green's shoulders, and said, "You lose one, you win another."

With the approval of Schary and Houseman, Rózsa had written and recorded an unusual overture, containing the chief character motifs of his score, to precede the film's main title. To this day, Rózsa is so angry at Green for scrapping it and filming the Tchaikovsky work in its stead that he will not utter Green's name, referring to him only as Metro's "music director" (*Films and Filming,* May 1977, p. 24).

Metro leased a legitimate Broadway theater, the Booth, for the June 1953 premiere, an unusual booking calculated to suggest that the film was to be viewed with the same cultural expectations one would bring to an all-star stage production.[17]

The studio also decided to exploit the craze for wide-screen films by blowing up the 35-mm. print well beyond its conventional ratio, thereby cutting off the top and bottom of the frame. In Mankiewicz's view, this occasioned "an opening-night disaster, with Edmond O'Brien's head completely cut off the screen, at one point, as well as the heads and feet of anyone going up the steps of the Senate."

Mankiewicz had already quarreled with Dore Schary over the studio's cutting of Antony's lines after his funeral oration and the subsequent murder of Cinna, the poet. "Shakespeare is not Leonard Spigelgass,"[18] Mankiewicz recalls yelling at Schary in the course of a telephone conversation from a summer house Joe had rented in Westport, Connecticut, to the studio head in Los Angeles.

The blown-up print, however, was the last straw. Mankiewicz engaged seventy-two-year-old Nick Schenck, the "silver-haired and deadly" president of Loew's and financial controller of MGM, in a "screaming fight worse than any I had had with Mayer." It ended with Schenck's ordering Mankiewicz out of his office and delivering the oft-used film executive's threat, "You will never work in this business again!" (Actually, the fight with Schenck had no significant repercussions.[19] Mankiewicz signed to direct *Julius Caesar* independent of his personal contract with Metro, which had been terminated several months prior to the Schenck quarrel.)

To add insult to injury, the Venice Film Festival board rejected

---

[17]The French have, in fact, classified Mankiewicz's pictures as *théâtre filmé*, and Mankiewicz has happily accepted this designation. Joe's interpretation of it is not that his films are merely photographed stage plays, although *Julius Caesar* comes very close to being one, but that his own screenplays, such as *All About Eve*, could be performed on stage as well because of their rich dialogue. Although Mankiewicz attempted to avoid using traditional stage business in *Julius Caesar*, the wind, lightning flashes, and other effects of the conspiratorial storm scene are artificial and hoary stage hokum, as are the death scenes of Cassius and Brutus.

[18]A screenwriter *(I Was a Male War Bride)* and a close friend of Schary's. Schary subsequently directed Spigelgass's Broadway hit, *A Majority of One*.

[19]Although unable to block Mankiewicz's future employment, Schenck got a measure of revenge by exacting an astronomic price for Metro's star Ava Gardner from United Artists for Mankiewicz's subsequent film, *The Barefoot Contessa*.

the film, calling it anachronistic. Apparently, the Venetians believed Shakespeare's allusions to books, clocks, hats, and angels to be the invention of Hollywood vulgarians.[20] The board chose *The Kentuckian* instead, a conventional film directed by and starring Burt Lancaster; the choice deepened Mankiewicz's scorn for film festivals.[21] Most of the aggrieved parties' feelings were mollified by the preponderance of laudatory reviews that *Julius Caesar* received. Typically, the majority of the critics mistook the high-minded intention of filming Shakespeare for a genuine cinematic achievement.[22]

On March 5, 1953, after a two-week bout of heart trouble complicated by uremic poisoning, Herman Mankiewicz died at the age of fifty-five. "I remember the night Herman died," says Joe's younger son, Tom; "Dad was so moved, so upset." Joe's older son, Chris, says, "For my father to open that closet of memories about Herman is either painful or hilarious."

Perhaps that night Joe recalled his promise to his improvident older brother, whose health had been broken by drink and a serious auto accident, that he would provide a college education for Herman's youngest child, Johanna, in the event of Herman's death. Perhaps to keep alive the memory of how often he had repaid Herman's initial help in bringing him to Hollywood, Joe preserved a sheaf of Herman's I.O.U.'s, salvaged from the 1952 fire of the Bekins moving van that was transporting all of Joe's carefully collected Hollywood memorabilia to New York. (Only one charred filing cabinet survived.)

"I remember vividly the last time I saw Herman," says Joe. "He was full of praise about *Julius Caesar*, which he loved. Quite under-

---

[20]In an odd concession to ancient Roman lighting sources rather than to the text, Metro's art department had an oil lamp flicker at the appearance of Caesar's ghost, when Brutus exclaims, "How ill this taper [candle] burns! Ha! who comes here?"

[21]Three years earlier (1950), the Venetians had told Darryl Zanuck, prior to the festival, that they could assure him only of getting a special citation for *No Way Out* because their first prize had already been awarded. Zanuck refused to enter the film, and Mankiewicz, despite his fondness for honors, has been disenchanted with film festivals ever since.

[22]Philip Hope-Wallace of the *Manchester Guardian* pinpoints *Julius Caesar's* failing in writing, "It is not pictorially of much interest. It does not exploit the cinema's special qualities, save those of intimacy, to any notable extent: it is dependent absolutely on the text and the spoken effect of the scenes, and it makes no concessions whatever to the supposed inability of mass audiences to follow this" (November 4, 1953).

standably, he found it much easier to like my direction than to like my writing." As Joe often told his New York friend Nancy Green, "Everyone else has a mother or father complex, but I have a 'Herman complex.' "

SHORTLY AFTER MANKIEWICZ COMPLETED FILMING *JULIUS Caesar* in mid-October 1952, he hurried back to New York to prepare for his first theatrical endeavor, staging a new production of *La Bohème* for the Metropolitan Opera.

Rudolf Bing, the Met's new managing director, had established an elite corps of theater directors, including Garson Kanin *(Die Fledermaus)* and Alfred Lunt *(Così Fan Tutte)*, who were to bring their innovative talents and theatrical know-how to bear on the stodgy acting and staging that prevailed at the Met.[1] Bing was also breaking with the Met tradition of performing operas only in their original language. The translation of *La Bohème* into English was entrusted to another figure from the film industry, Howard Dietz, long the head of MGM's advertising and publicity department in New York. Simultaneous to his work at Metro, Dietz had turned out stylish and unforgettable lyrics for a series of revues and musicals with composer Arthur Schwartz, as well as to write the witty adaptation of *Die Fledermaus.* The Strauss operetta turned out to be the box-office triumph of Bing's first season (1950).

---

[1]In an unpublished background interview with Time-Life staffers Dorothea Bourne and Carter Harman, Mankiewicz claimed that Bing had originally offered him both *Fledermaus* (1950) and *Così* (1951), the first two productions of Bing's tenure done in English translation, but because of his film commitments to Fox, Mankiewicz had been obliged to decline.

The fee for directing at the Metropolitan was low ($2,000), the prestige great, and the obstacles enormous. Mankiewicz's own musical and theatrical inexperience was compounded by the limited rehearsal time at the Met,[2] the necessity of preparing different casts in both English and Italian versions, and the acting limitations of his singers.

Mankiewicz set out to put the Bohemianism back into *La Bohème* and do battle with the sentimental tradition that he felt had transformed Puccini's lusty young people into decorous "eagle scouts" palatable to the Met's "white-gloved" patrons.

In line with his view that the unchaste Mimi was on the make for Rodolfo, who was not above a "quickie" (based on *Bohème*'s source, Henri Murger's novel *Scènes de la vie de Bohème*), Mankiewicz devised an unconventional first-act curtain. Rather than have Rodolfo (Richard Tucker) rush offstage with Mimi to join his pals at the café, Mankiewicz had him deliberately close the attic door at the end of the love duet, and then brought the curtain down on the couple's passionate embrace as they moved toward the bed.

In Act II Mankiewicz seated the feuding lovers Musetta and Marcello back to back at adjoining café tables, which instantly defined their relationship and allowed for a great deal more temperamental byplay than their usual placement at opposite sides of the stage. In the third act Mankiewicz banished the traditional tree, with its convenient bench for the lovers' reunion, in favor of cartons of cargo more germane to the customs barrier called for in the libretto. He also forbade the customary falling snow, which he felt contributed antithetical beauty and cheer to the bleakness of the score and the situation.

Rather than have the usual bed and pillows brought out for Mimi's death scene, Mankiewicz had her placed in the garret's one comfortable, worn leather chair by the stove. For additional warmth, Musetta gives Mimi her treasured white fur muff. Mankiewicz inventively timed it so that the muff fell from Mimi's lap and rolled across the floor, not at the moment of her death, but on cue, so that Rodolfo recognizes her death and utters his agonized "Mimi" to Puccini's fateful chords.

---

[2]Mankiewicz claims that he had only ten rehearsals with the English-singing cast and that the second full run-through with the orchestra was the first performance. The first stage rehearsals were sung in competition with noises of the carpenters and painters working on the stage.

The cast expressed delight with these novelties, as did the management. However, Howard Dietz's wife, the noted costumer Lucinda Ballard, was apprehensive. She thought "Joe was too anxious to [do] clever tricks and to move people around" and acknowledges that this called attention to the fact that it was too inventively directed.

Olin Downes, the *New York Times* music critic whose review was considered the most important, delivered Joe's worst notice. Downes only "congratulated" Mankiewicz for his direction of the first act. "Here were real people acting naturally, simply, eloquently, with no superfluities or conventional operatic mannerisms."[3] Of Act II Downes commented, "Puccini and his librettist[s] are much better stage directors than Mr. Mankiewicz," and "the fooling of the Bohemians in the last act was not lively, as it was confidently predicted it would be." Downes dismissed the rest of the production by saying, "There are few details of the stage business which differ importantly from the accepted formulas."

Poor Howard Dietz received a far worse critical trouncing for his witty, rhyming lyrics, which were generally denounced as doggerel. Dietz's "English version" was dropped after only six performances, and the matinee premiere on December 27, 1952, was the last time that the original cast performed together. Mankiewicz laments, "It's like blowing a perfect smoke ring to direct an opera at the Met. If they miss the opening, they never see the smoke ring."

The first performance of *Bohème* was also the last in which Rodolfo and Mimi remained behind at the end of Act I to indulge their carnal appetites. In deference to the prudishness of the Met's patrons, Bing demanded that the loving couple once more race off to join their *amici* at the Café Momus, and before long, falling snowflakes and the dear old tree were back in Act III.

Although Mankiewicz finally withdrew his name from the production after many seasons, the Metropolitan only replaced Rolf Gérard's sets[4] for the 1952 production in 1977 by importing inferior replacements from the Chicago Lyric Opera. For twenty-four years Mimi's

[3]*New York Times*, December 28, 1952.
[4]Mankiewicz contributed a typically eloquent and witty essay titled *"La Bohème: Decor and Decorum,"* on Gérard's designs and his own directorial innovations, for a catalog of the theater work of Rolf Gérard.

muff still rolled across the stage, though sometimes, because of the corpulence of the soprano, there was no lap for it to fall from, and it was posthumously "flung into the air," wrote Mankiewicz, "much like a football."[5]

Although Mankiewicz told an interviewer, during rehearsals of *Bohème*, that he planned to go to Hollywood in February 1953 to make *Jefferson Selleck* for Metro and return to New York in May, these plans went awry. Dore Schary thought Joe's idea that Spencer Tracy, as Selleck, should not age throughout the film ("always seeing himself as he is, not as he was," according to Mankiewicz's screenplay) was "an interesting idea" but difficult to bring off. Moreover, he thought the screenplay itself "didn't work, as it was too narrative and too turgid. No one gave much of a shit about Jefferson Selleck." When Schary pronounced the script unworkable, Mankiewicz indignantly informed him that he himself "would decide if it was a [feasible] screenplay or not, and," he reports, "we called off the contract."

The press release that appeared in the *New York Times* on April 13 announcing the termination of Joe's MGM deal said that "in exchange for permission to proceed with the formation of Figaro, Inc.,[6] the independent company that he is originating in New York, Mr. Mankiewicz has agreed to make one picture for Metro." Presumably, after Mankiewicz's furious quarrel with Nick Schenck in June over the projection of *Julius Caesar*, MGM was eager to let him out of this commitment.

One month later the *Times* announced that United Artists (UA) would finance two pictures to be produced by Figaro.[7] "*The Barefoot Contessa*, based on a story Mr. Mankiewicz originally had planned on doing as a novel, will be his first undertaking," the *Times* reported. "He will seek a new personality to introduce as the Hollywood glamor girl

[5]Joseph L. Mankiewicz, "*La Bohème:* Decor and Decorum."

[6]Mankiewicz says he chose the corporate name because, like the enterprising rogue, "Figaro was going to do a little bit of everything. I also liked a theme from Mozart's *Le Nozze di Figaro.*" This theme became the firm's logo music; *Bohème's* designer, Rolf Gérard, drew a courtly Figaro that served as the corporate logo.

[7]Mankiewicz was one of the first big Hollywood names the new UA management was able to sign. Figaro, Inc., was later to be joined by Burt Lancaster's independent company, Hecht-Hill-Lancaster. Since United Artists had no studio facilities to maintain, its overhead charges to the independent producer were considerably lower than those of the major film companies. Unlike the majors, UA also offered their name directors and producers a large measure of autonomy during filming.

in the story who lands a titled European for a husband and then has to support him."[8]

The actual screenplay of *The Barefoot Contessa* ends quite differently, and after considering for the title role a series of unknowns, a series of newcomers (among them Rossana Podesta and Joan Collins), and Elizabeth Taylor, Mankiewicz and the heads of United Artists, Arthur Krim and Robert Benjamin, decided on Ava Gardner.

Unfortunately for UA, Gardner was under contract to MGM, and in retaliation for Mankiewicz's tongue-lashing, Nick Schenck said he would not loan her out. He eventually relented but demanded an extortionary $200,000 plus 10 percent of *The Barefoot Contessa*'s gross over $1 million for Gardner's services.[9] Krim and Mankiewicz, setting up the production in Rome, fumed at the cost but decided to meet it.

In *The Barefoot Contessa*, Mankiewicz attempts a sardonic deflation of the Cinderella myth of movie stardom. He tries for an exposé of the movie business similar to his exposé of the Broadway jungle in *All About Eve*.

Harry Dawes (Humphrey Bogart) stands in a downpour at a Rapallo cemetery for the funeral of Contessa Torlato-Favrini. His reminiscences, by way of narration and flashback, and those of two other mourners, Oscar Muldoon (Edmond O'Brien) and Count Torlato-Favrini (Rossano Brazzi), chronicle the brief life of the contessa.

The tale begins in a tawdry Madrid nightclub, where Kirk Edwards (Warren Stevens), a ruthless movie tycoon, has brought his entourage: Dawes, a veteran Hollywood writer-director in disrepute for his alcoholism; Muldoon, a sweating, sycophantic publicist; and Myrna (Mari Aldon), a blonde hooker. They are seeking a "new face" for a film Edwards is producing and have come to see the *boîte*'s star attraction, Maria Vargas (Ava Gardner). Maria, a fiercely independent creature, refuses the blandishments of Edwards and Muldoon but succumbs to the gentle entreaty of Dawes, who prevails on her to make a screen test in Rome. The test is a triumph, as is her first starring vehicle, under Dawes's guidance. Maria Vargas is renamed Maria D'Amata.

Maria defends her father in court; he had murdered her harridan

---

[8]*New York Times,* May 12, 1953.
[9]Ava Gardner received only $60,000 of this sum.

mother, and Maria's eloquence gets an acquittal for him and favorable international publicity for herself.

After three pictures Maria is firmly established in Hollywood as a star, but success has not brought her contentment in her private life. Her secret affairs are with brutish types—a neurotic pattern of "rutting in the dirt" and social nonconformity that originated in her burrowing in the earth—barefoot—for shelter during air raids in her youth.

Kirk Edwards throws a party in Maria's Beverly Hills home for Alberto Bravano (Marius Goring), a South American sybarite. Bravano wants Maria to ornament his yachting party on an impending Riviera cruise. In his campaign to snare her, he enlists the services of Muldoon, who wants to become his publicist. Bravano picks a public quarrel with Edwards. When Edwards orders Maria to reject Bravano's invitation, she feels reluctantly obliged to assert her independence and accept it.

Maria becomes an aloof member of Bravano's party of boring "international set" figures; she rejects his advances, preferring fugitive alliances with earthier types like her dance partner at a gypsy encampment. When Bravano upbraids her later at a gambling casino, a bystander, Count Torlato-Favrini (Brazzi), who has been enraptured by her gypsy dancing, gallantly slaps Bravano and spirits Maria away to his ancestral palazzo.

The bachelor count, oppressed with loneliness and obsessed by the impending extinction of his family name, determines to marry Maria (who loves him in return), despite the warnings of his widowed sister (Valentina Cortesa) that they are doomed to be the last of their noble line. Director Dawes also has premonitions of disaster as he watches the couple's chaste courtship. He is disturbed by the weird fulfillment of Maria's longstanding Cinderella fantasy for which she has now found her "Prince Charming." But he cannot find it in himself to deny her happiness, and he gives her in marriage to the count.

Some months after the wedding, Maria confides to Dawes that the count had waited until their wedding night to reveal to her he was rendered impotent by a war injury. Her remedy for his melancholy is to provide him with an heir, sired by his chauffeur. Dawes is skeptical of Maria's confidence that the count will welcome the news of her pregnancy. He follows her back to the palazzo but arrives too late; the count has shot her.

The larger than life-size sculpture of Maria, commissioned by the count as the official portrait of the last Contessa Torlato-Favrini, now serves as her tombstone.

The device of multiple narrators necessary to complete a biographical portrait is common to both *All About Eve* and *The Barefoot Contessa*, but in the melodramatic, less witty *Contessa*, the nearly nonstop speech, which flows from narration to dialogue and back, grows wearisome. Unlike the framing device of the awards ceremony at the beginning and near the end of *Eve*, *Contessa*'s narratives proceed from, and necessitate a continual return to, the funeral. These obsequies become unintentionally emblematic of a film that expires in talk.

Mankiewicz's observations about life and film through Dawes, his mouthpiece, have considerably more vitality than his passive main characters, Harry and Maria. As in most of Mankiewicz's work, his contemptible and conniving figures are more arresting than his admirable characters. In this case, they are the supporting roles of the South American tycoon played by Marius Goring and Edmond O'Brien's smarmy publicist. Mankiewicz has given each of them a showpiece monologue. Goring, as Alberto Bravano, revels in confessing the selfish pleasures he derives from his conspicuous consumption. (This outburst provides the scandalous climax to a party scene that compares unfavorably in authenticity of milieu to the famous soirée in *All About Eve*, although Mankiewicz was more familiar with Hollywood bashes than Broadway parties when he wrote and directed *Eve*.)

Edmond O'Brien is superb as the constantly sweating Oscar Muldoon, whose frantic long-distance telephone tactics, trying to forestall the bad publicity from Maria's intervention in her father's murder trial, is "the scene that got me the Oscar," according to O'Brien. The role of Muldoon, a combined portrait of two former aides of Howard Hughes (John Meyer and Walter Kane),[10] was written especially for O'Brien, whose hilarious imitation of Martin Gabel's "Jewish Cassius" (from the Mercury Theatre production), while running his lines as Casca, had delighted Mankiewicz between takes of *Julius Caesar*. "I want you to play an Irish Jew," was the way Mankiewicz outlined the role of Muldoon to O'Brien on the phone. "What the fuck is that?" O'Brien inquired. "It's the Jewish Casca you used to do," Mankiewicz reminded him.

---

[10]Meyer, like his fictional counterpart, Muldoon, transferred his services to a foreign plutocrat, Aristotle Onassis. Walter Kane's habit of fingering a rosary in moments of stress was ordered deleted from the script by the Production Code office prior to filming.

The Barefoot Contessa has acquired a legendary status among French critics and *cinéastes*. In the opening dialogue of Louis Malle's *Le Souffle au Coeur (Murmur of the Heart)* (1971), the two points of reference for evoking the year 1954 in France are Dien Bien Phu and *La Comtesse aux Pieds Nus*. François Truffaut has included his rave review of *Contessa* in an anthology of his film criticism.

Whether Ava Gardner's extraordinary beauty, in her striking costumes by Fontana, compensates for her often vacuous and monotonous performance, featuring a false and later abandoned Spanish accent, was improved by dubbing for the French viewer or distracted from by the subtitles is conjectural. John O'Hara, writing in *Collier's*, asserted that "Miss Gardner is the most unconvincing cold fish in piscatorial or pictorial history."

Ava Gardner is alleged to have told Mankiewicz at the start of filming, "Hell, Joe, I'm not an actress, but I think I understand this girl. She's a lot like me."[11] Although Mankiewicz subsequently described Ava Gardner as "a true child of nature" to lure Michael Redgrave to a party in her honor, very little of her primitive abandon comes through in *The Barefoot Contessa*.

Mankiewicz admits that this was one of his rare failures to get an exceptional performance from even an undistinguished actress (as he had from Darnell or Tierney). "I don't think I was as much help to her as I would have liked. . . . It was almost unforgivably stupid of me not to recognize how really nervous and sensitive she was. She was aware that this was a tremendously difficult part, and she was terribly insecure about her ability to do it. I think I failed her, in one respect, because I didn't give her enough security. I remember once, in the course of a rehearsal with Bogie, I kidded her about not getting up, by saying, 'You're the *sittingest* actress I've ever worked with,' or some such stupid remark, and she never forgave me for it. I heard, years afterward, that she always remembered it and resented and disliked me for it. I'm truly sorry about it. I made a stupid joke which I thought would make her laugh and relax, and it had just the opposite effect. I very rarely make that mistake. I think she never really trusted me after that."

Edmond O'Brien says, "There was some failure in their relationship, and [it] got in the way of [Joe's] opening her up," but he attributes

---

[11]David Shipman, *The Great Movie Stars: The International Years*, St. Martin's Press, 1972, p. 174.

Ava's distraction to the constant attendance of her paramour at the time, the famed matador Dominguín.

The Barefoot Contessa was Mankiewicz's first color film, shot by the masterful English cameraman Jack Cardiff, and it contains scenes that haunt the memory. The neatly composed umbrella-carrying and raincoated figures in the opening cemetery scene are as majestic as Resnais's formal garden grouping in *Last Year at Marienbad*. The film's great tour de force is its second scene, which conveys the torrid impact of Maria's flamenco turn without showing any of her dance. This is achieved by a clever series of intercut vignettes of figures in the night-club audience. Mankiewicz cuts from the adoring glances of a busboy to the disdainful ones of a group of plump *señoras*. The patent lust of a table of young men is contrasted with the averted yearning of a distinguished-looking monocled man meticulously removing his glove. The discordant note, which gives the sequence the sardonic Mankie-wicz touch, is a bit of freely acknowledged self-plagiarism from a bistro scene in the author's *House of Strangers*—a young girl weeping at the proposition of her gross, older companion.

Various legends about the origins of *The Barefoot Contessa*, a film about a movie-star legend, have accrued to it over the years. Two tales, which Mankiewicz states "have no validity whatsoever," are attributed to women with whom he had some romantic involvement.

Doris Vidor, a noted social figure in Hollywood and New York as the daughter of Harry Warner and the wife of directors Mervyn LeRoy, Charles Vidor, and, briefly, Billy Rose, is said to have told Mankiewicz at a dinner party of the spectacular rags-to-riches rise of a certain European actress. When she later saw a screening of *The Barefoot Contessa*, she commented to Mankiewicz that she was de-lighted her story had been inspirational, to which Joe retorted, "What story?" In 1960, when Mankiewicz was harassed by a plagiarism suit on the film, he supposedly phoned Mrs. Vidor to request that she repeat her story for use as testimony. "What story?" asked Doris, feigning ignorance.[12]

In 1956 Linda Darnell confided to producer Sam Marx, a close friend of Mankiewicz from his years as head of MGM's story depart-

---

[12]When queried about this incident, Doris Vidor enigmatically wrote back, "I really don't have any story to tell you about *The Barefoot Contessa*. I think you should talk to Mr. Mankiewicz, and if he wants to tell you about it, it's all right with me."

ment, that the script of *The Barefoot Contessa* was written in her bedroom, with Mankiewicz reading Harry Dawes to her Maria. Sobbing, she claimed that Joe had left for New York to set up the deal with United Artists and had promised to contact her as soon as the contracts were drawn up, but the next she heard of the project was when she read in the trade papers that Ava Gardner had been signed for the part.[13]

Mankiewicz says that his affair with Darnell had ended by the time he left California for New York in 1951 and that he neither mentioned the script to her nor considered her for the part, having run into her only once thereafter. Although Joe spent the summer of 1952 on the coast making *Julius Caesar*, the year Darnell was officially divorced, he says that *The Barefoot Contessa* was written mostly in Glen Cove, Long Island, in 1953.

The film was hit with two plagiarism suits. One was quickly dismissed, but the second went to court in 1960, six years after the film's New York premiere. This lawsuit was brought by the female author of an unpublished novel, *The Cannibale*, based on the life of Anne Chevalier, a former cooch dancer at the Ziegfeld Follies who was discovered by Murnau and cast as the native girl, Reri, in his film *Tabu*. Although Mankiewicz had never read the book, the author had sent the manuscript, in the 1940s, to both his studio (Twentieth Century–Fox) and his agency (William Morris), so there existed the possibility that a synopsis of it had reached his desk. The author employed as her expert witness the film historian Richard Griffith to cite the parallels between Reri's career and the fictional Maria D'Amata. John Springer, Mankiewicz's publicist at one time and a noted film buff, reeled off a string of case histories of stars of humble origin who were discovered in similarly obscure places.[14] (Mankiewicz wryly mused, after the charges were dismissed, that the unfavorable publicity of such suits invariably makes headlines, while the news of one's exoneration

---

[13]Darnell also confessed to Marx that, regardless of Mankiewicz's perfidy, if he were to send for her, she would come running back to him. It may be that her allegations about *The Barefoot Contessa* are part of the wishful fantasy of a reunion with Joe that she longed for.

[14]The suing author contended that Mankiewicz had written nothing original for the screen. Curator Griffith said this was corroborated by the records of the Museum of Modern Art. John Springer inquired whether he had ever heard of *Million Dollar Legs*, one of the two Mankiewicz films in the museum's collection, and Griffith admitted he had not realized that Mankiewicz was the coauthor of it, as well as the author of the original story on which it is based.

is rarely reported or is buried in a tiny squib of print.)

Mankiewicz contends that the prototype for Maria Vargas was actually Margarita Cansino, who was discovered doing Latin American dances in Agua Caliente by Nick Schenck. Margarita was renamed Rita Hayworth and signed to a Fox contract in the mid-thirties; she later married the Moslem prince Ali Khan.

The Barefoot Contessa is largely a *drame à clef* populated by gossip-column figures. There's an Elsa Maxwell type; an amalgam of the South American playboys Trujillo, Patino, and Pignatari; a Zanuck-like, cigar-smoking casino habitué; and a Howard Hughes type in the character of Kirk Edwards.

The original script's thinly disguised references to Hughes were unmistakable:

> HARRY: That's what a man looks like whose grandfather made good, whose mother left him with two hundred million dollars, whose father ran away and hid from the world . . . poor little rich boy. . . . His money came from a patent on a valve in a stamping machine [Hughes's came from the patent on an oil-well drilling bit] and his heart was a valve in a stamping machine. Why did Kirk Edwards want to produce movies? The answer is more simple than anyone thinks. Because he wanted girls.

> MARIA: I have heard of him. He is the owner of Texas.

> HARRY'S VOICE: The next stop in Kirk's wooing was a literal kidnapping of Maria. I do not exaggerate. This was routine procedure with Kirk. . . .

"It's one of the legends that Howard Hughes put Gina Lollobrigida under contract and then locked her in a house," says Mankiewicz. The above narration accompanies a silent scene, later cut from the film, of Kirk Edwards being chased out of the Roman villa in which he has imprisoned Maria. A series of "heavy objects" crashing through the villa's glass doors precede Edwards's hasty retreat, mopping the blood from his face. In 1943 Ava Gardner, who had been ensconced in a Hughes hideaway after divorcing Mickey Rooney, ended a quarrel by knocking Hughes unconscious with a heavy ashtray.

> HARRY'S VOICE: Kirk didn't possess a home, really. He lived mainly in his office, and he maintained a half-dozen tiny apartments as hideaways.

After all, his life was that of an alley cat—and he always had an available furnished alley to go to.

When Hughes's lawyer, Greg Bautzer, got hold of a copy of the script, he phoned Mankiewicz in New York and intimated a possible libel suit by saying, "Joe, we've got to do something about this. Howard likes you, and it's a marvelous script, but you're cutting a little too close to the bone, and Howard doesn't like that." Since *The Barefoot Contessa* was the first big venture for the new heads of United Artists, Robert Benjamin and Arthur Krim, they asked Joe to screen the film for their law partner, Louis Nizer, a film attorney and expert on libel cases. Nizer's terse judgment was, "You had better listen to the man. He's got a case."

Mankiewicz recalls that he flew to Los Angeles and met with Hughes and Bautzer the following morning in Hughes's bungalow "hideaway" at the Beverly Hills Hotel. Over orange juice and steak (then the Hollywood breakfast vogue), Mankiewicz says, "I had to maintain the fiction that I hadn't been thinking of him at all. He accepted that fiction as a friend, but pointed out that other people might not feel the same way."

Soon after the two-hour meeting, Mankiewicz phoned his film editor, William Hornbeck, and asked him to try to explain to Bautzer the logistics of making the requested changes in the sound track in the two weeks remaining until the film's scheduled release date. With the negative and the prints being made in London, the sound track and other components for looping in New York, Bogart in California and Gardner in South America, the changes were impossible.

Hughes and his representatives cut right through this seemingly insoluble dilemma. The major obstacles, travel and distance, were no barrier to Howard Hughes, who had TWA at his disposal. Armed with introductory letters to officials at every necessary airport giving him the right to bump passengers from any filled TWA flight he required, Hornbeck proceeded at breakneck pace to make all the demanded changes and deletions (most of the lines quoted above). Thus Kirk Edwards was converted from "a Texas tycoon" to "a Wall Street lion."

Compensating for these minor losses, Mankiewicz crammed *The Barefoot Contessa* with his contemptuous observations of the venal idiocies of those figures in the movie industry he despises most after studio heads—producers and exhibitors.[15] Commenting on the extravagance of international talent scouting "for what is called, delicately, a new face," necessitating overnight hops from Rome to Madrid by private plane, Dawes/Mankiewicz notes, "I've known movie producers who would travel even further for a good smoked whitefish." Mankiewicz's favorite dig is the exit line he gives to an exhibitor: "Well, it's a wonderful art we're doing business in, gentlemen. Everybody be happy."

The exploitation of the poor by the rich is exemplified by the conscienceless Bravano, whose iron-fisted control of his nation's government and its news media frees him from fear of social reprisal. It is Bravano, the supreme exploiter, who voices Mankiewicz's long-held grievance toward American economic inequality, previously enunciated in *A Letter to Three Wives* and *People Will Talk*. Justifying his own tax dodges, Bravano excoriates the American tycoon's millions in tax-exempt bonds and oil wells, "whose power of production your government so generously protects, while it refuses similar benefits to the human brain."

Mankiewicz devotes his most splenetic attack to "the phenomenon of this day and age, called—don't confuse it with your local café society—'the international set,'" which yearly convenes on the lovely Riviera coast "the way an annual fungus gathers on a beautiful tree."

It is not fully explicable why Mankiewicz is so outraged by these harmless hedonists whose clothing and social gatherings provide escapist diversion (similar to the dizzy-heiress and fashion-show fluff he produced for MGM) for the masses who avidly read about them in the society columns. Mankiewicz comments, "The jet setters essentially fulfill their own dreams, not other people's. They, themselves, take their own lives very seriously. They really are the rich scum of the earth and I detest them." Joe's detestation of them may have to do with his hatred of social hypocrisy (he refers to them as "the pretenders, leading lives of pretense") and his feeling that privileged social status should be the exclusive province of the meritocracy—those, like himself,

---

[15]Penelope Houston traces the phenomenon of Mankiewicz overloading his scripts with comments on too wide a range of disparate issues from *All About Eve* to *People Will Talk* to *The Barefoot Contessa:* "Joseph Mankiewicz, one begins to think, looks on a film as a sort of expanding suitcase . . . and in *The Barefoot Contessa* the suitcase has split wide open under the strain" (*Sight & Sound,* January–March 1955, p. 146).

whose career achievements have earned them a place in the sun.

There is, however, a curious element of fascination mixed with his contempt when he reveals, "I would love to be invited to spend a weekend at the Comte de Paris's château. I'd like to spend a *month* at the palace in Monaco . . . and I wish I'd been at that incredible outrage that took place recently at Versailles."[16]

Although a much sought-after celebrity in New York theater and literary circles in the 1950s, Mankiewicz denies that his own party guest lists, at the elegantly furnished East Side townhouse he occupied after Rosa's death in 1958, comprised many of the very society figures he claims to abhor. He maintains that the only party of this type at his house was one he cohosted with fellow screenwriter and wit Harry Kurnitz, whose guests from the international set "were people I met for the first and last time," and that Jeanne Vanderbilt, whom he courted at the time, and her circle "could not be considered part of the jet set I am talking about."

Mankiewicz admits that "one of the gaps in my research is that I've met and known so few of the international set," and though quite a contingent from "the so-called Italian nobility worked as extras for me in *The Barefoot Contessa,*" most of his knowledge of the breed comes from "reading and hearing from friends who do know them." Perhaps that is why the sad spectacle of the champagne-guzzling Pretender and his dumpy, common, imbecilic wife badly playing after-dinner word games devised by Bravano's Elsa Maxwell–type hostess seems dully caricatured.

When the *Barefoot* company assembled in Rome, just after the beginning of the new year in 1954, Bogart took aside his old friend O'Brien, who had pulled him out of a number of scrapes on the Sunset Strip, in order to get a line on Mankiewicz's working methods. "He likes to shoot long master shots, because how they play determines for him where his coverage will be," O'Brien related.

"Oh shit," Bogie retorted. He confronted the director at the first evening's cast party. "I understand you like to shoot long scenes," Bogie snorted. "Well, I've made about a hundred pictures, and I never studied any lines in my life." Then, giving Mankiewicz a long,

---

[16]The theatrical fund raiser held in late November 1973, featuring a competition between the fashion creations of French and American designers, with Liza Minnelli performing and modeling Halston's clothes. Most of European and American high society were in attendance.

challenging look, "You understand what I mean?"

"Well, you're going to have to study this time, Bogie," said Joe very quietly, after staring Bogart down.

"All right," Bogart blithely replied, and subsequently he was letter perfect, except for an occasional scene with his costar.

According to Bogart's biographer, Joe Hyams, "Bogie didn't like Ava Gardner, and made no attempt to conceal it. He complained that as an actress she gave him nothing to work with. Consequently, when he felt a scene between them was going poorly he'd deliberately muff his lines in order to get a retake."[17]

Accounts of Mankiewicz's relations with his stars vary between Edmond O'Brien and Marius Goring, who spent a great many evenings with Mankiewicz during the filming as Goring's wife and Rosa had much in common as German-speaking actresses.[18] Goring says that Mankiewicz was "impatient and intolerant" of Bogart, "did his best to provoke him," and "was much happier working with Ava." Goring's view may be biased because of his distaste for Bogart's obscene conversation ("there's nothing more boring than a man who uses 'fucking' in every sentence"), excessive drinking, and dependence on *schtick*, such as his noted cheek tremor to indicate suppressed anger, which led Goring to refer to him privately as "Humphrey Bogus."

O'Brien, on the contrary, thinks Ava Gardner felt a suppressed hostility toward her on Joe's part because he felt she was an "inaccessible" actress. O'Brien recalls that the production company "had a terrible time with Ava in Rome, as she loves to stay out late because of her chronic insomnia." Bogart's wracking cough, caused by his constantly smoking unfiltered Chesterfields, presented another problem, and O'Brien recalls that "many takes were printed simply for the lines Mankiewicz could get between the coughs."

Mankiewicz admits that "Bogie wanted you to be afraid of him a little. He made perfectly sure that you knew he was going to be an unpredictable man. . . . I caught on to that, and I played my own little game of keeping him off balance by never giving him his opportunity. You forestall it by kidding him out of it."[19]

---

[17]Joe Hyams, *Bogie*, New American Library, 1966, p. 170.

[18]Goring says that his wife encouraged Rosa Stradner to attempt a comeback in the German theater, but nothing came of it.

[19]These and the subsequent quotes on Bogart are drawn from an interview between Mankiewicz and Michael Houdley that appeared on BBC-TV's *Omnibus* tribute to Bogart (January 1972).

Revealingly, Mankiewicz links both himself and Bogart to the role of Harry Dawes as an iconoclast. "Bogie was the iconoclast loose in a society that dealt in icons, which is Hollywood. The cynicism that the part required was his by nature. When you've been through the Hollywood mill, you've been through the mill of mills. . . . It was my cynicism, it was his cynicism. It was the cynicism of anyone who had worked in the theater, and in the world of theater folk, and had lived among them and been hurt by their standards and had been forced to compromise to their standards, and who had also been rewarded according to their standards. This does something to you. The rewards very often can be as damaging as the lack of reward in the theater, and by theater, of course, I mean the all-encompassing definition of theater —the carnival right up to grand opera. Bogie was Harry Dawes and I was Harry Dawes. . . . It was one of the two or three parts in his career . . . that caught him intellectually and emotionally."

" 'The whole thing is very adult, very exciting,' said Bogart, who was so enthusiastic about the film that one might have thought it was his first big break," writes biographer Hyams.

"It was not really a very good part for Bogie," Edmond O'Brien comments more pragmatically. "Audiences wanted to see him romantically involved with the girl."

As a newly independent producer-writer-director, Mankiewicz was freed at last from the editorial strictures of the front office and proceeded to indulge his tastes. Now if he wanted to repeat a scene from a different point of view, as he had wanted to do with Eve's speech on applause, he could and did so, with Bravano's denunciation of Maria at the casino and the count's retaliatory slap.

He now gave himself free rein to explicate every character's motivations psychologically, as in the superbly written but interminable balcony scene in which Dawes dispenses his wisdom about the limits of a director's ability to mold a star performance, and Maria, too helpfully, contributes her explanation of why she goes barefooted. As Arthur Knight commented, "Mankiewicz has psycho-detected them all so well that he not only explains them to us, he insists they explain themselves to us."[20]

The only area in which Mankiewicz still felt inhibited was in challenging long-held sexual taboos. He attributes the necessity of

[20]Arthur Knight, *Saturday Review*, October 16, 1954.

resorting to a mawkish "Laura Jean Libbey"[21] ending to the strictures of the fifties movie censorship code, which prevented him from depicting the count as a covert homosexual. (Actually, the count's impotence is not the Laura Jean Libbey contrivance that Mankiewicz denigrates but a replication of the war wound suffered by Jake in Hemingway's *The Sun Also Rises*.)

Mankiewicz claims that he wanted to have Maria catch the count in bed with his chauffeur, but he surely could have found a more surreptitious way of intimating the count's sexual preference, although the film's structure would have been vastly altered. In the more sardonic ending, Mankiewicz currently posits, the count would have wanted Maria as an ornament and cover for his sexual activity. He then would have murdered her to prevent her revealing this truth, rather than out of the passionate but frustrated attraction and pride that prompt this act in *The Barefoot Contessa* as it was filmed.

Although Mankiewicz was the perpetrator of a landmark in movie double entendres in the following exchange from *A Letter to Three Wives*—

> MRS. MANLEIGH: Sadie may not realize it, but whether or not she thinks she's listening, she's being penetrated!
> GEORGE: It's a good thing she didn't hear you say that.

—he admires Lubitsch's type of sexual innuendo more than the graphic depictions of sexual encounter that are now commonplace. It seems likely, therefore, that Mankiewicz's self-censorship, as much as fear of any regulatory agency's condemnation, served to inhibit *The Barefoot Contessa*.

Mankiewicz eagerly tells how Fellini, one of the few current directors whose work he likes, expressed his admiration for *The Barefoot Contessa* and acknowledged that it had inspired his own study of decadent society, *La Dolce Vita* (1960). Mankiewicz neglects to mention how his work was successfully redone ten years later by Frederic Raphael and John Schlesinger in their more sophisticated *Darling* (1965). That film launched a new film star, Julie Christie, in the title role as a promiscuous cover-girl Cinderella who winds up luxuriously trapped in the celebrity of a dissatisfying marriage to an Italian prince.

---

[21]The author of many popular sentimental novels of the teens and twenties, such as *Lovers Once but Strangers Now* and *When His Love Grew Cold*.

"Understand you're apprehensive because you've never done musical comedy"   12

*T*HE BEST MOVIE MUSICALS HAVE USUALLY BEEN ORIGINALS rather than film versions of stage hits. But the popularity of the award-winning *Guys and Dolls*, which ran on Broadway for three years after its 1950 opening, made it an eagerly sought commodity among the Hollywood moguls ever in pursuit of a presold title they could repackage with movie stars.

In 1954 the winner of the spirited bidding for *Guys and Dolls* was seventy-two-year-old Samuel Goldwyn, the pioneering Hollywood producer. He shelled out $1 million plus 10 percent of the gross for the rights, a sum previously paid for only two other Broadway successes, the comedies *Harvey* and *Born Yesterday*. Goldwyn may have had the inside track, since he had earlier commissioned *Guys and Dolls'* composer, Frank Loesser, to write the score of his soporific but successful *Hans Christian Andersen* (1952).

Goldwyn's choice of Joe Mankiewicz to write and direct *Guys and Dolls* was no more unlikely than the selection of Fred Zinnemann that year to direct the film version of *Oklahoma!* Although neither man had directed a musical before, both were "hot" because of their recent successes.[1] The announcement of Mankiewicz's signing a contract that offered a percentage of the profits in addition to

---

[1]Zinnemann had made *High Noon* in 1952 and *From Here to Eternity* in 1953.

a substantial salary appeared on July 9, 1954, less than three months after filming of *The Barefoot Contessa* was completed in Rome.

While such names as Burt Lancaster and Cary Grant were rumored to be Goldwyn's choice for the leading role of Sky Masterson, the producer determined on an authentic musical star, Gene Kelly. Kelly, still smarting from his recent MGM fiascos, the disastrous *Brigadoon* and his shelved ballet film, *Invitation to the Dance,* was extremely eager for the part. As in the case of signing Ava Gardner for *The Barefoot Contessa,* the stumbling block was Metro's corporate chief, Nick Schenck. According to Kelly's biographer, Schenck was nursing an old feud with Goldwyn and he declined to loan out his star, despite a personal appeal by Kelly and his powerful agent, Lew Wasserman, who flew to New York to beg Schenck to reconsider.[2]

Having failed to land a qualified song-and-dance man, Goldwyn put in a bid for Marlon Brando, aware that Brando's performance in *On the Waterfront* (released in October 1954) would doubtless make him the year's most lauded and publicized film star.

When Brando declined, Goldwyn, knowing Brando's confidence in Mankiewicz, sent Joe an urgent cable: "CAN'T YOU HELP?" In turn, Mankiewicz wired Brando, "UNDERSTAND YOU'RE APPREHENSIVE BECAUSE YOU'VE NEVER DONE MUSICAL COMEDY. YOU HAVE NOTHING REPEAT NOTHING TO WORRY ABOUT. BECAUSE NEITHER HAVE I. LOVE, JOE."

Buoyed by Mankiewicz's encouragement, Brando decided the light-comedy role would extend his range and help modify the industry's belief that he was only effective in heavy dramatic parts. He was further assured that his songs would be dubbed by an accomplished singer.

Brando was eventually prevailed upon to take voice lessons and make a test recording of the score. Frank Loesser knew that it would have been difficult to dub in a singer who could match Brando's high-pitched speaking voice, and he was mindful of the fact that Robert Alda, who created the role of Sky Masterson on Broadway, was not a great singer either. After listening to the playback, Loesser claimed that Brando had "a pleasing, husky baritone quality." Brando's reaction was that his voice "sound[ed] like the mating call of a yak." Nevertheless, "BRANDO SINGS!" was to be the slogan of the *Guys and Dolls* publicity campaign.

---

[2]Clive Hirschhorn, *Gene Kelly,* Henry Regnery Co., 1975, p. 245.

Goldwyn's great mistake was that he remained as deaf as Schenck to the appeals of Frank Sinatra, the star ideally suited to the role of the sharpie gambler and best capable of singing Frank Loesser's rapturous songs. Sinatra, who had also lost out to Brando for the lead in *On the Waterfront*, was determined to be in *Guys and Dolls* even if it meant taking the supporting role of Nathan Detroit. Nathan is the perennially broke and frantic comic foil to the younger romantic lead, Sky, who is invariably lucky with both dice and dames. (In the Broadway show the role was perfectly portrayed by the Jewish character actor Sam Levene.) Sky's courtship of the virginal Salvation Army sergeant Sarah Brown is counterpointed by Nathan's fourteen-year engagement to Adelaide, an aging nightclub chorus girl. Adelaide is as desperate for her ever promised, always postponed marriage as Nathan is to find a safe location to hold his high-stakes crap game.

That the role of Nathan Detroit required a Jewish comic to croak only one song ("Sue Me") was no deterrent to Sinatra. Because both he and Mankiewicz were handled by the same agent, Bert Allenberg, Sinatra wangled a personal interview with the director at Joe's Beverly Hills Hotel bungalow. This personal appeal by a star of Sinatra's stature was persuasive, and Mankiewicz gave him the role against his better judgment. By consenting to the miscasting of Brando and Sinatra, Mankiewicz killed any chance of his *Guys and Dolls* equaling the impact of George S. Kaufman's masterful Broadway production.

Despite this capitulation to Goldwyn's insistence on box-office names for the leads, Mankiewicz wanted to retain a number of key creative figures from the original production. He enthusiastically agreed to have Michael Kidd reproduce his acclaimed choreography, and he insisted that Vivian Blaine re-create the role of Adelaide, despite Goldwyn's preference for Betty Grable as a bigger movie name and a telephone request for the part from Marilyn Monroe, about which he deliberately neglected to tell Goldwyn.[3] Neither the choreography nor the comedienne's performance was very successfully transferred.

---

[3] In addition, Mankiewicz retained two of the Broadway show's most distinctive supporting players—B. S. Pully as the bullying thug Big Jule, and Stubby Kaye as Nicely-Nicely, one of Nathan's henchmen. Kaye had garnered raves for his evangelistic solo, "Sit Down You're Rockin' the Boat," and his fine tenor tops the trios "Fugue for Tinhorns" and "Guys and Dolls."

While making the film, Mankiewicz said, "This isn't the ordinary musical with spectacle numbers. The beauty of *Guys and Dolls* is that the dances and songs flow right out of the action. It's all part of the story."[4] Prior to the picture's release, Joe said, "Mike Kidd's choreography has been a tremendous help from the beginning. If the picture does come off, I think our overlapping will have something to do with it."[5]

Kidd's cartoon balletics do work well in the opening sequence, establishing the Times Square milieu of Runyon's knavish low-lifes, and are comically integrated into a Cuban nightclub scene. But Kidd's famous crapshooters ballet, which introduces the gambling scene in the sewer, simply impedes the film's action and reminds one that often the most exciting theater dances lose their pattern and pertinence when chopped up into angled shots and transferred to the flat screen.

The failure of Vivian Blaine's nightclub numbers has much to do with cleaning up Kidd's raunchy striptease for "Take Back Your Mink" and the substitution of the uninspired and redundant "Pet Me Poppa" for the show's country spoof, "A Bushel and a Peck." Despite the mildly suggestive lyrics of these songs, one would never know from the demure chorus line of Goldwyn Girls, the bright sets and costumes, and the club's neat proscenium arch that Adelaide performed her burlesque turns in the sleazy Hot Box Club.

Perhaps the film version of the hilarious sneezing aria, "Adelaide's Lament," fails to be amusing because Vivian Blaine played it too often in the theater. As Gary Carey unkindly, but not inaccurately, writes of Blaine, ". . . she overplays the role by rote. And Mankiewicz doesn't help. In misguided appreciation of her big comic scenes, he almost pushes the camera down her throat."[6] Moreover, the squeaky voice and Brooklyn accent, which Blaine affected for the role, become irritatingly artificial as the film progresses.

The unlikely casting of Jean Simmons, another untrained singer, in the soprano role of Sarah Brown proved to be an inspired choice. (Simmons only discovered she had not been the first choice for the part after the first day's rushes, when Goldwyn cradled her face in his hands and told her, "I'm so glad I couldn't get Grace Kelly.") Simmons's skillful transition from the prim and proper reprover to a tipsy, lovesick

---

[4]*New York Times*, April 10, 1955.
[5]Howard Thompson, *New York Times*, October 23, 1955.
[6]Gary Carey, *Brando!*, Pocket Books, 1973, p. 132.

importunist justifies Mankiewicz's calling her "the dream . . . a fantastically talented and enormously underestimated girl. In terms of talent, Jean Simmons is so many heads and shoulders above most of her contemporaries, one wonders why she didn't become the great star she could have been. . . . It's true, it's not that important to her. It doesn't seem to matter to her as much."

Were Mankiewicz less discreet, he might have added that Jean Simmons's gentle sweetness and beauty are as captivating off the screen as on and that his appreciation of her extended beyond her performance as Sarah Brown. "Yes, I was aware that he was in love with me," Simmons shyly says, "and I think I was with him, really, which I've never admitted to anybody."

There was little love lost, however, between Brando and Sinatra. The passage of time and Mankiewicz's subsequent friendship with Sinatra (who in 1968 lent Mankiewicz his home in Palm Springs and showered presents and medical attention on Joe's adored young daughter, Alexandra, when she became sick) may have blunted his memory of the tensions and hostilities between the male stars during the filming of *Guys and Dolls.*

"I do remember that Marlon's first day was very difficult for him," says Mankiewicz. "He was playing a scene in a [restaurant] booth with Frank, and he was having a difficult time getting the rhythms of Masterson down. The first day he had trouble; from then on he had none."[7]

As for Sinatra, Joe says, "I think he was a little apprehensive that Marlon was going to go 'Actors' Studio' on him, but he got over that pretty soon.[8] There were a couple of tense moments with Frank. There were times when he didn't want to say the lines as they were written, but he did deliver them. I don't think I wound up as Frank's favorite

---

[7]"After eight or more takes, Sinatra, who was obliged to eat cheesecake during Marlon's dialogue, slammed his fork on the table, sprang to his feet, and yelled at Mankiewicz, 'These fucking New York actors! How much cheesecake do you think I can eat?' and he walked off the set. Mankiewicz called for a five-minute break to ease the tension" (Carlo Fiore, *Bud: The Brando I Knew,* Delacorte Press, 1974, p. 144).

[8]Frank Sinatra is an instinctive, rather than trained, actor, who prefers his "first impulse" takes and loathes repetition of a scene, the perfecting process on which Brando dotes. Although Mankiewicz says that Sinatra did not pull his well-known "one take and that's it" routine on him during the filming of *Guys and Dolls,* Hollywood critic James Bacon quotes Sinatra telling Joe, "When Mumbles is through rehearsing, I'll come out" (*Hollywood Is a Four-Letter Town,* Henry Regnery Co., 1976, p. 203).

director, mind you. I didn't feel the hostility. We weren't buddy-buddy. But he was on time, he did his job.[9] When we became friends later, we never mentioned the film. . . . I think that he did the best he could under the circumstances, but he doesn't have the equipment to be that kind of Sam Levene Jew. Why should he?"

Sinatra did have the vocal equipment to show up Brando's inadequacies as a singer. According to Brando's friend and biographer, Carlo Fiore, who was on the *Guys and Dolls* set as Brando's stand-in, Marlon was outraged by Sinatra's balladeering and told Mankiewicz, "Joe, Frank's playing his part all wrong. He's supposed to sing with a Bronx accent. He's supposed to clown it up. But he's singing like a romantic lead. We can't have *two* romantic leads."

"I agree with you," Mankiewicz said. "What do you suggest I do about it?"

"Tell him!" Marlon said. "Tell him!"

The notion of "telling" Sinatra how he should sing a song brought a wry smile to Joe's lips. "*You* tell him," he said, and walked away.

Marlon was dumbstruck for a few seconds. When he recovered, he said, "It's not *my* job to tell him. It's the director's job. I'm never going to work with Mankiewicz again."[10]

What damages the film as much as the mismating of singing voices is the expansion of Nathan Detroit's role from a supporting part in a comic subplot to a starring role worthy of Sinatra and the equal of Brando's.[11]

Regis Toomey, an old friend of Joe's from Paramount days, played the role of Arvide, Sarah's paternal confidant in the mission. Toomey says the company split into factions, with Sinatra confining

---

[9]One of Mankiewicz's sons says, "Sinatra did a great seduction job on my father till they started to shoot. He finished the picture hating Sinatra and always used him as an example of bad actors who would blame someone else for blowing a line with such excuses as, 'There's an extra talking back there.' In contrast, when Marlon made a mistake, he would say, 'Sorry, Joe. I blew it. Can we do it again?' " Mankiewicz denies these remarks by saying, "It sounds like a cheap shot. I don't think Sinatra would blame himself, and I don't think Brando would say anything if he goofed."

[10]Fiore, *Bud: The Brando I Knew*, pp. 146–47.

[11]Not only are the spats and reconciliations of Nathan and Adelaide lackluster in the film, but a protracted scene between Sinatra and Blaine in Adelaide's dressing room, following a long scene between Brando and Simmons in the mission house, illustrates the dogged symmetry of Mankiewicz's script that accounts for the film's frequently leaden pace.

himself to his entourage and deliberately snubbing known friends of Mankiewicz. "Sinatra was snotty and very difficult, as he really didn't want to do [his part]," says Toomey. "He can be very cruel and disagreeable. Joe had an awfully hard time on that picture. He had to keep himself reined in all the time, because Sinatra didn't speak to Brando; they had intermediaries.[12] Joe had to keep his cool on account of Goldwyn, but I thought a number of times he was going to blow his top."

On the subject of his producer, Mankiewicz admits, "Goldwyn was tyrannical. I suppose I worked as well with Sam as anybody could. I hate to fall into those Hollywood clichés about 'Goldwyn has taste.' In a kind of crazy way, he did have taste. He didn't know anything about a script. Certain things rubbed him the wrong way. For example, in the opening 'Fugue for Tinhorns,' he didn't like the idea of them all singing at once because he couldn't understand what each of them was saying. Loesser wasn't about to try and explain a fugue to him. Those were the sort of things you had to overcome. . . .

"He wanted to know everything that was going on. When we had to come up with a new song in a hurry[13] [an unnecessary ballad for Sinatra, "Adelaide"], Loesser, Sinatra, Kidd, and I were beating our brains out. We didn't tell Sam we were meeting, and he raised holy hell for our meeting without him. Shaking his finger at us, he said, 'I want you to know I am not the kind of producer who slips the money under the door!' That is, he wanted to bring his money in and know what it was being spent for."

Of the inferior new songs (whose inclusion forced the removal of three of Loesser's most touching ballads, "I've Never Been in Love Before," "My Time of Day," and "More I Cannot Wish You"),

---

[12]Brando's Oscar for his role in *On the Waterfront,* won during the early filming of *Guys and Dolls,* may have been another source of Sinatra's hostility. After the completion of *Guys and Dolls,* Sinatra termed Brando "Mr. Mumbles, the most overrated actor in the world" (René Jordan, *Marlon Brando,* Pyramid Books, 1973, p. 67). Brando fired back, "Frank is the kind of guy, when he dies, he's going to heaven and give God a bad time for making him bald" (Carey, *Brando!* p. 132).

[13]The rush was to make a start date in January 1955 so that the film could be in distribution for the Christmas holidays. Mankiewicz's appendectomy on February 8 postponed the commencement of shooting until mid-March, but the film was ready for release in early November.

Mankiewicz simply comments, "I didn't like 'Pet Me Poppa,' though Goldwyn did, but 'A Woman in Love' is a very good song." It is catchy but also irritatingly simpleminded in comparison to Loesser's more sophisticated love songs. It did, however, garner a lot of radio air play at the time of the picture's release, and in a variety of orchestrations, it serves well to romantically flavor and interconnect the five sequences composing Sky and Sarah's overnight trip to Havana and back.

The expanded courtship sequence features a comic brawl in a Havana nightclub (retained from the stage play but shot like a barroom brawl in a Western) and Sarah getting amorously drunk on rum-laced milkshakes. It is quite possibly the best part of Mankiewicz's production, although all of the Brando-Simmons scenes are made pleasurable by the actors' interplay. Brando and Simmons had become friends during the course of their previous film together, the boring *Desirée* (1954), and their charming "chemistry" triumphs over their generally overwritten scenes and some of Mankiewicz's more unfortunate dialogue, such as Sarah's line about the tune of "A Woman in Love": "But now it's playing inside me all true and honest as though my heart were beating the drum." Earlier, the lay analyst Mankiewicz has Sarah sarcastically declare, "I'm nothing but a repressed, neurotic girl—I've read two whole books on the subject—who is abnormally attracted to sin and therefore abnormally afraid of it."[14]

Mankiewicz told an interviewer shortly before the film's release, "Many writers have tried to reproduce Runyonese, but it is just about impossible.[15] There's a lilt and rhythm that baffles you. In the Havana sequence, which I had to rewrite some, I [made] Sky's speech closer to normal and less like Runyon—basically because Runyonese isn't an exportable product; it can't be transplanted away from Broadway."[16]

Despite this disclaimer, Mankiewicz was so adept at inventing

---

[14]Mankiewicz's invention of Sarah's nervous habit of undoing a button of her uniform or suit jacket ("You're all bundled up, except for a button," says Sky, protectively closing it) is a much subtler symbol of Sarah's sexual ambivalence.

[15]Andrew Sarris wrote of the film, "Mankiewicz has made a mistake in naturalizing some of the dialogue: the heaviest scenes are those in which people talk like people" (*Confessions of a Cultist,* Simon & Schuster, 1970, p. 18. Reprinted from *Film Culture,* Winter 1955).

[16]*Cue,* October 22, 1955.

Runyonisms that he frequently overloaded his script with them, and there are moments when one wants to scream at the next malapropism. Mankiewicz himself acknowledges that on seeing the film again in 1972, he found it "too slow and too talky. That's a case where they should not have done as much talking as they did."

As first-time librettists of musical comedies learn to their dismay, the best "books" are the most minimal. Mankiewicz inflated the tight Jo Swerling–Abe Burrows script in an attempt to make the characters three-dimensional, but the result is that the film's two and a half hours are too often merely ponderous.

Mankiewicz had the famed theatrical designer Oliver Smith fashion highly stylized, clearly painted sets for this "musical fable of Broadway," as the show was billed.[17] However, as the critic Howard Thompson observed, "For all the movement, the artificial sets suggest theatrical enclosure,"[18] and Jean Simmons thinks "the style got confused in the disparity between the sets and performance." (Particularly jarring is the juxtaposition of real police cars and other vehicles against the abstract backdrops of Times Square's signs.)

Mankiewicz attributes some of the picture's problems to Goldwyn's insistence that the film be shot in CinemaScope, which he calls "the dollar-bill proportion." Says Mankiewicz, "When you've got to fill the CinemaScope screen, everything spreads out. . . . On that screen you had twice as many gangsters than you had on stage, twice as many twirls, and twice as many intricacies."

For the joyous double wedding of the principals at the end of the film, Mankiewicz made a significant departure from the stage play's final comic twist. In the play Sky joins the Save-A-Soul mission and plays Arvide's drum in the mission band. In the film version Sky does not give up his striped suit for the mission uniform.[19] "I insisted on that," Mankiewicz declares. "Sky would never have

---

[17]The sewer set of colored pipes is nearly a replica of Jo Mielziner's for the Broadway production.

[18]Howard Thompson, editor, *The New York Times Guide to Movies on TV*, Quadrangle Books, 1970, p. 86.

[19]Mankiewicz partially preserves the conversion by having the repentant crook Nicely-Nicely (Stubby Kaye) appear in Salvation Army uniform at the wedding finale. This switch is consistent with Nicely-Nicely's previous evangelical exhortation to his fellow gamblers in the song "Sit Down, You're Rockin' the Boat."

gone into the Salvation Army, nor would Sarah have wanted such a man."

What *Guys and Dolls* essentially lacks is the pace and pep that propelled it on the stage. Logic, intelligence, and care are Mankiewicz's contributions to his first and last film musical, but the exuberance of the show is gone.[20]

---

[20]*Guys and Dolls* does have its partisans. Andrew Sarris called it "the most entertaining musical from Hollywood since *Singin' in the Rain.*" Hollis Alpert in *Saturday Review*, November 12, 1955, wrote, "This is one of the great ones . . . kept in its proper size, unlike *Oklahoma!* The production numbers are not elaborate, but they are expert, charming, and immaculately executed."

The unquiet American

"You know, for people as expert with them as you are, the use of certain words should be licensed—like guns."

(The American)

*E*NCOURAGED BY THE PROSPECTS OF *THE BAREFOOT CONTESSA,*[1] United Artists made a new deal with Figaro. On January 18, 1955, while Joe was at the Goldwyn studio preparing *Guys and Dolls,* UA announced that Figaro would make four more films for them over the next three years, two of which were to be written and directed by Mankiewicz. The first of these was to be *The Story of Goya,* to be filmed in Spain after the completion of *Guys and Dolls.* In mid-October 1955 the deal was expanded to nine pictures (five by Mankiewicz) to be made within four years. Joe clearly needed help to fulfill this commitment. He prevailed upon Robert Lantz to give up his talent agency and installed him as executive vice-president to run Figaro's office in New York.

There were two unusual features in the nine-picture deal. The first

---

[1] *"The Barefoot Contessa* was successful," says Mankiewicz. "UA got hung up on some dreadful deal for European financing which had nothing to do with Figaro's share. To get *lire,* they made a deal with Rizzoli and Bob Haggiag, and they had to give away a great deal of their share [of *Barefoot Contessa*'s European earnings] for the *lire.* UA didn't even have their own distribution outlet in Italy. The film turned a big profit domestically. [*Author's note:* Not according to *Variety*'s list of big domestic grossers.] [Ava] Gardner's salary was very small by today's standards. That [price] was just Nick Schenck trying to destroy me. I must say for Arthur Krim, he just gulped and said, 'Pay it.'"

was that two of the non-Mankiewicz projects were to be produced "as stage plays before adaptation to the screen to gain the enhanced value of a Broadway presentation." The second feature was a provision for the development of young writers, producers, and directors.

Figaro's only theatrical venture was an ill-received coproduction, in October 1957, of Carson McCullers's *The Square Root of Wonderful.* In 1960 Mankiewicz did take an option on the novel *A Fine and Private Place,* a fantasy about two dead people conversing in a graveyard, by an eighteen-year-old author named Peter S. Beagle. Mankiewicz was to have written the stage version, but nothing came of the project after Twentieth Century–Fox bought out Figaro in early 1961.

Mankiewicz moved to utilize the talents of two outstanding television directors, George Roy Hill and Robert Mulligan, who have since made names for themselves in the movies.[2] Hill and his producer-partner, Jerome Hellman, made a deal with Figaro to produce a film called *The Harrigan Story,* about "an American Marine who went into Haiti," in Mankiewicz's synopsis, but the project never went beyond the stage of script revisions.[3] No Figaro production for Robert Mulligan was ever announced.

The project that became the only non-Mankiewicz[4] film for Figaro was brought to the company by Walter Wanger, Joe's old acquaintance from his years at Paramount. (Wanger had become a prolific independent producer. Some of his more notable films were John Ford's *Stagecoach* and *The Long Voyage Home* and Fritz Lang's *You Only Live Once.*) Wanger's property, *I Want to Live!* (1958), was a brutal melodrama about a real-life prostitute, Barbara Graham, whose execution in California had been highly publicized. The script claimed that she was framed for a murder and railroaded to the gas chamber.

Mankiewicz took credit as executive producer of *I Want to Live!* but he gave the final cut to the director, Robert Wise, and participated

---

[2]George Roy Hill has directed the hit films *Butch Cassidy and the Sundance Kid* and *The Sting.* Robert Mulligan directed *To Kill a Mockingbird* and *Summer of '42.*

[3]Figaro publicist Mike Mindlin says that he sat in on one of the *Harrigan Story* script conferences, and that Hill, Hellman, and he "were in absolute awe of Mankiewicz's mind. It was just breathtaking how fantastic he is with *other people's* scripts. When Joe's serving in all three capacities [producer, director, writer], the writer always wins. He takes from himself what he would never accept from anybody else."

[4]Joe's nephew Don Mankiewicz received coauthor credit for *I Want to Live!* by revising Nelson Gidding's screenplay.

only to the extent of approving the picture's script and budget and giving Wise his opinion of the rough cut. (Privately, Mankiewicz takes credit for the innovation of John Mandel's jazz score, just as he maintains that he introduced atonal music to movies with Franz Waxman's score for *Fury.*)

Susan Hayward won an Academy Award for her performance as the film's tough-talking, desperate B girl, and the harrowing depiction of Graham's gas-chamber execution is one of the strongest indictments of capital punishment in American film.

"It turned out to be an eminently successful film for UA and us," says Mankiewicz. "In fact, it was the most successful Figaro film. With the exception of *I Want to Live!* Figaro never accomplished what it set out to do."

If the company failed to realize Mankiewicz's great ambitions, it was not for lack of financial encouragement. NBC-TV was as eager as United Artists for the artistic prestige that association with Joseph L. Mankiewicz conferred. On June 1, 1956, the *New York Times* announced that NBC had acquired ownership of 50 percent of Figaro for an undisclosed amount of money.

Joe advised a friend, Nancy Green, to sell her RCA stock, if she owned any, since their television branch was foolish enough to spend $1 million for half of his company. Figaro publicist Mike Mindlin claims that "NBC gave Joe over $1 million in development money . . . though he assured Robby Lantz and me that we were going to produce the projects we brought in."

NBC's president, Robert Sarnoff, said that "Figaro is furnishing the consultation services of Mr. Mankiewicz and others on Figaro's staff to NBC" and that the film company was "granting to NBC . . . a favored position [that is, first refusal] in connection with all motion pictures produced by Figaro."

Mankiewicz says, "I knew NBC expected us to do things in TV that I didn't have too much intention of doing." The only idea that he offered to NBC, which the network failed to implement, was to produce a series of nationwide, televised competitions among amateur and regional theater groups to be judged by a panel of distinguished American theater figures.

Nancy Green comments that NBC was in a "period of name collecting, a form of artistic legitimization that CBS later attempted by signing Mike Nichols in the sixties and Joe Papp in the seventies, with no true lien on the services of the name involved." Mike Mindlin says, "Joe was to function in some vague way as an adviser, but he never really did."

In Mankiewicz's view, television was for fledgling directors like Hill and Mulligan, not for established names like himself. Mike Mindlin says, "He had complete contempt for noncreative executives," whose deficient esthetic sense apparently extended to their choice of clerical personnel. "Let's never have a meeting at UA again," Joe said to Mindlin one day. "I can't stand those pimply-faced secretaries."

The question of Joe's next film for Figaro grew in urgency as titles previously announced to the press were abandoned. *"The Story of Goya*[5] never got beyond the talking stage," says Mankiewicz, "while *Twelfth Night* I wanted to do very much with Audrey Hepburn playing both Viola and her twin brother and Danny Kaye as Aguecheek. . . . It was a question of availability. Hepburn wasn't available when I was."[6] Instead of the Shakespeare comedy, Mankiewicz turned to adapting Graham Greene's new, highly controversial novel, *The Quiet American.*

Mankiewicz has called his *Quiet American* (1958) "the very bad film I made during a very unhappy time in my life,"[7] the period of his wife's degeneration culminating in her suicide. Jean-Luc Godard, then a film critic, named it the best picture of 1958.[8] Robert Lantz speaks of the "unpardonable arrogance" of reversing the ending of Graham Greene's novel, and the film's publicist, Mike Mindlin, views the entire production as a willful "two-year exercise in self-destruction for Joe."

The publication of Greene's novel in 1956 had occasioned an extraliterary furor over its pro-Communist, anti-American slant. The book condoned the assassination of a young American political naïf for his dangerous meddling in the 1952 Vietnamese conflict between the French and the Communist Viet Minh by trafficking with a "Third Force."

The film closely preserves the triangular conflict between the

---

[5]United Artists did eventually produce a film biography of Goya. The atrocious result, *The Naked Maja* (1959), starred Anthony Franciosa as Goya and a clothed Ava Gardner as the Duchess of Alba, the inspiration and model for the title painting.

[6]Other unproduced Figaro projects include *Showcase,* a novel by Martin Dibner about the cutthroat business of a large department store; a Western, many times rewritten by the black playwright Louis Peterson *(Take a Giant Step);* and a script about the atomic bomb titled "Manhattan Project."

[7]Quoted by John Russell Taylor in *Joseph L. Mankiewicz—An Index to His Work,* British Film Institute, 1960.

[8]*Cahiers du Cinéma,* No. 92, February 1959.

American[9] (Audie Murphy) and a cynical, middle-aged English journalist, Fowler (Michael Redgrave), for the favor of Fowler's compliant native mistress, Phuong (Georgia Moll). Whereas Greene benignly reunites Fowler and Phuong after the Englishman has set up the American's assassination, Mankiewicz makes Fowler the dupe of a Communist conspiracy to implicate the American and leaves Fowler rejected by Phuong and guilt-ridden over his perfidy.

Both the novel and the film end with the same last line of Fowler's: "I wish there existed someone to whom I could say that I was sorry." The difference is that by removing Greene's prefatory "Everything had gone right with me since he [the American] had died," Mankiewicz transforms the novel's vague regret into the prospect of a chillingly moribund future for Fowler, a man isolated by his guilt and unwilling to seek the consolation of the Church.

Many critics[10] thought Mankiewicz changed the ending to avoid angering both American exhibitors and Figaro's financing distributor, United Artists.[11] Lantz claims that Joe boasted of his projected transformation in these words: "I will tell the whole story anti-Communist and pro-American." Mankiewicz now denies these assertions. He contends that he made the alteration because he was interested in dramatizing how "emotions can very often dictate political beliefs."

Vigot (Claude Dauphin), the French police chief investigating the murder, speaks for Mankiewicz when he says that Fowler's real motive is "jealousy [of] a younger, stronger, more promising, more attractive man." Fowler has unconsciously disguised his jealousy, Mankiewicz explains, "as a noble, political sacrifice." This revelation is the

---

[9]The character is named Pyle by Graham Greene, suggesting "a pain in the ass," but remains unnamed in the Mankiewicz version.

[10]Pauline Kael in *Kiss Kiss Bang Bang* (Bantam Books, 1969, p. 422) referred to "the offending compromises of the last reel," and the reviewer of the English *Daily Herald* said that "the wrong man has been murdered, not to point a tragedy, but to please the American box office" (March 28, 1958). David Robinson in *Sight & Sound* (Spring 1958) said, "It was predictable that an American [adapter of Greene's anti-American novel] . . . might be tempted into distortion. But to have treated the novel in this audacious manner must elicit a kind of admiration. It seems a much more clever way to impose an ideology to redirect the writings of its critics rather than to suppress them directly (like Communists or Catholics)."

[11]Mankiewicz asserts that UA was a courageous and independent organization that gave him full authority and the final cut. He says the film was made prior to UA head Arthur Krim's involvement with the Democratic administration, so there was no restriction placed on his following Greene's thesis if he wished.

basis of a sluggish explanatory sequence that slows down the end of the film when it most needs momentum. But to Mankiewicz the scene redeems the conclusion, "because in the book the motivation doesn't make sense about why he turned the American over to the Communists."

In order to enlighten Fowler and the audience, who have been equal dupes, Mankiewicz retains the evidence employed by Greene to indict the American and turns it back upon the author. Mankiewicz terms the novel "a terribly distorted kind of cheap melodrama in which the American was the most idiotic kind of villain." In his research Joe found that there was no such thing as "Dialacton," the white, powdered, plastic explosive in which Greene has his American trafficking. Greene had mistaken the puttylike explosive Melenite, colloquially termed by the French *le plastic* and used extensively by them during their occupation of Vietnam, for the material we generically term *plastic* (*matière plastique* in French). In the film Mankiewicz comments on Greene's gullibility by having Vigot condemn Fowler for accepting the planted evidence (an empty container of "Dialacton" as the explosive and a bicycle-pump mold as the detonator) furnished by a Chinese agent as proof of the American's guilt.[12]

On January 28, 1957, the day *The Quiet American* began location shooting, the Saigon correspondent for the *Times* (London) prematurely filed a dispatch proclaiming the screen adaptation a "travesty" of Greene's novel.[13] Greene retorted in a letter, "If such changes as

---

[12]The original shooting script contained another link between Greene and Fowler. Mankiewicz found in the novel that Greene had used the same jibe twice, in different contexts, so he had the American use this slip against Fowler: "I remember you were criticizing the overcleanliness of American girls—you said you couldn't imagine them 'a prey to untidy passion.' You liked that phrase. So you used it a week later about a Vietnamese accountant and his wife."

[13]The *Times* dispatch of January 9, 1957, which sparked Greene's letter, inaccurately attributed several political postures that did not exist in the script and put forth the absurd notion that Mankiewicz and his crew were spending their eight weeks of location work in Vietnam like a second unit crew "tak[ing] views of Saigon and the surrounding countryside." The portion that doubtless piqued Greene reads, "Hollywood's version will be a safe one—that of the triumphant emergence of the democratic forces in the young and independent state of Viet Nam backed by the United States, accompanied by the downfall of the British and French imperialists. The Viet Namese heroine, after the death of the American whom she loved, acts like a good nationalist by rejecting the cynical opium-smoking Englishman in favour of a politically irreproachable Viet Namese husband."

your Correspondent describes have been made in the film of *The Quiet American* they will make only the more obvious the discrepancy between what the State Department would like the world to believe and what in fact happened in Viet Nam. In that case, I can imagine some happy evenings of laughter not only in Paris but in the cinemas of Saigon."[14] This prophecy by a renowned writer that the film would be laughable "extremely disturbed" Mankiewicz, according to Claude Dauphin. Dauphin says that Joe had several meetings in Saigon with the opium-smoking French journalist and his young Indochinese wife who had served as Greene's models for Fowler and Phuong. Dauphin says that Mankiewicz urged them to write to Greene and encourage him to revise his derogatory opinion of the film version of his novel.

Mankiewicz maintains that Greene wrote his novel "in a fit of great pique" at the U.S. State Department for refusing him a visa. Beyond Greene's factual error over the term *le plastïc,* Joe believes that the novelist's clinging to a plot based on a mistaken premise "shows how deeply the childish emotion of pique can affect a man's writing and his political beliefs."[15]

Greene did not perceive that Mankiewicz had turned Fowler into a satire of his creator. In 1961, when Michael Redgrave was rehearsing Greene's play *The Complaisant Lover* in Philadelphia, Greene reproved him for having turned Fowler into "a buffoon." Redgrave was understandably bewildered by this disparagement since he had managed the feat of making a bitter and selfish neurotic into a deeply sympathetic figure.

In fact, Mankiewicz told the critic Arthur Knight that the character of Fowler had been the source of his attraction to Greene's novel, despite his reservations about its content. "I've often wanted to do a picture about one of those ice-blooded intellectuals," says Mankiewicz, "whose intellectualism is really just a mask for completely irrational passion."[16] Moreover, Mankiewicz corroborates the audience's prefer-

---

[14]The *Times,* January 29, 1957. Michael Redgrave's letter, defending the film against the inaccuracies of the January 9 dispatch, was printed above Graham Greene's snide but prophetic comments.

[15]His condemnation of *The Quiet American* aside, Mankiewicz describes Graham Greene as "an author I admire tremendously. I love the way he divides his work into 'entertainments' and serious novels." Mankiewicz has taken to doing this himself, terming *Sleuth* his first "serious work" since *Suddenly, Last Summer* and contrasting it with his previous "entertainment," *There Was a Crooked Man. . . .*

[16]*Saturday Review,* January 25, 1958.

ence for the perfidious Fowler over the virtuous American by stating, "I consider him the hero. He is right in all his political observations." Fowler also narrates the film and gets the best lines. Fowler's frequent potshots at American materialism are highly Greene spirited but are phrased with a stinging eloquence that is distinctively Mankiewicz's. Joe's own bit of material extravagance was imported rather than domestic—a Vuitton trunk that converted into a writing desk, which he asked Claude Dauphin to order in Paris for Saigon delivery. The distinguished actor attempted to dissuade Mankiewicz from the purchase; the trunk cost too much and Vuitton couldn't provide the dimensions he desired. But Mankiewicz, who has a penchant for luxury gadgets, was not deterred.

Redgrave's subtle portrayal of Fowler throws Audie Murphy's inadequacies as the American into sharp relief. Had Mankiewicz succeeded in casting his original choice for the American, the accomplished Montgomery Clift,[17] it seems certain that our sympathy for the rivals would have been more equally divided.

Murphy does have some of the right qualities for the part—a charming guilelessness and good looks. However, his wooden stance, his awkward gestures, and his hopeless, drawling delivery of Mankiewicz's lines belie the character's academic upbringing and Princeton polish. In his own gauche way, he is as much a nurd as Greene's caricature. Murphy, a much celebrated and decorated hero for his bravery under fire in World War II, was bedeviled by the trauma of combat. Saigon intelligence reports that he might be killed or kidnapped led him to carry one or more loaded .45s at all times. He slept with one under his pillow and would clutch it on awakening from his frequent nightmares. Putting him back to sleep required the comforting of the bodyguard chum he kept in constant attendance.

Sir Michael hated Audie's pistols, and Murphy was intimidated by Redgrave's vast acting experience and polished technique. Murphy's tension was so great in their scenes together that Redgrave became

---

[17]Laurence Olivier had tentatively agreed to play Fowler opposite Montgomery Clift but bowed out rather than appear with Audie Murphy. Robert Lantz attributes the loss of Clift and Olivier to Mankiewicz's refusal to send out early drafts of the script while he was revising it. Claude Dauphin says that Clift was still recovering from his serious auto accident suffered on May 13, 1956; his injuries from it had necessitated plastic surgery to repair his face. Mankiewicz says that Clift very much wanted to do the part. (*Author's note:* Clift did make *The Young Lions* in 1957, but I have not been able to determine when he committed himself to that picture.)

distracted by his fixed stare and asked Mankiewicz if he would tell Murphy to blink occasionally.

Redgrave understood Joe's reluctance to broach this matter to Murphy, but he was mystified when Mankiewicz refused to allow any cuts in Fowler's speeches. Redgrave, an exquisite writer himself whom Mankiewicz termed "a semantic philosopher" because of their occasional discussions of language, was simply following Joe's earlier instructions. When Mankiewicz cast Redgrave in New York, he remarked, "The script's rather overlong, so if you see any places where we can do some cutting advantageously, make a note of them." Redgrave complied in Saigon, only to be silenced by Joe's retort, "I'm not under contract to do a ninety-minute picture!"[18]—a closed-minded decision that Redgrave feels was "very damaging" to the film, as Mankiewicz was obliged to cut a great deal of valuable footage in order to preserve the plethora of dialogue.[19]

Redgrave found Mankiewicz equally grudging with praise. His spirits were buoyed only once, and at second hand, through Joe's pseudoaristocratic assistant, the Polish "Count" Michael (Misha) Waszynski. Waszynski confided that "Joe has only tried to foretell an Academy Award once before (Edmond O'Brien's for *The Barefoot Contessa*), and he says you are going to get one for this." (This augury proved inaccurate. Redgrave was not even nominated, and the award went to David Niven for *Separate Tables*.)

Redgrave found Mankiewicz unusually reclusive during the making of the film, retreating to his trailer between setups and holing up in his suite at the Majestic at night. Prior to the commencement of shooting, Mankiewicz did put in an appearance at a cocktail party. There publicist Mike Mindlin introduced his Vietnamese date, one Mademoiselle Phoque (pronounced "fuck"), to his chief:

MINDLIN: I'd like you to meet Miss Phoque.
MANKIEWICZ: *(looking her over and turning to Mindlin)* Oh really? What year?

---

[18]Mankiewicz is enormously finicky about every word and punctuation mark in his scripts. He bawled out Cliff Robertson on the set of *The Honey Pot* for adjusting dialogue to fit his own speech. Of all the actors I have spoken to who have worked with Mankiewicz, only Cary Grant *(People Will Talk)* said he was allowed to make minor changes to suit his comfort.
[19]Mankiewicz only managed to reduce his shooting script to a feasible length by cutting all of his detailed stage directions and retaining only his dialogue.

In addition to the inept performances delivered by Audie Murphy and the pretty Italian discovery Georgia Moll (Phuong),[20] a number of unusual problems affected the production during the eight weeks of shooting in Saigon and environs.

After the first night's filming of the colorful Tet New Year festivities, which provide the opening sequence of the film, Mankiewicz returned to his quarters at the Majestic Hotel to be greeted, like Fowler, by the police. They played Joe some tape-recorded threats gathered by their agents, who had been tailing known Viet Minh operatives in the immense crowd drawn by the film crew. The tapes pieced together a plot, planned for the next evening, to topple the tall ladder used by "the man with a face like a frog who smokes a pipe." Mankiewicz was not to be deterred. He announced, "I can't see a frigging thing if I don't go up the ladder. I don't think they're going to shoot me; it would be stupid. Besides, there should be some way of protecting the ladder," and he resumed his perch the following night. Luckily, he observed nothing more than a few minor scuffles on the fringes of the crowd below.

The incident at the Cao Dai ceremonies outside their exotic cathedral in Tay-Ninh had greater repercussions. "As the festival began, all was sweetness, light, and color," *Time* magazine reported.[21] "The camera ground away, Vestal Virgins, bishops, boy scouts and cardinals of both sexes thronged together in full ecclesiastic panoply on the great Square of the Universe." "What Mankiewicz and his company didn't know" was that the Cao Dai's pope was in exile in Cambodia and his disciples were furious over his absence. Moreover, the *Quiet American* crew had brought along papal robes for the actor playing the Cao Dai spokesman, which led the mob to believe that a new pope was being installed to satisfy the dictates of the production. *Time* reported that "quite suddenly the crowd turned hostile. 'We

---

[20]Figaro publicist Mike Mindlin says that he had recommended the ravishing and more authentically Asian France Nuyen to Mankiewicz on the basis of a tip from model Dorian Leigh and a portfolio of dazzling photos by Halsman. Mankiewicz flew to Rome to test her, but the results made her "look like Minnie Mouse," according to Mindlin, who thought the test demonstrated amazing visual ineptitude on Joe's part as supervisor. In 1958, when *The Quiet American* was released, Nuyen became Joshua Logan's discovery in the stage version of *The World of Suzie Wong* and his film of *South Pacific.*

[21]*Time,* February 25, 1957.

want our Pope,' they shouted in Vietnamese, shaking their fists in the faces of the bewildered Americans. As the clamor rose, the Vestal Virgins whipped out huge banners bearing the same demand in English.[22] 'This is not religious,' muttered one bewildered movieman, 'this looks political to me.' At last, as suddenly as it had begun, the disturbance was over, and the frenzied crowd disappeared from the square, leaving behind them a cloud of yellow dust kicked up by the stamping of thousands of frantic feet."

When the crew returned to Tay-Ninh the next day for additional shots inside the cathedral, they found the vice-pope and his retinue had vanished, and those Cao Daists who were on hand refused to cooperate. Ultimately, the setting was replicated and the sequence completed at Cinecittà in Rome, where most of the film's interior scenes were filmed.

While the glare of the midday sun posed depth-of-field problems for the cinematographer and occasionally necessitated early breaks in the filming, the Saigon heat was omnipresent and caused Mankiewicz to lose a great deal of weight. This condition was noted with concern by his intimates and was ultimately remedied by his wife when Joe arrived at the splendid villa she had readied for their reunion in Rome.

Rosa was again losing her mental health at the time, and her excessive use of alcohol and barbiturates aggravated her condition. Michael Redgrave recalls that at a party given by the Mankiewiczes in honor of Ava Gardner, his own fatigue was so great that he asked if he might lie down; he awoke to find Rosa holding him, covering him with "luxuriant" kisses, and muttering, "Joe doesn't mean it, you know," or something to that effect.

Rosa was less conciliatory about her own relations with Joe. Having been long complaisant about her husband's infidelities, she became openly furious about an affair she alleged he had had in Saigon with a member of the production staff. After she suicidally slashed her wrists, Joe asked his sister, Erna, who lived in Rome, to accompany Rosa to a clinic in Vienna for treatment while he completed production of the film.

---

[22]Leslie Mallory wrote, in the *News Chronicle* on March 20, 1958, that when the backs of the banners with sacred inscriptions were reversed, they displayed such slogans as "Shoot the Government." "When the Vietnamese government demanded they cut the scene from the picture, Mankiewicz said, 'Why should I? Nobody in America can read the language anyway, so what difference does it make?' They argued for two days and Mankiewicz eventually won."

Throughout the Vietnamese phase of the production, there were already many American military and civilian personnel in Saigon. Among them was the prototype of the Peace Corps field workers, the American Friends of Vietnam. The kindly ministry of the Friends led Mankiewicz to term them "an idealistic bunch of kids . . . who couldn't set off a firecracker on the Fourth of July," though their medical help in the villages was "a great irritant to the Viet Minh." Based on his acquaintance with some of them made on an earlier trip to Vietnam in mid-1956, Mankiewicz altered Greene's portrait of the American, "making [the character] both more credible and true to the earnest, hard-working, apolitical types that he had found in Indo-China."[23]

The innocence that Mankiewicz proclaims for the American, through Inspector Vigot's exonerating eulogy, is perplexing. Why should the American authorities want the American deported, and why should the Communists want him assassinated, if his activities are truly innocent? Mankiewicz admits "it is probably not awfully clear in the film" that he saw the Third Force, with which the American fraternized, as a bulwark of social stability and the only defense against a Communist takeover. Throughout the film he does have the American laud this faction's potential for social salvation, but at the end of the picture, the knowledgeable Vigot declares that his association was limited to "two brief talks" with the Third Force's military leader.

For a master of puzzles like Mankiewicz, who is usually so conscientious in explicating more than is necessary, this is an unusual lapse. It is also one of the consequences of his having twisted the Greene source material to his own ends.

Equally curious is the American's allusion to his Princeton acquaintance with "a very prominent Vietnamese living in exile. It was from him and not from a book that I learned about the Third Force, the Vietnamese people." "Who was he?" asks Fowler. "You know— or you should know—as well as I," responds the American, "because if all goes well, if Vietnam becomes an independent republic with a government freely chosen by its people—this man will be its leader."

We now know that this leader "discovered" at Princeton by John Foster Dulles and installed as a puppet president was none other than Ngo Dinh Diem, who just happened to be in office while *The Quiet American* was being shot in South Vietnam. A member of the production staff contends that at the time Mankiewicz was "brainwashed" by

[23]Arthur Knight, "One Man's Movie," *Saturday Review*, January 25, 1958.

prominent American Friends of the Diem regime, among them Angier Biddle Duke.[24] However, Christopher Mankiewicz recalls his mother saying that his father's cables often contained code words meant to indicate that everything favorable he said about the production meant the exact opposite. Therefore, it seems likely that Mankiewicz was suspicious of someone intercepting his cables and that he was obliged to "play ball" to secure the regime's assistance. Today Mankiewicz denounces Diem as "a thoroughly corrupt man" whom the CIA was "watching and abetting." That Mankiewicz, who has harsh words for Greene's gullibility, was himself duped or pressured into paying tribute to Diem is ironic, but perhaps an inevitable result of a foreigner's attempting an assessment of the intricacies of Vietnamese politics in the mid-fifties.

The ultimate failure of *The Quiet American* has less to do with the distortion of Greene's novel and more to do with the failure of Mankiewicz to realize his ideas in cinematic terms. It is not simply a miscalculation in form and tempo to place two brilliantly written but ponderous scenes (between Fowler and the American and then Fowler and Vigot) back to back at the end of the film. The problem is that both are essentially set pieces for the stage rather than the screen. The verbal revelations of the latter scene especially cry out for illustration, but Mankiewicz, despite his predilection for the flashback and for scenes recapitulated from a different angle, did not seize the opportunity.

An alternative to the second, lengthy confrontation scene would have been to intercut the battle of wits between Vigot and Fowler throughout the film, as Greene did in the novel.[25] Mankiewicz chose to make the body of the film one long flashback (identical to the form of *House of Strangers*) sandwiched between Fowler's identification of the American's corpse and the admission of his guilt.

A distinctive and irritating Mankiewicz trait in a work so auda-

---

[24]As related in Emile De Antonio's documentary film on American involvement in Vietnam, *In the Year of the Pig* (1969), "The American Friends of Vietnam, whose members included such distinguished liberals as Max Lerner, Arthur Schlesinger, Jr., Joseph Kennedy, and Senator John F. Kennedy, formed both a potent lobby and a favorable climate of opinion for President Diem."

[25]This alternative may have been Mankiewicz's original intention. Mike Mindlin, the film's publicist, read Mankiewicz's original script, which he found "incredibly complicated" with an enormous number of flashbacks, one of which contained a dream sequence within a flashback.

ciously heedless of commercial or popular appeal is his distrust of the intellectual audience for which the film was written. When Fowler betrays the American, it is not with a Judas kiss but with a too apt quotation. The signal to alert the assassination squad is his taking a book to the window,[26] and Fowler, by pure chance, opens to the page of *Othello* where Iago reveals,

> Though I perchance am vicious in my guess,
> As, I confess, it is my nature's plague
> To spy into abuses, and oft my jealousy
> Shapes faults that are not . . .

In the picture's final scene, after Fowler has humiliated himself by pursuing the dismissive Phuong on the dance floor of a crowded club, a fellow English journalist recapitulates the scene as it might appear in print:

> The celebration of Chinese New Year was briefly interrupted last night in a Cholon restaurant by a shabbily dressed middle-aged Caucasian who appeared suddenly on the dance floor, unshaved, unwashed and unwanted, and made a public nuisance of himself by haranguing a young Vietnamese girl.

This is meant to be sobering to Fowler, but its effect is patronizing to the audience in its repetition of what has already been witnessed.

Jean-Luc Godard accurately, if awkwardly, terms *The Quiet American* "an ultra-talkative, rather pretentious, slightly flabby although studded with good intentions, in other words, very literary film."[27] Godard also has a provocative notion about the paradox of Mankiewicz's "mental agility." He speculates that "in the end, too much intelligence limits the scope of a film, or, more precisely, its effectiveness."[28] Calling Mankiewicz "the most intelligent man in all

---

[26]In Mankiewicz's previous draft of the scene in his shooting script, Fowler makes the appropriate quote from a poem by Arthur Hugh Clough ("And if I should chance to run over a cad / I can pay for the damage if ever so bad") that Greene had used in his novel. In a voice-over narration in the film, Fowler/Mankiewicz self-consciously acknowledges that the device of taking a book to the window "smacked suddenly of cheap melodrama." At once, Mankiewicz slaps Greene and disarms any potential criticism for his having used Greene's shopworn device.

[27]*Godard on Godard*, translated by Tom Milne, Viking Press, 1972, p. 82ff.

[28]Godard may have had in mind such a brilliant speech as the indictment of French military tactics as a doomed relic of nineteenth-century colonial strategy, delivered by a sodden American journalist (Bruce Cabot). While admirable as political observation, this set piece scarcely forwards the film's action.

contemporary cinema" and "the Giraudoux of the camera," Godard goes on to complain that Mankiewicz "is too perfect a writer to be a perfect director" and laments the "fantastic film Aldrich—not to mention Welles—would have made of this fine script *which improves 100% on Graham Greene's novel"* (author's italics).

Predictably, Greene took an opposing comparative view of the film. Greene wrote, "The most extreme changes I have seen in any book of mine were in *The Quiet American;* one could almost believe that the film was made deliberately to attack the book and the author, but the book was based on a closer knowledge of the Indo-China war than the American director possessed, and I am vain enough to believe that the book will survive a few years longer than Mr. Mankiewicz' incoherent picture."[29]

Apparently, Mankiewicz employed the English cameraman Robert Krasker to impart the atmospheric chills he had given the Belfast and Vienna locations of Carol Reed's black-and-white political thrillers, *Odd Man Out* (1947) and *The Third Man* (1950). Contrary to Pauline Kael's claim that Krasker's cinematography "may explain why this Mankiewicz film has some camera movement,"[30] Mankiewicz maintains that *he* always calls the shots.

The ultimate chills from *The Quiet American* came with its negligible box-office returns. Mankiewicz characteristically kidded about the impending disaster by predicting to his publicist that Selznick's unsuccessful remake of *A Farewell to Arms* (which was concurrently filmed at Cinecittà) would gross more in California than *The Quiet American* would in both the United States and Canada. More soberly, he confided to critic Arthur Knight, "What is intriguing to me isn't necessarily intriguing to millions of potential moviegoers . . . and I'm worried as hell about how the public is going to take to my *Quiet American."*[31] As it turned out, they didn't.

---

[29]"The Novelist and the Cinema—A Personal Experience," in *International Film Annual,* No. 2, edited by William Whitebait, Doubleday & Co., 1958, p. 55.
[30]Kael, *Kiss Kiss Bang Bang,* p. 423.
[31]*Saturday Review,* January 25, 1958.

Sudden death,
sudden rebirth   14

LATE IN 1956, BEFORE MANKIEWICZ FLEW OFF TO SAIGON, ROSA
pleaded with him to cable her as soon as he arrived. Joe dismissed her
fears as foolish, saying that if the plane crashed, his name was prominent enough to be noted by the newspapers. To put her anxious mind
at rest, he did wire her, "ARRIVED SAFELY, SO THEY TELL ME."

On March 22, 1958, Mankiewicz says, an early edition of the
New York Times printed that he had been killed in the crash of
Mike Todd's private plane. Todd had, in fact, persuaded him to
make the flight from Los Angeles to New York in order to discuss
the possibility of Mankiewicz's writing and directing Todd's projected film of *Don Quixote*. But Joe's sister-in-law, Sara, alarmed by
the severe lightning and thundershowers that swept Los Angeles on
the evening of March 21, convinced him to make the trip on a
commercial airliner.

Nineteen fifty-eight was not to be the year of Joe's death but of
Rosa's. Her final decline had begun in Rome during the completion of
The Quiet American in the late spring of 1957. That summer, upon
her release from a clinic in Vienna, where she had been comforted by
the visits of Dr. Frederick J. Hacker, her Austrian compatriot and
psychiatrist friend from Menninger's and Los Angeles, Rosa was met
by her sons, who had been traveling in Europe on their summer vacation. Rosa's mother and Joe met them, and the family motored in a

rented Mercedes to Salzburg, where Rosa's mother lived, spending a night at the nearby Schloss Fuschl, where the Mankiewiczes slept in the former room of Nazi foreign minister von Ribbentrop.

In late July, Rosa flew back to the United States to complete her recuperation at a clinic in Connecticut so she could be out in time to see Chris and Tom before they departed for their respective prep schools. The country club ambience[1] had been recommended by Lawrence Kubie, the psychiatrist who had been treating her since the early fifties. (Dr. Kubie was a fashionable New York practitioner who had treated many famous people in the arts, such as the then troubled Vladimir Horowitz.)

Rosa's psychological maladies had been severely aggravated by a traumatic hysterectomy in the mid-fifties. It is, of course, conjectural whether her outbursts in Rome were related to her own fear of aging and loss of sexual attractiveness or to the fact that Joe's alleged mistress was a younger and far less physically prepossessing woman than the voluptuous Rosa.

It is unlikely that Rosa rationalized her husband's infidelty in the manner of his fellow writer-director Richard Brooks. Brooks maintains that "Joe is a romantic in many ways, especially with women. He has to be in love to function. He is tortured by the women he marries, and he is always in love, after he's married, with some other woman besides his wife. John Huston was the same way, as was Clifford Odets. They have to love with the excitement, the indecision, and the absolute torture that lifts them from the earth. When it's settled by marriage, they become dead souls and their juices are drained. Under stress, their minds were bright and they were quick, their whole chemistry was right. [These types of men are happiest] in pursuit, like that of an ephemeral idea in a story. In this way their personal and professional lives are intertwined."

Rosa may have comprehended this need somewhat, and, perhaps significantly, Rosa and Joe maintained separate bedrooms in both Los Angeles and New York, although this may have been as much because of Rosa's being a later riser than Joe, as he would be at work while she was still breakfasting in bed, reading the papers, and making her morning phone calls.

Dr. Hacker says, "To my knowledge, Rosa and Joe separated

---

[1]Described by Adelaide Wallace, Mankiewicz's former secretary.

about five or six times. I mean separations for more than a few days. Most of [these separations] lasted for several weeks—one of them for over half a year. During these periods, however, they would frequently visit each other, but I know for sure that they didn't live together. . . . [Joe] was advised many times to separate or get a divorce. He always promised [he would the] next year or that he would only remain until the particular crisis was over. So it was always clear the attraction she held for him, although I'm sure that he was not entirely faithful during those periods. She had a very strong hold over him, and [he had an exaggerated sense of responsibility] undoubtedly."

Christopher Mankiewicz says that few people tend to remember his mother's better side, her "bright, sunny, and good-humored" nature, and "the good times" and "the great instinctive rapport and respect" that held his parents together. (Dr. Hacker describes her as "a very devoted mother.")

To illustrate the "Jekyll-Hyde" quality of his mother's nature, Christopher recalls the occasion of his parents' fifteenth anniversary party with their sons in Venice, after the completion of *The Barefoot Contessa* in 1954. Only twenty minutes after his father had given his mother an impressive piece of jewelry as a gift, Rosa began hurling abuse, and Joe lamented, "Wouldn't it be nice to suspend hostilities for once at a time of celebration?"

Prior to her recriminations during the filming of *The Quiet American* in Rome, says Dr. Hacker, "Rosa, strangely enough, never reacted to [Joe's other infidelities] with particular vigor." He concedes, however, that Mankiewicz's liaisons often "coincided" with Rosa's difficulties and "may have played a role in" them. In turn, Joe's affairs were "undoubtedly" a form of escape from his unhappy home life. However, "there were many other things to which [Rosa] reacted more strongly," says Dr. Hacker, "namely [Joe's] preoccupation with work, presumably neglect, lack of understanding, and [that sort of thing]."

A woman friend prominent in the Broadway theater recalls that once, in response to Rosa's grieving that she was unable to keep a maid or fulfill her husband's household demands in New York, she told Rosa, "Joe is very attractive and lots of fun, but either you go to see a psychiatrist and tell him you're a masochist, or you make up your mind to get a divorce. You can't go on like this. You tell me he has affairs with other women and tells you about them. That you have to have hot coffee and hot food for anyone who comes into the house at any hour of the day or night. You wait on him hand and foot and you don't get anything for it, so it makes no sense."²

Dr. Hacker says that "Joe, like many charming, sweet, applause-hungry people, always had the need for a very strong and solid and, at times, even sadistic kind of person. Rose was his superego or conscience. . . . She was an extremely headstrong and decisive individual, very much in contrast to Joe, who always saw all sides of the picture. She made a quick decision, usually not the right one, and then polarized every issue very easily as 'good' or 'bad.' Strangely enough, this [decisiveness] had a great attraction to Joe, and he depended a great deal on that type of approval, [which,] just because of [his need,] was [often] withheld [by Rosa]. He could never do anything that would please her. . . . I would say it was a kind of masochistic submission to the judgment of somebody who at least was decisive, [although] Rose was not nearly as bright nor one-fifth as educated as Joe, and certainly didn't have his sophistication nor his ability to express herself."³

The implication of Christopher Mankiewicz's quotation of his father's frequent lament, "There are no creative producers left. How I'd love to have a really strong producer, someone I could communicate with or relate to," is that Joe yearns for a Rosa-like substitute whom he could respect on a creative level. "He says it's something he desperately needs, but look at the people he gets involved with. On the one hand, he'd love to run everything, but when he wants to be rational or practical, he says, 'Of course, I can't. It's exhausting. I don't have enough time.' As Doc Erickson, Mankiewicz's production manager in

---

²Christopher Mankiewicz disputes the characterization of his mother waiting on his father "hand and foot" by saying that "she was as regal as a Habsburg" and most likely would have rung for a servant. Chris also says that his father would rarely bring home unexpected guests.

³Christopher Mankiewicz says that while his mother was certainly less educated than his father she was probably more sophisticated. Former story editor and producer Sam Marx says, "When Joe has a friend or woman he likes, like Rosa Stradner, he will ascribe to her an intelligence matching his own." Curiously, the stories Marx tells to illustrate this assertion seem more like put-downs than praise. The first of Marx's anecdotes is Joe's often repeated crack, "My wife is all for religious tolerance. She feels every person should worship in any Catholic church of his choosing." The second is the story Mankiewicz told Marx of Rosa's reading *Gone with the Wind.* "Being fresh from Austria, she knew nothing about the American Civil War," says Marx. "According to Joe, she looked up in the middle of the book and said, 'If the South loses, I'll die.'" Mankiewicz acknowledges the incident but contends that Rosa was reading Woodward's *History of the United States,* which he had brought for her to study.

the sixties, observes, "Joe is very quick and perceptive in finding what's wrong with other people's work. . . . But self-criticism is quite another matter, and he doesn't accept criticism from anyone."

During the Mankiewiczes' first years in New York, Joe usually deferred to his wife's social ambitions. Reclusive by nature, Mankiewicz was aggravated at first by Rosa's desire to give big parties. In time he began to enjoy the society of such well-established and well-heeled figures as New York's Governor (1954–58) W. Averell Harriman and the publishing world's Harold Guinzburg (Viking) and Bennett Cerf (Random House) and their wives. While he had been irked initially by Rosa's desire for a chauffeured limousine and custom-made clothing, he would later tell their family friend Nancy Green, "Goddamn it, I make as much money as so-and-so, even with taxes, and I want my wife to have a chauffeur and be able to go to Mainbocher."

"In the later days," says Dr. Hacker, Rosa's opinionatedness "became so absurd that nobody could pay any attention to it at all. [Her views] became exaggerated, repetitive, and purely prejudicial. At that time, [the Mankiewiczes' last] estrangement [began], and then it became quite obvious that she was an ill person whom one had to care for rather than take very seriously. . . . [After she had been hospitalized several times in the East Joe] felt that she had antagonized so many people that, in the later phases of her life, she had hardly any friends. [There was] nobody who could care for her, and therefore he could not abandon her. . . . [Even in their Hollywood days] there were often very rough times, because for a while she took a very antagonistic attitude toward his work. She disliked it very much and tried to block it. [Her tactic] was to have major attacks of one kind or another, particularly of drinking, just when he started work or when there was a particularly crucial phase [of work].[4] . . . He then became, at times, ruthless with her."

On occasion Rosa would retaliate. At a dinner party at Cole Porter's one evening, Porter turned on his favorite television quiz show.

---

[4]Dr. Hacker further explains that Rosa was terribly frustrated. He says, "There was a tremendous amount of [professional jealousy between wife and husband]. In Rosa's view, she had given up a tremendous career for Joe, whom she accused of wanting to cast her in the role of a hostess, a housewife, and a mother. She made him responsible, irrationally it always seemed to me, for having ruined her professional career and was very jealous that he had one and that she was just Mrs. Mankiewicz, instead of being the big star that she had been at one time."

"Joe would answer the questions before the contestant," says Nancy Guild, so Rosa turned on him and said, 'Do you think anyone's interested in how much you know? We're trying to watch the show!' " "I thought it was a very ugly scene," Guild comments, "but she was bored with his penchant for showing off intellectually."

Nancy Green says that she, like the Mankiewicz family friends Alfred Katz[5] and Jessica Tandy, "became quite protective of Rosa because I thought she was so vulnerable. I became quite upset by people making fun of her, which they did a great deal." For example, one evening a terrified Rosa begged Nancy Green to come over to the apartment so that she might show her a threatening message, written in a strange hand, which Rosa had found in her bedside engagement book. "It was during the Jelke trial,[6] and someone had written, 'Beware the Ides of March. Beware of Jelke,' or something to that effect. Rosa decided someone evil or crazy was trying to do her in. . . . Two or three weeks later we learned that John Steinbeck and Quentin Reynolds had done it as a prank at a dinner party the Mankiewiczes had given.

"Things worried Rosa more, petty things. She made things a little more dramatic and terrifying by her projecting, but she was an actress once. . . . Like anyone who's in constant need of help, she became something of a liability. . . . She was terrified by the fact that she could never take another sleeping tablet. It seems that while on a trip to see her mother, she had gotten very ill from [sleeping pills] and had been hospitalized. The pills had begun to affect her reason, as they do if you take too many." Doctors gave warning and Rosa promised to quit, but Mankiewicz's niece Johanna says that her uncle and many others knew that Rosa had Dorothy Kilgallen's and Judy Garland's fatal habit of "drinking and taking pills at the same time." Rosa, as Herman had, was becoming "almost a total dependent, a liability, and a burden on [Joe]."[7]

For the summer of 1958, the Bennett Cerfs had found the Mankiewiczes a house for rent, near theirs, in Mt. Kisco, New York. "It was

---

[5]Alfred Katz, a publicist, was an associate of Angier Biddle Duke, the head of the International Rescue Committee (IRC). Rosa Stradner devoted a great deal of her time to the activities of the IRC, which included aiding the evacuation of protesters of the Russian suppression of the 1956 Hungarian uprising.

[6]Minot (Mickey) Jelke III, an heir to a margarine fortune, was tried in March 1955 and convicted of heading a call-girl ring.

[7]Dr. Frederick J. Hacker speaking of Herman Mankiewicz.

one of the happiest summers they ever had," says Addie Wallace. "They had this lovely house [it belonged to investment banker Gilbert Kahn], and the boys were working and learning to drive."

According to the Associated Press account, "Mankiewicz said he had last seen his wife on Friday night [September 26] when he left for New York to work on a forthcoming Broadway play [*Jefferson Selleck*]. 'She appeared to be in good spirits at the time,' he added."[8]

That Saturday morning Mankiewicz phoned his niece Johanna ("Josie"), who had just returned from a European trip Joe had given her, in the tradition of his father, on her graduation from Wellesley. Joe told Johanna he had called Mt. Kisco but had received no answer and was worried. He asked Josie to join him at the Park Avenue apartment. After persistent phoning, they finally reached the caretaker in Mt. Kisco at about 2 p.m. He assured them that Mrs. Mankiewicz was sleeping and that everything was all right. "Joe said that didn't sound right and that he [the caretaker] should try to wake her," Johanna recalled. "[We] drove to Mt. Kisco together, but by the time we got there, [I had the feeling] that she was dead, as no one had seen her, and there was something ominous about Bennett Cerf's limousine parked outside in the driveway. Uncle Joe said, 'You go upstairs.' I went up and discovered her body, which is something I have always deeply resented his making me do."

The AP reported that "a caretaker had found the body lying on the floor next to a writing table. A note, which police said couldn't be deciphered, was close by the body. [Mankiewicz says the note was written to Dr. Kubie, Rosa's psychiatrist, but he will not disclose its content.][9] Police list the death as natural, pending an autopsy." The report of the Westchester County medical examiner declaring Rosa, aged forty-five, "a suicide through an overdose of sedatives," did not appear for two months (November 25), thereby permitting a Catholic burial.[10]

---

[8]Associated Press report dated September 27, 1958, published in the *Los Angeles Times,* September 28, 1958.

[9]The *New York Times* of September 28, 1958, reported that the note was found clutched in Rosa's hand and, though most of it was indecipherable, "Mrs. Mankiewicz indicated that 'she was tired,' the police reported."

[10]The original autopsy, conducted on September 28, 1958, by Dr. William G. Best, the assistant medical examiner of Westchester County, failed to establish the cause of death. The *New York Times* of September 29 reported that "Dr. Best said

"That night [September 27] there was, surprisingly, a kind of gay dinner party at the Cerfs'," said Johanna. In the early hours of Sunday morning, family friends, like Nancy Green, were awakened by phone calls announcing that Rosa had finally done it. ("Rosa had so often spoken of suicide that no one took these announcements seriously," says Dr. Hacker, "though she had made several attempts in the past.")

Mrs. Green, like many of Rosa's family and friends, found her sadness mitigated by relief. "I thought, that poor, tortured soul was finally at peace," she says. "The agent Mark Hanna, Rosa's great friend, had died only six weeks before [August 14], which may have been a contributory factor."[11] However, she felt that Joe seemed deeply conflicted between "the fear of his unexpected freedom" and his guilt over being providentially relieved of his tormenting burden.

After Rosa's death Mankiewicz, who had often used his own successful analysis in the early forties, "as a kind of aggressive weapon against Rose,"[12] contrasting his "cure" with her dragged-out analysis during the last sixteen years of their nineteen-year marriage, returned to treatment with Dr. Edmund Bergler. (Bergler's main contribution to psychiatric literature, according to Dr. Hacker, "was the description of how people destroy themselves by too much guilt and self-blame.")

"The only time I ever saw Uncle Joe betray true emotion was at the cemetery," said Johanna. "Three people [presumably Mankiewicz and his sons] threw dirt on the coffin. Joe went back, sank his spade in the earth, and sat down. Then, almost immediately, he stood up and said, 'Enough! Let's go.' It was heartbreaking. He was putting an end to it—her death, her life. It was all over, and he'd had enough. He couldn't sit there another minute."

The only thing that Mankiewicz will say of Rosa Stradner, fifteen

---

there were no obvious indications that Mrs. Mankiewicz had taken an overdose of sedatives, although some were found in a medicine cabinet." On September 28 Dr. Best "said that a week would be required to complete a chemical analysis," but his finding of suicide by an overdose of sedatives did not occur until November 25, while Mankiewicz was in Europe.

[11]"Mark, over the years, has always meant very much to [Rosa] as a friend, [in terms of] his affection, his kindness, his devotion and loyalty when she needed it most," said Mankiewicz in his eulogy at Mark Hanna's funeral.

[12]Dr. Frederick J. Hacker. In 1943, in an attempt to curb what Mankiewicz terms his "neurotic gambling," Joe underwent psychoanalysis by Otto Fenechal, a colleague of Freud's and the author of the standard text *The Psychoanalytic Theory of Neurosis.* As with Rosa, Dr. Hacker never had a professional relationship with Joe.

years after her death, is, "Easily the most important influence on my life was my wife of nineteen years, who is now dead."

Although a film project would inevitably interfere, Mankiewicz never lost his ambition to work in the theater.

In an interview published on October 23, 1955,[13] prior to the release of *Guys and Dolls*, Mankiewicz announced that he was going to direct *Maiden Voyage*, a play by his friend Paul Osborn. Mankiewicz's description of the work as "a very charming play about American high society" did not reveal that it was populated with mythological figures from *The Odyssey*. The plot concerned Zeus's disapproval of his daughter Athena's love affair with the mortal, married Odysseus, who is old enough to be her father. Under the stewardship of the dynamic promoter Billy Rose, Mankiewicz cast Claire Bloom as Athena and Lorne Green as Zeus and supervised Oliver Smith's set designs and Lucinda Ballard's costumes.[14]

Neither Paul Osborn nor Mankiewicz remembers why Billy Rose canceled the production, but *Maiden Voyage*'s subsequent failure to make it to Broadway (under a different producer it closed in Philadelphia in March 1957) suggests that Rose may have foreseen that the play was a poor risk.

Mankiewicz's next theatrical opportunity occurred in early October 1957, when he went to Princeton, New Jersey, to inspect the troubled tryout of Figaro's production of Carson McCullers's play *The Square Root of Wonderful*, a work quite as dreadful as its title. Mankiewicz says, "I never had a great deal of faith in the project, but I liked Robbie's [Lantz] enthusiasm. Naturally, I supported him in it. . . . I

---

[13]Howard Thompson, *New York Times*, October 23, 1955.

[14]Costumer Lucinda Ballard recalls that Mankiewicz asked her to supply miniature pencil "roughs" of her designs, just as she had done for Elia Kazan on such productions as *A Streetcar Named Desire* and *Death of a Salesman*. Miss Ballard complied, but she could tell that Mankiewicz was less than elated by what she submitted. When she mentioned Joe's lack of enthusiasm to her studio mate, the famed set designer Oliver Smith, he recommended that she switch to full-size color renderings on bristol board covered in cellophane. Smith said that, in his experience, Hollywood producers and directors had a curious fondness for viewing sketches on the floor and tromping on them as they deliberated. Mankiewicz could never have guessed that this observation was the source of Miss Ballard's hysterical outburst of laughter when she and Smith later visited Mankiewicz, and his foot inadvertently touched one of her drawings spread out on his living-room floor.

was abroad. I came back just in time to attend the out-of-town tryout in Princeton."

Robert Lantz, who was coproducing the play with Arnold Saint Subber, says that "Joe tried to be sensible, constructive, and practical. He thought he could help Carson as he had aided screenwriters, but greater men than Joe Mankiewicz[15] have failed, trying to help Carson. No one is on her level, therefore no one can help. . . . Carson asked him to revise the play,[16] but when she looked at his revisions, she said, 'That doesn't work,' and couldn't explain why not. All of Carson's [dialogue came from] instinct and inspiration. Joe's comes out of real, professional know-how, and he couldn't understand her no's unaccompanied by reasons.

"Joe was in favor of letting José Quintero [the play's director] go," says Lantz, "and Saint Subber and I assumed that Joe would be prepared to take over. But Joe said, 'I haven't got the time [Mankiewicz says he was busy cutting *The Quiet American*] or inclination' . . . and he felt strongly that it would look like a power play for him, as a producer, to assume control after consenting to the firing of a distinguished director."

According to Lantz, Saint Subber was banking on Mankiewicz's loyalty to Anne Baxter, the star of *Square Root,* and assumed that if he and Lantz could not find a top-flight replacement for Quintero, Joe would come to the rescue to protect Figaro's investment. While Quintero knew the play had great problems, he was certain that Mankiewicz's literary style made him an unsuitable play doctor for McCullers's text. Quintero, therefore, relinquished his directorial assignment with relief and was replaced by the lesser-known George Keathley, a client of Quintero's and McCullers's agent, who had directed some of Tennessee Williams's plays outside New York.

The Square Root of Wonderful opened in New York at the National Theatre on October 31, 1957. It proved an unhappy Broadway debut for George Keathley and a tormenting eight weeks of performing to hostile theater parties for Anne Baxter. For the first time a work by

<hr>

[15]For example, Tennessee Williams attempted to help his friend McCullers by rewriting a portion of her dramatization of *The Member of the Wedding,* but it jarred with the rest of the script and had to be scrapped.

[16]Carson McCullers, in her acknowledgments in the published version of *The Square Root of Wonderful* (Houghton Mifflin, 1958), lists Mankiewicz among those she thanks for "their very able and talented contributions" to the play.

Carson McCullers was panned by every New York critic except the *World Telegraph*'s.[17]

A year later, in October 1958, Mankiewicz once again attempted to doctor a show in trouble on the road. The play was *The Man in a Dog Suit,* which had been coauthored by William Wright, Joe's old friend and former housemate, and it starred Joe's close friends Hume Cronyn and Jessica Tandy. As a distraction from Rosa's death and as a favor to the Cronyns, Mankiewicz went to Philadelphia to try his hand. "He tried to help and did some rewriting," says William Wright, "but his suggestions were not better, only different, and we took damned few. He didn't attack the basis of the problem—he just gave us icing when the problem was the cake."

Rather than tinkering with *The Man in a Dog Suit,* Mankiewicz would have done better to have concentrated his efforts on his own play, *Jefferson Selleck.* Despite Dore Schary's dismissal of Mankie-

---

[17]Mankiewicz says that the veiled but cutting reference to him in Wolcott Gibbs's *New Yorker* review (November 9, 1957, pp. 104–5) was attributable to the "unending vendetta which Wolcott Gibbs and John O'Hara conducted against [me]" for rewriting their friend Scott Fitzgerald's dialogue for *Three Comrades.*

Gibbs wrote, ". . . but the frequent occasions when the author's muse deserts its homeland wings, or flaps west to Hollywood are even worse. When this Choctaw mood sets in, we get such passages as:

> "You never told me you were married."
> "You never asked me."
> "What was she like?"
> "She was very beautiful."
> "What—"
> "She died."
> "Oh."

or:

> "Do you believe in God?"
> "I do tonight—altogether."

or even:

> "I love your body. I love the wisdom in your funny heart. I love you period."

"For one reason or another, I decline to believe that Mrs. McCullers wrote these horrid lines herself, preferring to attribute them to some skulking litterateur in the ranks of the management."

Gibbs's "one reason or another" was doubtless the gossip that Mankiewicz was rewriting McCullers as he had Fitzgerald. Yet the examples Gibbs cites seem quite consistent with the banality of much of McCullers's text.

The fact that Mankiewicz still remembers Gibbs's personal attack after fifteen years suggests the impact that it had upon him, and it may well have contributed to his fear of having a play of his judged by the Broadway critics.

wicz's screen adaptation of the novel in 1953, Joe's fascination with the material endured. Some years later he discussed with Henry Fonda the prospect of turning *Jefferson Selleck* into a stage play with Fonda in the title role. Fonda was a particular devotee of the novel because Carl Jonas's fictional town, Gateway, was actually Fonda and Jonas's home town—Omaha, Nebraska. "Most of those people were as familiar to me as they were to Carl Jonas," says Fonda. "Joe eventually sent me this huge script, which must be the longest play that has ever been written. He said, 'I know it's too long, but I just kept writing, and I'll edit it.' "

On the strength of the material[18] and the names of Fonda and Mankiewicz, David Merrick took an option on *Jefferson Selleck* and engaged Oliver Smith to design the scenery. A few weeks after Rosa's death, Merrick gathered Mankiewicz, Fonda, and Smith to determine how, or if, they should proceed with the venture. "We all agreed it was unproducible," says Fonda. "It was not just a question of its extreme length, but its concept. I felt it was impossible for the narrating title character, who was fifty-five years old, to play a scene as an eighteen-year-old. Not even a protean actor could accomplish that without a change of wig and wardrobe. . . . We all agreed it was foolish to go on, and Joe accepted the group's verdict. He said, 'I'm going to get on a boat and rewrite it,' as he was going to Italy on a long cruise to recuperate from the strain of his wife's death. Then he learned on landing that his agent, Bert Allenberg, had died.[19] To my knowledge, he never went back to work on that script."

---

[18]Joe's hypercritical niece described the work as "a good play, awfully well written." But Mrs. Arthur Hornblow, Jr., the wife of the noted film producer, says, "*Jefferson Selleck* was a very dull novel, so Joe's play was better, but it couldn't be that much better than its source. . . . He thought he would hold up a mirror to a dull section of America, so he held up the mirror and it reflected a dull section." "There was not that much point in his having taken the trouble to dramatize it," concurred Arthur Hornblow, Jr., the producer of *Ruggles of Red Gap, Midnight,* and *The Asphalt Jungle* and a longtime friend of Mankiewicz in New York.

[19]Bertram Allenberg died of a cerebral hemorrhage on November 27, 1958, in Hollywood, at the age of fifty-nine. He had been Mankiewicz's agent for twenty-five years, succeeding Myron Selznick in 1933. "Myron took me on only because I was Herman's kid brother," says Joe, "and I was the least of [his] clients. I was getting $200 a week, at the most, when Myron [let me go]. I'd become a friend of Bert's and wanted him to represent me, and Myron didn't object." Mankiewicz calls Allenberg "one of the two or three most honest men in the business, and one of my dearest friends. He was a brilliant agent. He was responsible for Sinatra's getting *From Here to Eternity* and, as Danny Kaye's agent, contributed substantially to his successful career."

Mankiewicz's continual disparagement of Hollywood and asser- tion that he was abandoning films to devote himself to the theater were viewed with increasing skepticism by many theater people. George S. Kaufman, who genuinely loathed the movies and had been the most prolific coauthor and director on Broadway since the twenties, was understandably piqued by Joe's claiming the theater as his domain with no substantiating credits. One day in the late fifties, the sickly Kauf- man, who had been regularly announcing his impending death, told Moss Hart, his former partner and Mankiewicz's friend, "I've changed my mind about wanting to die." Hart delightedly inquired, "Why is that, George?" Kaufman replied, "I intend to live until Joe Mankiewicz has done his first play on Broadway."[20]

Mankiewicz left for Europe in early November 1958 and returned in time to spend the Christmas holidays with his sons, home from school, and Johanna, who had moved into the Park Avenue apartment in his absence.

To start off the new year of 1959, Mankiewicz decided to rid himself of his memories of the last years with Rosa. He gave up the

---

[20]Mankiewicz's subsequent playwriting venture was an adaptation of a play he had read in its original German—*The Meteor*, by Friedrich Dürrenmatt (author of *The Visit*). This tragicomedy or "metaphysical farce" concerns a famous writer, sick to death of the human condition, whose death wish is granted only to those with whom he comes in contact. Dürrenmatt describes the protagonist as a man who loses "all respect for human laws and sets about the systematic destruction of everything and everybody around him. His weapon is truth without mercy" (Sam Zolotow, *New York Times*, July 13, 1966). David Merrick announced plans to produce the play under his foundation's sponsorship in the fall of 1967.

On August 14, 1968, two years after the first announcement of *The Meteor's* production, the *New York Times* announced that Paul Rogers, the year's Tony Award winner for his role in Pinter's *Homecoming*, would play the leading role of the loathsome writer. A production date was said to be contingent on finding a director for the play, because Mankiewicz was occupied with such film projects as *There Was a Crooked Man.*...

As late as 1972, Mankiewicz was discussing the revision of his typically overlong first draft of the play with the producing team of playwright Edward Albee and Richard Barr. Mankiewicz says that although Dürrenmatt's publisher had praised his free adaptation as "superior to the original," the rights to the work were held by the producer Leo Kerz, who refused to relinquish them, so the Albee-Barr production talks were halted.

The opinion of those people (whom the author has spoken to) who have read Mankiewicz's adaptation has been uniformly disparaging, and the first production of the work in English, translated by James Kirkup and performed by the Royal Shake- speare Company in 1966, was unfavorably received by the English critics. Nonetheless, Mankiewicz still speaks of doing both *The Meteor* and *Jefferson Selleck*.

apartment in favor of a splendid townhouse nearby on Seventy-first Street off Lexington Avenue ("the only way to live in New York," says Joe) and took up residence in the Hotel Stanhope until work on the townhouse was finished. He entered into short-term therapy with Dr. Bergler and began seeing Jeanne Vanderbilt, an attractive, socially prominent, culture-conscious divorcée who had been married for ten years to the millionaire sportsman Alfred Gwyn Vanderbilt.

Forsaking Figaro, Mankiewicz once more accepted the offer of a powerful producer, Sam Spiegel, whose previous credits included the hugely successful films *The African Queen* (1952), *On the Waterfront* (1954), and *The Bridge on the River Kwai* (1957). Spiegel offered Mankiewicz the direction of the film version of *Suddenly Last Summer*, a shocking one-act play by Tennessee Williams that had premiered in January 1958 as part of the double bill *Garden District* and become "the most talked about Off-Broadway production of the 1957–58 season."[21]

Suddenly Last Summer is a southern gothic horror tale much like Williams's 1948 short stories of homosexual martyrdom, "One Arm" and "Desire and the Black Masseur." A wealthy harridan, Violet Venable, attempts to bribe Dr. Cukrowicz, a young psychosurgeon from a New Orleans mental hospital that is desperately in need of funds, into lobotomizing her niece, Catherine Holly. Violet wants the operation performed in order to prevent Catherine from defiling the memory of her son, the poet Sebastian. Catherine has been babbling obscenely about Sebastian's death the previous summer. The climax of the play occurs when Catherine overcomes her memory block to recall, in a horrific monologue, that the pederast Sebastian had been dismembered and partially devoured by a band of starving Spanish urchins, some of whom Sebastian had courted.[22]

---

[21]Nancy M. Tischler, *Tennessee Williams: Rebellious Puritan*, Citadel Press, 1961.

[22]Presumably, Sebastian's wounds are meant to recall the torture of Saint Sebastian, whose body was pierced with arrows, just as Catherine's truth-telling monologue parallels the learned speech of Saint Catherine of Alexandria, whose eloquence cowed the Emperor Maximin II. In the Renaissance wealthy homosexual patrons and prelates would often have their lovers painted as the nude Saint Sebastian, since the iconography of the arrow-pierced body of the martyr made possible the public display of these portraits.

In the film, Sebastian's studio, which Mrs. Venable shows Dr. Cukrowicz ("It was formerly the *garconnière* where the young men of the family could go to be private"),

The high standing of Williams's work and the challenge of guiding Katharine Hepburn (Violet Venable) and Elizabeth Taylor (Catherine) through these great roles were among the elements that attracted Mankiewicz to this film project. The audacity of tackling material that touched on such movie taboos as an oedipal relationship, homosexuality, psychosurgery, and cannibalism was doubtless an added inducement. (In 1973 Mankiewicz described *Suddenly Last Summer* as "a badly constructed play based on the most elementary Freudian psychology and one anecdote [the final horror story].")

The preliminary work on the script of *Suddenly, Last Summer* went swimmingly. "I remember working very nicely with Gore [Vidal], in New York, on the screenplay," says Mankiewicz.[23] "Then going to London, since Sam [Spiegel] had asked me to make some changes, cuts, and revisions. I can remember Tennessee, in Sam's suite at the Connaught, even complimenting me on a particular line of dialogue I wrote [for Mrs. Venable], 'All poets, whatever age they may seem to others, die young,'" which Williams thought captured his style.

Problems began with the filming of Montgomery Clift's first scene. In this scene Dr. Cukrowicz (Clift) is trying to perform delicate brain surgery in the state hospital's dilapidated operating theater. During the operation the lamp above the operating table flickers off and on and the viewers' gallery rail snaps, distracting the surgeon and infuriating him.

Suddenly's cinematographer, Jack Hildyard, thought that Clift's difficulty in remembering his lines and inability to hit his marks were

---

contains a painting of Saint Sebastian, as well as several other studies of male nudes, indicative of Sebastian's homosexual proclivities.

Tennessee Williams's *Memoirs* (Doubleday, 1975) details the autobiographical elements that the playwright transmuted into *Suddenly Last Summer*. Both the violence that Williams encountered in his own homosexual pursuits and the lobotomy of his beloved sister, authorized by their mother, whose sensibilities were offended by her disturbed daughter's obscene speech, are incorporated into this play.

[23]The screen credit reads, "Based on a play by Tennessee Williams, written for the screen by Gore Vidal and Tennessee Williams." Mankiewicz says, "I think Tennessee wrote a first draft, [although] I'm not sure." Williams says that he had nothing to do with the film. The final shooting script preserves almost all of the play's dialogue, although several scenes have been relocated from the jungle garden of Mrs. Venable's mansion, where the entire play takes place, to the mental hospitals where Catherine is incarcerated. Mankiewicz's concessions to Hollywood conventions include a reprise of the famous Taylor-Clift embrace from *A Place in the Sun* and the suggestion of a "happily-ever-after" ending as the doctor and his cured patient go off hand in hand.

attributable to first-day nerves and a lack of familiarity with the English crew. However, as the production went on, it became evident that Clift's problems were chronic and caused by drugs, drink, and depression.

Mankiewicz will volunteer only that Clift "was on all sorts of tranquilizers" and "was in bad shape." Joe does mention that Clift slept over in his suite at the Dorchester on several occasions, where one can infer that Clift had passed out, as he had more publicly on the flight to London to make the film and in limousines conveying him and members of the company to several social functions.

Contrary to reports in several recent books on Katharine Hepburn that her dislike of Mankiewicz stemmed principally from his maltreatment of Clift during the filming, Joe says that "Elizabeth Taylor was Monty's closest friend, and Elizabeth and I worked desperately to keep Monty going. I had all sorts of scenes with Monty—scenes with me comforting him and his sort of relying on me."

William Hornbeck, the editor of *Suddenly, Last Summer* and of all three Figaro films, had known Clift from the time he edited *A Place in the Sun* (1951), and his friendship with Clift, like Elizabeth Taylor's, began during work on that picture.

Both William Hornbeck and Jack Hildyard attest to Mankiewicz's great solicitude toward Clift. Knowing of Hornbeck's friendship with the tormented star, Mankiewicz prevailed on his editor "to sit in [Clift's] dressing room and chat with him to see what he was doing to get into 'this condition,' " says Hornbeck. "Though I could never fathom the source, Joe thought he was either smoking or taking dope or drinking by putting booze into his orange juice. . . . Mankiewicz would often ask me, 'What's wrong with him? He acts like he doesn't hear [me].' "

To illustrate the perversity of Clift's behavior during the filming of *Suddenly, Last Summer*, Hornbeck tells the following stories: "Monty had told Mankiewicz he wouldn't dub the lines of a scene, and we needed the lines very badly, as, on the original track, you could hear the sound of automobiles, though it was an interior scene. I was delegated to somehow get [Clift] to do it. I told him, 'You don't have to do it for Joe, do it for me.' Monty said, 'I don't want to do them,' and I replied, 'Joe is going to get awfully mad at me if you don't.' I asked, 'What harm [did he feel there was in repeating the lines]?' and Monty claimed, 'The lines in the picture are better.' I said, 'They're not better.

They have noise behind them, and we can't use them!' He said, 'Well, they'll have to be fixed some other way.' Then he did the strangest thing. He lay down and rolled around on the floor like a naughty child. He was so infantile and so nasty that I grew very irritated with him. I said, 'It's really a shame you can't behave like an adult.' He finally did the lines, but we parted kind of at odds. When I returned home the next day, I found that he had sent me a pound of caviar, by way of an apology.

"One morning Monty came into the cutting room at eight-thirty, and I knew his call was at nine. When it got close to that time, I reminded him, 'Monty, you should be out on the set.' He replied, 'I want them to think I'm late this morning.' [Hornbeck adds that Clift was often tardy in arriving for his morning calls.] I said, 'You will be, if you sit here.' At nine-fifteen I sent my assistant out to notify them where Monty was closeted. When [Clift finally] arrived on the set, he told Mankiewicz, 'I've been here since eight-thirty!' "

Considering his condition, Clift's performance as Dr. Cukrowicz, though slightly cloddish and sometimes oddly crouched or thick of tongue, is typically sensitive and appealing. The curiosity of his performances in *Suddenly, Last Summer* and in the title role in *Freud* (1962) is that, while playing a judge of sick psyches, the fearful-eyed and tremulous Clift appears in both pictures as the actor most in need of psychiatric care.

Katharine Hepburn was always punctual. But in her own domineering way, she proved as great a trial to Mankiewicz as Montgomery Clift.

Mankiewicz's friendship with Hepburn dated from the early forties, when he produced her great successes at MGM, *The Philadelphia Story* and *Woman of the Year*. An engraved silver box and inscribed dictionaries from this period attest to Hepburn's admiration for Mankiewicz. But on *Suddenly*, Joe says Hepburn presented herself to him as a "grande dame of the theater." She was fresh from her appearances in Shakespeare productions with an Old Vic troupe touring Australia and the American Shakespeare Festival.

"Hepburn likes to fight, which everybody knows. It's her way to release tension," says director Michael Bennett,[24] who choreographed Hepburn in the 1971 musical *Coco*. "Katharine would take over any-

[24]Jerry Tallmer, *New York Post*, September 20, 1975, p. 13.

one, if she had the chance," says Jack Hildyard, who had previously photographed Hepburn in *Summertime* (1955).

Mankiewicz had had an early taste of the grande dame's hauteur when the 1950 production of *As You Like It*, starring Hepburn, came to Los Angeles on its post-Broadway tour. Hepburn phoned Mankiewicz and said she was leaving a pair of seats in his name for a series of performances, as she did not wish to know in advance which one he would attend, though she would appreciate his coming backstage on the evening that he saw the play. Mankiewicz dutifully attended and was kept waiting at length with Hepburn's other backstage visitors until the star had had sufficient time to disguise her beauty by smearing her face with cold cream to receive her guests à la Margo Channing. "I didn't like the show very much," says Mankiewicz, "but I kept telling her how wonderful she was and how marvelous the production was. Many years [before], Moss Hart taught me that when you go backstage out of town [during a tryout], you tell the truth; in New York [when the show has been "frozen"] you lie. Kate kept insisting that there must have been something I didn't like. I said, 'No, no. Everything was just marvelous.' She kept after me for so long that I finally capitulated. I knew they'd been on the road forever with this production, and they had been playing vast arenas like the Kansas City Auditorium, and so they were all shouting a bit. For an intimate theater like the old Biltmore in downtown Los Angeles it was a little loud, and I told her so. She suddenly froze and said, 'You film people think everything is too loud!' I had fallen into the trap . . . the actress's ploy."

Mankiewicz was not about to be taken in again. As he explains it, "Kate wanted very much to direct herself in *Suddenly, Last Summer*. This is a battle I don't think a director can ever afford to lose, because the first time I lose that battle, then I must give up directing. I refused to lose that battle, and I insisted on the performance being played my way."

While Hepburn had boned up on Tennessee Williams's work and was certainly familiar with the role of Mrs. Venable and the subject matter of *Suddenly, Last Summer* before she accepted the part, it appears she had second thoughts about it after production began. Hepburn's producer-writer friend Chester Erskine tried to persuade her that not only was Mrs. Venable the best-written role but that it was a character part, rather than the lead, which justified her taking second billing to another actress for the first time in her career. In turn,

Hepburn protested to Erskine that she found the role "unsympathetic and wanted to play the woman as insane in order to distance the role or remove herself from identification with it."

The struggle between the director and the star began with the filming of Hepburn's entrance. She descends in a thronelike private elevator to greet Clift. Designer Oliver Messel's gilded, ornately carved elevator cage nestled between two white metal palm poles, and Gore Vidal's amusingly imperious dialogue ("My son Sebastian always said, 'Mother, you look like . . . the goddess descending from the machine.' . . . Are you interested in the Byzantine, Doctor?") are sufficiently bizarre, yet Hepburn wanted to kick the elevator gate open with a great flourish to suggest Mrs. Venable's lunacy. Since Violet Venable's collapse into regressive dementia, when she mistakes the doctor for her dead son, occurs only at the end of the film, Mankiewicz knew Violet's behavior should be confined to haughty eccentricity until this climax. To placate Hepburn, Mankiewicz consented to shooting the scene her way and his, although he never had any intention of using her version.

Throughout the film, Mankiewicz was obliged to pacify his shrewish Kate. Mrs. Donald Ogden Stewart, the wife of Hepburn's old screenwriter friend, recalls a typical argument, off the set, with Hepburn telling Mankiewicz, "If you only knew what it means to me when I have to say those things!" Joe soothed, "That's the play, and that's what we have to do."

If Hepburn's friend and chronicler Garson Kanin is to be believed, Violet Venable's self-delusion in maintaining that her son was chaste and her denial that she had helped lure attractive young men for him were not so far removed from Hepburn's own refusal to acknowledge the existence of homosexuality. Kanin contends that in a Paris hotel suite in 1961, more than a year after *Suddenly, Last Summer*'s release, he and Spencer Tracy described homosexual acts in laborious detail to Hepburn, who maintained her firm disbelief in the existence of such ridiculous practices.[25]

What evidently precipitated Hepburn's final blowup with Mankiewicz was an ingenious and apt transformation in her appearance he devised with his cameraman Jack Hildyard. "When she [Mrs. Venable]

[25]Garson Kanin, "The Private Kate," *McCall's*, February 1970, pp. 109–10. This anecdote does not appear in Kanin's subsequent memoir, *Tracy & Hepburn* (Viking Press, 1971), although the rest of the article is incorporated.

spoke of her son," Mankiewicz explains, "we had her look as young and as beautiful as was possible, which with Kate was then still very possible [with the aid of diffusion lenses]. At the end, I remember we shot her hands [first opening and later closing her son's empty composition book from his fatal summer] after Catherine has told the truth. I wanted them to look like an old woman's hands. Kate didn't like that close-up nor the last one of her before she went to the elevator.[26] I wanted her suddenly to look old. In other words, the destruction of the legend about Sebastian, her son, destroyed her illusion of youth. I think Kate sensed what Jack and I were up to [that is, removing the diffusion lenses and making her lighting harsh], and she didn't like what I was doing." Hepburn wanted to preserve the illusion of her screen beauty, and the comparison of her seamed and freckled hands and face juxtaposed with close-ups of the gorgeous Taylor is especially unflattering.

The upshot was that after her final day on the film, Hepburn contemptuously spat at Mankiewicz in front of a shocked assemblage on the sound stage and then repeated this unladylike gesture in the producer's office by way of a farewell to Sam Spiegel.

"To the best of my knowledge, she never saw the film," says Mankiewicz. People tell me that she refused to see it." If, in fact, Hepburn never has seen *Suddenly, Last Summer,* she has missed one of her most extraordinary performances. Tennessee Williams, who has publicly denounced the picture,[27] thought that Hepburn and Taylor were miscast and told a biographer that "he sensed that Hepburn was unhappy with her part."[28] However, Garson Kanin quotes Williams as having written, "Kate is a playwright's dream actress. She makes dialogue sound better than it is by a matchless beauty and clarity of diction, and by a fineness of intelligence and sensibility that illuminates every shade of meaning in every line she speaks."[29]

Williams's testimonial accurately describes Hepburn's scintillat-

[26]The unflattering, nonfiltered Hepburn close-ups are actually three reaction shots of her face and two of her hands during Taylor's speech.
[27]In 1972 Tennessee Williams told a *Village Voice* reporter that the film "made me throw up." He commented to a biographer, Nancy Tischler, shortly after the film's release in December 1959, that in the film there were "unfortunate concessions to the realism that Hollywood is too often afraid to discard. And so a short morality play, in a lyrical style, was turned into a sensationally successful film that the public thinks was a literal study of such things as cannibalism, madness, and sexual deviation" (Tischler, *Tennessee Williams: Rebellious Puritan,* p. 257).
[28]Tischler, *Tennessee Williams: Rebellious Puritan,* p. 257.
[29]Kanin, *Tracy & Hepburn,* pp. 223–24.

ing recitations in *Suddenly, Last Summer,* in which her mannered speech perfectly suits Williams's fevered prose. Even Mankiewicz, who now terms Hepburn "the most experienced amateur actress in the world," most of "whose performances . . . though remarkably effective . . . are fake," and "who now can't turn off the tears," concedes she gave "a damned brilliant performance" in *Suddenly.*

Mankiewicz is deservedly proud of the performance he obtained from Elizabeth Taylor and of the remarkable flashback sequence he devised to illustrate her narration of Sebastian's death.

The only real deficiency in Taylor's performance as Catherine is that she never allows us to feel any ambiguity about her sanity. Catherine's traumatic experiences, her forced isolation, punitive treatment, and sedation in the asylum, and the impending threat of a lobotomy sanctioned by her family might well have turned her into the violent creature her aunt told the surgeon she was. But Taylor plays Catherine's attempts at escape and suicide so that they appear perfectly rational. As Dr. Cukrowicz and the audience perceive from the outset, it is Mrs. Venable who is demented and vicious and Catherine who is reasonable and kind. In consequence, the suspense is negligible, and the melodramatic story seems to be nothing more than a delay before Catherine's exoneration.

Mankiewicz insists that "it was the best screen performance Elizabeth Taylor ever gave," and many critics agree. As she had demonstrated in the role of Maggie in *Cat on a Hot Tin Roof* (1958), Taylor's film role previous to *Suddenly, Last Summer,* Tennessee Williams's tormented heroines are well suited to her talents, provided that she receives the guidance of painstaking directors like Richard Brooks *(Cat)* and Mankiewicz.

Suddenly's flashback sequence is the most imaginative in any of Mankiewicz's films. The bleached quality of the black-and-white print is the perfect correlative to the "bone white sun" refrain from Catherine's monologue. Catherine's long-repressed, painful flashes of memory,[30] brought forth with the aid of Dr. Cukrowicz's "truth serum"

---

[30]For Catherine's first, unsuccessful attempt to recall Sebastian's death, Mankiewicz employed an aural rather than a visual flashback. Catherine manages to recapture a passage from the urchins' "cacaphonous music," the steel-band processional that we hear in its entirety when she remembers the complete event at the end of the film. Mankiewicz's claim that Sidney Lumet's use of subliminal flash cuts in *The Pawnbroker* (1965) derives from the flashback sequence in *Suddenly, Last Summer* is not substantiated by the released film.

(sodium pentathol), are conveyed in a series of dissolves. Mankiewicz and his editor alternate back and forth between light and dark close-ups of Taylor's face, which they move from the center to the edge of the frame to reveal images of the summer's events as they become clear to Catherine again. Mankiewicz symbolically repeats the image of the skeletal angel of death, a statue twice seen in the Venable "jungle garden," by having Sebastian, in his flight from the pursuing urchins, run past a seated skeleton in a cloak. As Catherine follows, we see that this phantom is actually a cloaked old woman peddler. Then, as Catherine witnesses the cannibal rite, performed in the ruins of an ancient temple, the skeletal statue briefly supplants Catherine at the right edge of the picture frame.

Sebastian's imploring hand, the only part of his body that protrudes from the dark horde of his devourers, is a memorable image that was subsequently employed by director John Boorman for *Deliverance* (1972), in which the final, nightmarish shot is of a corpse's hand jutting from the river.

This discreetly suggestive sequence of procurement and cannibalism and some "snake-pit" shots of the lunatics at the mental asylum are Mankiewicz's only visual concessions to the audience's voyeuristic appetite. Except for the ending, Mankiewicz refused to illustrate the long speeches in which Catherine and Mrs. Venable relate their memories to Dr. Cukrowicz. Mrs. Venable's lengthy prattle about her wondrous son and her trip with him to view the savagery in the Encantadas, shortly followed by Catherine's confession, which tells of her seduction by a married man and her maltreatment at the asylum, though brilliantly scored, paced, and performed, form a talkathon unalleviated by imagery or physical action.

The expectation of the executives of Columbia Pictures, the company distributing the film, was that the picture was too rarefied and highbrow to be commercial. At best, they hoped for a *succès d'estime*, with critical accolades for the performances and for the screenplay's fidelity to Williams's text.

Sam Spiegel attributed Williams's giggling through a private screening at Spiegel's New York apartment to the playwright's inebriation. But the producer could not so easily discount the numerous reviews that disparaged the film as ludicrous claptrap or hothouse melodrama. Spiegel was "extremely depressed" by these notices, according to reports that reached Christopher Mankiewicz.

To counter the negative reviews and the film's inexplicit content, Spiegel and Columbia's publicity department devised an ad campaign featuring Elizabeth Taylor spilling out of a low-cut white bathing suit with the copy line, "Suddenly last summer, Cathy knew she was being used for evil." The *zaftig* bathing beauty proved as magnetic a lure for the movie-going public as she did, in the film, for the young men Sebastian coveted at the public beach. Williams's reputation for perversity, combined with the critics' denunciation of the film's subject matter, served to rouse the public's curiosity. *Variety* lists the net return to Columbia as $6,375,000, exclusive of foreign revenues, which may well have doubled this figure.

Christopher Mankiewicz says that his father "was very upset at the injustice" of his not receiving an Academy Award nomination for direction, since both Elizabeth Taylor and Katharine Hepburn were nominated for the Best Actress award.[31] Nonetheless, the actresses' outstanding performances and *Suddenly, Last Summer*'s great commercial success dimmed the movie moguls' memory of Mankiewicz's previous fiascos in the fifties and made him, once more, one of America's most sought-after directors.

---

[31]Just as Bette Davis and Anne Baxter split the Best Actress vote for *All About Eve*, the nomination of both Taylor and Hepburn for *Suddenly, Last Summer* doubtless aided the victory of Simone Signoret for her role in *Room at the Top*. William Wyler took the directing award for *Ben-Hur*, a film Mankiewicz detested.

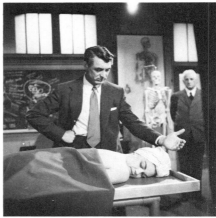

Mankiewicz demonstrates the anatomy lesson for Cary
Grant in *People Will Talk* (1951), and Grant follows Joe's
instructions, with Finlay Currie looking on in the background. *Courtesy Movie Star News*

Directing Jeanne Crain in *People Will Talk*, Mankiewicz's change of facial expression foreshadows his later
crack, "I don't like the name Deborah [Crain's character],
and I don't like Jeanne Crain." *Courtesy Movie Star News*

Mankiewicz and Ethel Barrymore present Walter Hampden with a scroll honoring his fifty years in the theater. Hampden was playing the English ambassador, Sir Frederic, in *Five Fingers,* Joe's last picture under his Fox contract, which terminated in the autumn of 1951.

Rosa looks furious while Mankiewicz feigns a smile. His mesmeric eye pop is caught by the photographer. Joe most likely caught hell at home after this formal occasion.
Courtesy Christopher Mankiewicz

In a preproduction rehearsal conference during the summer of 1952, a slippered but gloveless Mankiewicz confers with three stars of *Julius Caesar:* John Gielgud, Greer Garson, and Deborah Kerr. *Courtesy the Memory Shop*

It is unlikely that director Mankiewicz or MGM's production chief Dore Schary actually took much interest in the cinex strip that Joseph Ruttenberg, *Julius Caesar*'s veteran photographer, is showing them. The cutter's glove on Joe's right hand covers the painful skin ailment often brought on by the pressures of production.

Mankiewicz giving a pointer during *Julius Caesar*. That is a technician, not a Roman bust, behind the camera.

Courtesy Adelaide Wallace

Mankiewicz showing Brando how to rage over Caesar's murder in the "Oh, pardon me, thou bleeding piece of earth" soliloquy. John Gielgud had already provided private instruction.

Courtesy the Museum of Modern Art/Film Stills Archive

Brando relaxing while Mankiewicz instructs him in delivering Antony's funeral oration. *Courtesy Adelaide Wallace*

The last day of filming *Julius Caesar.* Mankiewicz shows his puny force of warriors in the Battle of Philippi how to bear a shield. (Note the "plains" of Hollywood's Bronson Canyon in the background.) *Courtesy Adelaide Wallace*

The Mankiewicz family returns home on the *Cristoforo Colombo,* after the completion of *The Barefoot Contessa* in late summer 1954. LEFT TO RIGHT: Christopher, Joe, Rosa, and Tom. *Courtesy Christopher Mankiewicz*

Mankiewicz was much closer to Jean Simmons (in her Salvation Army costume) during the filming of *Guys and Dolls* (1955) than this photograph would indicate. Notice the odd juxtaposition of the real wet pavement and taxis against the stylized Times Square backdrop.

Mankiewicz and *Guys and Dolls* choreographer Michael Kidd looking rather pleased with themselves. Perhaps Brando's dancing is the source of their glee. *Photograph by Phil Stern, courtesy Adelaide Wallace*

Frank Sinatra speaks to his director during a setup on *Guys and Dolls.*
Sinatra's rivalry with Marlon Brando limited their exchanges to the script's
dialogue.   *Photograph by Phil Stern, courtesy Adelaide Wallace*

Mankiewicz instructs the
American (Audie Murphy) how
to react to his sabotaged car in
The Quiet American. Because of
the uprising of the Cao Daists in
Vietnam (1957), the shooting
was moved to Cinecittà Studios
in Rome. This set is a mock-up of
a Tay-Ninh exterior.

Mankiewicz giving a Viet-
namese girl a piece of "business"
during the opening Tet New
Year sequence of *The Quiet
American,* on location in Saigon,
January 1957.

A family gathering at New York's Plaza Hotel during the Christmas holidays in 1958. On the far right are Herman's daughter, Johanna (Josie, Joe's hostess in place of his deceased wife, Rosa), and Joe. To their right are Myra Fox, Josie's cousin, Tom Mankiewicz (in from Exeter), Anne Adler, Josie's closest friend and roommate at Wellesley, and Christopher Mankiewicz, an undergraduate at Columbia, Joe's alma mater.   *Courtesy Mrs. Sara Mankiewicz*

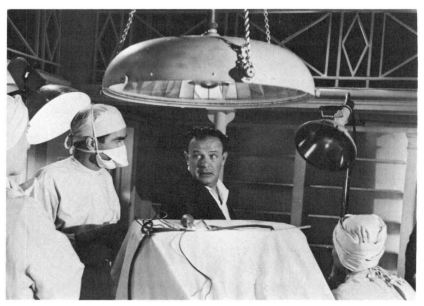

Mankiewicz under the faulty operating theater lamp. The masked surgeon, Montgomery Clift, was unusually shaky in this first filmed sequence of *Suddenly, Last Summer*, at Shepperton Studios in London, 1959.

The master of all he surveys contemplates Cleopatra's triumphal entry into the massive Roman Forum set on a fortunately sunny day at Rome's Cinecittà lot.

Courtesy Cinemabilia

Happy days early in the production of *Cleopatra* (October 1961). Joe's fellow pipe smoker, on the left, is his buddy Hume Cronyn. The smiling chap behind the sunglasses is Richard Burton. *Courtesy Adelaide Wallace*

Rex Harrison often drove Mankiewicz to distraction with his nit-picking. In this shot, as Caesar, he appears to be questioning the authenticity of Antony's (Burton's) medallion, early in the filming of *Cleopatra* (October 1961). Christopher Mankiewicz, in the center, took off a term from Columbia University to work on the film as an assistant director.

Courtesy Adelaide Wallace

Mankiewicz instructing his attentive Cleopatra (1961). Note the prominent tracheotomy scar below Elizabeth Taylor's neck.   *Courtesy Adelaide Wallace*

Script supervisor Stanley Scheuer holding a portion of the script for a mock argument in a comic publicity shot between Martin Landau (Rufio) and Mankiewicz.   *Courtesy Stanley Scheuer*

It is a matter of conjecture as to what prompted the interesting facial expressions of *Cleopatra*'s principals. The scene, shot in late January 1962, was the first between Burton and Taylor, but Mankiewicz already knew of their off-screen liaison.

Poker expert Mankiewicz stacks the deck for Cecil Fox (Rex Harrison) and his always-victorious opponent McFly (Cliff Robertson) for a long take in *The Honey Pot*. The clapstick reveals the film was then titled *Anyone for Venice?* (autumn 1965, Rome's Cinecittà Studios). *Courtesy the Memory Shop*

Mankiewicz directs Rex Harrison as the dying prospector in the Texan "desert dream fantasy," a scene that was cut from the released version of *The Honey Pot* but shown at the film's London premiere in March 1967.

Courtesy the Memory Shop

Proud papa Joe shoulders his first daughter, Alexandra, from his union with his third wife, Rosemary Matthews. Circa 1968.

Courtesy Mrs. Sara Mankiewicz

Joe mugs for the camera. Swaddled Alexandra is poised in her perambulator.

Courtesy Mrs. Sara Mankiewicz

Mankiewicz gestures in the sweltering heat of Joshua Tree National Park's desert while filming *There Was a Crooked Man* . . . in 1969, with Kirk Douglas. The film's juvenile, Michael Blodgett, is on the left.

Laurence Olivier, as the imperious Andrew Wyke in *Sleuth*, imitates his director's clutching gesture. The mechanical mandarin, left corner, has got it down pat.

JUST AS MANKIEWICZ HAD RETURNED TO MGM AFTER AN ACRIMO-nious departure and nearly a decade's absence, when a new regime had taken office, so he once again signed a contract to write and direct films for Twentieth Century–Fox.

Darryl F. Zanuck, whose dictatorial insistence on final cuts had led to Mankiewicz's severing his ties with the studio, ended his reign as Fox's production chief in 1956 to pursue a career as an independent producer based in Paris. His independent production deal was not the common severence agreement concluded by film studios with a depart-ing production chief. A principal shareholder in Fox, Zanuck was able to compel the company to distribute his DFZ productions. These European films featured a succession of Zanuck's protégée-companions whom he was determined to make into movie stars. Invariably, the pictures—and the protégées—proved to be dismal failures.

Even before his departure from the studio he ruled, Zanuck had begun his series of European discoveries with the untalented Bella Darvi, whose last name was a conflation of Darryl and Virginia, the name of Zanuck's tolerant wife. After Darvi had flopped in such pic-tures as *The Egyptian* (1954) and *The Racers* (1955), Zanuck retired her, although he felt obliged to pay off her heavy gambling debts at the casinos to which he had introduced her.

Zanuck's next protégée, the first companion of his Parisian exile, was Juliette Greco, who had already made a name for herself by singing in fashionable Paris *boîtes*. Zanuck began her film career with roles in such major Fox productions of his as *The Sun Also Rises* (1957) and *The Roots of Heaven* (1958) and eventually starred her in his independent DFZ turkeys *A Crack in the Mirror* (1960) and *The Big Gamble* (1961). Zanuck's "star treatment" was equally ineffectual in launching the careers of his subsequent mistresses, Irina Demick and Genevieve Gilles, but he persisted in his sodden folly until Gilles's embarrassing failure in *Hello–Goodbye* (1970).

The first of Zanuck's independent productions was to be the heavily publicized *De Luxe Tour*, a travelogue-romance based on a novel by Frederic Wakeman. During the summer of 1957, Zanuck and his entourage spent a small fortune filming background footage and scouting locations in a converted B-25 bomber flown by the celebrated stunt pilot Paul Mantz. After many writers had tried to produce a satisfactory screenplay, Zanuck was obliged to turn to Mankiewicz for help. "[Zanuck] was scrounging around trying to get anyone to do anything for him," Joe recalls, and Mankiewicz's rejection of *De Luxe Tour* doubtless exacerbated an already antagonistic relationship at a desperate point in Zanuck's career. Zanuck abandoned the picture, but it is unlikely he forgot Mankiewicz's refusal.

A property offered by Fox's new production chief, Buddy Adler, was much more to Mankiewicz's taste for prestigious projects. The material he was asked to adapt and direct was Stephen Vincent Benét's epic Civil War narrative poem, *John Brown's Body*.[1]

Mankiewicz was delighted with the prospect that a film of *John Brown's Body* could be released in time to commemorate the 1961 centennial of the commencement of the Civil War. He was particularly fond of the work and says he planned "to use a great deal of Benét's text," probably as linking narration between Mankiewicz-written scenes. "I love *John Brown's Body*," says Mankiewicz. "I really wanted it to be an important film." Although Mankiewicz says he intended the

---

[1]Interest in Benét's work, which had dwindled after the poem had won a Pulitzer Prize in 1929, had been revived by a successful staged reading of the work, directed by Charles Laughton in 1952. The play starred a quartet of name actors headed by Tyrone Power. Like its predecessor, *Don Juan in Hell*, the production had a triumphal national tour that culminated in a critically heralded run on Broadway and a two-record album.

film to run only about two and a half hours, the Fox brass (principally, Fox's president, Spyros Skouras, who monitored budgets in New York and dictated to production chief Adler at the studio in Los Angeles) must have been scared off by the scope of Mankiewicz's projected treatment since, according to Joe, they decided the picture would be too expensive.

Mankiewicz believes that Fox's decision to cancel was also based on the old Hollywood bugaboo that Civil War films are ipso facto commercial liabilities, despite the enormous success of *Gone with the Wind.* "Mr. Skouras and Mr. Buddy Adler [may have] remembered Thalberg's great dictum when he turned down *GWTW* for MGM," says Joe, "which I heard when I wanted to do [the film] with Gable and Crawford. Louis Mayer sent for Thalberg, who told him, 'Forget it. No Civil War picture ever made money.' He said that because [Thalberg] had just done one with Marion Davies, *Operator 13* [1934], which went on its ass.² This mystique lingered in Twentieth's mind, so *John Brown's Body* [was buried]."

Ironically, while Fox had shifted Mankiewicz away from a Civil War epic because it was too costly, they next gave him the even more massive job of condensing Lawrence Durrell's *Alexandria Quartet* into a single film to be called *Justine.* While Durrell's *Quartet* had become the rage of literary cultists with the British publication of the first novel, *Justine,* in 1956 and had gained in popularity through the release of the fourth volume, *Clea,* in 1960, it is doubtful that anyone at the studio above the story editor was familiar with the scope of the entire work. More than likely, the studio hoped that Mankiewicz, a specialist in complex feminine psychology, would be able to reduce the convoluted tale of the novel's femme fatale, Justine, whose devious history is revealed from the points of view of a number of her intimates, into a vehicle for a star and her satellites in the mode of *All About Eve.* (In fact, Mankiewicz and his producer, Walter Wanger, had Elizabeth Taylor in mind for the role.)

Mankiewicz's dismay over the cancellation of *John Brown's Body* ended when he got the dream assignment of tackling Durrell's labyrinthine masterwork. The great challenge for Mankiewicz was to find a

---

²MGM ultimately got to distribute *Gone with the Wind* in exchange for loaning out Clark Gable to David O. Selznick, the film's producer.

cinematic equivalent for the space-time-relativity structure employed by Durrell in the novel.[3]

Durrell's protagonist and principal narrator is Darley, the young Anglo-Irish schoolteacher and would-be novelist. While the novel charts Darley's intellectual and emotional maturation into artistry, both Darley's and Mankiewicz's fascination lies in determining the "truth" about the fabulously rich, beautiful, and mysterious Justine, the dark lady with whom Darley has had a short but unforgettable love affair.

In kaleidoscopic fashion the novel and Mankiewicz's incomplete screenplay present a contradictory series of revelations about Justine as she is perceived by her sophisticated coterie in Alexandria, the "dream city" of lust and intrigue. The major revelation is that Justine and her husband, Nessim (possibly her true love, despite her strategic infidelities), are involved in a Coptic plot against the Moslems to arm the Zionist forces in Palestine. The psychosexual relations of almost every conceivable variety masking this political conspiracy provided Mankiewicz with subject matter of especial fascination.

The material also offered Mankiewicz the opportunity to use his favorite techniques—numerous flashbacks and several narrators with different points of view, employed to assemble a composite portrait of the subject. As Mankiewicz wrote in his screenplay treatment, "The problem [is] not only the multiplicity of the flashbacks, but also the necessity for them 'to interlap and interweave' [Durrell's description], while at the same time contributing to the progress of a straightforward, dramatic story line."

Mankiewicz expounded on this problem of storytelling in 1973, thirteen years after wrestling with it. "If you set out to [write] a film in which you hear about a woman from four points of view . . . the fact that none of the four is true [should] hit you with a jolt, [and] each of those four [stories] had better be pretty well told, so at no point does the audience say, 'I'm being misled here.' You've got to keep an audience in the state of mind, 'At last I'm hearing the truth because

---

[3]In *The Novel Now* (Faber & Faber, 1971, p. 97) novelist Anthony Burgess provides an accurate description of the work by writing, "[as] one novel of the *Quartet* [is] concerned with time, and the other three with the 'three sides of space' we can never see the whole of any given character or event in one novel alone."

this all makes sense,' and end up [with them] saying, 'For Chrissake, it was [all] wrong.' " This statement suggests that Mankiewicz was in the process of changing his view of character revelation from the psychologically explicable (Eve, Maria Vargas, Fowler) to the ultimately enigmatic (Justine).

Mankiewicz's apparent "solution," on the basis of approximately half of the first-draft screenplay that he completed, was progressively to fill in the beginnings or endings of scenes we have previously witnessed, that is, showing us what "really" happened before or after the narrating character had entered or left a given scene.

What Mankiewicz evidently had not solved was how to condense the entire *Quartet* into even an exceptionally long feature-length film. The half-completed first draft ran 674 typed, triple-spaced pages and represented only 76 pages of Mankiewicz's 151-page "Treatment Outline." In his introduction to this treatment, Mankiewicz acknowledged "that the screenplay . . . is at least twice too long," because of repetitions, some of which, he claimed, "were deliberate and dramatically valid."

Mankiewicz is a hapless editor of his own work because of his propensity to articulate every scene. He has no faith in the eloquence of scenes with little or no dialogue, and so in refining his work, he tends to expand rather than contract. (The most recent example of this quirk was his half-hour tribute to Bette Davis in 1977, which he intended to reduce from his original ten-minute speech to each speaker's allotted three minutes.)

Mankiewicz issued a valid disclaimer in stating that his outline would be "literally unintelligible to anyone who has not read carefully all four of Durrell's books." Since this warning "effectively eliminated everyone at the studio with the exception of Richard Zanuck [Darryl's son and heir apparent]," Mankiewicz was obliged to content himself with the enthusiastic reaction of *Quartet*'s author, Lawrence Durrell. "Larry said it was all there," says Mankiewicz, "though I did leave out Scobie [an English pederast scoutmaster employed by the Egyptian police], didn't I?" (The extreme length of Mankiewicz's projected treatment and first draft of *Justine* recalls the inordinate length of his stage version of *Jefferson Selleck* and forecasts his subsequent protracted screenplays for *Cleopatra* and *The Honey Pot*. Both of these films ultimately suffered damaging cuts as a result of their excessive running time.) In retrospect, Mankiewicz says, "I don't think my *Justine* would have cost what the final *Justine* cost," referring to the unfortunate version that Fox released in 1969.[4]

The partial screenplay of *Justine* contains more of Mankiewicz's own observations and apposite autobiographical material than practically any of his realized films. For example, an exchange between Pursewarden, an established author, and Darley, his admirer and would-be emulator, is reminiscent of Max Beerbohm's drawings of the elderly famous speaking in balloon captions to their younger selves, had Max included Joe in this series:

> PURSEWARDEN: We are bondsmen, you and I, fellow writers, heavy with a sense of different, deep, personal failure.
> DARLEY: Your writing has brought you the promise of financial security. Your name has acquired a reputation bordering on greatness—has no happiness come with all that?
> PURSEWARDEN: You'll find yourself more and more wanting in true greatness—while your name gets bigger day by day like some disgusting poster. You'll find yourself walked with and talked with and slept with—as a reputation bordering on being a man but not a man. You'll find your bloody name covering you like a tombstone.

A commemoration of "Pop" Mankiewicz's philosophy is contained in the following reproof:

> JUSTINE: Never say that word [*poor*]. My father was a scholar of great wisdom and no wealth. He forbade the word in our house except to describe the economic condition. The *poor* human is the mediocre one, the one who has failed.

Even the favorite Mankiewicz notion of the desirability of interracial marriage is put forth by his wise and cynical mouthpiece, the writer Pursewarden:

> LORD ERROL: Still, it seems one must choose.
> PURSEWARDEN: Not if the choice is between black and white. Why? . . . My own feeling is that the world will be unable to know peace or plenty until the inevitable day when our skins are one rather attractive beige color and our flags nonexistent.

---

[4]Fox eventually assigned the film, written by Lawrence B. Marcus, to director Joseph Strick, in the mistaken belief that the man who had tackled as vast a work as Joyce's *Ulysses* could make a film out of Durrell's epic novel. Almost all of Strick's work, filmed on African locations with an international cast, was scrapped. With inadequate time to prepare, George Cukor was given the hopeless task of reshooting the entire film on the Fox lot. The result was a gorgeous but nearly incomprehensible picture.

During the winter of 1960, Mankiewicz was basking in the comfort of Hume Cronyn's Bahamian retreat, Children's Bay Cay, delighted with his daily progress on the script of *Justine* and the company of Jeanne Vanderbilt.

In London at the same time, *Justine*'s future producer, Walter Wanger, and Mankiewicz's employer, Twentieth Century–Fox, were losing millions trying to film Wanger's long-delayed production, *Cleopatra,* starring high-priced Elizabeth Taylor. (Taylor became committed to *Cleopatra* only when Fox accepted what she expected would be a prohibitive demand for a $1 million fee, against 10 percent of the gross, the first such salary in motion-picture history.) Taylor's fragile health, repeatedly shattered by London's inclement weather and the freezing sound stages of Pinewood Studios, a ludicrous script manufactured by a series of writers, and the perfectionist demands of the director, Rouben Mamoulian, had already cost $1 million more than the film's $6 million budget, and only ten and a half minutes of the film had been shot.

Cleopatra already had a history of problems. In 1958 Wanger had initiated the project, and John De Cuir, *Cleopatra*'s art director, had begun building the ancient city of Alexandria on Fox's back lot. When Fox sold this valuable Beverly Hills real estate to the future builders of Century City, preventing the construction of the exterior sets, Mamoulian welcomed the opportunity to shoot *Cleopatra* in Rome, with locations in Egypt.

De Cuir once more began erecting Egyptian temples, this time on the site of the present Rome airport, and began extending lakes to accommodate galley ships. But one of Fox production chief Buddy Adler's last acts, prior to his death from cancer in 1960, was to order a halt to the construction in Rome and to transfer the production to London.

Bob Goldstein, Fox's London-based European representative and Adler's successor, had prevailed on Spyros Skouras to take advantage of Great Britain's Eady Plan (which granted financial incentive to foreign filmmakers) and Fox's frozen assets in England. (Goldstein was the producer of Fox's notorious *Snow White and the Three Stooges* [1961]. Mankiewicz describes him as "only capable, with difficulty, of ordering a ham sandwich.") The ensuing disaster was, of course, blamed on the dead Adler by the surviving Fox executives.

In order to stifle any opposition from Mamoulian, the decision to shift the production was made without consulting him. The director's only purpose in flying to London was to remedy the unsatisfactory screenplay by English novelist Nigel Balchin. To Mamoulian's surprise, he was met at the airport by John De Cuir, whom he thought was busily engaged in supervising and designing the sets in Rome. In the course of their drive into town, Mamoulian caught a distant glimpse of palm trees ludicrously dotting the suburban London landscape. According to De Cuir, Mamoulian turned as green as the lush English grass, asked the driver to stop the car, and proceeded to vomit over the railing of the parkway for the next fifteen minutes, incredulous and furious at the Fox management's double-cross.

Mamoulian was to receive another blow from Elizabeth Taylor, but De Cuir maintains that Mamoulian had set himself up for it by making two fatal mistakes. The first was in rejecting the first twenty-five pages of a new script of *Cleopatra* by none other than Lawrence Durrell, who, according to Walter Wanger, had previously insisted that he "would have nothing to do with movies or Hollywood." De Cuir terms Durrell's work "absolutely sensational, dazzling," and doubtless it was, in comparison to the tripe fashioned by Nigel Balchin and rewritten by Dale Wasserman *(Man of La Mancha).* But Mamoulian would have none of it, denouncing Durrell's pages as "absolute crap . . . nothing but sensationalism," and steadfastly refusing "to be associated with a man who thought and wrote that way."

Mamoulian's second error was in assuming that he had Taylor firmly in his corner and Skouras in his pocket. Filming began on September 28, 1960, and was suspended on November 18, with Taylor frequently bedridden by viruses or sickened by the script. Mamoulian stalled, waiting for Fox's veteran screenwriter Nunnally Johnson to come up with a suitable screenplay, but Fox demanded that shooting resume on January 3, 1961. Mamoulian had frequently tendered his resignation, secure in the belief that Skouras, who had engaged him, would never accept it. Skouras's patience, sorely taxed by the production's mounting costs and his studio's series of box-office flops, was wearing thin. Mamoulian quit once too often. When he resigned on January 18, he believed that he had the wholehearted support of his star. "What he didn't know" was that Skouras had privately contacted Taylor, who strongly urged that Mamoulian be replaced by Mankiewicz, in whom she had great confidence after *Suddenly, Last Summer.* In turn, Skouras leaped at the idea of hiring Joe, who was not only a director respected by Taylor, but an elegant writer capable of fashioning a satisfactory shooting script.

Producer Wanger, not wanting to interrupt Joe's work on Wanger's next project, *Justine,* was opposed to the idea. So was Mankiewicz, who, when contacted in the Bahamas, flatly declined the offer. Skouras was determined to have him at any price. (In the movie business an outright refusal provides the greatest possible incentive to escalate an offer, especially when a studio is in desperate need of a particular talent.) Skouras contacted Charles Feldman, Mankiewicz's agent at the time, and pleaded with him to summon his client to a face-to-face meeting. Scenting big money, Feldman prevailed on Mankiewicz to return to New York for a parley with Skouras.

During lunch at the Colony, Skouras asked Mankiewicz to name his own figure. "I said I was earning as much money as I wanted to earn, writing what I loved writing, which was *The Alexandria Quartet,*" says Mankiewicz. "Skouras and Feldman both tried to come up with some way of getting me a lot of money tax free . . . a fabulous villa in the South of France or a big yacht." Pleading ignorance of such tax-free schemes, Mankiewicz insisted that they confer next day with his lawyer, Abe Bienstock, at Joe's townhouse. At this meeting Feldman broached the tax-free gift of a huge yacht, and according to Joe, Bienstock commented, "I think it would be a wonderful gift because I enjoy cruising on yachts, and I would love to be Joe's guest. But it wouldn't be as much fun to be a yacht-party guest if Joe wasn't there, and he won't be, because he'll be in a federal penitentiary for income-tax evasion. That is the last I want to hear of tax-free gifts under any circumstances whatsoever."

Skouras was undeterred and suggested a capital-gains deal whereby Fox would acquire Joe's services by buying his company, Figaro, Inc. Mankiewicz told Feldman that he didn't want to give up *Justine,* but Feldman persuaded him that he could still do the Durrell work after *Cleopatra* and that this offer was probably the only opportunity he would ever have to make real "keeping money," as opposed to his usual highly taxed salaries. His advice to Joe was, "Hold your nose for fifteen weeks and get it over with."

The asking price set by Mankiewicz's representatives for Figaro was a steep $1.5 million. The desperate Skouras agreed. The hitch was that NBC, which owned 50 percent of Figaro, demanded half the booty, and Joe had no interest in parting with any of it. If Fox wanted him that badly they would simply have to pay NBC an equal $1.5 million. Skouras wound up forking over $3 million, in addition to Mankiewicz's salary and expenses—surely the highest sum ever paid for the services of a director.

Mankiewicz flew to London on February 1, four days after the announcement of his engagement as writer-director, to conduct the salvage operation.

Production designer De Cuir and producer Wanger met Mankiewicz at the airport. De Cuir describes him as appearing "very dour and sad" on his arrival. Joe's gloomy mood was not alleviated by his trip to Pinewood. He viewed the ten and a half minutes of film Mamoulian had shot and pronounced them unusable. The footage included a conventional scene of Cleopatra's introduction to Caesar (Peter Finch) by being unrolled from a carpet, and a weird symbolic chase scene between Antony (Stephen Boyd) on a stallion and Cleopatra on a mare. Mankiewicz found it equally bizarre that Mamoulian had, inexplicably, shot thousands of feet of wardrobe tests with an unnecessary sound track. Mankiewicz next inspected John De Cuir's sets, the exteriors already corroding from winter storms, and proclaimed them "a garish disaster."[5]

The major problem area that Mankiewicz was saddled with was the script, which he called "unreadable and unshootable," a pretentious fairy tale about "a virgin who could only be deflowered by a god," filled with "ornate cat symbolism."[6] He begged for time to write a new script from scratch. With overhead expenses running at $45,000 per day, even with the production shut down, and the insurance companies contesting the studio's compensatory claim for losses resulting from bad weather and Taylor's illnesses, Fox allowed Joe only two months for preparation. Shooting was scheduled to resume on April 4. The company did provide for some high-priced collaborative help in writing the new screenplay by permitting Mankiewicz to engage Lawrence Durrell and Sidney Buchman, formerly a top Hollywood screenwriter *(Theodora Goes Wild, Mr. Smith Goes to Washington)* before his

[5]De Cuir says that Mankiewicz later tempered this appraisal by saying that there were "too many sets and that they were overbuilt." "When I pinned him down," says De Cuir, "he accepted them all, and agreed that there would be no tearing down or remodeling." Mankiewicz says that he still has no idea what scene required an elaborate underwater tank set.
[6]Dick Sheppard, *Elizabeth*, Doubleday, 1974, pp. 257 and 261.

blacklisting and subsequent emigration to London.

Mankiewicz closeted himself in a comfortable suite at the Connaught Hotel and buckled down to a crash program of round-the-clock writing with his colleagues. However, the urgency of their labor was curbed by the alarming news on March 4 that Elizabeth Taylor was in critical condition with lung congestion brought on by a case of flu. After five days the crisis had passed, but though *Cleopatra*'s star was out of danger, she needed a long period of recuperation in a warm climate and cosmetic surgery to conceal the scar on her throat left by the tracheotomy performed to aid her breathing.[7]

Fox had no choice but to shut down the production. The dismantling of $600,000 worth of sets at Pinewood began on March 14 and signaled the end of Fox's costly London folly. Having already invested over $6 million, the entire budget for the London production, only $2 million of which could be recouped from insurance, Fox might well have considered abandoning the ill-fated project. But the newspaper scare headlines over Taylor's illness had produced a tidal wave of publicity and renewed public sympathy for the woman previously reviled as a home wrecker for "stealing" Eddie Fisher from Debbie Reynolds. Hollywood's forgiveness and its joy at Taylor's recovery and return to the film colony were expressed in awarding her an ill-deserved but long-withheld Oscar for her performance in the trashy film version of *Butterfield 8.*

Not only was Fox holding a commitment of the world's most publicized movie star, but Skouras was faced with the not inconsiderable item of the Figaro buy-out for securing Mankiewicz's services, which he was obliged to justify to Fox's board of directors and their bankers. Moreover, Wanger and Taylor were enthusiastic about the psychological orientation that Mankiewicz had devised for the new screenplay. Skouras was equally mindful of the $40 million domestic grosses of such historical epics as Paramount's *Ten Commandments* (1956) and Metro's *Ben-Hur* (1959). He was desperate for a similar blockbuster to wipe out the memory of his string of failures and to refill the company's coffers.

Symptomatic of Skouras's panicky indecisiveness was that on April 19, little more than a month after he had announced a September start date in Rome for *Cleopatra*'s resumption, he changed his mind

---

[7]Despite cosmetic surgery, the scar on Taylor's neck is visible in *Cleopatra.*

and ordered the production shifted to Hollywood for a summer start. While two boatloads of sets and costumes from England were being shipped to California through the Panama Canal and John De Cuir once more began plans for the construction of sets on the Fox lot, Mankiewicz abandoned his concentrated writing efforts in order to scout suitable locations in the vicinity of Rome and along the Nile in Egypt.

Mankiewicz returned to Hollywood on June 12, enthusiastic about the Italian locations he had found, but not eager to shoot in Egypt. On June 30 Skouras once more reversed his decision and agreed to let Mankiewicz make the film in Rome. The financial considerations that prompted this switch were the tax status of Elizabeth Taylor's production company, incorporated in Switzerland, which mandated European rather than American production, and the fact that Fox's sound stages and reduced back lot were committed to the company's television series and the production of George Stevens's *Greatest Story Ever Told*. (Ironically, Fox later dropped Stevens's "biblical," realizing that with their huge losses they would be hard-pressed to finance more than one expensive epic. Consequently, Fox's lot was nearly idle while *Cleopatra* ran up huge construction bills at Cinecittà, and an unusually stormy Roman autumn created costly delays in production while the weather in Los Angeles was balmy.)

The decision to shift the production to Rome left designer De Cuir and production manager "Johnny" Johnston less than three months to build, staff, and organize the mammoth production. (On the comparable Roman production of *Ben-Hur*, even though the screenplay was being daily rewritten by Christopher Fry throughout the filming, Metro spent a year in preproduction, working from a blueprint script that detailed all the requisite sets and locations.)

The Mankiewicz-Buchman-Durrell collaboration on the screenplay ended about the time of the termination of the London production. Apparently, Mankiewicz was dissatisfied with Durrell's contribution, but Buchman was instructed to complete an outline of the entire picture. Although Mankiewicz had suggested such distinguished playwrights as Lillian Hellman and Paul Osborn as capable of completing the script, on April 29 Walter Wanger shelled out $75,000 to engage Ranald MacDougall, a distinctly inferior talent, whose most distinguished credits were such forties films for Warner Brothers as *Mildred Pierce* (1946), *June Bride* (1948), and *The Hasty Heart* (1949). He had the reputation, however, of being "an extraordinarily fast writer."[8]

MacDougall plunged into research and roughed out a "dummy" screenplay following Buchman's outline. Wanger assured MacDougall that he would be given ample time to polish his very rough draft, but Mankiewicz was not about to have a writer like MacDougall furnish the dialogue for his grand concept. While MacDougall slaved away at his office on the nearly empty Fox lot, he was unaware that Mankiewicz was writing his own script from the Buchman outline and MacDougall's rough draft. MacDougall did not learn that Mankiewicz had usurped sole credit for the screenplay until production in Rome began on September 25 and it was announced that Joe had completed a draft of the first half of the film (the "Caesar and Cleopatra" portion) during two months of preproduction work in Rome.

Mankiewicz's dilemma was how he could possibly polish and complete his screenplay while directing such an enormous production. Moreover, although Walter Wanger retained his percentage of the film's potential profits, since the idea of *Cleopatra* as a film and Taylor in the title role was his, he was the producer in name only. Skouras had lost all faith in Wanger after the London fiasco and now bypassed him by dealing directly with Mankiewicz as the man in charge. (In fact, Wanger was allowed to remain with the production only because of Mankiewicz's appeal that he be retained.)

Mankiewicz pleaded for a postponement until he had completed the screenplay, but Skouras was adamant, declaring that Fox's board would never sanction paying Elizabeth Taylor to sit around collecting $50,000 a week in salary plus $3,000 for expenses. Mankiewicz's rebuttal was that even if it took him ten weeks to finish, $500,000 to Taylor would be a pittance compared to what it would cost the production to fly blind without knowledge of what actors, sets, and costumes would be required for the second half of the picture.

Mankiewicz was trapped. Not only had he indentured himself to Fox by selling them his company, but he had persuaded Rex Harrison to play Caesar and Richard Burton to play Antony solely on his reputation as a writer, since there was no polished or completed script to show them. Fifteen weeks of "nose holding" had already stretched to eight months prior to the start of filming, and now Mankiewicz was obliged to keep the once lucrative bargain he had made, but at a terrible

---

[8]MacDougall's self-characterization in a 1972 interview with the author.

personal cost. The decision to begin on the start date meant that Mankiewicz would have to undertake the superhuman task of producing and directing by day and writing by night and on his days off (Sundays only at the outset, because a six-day work week had been scheduled to expedite filming and get the most out of the stars who were drawing big weekly paychecks).

Skouras's refusal to heed Mankiewicz's sound advice proved to be one of the most expensive mistakes in the history of motion pictures. It precipitated *Cleopatra*'s massive cost overrun that nearly bankrupted Twentieth Century–Fox and toppled Skouras and his aides from their posts. What should have been as obvious to Skouras as the folly of starting production without a completed script was that Mankiewicz's rough draft of the Caesar and Cleopatra portion was in itself a very long film.[9] Mankiewicz's concept that Antony's behavior was predicated on his sense of inferiority to Caesar and the contrast between Cleopatra's relationships with the older Roman ruler and his younger successor could only be realized if the film covered the full twenty years from Cleopatra's introduction to Caesar, at the age of nineteen, to her suicide at thirty-nine, following Antony's death. This span encompasses the time frame and events of three famous plays with which Mankiewicz was obliged to compete, namely, Shaw's *Caesar and Cleopatra* and Shakespeare's *Julius Caesar* and *Antony and Cleopatra.*

The situation was quickly grasped by a Fox executive referred to only as "the Boat" (the Deep Throat of *The Cleopatra Papers,* a collection of letters and telegrams exchanged by the film's publicists, Jack Brodsky and Nathan Weiss, corresponding from the battlefields of the filming in Rome and the front office in New York). On October 18, less than a month after the start of production, the Boat was dreaming greedily of making two blockbusters out of the material, each costing $10 million. The pictures would simply be released in successive years, just as Fox eventually did with Richard Lester's *Three Musketeers* in 1974 and 1975.

However, Skouras and his production chief, Peter Levathes, were

---

[9]This may be an unfair judgment, because in Walter Wanger's published diary of the production he notes that as late as August 4, near the time that Skouras must have insisted on a September start date, "Peter Levathes [Skouras's designate as head of film production] has been pressing me for the script, which I have refused to give him . . ." (*My Life with Cleopatra,* Bantam Books, 1963).

getting cold feet after less than a month of filming and were quite willing to settle for one good film. Even though they had spent a tidy sum ($50,000) buying Richard Burton out of his Broadway musical hit, *Camelot,* and had contracted him for a substantial salary to play Antony, they were willing to take the loss on these expenditures. On October 20, according to *The Cleopatra Papers,* "Skouras and Levathes asked [Burton] whether he'd mind terribly if they finished the picture when Caesar is killed. 'I told them I'd sue them until they're puce,' Burton told publicist Brodsky."[10]

Cleopatra's $10 million projected budget was a considerably higher figure than Skouras and Levathes wished to convey to their board and bankers. In fact, Skouras wanted to report only an $8 million dollar budget for *Cleopatra* to his board, that is, only $2 million more than the budget of the abortive English production. Confidentially, production manager Johnston had given Mankiewicz a necessarily rough, estimated budget of $14 million based on the incomplete script. Therefore, when Skouras demanded that Joe agree to a phony figure for the Fox board's benefit, Mankiewicz flatly refused to be a party to it, maintaining, with Wanger, that $10 million had already been committed to the project.

The acrimonious exchange over the unknown budget was to set the pattern for the production, with Skouras and Levathes periodically flying to Rome or dispatching managers like Sid Rogell in futile efforts to limit the spiraling costs. But Mankiewicz knew just how to handle them. As John De Cuir describes the ritual, the Fox executives would arrive on the vast sound stages of Cinecittà, dwarfed by the enormous sets. "Mankiewicz would greet them and just take them apart. He would cut them up into little pieces halfway across the sound stage. Then [in the screening room] he would lead them right into the trap by asking them how *they* would cut a sequence, and [then] he would show them how he intended to accomplish [it]."

The burden of dealing with the Fox chieftains only added to the

[10]Jack Brodsky and Nathan Weiss, *The Cleopatra Papers,* Simon & Schuster, 1963, p. 7. Although Richard Burton had made a hit in *The Robe* (1953), Fox's first picture in CinemaScope, his eight films before *Cleopatra* had all flopped. Skouras was bitterly opposed to hiring him to play Antony, as it entailed buying him out of *Camelot* for $50,000, but Mankiewicz fought to have Burton and won.

enormous pressures that daily depleted Mankiewicz's energy. The day that filming began, only one of the picture's sixty sets had been completed to Mankiewicz's satisfaction and the exterior locations became a continual source of aggravation.

The basic plan was to film the big exterior scenes, such as Caesar's arrival at Alexandria and Cleopatra's triumphal entry into Rome, during the usually splendid Roman autumn. The difficulty in shooting at Torre Astura, near Anzio, which had been selected as the site for the huge outdoor set of the palace square and the harbor of Alexandria, was that the designers had chosen the location while riding in a speed boat along the Italian coast. "Nobody took the time to go ashore," says "Doc" Merman, "where they would have discovered a hidden sandbar right in front of where they had built a huge pier for Caesar's landing." The scouts were so delighted at being able to rent Prince Borghese's unobstructed private beach that they also neglected to discover that the waters near Anzio still contained mines set to deter American invaders during World War II, and that in peacetime war games, NATO maintained a firing range nearby that would make sound recording on the location frequently impossible. In addition to the difficulty of constructing a glass (a pane on which was painted such landmarks of ancient Alexandria as the wondrous Pharos lighthouse) to accommodate a panoramic shot of the harbor for the vast dimensions of the 70-mm., Todd-AO film ratio, the Alexandria sequence became a time-consuming and expensive headache for a production whose cast and crew cost an average of $67,000 per day, by Walter Wanger's calculation.

The problem of Caesar's landing was minor compared with the difficulties encountered in filming Cleopatra and her son Caesarion's triumphal entry into the Roman Forum, perched thirty feet in the air atop an enormous sphinx drawn by three hundred black slaves. The scene was intended to be one of the film's most spectacular highlights. It is an elaborate production number containing African tribal dancers, clouds of colored smoke, streamered arrows shot by archers, showers of golden coins, and doves flying out of breakaway pyramids. These were but a few of the divertissements suggested by the script and press releases (many more were contemplated and several were shot), all choreographed by veteran Hermes Pan as the lavish prelude to Cleopatra's Forum entrance on the sphinx before a crowd of nearly six thousand extras.

Mankiewicz's original requirements for the scene were even more grandiose, including obstreperous animals, later cut from the sequence, all of which had to be regrouped and whose excrement had to be removed every time an actor blew his lines, as Rex Harrison did constantly on his first day of shooting. In addition, Elizabeth Taylor was terrified of heights and fearful of reinjuring her back, which previously had been repaired by a spinal fusion operation, and refused to descend the railless stairs of the sphinx to greet Caesar.[11]

To top off this infuriating series of setbacks, gusty winds played havoc with the processional, and daily downpours made a swamp of the Forum set. By the end of October, the triumphal entry was declared a washout, and the completion of it was postponed until the spring.

By October 20, three and a half weeks after the start of filming, Mankiewicz finished writing the first half of the script, which ran 197 pages. By November 1 he was begging the studio to institute a five-day work week, permitting him an extra day to write. To induce Fox, he assured his bosses that Taylor, Burton, and Harrison had agreed to take commensurate salary cuts for the shortened work week. Peter Levathes cabled back an obdurate refusal, adding, "We are the laughingstock of the industry; that is the greatest disaster in show business."[12] But by November 23 Mankiewicz had his five-day week and a switch to "French hours" (12 to 8 P.M.), which meant that he could hold production meetings in the morning and work with a sober company that had not imbibed too much wine during the lunch break.

Considerable friction had developed over the contemptuous manner in which the English and American crew members were treating their Italian coworkers. Mankiewicz assembled the English-speaking crew members in a projection room and laid down the law by saying, "You've forgotten something. You are guests in *their* country. Just imagine what it would be like if *Cleopatra* were an Italian film shooting at Fox, and they bossed you around in the manner you are treating them!"

Previous to the midday starting time, Joe was considerably more

---

[11]When the entry scene was reshot in the spring, this problem was remedied by having Cleopatra and Caesarion lowered down the steep steps on a litter borne by the Nubians. The overhead crane shot from behind the sphinx and Cleopatra's descent, shot from below, are even more breathtaking than the preceding pageantry.

[12]Wanger, *My Life with Cleopatra*, entry of November 4, 1961.

permissive toward Taylor, who frequently arrived late—and without apology—from her long, wine-filled lunches. Whereas in one breath Rex Harrison says, "It was all going like an ordinary film. We were getting three minutes [of screen time] a day, and Elizabeth was turning up more or less on time," in the next he says, "The reason [Joe and I] know each other so well is the prodigious number of man-hours we spent on the set waiting for Elizabeth. Joe controlled his irritation, as I did, purely selfishly, for I knew if I hadn't, I wouldn't have been able to play the scene. We had to keep our cool. The moment she appeared, the lights went up, and boom, you were in the scene. There was no question of messing about, but she always had some excuse [for her lateness]."

Harrison fails to mention some of his own delaying tactics. One morning, to demonstrate his irritation at the eleventh-hour schedule changes that were made to accommodate Taylor, who was not obliged to perform during the first two days of her menstrual cycle, Harrison failed to appear for his call. When Christopher Mankiewicz was dispatched to fetch him from his villa, Harrison appeared in his bathrobe and blithely fibbed that he had not been notified that he was needed.

Christopher, who was working as a second assistant director, says he was "surprised that such a strong-willed figure [as his father], who usually has very precise ideas about what to do, was so nondecisive in directing *Cleopatra*." At first, Christopher thought it was a conscious decision on his father's part "to pacify everybody and not to do battle with the considerable egos of Rex and Elizabeth." Chris says, "I waited for the day he'd get ticked off and really tell her off, what with a hundred people just sitting around waiting for her, while such huge sums were being spent. I finally attributed it to the fact that his condition was so weak during that picture that perhaps he lacked the strength or desire to engage in a dispute. I have never seen such directionless behavior on his part toward other people, and if ever there was a picture that needed a dictator to shape it up, it was this one."

Actor Roddy McDowall holds a more laudatory opinion of Mankiewicz's seeming passivity. He says, "Joe is a man of incredible patience, tenacity, invention, and wit. He always made time to talk and to care. He was so patient and funny. . . . He didn't make the actors suffer for what must have been heartbreaking to him."

Other accounts would indicate that Mankiewicz's response to the intolerable pressures that beset him was to adopt an outward insouciance. Sam Marx, who was in Rome completing an "antiquity" of his own, the low-budget *Damon and Pythias,* recalls running into Wanger and Mankiewicz, "happy as larks," taking an evening stroll on the Via Veneto. "Knowing [the production] was teetering on the brink of disaster," Marx said, "'I can't get over how happy you two guys are.' Joe replied, 'Why shouldn't we be? We are probably the only two men in the world who will ever have $25 million to make a movie.'" Jack Brodsky quotes Mankiewicz as telling Taylor, during the conflict over the six-day week, "Let's just not show up. What can they do, fire us?"[13]

By Christmastime, Brodsky reported that Mankiewicz had completed writing the first fifty pages of the second half of the film and that they were "fabulous." Such raves had not always greeted Joe's daily handouts of his nighttime labors. One day Rex Harrison stopped by Mankiewicz's trailer and used the tactful ploy of saying, "Joe, this dialogue is simply dreadful. Now, I know you didn't write this, but we have to do something about it because I simply cannot speak these lines."

The problem was not confined to some unacceptable lines for Caesar, however, but was considerably larger. As Chris Mankiewicz comments, "For the first few months, the original script was shot as it was. As this first draft kept going on and on, no one had a chance to step back and say, 'Now let's cut the first draft down and make it into a second draft.' [Joe] should never have been permitted to shoot all [that he had written]." Mankiewicz was not unaware of the problem. When he gave friends the script to read, he told them, "It's too long, but I don't have the time to make it short." As Spyros Skouras commented to Walter Wanger, after yawning through a screening of fifteen or twenty reels of this material, "I wish to hell I'd never seen you in my life."[14]

By mid-January there were some fresh faces on the set. To prepare the battle scenes, Andrew ("Bundy") Marton, the second unit director responsible for such famous action scenes as the chariot race in *Ben-Hur,* was brought in to replace Ray Kellogg. C. O. ("Doc") Erickson arrived to take over the ailing Johnny Johnston's impossible job as

---

[13]Brodsky and Weiss, *The Cleopatra Papers,* p. 13.
[14]Sam Marx recounting a comment overheard by his son, Richard, one of whose duties as an assistant editor was to supervise executive screenings of *Cleopatra.*

production manager. In turn, Fox sent in its representative, Doc Merman, as executive production manager in an attempt to hold down the skyrocketing budget. However, the "Doctors" had as little success in controlling Mankiewicz, whom they merely soothed, as they did in quelling the price-gouging and outright thievery that was making *Cleopatra* an annuity for many Italian entrepreneurs. "There were cases of massive stealing," says Chris Mankiewicz, "with many thousands of dollars being siphoned off by the Italian production managers. Meetings were held and all the thievery was exposed, but no one was fired, because no decisions were taken."

Joe Mankiewicz describes his situation by saying, "I was down in the hold of this ship shoveling coal like an s.o.b., but there was no one on top steering. Walter [Wanger] was a very tasteful, wasteful gentleman. He knew very little about the economy of producing. . . . Not since Marco Polo came back from China had there been the advent of such riches in Italy. One of the Italian production managers became a millionaire from *Cleopatra.* Lots of money was stolen, but [Wanger] just 'didn't know' about them and didn't stop them."

Richard Burton had spent the best part of three months restlessly idling about the cafés of the Via Veneto, cooling his heels for $250,000 (his three-month guarantee), and was about to go on even more high-priced overtime when he appeared in his first scene with Elizabeth Taylor on January 22, 1962. Although Burton had facetiously commented before his departure for Rome, "I've got to don my breastplate once more to play opposite Miss Tits," the great stage actor, wit, and womanizer evidently formed a different opinion while he was observing Taylor at close range for the first time.

On January 26 Mankiewicz confirmed to Wanger the rumors that were shortly to become the favorite gossip item of the world press in the subsequent six months of *Cleopatra*'s filming. The saga of Liz and Eddie and Richard and Sybil, the tabloids' favorite real-life soap opera, became an added drain on Mankiewicz's sorely taxed energies, much as he enjoyed his role as confidant and marriage counselor to the participants. Roddy McDowall (Octavian), a close friend of Taylor's from their days as child actors in Hollywood and a pal of Burton's from their year together in *Camelot,* began calling Joe "Father Flanagan, because he had everybody's problems to deal with." (One example of Mankiewicz's ministrations was the night a panic-stricken Eddie Fisher phoned Joe to report that his wife had taken an overdose of sleeping pills. Mankiewicz raced over to their villa and forced Taylor to tell him how many pills she had swallowed. When she groggily admitted taking only four, Mankiewicz pacified Fisher and told Taylor to take the next day to sleep it off.) But by the spring, when the scandal had been raging for several months, Burton became fed up with Joe's counseling services and snapped at Tom Mankiewicz, "I'm so goddamned tired of your father playing psychiatrist."

Tom Mankiewicz had arrived in Rome to work on the film after completing his spring term at Yale, while his brother Christopher had gone back at the end of January to resume his studies at Columbia. Before his departure, Christopher committed an inadvertent but damaging indiscretion. In praising Taylor's beauty, he told her he could not comprehend Irene Sharaff's complaints about her figure. (Sharaff had legitimate cause to gripe about Taylor's fluctuating weight. She had designed a fabulous collection of fifty-eight costumes with an emphasis on décolletage, and whenever Taylor put on weight, bothersome and intricate refitting became necessary.)

Some of the picture's detractors commented that Taylor's constant costume changes were the most variable element of her performance and the most awesome spectacle in *Cleopatra*. The oddity is that as Taylor sheds both weight and her elaborate eye makeup through the course of the film, she appears to grow younger rather than older.

While Taylor lost weight, Mankiewicz was losing his grip from exhaustion. "I was very, very lucky to be in the first half of the picture," says Rex Harrison. "Joe hadn't reached his climax of despair at that point." Harrison is referring to the state of nervous exhaustion that Mankiewicz had attained by the end of February. As Wanger noted in his diary on February 26, "JLM is in bad shape. . . . He is distraught and overloaded with work." Mankiewicz's doctor insisted that he play seven holes of golf in the morning for exercise and relaxation. But the grind of production meetings morning and afternoon, in addition to the shots and pills that got him through the days of directing and the nights of writing, had begun to take their toll. Mankiewicz describes his horrifying regimen. "Someone would wake me up at five-thirty or six in the morning, and I would gulp down a Dexedrine. I was given a shot after lunch to keep me going through the afternoon. Then I was given a shot after dinner so I could write till two in the morning, and then I got a final shot at two so I could go to sleep."

Wanger sent for Ranald MacDougall in Hollywood to draft the

as-yet-unwritten battle scenes of Moongate (the main entrance to Cleopatra's besieged palace) and Actium (Antony's naval Waterloo). Although MacDougall was still bitter at having been made to labor in vain on his unused screenplay of *Cleopatra* and had demanded an exorbitant price for his reengagement, he says that Mankiewicz "won my heart" at their first encounter on February 28. "He was very charming and humble for the first and last time," says MacDougall. "He threw his arms out, saying, 'Thank God you're here. I've gone dry.' I recalled the horror of my own brief dry spell and related to him as a writer for the first time, as I was aware that he'd bitten off far more than he could chew."

Wanger wrote that he screened only two hours and eighteen minutes of the edited film for MacDougall and that the "magnificent" performances of *Cleopatra*'s stars outweighed all the griefs of the production.[15] MacDougall's recollection is that he viewed five and a half hours of the film, excluding Cleopatra's triumphal entry and without having yet reached Caesar's assassination. MacDougall claims that Wanger admitted the film was "overblown and long" and sought MacDougall's advice on how to fix it. MacDougall's view was that, besides such incidental problems as the difficulty of matching "a plump Elizabeth walking through the palace" with her much slimmer figure in later close shots, the "ponderous dialogue" made the picture seem "interminable." MacDougall felt that Mankiewicz had padded his friend Hume Cronyn's role as Sosigenes, Cleopatra's tutor, in an attempt to establish Cleopatra's credentials as an intellectual, and that the "wandering discourses and philosophical exchanges" were not only anachronistic but boring. Wanger claimed that Mankiewicz was well aware of the need for severe condensation of this material: "He's already faced it. He knows."

However, MacDougall says, "Joe didn't want to know. . . . He was semi-mad at that point, riding something he couldn't get off. Reality and he had parted company, and though it was hard to talk to a thoroughly exhausted man at the end of the day, he had a manic sort of extra dimension from lack of sleep."

As evidence of just how foggy Mankiewicz's brain had become, MacDougall says, "He showed me one page on which he'd written one sentence fifteen different ways." MacDougall simply refined his version

---

[15]Wanger, *My Life with Cleopatra,* entry of February 28, 1962.

of the Moongate sequence from the script he had completed in September and submitted it to Mankiewicz. As another example of Joe's state of mind, MacDougall cites Mankiewicz's contemptuous and arbitrary insistence on giving John Valva, Roddy McDowall's close friend, an "in joke" character name in the script, Valuvus. Joe's decree, over MacDougall's heated protest, automatically gave Valva a salary and living expenses for the run of the production, although his only significant appearance in the film is as the Roman soldier who refuses to engage Antony in single-handed, suicidal combat.[16]

By April 5 Wanger noted that they had "more than one-half the picture in the can, [having] filmed 802 scenes and 213 pages of script." On that day publicist Jack Brodsky, at the behest of the Associated Press, came on the set to ask Joe if he had any comment on the front-page story in an Italian paper that Burton was merely acting, under Joe's orders, as Elizabeth's consort in order to cover up the real romance between Mankiewicz and Taylor. Burton, acting out his characterization in an Italian paper as "a shuffle-footed idiot," dumbly inquired, "Duh, Mister Mankcavitz, sir, do I have to sleep with her again tonight?" Joe replied to Brodsky, "The real story is that Richard Burton and I are in love and Elizabeth Taylor is being used as our cover-up." He authenticated this assertion by kissing Burton on the mouth and walking off the set.[17] This jest made headlines in several Italian newspapers, although the yellow press in London was obliged to suppress it because of the prevailing ban on printing homosexual allegations.

Such vicissitudes as Taylor returning home alone from a weekend in late April with a black eye and a bruised nose, which made her unphotographable for two weeks, Mankiewicz's being bedded with a strep throat and fever in early May, and the Roman winds of April hampering exterior shooting were forgotten in the celebration that capped the completion of the sequence of Cleopatra's entry into the Forum on May 9.

---

[16]Roddy McDowall disputes the claim that John Valva was paid for a long period of time because of his being given a character name in the script. Whatever the facts of the matter, Mankiewicz may have been doing McDowall a well-earned favor, both for exploiting him as the dyed blond, effeminate Octavian and for McDowall's invaluable aid as a sympathetic intermediary between Mankiewicz and his close friends Taylor and Burton.
[17]Brodsky and Weiss, *The Cleopatra Papers*, p. 62.

Although the production team was greatly relieved that the six thousand Italian extras had cheered Taylor, rather than jeering at her in the fashion of the Vatican press, Mankiewicz denounced the footage in a postmortem conference after a screening of the sequence. Joe's relations with *Cleopatra*'s cinematographer, the cranky Leon Shamroy, Fox's senior cameraman who was obsessed with his visual imagery to the exclusion of Mankiewicz's dialogue, were stormy from the outset of the production. One of Shamroy's most irritating traits was that whenever Mankiewicz suggested an interesting shot or angle, "Shammy" would always reply that he had already done it in a previous picture. On this occasion, however, Mankiewicz was furious that his staff had not followed his recommendation that the crowd of extras be mobilized, as in DeMille's epics, by costumed assistants who would be responsible for checking the costuming, makeup, and movement of the extras in each of their platoons. Instead, directions had been relayed to the extras via loudspeaker, and the results were visible wristwatches, wigs on backwards, and frequent gaps in the crowd, which was meant to fill the Forum entirely. Mankiewicz moaned, as he was to do for much of the filming, that no one but he truly cared and that he had to be responsible for everything himself—an impossible task.

By the end of May, Mankiewicz had wrapped up most of the mausoleum scenes between Antony and Cleopatra, including her suicide by asp bite (on the wrist rather than the breast, in Mankiewicz's decorous version). At this point Mankiewicz had completed enough of the screenplay so that he no longer had to write at night. However, Wanger anticipated with dread the impending arrival of Fox's production chief Levathes and two fellow executives on June 1. He was fearful that with five hours and fourteen minutes of edited film[18] and the completion of Cleopatra's death scene, the "Big Three" were coming to shut down the production. Many of the film's most spectacular scenes remained to be filmed on Italian locations. These included the opening Battle of Pharsalia, the big naval battle at Actium, the arrival of Cleopatra's golden barge at Tarsus, and Antony's single-handed confrontation with Octavian's legions (to be shot in Egypt). Comple-

---

[18]The specificity of the film's running time, as noted by Wanger in his diary entry of May 30, calls into question MacDougall's assertion that he had seen five and a half hours of edited footage on February 28, unless the "Caesar and Cleopatra" half had been greatly reduced in the interim.

tion of these sequences, crucial to both the script and the public's expectation of spectacle, was conservatively estimated by the production staff as requiring three more months, concluding on August 31. (Elizabeth Taylor had already termed the endlessly protracted production "Suddenly, Next Summer.")

The Big Three had different necessities in mind. They were concerned only with plugging the greatest drain on Fox's nearly depleted cash reservoir. Fox's 1961 losses totaled $40 million, with the production of *Cleopatra* accounting for half that sum. The company's only hope for future earnings was to get Zanuck's *Longest Day*, an all-star Normandy invasion epic, and the scandalously ballyhooed *Cleopatra* into release as quickly as possible. Levathes also had designs on succeeding Skouras as president of Fox, and he had surreptitiously marshaled support from some members of the board of directors.

In a series of hard-nosed and foolhardy ultimatums issued in the course of their five days in Rome (June 1–5), the "Three Wise Men," as Wanger sarcastically termed them, canceled the filming of the Battle of Pharsalia (which was eventually filmed twice, as it is the background of the film's first scene),[19] summarily fired Wanger, and demanded that Taylor's salary be terminated on June 9 and that all photography be halted by June 30.

Mankiewicz told the dictatorial execs that if they instituted these edicts, they would wind up with "the first indoor movie ever shot in Todd-AO." He stormed out of the second evening session after novice Levathes had the gall to claim that Joe did not know what he was doing or how to make a movie. In turn, Wanger told Levathes, "Pete, don't let failure go to your head."[20]

Mankiewicz refused to sign the memorandum of understanding, which Levathes had drawn up, agreeing to the termination dates. Instead, he fired off a cable to Judge Samuel Rosenman, a celebrated jurist and Democratic bigwig who had been named Fox's chairman of the board during the winter in order to bolster Skouras's toppling regime. Joe recognized the futility of trying to explain in a telegram that the meeting between Cleopatra and Antony on board her royal

---

[19]The Fox executives may have been shamed into coming up with meager funds for a cut-rate Battle of Pharsalia when Rex Harrison, who recognized the importance of the opening scene, offered to pay for it himself.

[20]Brodsky and Weiss, *The Cleopatra Papers*, p. 116.

barge at Tarsus (to be shot on location at Ischia) is the night that Antony first beds Cleopatra and becomes emotionally ensnared. Mankiewicz simply wired that if Taylor was not made available to him, the ensuing scene would represent "the most expensive *coitus interruptus* in history." Rosenman got the point, and Taylor was allowed to work through June 23, which permitted her to do the location scenes at Ischia (where the Battle of Actium was also filmed), though Mankiewicz was not permitted to do the shot he wanted of Cleopatra making her final progress to the mausoleum.

On June 26 Skouras was forced to resign as president of Fox. Four days later, when Mankiewicz was informed that the studio remained adamant about canceling the conclusion of the Battles of Pharsalia and Philippi, Joe threatened to resign. His wire to Judge Rosenman, Skouras, and Levathes concluded, ". . . FOR MY PART, I HAVE EXHAUSTED SUCH ENERGIES AND TALENT AS I POSSESS, AND THE PROSPECT OF A FLOW OF SIMILAR PRONUNCIAMENTOS IN THE MONTH AHEAD IS ONE I CANNOT FACE. NOR WOULD I WANT TO FACE THE FILM I COULD NOT ASSEMBLE PROPERLY MUCH LESS TURN OVER WITH PRIDE. WITH MUTUAL APPRECIATION OF RESPONSIBILITIES, AND SUGGESTING THAT MINE TOWARD THE STOCKHOLDERS IS NO LESS THAN YOURS, I SUGGEST THAT YOU REPLACE ME SOONEST POSSIBLE BY SOMEONE LESS CRITICAL OF YOUR DIRECTIVES AND LESS DEDICATED TO THE EVENTUAL SUCCESS OF CLEOPATRA." Mankiewicz eventually got his way, and he hastily shot the end of both battles to provide a parallel link between the first and second halves of the film.

The desert location scenes to be shot in Egypt were also rescheduled. From July 18 to 28, amid extreme heat, riots between extras and students who wanted their jobs, and the failure of much crucial equipment to arrive, the filming of *Cleopatra* was completed in the primitive village of Edkou, an hour from Alexandria.

Cleopatra, which Mankiewicz describes as "the hardest three pictures I ever made," wound up with its writer-director not only physically and mentally exhausted, but a temporary cripple. As Mankiewicz describes the accident, "It was one of those things that was going to happen out of sheer percentage. While we were winding up in Alexandria, the nurse that was giving me shots had covered every square inch of my ass. One happened to hit the sciatic nerve, and I just couldn't walk. I was in agony and had to get around by hobbling on a cane . . . or by wheelchair. [In order to get to the location] I was lifted into a jeep, while my son Tom rode alongside me on an Arabian mare." Designer John De Cuir remembers the sight of Mankiewicz "being carried on a stretcher across the sands of Alexandria, all scrunched up and frantically scribbling on a pad. I asked, 'How's it going?' and he replied, 'I'm writing the last page.'"

Mankiewicz's belief that the exhausting filming had concluded with the Egyptian locations proved to be only wishful thinking. On July 25 Darryl F. Zanuck, a large shareholder because he was made the first head of production when Twentieth Century merged with Fox in 1935, maneuvered himself into taking over the presidency of the company, succeeding Spyros Skouras. On Saturday, July 28, "Bundy" Marton, the second unit director, subbing for the ailing Mankiewicz who had returned to Rome on the twenty-fourth, wrapped up the Egyptian location scenes. The actual filming of *Cleopatra* had consumed ten months, and Mankiewicz's anticipated fifteen-week commitment had stretched to a year and a half.

While Mankiewicz was supervising the editing of *Cleopatra* and attempting to recuperate, a rejuvenated Zanuck was executing massive power plays. He had his son Richard close down the Fox studio in Los Angeles, retaining only minimal facilities. The move axed innumerable department heads and longtime Fox employees. Zanuck was chiefly preoccupied with editing his own epic, *The Longest Day,* for a lavish September premiere in Paris. The immediate box-office success of Zanuck's $10 million, three-hour "dreary documentary," as Mankiewicz calls it, which featured twenty-five stars (including cameos by Richard Burton and Roddy McDowall, moonlighting from *Cleopatra*) in talky vignettes alternating with battle scenes, temporarily sustained Fox's shaky finances and "revived all of [Zanuck's] ego but none of his talent," says Mankiewicz.

It was from this position of newfound corporate authority and commercial security that Zanuck summoned Mankiewicz to Paris and, on October 13, viewed his "rough cut" of *Cleopatra,* on which Joe had been laboring for over two months. There are conflicting reports about the running time of the rough cut and Zanuck's reaction to it. Mankiewicz contends that at Zanuck's insistence he had cut the picture to four and a half hours,[21] although he strongly felt the film should have

---

[21]One newspaper account of the period corroborates Mankiewicz's claim. A Paris date-lined article by Robert Walden in the *New York Times* of October 24, 1962, notes

been divided into two feature films of two and a half to three hours in length. Mike Mindlin, Joe's former publicist at Figaro, recalls running into Mankiewicz and Hume Cronyn in Paris at the time. "Oh, Mike," called Joe as he was getting into a car, "Zanuck just saw the picture and he thinks it's terrific."[22]

On the contrary, Zanuck told his biographer, Mel Gussow, although he had anticipated simply approving the picture, he was "shocked" after screening the first cut. "I asked to see the sequences that had been cut," said Zanuck, "and decided that some of them should be restored, but I found to my astonishment that no loops had been made for certain of the eliminated episodes. . . . I was powerless. . . . In other words, Mr. Mankiewicz obviously considered the picture finished when he brought it to me." Mankiewicz terms the charge that he had, in effect, brought Zanuck a final cut of the film "ridiculous." He says, "It would have been absurd to prepare all of the out-takes for dubbing, because loops could be easily prepared." He claims that the version he showed Zanuck "had been cut for length only."

Production designer John De Cuir says that at the meeting subsequent to the screening, concerning reshooting certain sequences and creating new bridging material, "Darryl kept intoning, in not too happy a voice, 'Seven and a half hours!' " De Cuir says that Zanuck, rather than restoring sequences, demanded that the film "be cut to three hours and fifteen minutes.[23] When Joe managed to cut out only thirteen minutes, Zanuck took the picture away from him and brought in his right-hand man, Elmo Williams, a fine cutter who had saved many pictures [for example, *High Noon*]. Elmo looked at [*Cleopatra*] like a

---

that the "tentative rough assembly of 'Cleopatra' . . . ran four and a half hours." However, in a *Time* magazine interview (November 2, 1962), Mankiewicz said, "I showed [Zanuck] the first half of the picture."

[22]An article in the *New York Herald Tribune* of October 31, 1962, states, "Mr. Zanuck told Mankiewicz that 'it was beautifully acted, beautifully directed, and beautifully staged,' but added later that he wasn't satisfied with certain physical aspects of some battle scenes" (Mel Gussow, *Don't Say Yes Until I Finish Talking*, Doubleday, 1971, p. 255).

[23]De Cuir says that three years later, when he was working again with Mankiewicz in Rome on *The Honey Pot*, "Joe said to me, 'I know you're going to see Darryl in Paris, and I know they still have those clips. Why not try it in the seven-and-a-half-hour version?' It broke my heart. Three years later he was still trying to get back those scenes he believed in so deeply." De Cuir says that a year later he did propose the restoration to Zanuck, "as, at that point, the picture had earned back its cost and was making a bit of money. Zanuck said, 'Oh, c'mon. That's a closed subject.' "

butcher deciding how many steaks he could get out of a side of beef. In a matter of forty-eight hours, he had whittled it down to the running time Zanuck had requested."

Mankiewicz had no inkling of Williams's "butchery" for eight days after the screening. Although Zanuck had praised Joe at the screening, he canceled his meeting with Mankiewicz scheduled for the following day, when they were to discuss the film in detail, and departed Paris, "leaving me with a large amount of omelette on my face," as Mankiewicz later described his mortification.[24]

On Monday, October 22, Mankiewicz received a letter from Zanuck, dated October 21, specifying that he was to "have no further part in editing *Cleopatra,* and terminating his services after he had completed redubbing some scenes with Taylor and Burton, which he was preparing to do with them in Paris."[25] On Tuesday, the twenty-third, Zanuck publicly announced his firing of Mankiewicz. That evening Joe fought back by declaring, "I intend, by every means available, to regain the usurped right to finish my work, and hopefully, to prevent *Cleopatra* from becoming 'The Longest Night.' "[26]

Cleopatra's stars rallied to their director's defense. Elizabeth Taylor said, "What has happened to Mr. Mankiewicz is disgraceful, degrading, and particularly humiliating. I am terribly upset. He's done a marvelous job. Mr. Mankiewicz has put two years of his life into *Cleopatra,* and the film is his and Mr. Wanger's. Mr. Mankiewicz took *Cleopatra* over when it was nothing—when it was rubbish—and he made something out of it. He certainly should have been given the chance to cut it. It is appalling."[27] Richard Burton commented, "It is just a matter of good manners. What was done was vulgar. You can easily see where my loyalties lie.[28] I think Mr. Mankiewicz might have made the first really good epic film. Now *Cleopatra* may be in trouble."

On October 25 Zanuck issued the following snide rebuttal: "In exchange for top compensation and a considerable expense ac-

[24] *Variety,* October 31, 1962.
[25] *Ibid.*
[26] Robert Alden, *New York Times,* October 24, 1962.
[27] *Ibid.*
[28] Zanuck later retorted to Mel Gussow, his biographer, "Obviously Richard Burton had forgotten that [while he was performing in Zanuck's *Longest Day*] he . . . urged me to go to Rome to sit on the set to get Mankiewicz moving and scare hell out of him" (*Don't Say Yes Until I Finish Talking,* p. 256).

count,[29] Mr. Joseph Mankiewicz has for two years spent his time, talent, and $35 million[30] of Twentieth Century–Fox's shareholders' money to direct and complete the first cut of the film *Cleopatra.* He has earned a well-deserved rest."

In an article in the *New York Herald Tribune* on October 26, Hollywood correspondent Joe Hyams printed scorching excerpts from writer-director Billy Wilder's "Dear Darryl" telegram, declining Zanuck's invitation to direct a picture for Fox. Wilder was deeply incensed by Zanuck's summary dismissal not only of Mankiewicz but also of his esteemed former partner, Charles Brackett *(The Lost Weekend, Sunset Boulevard),* a writer-producer whose contract to make a film for Fox had been abrogated by Zanuck's shutting down the studio and refusing to honor any deals made by the Skouras-Levathes regime. Wilder wired, "YOU'VE BEEN TOO LONG AND TOO FAR AWAY TO KNOW THAT A WAVE OF DISGUST HAS SWEPT OVER THIS TOWN SINCE THE BRUTAL AND CALLOUS DISMISSAL OF PEOPLE, EVEN THOUGH THEY HOLD PERFECTLY LEGAL CONTRACTS. THE 'LET THEM SUE' ATTITUDE IS REPREHENSIBLE. NO SELF-RESPECTING PICTURE-MAKER WOULD EVER WANT TO WORK FOR YOUR COMPANY. THE SOONER THE BULLDOZERS RAZE YOUR STUDIO, THE BETTER IT WILL BE FOR THE INDUSTRY."

The *Herald Tribune* article also quoted the distinguished film director William Wyler, a member of Fox's new board of directors, as saying, "Speaking as a fellow director—not as a member of the Fox board—I was sorry to see Darryl F. Zanuck take the picture away from Mankiewicz."

In response to the Friday morning article in the *Herald Tribune,* Zanuck hastily called a press conference in the Twentieth Century–Fox board room. Zanuck explained his action by claiming that Mankiewicz had demanded complete control of *Cleopatra,* a right that Zanuck reserved to himself. "I, in turn, refused him that control, but

---

[29]Later detailed by Zanuck as $260,000 in salary and $60,000 in expenses, over and above $1.5 million in capital gains from Fox's purchase of Mankiewicz's half interest in Figaro, Inc. Mankiewicz told columnist John Crosby, "This hasn't been a remunerative experience for me. Actually, I will make less out of this picture than any picture I've made in the last ten years" ("Crosby Abroad," *New York Herald Tribune,* October 1962).

[30]John Crosby wrote in his *New York Herald Tribune* column filed from Paris that two days before this announcement, Zanuck had put the cost of *Cleopatra* at $32 million and therefore had "upped the ante $3 million in a matter of 48 hours."

I left the door open—wide open—and offered to meet with him at any time and debate the points of difference. I would rather go back to another job than leave picture making totally in the hands of an artist." Further, Zanuck said that although he admired Mankiewicz's direction of the film's major scenes, he disliked the continuity of Mankiewicz's version, which he felt was marred by "extraneous" minor scenes. He termed *Cleopatra* "this monster hanging on my shoulder," and said, "I can't afford the luxury of more talk" because the interest charges on the film were costing his company $7,000 a day. He blamed Mankiewicz for wasting at least $7.5 million by misscheduling Richard Burton, "who worked only one of his first seventeen weeks in Rome and [Roddy] McDowall, who appeared only once in four months. His greatest extravagance was in ordering sets built at exorbitant overtime costs which were then left unused for months."[31]

Pressed by reporters to explain Mankiewicz's proprietary intransigence, Zanuck said that Mankiewicz had exercised more authority than any film director in history[32] and speculated, "I think that after a year and a half of directing Caesar and Cleopatra and Mark Antony, some of the tinsel must have rubbed off on him."[33] Zanuck tried to brush off this remark as being merely facetious, but it served to infuriate Mankiewicz. Reached by phone in Paris, Mankiewicz told a *New York Times* correspondent that he had never demanded complete control of the film, only the opportunity to complete his first cut. He bitterly added, "Mr. Zanuck had nothing whatsoever to do with the production. The fact is, he can't wait to 'save' the picture."[34]

Mankiewicz saved his major rebuttal for his own press conference, which he convened at his East Side townhouse on Tuesday, October 30, after his return to New York. Joe denied any immediate plans to sue Zanuck or Fox for breach of contract, although he said he had discussed the possibility with his lawyers. "It's not a question of legality,

---

[31] *Time*, November 2, 1962, p. 47.

[32] To pinpoint the blame for the mismanagement that had allowed Mankiewicz such free rein, Zanuck announced at the press conference that Peter Levathes, Skouras's longtime protégé, who had already been demoted from head of film production to president of Fox's television department when Zanuck took office, had left the company.

[33] The account of Zanuck's press conference is drawn principally from William G. Wing's article in the *New York Herald Tribune*, October 27, 1962.

[34] Eugene Archer, *New York Times*, October 27, 1962, p. 14.

it's a question of morality," he emphasized. "I'm much too old a cotton picker not to know the score. I know what 'Old Marse' will do with the cotton in the end. I've been through the mill too many times not to know. Mr. Zanuck is the boss. He's like the rich little kid who owns the football and can pick it up any time he wants to and go on home. But, hell, not to be permitted to discuss the film I made? I spent two years working on the picture, but Mr. Zanuck, who hasn't even read the completed script, refused to listen to or discuss my ideas on it, although I volunteered to meet him any time, anywhere. . . . Now I think I've as much chance of being invited to see what's being done to the movie as there's a chance of Castro inviting all of us down to swim at the Havana Hilton." Getting even for Zanuck's "tinsel" crack, Mankiewicz compared Zanuck's own "high-handed method" to Khrushchev's behavior at the UN, by saying, "He's pounding a table with his shoe."

Mankiewicz then traced the film's inordinate cost to "the idiotic decisions . . . made by many different people," such as the studio edict to begin filming without a completed script, "because the attitude was, 'The girl's on salary; let's get something on film,' a costly blunder [which he had cautioned against]. *Cleopatra* was first conceived in emergency, shot in hysteria, and wound up in blind panic, but any effort to saddle blame on Miss Taylor for the cost is wrong. . . . Miss Taylor may have had problems of illness and emotional problems, but she didn't cost Twentieth any $35 million!"

Mankiewicz said that he did plan to take "a long rest," not because of Zanuck's recommendation but in order to recuperate. He concluded by saying that the experience of making *Cleopatra* had left him with "a deep distaste for the making of films, other than those areas that have to do with the creative side. After more than thirty years, I thought I'd seen all the infighting and dirt," but *Cleopatra's* production exceeded all his experience of nastiness. He also announced that Zanuck's dismissal had effectually terminated his contract with Fox and regrettably freed him from his commitment to write and direct his dream project, *Justine.*[35]

During the course of filming *Cleopatra*, Mankiewicz had come to

---

[35]The account and quotes from Mankiewicz's press conference are drawn from articles of October 31, 1962, in the *New York Herald Tribune* (unsigned), by Eugene Archer in the *New York Times*, and by Atra Baer in the *New York Journal American*.

rely on the assistance of Rosemary Matthews, an efficient staff member on the set. The pert Miss Matthews, whose father was an English archdeacon and whose mother was a distinguished ophthalmic surgeon, had become acquainted with Mankiewicz in 1954, during the filming in Rome of *The Barefoot Contessa.*

According to Addie Wallace, Joe's former secretary, Miss Matthews graduated from drama school in England and was eventually brought to Rome by her more extroverted actress sister, Pamela. Rosemary found work as a production secretary on *William Tell,* a never completed Errol Flynn picture being shot in an Alpine location. In lieu of their paychecks, which were not forthcoming, Flynn and his producer attempted to pacify the crew with token sums for expenses and gambling at a nearby resort. Rosemary Matthews saved what she could until she had enough money to get back to Rome. On her return she sought a job through her friend Michael Waszynski, Joe's associate producer. Waszynski thought that Rosemary's fluency in Italian would make her a valuable aide to Rosa, in charge of instructing the Mankiewicz villa's staff. There Rosemary grew fond of Joe, and after he returned to the States to direct *Guys and Dolls,* she would frequently write him letters marked "personal."

Evidently, Mankiewicz reciprocated her fondness, for when Miss Matthews and Figaro's production manager, Johnny Johnston, were discharged from Robert Rossen's European production of *Alexander the Great* (1956), Mankiewicz helped arrange for her emigration to the United States. After she had found an apartment in Santa Monica, Miss Matthews stayed on in Los Angeles to assist Johnston on *I Want to Live!,* and then she organized the complex logistics of *The Quiet American* company's trip to Saigon. On this film she again served as Johnston's secretary-assistant throughout the production.

On *Cleopatra* Rosemary Matthews served in the capacity of a production assistant, and she took charge of supervising the voluminous number of production reports and getting cables sent through the labyrinthine Italian system. According to Walter Wanger's diary, Rosemary and her sister, Pamela Danova (then married to the handsome actor Cesare Danova, who played Appolodorus, Cleopatra's devoted servant and displaced lover), became Joe's best intelligence-gathering source; they kept him abreast of all the *Cleopatra* company's doings on and off the set.

Mankiewicz's relationship with Jeanne Vanderbilt had terminated, and at that point (following the humiliating battles with Zanuck), says his confidant Hume Cronyn, "he mistrusted everything about himself and his whole emotional functioning." Although Mankiewicz mistrusted committing himself to any woman, Rosemary Matthews had grown so indispensable to him during the trials of *Cleopatra* that friends such as Irene Mayer Selznick thought that at this stage of his life a union with a devoted if less glamorous woman would be the most sensible decision he could make.

On December 14, 1962, Mankiewicz married Rosemary Matthews before a New York judge. The wedding party was small. "I had my lawyer, my doctor, and my friends," said the groom, referring to attorney Abraham Bienstock, Dr. and Mrs. Edmund Goodman, Mr. and Mrs. Arthur Hornblow, Jr., and Addie Wallace ("the mother of the groom," quipped Mrs. Hornblow). Rosemary's father and mother and an aunt flew over from England to attend. Also in attendance were Joe's niece Johanna and her husband, Peter Davis (*Hearts and Minds*), as well as Joe's musicologist son Christopher, who says he was reproved by the bride for selecting Mendelssohn's wedding march rather than Wagner's.

Just a week before the wedding, the *New York Times* had printed the surprising announcement that "Mankiewicz will probably rejoin the production [of *Cleopatra*] for additional shooting, as he had recently had an 'extremely constructive' conference with Mr. Zanuck." On December 26, while Joe and Rosemary were honeymooning in the Caribbean, *Variety* confirmed the reconciliation in an item headlined, "Zanuck and Mank End Tiff on Cleo."

The rapprochement between the antagonists was purely pragmatic. Zanuck and Elmo Williams found that having cut the film to half its original length, there were now significant gaps in the continuity that had to be bridged. "Darryl was against bringing Joe back," says John De Cuir, "but I pleaded, 'It's Joe's picture. It's his material. There isn't a writer-director in Hollywood who can wade into that complex mess and do that patchwork.' Elmo agreed, but Darryl resisted. The decision was made that they would lay out the continuity. With Elmo serving as watchdog, Joe would not be allowed to shoot anything but the structure outlined. It was really a Gestapo [tactic]." Zanuck promised Mankiewicz that he would "bend over backwards artistically" so he would not be obliged to assert his authority.

Mankiewicz describes their relationship as "businesslike." He justifies his return to the picture by the obligation he felt to direct Harrison and Burton personally in their scenes. In retrospect, however, he deplores his capitulation, saying, "When he fired me, I should have stayed fired. It was a mistake to have shot those retakes, because it implied approval by me of what he had done to the film, and this was something I deeply regret having done. Had I stuck to my guns, I might have had a better chance of taking my name off [*Cleopatra*] as its director. I tried to."

Besides wanting to polish the truncated version bearing his name as writer-director, Mankiewicz also had the ulterior motive of restoring some of the cuts that Zanuck and Williams had inflicted. He was partially successful, managing to restore bits of Sosigenes (Hume Cronyn) tutoring Cleopatra, but almost all of the key supporting characters, such as Antony's confidant, Rufio (Martin Landau), and Octavian (McDowall), had been cut to the bone, and their significant commentary on the central characters was thereby lost.

In Mankiewicz's view, "the person who suffered most in the cutting of the film was Dick Burton. He gave a brilliant performance and a lot of his most marvelous scenes were never shown." Mankiewicz might have foreseen this butchery in Zanuck's strange comment, at his first viewing of the film. "If any woman behaved toward me like Cleopatra treated Antony, I would cut her balls off." Mankiewicz realized that Cleopatra's domination of the formerly powerful Antony was not so different from the manner in which Juliette Greco and Irina Demick had driven the infatuated Zanuck to drink ("He'd become the kind of figure Emil Jannings [*The Blue Angel*] used to play," says Mankiewicz of Zanuck in his Parisian exile), and that seeing such a situation dramatized was consequently intolerable to Zanuck.

On February 14, 1963, in the chilly climate of Almeria, a wild, mountainous region of southeastern Spain, Mankiewicz began to film the opening scene of *Cleopatra* again by restaging the Battle of Pharsalia sequence on a hilltop overlooking a dusty, windswept plain. He had been as displeased as Zanuck with the original, cheap version he had been obliged to shoot hastily "with 180 dummies of dead soldiers and their horses and only eight live soldiers and four real horses," which he cranked out just before the end of production in Italy the previous summer.[36] Even the more extensive Almeria version has nowhere near

---

[36]While Mankiewicz may well have been displeased with the limited resources made available to him for this first Battle of Pharsalia, the decision to use fiber-glass

the impact of the scene he had originally scripted, in which the camera moves with a shepherd who, in driving his flock over a verdant hill, plunges into the carnage of the Pharsalia battlefield. Moreover, Mankiewicz could not begin the film as he had intended by introducing Antony as the worshipful subordinate to Caesar, because in February, Richard Burton was busy filming *The V.I.P.s* with Taylor in London. Instead of Caesar instructing Antony in how to administer Rome in his absence while he goes off to settle the dispute over the rulership of Egypt, the hastily revised version shows Caesar dispatching Rufio (Landau) and Candidus (Andrew Faulds), who were obliged to divide up Antony's dutiful lines.

A portion of the first day's filming was devoted to posing Zanuck riding up and down on the high crane for an NBC-TV documentary titled *The World of Darryl Zanuck*. When asked if he would participate in this film, Mankiewicz said, "Yes, provided you call it *Stop the World of Darryl Zanuck, I Want to Get Off*. As soon as the documentary crew had enough shots of the cigar-smoking tycoon giving the appearance of directing the camera from on high, Zanuck got into his helicopter and flew away. It was as well that Zanuck was not on hand to witness the expensive goof perpetrated on the first shot. The French cameraman misconstrued Mankiewicz's calling "Rex" to be the cut, and so the elaborate panoply of unloosing six hundred riderless horses, igniting funeral pyres, and shackling lines of captured soldiers had to be set up again with commands for the multilingual assemblage given again in six languages. "By the time the horses had been corralled," says

---

dummies instead of real horses was Joe's, according to Ranald MacDougall. MacDougall enjoyed poring over the mountains of production memos to while away his spare time at Cinecitta. In the course of his browsing, he learned that Mankiewicz had argued that the dead horses would have to be simulated, because even when horses had been knocked out by anesthesia, their chests still heaved in breathing, which would ruin the "horrors of war" effect he desired.

An aide proposed that since they had imported a vast number of horses from Yugoslavia for the production, a sufficient number of them could be killed, providing Mankiewicz with actual dead horses for his battle scene. A wiser head cautioned that the ASPCA might learn of this scheme, since the studio was swarming with journalists clamoring for gossip. Therefore, the decision was made to make the carcasses out of fiber glass. Unhappily, the plaster cast model for the dead horses was made from the scrawniest specimen in the stable, his exposed rib cage revealing his emaciation. MacDougall's curiosity over the source of the skins and manes that the wardrobe women were busily sewing on to cover the fiber-glass forms was quickly allayed—the Yugoslav horses were being systematically butchered in order to furnish them.

Martin Landau, "the wind had come up, and they never again got the shot nearly as well." At the cost of $500,000, Mankiewicz finally captured a suitably impressive establishing shot of the battle's aftermath, but without any close-up details, most of the elaborate scene becomes merely the backdrop for Caesar's commentary on the futility and waste of combat and the following dispatch of his officers on the guardianship of Rome:

> RUFIO: . . . Caesar's word will be law.
> CAESAR: Well, be sure to have at least three legions with you always—they help keep the law legal.

This scene is characteristic of Mankiewicz's intention of making *Cleopatra* "an intimate epic" (an oxymoron in Todd-AO), humanizing his legendary characters by focusing on their private lives and confining the spectacle to intermittent set pieces. (Mankiewicz's personal distaste for obligatory DeMille-like spectacle scenes is demonstrated by the ironic wink that Cleopatra gives Caesar to conclude her triumphal entry scene and by the nearly comic repetition of ballistas catapulting fiery missiles in the battles of Moongate and Actium.) Zanuck's instinct was to condense the talk-filled narrative in order to feature the spectacles, and reducing the film by three and a half hours did serve to give the battles and pageants far greater prominence than Mankiewicz had intended. As a *Newsweek* critic later observed, ". . . all that remains are high points. At six hours, *Cleopatra* might have been a movie. At four hours, it is the longest coming attraction for something that will never come."[37]

After completing the location work in Almeria, Mankiewicz returned to London for eight consecutive days of filming with Burton. These retakes principally concerned shooting new, abbreviated versions of Antony's leave-takings from his undesired wife, Octavia (Jean Marsh), and his faithful companion, Rufio.[38]

On March 5, 1963, at the Pinewood Studios where Mankiewicz

---

[37]*Newsweek,* June 24, 1963.

[38]Because the scene of Rufio's suicide is eliminated in this new version, it is unclear to the audience, when Antony discovers Rufio's body, whether he has taken his own life or been killed by Antony's deserting legion. After *Cleopatra's* opening, producer Wanger said he was "appalled" by the scene of Antony dining with Octavia, which was written and inserted under Zanuck's order. "It gives absolutely no new information," said Wanger, "and stops cold the second half of the picture."

had first taken over Mamoulian's production two years earlier, the filming of *Cleopatra* was finally completed.

Mankiewicz spent most of the next three months in Los Angeles supervising all postproduction phases of the film, including integration of the new footage and the melodiously romantic score by Alex North. North was selected as the film's composer primarily on the basis of Mankiewicz's sons' enthusiasm for his great score for Kubrick's epic, *Spartacus* (1960). Although Christopher, the Mankiewicz family's most knowledgeable music buff, was disenchanted with North's score for *Cleopatra*, Mankiewicz was so delighted with it that he made the unusual gesture (for him) of contributing extensive liner notes for the sound track album.[39]

Generous in his commentary on Alex North's score, Mankiewicz was niggardly in granting any screenwriting credit to Sidney Buchman or Ranald MacDougall. Since Buchman was unofficially blacklisted and living in Europe, MacDougall brought the issue before an arbitration panel of the Screen Writers Guild. When Walter Wanger asked Mac-Dougall to withdraw his protest and informed the Guild that no treatment by Buchman existed, MacDougall sent the abitrators his personal copy of the Buchman outline. The result was "an unpleasant arbitration for Mankiewicz and Wanger," according to MacDougall, who followed up by "vindictively" submitting his original 350-page script (misattributed to Mankiewicz on the title page), which Mankiewicz had used as the basis for many scenes. As usual, Joe had completely rewritten MacDougall's dialogue, as he had Michael Wilson's for *Five Fingers*.

The first decision handed down by the Guild's arbitration panel was that the title credit should list the screenwriters in the sequence of their work on the film, which was Buchman, MacDougall, and Mankiewicz. When this judgment was protested, a second panel gave Mankiewicz the top credit of the trio of writers. Moreover, the Screen Writers Guild, in a well-merited and face-saving gesture, honored Mankiewicz by presenting him with their annual Laurel Award for outstanding achievement in his career as a screenwriter.

Mankiewicz described his arrival in the pandemonium of the huge crowds surrounding New York's Rivoli Theatre on the evening of June

---

[39]These notes provide a valuable elucidation of many points in Mankiewicz's conception of *Cleopatra* that are unrealized in the version of the film that was released.

12, 1963, for the benefit world premiere of *Cleopatra* as the equivalent of "being carted to the guillotine in a tumbrel."

The next days' reviews in the New York press and the subsequent notices by the magazine critics were, predictably, hatchet jobs. While the public was panting to see Taylor and Burton's love scenes (which were disappointingly tame), the critics were just as eagerly waiting to denounce the obscenely expensive, scandal-ridden, and overpublicized film as worthless. Only Bosley Crowther of the *New York Times*, Mankiewicz's staunch fan, for whom Fox had set up a private screening, praised the film as "stunning and entertaining." While acknowledging how "abysmally engineered the planning and the making" of the film were, Crowther maintained that "by the grace of a rare script, writing, and direction," Mankiewicz had brought off the "dumbfounding and unbelievable" feat of making it a genuine "piece of entertainment."[40]

Of all the unfavorable reviews the film received, few were as scathing as that of the new film critic of the *Times*'s rival paper, the *New York Herald Tribune*, Judith Crist, who was desperately trying to make a name for herself after being promoted from second-string drama critic. Crist's review, titled "CLEOPATRA: A Monumental Mouse," so provoked Fox's head of publicity that he threatened Jock Whitney, the *Tribune*'s publisher, with withdrawal of all of Fox's advertising from the paper. Fox did not follow through on this threat, although it did cancel its table at the 1963 New York Newspaper Women's Club ceremony granting Crist its Front Page Award for her "fearless" review. In a gesture of noblesse oblige, Mankiewicz personally paid for the table anyway, and ten years later (November 1973) served as Mrs. Crist's honored guest at one of her Tarrytown (New York) Conference Center weekends, where a mini-retrospective of his films, along with his commentary, was shown to an audience whose members paid $100 or more for the privilege of attending. (Judith Crist's subsequent reviews of *Cleopatra* in *TV Guide* are a great deal more temperate, even verging on the favorable.)

In the midst of the critics' carping about many of *Cleopatra*'s genuine deficiencies, such as the less than "infinite variety" displayed by the often shrill and shallow performance of the technically ill-equipped Elizabeth Taylor as Cleopatra, few reviewers dealt with the

[40]*New York Times*, June 13, 1963.

film as superior to most previous historical epics. Only Richard Roud, in the *Manchester Guardian,* who overstated his case by calling *Cleopatra* inferior to such epics of the period as *El Cid* (1961) and *Barabbas* (1962), and Michael Wood, who was more objective in his perceptive 1975 study, *America in the Movies,* discussed the film in its generic context.

Wood's thesis is that *Cleopatra* was "a perverse project" in that it "has all the ingredients of a great elegy . . . and hardly any of the elements of an epic," which by Wood's classical definition only "thrive[s] on historical success" and must embody "an extravagant victory against all odds."

Given the facts of Antony's desertion of his troops at the naval battle of Actium and the famous love-death suicides of Antony and Cleopatra, it is difficult to see how Mankiewicz could have reworked the story of tragic love into any kind of a triumph, although Cleopatra's fatal act serves to thwart the villainous Octavian's ambition to degrade her by returning her to Rome as his captive. Moreover, the final image of Cleopatra lying in state on a catafalque dressed in the golden raiment of her triumphal entry into Rome is meant to link her with the similarly gilded figure of the embalmed Alexander the Great in his tomb, the shrine that inspires Cleopatra and Caesar's "one world" Alexandrian dream of international union and peace.[41] Cleopatra's obsession with achieving this goal comes into conflict with her personal devotion to her Roman lovers and leads first to Caesar's assassination and then to Antony's defeat.

Despite Zanuck's massive cuts, Mankiewicz managed to preserve his script's imagery of golden imperial symbols, which includes the gilded statue of Caesar as a god (which Cleopatra has erected outside her palace) and Cleopatra's gold necklace of commemorative Roman coins bearing Caesar's profile, which Antony feels obliged to unclasp before he can first go to bed with her. (This necklace ends up as a piece of booty thrown about by Octavian's conquering soldiers when they

---

[41]Asked if this "one world" theme was derived from the ideology of Wendell Willkie, the 1941 presidential aspirant whose candidacy Mankiewicz supported, Joe replied that, on the contrary, he had taken this idea directly from the Durants' study of Caesar and Cleopatra in their *Story of Civilization* series. *Newsweek*'s critic accurately noted that the idealistic statements in which these ambitions are couched, as Cleopatra and Caesar seal their marital and political pact by Alexander's tomb, attempt to blunt the totalitarian implications of this dream of world conquest and rulership.

invade Cleopatra's palace near the end of the film.) Mankiewicz also uses the transfer of another piece of gilded jewelry as a connecting device throughout the film to exemplify the transience of power. A ring has been given by Caesar's daughter to her husband, Pompey, whom Caesar has defeated in the opening Battle of Pharsalia. When he pursues Pompey to Egypt, Caesar is presented, to his dismay, with Pompey's decapitated head and the ring, which he places on a gold chain around his neck as a memento mori. In turn, Caesar gives it as a trinket of succession to Caesarian, his son by Cleopatra, and when Octavian later arrives in Alexandria wearing it, Cleopatra instantly realizes that Octavian has murdered her son, despite his assurances that the boy is safe. Cleopatra's awareness that the last of her line is dead leads directly to her decision to take her own life.

Another of *Cleopatra*'s imaginative linking devices was the use of matching dissolves from faded illustrations, painted in the style of ancient Roman frescoes, to vivid, freeze-frame, establishing shots of a scene that swiftly flow into motion. This cinematic technique of bringing antiquity to life or receding back into its artifacts was similarly employed by Fellini in his *Satyricon* (1970).

Michael Wood suggests that the difficulties of *Cleopatra*'s production permeated "the mood of the finished film." More precisely, Mankiewicz's fatigue is evidenced in his increasingly stilted writing[42] and enervated direction of the second half of the film, combined with

---

[42]Although Mankiewicz felt that he had found a style for the dialogue that skirted both the "pseudo-archaisms" of most historical films and the contemporary idiom, there are some notable lapses into the latter, such as Cleopatra's lines to Caesar, "We've gotten off to a bad start, haven't we? I've done nothing but rub you the wrong way."

While the critics jumped on Antony's comment on Cleopatra's triumphal entry, "Nothing like this has come into Rome since Romulus and Remus," few singled out Mankiewicz's superb lines for Antony before and after his bungled suicide:

ANTONY: *(staring at his sword)* I've always envied Rufio his long arms. *(After stabbing himself and rolling down a short flight of stairs to drive the blade home, Antony finds himself badly wounded but still alive.)*
   The ultimate desertion—I from myself. Else how could I have missed what I must have aimed for all my life?

Penelope Houston, writing in *Sight & Sound* (Autumn 1963), accurately describes the script as "not achiev[ing] anything like a consistency of tone. . . . Much of the script is of the order known as 'literate'—that is to say, the sentences are very carefully grammatical and just a little too long for some of the actors to speak with ease or conviction."

the ever more listless performances of Burton and Taylor, who were preoccupied and embroiled in the domestic ramifications of their endlessly publicized affair.

Rex Harrison's suave authority as Caesar and his unique ability to make Mankiewicz's dialogue sparkle successfully carry the first half of the film.[43] Contrary to Mankiewicz's assertions, Darryl Zanuck's intuition that something was radically wrong with the second half of the film was likely a sound one. However, Zanuck's diagnosis was that the fault was attributable to the weakness of Antony's character. An examination of the screenplay suggests that the real weakness lies in the frequent banality of Mankiewicz's prosaic approximations of the poetry of Shakespeare's tragedy, which served to elevate Antony and Cleopatra to the level of sublime creatures.[44] The consequent truncation of Antony's role renders Burton considerably less an object of our sympathy and more a scenery-chewing, self-pitying lush.[45] Similarly, the cutting of Octavian's part leaves McDowall as a peroxided, effeminate ranter, rather than the ice-cold schemer masking an envy of Antony as great as Antony's sense of inferiority to Caesar.

---

[43]The first half is also leavened by frequent quips and an air of high comedy, while the second half, for the most part, turns dully solemn.

Rex Harrison said in a 1972 interview with the author that Caesar was his favorite film role. In 1977, while in rehearsal for *Caesar and Cleopatra*, he disparaged Mankiewicz's dialogue in comparison to Shaw's in a *New York Times* interview. Harrison lacked his customary vitality, and the Broadway production failed dismally, yet his Caesar in *Cleopatra* was an expertly Shavian-style performance.

Mankiewicz's intention was to modify Shaw's concept of an elderly, sexless, and pedantic Caesar (that is, Shaw himself) molding a kittenish, schoolgirl Cleopatra into regal womanhood. Ironically, Harrison's sophistication opposite the physically mature but girlish-mannered Taylor has the effect of replicating the Shavian situation.

As in Shaw's play, Caesar is beneficent to his enemies, while Cleopatra has an appetite for personal vengeance. Mankiewicz's major change is to make Cleopatra combative with Caesar from the time of their first encounter and also the object of his sexual attraction. Although Mankiewicz attributes to Cleopatra an intelligence and emotional complexity equal to Caesar's, Taylor's performance belies these attributions.

[44]"At the end," wrote Penelope Houston, "the dialogue seems drastically inhibited by an awful awareness that it must risk comparison with Shakespeare and gropes helplessly after a tragic idiom of its own" (*Sight & Sound*, Autumn 1963).

[45]Shots of Antony, goblet in hand, are as frequent as scenes in which Caesar declines a drink. Antony's weakness for wine is continually commented on and is the source of Cleopatra's satiric pageant showing Bacchus wining and wenching, at the banquet for Antony on board her royal barge. The parallel between Antony's rivalry with Caesar and Joe's with Herman is slightly altered by giving the younger, overshadowed Antony the attribute of Herman's alcoholism.

Because the eliminated three and a half hours of *Cleopatra* remain stored in Fox's vault and are thus unviewable, it is impossible to verify John De Cuir's claim that "the best of Joe's work was cut out" or Mankiewicz's contention that Richard Burton's performance was obliterated.

The extraordinarily long four-hour-and-three-minute version that opened at the Rivoli had twenty-two minutes deleted early in its run, following the savage reviews, but this loss was minor in comparison to the cuts made to reduce the film to three hours in a 35-mm. print after it had played its first-run engagements. This print is the only version now available for revivals, and Mankiewicz bitterly describes the progressive butchery of his intricately structured work as watching it "being whittled into banjo picks."

As for the widely quoted figure of $40 million, which *Cleopatra* is alleged to have cost, in April 1964 a Fox executive announced *Cleopatra*'s negative cost as $31 million and $44 million as the figure at which the film would break even. Several knowledgeable sources like Doc Merman insist that *Cleopatra* has not only broken even but earned a bit of money, while later Fox pictures such as *Hello, Dolly!* (1969) and *Tora! Tora! Tora!* (1970) have lost astronomical sums. Merman scoffs at all the published figures of *Cleopatra*'s cost, saying that they undoubtedly contain every Fox write-off, including Darryl Zanuck's laundry bill.

While *Cleopatra* served to make Burton and Taylor the most sought-after and highly paid team in the movies, its critical reception severely damaged Mankiewicz's professional reputation and self-esteem.

Joe and his newly pregnant wife sought a country retreat away from New York's social demands and publicity, where he could hide his humiliation and regain his vitality. No house and grounds captivated his exacting taste except one that was not on the market. This was the idyllic estate of Donald Klopfer, Bennett Cerf's partner in Random House, which featured symmetrical ponds and overhanging willow trees on either side of the path from the residential house to a converted barn that served as an imposing library-office.

During a party at the Klopfers', Mankiewicz begged his host to notify him if he ever considered giving up the property, but Klopfer assured him that there was little likelihood of this happening. Joe's timing proved to be propitious, as little more than a week after the party, Mrs. Klopfer decided that she no longer cared to compete with Phyllis Cerf as the social doyenne of the Pound Ridge area.

Mankiewicz's luck seemed to be changing for the better. In succession, he acquired his dream house, his wife gave birth to Alexandra in April 1966, the daughter he had always longed for, and the isolated study proved the perfect place to begin writing again.

With all the awards and certificates for his successful films covering the available wall space, Mankiewicz's only framed mementos of *Cleopatra*— two *New Yorker* cartoons—were deliberately placed in the study's bathroom, just above the toilet. One cartoon typifies the hopeless position in which Mankiewicz found himself during the production. Two prisoners in a dungeon are chained to their cell wall with their arms manacled above their heads. One convict turns to the other and announces, "Now here's my plan." The second drawing shows two matrons standing on a suburban railway platform, with the famous poster of Harrison and Burton behind the reclining Taylor in the background. The poster proclaims, "The Motion Picture the World Has Been Waiting For." In the caption one matron says to the other, "What annoys me is that I *know* I'm going to see it."

"It has always been my belief that Ben Jonson botched the finish of his play"

"Scripts. What else is there? Starting when you're a kid—what you're going to be when you grow up. Then for the rest of your years . . . a brand new script every day. Once in a while it plays the way you write it. But most of the time, life—or other people's scripts—louse it up. . . . In my business [the movies], after a while you find yourself writing fewer and fewer of your own—about yourself, that is."

(cut from the first draft of THE HONEY POT*)*

*T*HE OBSERVATION THAT "LIFE LOUSES UP OUR SCRIPTS"—OUR plans for careers, romances, or even for a single day's activity—is one of Joe Mankiewicz's most frequent laments.

The Honey Pot (1967), Mankiewicz's last screenplay to date, was written, in part, to illustrate this personal maxim. The plot is patterned on Ben Jonson's Elizabethan comedy *Volpone,* as updated by Thomas Sterling in his novel *The Evil of the Day* and as dramatized by Frederick Knott in his play *Mr. Fox of Venice,* based on Sterling's novel.

The intricate pattern of reversals of expectation woven into Mankiewicz's final shooting script is partially obscured by the nineteen minutes cut from the film after the fiasco of its gala London premiere.[1] Even with this substantial reduction, *The Honey Pot* moves sluggishly for most of its two hours.

Of far more drastic consequence, in Mankiewicz's view, was his abandoning the novelties of his first script, among them a series of laudatory memos from a theater-chain owner that commented on the

---

[1]The film ran 150 minutes in London, 131 minutes at its New York premiere, and is presently 121 minutes in the version shown at revival theaters. The most widely seen version on NBC-TV is labeled "edited for television"; it is the two-hour version, with 10 to 15 minutes cut, including one of Mankiewicz's favorite gags—the Hollywood actress expressing amazement that a seventeenth-century play, *'Tis Pity She's a Whore,* was written by John Ford, whom she thought of only as a movie director.

action, and what Mankiewicz terms "the Pirandellian device" of a running battle between the actor playing Cecil Fox and a theater manager over these intrusive commentaries.

"In many ways, the first draft I sent over to United Artists was the best script I've ever written in my life," says Mankiewicz. "It had in it many things that have never been done on the screen—things that I would like to do today. It was a 'self-censoring' film in which memos were suddenly slipped in front of the projector, based upon the [hypocritical] morality of the American people."

For example, the stated policy of Archimedes A. Bluebird, president of Blauvogel International, is "to bring to our community theater [a neighborhood Blauvogel Flagship of Family Entertainment] the same standards of morality which the average family has in its own home!" (As Mankiewicz's mouthpiece, Fox snidely retorts to this credo, "If Mr. Bluenose succeeds, the police will close down every cinema in the world!")

Following an introductory scene in which McFly, a gigolo for Rome's Eternal City Escort Service, pockets his chit marked with a $50 tip and departs the sleeping figure of a matron "with the features of a baking contest winner—her contact lenses safely parked on the night table," this memo appears on screen:

SUBJECT—PRODUCT MORALITY ANALYSIS
. . . it should be made even more clear that while acting as this lady's guide, they were caught in a rainstorm and had to dry their clothes. The fact that he is now applying for honest work [as Fox's secretary] is morally helpful.[2]

Following an extended poker game between Fox and McFly, during which Fox vainly tries to cheat the former Las Vegas dealer, this memo appears:

Obviously no expense spared here in providing authentic fine points of poker. As a result, the scene is both entertaining and truly educational. Tie-ups should be made with schools, teacher groups, etc.

---

[2]Mankiewicz is satirizing Hollywood censorship, which began with the Production Code issued by the Hays Office in 1930 and was made even more restrictive by the strictures of the Catholic Legion of Decency, founded in 1934. Mankiewicz still derides inane rulings that required that married couples be shown sleeping in separate beds and that served to veto a Metro script titled *Infidelity*. Only *Fidelity* was deemed acceptable, though F. Scott Fitzgerald's screenplay was never filmed.

Later, Lone Star fantasizes Fox as a grizzled prospector dying in the desert. After tenderly cradling him in her arms, she displays her true pioneer spirit ["ambition, guts, and above all, greed"], shouts, "Are you dead, you bastard?" and proceeds to tear open Fox's gold-filled saddle bags. A memo follows:

> Solid values here. Recalling to our audience what our pioneers went through for their beliefs—and how their women stuck [by them] to the end. My wife is crazy about the cowgirl outfit [Lone Star's ludicrously spotless, white-fringed "Hollywood" costume].

UA's head, Arthur Krim, would have none of this. Mankiewicz conjectures that "*au fond*, Mr. Krim was a little scared of the exhibitors' reaction." Some time later, Joe mused, "In a crazy way, I don't think it was a question of hitting Arthur Krim or any of them where they live, so much as they are terrified of fantasy as such. He [Krim] wanted all of that eliminated, not because of its *content*, but because of its *style*. . . . I think this was the first projected film in which the actors about to appear on the screen are heard before they appear, screaming about not being allowed to get on, arguing about not being interrupted. In other words, the Pirandello pattern of the stage being used on the screen." For example:

> THEATER MANAGER: Get off the sound track. You haven't even been established as a character yet!
> FOX: You're drooling away precious footage.

"In films," Mankiewicz elaborated, "you have to break through what the financiers believe to be the audience's capacity to understand, and the men who put up money for films say that the last big hit is what the audience can understand—nothing different. They do not want anything new. If anything new comes along, it is rammed down their throats, and they are delighted when it fails."

Mankiewicz did film, and later scrap, the three dream sequences of the covetous women fantasizing Fox's death and their inheritance. The elimination of these scenes—the "scripts" that are subsequently "loused up" by reality—is the major disfigurement of Mankiewicz's grand design.

In one of them, the actual meeting between Princess Dominique (Capucine) and Fox (Rex Harrison) begins with exactly the same dialogue that she had imagined in her fantasy of Fox's death-bed contrition for having once propositioned her aboard his yacht, at which time she had scornfully rejected the pleasure craft as the price of her consent. However, the irony lost with the cutting of this prelude hardly diminishes the impact of the scene that follows, which is surely one of the most viciously cynical depictions of a sexual conquest in Mankiewicz's or the cinema's canon.

> DOMINIQUE: Is that why—as you wrote—my forgiveness is so important to you?
>
> FOX: Because of all women, my experience with you was the one I regret most—perhaps the only one I regret at all.
>
> DOM.: *(gently)* I have forgiven you.
>
> FOX: (*as if not hearing*) Because—at the time—it was impossible for me to concede, with my big yacht and many millions, that there was anything or anyone I couldn't have . . .
>
> DOM.: (*comfortingly*) I promise you, you're forgiven.
>
> FOX: And because—now—with an even bigger yacht and even more millions—(*He brings his head forward. His eyes glitter at her. Calmly*) I know damn well there *isn't* anything—or anyone. Isn't that so—your Highness?
>
> (DOMINIQUE *stares at him, numbly. She rises slowly.*)
>
> DOM.: Of course. You couldn't care less, could you, about being forgiven —for anything. . . . (*harshly*) What guarantee will you give me—that I will be the one? [that is, his heir]
>
> FOX: None.
>
> (DOMINIQUE *nods. She crosses slowly to close the curtains.*)
>
> FOX: Leave the light as it is. Come and sit down.
>
> > [I don't like being repulsive in the dark. (First draft)]
>
> (*He indicates the ottoman beside his chair. Submissively, impassively, she sits. He eyes her for a moment.*)
>
> FOX: It isn't easy for a man—when a woman needs him more than he needs her.
>
> (*Then, starting at the very top of her dress, with great deliberation, he begins to unbutton the front of it. . . .* MCFLY *enters.* DOMINIQUE *leaps up, turns away, and buttons her dress quickly.* FOX *stifles his irritation.*)

Mankiewicz did, however, delete for Krim a number of symbolic dreams reminiscent of those in Bergman's *Wild Strawberries*.[3] Their

---

[3]Mankiewicz used to scoff at Ingmar Bergman's symbolic dream sequences and devices in *The Seventh Seal* and *Wild Strawberries* as pretentious and old-fashioned derivatives of cinematic German expressionism of the twenties. Of late, he has shifted his scorn to such critical favorites of American film critics as Antonioni and Bertolucci.

reception was prophesied in one of the scrapped Bluebird memos:

> Talk, talk, talk. When is this girl [Nurse Watkins] going to start regenerating this boy [McFly]? The phone call was just a phony excuse for that artsy dream sequence. Chop it out! This kind of nonsense we don't have to take from American directors.

"I had this meeting with UA," Mankiewicz recalls. "I had just come out of this two-year depression that I had been in [following *Cleopatra*], and for the first time in my life I wasn't sure. . . . The fact remains that with *The Honey Pot* I was terribly insecure and shot the wrong script. I just shot the comedy-mystery they wanted . . . [that is,] the 'straight' part of the script and not the part that I really thought was original." Mankiewicz's contention that he "wouldn't have had any trouble in cutting [the long first draft] down" is somewhat questionable when his history of producing overlong scripts for his own productions is considered.

Rex Harrison recalls that when Mankiewicz first sold him on the project, while he was stopping at the St. Regis in New York after collecting his Oscar for *My Fair Lady,* the voluminous script filled a large suitcase. Harrison remembers, "Joe was rather loath to show it, as almost no one had seen it." As Harrison became progressively intrigued, Mankiewicz, buoyed by his interest, kept postponing his dinner until the better part of the evening was consumed just reading through the script. Harrison does, however, corroborate Joe's view that "the film we shot was certainly neither as unusual nor as clever as that original script," and appreciates its Mankiewiczian hallmark—"it was a very ambitious idea."

When filming began in Rome at Cinecittà on September 20, 1965, Harrison, a veteran of three previous Mankiewicz films and a friend since his years as an imported Fox contractee in the forties, found Joe, as a director, "a changed man." Harrison, who had marveled at Mankiewicz's unruffled poise during the making of *Cleopatra*, notably when they had to spend frustrated hours waiting for Elizabeth Taylor to arrive, now found him "far less relaxed . . . much more easily irritable, and less tolerant of everything.[4] It was then I began to realize

---

[4]Harrison himself was a prime source of irritation to Mankiewicz. While Joe acknowledges that, as a writer, he would rather "have Rex Harrison play my high comedy than any other actor in the world," as a director, he describes Harrison as an egotistical "cunt" and "a very difficult man to work with. He gives everybody problems

what had happened to him over *Cleopatra."* John De Cuir, who designed both films, said that "coming back to Rome [three years later] reawakened all his memories of *Cleopatra,* all the heartaches and problems."⁵

Costar Cliff Robertson found Mankiewicz "extra-guarded . . . because of the *Cleopatra* experience, always holding his armor a little high." When Robertson, a regular in live television drama and oriented toward the budgetary economies the video medium enforced, had the temerity to suggest that Mankiewicz take advantage of a complex lighting setup to shoot a subsequent scene in which he again walks to the palazzo's private elevator, Joe turned to Rex, laughed, and said, "No, son, we're not doing television now." "Joe likes the style of a big movie," says Robertson. "He's not oriented to such a pecuniary logistic because he's used to movies being done the way they were in the olden days." The filming of *The Honey Pot* required five months, an exceptionally long period for a film shot mostly in interior sets.

The Honey Pot represented not only a comeback attempt from the career-shattering experience of *Cleopatra,* but a return as well to the genre of Mankiewicz's greatest successes and expertise—the elegant drawing-room comedy. Mankiewicz's post-*Cleopatra* cracks about wanting to shoot his next film in a phone booth or anything with four walls are symptomatic of his longing for the familiarity of a theater piece shot principally on sound-stage interiors. The wittiest of the film's many working titles, *Anyone for Venice?,* is indicative of Mankiewicz's inclination. ("Tennis, anyone?" was a classic drawing-room comedy entrance line.)

Rarely in a contemporary film have as many opening and closing doors been photographed. At a faster tempo, the device is indigenous to stage farce from Feydeau to George Abbott, but Mankiewicz's

---

and he knows it. Everybody knows it." Robert Lantz refers to the "love-hate" relationship between Harrison and Mankiewicz and describes the "bloody" clashes between them on all four films that they made together. "There is enough residual contempt [between them] to last a lifetime," says Lantz. "Rex, in rehearsal, is impossible with directors and actors." Both Lantz and Mankiewicz's wife begged Joe, for the sake of his health, not to turn to Harrison should Laurence Olivier be felled by illness during the making of *Sleuth* (1972).

⁵On December 4, 1965, Italy's president awarded Mankiewicz an Order of Merit, as compensation for his travail and in gratitude for his having made four films in Italy. Joe was the first American to receive the honor, which granted him the title *Commendatore.*

scrupulous observance of the convention, beyond heightening the mystery of McFly's inventory of the rooms in the palazzo, most likely derives from the predilection of Lubitsch, Joe's idol, for investing a closing door with suggestions of sexual intimacy. Such early lessons from the master take root and are difficult to abandon. Robert Lantz believes that by forcing his client to view and analyze the editing of a number of current films prior to making *Sleuth* (1972), he helped persuade Joe to renounce "the old-fashioned movie-making approach where everything had to be [painstakingly] established."

Mankiewicz fired his original *Honey Pot* cinematographer, Pietro Portalupi, after the first week and engaged a younger man, Gianni Di Venanzo, famed for his work with Antonioni (*La Notte, L'Eclisse*) and Fellini (*8 ½, Juliet of the Spirits*). Di Venanzo "promptly reversed the lighting pattern [of his predecessor], and though comedy is usually brightly lit, decided on diffused lighting, deploying only baby spots to get his emphases."[6]

Cliff Robertson says, "I never saw a man do more with less light. He gave the film a sense of mystery and resplendence." Mankiewicz considers him possibly his favorite cinematographer among the many great ones he has worked with (Arthur Miller, Robert Krasker, and Jack Cardiff among them).

Sadly, the forty-six-year-old Di Venanzo died some weeks before the picture was completed, of hepatitis incorrectly diagnosed as food poisoning. He was succeeded, for the remainder of the filming, by his camera operator, Pasqualino De Santis,[7] but the event, according to Robertson, "cast a pall over the whole set."

Although the homicide and suicide in *The Honey Pot* are treated cavalierly, with the murderer and his victim happily reunited in the afterlife, the reality of death surrounded the production. The schedule was altered to permit Susan Hayward to fly back to the States to attend to her gravely ill husband, who soon died. Rachel Roberts, at the time Rex Harrison's wife, attempted suicide by a barbiturate overdose after she was rejected for the part of the English nurse in favor of Maggie Smith. Mankiewicz was awakened in the middle of the night by the distraught Harrison. As a veteran of such crises, Joe forsook his sleep to comfort his star and keep his misfortune out of the newspapers.

---

[6]Melton S. Davis, *New York Times,* December 5, 1965.

[7]De Santis has since become a top Italian cinematographer and won an Academy Award for his work on Zeffirelli's gorgeous *Romeo and Juliet* (1968).

If *The Honey Pot* is filled with misleading clues about the identity of the murderer, it is equally full of revealing ones about the identity of its author.

The film's great set piece is Fox's speech on time, "Fox's religion," according to Mankiewicz, and "the one obsession common to all mankind," according to Fox. Mankiewicz says the following speech "is one of which I'm very proud":

> *(The various clocks strike.* FOX, *at the mantel, glowers morosely at* MERLE's *magnificent modern clock—encased in glass—with dials showing the time in major cities throughout the world.)*
>
> FOX: Damn clocks. The sun's just coming up in Bangkok.
>
> SARAH: It's getting late in Venice.
>
> FOX: Bangkok, too. What makes you think sunrise is only early, Mothbrain? It's damn late—everywhere.
>
> *(He turns toward the bar. His eyes fall on the hourglass filled with gold dust. He picks it up, carries it with him tenderly. He turns it over.)*
>
> FOX: Listen . . . not a sound. There is nothing like gold to pass the time—there never has been. Watch . . . see the color of time. Golden. *(He fixes a drink, and drinks.)* How little you people value time—you little people. Like everything else, you'll choose what's more—not what's better. Even time. You'll pray to live one hundred long, miserable years—you'd feel cheated if all you got was, say, fifty of the best. Quantity, *si*—quality, *no.* Venice is tiny and precious; Los Angeles, gigantic and terrifying—who wants it? Most people, that's who. *(another drink, a stiffer one)* There's *good* time, and *bad* time, you know—does a clock give a damn what kind it measures? No. But we do—we *special ones.* We slow down for the good—we sip it, second by second, like a great wine—and we speed up the bad. You little people—you chumps—swallow time like hamburger. A hundred years of well-done hamburger—you'll all settle for that. *(another drink, which he carries toward her)* If I were to tell you that, for me, these ten minutes of my life will be fuller, and richer, than the next ten years for any chump in Paris, London, Rome, New York, or Bangkok—would you know what the hell I was talking about?
>
> SARAH: Honestly—no.

Mankiewicz, viewed by many of his colleagues as justly snobbish because of his superior intellect and accomplishment,[8] is quite forthright about his elitism. "I don't believe in the equality of people," he

---

[8]Cliff Robertson, for one, terms him "a delightful snob."

says. "All people are born equal, but that equality ceases within five minutes after they are born—depending on the roughness of the cloth they are wrapped in and the color of the room in which they are put; the quality of the milk they drink and the gentleness of the woman who picks them up."

He expands his argument to inveigh against the egalitarian principle of the ballot box. "I don't see why democracy should suddenly equalize literacy and illiteracy. I believe that people should have to qualify for voting privileges. Each person should have a vote, but some should count for more than others because some people know more than others and are better qualified to vote."

The same principle animates his condemnation of the membership "of what is fatuously termed the Motion Picture Academy of Arts and Sciences," which he finds polluted by the inclusion of biased studio heads, publicists, and ill-informed figures on the periphery of the business. Mankiewicz fancifully muses about forming a genuine "academy" of his peers—fellow Oscar winners for writing and directing—to vote on the annual recipients of these awards. Mankiewicz's own criterion for those with whom he prefers to associate is proclaimed in Fox's line, "Now, as you know, wherever in the world individuals of great talent —or those who have otherwise deviated from the normal—meet, there is an instant, instinctive recognition."

As the work-at-home *grand seigneur* of his own Westchester County, New York, estate, Mankiewicz views the existence of his neighboring suburban commuters with aristocratic condescension. "Christ, I watch them leave here—fifty thousand of them every day drive into the city. The wives are hanging around the supermarket. They're getting fucked by the laundryman or the milkman. The fifty thousand men come back five days a week, and Saturday it's the golf course and boozing."

One of Joe's favorite jokes in *The Honey Pot,* which he feels went unappreciated, is the tag to the scene in which the foolish police inspector Rizzi and his family sit spellbound watching *Perry Mason,* ludicrously dubbed for Italian television. At the conclusion of the show, Rizzi exclaims with awe, "A great genius. If it were not for Signor Perry Mason—every week, in America, an innocent person would be convicted of murder."

Mankiewicz's personal contempt for television is voiced by Fox, who terms TV entertainment "for the witless and undemanding," comparable to the Elizabethan hoi polloi's barbaric pleasure in witnessing the "torturing [of] lunatics and animals—bear baiting. . . . The Elizabethan elite, however, for their more exclusive entertainment, baited each other. People baiting"—a favorite Mankiewicz sport.[9]

The pursuit of wealth—the trait common to all of *The Honey Pot*'s characters—is a significant preoccupation of Mankiewicz himself. "I know money, McFly," says Fox early in the proceedings, "there's never enough." The assertion parallels a conversation in a limousine carrying Mankiewicz, fellow writer-director Moss Hart, and publisher Bennett Cerf to a Broadway opening. The subject discussed by these three very affluent men was what it would be like to have really vast wealth. "Wouldn't it be fantastic!" Mankiewicz exclaimed, much to the chagrin of his niece, Johanna, riding up front, who thought the low-incomed chauffeur might rightfully assault them.

The running poker game[10] between Fox, the aggressor and perennial loser, and the wary cardsharp McFly has nostalgic echoes for Mankiewicz. Brother Herman was a chronic loser at the big Saturday night Hollywood poker games.[11] The top film executives, who knew what a bad but inveterate player he was, would frequently get him to do script work to pay off his $1,000 or more evening's debt. Joe, after practice at smaller stakes, also worked himself up to the big tables and the large pots with as little success as Herman, and comparisons of

---

[9]For example, when Mankiewicz read in a gossip column that a wedding might be in the offing between his youngest son, Tom, and the actress Tuesday Weld, he phoned Tom and said, "Just consider the euphony of the name Tuesday Mankiewicz."

[10]The master shot of the heavily expository first poker match was an unusually long five-minute take. Both Cliff Robertson and Rex Harrison remember its extreme intricacy. Harrison recalls, "Not only was Joe's dialogue fairly hard to keep flowing correctly, but playing poker at the same time was a bit like patting your stomach and rubbing your head. I managed to get them [both] finally, but it was hard to do."

[11]In Hollywood a widely told story, possibly apocryphal, of Herman's seriousness as a poker player and his outrageous sense of humor concerns his reformation of a movie tycoon's bratty son who constantly meddled in the weekly big-stakes poker game at the film mogul's home. The rest of the players were equally irritated by this kid's wandering around the table, picking up chips, and asking questions, but no one had the temerity to reprimand the host's son.

One evening Herman took the boy by the arm and led him outside the card room. Herman shortly returned, but the boy never bothered the players for the rest of the evening. The guests were incredulous and begged Herman to tell them how he had handled the boy—thrashing, tongue-lashing, hypnotism, or what? "Easy," said Herman. "I just found a private spot on a back stairway and taught the kid to masturbate. He took to it like a duck to water."

gambling to the movie business abound in *The Honey Pot.*

The Honey Pot is the most flagrant example of Mankiewicz's penchant for expository pedantry. This obsessive elucidating of every moment of his scripts is most likely the result of his snobbish distrust of his audience's retentive intelligence. The view of the gifted comedy director Mike Nichols is pertinent to this problem. "Any good movie is filled with secrets," said Nichols in an interview at Brandeis University. "If a director doesn't leave anything unsaid, it's a lousy picture. If a picture is good, it's mysterious, with things left unsaid."[12]

Mankiewicz is not content simply to establish the analogue to *Volpone* by having Fox witness a private performance of the play (interrupted at the point he intends to depart from Jonson's plot) in the film's opening sequence. Rather, he finds it necessary for three characters (McFly, Watkins, and Rizzi) to recognize the parallel, with McFly making textual comparisons as if he were a talking crib sheet. If one knows the general contour of *Volpone,* these references are unnecessary, and if one is ignorant of it, they are simply a confusing distraction.[13]

Another spate of expository reiteration is equally tiresome. Bosley Crowther, an important Mankiewicz devotee while chief film critic for the *New York Times,* points out that "in the pursuit of [the nurse's] intrusion, Mr. Mankiewicz both helps and hurts the overall attraction and development of his film. For what he gains by the dexterity and subtle caginess of Maggie Smith as the inquisitive observer, he loses in his too strong emphasis upon her involvement and persistence in probing what's going on."[14]

Nurse Sarah Watkins's initial recognition of who killed her mistress is conveyed brilliantly through totally cinematic means. Mankiewicz sets up the scene early in the film by showing, in a seemingly pointless shot, the gondolier laboriously counting, on the stairs to the palazzo, the coins McFly has given him as fare for transporting him

---

[12]Quoted by Herman G. Weinberg, *The Lubitsch Touch,* E. P. Dutton, 1968, p. 65.

[13]In comparing his screenplay to his sources (the Sterling novel and the Knott play), Mankiewicz says, "The form of *Volpone* was not in either of them—they just referred to it. They didn't have the actual frame of the play that I started with."

[14]*New York Times,* May 23, 1967, p. 52. The generally enthusiastic reception of the film on television, even with the cuts inflicted, is partially due to the aid of these recapitulations after the distraction of long halts for commercials.

and Watkins home from their date. In her realization scene, Watkins closes her fist, in imitation of Mrs. Sheridan's gripping her roll of quarters, the remembered sound of the gondolier's coin clinking recurs on the sound track, and (via a quick cut of the gondolier scene) she recalls the oddity of the gondolier laboring to count the fare. No oddity at all, if McFly had paid him with Mrs. Sheridan's quarters—as he must have!

Regrettably, Mankiewicz mars this ingenious stroke of compression by having Sarah subsequently confide her realization, at length, to both McFly (to demonstrate her love for him) and Fox (to tenuously motivate his suicide because McFly now has possession of this misconstrued evidence). The repetitious testimony protracts the "one genuinely charming and touching scene" (according to Crowther) between Rex Harrison and Maggie Smith, two English masters of high comedy technique, whose brilliant interplay gives Mankiewicz's text the true luster it requires.[15]

The scene not only contains Fox's speech on time, but begins with an astonishing "private moment"—a solo balletic bedroom turn by Fox (Harrison cleverly intercut with a dancer double), whose one frustrated ambition has been to be a ballet dancer, performed to Ponchielli's "Dance of the Hours." Fox continually plays a record of this piece, which fuses his secret ambition with his obsession about time, and Mankiewicz cleverly builds up to this virtuoso display by foreshadowing shots of Fox doing barre exercises or danced entrances.

One of the surprising disappointments of *The Honey Pot*, noted by many critics, is the lackluster performances of the three lady predators, played by the unflatteringly photographed trio of the aging Susan Hayward, Edie Adams, and Capucine, in the hands of a famed director of women. Partially this is because of the sizable cut in the film that gave these characters some background by showing each woman in her native milieu and her distinctive dream of inheritance from the expiring Fox.

Partially it is a matter of casting. Capucine was a "special friend"

---

[15]Rex Harrison commented, "It's nice when the ball comes back, as with Maggie Smith. The ball comes back so rarely in most of my screen work. . . . You [generally] have to hit as though there wasn't a ball there." After notable supporting roles in *The Pumpkin Eater* (1963) and *The V.I.P.s* (1963), Maggie Smith was given her first substantial part by Mankiewicz in *The Honey Pot.*

of Charles Feldman, Mankiewicz's agent at the time and the film's packager.[16] Anne Bancroft was originally announced for the role of the dumb Hollywood star, played by Edie Adams, but she abdicated it for a more prestigious stage role in *The Devils*. Although Edie Adams is known for her impersonations of film stars, such as her "dumb blonde" takeoff on Marilyn Monroe, her performance never transcends the caricature of her nightclub routine. Susan Hayward was suffering a private grief, as previously noted. Even so, her delivery of such lines as "Forget the wrap, I think I'll just turn on a little heat of my own," or "Hold on to your crown, Highness—and your bottle, Lowness," compares unfavorably with Bette Davis's zestful readings of similar lines in *All About Eve*.

Mankiewicz's observations on the social targets he aimed at with each of these women are more interesting than the figures themselves. (An English critic, Alexander Walker, called the uncut version Mankiewicz's "Letter to Three Bitches.")[17]

Merle McGill's (Adams) lines, "You know what would be wonderful? If life was like a movie script. . . . They take out all the terrible part of life—the living of it. You want—dissolve—you've got," derive from Mankiewicz's observation that this infantile demand "is the real

---

[16] *The Honey Pot* is billed as a Charles K. Feldman / Famous Artists Productions / United Artists production, with Mankiewicz, as is his preference since his Metro days, taking no credit as the film's producer, a title he despises. His contempt for the producer's function is best illustrated by an allegory he says he wrote "when [he] was very young" and which he recounted to the delight of an audience at the Tarrytown Conference Center on November 24, 1973.

Titled "What Does a Producer Do?" the fable concerns a writer, a director, and a producer scouting locations who find themselves lost in the Mojave Desert. At the point at which they decide to split up and each search for a return route, utilizing their individual talents, the writer comes upon a rock. Pushing it aside, he discovers an enormous can of tomato juice, chilled by being shielded from the sun.

"With his last bit of strength, he holds it up and says, 'I, the writer, have found the substance and the sustenance whereby we can exist. Come quickly!' The other two rush over.

"The director takes out his pocket knife, with his last remaining strength, and says, 'I, the director, will now open the can of tomato juice so that we can all drink from it and go on,' which he proceeds to do. As he and the writer fall exhausted, the director is about to raise the tin to his mouth when the producer says, 'Stop! First, I, the producer, must pee in it.' "

Mankiewicz defines an associate producer as "a mouse studying to become a rat."

[17] Alexander Walker, "Four Women and a Mankiewicz," *Evening Standard*, March 28, 1967.

sickness that Hollywood gives its most successful residents."

Princess Dominique (Capucine) is a member of the international jet set that Mankiewicz claims to despise. He lampooned them earlier in *The Barefoot Contessa,* and at the time of *The Honey Pot'*s London premiere, he said they would be the subject of his next film or play. "They create their own importance, but, in fact, they're like an appendix. Once they served a purpose, but now no one knows what they're for."

"Mankiewicz reserves his full admiration [deservedly] for Maggie Smith," whom he characterizes as "the unthrusting, emotionally honest, no less sexually fulfilling female [than traditional movie siren types]. After all, I should know about her, I married one," said Mankiewicz, referring to his present English wife, Rosemary Matthews.

One of *The Honey Pot'*s few broad farce scenes has its origin in a bit of fakery that Louis B. Mayer performed during Joe's Metro days. When Lone Star invades Fox's "sick room" with a Mutt and Jeff team of ambulance attendants, Fox feigns a nearly simultaneous heart attack and rigor mortis to prevent them from carrying him off.

Mayer employed the ruse when Myrna Loy refused a script despite Mankiewicz's persistent cajoling on Mayer's behalf. Loy recalls that Mayer conveniently "expired" on his office couch, and that while his attendants hovered over him, she and Joe stood by, in a corner of the room, until Mankiewicz's nonstop jokes made her burst out laughing. Her hilarity was curbed by a frantic aide who implored, "Myrna, for God's sake, get some ice!" She complied by scurrying to Mayer's office bar and finally managed to locate a filled bucket in a closet overflowing with gift bottles of Southern Comfort. When Mayer "came to" an hour later, he berated her unseemly mirth by saying, "You wouldn't have cared if I *had* died!"[18]

Mankiewicz's version is somewhat different. He recalls that after Loy had entered Mayer's office, there was the familiar announcement of a heart attack and an urgent summons made for Mayer's physician, Dr. Jones. After the doctor's ministrations, Loy submitted to accepting the script, saying, "Oh, for God's sake, Louie, don't let it have this effect on you. It's only a part." Mayer groaned, "No, no. You're only saying that to make me feel better." Loy remonstrated, "Honestly, I'll play it, I *want* to play it," and left the office mortified at the catastrophe

---

[18]Recounted by Myrna Loy in a 1972 telephone interview.

she had precipitated. The moment she closed the door, Mayer leaped off the couch and briskly inquired of his secretary, Ida Koverman, "O.K., who's next?"

Mankiewicz confesses, "I have no way of knowing whether her version or mine is accurate," but asserts that Mayer's bar was actually stocked with cream soda because "he only gave liquor as gifts to those who were not under contract [to MGM]" and therefore kept none on the premises.

Cliff Robertson early concluded that it was as well "not to cross swords" with a man who filled in his crossword puzzles with a fountain pen, as Mankiewicz does. "He's extremely jealous of his words," Robertson recalls. "Even for an infinitesimal change, you had an infinitesimal chance of getting it made." Robertson also suspected that behind the "Cheshire grin" of the director who patiently smoked his pipe with an attitude of "this too shall pass" while the actor fervently appealed to change an *and* or a *but*, there remained "the playfulness of a little boy."

This intuition was ultimately borne out. Actors away from home develop cravings for favorite domestic delicacies. Edie Adams satisfied hers by flying in Chasen's chili for a cast party, but the English contingent, headed by Maggie Smith, yearned for a particular pork sausage unobtainable in Rome. When Robertson embarked for a long weekend in London, Smith, the script girl, and the English members of the crew all pressed money on him to purchase the prized "bangers." Robertson faithfully returned with seven pounds of sausage in tow, but made the innocent mistake of storing them in the accommodating Mankiewicz larder for Joe to deliver, since Robertson had no call the next day.

Robertson assumed that Mankiewicz had dispensed the sausages to their commissioners and was moderately surprised that no one ever bothered to thank him for his efforts. Three weeks later Maggie Smith took the initiative and kiddingly chastised him for his negligence with, "I wasn't going to bring it up, you s.o.b., but . . ." When confronted, Mankiewicz replied, "Yes, they were delicious," with a wry, "nobody asked me" expression of innocence, though Mrs. Mankiewicz later informed Robertson they had been her gourmet husband's daily breakfast treat. The Britons, accustomed to wartime privation, accepted their loss as part of Joe's "raffish sense of humor."

Unawed by the precedent of a great playwright and unruffled by the unfavorable comparison of his *Cleopatra* to those of Shaw and

Shakespeare,[19] Mankiewicz, in *The Honey Pot*, puts forth the impish notion that Ben Jonson's classic can be improved upon. "It has always been my belief," he has Fox boast, "that Ben Jonson botched the finish of his play. Mosca could never outsmart Volpone—not in a million years."[20] The fact that McFly/Mosca does triumph over Fox/Volpone in the end does not invalidate the conceit of Mankiewicz as the superior play analyst implied in that remark.

McFly says sarcastically to Fox, "I can't wait to hear your finish. In the original, you remember, they both wind up in jail." In turn, several critics disparaged Mankiewicz's finale. Among them, Richard Schickel remarked that "unable to provide one satisfactory ending . . . Mankiewicz gives us three conclusions, each softer than the last."[21]

Mankiewicz's private back-patting via Fox's alternately self-congratulatory and irascible voice-over commentary, which serves to facilitate each twist, is quite enjoyable, although Mankiewicz calls the interspersed narration "a hangover from the earlier script."

These are the highlights of the running commentary:

FOX'S VOICE: Obviously, this is not the finish I had in mind. But I would suggest not reaching for your hats. It's still my script they're playing. Revised, of course.

There was no reason for Dominique to reveal that my hourglass was a copy—and the gold dust fake. It contributes nothing to the plot—merely changes and cheapens my finish.

(*Ending #1, as* MCFLY *signs over to* SARAH WATKINS *what he mistakenly thinks is Fox's worthless will, without realizing that since Fox was Sheridan's common-law husband, his estate inherits her fortune.*) Genius . . . genius. Machiavelli couldn't have thought of that.

---

[19]In Aaron Latham's *Crazy Sundays* (Viking Press, 1971, p. 121), "Edwin Knopf says of Mankiewicz, 'It is both Joe's strength and his weakness that he thought he could rewrite anyone.' George Oppenheimer sums up the producer as follows: 'Joe thinks he's Shakespeare.' "

Mankiewicz deeply resents Oppenheimer's crack and retorts that in the main titles of his film of *Julius Caesar* there was no such credit as "Written by William Shakespeare with additional dialogue by Sam Taylor" (referring to Taylor's 1929 production of *The Taming of the Shrew*, starring Mary Pickford and Douglas Fairbanks).

[20]The tenor of this quote recalls Mankiewicz's cocky, though insightful, disparagement of Shaw's *Caesar and Cleopatra.*

[21]*Life*, July 14, 1967, p. 12.

(*Ending # 2, as* MCFLY *rejects* SARAH *'s proviso that she will return the inheritance to him if he marries her and returns to law school*)
At least we'll be spared that closing panorama of beauty where they walk together across St. Mark's Square into the dawn over Venice.

Of course, that is precisely the closing shot of the film, though the rarely seen wintry gray and wet paving of the square provides a visual fillip congruent to Mankiewicz's designation of the film as "a winter comedy" in deliberate contrast to the lush travelogue view of Venice in David Lean's *Summertime.*

The "heavenly" high angle from above the square and the omniscient banter of Lone Star and Fox in their afterlife reunion resemble the gilded-cloud commentary of the gods on the mortals below in Giraudoux's *Amphitryon 38.* It provides the summation of Mankiewicz's sweet-and-sour philosophy of frustrating fate:

(*Ending # 3, as* MCFLY *capitulates to* SARAH *'s terms and catches up with her after a pursuit across the piazza*)
FOX'S VOICE: What's happened—no! I *will not* have it! *Why* must the commonplace always win in the end? *Why* must we, in the end, satisfy always the limited tastes and desires of the vegetating average man?
LONE STAR'S VOICE: Ceece [her nickname for Cecil]—stop yellin' so loud.
FOX'S VOICE: (*thundering*) It's *my* story—and I want it to finish *my* way!
LONE STAR'S VOICE: But it didn't. Neither did mine, you know. And it's kinda nice for young people to get together at the end.
FOX'S VOICE: "Nice."
LONE STAR'S VOICE: (*gently*) Ceece. Let the folks go home, now.
FOX'S VOICE: (*wincing*) "Folks." (*wistfully*) D'you know what *would* be nice, Lone Star? If—just once—the bloody script turned out the way we wrote it.

"Why not just call it 'Joe Mankiewicz's First Western'?" 17

*W*ITH THE COMMERCIAL AND CRITICAL FAILURE OF HIS "COME-back" film, *The Honey Pot,* and the illness of his agent, Charles Feldman (who died in 1968), Mankiewicz saw his career lapse into a limbo of agent hopping.

Mankiewicz signed first with an Englishman, Richard Gregson, who was soon obliged to give up his choice client list when he decided to become a film producer. Joe's contract was then inherited by the young turks of CMA, Freddie Fields and David Begelman, who had acquired a reputation for their aggressive assembly of director-writer-star packages. Their representation of Mankiewicz proved short-lived. Joe then turned to Robert Lantz, the former Figaro executive who had returned to his elite talent agentry, and said, "I'm coming home!"

A chance shipboard friendship served to change Mankiewicz's fortunes, eventually returning him to Hollywood after a thirteen-year absence.[1] The admiring patron who sought his wisdom and companionship was Kenneth Hyman, an expatriate who was disconsolate over having to return to the States. Hyman had abandoned his English residence and career as a successful producer (*The Dirty Dozen* [1966]

---

[1]Mankiewicz had been in Los Angeles during the spring and summer of 1961, when it seemed *Cleopatra* would be shot on the Fox lot, and again in 1963 to supervise *Cleopatra*'s scoring.

was his most recent and most financially successful picture) to head production at Warner Brothers, which had been acquired by his father's company, Seven Arts.

Mankiewicz bolstered young Hyman's spirits by painting a bright picture of the pleasures of power and the opportunities for innovation that his new post would afford him.[2] Joe was also tactful or adroit enough not to push any projects of his own. Hyman was so captivated by Mankiewicz's charm, knowledge, and reputation that, after taking office, one of his first moves was to sign Joe to a multiple-picture directing deal at Warner–Seven Arts.

The first project that Hyman offered Mankiewicz was a film biography of Shakespeare's life and times (variously titled *The Bawdy Bard* and *Will*), to be scripted by Anthony Burgess, the distinguished British author of a well-received novel about Shakespeare, *Nothing Like the Sun* (1964).[3] Under Mankiewicz's supervision, *Will* mushroomed in length to three and a half hours, plus an intermission, and its estimated budget escalated to between $13 million and $14 million, which made it a prohibitive risk.[4]

At the same time, a new script by the New York wits Robert Benton and David Newman (Warners' hottest writing team by virtue of their first screenplay, *Bonnie and Clyde*) was making the rounds of

---

[2]When Mankiewicz, in the mid-fifties, had been offered a similar opportunity to head production at MGM, which was floundering, he says that he stipulated he would only take the post if he could run the studio from New York. In view of Metro's huge lot in Culver City, his proposal was rejected.

[3]Anthony Burgess says that early in 1968, when he arrived in Los Angeles to begin work, the Shakespeare film was to be a musical, as the vogue for musicals in the film industry was still great. This concept, known as *The Bawdy Bard*, was supervised by actor-producer William Conrad (TV's *Cannon*), but when Mankiewicz entered the project, he scrapped the idea of a musical in favor of a drama dealing with his favorite subjects—theater people and theater history.

Burgess describes Mankiewicz as "a true gentleman with an immense literary knowledge of Elizabethan literature" who "didn't niggle with and was highly respectful of words." By working out all the shots of the film in his head, Mankiewicz was of incalculable aid to Burgess in writing the script, though Burgess was fearful that Joe "would be a bit too Anglophile," while the script really required a director "less respectful of Shakespeare."

[4]Ken Hyman's judgment of the commercial prospects of *Crooked Man*, as opposed to those of *Will*, was so optimistic that, according to screenwriters Benton and Newman, he encouraged the writing of a script that would cost no less than $5 million. They contend that the eventual cost of *Crooked Man* was $8.5 million, which paid for a massive prison set built in Joshua Tree National Monument Park at a reported cost of $300,000, seven weeks shooting at this desert location, and countless postproduction expenses in reediting the film for its long-delayed release.

producers and directors on the Burbank lot. Hyman, a devotee of screen brutality (witness *The Dirty Dozen* and *The Hill* [1965], a harrowing study of a barbaric English military stockade in an African desert), had proposed to Benton and Newman that they unite their common enthusiasm for bloodletting by making a film that would combine two movie genres—the prison-break picture and the Western.

The team had waxed enthusiastic over the notion and had plunged into research on prison conditions of the 1880s, eventually turning out a screenplay entitled "Hell." Hyman collected various opinions on this script around the studio and urged Benton and Newman to incorporate the suggested changes into a second draft. This version, which they considered inferior, also made the rounds in search of a suitable director, but there were no takers.

Eventually, on the night of the Screen Writers Guild awards ceremony honoring the team for *Bonnie and Clyde*, Hyman casually announced to the delighted prize winners, "I've got a surprise for you. Joe Mankiewicz has read your script and wants to do it."

The writers' elation was bolstered by Mankiewicz's preference for their original script ("Jesus, m'boys, this is what I was talking about. Why didn't you show this to me in the first place?"). Their confidence in their new mentor was instantly reaffirmed by his characterization of their script as "very Dickensian"—their precise intention in populating the picture with a cast of eccentric characters bearing connotative names. In the view of C. O. ("Doc") Erickson,[5] Benton, Newman, and Mankiewicz's devotion to fleshing out each of these supporting figures expanded the script to an unfeasible running time[6] and ultimately detracted from the main conflict between the film's protagonists, Pit-

---

[5]Erickson remained as Mankiewicz's executive producer–production manager from *Cleopatra* through *Crooked Man*, including Joe's dreadful, expensive all-star film for a Xerox-sponsored series on ABC-TV on behalf of the United Nations. Mankiewicz had the ungrateful task of directing Rod Serling's updated version of *A Christmas Carol*, titled *A Carol for Another Christmas*. It starred Sterling Hayden as Grudge, an embittered isolationist "hawk" reformed by liberal platitudes and such horrors of war as the aftermath of Hiroshima. Mankiewicz shot the film in a New York studio in October 1964, prior to making *The Honey Pot*. The film went $200,000 over its $400,000 budget.

[6]Although two of the preliminary stories filling in the backgrounds of the cellmates (Ah Ping and Floyd Moon) were deleted from the script just before the commencement of shooting, for reasons of cost and running time (they are simply alluded to in the revised text), the completed film's rough cut ran 165 minutes. Exhibitors prefer the average film to run no longer than two hours to facilitate two evening performances, and therefore *Crooked Man* was eventually cut to 125 minutes.

man and Lopeman (Kirk Douglas and Henry Fonda).

The revisions started in Mankiewicz's bungalow at the Beverly Hills Hotel and continued for six months back on the East Coast, with Benton and Newman traveling once or twice each week up to Mankiewicz's study in Bedford to show the director their new material. Erickson describes Benton and Newman's role in the rewriting as that of "students learning from the master. Joe likes nothing better than the role of professor."[7]

He also enjoyed his role as raconteur of Hollywood lore to a pair of captivated fledglings, and several situations in the script prompted a number of his best stories.

"On the second day we worked with him," Robert Benton recalls, "we had written, 'CUT: to an exterior plain. A herd of cattle and six cowboy rustlers riding at night.' " The ensuing debate over how many head of cattle constituted a herd prompted a favorite tale of Joe's about his early days at Paramount. Two of his mentors were the lot's ace "spitball" artists, the team of Grover Jones and Bill McNutt, who taught young Mankiewicz the art of "winging it" at story conferences.

As Mankiewicz tells it, Jones and McNutt were pitted opposite Sam Jaffe, the brother-in-law of Paramount studio chief Ben Schulberg, and the studio's cost-conscious production manager. The issue was an opening scene description they had written for a Western to be directed by Victor Fleming.

> JAFFE: Sit down, gentlemen, and have a cigar. Now, gentlemen, I know that you appreciate, as much as I, the value of money, and we want to get every bit of value on the screen that we possibly can, but at the same time, we don't want to go crazy with money. Now, for example, you say here, "FADE IN—Scene 1: As far as the eye can see, milling longhorn Texas cattle." Is that right, gentlemen?
>
> JONES AND MCNUTT: That's right, Sam.

---

[7]While supervising Benton and Newman's revisions, Mankiewicz was engaged in writing his own screenplay, an adaptation of *Couples,* John Updike's 1968 best seller. (Mankiewicz had committed himself to write and direct *Couples* before Warner–Seven Arts had offered him a multiple-picture deal and assigned him to *Will.*) Only half of the screenplay was completed, but Mankiewicz already had the notion of casting such actual couples as Burton and Taylor and Newman and Woodward.

Mankiewicz claims that he had passed his deadline for delivery of the script and Wolper would not grant him an extension to complete it as he wished. Doc Erickson says that Joe lost interest in the script and was glad to negotiate his way out of the assignment.

JAFFE: Now tell me, gentlemen, how many is that "as far as the eye can see?" Twenty thousand? Thirty thousand? Forty thousand?

JONES: We didn't really mean it that way, Sam. We just meant a lot of Texas longhorns.

JAFFE: First of all, do they all have to be Texas longhorns? Because a Texas longhorn cow costs $60 a day to rent. A shorthorn costs $30 or $40. Couldn't we have up front the longhorns and in back the shorthorns?

JONES: Yes, Sam, that's very possible.

JAFFE: You see, we're making great progress. Already we're cutting down thousands of dollars. Now, gentlemen, instead of a plain, what about a ravine with two sides? Already, you don't have to have ten thousand, you could have maybe four thousand. You can still fill the ravine. That's your idea, isn't it?

JONES: Yeah, that's possible.

JAFFE: Or, if you're really clever, you could even use the side of a hill. Against the side of a hill, maybe six hundred cattle would fill the screen.

JONES: Yes, Sam, six hundred.

JAFFE: You see, gentlemen, this shows you the cooperation you get at a studio like Paramount. Here we sit like adult men, and we're already whittling down $40,000 or $60,000.

JONES: May I interrupt, Sam?

JAFFE: Of course, Grover.

JONES: Sam, a thought just occurred to me. Do you think by going to Texas you could get us a soundtrack of fifty thousand longhorn cattle?

JAFFE: A soundtrack only? Why, that's very simple. We could get the sound of a hundred thousand just by sending a sound man to Texas.

JONES: You think you could rent just two longhorn cattle?

JAFFE: Two longhorn cattle? We could buy them. You could own them. That would be a very easy thing to do. But why, Grover?

JONES: I think Bill and I could fade in on a tight two-shot of the two longhorn cattle, while, off screen, you *hear* fifty thousand. Then one longhorn cow turns to the other and says, "You know, you'd never think that fifty thousand longhorn cattle could make so much god-damned noise."

"And that's when Sam Jaffe said, 'This is an insult. Get out of my office,' and chased Jones and McNutt all the way down the hall."

Benton and Newman took the point, and *There Was a Crooked Man . . .* begins with the arresting nighttime close-up of the hooves of the bandits' horses swathed in burlap to muffle their sound.

The device of the brothel peephole in *Crooked Man,* through which Pitman's robbery victim spies him cavorting with two beauties, inspired Joe to regale his screenwriters with a tale of voyeurism at Metro in 1931—another little-known saga from the Mankiewicz fund of what he terms "Hollywood graffiti." It seems that following the extensive location shooting in Africa for their white-hunter film, *Trader Horn,* MGM had imported six black tribesmen to lend authenticity to the interiors being shot back in Culver City.

First, there was the problem of housing the blacks. To avoid riling tempers at the local hotels or apartment houses, it was decided that the Africans would be perfectly at home living on the sound stage's jungle set. It became clear, however, after a week had passed, that the natives' growing truculence was not over their domicile, but because they were horny.

A meeting of key MGM executives was hastily assembled to deal with this crisis. Calling upon the services of the prostitutes or starlets who regularly entertained the studio's visiting "firemen" seemed out of the question, so they summoned Metro's sole black employee— "Slickum," the studio shoeshine man—for advice. He highly recommended his nympho sister for the assignment, as he despised his brother-in-law. Apparently, this solution was satisfactory to all concerned, and peephole viewing of the nightly orgies on the jungle set became Metro's hottest, most exclusive attraction.[8] (The screenwriters' exotic touch of having a black madam [Claudia McNeil] as proprietress of the brothel in *Crooked Man* is possibly a tribute to Joe's tale.)

One of the major concerns during the Mankiewicz-supervised rewrite phase was to chart the progressive transformation of Lopeman from the role of puritanical sheriff, first seen ousting a prostitute from a hotel bedroom and refusing her blandishments, to the role of vengeful warden at the end of the film, when he returns to town in pursuit of Pitman and requests "the professional discount for lawmen" at the local brothel. (In the released version, Lopeman declines the black madam's hospitality.)

---

[8]Another version of this story appears in Samuel Marx's *Mayer and Thalberg* (Random House, 1975, p. 150). In Marx's version there are only "two native chiefs, each seven feet tall . . . imported from Kenya," and the chiefs refused the housing accommodations the studio obtained, preferring to live in more habitual quarters on the Metro lot. Marx makes no mention of the sexual services provided. Mankiewicz was not yet at Metro in 1931 and may have embellished the story while Marx was present, although he may be more discreet in discussing the matter.

Benton and Newman feel that they never satisfactorily accomplished the curious transformation of Lopeman, whose overt purpose is to capture and kill his adversary but who secretly wishes to be the amoral Pitman, whose cocksureness captivates both men and women. They wrote a scene in which Lopeman tries to elicit the secret of Pitman's magnetism from the attractive widow (Lee Grant) who has supplied Pitman with her bed and body, a change of clothing (her late husband's), and a horse to further his escape.

As David Newman recalls, "What would make a guy like that [Lopeman] turn into what he does [Pitman's emulator] . . . was something that Joe wanted us to do. It was the only instance I can recall that we never fully understood [what Mankiewicz required]. I don't think he did either, for he never articulated it well enough to make us understand. We wound up writing a scene that hit on all those numbers, but it had a lot of lines like Fonda saying, 'You mean some people are like this and some people aren't?' And Lee Grant would say, 'Well, you think what you want to think.' . . . What the scene really was, was our confusion about what the fucking point was. We just danced around it all the time, and it turned out very vague."

The scene has been completely cut from the released version of the film, and in place of this encounter, the widow simply denies to Lopeman that she has seen the fugitive; he sarcastically comments on the prison mule in her corral and rides off.

The psychological complexity of Lopeman's transformation was thus reduced to an ironic plot twist no deeper than the accident of Pitman's fatal snake bite at the end. In any case, Warners' desire to reduce the film to a conventional two-hour feature dictated that the film hasten to its conclusion after Douglas's death, rather than dawdle over Lopeman's delayed crisis of identity.

Mankiewicz's desire to graph Lopeman's conversion is consistent with his previous insistence on the fullest possible psychological explication of major changes in his character's behavior. What may account for Joe's unusual inarticulateness in attempting to explain to the authors Lopeman's conflicting admiration and hatred for Pitman is that several aspects of this dilemma reflect typical conflicts in Mankiewicz's own life.

The conflict of wishing to emulate or supplant an idolized figure, which is also central to *Letter, Eve,* and *Cleopatra,* is undoubtedly related to Joe's personal and professional rivalry with Herman. Similarly, while Mankiewicz had depicted the gradual abandonment of sexual inhibition by women in *The Ghost and Mrs. Muir, Guys and Dolls,* and *The Honey Pot,* he had never dealt with a male character going through such a change. His inability to chart the course for his writers may be related to his guilt at having taunted his older, more worldly, and extroverted brother for Herman's innate puritanism in failing to avail himself of the numerous compliant women who thronged the studios. (Although, since Joe was both younger and more physically attractive than his brother, this taunting may have been another way of competing with Herman's abiding reputation as the greater intellectual and wit. However, Joe claims that he was often called upon at Metro to rewrite love scenes in his brother's screenplays because Herman, he maintains, had no gift for creating romantic dialogue.)

Pitman's charm for men and women and his single-minded determination not to share his loot are not so far removed from Mankiewicz's own personality and his constant grumblings about the studios' 25 percent (or more) overhead charge and the movie exhibitors' larcenous withholding of the box-office take. At the same time, the emblem of Pitman's hypocrisy, his steel-rimmed fake glasses, may bear some relation to Mankiewicz's self-image as the shrewdest "whore" in the movie business, although similar spectacles were a notable and necessary appurtenance of his father, the erudite professor. In any case, the fact remains that Mankiewicz was attracted to the story of an idealist who sells out for a life of comfort on the proceeds of stolen loot—precisely Herman's view of the overpaid Hollywood screenwriter's lot.

Henry Fonda's view of *Crooked Man,* in retrospect, is that "it was a very good script, and it felt good shooting it. It just didn't work as a movie, and I'm very disappointed with it." Kirk Douglas, more analytically, says, "I thought the idea of the Western was brilliant, but the exchange of ideas came too late in the third act, when you need visuals and not talk . . . and the switch—his [Lopeman's] almost taking on my identity—was equally brilliant, but it started too late in the picture."

By jettisoning most of the film's psychological ballast, Mankiewicz caused the film's balance between the satirically funny and the painfully brutal to become quite tenuous. "The result is a piecework movie in which individual sequences work well but contradict each other until total moral confusion reigns," wrote Paul Zimmerman in *Newsweek*.[9]

Few critics were as emotionally incensed by *Crooked Man* as Pauline Kael, who jeered at the film as "a new low in cynicism" even in the era of spaghetti Westerns, termed Mankiewicz's direction the "Grand Rapids style of filmmaking," and labeled the creators "hacks" for failing to consider the damaging implications of their plot in terms of the present-day controversy over progressive prison reform.[10]

Kael's personal spleen toward Mankiewicz is revealed in her review of Benton and Newman's subsequent film, *Bad Company* (1972), in which a character named Big Joe, claiming that he has taught a young outlaw all his tricks, bellows Mankiewicz's favorite refrain, "I'm the oldest whore on the block [beat]." In David Newman's words, "It's our little homage, our little valentine to Joe. We love him."[11] Kael says that this "roaring, disgusted egomaniac" is, "as anyone who has ever seen Joe Mankiewicz on TV can perceive, a stunning caricature— maybe the funniest portrait we've had—of a big-time movie director. . . . The florid self-esteem of a brigand or a buccaneer may go to the heart of what makes a Hollywood winner."[12]

In the context of the series of betrayals Lopeman suffers throughout *Crooked Man*, the implications of the film's ending are no more profound than the truism that a streak of larceny exists in even the most virtuous of men. The twist is part of the corrective to the good-guy-versus-bad-guy mythology of the traditional Hollywood Western that

---

[9]January 4, 1971, p. 60.

[10]*New Yorker*, January 9, 1971, p. 65. Similar charges might be leveled against the cynical nihilism in the films of Robert Altman, except that Altman was one of Kael's pet directors and she despises Joe Mankiewicz.

Benton and Newman realize that their film might be taken as "a kick in the face to liberals and penologists," but they cite the conviction of New York City's commissioner of sanitation in the early seventies ("Marcus was [Mayor] Lindsay's great liberal") for being on the take as evidence that "just being liberal is no more proof of your morality than being conservative."

Although Benton and Newman think that part of the fun of the film's ending derives from the observation that a reformer's principles are often "only skin deep," they are annoyed at Pauline Kael for assuming that, because their favorite subject matter concerns the reasons unlikely people move into a life of crime, they are endorsing or advocating criminality as a way of life, or "that the subject matter of any creative work represents [the author's] philosophy of life." (This defense by Benton and Newman represents a condensation of their comments to the author and those that appeared in a "Rebuttal" column by Liz Smith in *Cosmopolitan*, January 1973, p. 110.)

[11]*Village Voice*, January 18, 1973, p. 76.

[12]*New Yorker*, October 7, 1972, pp. 139–40.

Mankiewicz and his writers had set out to administer.[13] Mankiewicz said, at the time of *Crooked Man*'s release in 1970, "I have to be cynical about the Western myth because it's really beginning to take over the country between Goldwater and Agnew. *Gunsmoke*'s values are Agnew's in many ways, and if you ever wanted to do the life of Agnew, you'd have to star James Arness. . . . Even the liberals are beginning to believe that there was something glorious about Wyatt Earp and Billy the Kid." (Although this comment was made precisely three years before Agnew's forced resignation from the vice-presidency, Agnew's hypocrisy as a "law and order" man actually on the take is congruent with the film's prophetically cynical outlook.)

Mankiewicz took a special, boyish delight in having Fonda sell out at the picture's end. When Joe confided this intention to his old colleague Elia Kazan, who was making *The Arrangement* on the Warner lot at the time, Kazan exclaimed, "Jesus Christ, you've picked the symbol of American middle-class morality. That's like spitting on the flag!"[14]

Mankiewicz also reveled in the varieties of homosexual conduct he now had the license to depict, from the domestic bickering of the long-married con men (John Randolph and Hume Cronyn), to the sadism of the rock pile foreman with an eye for the physique of youthful cons, to the decadent furnishings of the bedroom of the cologne-sniffing Warden Le Goff (Martin Gabel), which includes a miniature of Michelangelo's David, a blackamoor figurine lamp, and a tented Moorish bed.

Joe's prudery about bloodshed and nudity, even in this amoral film, is still evident. We are spared the sight of Cavendish being whipped and Moon killing a doctor and a guard with a scalpel.[15]

---

[13]It is also precisely the same ending invented six years before *Crooked Man* by writers William and Tania Rose for the ironic "payoff" to Stanley Kramer's *It's a Mad, Mad, Mad, Mad World* (1963). At the conclusion of this earlier comedy, the honest police chief (Spencer Tracy) makes off with the satchel of loot he has been trying to pry from the comic crooks' clutches during the entire film.

[14]Fonda contends that, prior to *Crooked Man*, Sergio Leone went a great deal further in playing against Fonda's traditional screen image by making him the black-suited, murderous villain in *Once Upon a Time in the West* (1969), in which he slaughters an entire family on his first appearance.

[15]This reticence caused *Newsweek*'s Paul Zimmerman to attack the film for its "bloodless, storybook violence" (January 4, 1971, p. 60). Studio head Ken Hyman was hoping for much more of the *Dirty Dozen, Bonnie and Clyde* blood baths that Benton and Newman's original script, "Hell," provided. Doc Erickson, the film's executive producer, recalls that in this version "the violence was so overdone that it was impossible for Joe to do it justice, so he toned down the violence and increased the humor."

Mankiewicz served as his own censor, much to the distress of several Warner executives, by cutting the obligatory sixties "pussy shot" of the schoolteacher emerging stark naked from the dining hall riot. "It was an obvious piece of hokum comedy," says Mankiewicz, "which films are filled with today, so I said, 'Screw it. That's not for me.'"

With justification, Pauline Kael terms the film "a movie pastiche" and contends that "everything in it is stolen from old movies and stood on its head." However, her statement that "the clichés are just as stale upside-down and presented as leering realism" is unjust. For "nonleering" realism Mankiewicz left a standing order that no manure was ever to be swept up from the set. "My Western," he said, "is going to be the first that has horse shit in every scene." He was also scrupulous in seeing that any visitor to the desert prison arrived covered in dust from the journey, and with an eye for the witty and telling detail, he showed the Chinese convict, Ah Ping, eating his soggy grub using the handle of his spoon in lieu of a chopstick.

Other reversals, such as Lopeman using a pile of warm manure instead of hoofprints as a means of trailing Pitman, and the half-crazed Missouri Kid (Burgess Meredith) growing marijuana in his cell are equally droll. Even more delectable is the pocket satire on black and white servant-master relations in the film's opening sequence. We watch a black cook, weary and disgruntled from a day of toil behind the stove, wipe the sweat off her brow and then tie back her bandanna to transform herself into a beaming Aunt Jemima stereotype, clucking cheerfully as she enters her employers' dining room with a platter of fried chicken. After the robbery she and her butler husband calmly eat their own supper behind an upturned table barricade, and when he is summoned to take part in the ensuing gun battle, she firmly detains him with the injunction, "Don't you go getting your black ass shot off for no white man." The tone of this opening sequence forecasts that the film will be a spoof throughout and makes the more straightforward, melodramatic episodes in the later prison scenes somewhat incompatible stylistically.

The filming itself had its share of hilarity and seriousness. As a gag, Mankiewicz one day ordered the production crew's dotty sweeper off the set for wearing a "John Goldfarb, Please Come Home" T-shirt. Joe explained that a lavish, catered buffet preview of that wretched, 1965 Shirley MacLaine comedy was the last occasion on which he had been invited back to the Twentieth Century–Fox lot. Asked for his reaction to the film, Mankiewicz had acidly responded, "I think you should release this supper and eat the picture!"

The grim event of the filming was the discovery that Hume Cronyn, Mankiewicz's great friend, was suffering from an optic cancer that required prompt surgery and would necessitate the removal of an eye. Observers report that while Mankiewicz was visibly stricken by the calamity, Cronyn gamely insisted not only on completing his scenes in the hastily revised schedule, but on daily working for hours past the regular 5 P.M. "wrap time," despite Joe's protests.

Cronyn and the other veteran character actors in the cast are in top form under Mankiewicz's meticulous guidance. As Joe told Michael Blodgett, the film's only juvenile, "You'll be competing with a hundred and fifty years of scene-stealing experience" in the cramped prison cell, opposite Meredith, Cronyn, Randolph, Warren Oates, and Douglas.

Benton and Newman marveled at Mankiewicz's doing five progressively superior takes of a scene in which Burgess Meredith, being solicited to take part in the prison break by Douglas, makes the transition from a self-deprecator ("You don't want an old coot like me") to a haughty superior ("Look, pissant, this is the Missouri Kid you're talking to!"). To the writers' query about why he had proceeded beyond the third take, which seemed unsurpassable, Mankiewicz replied, "You have to know the actor. Some actors you have to keep pushing and pushing. Some go downhill after just one take." As he had earlier observed to Benton and Newman while viewing the progressively inferior screen tests of a young actor they were considering for the juvenile, "That's the thing about [the test's famous director]. He starts out with something great, and he's not satisfied until he makes it mediocre."

Prior to the signing of Douglas and Fonda, a vast number of casting combinations had been considered, such as John Wayne and Warren Beatty (a teaming some industry figures think would have been a stronger box-office draw). These casting conferences were paralleled by endless sessions devoted to selecting an appropriate title for the film to replace such working titles as "Hell," "Hang-Up," and "The Prison Story." Mankiewicz would laboriously print each title suggestion under the stars' names on a three-by-five card and then pass it around the room for the entire production team's reactions. At one point when the dilemma seemed insoluble, he facetiously quipped, "Why not just call it 'Joe Mankiewicz's First Western'?" Finally, Benton and Newman hit upon the nursery-rhyme idea appropriate to their spoofing fable.[16]

Industry observers commenting on the film's commercial failure attributed it as much to the fading allure of its "geriatric" stars, Douglas and Fonda, and their supporting "over-the-hill gang," as to its handling by Warners' new management,[17] headed by the former talent-agency head Ted Ashley, who was installed as production chief in late 1969, after Seven Arts sold Warners to the Kinney Corporation. Ashley and his cohorts kept *Crooked Man* on the shelf (or being reedited) for over a year after its completion.

Vincent Canby felt that "in the roles of Mr. Douglas and Mr. Fonda, who play variations on their mythical movie selves . . . one of the film's bothersome idiosyncracies is that it wants to utilize its myths and to work against them."[18]

Henry Fonda does not refer to his costar by name, but speaks of the "very external" type of actor "who gives you the feeling he isn't listening" and is more concerned with his handling of a prop cigar and which way to blow the smoke than with the scene's content and conflict.[19]

Mankiewicz concurs that there were many "nuances I wanted from Kirk, but he's just not geared to accept those things anymore. Kirk works in broad strokes and is only prepared to take a limited amount of direction—basic rights, basic wrongs, basic changes. Kirk has now become, I think, not so much an actor as he is a motion picture 'function.' He's prepared to act, direct, manage, produce, and distribute. He knows pretty much what he wants to do and what he's prepared to do. If this had been a more important film, I think I would have had a much tougher time."[20]

Kirk Douglas contrasts Mankiewicz as a director with Elia Kazan, with whom he had just completed *The Arrangement* prior to starting on *Crooked Man.* "Kazan is completely involved with you," says Doug-

---

[16]Allusions to the nursery-rhyme title are incorporated not only in the child-book letter drawings of the film's opening credits but also in the motifs of the stained-glass windows in the town's brothel—a very witty touch.

[17]The film received little promotional push and was unceremoniously premiered in New York on a Friday (Christmas Day 1970), traditionally the day weak releases are opened, because of the lower circulation and readership of Saturday newspapers.

[18]*New York Times,* December 26, 1970.

[19]Henry Fonda made these remarks in an interview with the author in the summer of 1972.

[20]Mankiewicz chooses to regard *There Was a Crooked Man . . .* as one of his "entertainments."

las, "while Joe is completely detached—an observer. After you finish a take, he'll generally make a wry comment."

"I was having fun," says Mankiewicz, and Benton and Newman affirm that "he really had a great time on the picture and was constantly funny." Kirk Douglas says, "I didn't think he was comfortable with the elements [the physical action, horses, and other Western appurtenances]. Joe is best with mental rather than physical gymnastics." Mankiewicz, on the contrary, recalls, that "when I staged a kind of good fight scene around the latrine, Douglas was full of praise and said, 'You did that like you've done Westerns all your life. You ought to do nothing but Westerns!'"

Vincent Canby, who admires the film's "smaller, more civilized confrontations, done with irony and wit," states that "Mr. Mankiewicz is not at his best in staging the big, brawling scenes of roughhouse and riot that erupt throughout the film," but conjectures, "that may be simply because they don't seem to fit into the main scheme of the movie."

As if to proclaim his "with-it-ness," Mankiewicz allowed Broadway composer Charles Strouse frequently to envelop *Crooked Man* with the pop sound of an aggressively repetitive and overorchestrated title ballad (egregiously sung by Trini Lopez, a star of Warner's Reprise records) and cinematographer Harry Stradling, Jr., to employ an abundance of modish zoom shots. Calling for a "Dutch angle" on a tableau of Oates and Meredith pretending to feed a dead guard (not used in the picture), Joe, aware of the criticism of the conventional camera work in his films, proclaimed, "Tell them Mankiewicz can tilt the camera too!"

No doubt Mankiewicz felt his favorable judgment of the work confirmed by English critic Tom Milne, in the *Observer,* who termed *There Was a Crooked Man* . . . "a Western Comedy of Manners" and found it "sane, civilized, and extremely funny, confounding the proposition that there are good and bad men in this world in a typically sour, sophisticated Mankiewicz manner."[21]

---

[21]November 1, 1970.

*M*ANKIEWICZ WARNED ME THAT OBSERVING HIM AT WORK ON the set would be unrewarding. He explained that his method was to take actors aside and whisper his instructions to them. He makes it a rule never to intrude himself even by calling "Action," but prefers to encourage the actors' concentration by keeping out of their line of vision and letting them take their cues from the clapstick boy's calling the take number, followed by the sound man's "Speed" or "Rolling." However, the prospect of watching the consummate actor's director guiding the consummate English actor, Laurence Olivier, opposite Michael Caine in *Sleuth*, Anthony Shaffer's two-character tour de force, was too tempting to miss.

As we rode out to Pinewood Studios, outside London, on a sunny first of May, 1972, in his chauffeured Rolls, Mankiewicz filled me in on the progress of the two-week rehearsal period and one week of filming that had taken place prior to my arrival. He attributed the loss of a large amount of rehearsal time to the complex makeup tests run on Michael Caine, who had to be physically transformed for the retaliation scene that provides the play's second-act twist. Only a perfect disguise of Caine's features would be effective.

I later learned that more time-consuming than the makeup tests had been Lord Olivier's turmoil over the premature announcement in the press of Peter Hall's succeeding him as director of the National

Theatre, which prompted incessant inquiries by the news media and stole a bit of his glory in leading the company he founded into its new South Bank plant in 1974.[1]

Mankiewicz reported with pleasure that Olivier and Caine were in awe of each other. Caine was understandably intimidated by the prospect of playing opposite the English theater's greatest reigning star, fresh (or possibly fatigued) from a triumph in the National's revival of *Long Day's Journey into Night*, and Olivier apparently was envious of Caine's status as a film star.[2] It quickly became evident that Caine's initial awe would give way to solicitous patience with his senior costar.

Watching the filming of a scene in the oak-beamed billiard room of the Wyke (Olivier) mansion, during which Wyke banks all the balls and Milo (Caine) never gets a chance to lift his cue stick, I realized that Olivier was experiencing difficulty remembering his lines. While sometimes failing to announce the color of the ball he was about to sink, as the script indicated ("Once more with balls," he quipped), Olivier was taking the trouble to sink most of his shots, even though the actual trick shots were to be inserts provided later by a professional billiards player.

Initially, I thought it was simply this complicated billiard-shot "business" that was interfering with Olivier's concentration. (Mankiewicz consulted the billiards pro, and though he thought the interjected announcements of the color of each ball were unnecessary, they appear in the film.) But in the days to come, Olivier's mortifying lapses —he repeatedly stopped takes with an "Oh, shit" or "Sorry, Joe" when he knew he had erred or "dried up"—became agonizing for the crew members, who, as the takes dragged on, tended to drift away from the set or turned their heads in embarrassment.

Although Mankiewicz was clearly pained by the delays incurred and could often be seen bitterly shaking his head like a losing coach on the sidelines, he was quick to dispel Olivier's own discouragement

---

[1]Delays ultimately postponed the opening of the new National Theatre until the spring of 1976. Although the largest of the building's three theaters is deservedly named the Olivier, its namesake has yet to appear with the company in its new home.

[2]Except for the filmed reproductions of his National Theatre successes in *Othello* and *The Dance of Death*, Olivier's last lead in a film had been in the little-known *Term of Trial* (1962), and in recent years his commercial film work had been relegated to choice but infrequent supporting roles in such epics as *Khartoum* (1966) and *Nicholas and Alexandra* (1971).

or mounting tension with an uproarious story from his fund of theater and movie lore. Mankiewicz (*Guys and Dolls*) and Olivier (*Wuthering Heights*) share the experience of having worked with the often irascible producer Sam Goldwyn. A scurrilous Goldwyn story was sure to cheer Olivier, and Mankiewicz's lurid depiction of the former titan as senile and homicidal toward those who nursed him in his wheelchair dotage was an unfailing laugh-getter.

Michael Caine has since related to me that at another "sticky point" in the filming, Olivier told Mankiewicz that Goldwyn's comment on the American devastation of Hiroshima was "That atomic bomb is dynamite!" In response Mankiewicz contributed his own favorite Goldwynism, delivered on the occasion of a revision of the *Guys and Dolls* script he had submitted to the producer. "I loved the rewrite," Goldwyn gushed. "Now the picture has warmth and charmth."

Olivier, who celebrated his sixty-fifth birthday during *Sleuth*'s fifth week of filming, and Mankiewicz, two years his junior, are contemporaries, and their relationship evidently was founded on mutual respect and admiration. "I've known him all my life," Olivier hyperbolized to a BBC-TV interviewer. "He's a marvelous director. He really knows the job. He's wonderful."

Despite Olivier's costly fluffs, Mankiewicz maintained that "there is no actor in the world who can do as much, from all his work in Restoration comedy, with a peruke and snuff box as Larry." The scene he was referring to is one in which Olivier models a Monsieur Beaucaire outfit and then a monk's cowl as possible costumes for Caine's burglary getup. Olivier's droll camping is countered by Caine's own deft drag bit; he extends a limp wrist and clutches a flapper's dress to his chest.

The pity, during the filming, was that Olivier, despite his fabled command of the most intricate dialogue, experienced unusual difficulty in delivering the ornate speeches that Anthony Shaffer wrote for Wyke, the has-been author who spouts paragraphs of the thirties thrillers he still writes. Olivier's struggle to remember his lines made the character's relish for high-flown speech difficult to believe and appeared to undercut the first half of the film, during which Wyke is supposed to be on the offensive, demolishing Milo with humiliating words and deeds.

At one point Olivier bounded off the set, hissing to playwright Shaffer that "there's no such word as *pulsing,*" in reference to the line

"What does my insurance company discover when it swings into action, antennae pulsing with suspicion?" This criticism had been preceded by a long-winded discourse from Olivier on the way *antennae* would be pronounced if Wyke had learned his Latin at an old-fashioned public school like the one that Olivier had attended. "It's going to be a long summer," muttered the ever candid Shaffer.

Such nit-picking might have alleviated one day's humiliation for Olivier, but the problem remained whether the editing would cover all of his gaffes. It seemed likely that some of his speeches would have to be dubbed in postproduction to give them the requisite authority and correct phrasing that seemed absent in some of the printed takes, in which he alternately rattled, hesitated, was inaudible, or affected a strident bluster to cover his discomfiture. Mankiewicz began to shorten the takes in order to accommodate this problem, and Olivier would sigh with gratitude after being informed by Joe at a given point in rehearsal, "That's the cut."

According to cameraman Oswald Morris, Olivier had hoped to memorize his lines during the truncated rehearsal period. Michael Caine told me that Olivier would come into his dressing room between setups and ask to run great stretches of the play. Caine would urge him to "forget about yesterday's and tomorrow's, and just concentrate on the pages we're shooting today." Caine also confided to Mankiewicz, echoing Churchill on the Nazis, "When he's [Olivier] not at your feet, he's at your throat."

At one point, I did manage to overhear a revealing bit of whispered coaching from the director. Olivier complained to Mankiewicz that he was baffled at whether to adopt "phase two" or "phase four" when he confronted the intimidating Inspector Doppler. Joe reassured him that "from now on we'll shoot in sequence." Mankiewicz later explained to me that these "phases" represented the adjustment or specific changes in Wyke's attitude to Doppler from

(1) amused condescension, with which he greets the yokel police inspector, to
(2) slight bafflement at the strange things that are happening, to
(3) anxiety as he realizes that very important pieces of circumstantial evidence are turning up ("It's getting to be very serious!"), to
(4) panic ("I don't care how many police cars there are, I'm going to run out of my own house").

Clearly Olivier was finding it difficult to shift from the long rehearsal process of the theater to the exigencies of filming. Olivier later described his difficulties with the role as "really terrible. It's been really very long. . . . I was terribly busy at the National [Theatre, so] I didn't have time to learn it before we started, and that's the only thing to do. . . . I don't think I've let the production team down more than once or twice by just frankly not being able to learn it," but he described his part as "very hard" to commit to memory because the "very clever author, Tony Shaffer . . . has written it as an author speaking in the way that an author would like to speak, and that's not a very colloquial way of speaking. . . . As they are not the words that immediately spring to mind, you've got to find them . . . and those long, alliterative lists of things are always difficult to put in the right order, as they derive from the author's struggle for the *mot juste* and abound in literary references."[3]

Yet when it came to handling a script direction as outré as feigning an old lady's voice while setting a dynamite charge, Olivier was incomparable. His technical mastery was on display most effectively in the reaction shots, shown in their entirety in the "dailies." While Caine tended to be wooden and opaque responding to dialogue or action off camera, Olivier, divorced from the responsibility of delivering lines, ran through a miraculous variety of facial expressions, his mocking spaniel eyes flashing semaphores of graduated contempt.

The result of lengthy, repeated takes, technical malfunctions, and the scrupulousness of Mankiewicz and his cameraman was that the production rapidly fell a week behind the original ten-week shooting schedule. Such "overage" inevitably prompts the producer to put pressure on the director to make up for lost time by cutting the script or decreasing camera coverage.

Mankiewicz tried to make clear to the producers that his films are ultimately made in the editing room and that he wanted to preserve some options by shooting different versions of a number of scenes. For example, he shot alternative entrances for Olivier and Caine into Wyke's house (one of Caine fondling Wyke's wife's raincoat on the coat rack in the hallway and another of Olivier menacingly locking the

---

[3]These quotes derive from an interview with Lord Olivier, "Inside the Maze," on the *Film Night* television program on BBC-2, telecast on January 26, 1973. (For purposes of clarity, I have restructured the last paragraph of Lord Olivier's statement on the intricacy of Anthony Shaffer's text.)

front door), as well as both verbal and nonverbal reaction shots of Olivier observing Caine's antics from a first-floor window as Milo struggles with clown's costume and entry ladder before the staged burglary.

One morning as I entered the sound stage with Tony Shaffer, Morton Gottlieb, the film's titular producer,[4] lolling in one of the antique chairs on the set, announced to the writer, "I think I've found some good cuts." "Splendid," Shaffer ironically congratulated as we passed by, saying to me sotto voce, "I know exactly what Joe will do with them." Later Mankiewicz's voice boomed from his trailer as he berated Gottlieb by shouting, "Get off my back, or I'll put Robbie [Lantz—the agent of both Mankiewicz and Shaffer] on yours."

Joe's moods were as variable as the London weather. Sunny mornings joking with the crew ("For the first time in motion picture history, I have hijacked the crane operator. Now take me to Cuba or Tel Aviv! This crew will not be released until Sam Spiegel and his yacht have been liberated") often degenerated into rainy afternoons of ill humor.

Some of Mankiewicz's problems were physical. No sooner had he recovered from the limp caused by a chronically troublesome "disintegrated disk" in his back than he fell backward and impaled the back of his thigh on the protruding nut of the camera mount's mobile steering column. Just as he had earlier disregarded his back in demonstrating for Michael Caine how he wanted him to swing and position a metal ladder, Joe went on working despite the pain from his leg. But by the next day his sallow color and hollowed features signaled that the bruise was more serious than anyone had at first suspected. In fact, the bruise had caused internal hemorrhaging, and a massive loss of blood necessitated a transfusion.

Undaunted, Mankiewicz showed up for work the next day and used an antique upholstered wheelchair that the prop man had rigged with a splint to elevate his injured right leg. Joe set about staging the tricky business of Olivier savaging his wife's wardrobe. But he did not get much beyond contributing the whimsical notion of having him rip

---

[4]Gottlieb, as one of the producers of the West End and Broadway productions of *Sleuth*, managed to gain his first film producer's credit on the picture, although the film's production manager handled most of his responsibilities. Mankiewicz's boss was actually Edgar J. Scherick, the film's executive producer, who made periodic visits to London and sent representatives to report on the production's progress in his absence.

her sweaters (rather than her "frillies" in the script) and making all their buttons pop off. At 10:30 A.M., two hours after he arrived on the set, Joe was wheeled off like Sheridan Whiteside in *The Man Who Came to Dinner,* and the production was shut down for a week to give the injured limb a chance to heal properly.

Just as troublesome as Mankiewicz's physical ailments and Olivier's memory were Joe's technical deficiencies as a film director. Having jokingly informed his eminent cinematographer, Oswald (Ozzie) Morris,[5] that he didn't know which end of the viewfinder to look through and that he was relying on Morris to break up what he had staged into shots, Mankiewicz devoted himself almost exclusively to the script and the performances. This was a practical impossibility; the camera ultimately must be placed and the actors positioned to accommodate the high aspect ratio of the Panavision lens. In each instance Morris would find a solution to accommodate the staging ("I must say we go through hell while it's happening," Morris commented to me) or oblige Joe to find an alternative angle more aesthetically pleasing or more helpful to the story point he wanted emphasized.

When I asked Mankiewicz about this in a subsequent interview, he offered a sharp rebuttal. "I *said* I know very few of the technical terms. I still don't know lenses. There's no reason why I should know lenses. But *I* placed every camera setup in *Sleuth,* which I think is a damned well-photographed film, and I told Ozzie Morris where I wanted the camera to be, what I wanted the camera to see, and how I wanted it to move. He then set up the camera, put on the proper lens to give me what he thought I wanted to see . . . and then I got behind the camera, looked through it, and said, for example, 'No, I want it smaller; I want it larger; I want it framed this way or I want it composed that way. After they made these changes, both Ozzie and the operator looked through the finder and said, 'This is exactly what the Guv wants,' and then lit it."

When I asked about his requesting Morris to break up his staging into shots, Mankiewicz replied, "I couldn't remotely have said that. . . . I did say, I always want you to speak up if you can think of a better

---

[5]Morris shot most of the recent big musicals done in Europe, such as *Oliver, Goodbye Mr. Chips,* and *Fiddler on the Roof,* for which he was awarded an Oscar. His innovations in color cinematography can be seen in John Huston's *Moulin Rouge* and *Moby Dick* and Franco Zeffirelli's *Taming of the Shrew.*

idea than mine." I directed [the film] shot by shot because, as you remember, I had to do it that way with very few long master scenes. Therefore, how could [Morris] break it up into shots?"

In an interview subsequent to the filming, Olivier tended to corroborate Mankiewicz by claiming, "He's technically marvelous. He flings the camera about in a most gifted sort of way, and he's always clever, always right, always true. . . . It's enormously tiring for Joe because he has to concentrate so much on willing unto himself ideas for hundreds of angles—he's got [to find] hundreds of angles on it to keep it moving with just two people."

"Timing of dialogue is tremendously important if you're going to get the best setups," said Morris in an interview with me halfway through the filming. "Joe times the dialogue as two people talking, not being photographed by a camera, and that is the difference. I'm not saying you can't get a good movie that way—you can, but it's not the 'perfect' movie."

Morris, who never stopped scrutinizing the lighting through his filter, which was screwed to his eye like a monocle, was as concerned about Joe's morale as he was zealous about the camerawork. "Joe desperately needs encouragement, and he always looks to me to approve what he's saying. If I nod my head, then he feels better."

Only he and Mankiewicz, Morris felt, were aware of the great challenge of shooting a two-character picture predominantly in the interiors of a single setting.[6] Having broached the problem at his first meeting with Mankiewicz and having gotten no immediate response, Morris realized that he had "obviously hit right on a tender spot." Morris then observed Joe " 'giving a lot of stick' to the props, wardrobe, and costume people," a sure sign that this evasion was preying on him. Eventually Joe began to broach the subject openly to Morris by asking questions.[7] Morris thought that Mankiewicz had at least absorbed the general principle, taught him by John Huston, that the director should, as much as possible, delay moving in close to the actors during the

---

[6]To my knowledge, the only parallel film to *Sleuth*, in terms of using two actors in one major set, is Irving Reis's undistinguished *The Fourposter* (1952), which came close to approximating a photographed stage play.

[7]Mankiewicz contends that his meeting with Morris to determine a photographic style for the film was scheduled during the preliminary two-week rehearsal period and that its cancellation was due to the disruption that occurred. (Olivier's and Caine's absence should have left them ample time for it.)

opening ten minutes of a picture, saving the move-ins for climactic heightening as the action progressed.

This strategy went out the window at the commencement of shooting. ("Once he starts work with the actors, he's a different man and completely forgets the camera," said Morris.) Mankiewicz did not begin ordering the camera to retreat until the fifth or sixth week of filming. "Now that we're into the meat of the film, he's starting to do it a bit, and I think it's slightly the wrong way round, but equally well I'm very glad he's doing it even now," sighed Morris.

Mankiewicz's version of what happened is just the opposite. He told me, "As a matter of fact, Ozzie used to come up to me often and complain, 'Don't you think we ought to show more of the set?' I said, 'Patience, we will, we will. We've got a whole half a picture to go.' Then in the second half, [Morris] said, 'Boy, am I glad we didn't blow this all in the first half.' "

Two incidents from the last day of shooting I observed point up the liability of Mankiewicz's ignorance of technical matters. The first concerned the shot of a lady's stocking being flushed down a toilet bowl (an incriminating clue that Wyke is frantic to get rid of). The trouble began the day before when the toilet would not flush properly, and Mankiewicz was irritated at the unnecessary delay.

In his vexation he disputed Morris's contention that they could not keep cutting back to the same size shot of the toilet. Morris wanted to employ a more dramatic, extreme close-up of the bowl. "I've got a slightly sadistic streak in me," Morris confided, "and if a director argues with me over something, and I think I'm right, I'll switch right onto his side and encourage him to do it. By doing that, he suddenly thinks, 'Why has he changed? Maybe he's right!' Tonight Joe said, 'You're absolutely right; we do need the close shot there.' "

The second incident involved a series of story-board sketches that Mankiewicz had ordered from one of the staff designers under Ken Adam, the gifted designer of the fanciful sets for the James Bond series. Not only were each of the rooms in the mansion distinctive, but among the vast array of antique mechanical games that lined the corridors and every corner of the great hall room, the sets were filled with all manner of eye-catching objects. Typical of these was a portrait of Wyke's wife, Marguerite, that bore an uncanny resemblance to Joanne Woodward (an "in joke," since the Paul Newmans are friends of Mankiewicz's) and a stuffed bulldog head ("No doubt Marguerite's favorite dog," quipped Tony Shaffer while pointing out to me Adam's most whimsical decorations).

After the unsuccessful toilet flush, Mankiewicz retired to his small trailer on the sound stage[8] and sent word that he was not to be disturbed—a tip-off to Morris that he was still uncertain about how to shoot the following "graveyard" scene. When Mankiewicz arrived back on the set and was informed that several of the setups could not be shot as sketched, he raged, "But I've memorized them." Then he began to harangue Ken Adam, who stammered that the sketches were only meant to be suggestive and that the artist could only imagine the eventual staging. Adam concluded his remarks by biting off the end of his cigar in exasperation.

Ozzie Morris thought that Mankiewicz's consultative method of filmmaking was inevitably a compromise. "You can always shoot it to make it work, so that it will join together, but it may not be in the most dramatic or exciting visual way." This is the area where the director versed in technical lore is at a great advantage in staging for the camera, but only a handful of these technical wizards possess Mankiewicz's expertise with script and actors. Robbie Lantz points out that Joe was pampered at the start of his directing career by Fox's army of technicians, who obligingly executed what he had roughly outlined. Lantz contrasts this ignorance with his former client Mike Nichols, who, even as a fledgling director, acquired comprehensive knowledge of camera lenses and the like.

Where Mankiewicz excelled was in embellishing a performance by refining the actor's tempo and bits of business. Watching Joe improve Caine's ladder burglary in clown's costume gave me great admiration of this particular skill. While watching Caine rehearse, Mankiewicz jotted on three-by-five cards the following:

—getting boot caught twice in ladder
—falling backward out of frame
—getting putty stuck on his hand
—using glass cutter the wrong way

---

[8]During the lengthy lighting setups, Mankiewicz habitually retreated for privacy to his spartan and stifling trailer. Like Olivier, he never appeared for lunch in the imposing wood-paneled studio restaurant but preferred a solitary meal of hot dogs and potato or egg salad in his handsomely appointed office near the set.

Mankiewicz then harmonized these new ideas with the actor's own impulses. The result was one of the film's comic high spots.

I was, however, surprised to find Mankiewicz's fabled articulateness in instructing actors often absent. Ozzie Morris commented that both Olivier and Caine were so fast on the uptake that they would frequently interrupt Joe without permitting him to complete his thought, not to mention his sentence. Then again, there were times when Joe would start a phrase and never complete it[9] and other times when his instructions tended to be muffled and woolly, his clenched pipe stem interfering with his verbal clarity, but indicative of his uncertainty or weariness.

Mankiewicz's perfectionism impelled him to make Tony Shaffer, also a compulsive polisher, do three revisions of the screenplay based on his international stage success. Said Shaffer, "Joe wanted me to dot every *i*, so everything would be spelled out for the denizens of Poison Wells, Pennsylvania [Mankiewicz's figurative hick town], and when I dropped something he liked, it always reappeared in the subsequent version."

Like Olivier, Mankiewicz seemed constitutionally more suited to the rehearsal process of the theater than to the irreversibility of filmmaking. Despite Joe's painstaking annotations of his script, "he doesn't quite know how it's going to go until he's worked it out with the actors," noted Morris, "and he will do anything to divert attention from himself onto any other aspect of the film in order to give himself time to think it through."

Sleuth premiered in New York and Los Angeles in late December 1972, having been rushed to completion in time to qualify for the annual awards and garner a portion of the big holiday box-office coin.

Despite the almost unanimously favorable critical response among the prominent American critics (Kael, Sarris, and Kauffmann were the

---

[9]Lord Olivier discusses this phenomenon in his BBC television interview: "He's got a quaint way, sometimes, of [verbally blocking], which is rather amusing to us, if we can guess what he's trying to do. Not, I may say, as incoherent as William Wyler, but [odd] for a man with the command of words that he's got, because he's a marvelous writer. . . . I think there's something habitual in the flow of words from the brain to the hand, so [that when he's] got to stop and use the larynx, I think it sort of gets [blocked]. It forms a sort of mental stammer. He talks marvelously to us except when he's anxious, and when he really wants to say exactly the right thing, he sort of corks up a little in a very sweet, charming, amusing way."

film's only major detractors) and the healthy grosses, Mankiewicz was weary and disgruntled when I met with him shortly after the film's release. He quipped, "I always used to say, jokingly, after *Cleopatra* that what I wanted was a picture with just two actors and a telephone booth. Well, I finally got it."

The film was an exhausting trial for him, and he confided to intimates in the course of making it that he might never do another film. (This may have been a self-fulfilling prophecy, because six years later, having failed to complete an adaptation of Dee Wells's novel *Jane* for Columbia Pictures, he has yet to make one.) When I asked him about this pessimistic prospect, he replied, "I'm still not quite sure I will. I would certainly never direct another film under those conditions."

"Those conditions" relate primarily to *Sleuth*'s executive producer, Edgar J. Scherick. (Scherick is a former ABC-TV programming executive who began to produce feature films in 1968, beginning with *For Love of Ivy,* financed by ABC under his Palomar Production Company. With new financing from Bristol Myers, after ABC's withdrawal from filmmaking, Scherick had two of the prestige pictures of 1972 in *Sleuth* and *The Heartbreak Kid.*)

Two nights before *Sleuth*'s first press screening in New York, Scherick decided that the film required an intermission. Mankiewicz had especially devised a long dissolve sequence of all the mechanical dolls in motion, accompanied by three Cole Porter songs, to convey the stage play's intermission break without bringing the film to a halt. Without notifying Mankiewicz, Scherick ordered the original negative, which was in England, to be cut, and after the imbroglio that ensued, Mankiewicz's version was restored from a grainy, dupe negative.

Comparing Scherick to Zanuck, his *Cleopatra* nemesis, Mankiewicz hooted, "This man doesn't know fuck-all. At least Zanuck knew the difference between a dissolve and a freeze frame. He doesn't know what it means to open up a print and recut a negative."

Mankiewicz's contempt for producers is boundless. He contends that their only function is to package the property and its name components. All the day-to-day chores of administrating the production are left to the production manager, while the producer asserts his ego by making asinine and destructive comments on the dailies.

Joe's despair reached new depths with the receipt of a formal letter from Scherick insisting that if Mankiewicz would not make the enclosed list of cuts he requested, Scherick would make them himself.

"It's happening to me all over again, only now it's happening on a film I was pleased with," Mankiewicz said wistfully while the battle raged. "Nunnally Johnson or John Huston would just have a drink and forget about it, but I can't. . . . I've always envied Nunnally, whom I adore as a person, the distance he kept from the film business, regarding it as just a way to make a living. Whether I mean to or want to, I always become deeply involved with what I do."

Scherick's most painful directive involved cutting the main title sequence,[10] which Mankiewicz considered one of his most imaginative and effective contributions, as it foreshadows the film's ending and comments on the action. The inspiration for the main titles came from the miniature tableaux illustrating each of Wyke's detective stories that Ken Adam had designed for the decor of Wyke's celler. Mankiewicz used close-ups of these miniatures behind the titles. At the end of the film, he dissolved the final long shot of Wyke and his fallen victim in his great hall from a freeze frame to one of these stage set models, implying that "Andrew's life has become one of his books . . . or the 'Ultimate Game,' the game I was playing. The idea is you play the game, whether it's love or murder or any game you play intensely, and at a certain point the game plays *you,*" Mankiewicz explained.

The critics subsequently seized upon the painted curtain descending on this tableau as Mankiewicz's way of labeling the film a theater piece, and Scherick was possibly as unhappy with the curtain as Mankiewicz became with the critics' limited perception of his intent. "I don't blame Ed Scherick, who is just an illiterate who went to Harvard," said the disgruntled director, "but I do blame the critics for not having [understood that] Mankiewicz used this frame to reveal [that] this [final curtain] is but one more proscenium [around] yet another play."

Another moment that irritated Scherick (rightly, I think) is the zoom in on the initials *M. T.* on Milo's partly concealed red sports car. This shot occurs after Doppler and Wyke depart from the freshly dug

---

[10]This cut would have meant eliminating John Addison's sprightly harpsichord overture. "When Ed Scherick first heard John Addison's overture, he was lifted out of his seat. Now he's heard it too often, so he wants to cut it," said Mankiewicz during the dispute. Scherick's contention was that, as is typical of Mankiewicz's work, the film was too long. However, a far better cut could have been made in the overextended sequence with the progressively boring Inspector Doppler.

grave in Wyke's garden. When I questioned Joe about this shot, he conceded that it was "a red herring of my own. I'm playing a game too, as the director, and I wanted the audience to think, 'Maybe Milo's body is under that grave,' at the end of the garden sequence."

Regrettably, the initials, rather than serving to implicate Wyke, tend to tip off the audience to Doppler's identity as Milo too soon. The play turns on this gimmick, and the producers even gave special billing in the cast credits to one "Alec Cawthorne as Inspector Doppler" in order to con the audience.[11]

When I first saw an actor on the set in the Doppler costume and makeup, the disguise was so convincing that I could scarcely believe it was, in fact, Michael Caine. In numerous takes Caine displayed consummate skill as a character actor; his characterization greatly surpassed Keith Baxter's very broad caricature of the inspector on Broadway (Baxter had originated the role in the West End). Oddly, Caine's impersonation proved less convincing in the film than on the set. The excellence of the makeup and the adopted West Country accent were betrayed by Caine's distinctive vocal timbre, laconic phrasing, and tilted stance in moments of relaxation.

Scherick also wanted Mankiewicz to cut some of the scene between Doppler and Wyke in the celler, though Mankiewicz contended that this dialogue was crucial because there are references to it in subsequent scenes. (None of these cuts was ever instituted, but Mankiewicz has yet to see any money from his percentage of the moderately successful picture, which has grossed $5.6 million in the United States and Canada.)

What Scherick may have sensed was that the film's real letdown came in the second half of the second act. Wyke's scurrying to find Milo's planted clues, although more harried in tempo, appears to be simply an inverted repetition of Doppler's methodical discovery of the circumstantial evidence he (Milo) has planted earlier in the act, such as fake bloodstains on the staircase or the phony grave in the garden. The letdown may also be due to the emphasis placed on Wyke's fatigue

---

[11]The fictional Mr. Cawthorne was issued his own dressing room at Pinewood, even though the set was generally closed to the press. To conceal further that the play has only two characters, the credits list the absent Marguerite as a role played by Eve Channing (an "in joke" homage to the rivals of *All About Eve*); also listed are the two police officers with whose arrival Milo threatens Wyke.

(or Olivier's) rather than on his genuine terror at being caught by the police. A greater sense of desperation might have given the sequence an urgency compelling enough to divert attention from the mechanical plot inversion.

While the film revealed no evidence of Olivier's difficulty with the text, his tendency toward a broadly theatrical rather than cinematic performance was reinforced by the camera's closeness and Caine's contrasting underplaying. When Milo piteously weeps for mercy as Wyke levels a pistol at his head, Caine's naked terror seems far more genuine than the superb mask of mortal humiliation that Olivier later affects when his sexual impotence is revealed.

Pauline Kael wrote that Olivier was wasted "in a gentleman-bitch George Sanders role" and contends that Olivier "tries to give it too much—his intensity and bravura are too frantic for this pseudo-civilized little nothing of a play."[12]

The more restrained and objective critic Stanley Kauffmann wrote, "Much fuss is being made about Laurence Olivier's performance as the author. He's good enough, surely, but not better than a dozen other English actors might have been. However, this is Lord O. in Entertainment, and we are all supposed to rave at Greatness Unbending. Michael Caine is far more impressive in the other major role . . . because he shows a greater range, not (as Olivier does) a smaller one."[13]

Mankiewicz commented, "I just thank God for the resourcefulness of Larry and Michael. There was nothing I called upon them for that they couldn't or wouldn't deliver with infinite variety and interest.

"You don't really direct an actor like Olivier—you edit him, you judge. . . . It's strenuous, but very exciting. . . . He's the most incredible 'institution' I've ever directed. He's had fifty years of acting behind him, so he has already played everything in every way. . . . You're not

[12]*New Yorker*, December 23, 1972, pp. 53–54. Kael might have noted that George Sanders's "gentleman bitch" characterization was played to perfection in Mankiewicz's *Ghost and Mrs. Muir* and *All About Eve*, although this persona was derived from Sanders's characterization of the cynical Lord Henry Wooton in *The Picture of Dorian Gray* (1945).

[13]*New Republic*, January 20, 1973, p. 26. I think that Kauffmann misses the point that most of the great English actors like Olivier, Gielgud, and Scofield have rarely been seen, outside the London theater, playing high comedy, at which they excel, and *Sleuth* provides a rare opportunity for a worldwide audience to see Olivier in such a role.

392 PICTURES WILL TALK

going to teach him anything new, but you can get a new combination from him with the same colors. I remember having supper with him one evening and asking what he would do at the National Theatre under Peter Hall. He asked me, 'What would you suggest, old boy? You see, I've played them all.'

"When [Caine] comes on the set, you sense his eagerness, his ambition. He wants to cut loose and be known as the goddamned good actor he *is*. You push and you prod him, and he's grateful for the prodding. He always comes up with things he hasn't tried before, and they work and it's marvelous. . . . I think Michael deserves a tremendous amount of credit for the overall level of performance in this picture, considering there was a set that could have exploded with tension many, many a day."

Although both Caine and Olivier were nominated for Academy Awards for Best Actor and Olivier won the accolade of the New York Film Critics Circle, Mankiewicz was peeved that the elitist National Society of Film Critics gave its prize to Al Pacino for *The Godfather* (Brando won the year's Oscar). Mankiewicz termed Pacino's performance "the very sincere gangster son of the gangster father, which Julie [John] Garfield played a dozen times. To compare Michael Caine's performance, let alone Larry's, with Al Pacino's . . . makes me despair not only of the so-called cinema as an art but of the people who evaluate the cinema."

Mankiewicz took a sly swipe at the critics' fancied expertise by commenting, as he presented the 1972 New York Critics Circle award to Ingmar Bergman for the screenplay of *Cries and Whispers,* that he had no idea the New York critics were so well versed in Swedish as to appreciate the subtleties of Bergman's script—implying that they had judged Bergman's screenplay solely from the subtitles.[14]

Negative reaction to *Sleuth* has much, I think, to do with the critics' essential dislike of the play's constant cleverness and ornate speech[15] and their foreknowledge of its symmetrical plot. As John

---

[14]Although formerly a detractor, Mankiewicz is now a great admirer of Ingmar Bergman's work. He is, however, bemused at the critics' double standard toward Bergman's loquacious films, since they invariably complain that Mankiewicz's pictures are overly talky. "The most talky director in the world is Mr. Ingmar Bergman," says Joe. "His people never stop talking, and they are fascinating. I love them."

[15]Regarding the quality of the writing that drew Mankiewicz to *Sleuth,* John Simon pays it just due in stating that "Shaffer's respect for verbal finesse, savoring of ultracivilized repartee, ability to blend psychologically revealing dialogue with wittily

Simon notes, "A known ending is as embarrassing for a thriller as the mark of Cain for a fratricide. It is especially damaging for a plot whose basic device is reversals, and which progresses by putting one switch-eroo in front of the other."[16]

Mankiewicz did his best to camouflage the improbability of both characters being such uniquely clever and well-matched gamesmen by contrasting the characters more sharply. Mankiewicz says of these revisions, "The most important change in *Sleuth* was in the character of Milo. In the stage version Milo was a stooge, particularly in the first act, where he did nothing but say, 'Yes, sir,' 'No, sir,' and never at any time asserted himself. Remember in the play the poor bastard was not only part Italian but also a Jew, which seemed to me rather simplistic, and when he did speak, he spoke exactly the same as Andrew [Wyke] spoke, in exactly the same language. None of the background of his growing up in the streets of London's East End was in the play, but by making him of Cockney origin, in terms of speech, he is clearly differentiated from Andrew." (Not to mention that the role is tailored to Michael Caine's Cockney origin, although he was Mankiewicz and the producers' third choice for the part, after Albert Finney was deemed too plump and Alan Bates turned down the role.)

"I wanted to bring more emphasis to the class struggle that took place, though Tony Shaffer felt it was implicit in the play." (For example, one of the great laugh lines in the film is Wyke's incredulous reiteration of Milo's line "Become English?" which is one of the few lines for which Mankiewicz claims personal credit.)

Shaffer added to the screenplay any number of vicious slurs for Wyke to make on Milo's "Dago" or "Wop" lineage and on his profession as a hairdresser. Throughout the early weeks of filming, Shaffer was avidly reading an anthology of period thrillers and adding to his script such racial slurs from it as "eye-rolling Darkie," "the swarthy Yid," and "the oily Levantine" to broaden Wyke's bigotry.[17]

Mankiewicz feels that the American critics have, by and large,

---

pyrotechnical hyperbole survive in the film version." In fact, they are enhanced, as Paul Zimmerman observed: "Mankiewicz' primary contribution lies in his respect for the script . . . with every line treated as an event" (*Newsweek*, December 18, 1972, p. 93).

[16]*New Leader*, January 8, 1973, pp. 20–21.

[17]These additions prompted Andrew Sarris to remark, "Unfortunately, Shaffer's script is too explicitly oriented to the race, creed, and color homilies of our venerable theater parties" (*Village Voice*, January 4, 1973). This is a mistaken assumption, for, as I point out, they were not in the play.

missed "the nuances" of Michael Caine's revealing lapses from his scrupulously adopted upper-class speech in significant moments of greed or terror. Mankiewicz calls these lapses into Cockney "one of the most brilliant bits of dialect usage that the screen has seen in a long time . . . but the critics are still looking for photographic effects. Performance means nothing."

What several of the film's critics have heavily dumped on is Mankiewicz's overuse of Wyke's collection of mechanical dolls and games for symbolic punctuation and cutaways from the photographic ping-pong of shifting back and forth from Olivier to Caine. John Simon finds the device the "one mildly irritating aspect" of Mankiewicz's direction, while appreciating that it "is meant to make the atmosphere more ominous and to introduce, as it were, further characters, even if they are mere automata or effigies."

This is the closest any critic has come to appreciating the various "relationships" between the puppets and his principal characters that Mankiewicz attempted to effect as the film progressed. He explains that "I winged the automata things on the set—they weren't in the script, but without the cutaways you would have been conscious of there being only two actors. . . . The little ballerina is obviously in love with Milo—waiting for Milo to come back downstairs . . . or turning her back when he is shot. The Piano Lady is obviously the doyenne of the house and possessive of Andrew. . . . In the dance of the dolls [the entr'acte] Wyke becomes the last dancing figure, and there was a strange relationship between the sailor and Andrew Wyke."

I confess I have yet to perceive clearly these connections in four viewings of the film, but I rather suspect these inanimate objects lose their visual potency through overuse, and that Mankiewicz's clever intent of cumulative effect through intercutting is not truly achieved.[18]

One nonmechanical figurine does have connotative reference both to *Sleuth* and to Mankiewicz's previous films. Dwarfed in its

---

[18]I find the automata most effective in the set pieces Mankiewicz invented for the entr'acte and in the finale, in which the dolls are photographed close-up from grotesque, expressionist angles to supply the film's mad and mocking final chorus. The film's most successful metaphoric combination of sound and sight is its superb opening sequence, which counterpoints Milo searching through a maze of hedges to find his host's "outdoor inner sanctum" with a reading of the labyrinthine denouement of Wyke's latest mystery novel being played on a cassette recorder.

isolated position of honor in the center of Wyke's broad fireplace mantel is the Edgar, a small china bust of Poe—the Mystery Writers Guild annual award. Mankiewicz often uses this tiny Edgar in ironic juxtaposition to the larger figure of Wyke's head in the foreground of a shot—suggesting that though Wyke's stature as an author of mysteries is less than Poe's, his ego is far greater. In the course of the film, Mankiewicz intercuts five close-ups of the statuette from different angles, with diminishing effect, to emphasize the discovery of significant clues (in the Doppler sequence) and relate *Sleuth* to the mystery genre that Poe pioneered. (Although the Edgar on Wyke's mantel in the film is actually Anthony Shaffer's for his play *Sleuth*, on the ledge above Mankiewicz's rustic hearth is yet another Edgar—the one Joe received for *Five Fingers*.)

Mankiewicz's most familiar device, used as a focal point in many of his films' most important interiors, is a dominating portrait of a character's forebear that becomes symbolic of the character's feelings of inferiority.

Despite Mankiewicz's fatigue and his running battle with Scherick, the sustaining comfort from his labor on *Sleuth* was that after thirteen years Joe Mankiewicz was once again the director of a hit picture. An Academy Award nomination for Best Director, which Mankiewicz thought an absolute impossibility, was the icing on the cake.

Prior to the Academy's announcement, the event that had raised Mankiewicz's flagging spirits most was a letter from the agent Irving Lazar ("the unofficial agent to all those who are hot," says Joe), which Mankiewicz received shortly after *Sleuth*'s opening. "The minute you release a picture and get a warm, friendly note from Irving Lazar the next day, you know you've got a winner," Mankiewicz chortled. "I'm as jealous of my 'oldest whore' theory as Andrew Sarris is of his *auteur* concept. Suddenly you get hot, and the wrinkles go out of your face, and you are a young beauty again."

Epilogue

THIS BIOGRAPHY CONTAINS DIFFERENT VERSIONS OF MANY EVENTS. At one time I rationalized these variations by saying that they were appropriate to a biography of a highly ambivalent man who always wanted to show the same scene from different points of view.

I now realize that if a biographer is primarily dependent on oral history, each person's memory of the past contains only a subjective portion of the truth, faded or distorted by time. The distortion is magnified because most of the people who consented to be interviewed for this book admire Joe Mankiewicz and retain vestigial affection for him. I must assume that many of the more than one hundred persons who failed to respond to my letter of inquiry, which was accompanied by Mankiewicz's letter of authorization, harbor negative feelings toward him. Their testimony would surely have altered and deepened this work, as would have access to Mankiewicz's personal correspondence, diaries, and files, which I was denied.

Although Mankiewicz acknowledges having had extensive correspondence with Karl Menninger, he heatedly denies ever writing the one letter to Menninger I had been told about that bears on his veracity. Dr. Frederick J. Hacker said that this letter was characteristic of Joe's brand of incisive humor and provided the conclusion of one of his favorite stories about Mankiewicz. The story concerns the traditional interview that Dr. Menninger had with relatives of his patients in order to obtain information pertinent to their history. On one of Joe's visits to see Rosa at the Topeka clinic, he readily submitted to Menninger's inquiry and provided the doctor with a number of vivid stories about his wife.

"At the end of the interview," according to Hacker, "Dr. Menninger customarily asked, 'Do you yourself have any difficulties?' Joe said, 'No, not particularly. I function all right. Of course, I'm not always very happy with myself because I have a tendency to prevaricate and tell tall stories and make myself appear in a good light.' Dr. Menninger responded, 'If you feel this is a major factor, maybe you should look into that sometime and have an analysis.' Joe said, 'I think that's very good advice. I've been considering it. Thank you very much,' and left.

"Six weeks later Dr. Menninger, who was a great moralist, wrote Joe an enraged letter saying, 'How dare you come here and take our time and waste yours by telling us a bunch of lies, because so many of the things you told us proved to be inaccurate.' Joe wrote back a masterful letter, in which he said, 'But, Dr. Menninger, why do you blame me for that? I told you [that was my problem], and it was precisely for that that you recommended treatment. You were quite right, so why do you expect me to be cured before treatment has begun?' "[1]

Mankiewicz said to me, in one of our last interviews, that he had never lied to me. I tried to let him off the hook by saying I assumed that, being a noted raconteur, he embellished the truth to improve his stories, and that oft-told tales frequently become factual through repetition. Was there no validity to accounts that differed from his? Generally not, I gather from his denials, especially if the story was unflattering.

I feel a great sense of loss at never having known the man Benton and Newman describe as "the wittiest, classiest person we've ever known," the delightfully happy and genial young man he used to be, according to his sister, Erna, and at so rarely glimpsing the vulnerable man behind the caustic facade that Hume Cronyn perceives. Whatever bitterness I feel toward being shut out by Mankiewicz, after devoting such a chunk of my life to writing about his, pales by compari-

---

[1]Although Mankiewicz denies the entire incident, Dr. Hacker, who "quotes" this story as an "anecdote," states that at one time he had a copy of the letter.

son with the pain and sense of betrayal felt by several longtime intimates whom Joe has dropped in recent years.

Addie Wallace, his devoted secretary of thirty-seven years, was discharged with the unconvincing explanation that he could no longer afford a secretary nor did he require her further assistance. (Mankiewicz currently has a secretary, and the socially eminent Mrs. William Paley has acquired the capable services of the sweet and intelligent Mrs. Wallace.)

Robert Lantz, Joe's friend of thirty years, was impersonally notified by telegram that his services as an agent were terminated because he had done nothing for Joe since he put Mankiewicz together with his client Anthony Shaffer on *Sleuth*. (Mankiewicz has subsequently bounced from the Hollywood agent Evarts Ziegler to ICM's New York film department head, Sam Cohen, without landing a job through them, and is now without an agent.) Mankiewicz also withdrew as a client of attorney Abraham Bienstock, another of his circle of close friends. How many remain besides the Hume Cronyns is conjectural, but it presages increasing isolation.

Once, by way of indirectly inquiring about Mankiewicz's own isolation from present-day society—his favorite satirical target—I asked him what he thought of Fellini's comments on the subject in his interview with Lillian Ross in the *New Yorker*. Fellini attributed the change in his films—from such social studies as *I Vitelloni* and *La Dolce Vita* to his later autobiographical extravaganzas—to the fact that his celebrity prevented him from mingling with the bus-riding populace, which had been his practice in the past. Mankiewicz evaded the analogue to his own hermetic existence by saying that Fellini delighted in putting on interviewers. (Of course, Mankiewicz has little personal knowledge of public transportation. Not only does he insist on the old-time production perquisite of a chauffeured limo, but once when Rosa requested the use of the family limousine to transport their sons, he thundered, "Goddamn it, let them take taxis like other children!") However, Mankiewicz's self-imposed seclusion is curious for a man who left Hollywood to escape the confines of what he termed "the ivory ghetto"—the film colony whose conversation was confined exclusively to movie deals, gossip, and "properties."

One phenomenon common to such writers as Mankiewicz and Edward Albee is the transient nature of their great, theatrical "bitch wit," which infused and energized their most notable work. The loss or abandonment of this delightful style may be related to these authors' serious intellectual pretensions and pomposity which arose with their great success and may be contrasted with Noël Coward, who, according to Kenneth Tynan, "never suffered the imprisonment of maturity" because of his open "pipeline to infancy, and all the imaginative exuberance that goes with it" (*New Yorker*, January 24, 1977). I think it is also, in part, because of the nature of that acidulous wit, which corrosively turns upon itself.

Mankiewicz's idle boast that "I could blow out of my nose" trifles superior to those of the prolific Neil Simon and Woody Allen is understandable in view of his vast congestion of ideas and opinions and the refinement of his literary style beyond the wisecracks and one-liners of his early comedies. Unfortunately, Mankiewicz has never capitalized on his unusual ability to play the devil's advocate on almost any issue for the sheer intellectual exhilaration of being provocative. Had he been able to tap this unique dialectic capability by surmounting his psychological block toward playwriting, he might well have become the contemporary American equivalent of Bernard Shaw, whom he rivaled in *People Will Talk* and the first half of *Cleopatra.*

As for Joe's unacknowledged rivalry with Herman, which I have traced through his later work, Dr. Frederick Hacker, a friend of both brothers' families, made the following observation: "[Joe] was in constant competition with [his] brother, who was a great wit [as a conversational artist] and who was by many people, as a result of a peculiar myth-making process, [considered] the more substantial, the more human, the accessible, and the more humane of the two, though I never could completely see it that way. . . .

"Joe, in many respects, contrary to what most people right now, mythologically, feel, was probably the more gifted of the two, as he was capable of a sustained creative attention that led to at least two, three, or four really great things, which his brother never was able to [achieve]."

Joe Mankiewicz's hatred of the motion picture business terms *industry* and *product,* when applied to what he had always considered an art form, are manifest in all of his work since the mid-forties. (Unhappily, Joe's public diatribes against "the industry" have grown as long-winded as his screenplays; he inappropriately included them in his tributes to Joe Youngerman of the Screen Directors Guild in 1975 and to Bette Davis, on the occasion of her 1977 Life Achievement Award from the American Film Institute. Carl Reiner, the M.C. at the Youngerman banquet, brought down the house following Joe's speech by commenting, "That was the problem of *Cleopatra*. It went on too long.")

Mankiewicz's belief that with the advent of "talkies" the screenwriter had an obligation to write dialogue as literate and eloquent as any playwright is noble, if sometimes self-defeating. The unique quality of his work (even the failures contain electrifying scenes) distinguishes it from the preponderance of American movies intended to appeal to the lowest common denominator of the filmgoing public. The self-proclaimed "oldest whore" is actually the American cinema's most fastidious courtesan.

The Films of
Joseph L. Mankiewicz

TITLING

THE DUMMY (FAMOUS PLAYERS–LASKY–PARAMOUNT) Director: Robert Milton. Supervisor: Hector Turnbull. Adaptation and Dialogue: Herman J. Mankiewicz, from the play by Harvey J. O'Higgins and Harriet Ford. Titles (silent version): Joseph L. Mankiewicz. U.S. release: March 9, 1929. Length: 6 reels, 5,357 feet. Cast: Ruth Chatterton, Fredric March, John Cromwell, Jack Oakie, Zasu Pitts.

MOMA/Film Stills Archive

CLOSE HARMONY (FAMOUS PLAYERS–LASKY–PARAMOUNT) Director: A. Edward Sutherland. Dialogue: John V. A. Weaver, Percy Heath. Adaptation: Percy Heath. Story: Elsie Janis, Gene Markey. Songs: Richard A. Whiting, Leo Robin. Titles (silent version): Joseph L. Mankiewicz. U.S. release: April 13, 1929. Length: 7 reels, 6,271 feet. Cast: Charles "Buddy" Rogers, Nancy Carroll, Harry Green, Jack Oakie, Richard "Skeets" Gallagher.

MOMA/Film Stills Archive

MOMA/Film Stills Archive

THE MAN I LOVE (FAMOUS PLAYERS–LASKY–PARAMOUNT) Director: William A. Wellman. Associate Producer: David Selznick. Story, Screenplay, and Dialogue: Herman J. Mankiewicz. Titles (silent version): Joseph L. Mankiewicz. U.S. release: May 25, 1929. Length: 7 reels, 6,669 feet (silent version, 6,453 feet). Cast: Richard Arlen, Mary Brian, Harry Green, Jack Oakie.

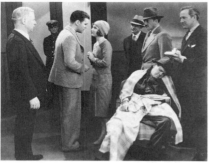

MOMA/Film Stills Archive

THE STUDIO MURDER MYSTERY (FAMOUS PLAYERS–LASKY–PARAMOUNT) Director: Frank Tuttle. Screenplay: Frank Tuttle, from a story by A. Channing and Carmen Ballen Edington. Adaptation: Ethel Doherty. Titles (silent version): Joseph L. Mankiewicz. U.S. release: June 1, 1929. Length: 8 reels, 6,070 feet (silent version 5,020 feet).
Cast: Doris Hill, Neil Hamilton, Fredric March, Warner Oland, Florence Eldridge, Chester Conklin.

MOMA/Film Stills Archive

THUNDERBOLT (FAMOUS PLAYERS–LASKY–PARAMOUNT) Director: Josef von Sternberg. Associate Producer: B. P. Fineman. Screenplay: Jules Furthman, from a story by Jules and Charles Furthman. Dialogue: Herman J. Mankiewicz. Titles (silent version): Joseph L. Mankiewicz. U.S. release: June 22, 1929. Length: 8 reels, 8,571 feet (silent version 7,311 feet).
Cast: George Bancroft, Fay Wray, Richard Arlen, Tully Marshall.

MOMA/Film Stills Archive

RIVER OF ROMANCE (FAMOUS PLAYERS–LASKY–PARAMOUNT) Director: Richard Wallace. Screenplay: Ethel Doherty. Adaptation: Dan Totheroh, John V. A. Weaver, from Booth Tarkington's play *Magnolia* (1923). Titles (silent version): Joseph L. Mankiewicz. U.S. release: June 29, 1929. Length: 8 reels, 7,009 feet (silent version, 7,082 feet).
Cast: Charles "Buddy" Rogers, Mary Brian, June Collyer, Henry B. Walthal, Wallace Beery.

THE MYSTERIOUS DR. FU MANCHU (FA-
MOUS PLAYERS–LASKY–PARAMOUNT) Director:
Rowland V. Lee. Screenplay and Dialogue: Florence Ryerson, Lloyd Corrigan, from the story by
Sax Rohmer. Comedy Dialogue: George Marion, Jr. Titles (silent version): Joseph L. Mankiewicz. U.S. release: August 10, 1929. Length:
8–9 reels, 7,663 feet (silent version,
7,695 feet).
Cast: Warner Oland, Jean Arthur, Neil Hamilton.

MOMA/Film Stills Archive

THE SATURDAY NIGHT KID (FAMOUS
PLAYERS–LASKY–PARAMOUNT) Director: A. Ed-
ward Sutherland. Adaptation: Lloyd Corrigan,
from the story "Love 'Em and Leave 'Em" by
George Abbott and John V. A. Weaver. Dia-
logue: Lloyd Corrigan, Edward E. Paramore, Jr.
Titles (silent version): Joseph L. Mankiewicz.
U.S. release: October 26, 1929. Length: 7 reels,
6,015 feet (silent version, 6,392 feet).
Cast: Clara Bow, James Hall, Jean Arthur,
Charles Sellon, Edna May Oliver, Jean Harlow.

MOMA/Film Stills Archive

THE VIRGINIAN (FAMOUS PLAYERS–LASKY–
PARAMOUNT) Director: Victor Fleming. Adapta-
tion: Howard Estabrook, from the play by Owen
Wister and Kirk LaShelle. Dialogue: Edward E.
Paramore, Jr. Titles (silent version): Joseph L.
Mankiewicz. U.S. release: November 9, 1929.
Length: 9 reels, 8,717 feet (silent version, 7,407
feet).
Cast: Gary Cooper, Walter Huston, Richard
Arlen, Mary Brian, Chester Conklin, Eugene
Pallette.

MOMA/Film Stills Archive

SCREENWRITING

MOMA/Film Stills Archive

FAST COMPANY (FAMOUS PLAYERS–LASKY–PARAMOUNT) Director: A. Edward Sutherland. Screenplay: Florence Ryerson, Patrick Kearney, Walton Butterfield. Dialogue: Joseph L. Mankiewicz. Adaptation: Patrick Kearney, Walton Butterfield, from the play *Elmer the Great* (1928) by Ring Lardner and George M. Cohan. U.S. release: September 14, 1929. Running time: 70 minutes.

Cast: Evelyn Brent (Evelyn Corey), Jack Oakie (Elmer Kane), Richard "Skeets" Gallagher (Bert Wade).

MOMA/Film Stills Archive

SLIGHTLY SCARLET (FAMOUS PLAYERS–LASKY–PARAMOUNT) Directors: Louis Gasnier, Edwin H. Knopf. Screenplay and Dialogue: Howard Estabrook, Joseph L. Mankiewicz. Story: Percy Heath. U.S. release: February 22, 1930. Running time: 70 minutes.

Cast: Evelyn Brent (Lucy Stavrin), Clive Brook (Hon. Courtenay Parkes), Paul Lukas (Malatroff), Eugene Pallette (Sylvester Corbett), Helen Ware (his wife), Virginia Bruce (Enid Corbett).

AMPAS

THE SOCIAL LION (PARAMOUNT–PUBLIX CORP.) Director: A. Edward Sutherland. Dialogue Director: Perry Ivins. Scenario: Agnes Brand Leahy, from the story "Marco Himself" by Octavius Roy Cohen. Adaptation and Dialogue: Joseph L. Mankiewicz. U.S. release: June 21, 1930. Running time: 72 minutes.

Cast: Jack Oakie (Marco Perkins), Mary Brian (Cynthia Brown), Richard "Skeets" Gallagher (Chick Hathaway), Olive Borden (Gloria Staunton).

ONLY SAPS WORK (PARAMOUNT–PUBLIX CORP.) Directors: Cyril Gardner, Edwin H. Knopf. Screenplay: Sam Mintz, Percy Heath, from the play *Easy Come, Easy Go* by Owen Davis. Dialogue: Joseph L. Mankiewicz. Film Editor: Edward Dmytryk. U.S. release: December 6, 1930. Running time: 77 minutes.
Cast: Leon Errol (James Wilson), Richard Arlen (Lawrence Payne), Mary Brian (Barbara Tanner), Stuart Erwin (Oscar), Anderson Lawler (Horace Baldwin), Charles Grapewin (Simeon Tanner).

MOMA/Film Stills Archive

THE GANG BUSTER (PARAMOUNT–PUBLIX CORP.) Director: A. Edward Sutherland. Story: Percy Heath. Dialogue: Joseph L. Mankiewicz. U.S. release: January 17, 1931. Running time: 74 minutes.
Cast: William Boyd (Mike Slade), Jack Oakie ("Cyclone" Case), Jean Arthur (Sylvia Martine), Wynne Gibson (Zella).

MOMA/Film Stills Archive

FINN AND HATTIE (PARAMOUNT–PUBLIX CORP.) Directors: Norman Taurog, Norman Z. McLeod. Scenario: Sam Mintz, from the novel *Mr. and Mrs. Haddock Abroad* by Donald Ogden Stewart. Dialogue: Joseph L. Mankiewicz. U.S. release: February 28, 1931. Running time: 78 minutes.
Cast: Leon Errol (Finley P. Haddock), Mitzi Green (Mildred), Zasu Pitts (Mrs. Haddock), Jackie Searl (Sidney), Lilyan Tashman (the "Princess"), Mack Swain (Frenchman with beard), Regis Toomey (Collins), Harry Beresford (N.Y. street cleaner).

AMPAS

406 PICTURES WILL TALK

MOMA/Film Stills Archive

JUNE MOON (PARAMOUNT–PUBLIX CORP.) Director: A. Edward Sutherland. Scenario: Keene Thompson, Joseph L. Mankiewicz, from the play by Ring Lardner and George S. Kaufman. Dialogue: Keene Thompson, Joseph L. Mankiewicz, Vincent Lawrence. U.S. release: March 21, 1931. Running time: 79 minutes.
Cast: Jack Oakie (Frederick Martin Stevens), Frances Dee (Edna Baker), June MacCloy (Eileen Fletcher), Ernest Wood (Paul Sears), Wynne Gibson (Lucille Sears), Harry Akst (Maxie Schwartz), Sam Hardy (Sam Hart).

MOMA/Film Stills Archive

SKIPPY (PARAMOUNT–PUBLIX CORP.) Director: Norman Taurog. Supervisor: Louis Lighton (uncredited). Scenario: Joseph L. Mankiewicz, Norman McLeod. Dialogue: Joseph L. Mankiewicz, Norman McLeod, Don Marquis. Adaptation: Percy Crosby, Sam Mintz, from the comic strip by Percy Crosby. U.S. release: April 25, 1931. Running time: 85 minutes.
Cast: Jackie Cooper (Skippy), Robert Coogan (Sooky Wayne), Mitzi Green (Eloise), Jackie Searl (Sidney), Willard Robertson (Dr. Herbert Skinner), Enid Bennett (Mrs. Ellen Skinner), David Haines (Harley Nubbins), Helen Jerome Eddy (Mrs. Wayne), Jack Clifford (Dogcatcher Nubbins).

MOMA/Film Stills Archive

NEWLY RICH (retitled *FORBIDDEN ADVENTURE*) (PARAMOUNT–PUBLIX CORP.) Director: Norman Taurog. Scenario: Edward Paramore, Jr., Norman McLeod, Joseph L. Mankiewicz, from the short story "Let's Play King" by Sinclair Lewis. Dialogue: Norman McLeod, Joseph L. Mankiewicz. U.S. release: July 5, 1931. Running time: 77 minutes.
Cast: Mitzi Green (Daisy Tate), Edna May Oliver (Bessie Tate), Louise Fazenda (Maggy Tiffany), Jackie Searl (Tiny Tim Tiffany), Virginia Hammond (Queen Sedonia), Bruce Line (King Max).

SOOKY (PARAMOUNT–PUBLIX CORP.) Director: Norman Taurog. Scenario and Dialogue: Sam Mintz, Joseph L. Mankiewicz, Norman McLeod, adapted from Percy Crosby's *Dear Sooky*. U.S. release: December 26, 1931. Running time: 85 minutes.
Cast: Jackie Cooper (Skippy Skinner), Bobby Coogan (Sooky Wayne), Jackie Searl (Sidney Saunders), Enid Bennett (Mrs. Skinner), Helen Jerome Eddy (Mrs. Wayne), Willard Robertson (Mr. Skinner).

MOMA/Film Stills Archive

THIS RECKLESS AGE (PARAMOUNT–PUBLIX CORP.) Director: Frank Tuttle. Scenario and Dialogue: Joseph L. Mankiewicz. Adaptation: Frank Tuttle, from the play *The Goose Hangs High* by Lewis Beach. U.S. release: January 9, 1932. Running time: 80 minutes.
Cast: Charles "Buddy" Rogers (Bradley Ingals), Richard Bennett (Donald Ingals), Peggy Shannon (Mary Burke), Charles Ruggles (Goliath Whitney), Frances Dee (Lois Ingals), Frances Starr (Eunice Ingals), Maude Eburne (Rhoda).

AMPAS

SKY BRIDE (PARAMOUNT–PUBLIX CORP.) Director: Stephen Roberts. Scenario and Dialogue: Joseph L. Mankiewicz, Agnes Brand Leahy, Grover Jones, from a story by Waldemar Young. U.S. release: April 29, 1932. Running time: 78 minutes.
Cast: Richard Arlen (Speed Condon), Jack Oakie (Alec Dugan), Virginia Bruce (Ruth Dunning), Robert Coogan (Willie), Charles Starrett (Jim Carmichael), Louise Closser Hale (Mrs. Smith), Tom Douglas (Eddie).

MOMA/Film Stills Archive

MILLION DOLLAR LEGS (PARAMOUNT–PUBLIX CORP.) Director: Edward Cline. Supervisor: Herman J. Mankiewicz (uncredited). Scenario and Dialogue: Joseph L. Mankiewicz, Henry Myers, from a story by Joseph L. Man-
(Continued)

MOMA/Film Stills Archive

kiewicz. Cameraman: Arthur Todd. U.S. release: July 8, 1932. Running time: 64 minutes. Cast: Jack Oakie (Migg Tweeny), W. C. Fields (the President), Andy Clyde (Major-Domo), Lyda Roberti (Mata Machree), Susan Fleming (Angela), Ben Turpin (Mysterious Man), George Barbier (Mr. Baldwin), Hugh Herbert (Secretary of the Treasury), Dickie Moore (Willie), Billy Gilbert (Secretary of the Interior), Vernon Dent (Secretary of Agriculture), Teddy Hart (Secretary of War).

AMPAS

IF I HAD A MILLION (PARAMOUNT–PUBLIX CORP.) Directors: Ernst Lubitsch (opening and sketches "The Clerk" and "The Streetwalker"), James Cruze ("The China Shop"), Stephen Roberts ("The Forger"), Norman McLeod ("The Three Marines"), Bruce Humberstone ("The Condemned Man"), Norman Taurog ("The Auto" or "Rollo and the Roadhogs"), William A. Seiter ("Old Ladies' Home"). Screenplay: Claude Binyon, Whitney Bolton, Malcolm Stuart Boylan, John Bright, Sidney Buchman, Lester Cole, Isabel Dawn, Boyce DeGaw, Walter DeLeon, Oliver H. P. Garrett, Harvey Gates, Grover Jones, Ernst Lubitsch, Lawton Mackall, Joseph L. Mankiewicz, William Slavens McNutt, Seton I. Miller, Tiffany Thayer, from a story by Robert D. Andrews. (Mankiewicz wrote "Rollo and the Roadhogs" and "The Three Marines" and contributed to other sketches and the framing story.) U.S. release: December 2, 1932. Running time: 88 minutes.

Cast: Richard Bennett (John Glidden), Gary Cooper (Gallagher), George Raft (Eddie Jackson), Wynne Gibson (Violet), Charles Laughton (Clerk), Jack Oakie (Mulligan), Frances Dee (Mary Wallace), Charles Ruggles (Henry Peabody), Alison Skipworth (Emily), W. C. Fields (Rollo), Mary Boland (Mrs. Peabody), Roscoe Karns (O'Brien), Lucien Littlefield (Zeb), May Robson (Mrs. Walker), Gene Raymond (John Wallace).

DIPLOMANIACS (RKO RADIO) Director: William A. Seiter. Producer: Sam Jaffe. Screenplay: Joseph L. Mankiewicz, Henry Myers, from a story by Joseph L. Mankiewicz. Music: Max Steiner. Songs: Harry Akst, Edward Eliscu. U.S. release: April 29, 1933. Running time: 76 minutes.
Cast: Bert Wheeler (Willy Nilly), Robert Woolsey (Hercules Glub), Marjorie White (Dolores), Phyllis Barry (Fifi), Louis Calhern (Winklereid), Hugh Herbert (Chinaman), William Irving (Schmerzenpuppen), Neely Edwards (Puppenschmerzen), Billy Bletcher (Schmerzenschmerzen), Teddy Hart (Puppenpuppen).

MOMA/Film Stills Archive

EMERGENCY CALL (RKO RADIO) Director: Edward Cahn. Producer: Sam Jaffe. Screenplay: John B. Clymer, Joseph L. Mankiewicz, from the story by John B. Clymer and James Ewens. U.S. release: June 24, 1933. Running time: 65 minutes.
Cast: Bill Boyd (Joe Bradley), Wynne Gibson (Mabel Weenie), William Gargan (Steve Brennan), Betty Furness (Alice Averill), Reginald Mason (Dr. Averill), Edwin Maxwell (Tom Rourke).

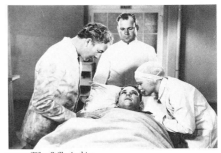

MOMA/Film Stills Archive

TOO MUCH HARMONY (PARAMOUNT) Director: A. Edward Sutherland. Producer: William LeBaron. Scenario: Joseph L. Mankiewicz. Dialogue: Harry Ruskin. Songs: Arthur Johnston, Sam Coslow. (The story has a number of correspondences to *Close Harmony* [1929], which Sutherland directed and Mankiewicz titled.) U.S. release: September 23, 1933. Running time: 76 minutes.
Cast: Bing Crosby (Eddie Bronson), Jack Oakie (Benny Day), Richard "Skeets" Gallagher (Johnny Dixon), Harry Green (Max Merlin), Lilyan Tashman (Lucille Watson), Ned Sparks (Lem Spawn).

MOMA/Film Stills Archive

ALICE IN WONDERLAND (PARAMOUNT) Director: Norman Z. McLeod. Producer: Louis L. Lighton. Screenplay: Joseph L. Mankiewicz, William Cameron Menzies, from the novels by Lewis Carroll. Art Director: William Cameron Menzies. Masks and Costumes: Wally Westmore, Newt Jones. Setting: Robert Odell. Music: Dimitri Tiomkin. Technical Effects: Gordon Jennings. Cameraman: Henry Sharp. Editor: Edward Hoagland. U.S. release: December 11, 1933. Running time: 90 minutes.

Cast: Charlotte Henry (Alice), Richard Arlen (Cheshire Cat), Roscoe Ates (Fish), William Austin (Gryphon), Billy Barty (White Pawn), Billy Bevan (Two of Spades), Gary Cooper (White Knight), Leon Errol (Uncle Gilbert), Louise Fazenda (White Queen), W. C. Fields (Humpty Dumpty), Richard "Skeets" Gallagher (White Rabbit), Cary Grant (Mock Turtle), Ethel Griffies (Governess), Sterling Holloway (Frog), Edward Everett Horton (Mad Hatter), Roscoe Karns (Tweedledee), Mae Marsh (Sheep), Polly Moran (Dodo Bird), Jack Oakie (Tweedledum), Edna May Oliver (Red Queen), May Robson (Queen of Hearts), Charles Ruggles (March Hare), Jackie Searl (Dormouse), Ned Sparks (Caterpillar), Ford Sterling (White King).

MANHATTAN MELODRAMA (METRO–GOLDWYN–MAYER) Director: W. S. Van Dyke, Jack Conway (uncredited). Producer: David O. Selznick. Screenplay: Oliver H. P. Garrett, Joseph L. Mankiewicz, from the story "Three Men" by Arthur Caesar. Photography: James Wong Howe. Songs, Richard Rodgers, Lorenz Hart. Editor: Ben Lewis. Special Effects: Slavko Vorkapich. Production: March 12–April 3, 1934. U.S. release: May 6, 1934. Running time: 93 minutes.

Cast: Clark Gable (Blackie Gallagher), William Powell (Jim Wade), Myrna Loy (Eleanor), Leo Carillo (Father Joe), Nat Pendleton (Spud), George Sidney (Poppa Rosen), Isabel Jewell (Annabelle), Murial Evans (Tootsie), Mickey Rooney (Young Blackie).

OUR DAILY BREAD (a viking production / united artists) Producer, Writer, and Director: King Vidor. Scenario: Elizabeth Hill Vidor. Dialogue: Joseph L. Mankiewicz. Photography: Robert Planck. Music: Alfred Newman. Editor: Lloyd Nossler. U.S. release: October 2, 1934. Running time: 74 minutes.
Cast: Karen Morley (Mary Sims), Tom Keene (John Sims), John T. Qualen (Chris), Barbara Pepper (Sally).

moma/Film Stills Archive

FORSAKING ALL OTHERS (metro–goldwyn–mayer) Director: W. S. Van Dyke. Producer: Bernard H. Hyman. Screenplay: Joseph L. Mankiewicz, from the play by Frank Morgan Cavett and Edward Barry. Photography: Gregg Toland, George Folsey. Music: William Axt. Editor: Tom Held. Production: September 25–October 22, 1934. U.S. release: December 25, 1934. Running time: 84 minutes.
Cast: Joan Crawford (Mary Clay), Clark Gable (Jeff William), Robert Montgomery (Dill Todd), Charles Butterworth (Shep), Billie Burke (Paula), Frances Drake (Connie), Rosalind Russell (Eleanor), Tom Ricketts (Wiffens), Arthur Treacher (Johnson).

moma/Film Stills Archive

I LIVE MY LIFE (metro–goldwyn–mayer) Director: W. S. Van Dyke. Producer: Bernard H. Hyman. Screenplay: Joseph L. Mankiewicz, from the short story "Claustrophobia" by A. Carter Goodloe, adapted by Gottfried Reinhardt and Ethel B. Borden. Photography: George Folsey. Music: Dimitri Tiomkin. Editor: Tom Held. Production: June 3–July 16, 1935. U.S. release: October 14, 1935. Running time: 81 minutes.
Cast: Joan Crawford (Kay), Brian Aherne (Terry), Frank Morgan (Bentley), Aline MacMahon (Betty), Eric Blore (Grove), Fred Keating (Gene), Jessie Ralph (Mrs. Gage), Arthur Treacher (Gallup).

moma/Film Stills Archive

FILMS PRODUCED

Library Performing Arts

THREE GODFATHERS (METRO–GOLDWYN–MAYER) Director: Richard Boleslawski. Producer: Joseph L. Mankiewicz. Screenplay: Edward E. Paramore, Jr., Manuel Seff, from the story by Peter B. Kyne. Photography: Joseph Ruttenberg. Musical Score: William Axt. Editor: Frank Sullivan. Production: November 27, 1935–January 3, 1936. U.S. release: March 7, 1936. Running time: 82 minutes.
Cast: Chester Morris (Bob), Lewis Stone ("Doc"), Walter Brennan (Gus), Irene Hervey (Molly), Sidney Toler (Professor Shape).

MOMA/Film Stills Archive

FURY (METRO–GOLDWYN–MAYER) Director: Fritz Lang. Producer: Joseph L. Mankiewicz. Screenplay: Bartlett Cormack, Fritz Lang, from a story by Norman Krasna and Joseph L. Mankiewicz (uncredited). Photography: Joseph Ruttenberg. Music: Franz Waxman. Editor: Frank Sullivan. Production: February 20–April 25, 1936. U.S. release: May 22, 1936. Running time: 90 minutes.
Cast: Sylvia Sidney (Katharine Grant), Spencer Tracy (Joe Wilson), Walter Abel (District Attorney), Bruce Cabot (Kirby Dawson), Edward Ellis (Sheriff), Walter Brennan ("Bugs" Meyers), George Walcott (Tom), Frank Albertson (Charlie).

MOMA/Film Stills Archive

THE GORGEOUS HUSSY (METRO–GOLDWYN–MAYER) Director: Clarence Brown. Producer: Joseph L. Mankiewicz. Screenplay: Ainsworth Morgan, Stephen Morehouse Avery, from the novel by Samuel Hopkins Adams. Photography: George Folsey. Music: Herbert Stothart. Editor: Blanche Sewell. Production completed: August 15, 1936. U.S. release: September 1, 1936. Running time: 102 minutes.
Cast: Joan Crawford (Peggy O'Neal), Robert Taylor ("Bow" Timberlake), Lionel Barrymore (Andrew Jackson), Franchot Tone (John Eaton), Melvyn Douglas (John Randolph), James Stewart ("Rowdy" Dow), Alison Skipworth (Mrs. Beall), Louis Calhern (Sunderland), Beulah Bondi (Rachel Jackson), Melville Cooper (Cuthbert), Sidney Toler (Daniel Webster), Gene Lockhart (Major O'Neal).

LOVE ON THE RUN (METRO–GOLDWYN–MAYER) Director: W. S. Van Dyke. Producer: Joseph L. Mankiewicz. Screenplay: John Lee Mahin, Manuel Seff, Gladys Hurlbut, from the story "Beauty and the Beast" by Alan Green and Julian Brodie. Photography: Oliver T. Marsh. Editor: Frank Sullivan. Production: August 19–September 12, 1936. U.S. release: November 26, 1936. Running time: 80 minutes.
Cast: Joan Crawford (Sally Parker), Clark Gable (Michael Anthony), Franchot Tone (Barnabas Pells), Reginald Owen (Baron), Donald Meek (Caretaker).

MOMA/Film Stills Archive

THE BRIDE WORE RED (METRO–GOLDWYN–MAYER) Director: Dorothy Arzner. Producer: Joseph L. Mankiewicz. Screenplay: Tess Slesinger, Bradbury Foote, from the play *The Girl from Trieste* by Ferenc Molnár. Photography: George Folsey. Music: Franz Waxman. Lyrics: Gus Kahn. Editor: Adrienne Fazan. Production: June 3–August 10, 1937. U.S. release: October 8, 1937. Running time: 103 minutes.
Cast: Joan Crawford (Anni), Franchot Tone (Giulo), Robert Young (Rudi Pal), Billie Burke (Contessa Di Meina), Reginald Owen (Admiral Monti), George Zucco (Count Armalia), Mary Phillips (Maria).

MOMA/Film Stills Archive

DOUBLE WEDDING (METRO–GOLDWYN–MAYER) Director: Richard Thorpe. Producer: Joseph L. Mankiewicz. Screenplay: Jo Swerling, Waldo Salt (uncredited), from the play *Great Love* by Ferenc Molnár. Photography: William Daniels. Music: Edward Ward. Editor: Frank Sullivan. Production: May 26–August 12, 1937. U.S. release: October 15, 1937. Running time: 87 minutes.
Cast: William Powell (Charlie Lodge), Myrna Loy (Margit Agnew), Florence Rice (Irene Agnew), John Beal (Waldo Beaver), Jessie Ralph (Mrs. Kensington Bly), Edgar Kennedy (Spike), Sidney Toler (Keough).

MOMA/Film Stills Archive

MOMA/Film Stills Archive

MANNEQUIN (METRO–GOLDWYN–MAYER)
Director: Frank Borzage. Producer: Joseph L.
Mankiewicz. Screenplay: Lawrence Hazard,
from an unpublished story, "Marry for Money,"
by Katharine Brush. Photography: George Fol-
sey. Music and Lyrics: Edward Ward, Bob
Wright, Chet Forrest. Editor: Frederick Y.
Smith. Production: September 7–October 26,
1937. U.S. release: January 20, 1938. Running
time: 95 minutes.
Cast: Joan Crawford (Jessie Cassidy), Spencer
Tracy (John L. Hennessey), Alan Curtis (Eddie
Miller), Leo Gorcey (Clifford).

MOMA/Film Stills Archive

THREE COMRADES (METRO–GOLDWYN–
MAYER) Director: Frank Borzage. Producer: Jo-
seph L. Mankiewicz. Screenplay: F. Scott Fitz-
gerald, Edward E. Paramore, from the novel by
Erich Maria Remarque. Photography: Joseph
Ruttenberg. Music: Franz Waxman. Songs:
Bob Wright, Chet Forrest. Editor: Frank Sul-
livan. Montage: Slavko Vorkapich. Production:
February 4–March 30, 1938. U.S. release: June
3, 1938. Running time: 100 minutes.
Cast: Robert Taylor (Erich Lohkamp), Marga-
ret Sullavan (Patricia Hollmann), Franchot
Tone (Otto Koster), Robert Young (Gottfried
Lenz), Guy Kibbee (Alfons), Lionel Atwill
(Breuer), Henry Hull (Dr. Becker), Charley
Grapewin (Local Doctor), Monty Wooley (Dr.
Jaffe).

MOMA/Film Stills Archive

THE SHOPWORN ANGEL (METRO–GOLD-
WYN–MAYER) Director: H. C. Potter. Producer:
Joseph L. Mankiewicz. Screenplay: Waldo Salt,
from the story "Private Pettigrew's Girl" by
Dana Burnet (previously filmed by Paramount
in 1929). Photography: Joseph Ruttenberg.
Music: Edward Ward. Editor: W. Don Hayes.
Production: March 28–May 6, 1938. U.S. re-
lease: July 15, 1938. Running time: 85 minutes.
Cast: Margaret Sullavan (Daisy Heath), James
Stewart (Bill Pettigrew), Walter Pidgeon (Sam
Bailey), Hattie McDaniel (Martha), Nat Pen-
dleton ("Dice"), Alan Curtis ("Thin Lips"),
Sam Levene ("Leer").

THE SHINING HOUR (METRO–GOLDWYN–MAYER) Director: Frank Borzage. Producer: Joseph L. Mankiewicz. Screenplay: Jane Murfin, Ogden Nash, from the play by Keith Winter. Photography: George Folsey. Music: Franz Waxman. Editor: Frank E. Hull. Production: August 20–October 3, 1938. U.S. release: November 11, 1938. Running time: 80 minutes.
Cast: Joan Crawford (Olivia Riley), Margaret Sullavan (Judy Linden), Robert Young (David Linden), Melvyn Douglas (Henry Linden), Fay Bainter (Hannah Linden), Allyn Joslyn (Roger Q. Franklin), Hattie McDaniel (Belvedere).

MOMA/Film Stills Archive

A CHRISTMAS CAROL (METRO–GOLDWYN–MAYER) Director: Edwin L. Marin. Producer: Joseph L. Mankiewicz. Screenplay: Hugo Butler, from the novel by Charles Dickens. Photography: Sidney Wagner. Editor: George Boemer. Production: October 5–November 3, 1938. U.S. release: December 16, 1938. Running time: 69 minutes.
Cast: Reginald Owen (Ebenezer Scrooge), Gene Lockhart (Bob Cratchit), Kathleen Lockhart (Mrs. Cratchit), Terry Kilburn (Tiny Tim), Barry Mackay (Fred), Lynne Carver (Bess), Leo G. Carroll (Marley's Ghost), Lional Braham (Spirit of Christmas Present), Ann Rutherford (Spirit of Christmas Past), D'Arcy Corrigan (Spirit of Christmas Future).

MOMA/Film Stills Archive

THE ADVENTURES OF HUCKLEBERRY FINN (retitled *HUCKLEBERRY FINN*) (METRO–GOLDWYN–MAYER) Director: Richard Thorpe. Producer: Joseph L. Mankiewicz. Screenplay: Hugo Butler, from the novel by Mark Twain. Photography: John Seitz. Music: Franz Waxman. Editor: Frank E. Hull. Production: November 20–December 28, 1938. U.S. release: February 10, 1939. Running time: 90 minutes.
Cast: Mickey Rooney (Huckleberry Finn), Walter Connolly (the "King"), William Frawley (the "Duke"), Rex Ingram (Jim), Lynne Carver (Mary Jane), Jo Ann Sayers (Susan), Minor Watson (Captain Brandy), Elizabeth Risdon (Widow Douglass), Victor Kilian ("Pap" Finn).

Movie Star News

MOMA/Film Stills Archive

STRANGE CARGO (METRO–GOLDWYN–MAYER) Director: Frank Borzage. Producer: Joseph L. Mankiewicz. Screenplay: Lawrence Hazard, from the novel *Not Too Narrow, Not Too Deep* by Richard Sale. Additional Dialogue: Lesser Samuels. Photography: Robert Planck. Music: Franz Waxman. Editor: Robert J. Kern. Production: October 19–December 28, 1939. U.S. release: March 1, 1940. Running time: 105 minutes.
Cast: Joan Crawford (Julie), Clark Gable (Verne), Ian Hunter (Cambreau), Peter Lorre (M'sieu Pig), Paul Lukas (Hessler), Albert Dekker (Moll), J. Edward Bromberg (Flaubert), Eduardo Cianelli (Telez), John Arledge (Dufond).

MOMA/Film Stills Archive

THE PHILADELPHIA STORY (METRO–GOLDWYN–MAYER) Director: George Cukor. Producer: Joseph L. Mankiewicz. Screenplay: Donald Ogden Stewart, from the play by Philip Barry. Photography: Joseph Ruttenberg. Music: Franz Waxman. Editor: Frank Sullivan. Production: July 5–August 14, 1940. U.S. release: December 26, 1940. Running time: 112 minutes.
Cast: Cary Grant (C. K. Dexter Haven), Katharine Hepburn (Tracy Lord), James Stewart (Macauley Connor), Ruth Hussey (Elizabeth Imbrie), John Howard (George Kittredge), Roland Young (Uncle Willie), John Halliday (Seth Lord), Mary Nash (Margaret Lord), Virginia Weidler (Dinah Lord), Henry Daniell (Sidney Kidd).

THE WILD MAN OF BORNEO (METRO–
GOLDWYN–MAYER) Director: Robert B. Sinclair.
Producer: Joseph L. Mankiewicz. Screenplay:
Waldo Salt, John McLain, from the play by
Marc Connelly and Herman J. Mankiewicz.
Photography: Oliver T. Marsh. Editor: Frank
Sullivan. Music: David Snell. Production: Octo-
ber 25–November 20, 1940. U.S. release: Janu-
ary 24, 1941. Running time: 78 minutes.
Cast: Frank Morgan (J. Daniel Thompson),
Mary Howard (Mary Thompson), Billie Burke
(Bernice Marshall), Donald Meek (Professor
Birdo), Marjorie Main (Irma), Connie Gilchrist
(Mrs. Diamond), Bonita Granville (Francine
Diamond), Dan Dailey, Jr. (Ed LeMotte), An-
drew Tombes ("Doc" Dunbar), Walter Catlett
("Doc" Skelby), Phil Silvers (Murdock).

Movie Star News

THE FEMININE TOUCH (METRO–GOLD-
WYN–MAYER) Director: W. S. Van Dyke. Pro-
ducer: Joseph L. Mankiewicz. Screenplay:
George Oppenheimer, Edmund L. Hartmann,
Ogden Nash. Photography: Ray June. Music:
Franz Waxman. Editor: Albert Akst. Produc-
tion: June 30–July 29, 1941. U.S. release: Octo-
ber 1941. Running time: 97 minutes.
Cast: Rosalind Russell (Julie Hathaway), Don
Ameche (John Hathaway), Kay Francis (Nellie
Woods), Van Heflin (Elliott Morgan), Donald
Meek (Capt. Makepeace Liverwright), Henry
Daniell (Shelley Mason), Sidney Blackmer
(Freddie Bond).

MOMA/Film Stills Archive

MOMA/Film Stills Archive

WOMAN OF THE YEAR (METRO–GOLD-WYN–MAYER) Director: George Stevens. Producer: Joseph L. Mankiewicz. Screenplay: Ring Lardner, Jr., Michael Kanin. Photography: Joseph Ruttenberg. Music: Franz Waxman. Editor: Frank Sullivan. Production: August 27–October 25, 1941. U.S. release: January 19, 1942. Running time: 112 minutes.
Cast: Spencer Tracy (Sam Craig), Katharine Hepburn (Tess Harding), Fay Bainter (Ellen Whitcomb), Reginald Owen (Clayton), Minor Watson (William Harding), William Bendix (Pinkie Peters), Ludwig Stossel (Dr. Martin Lubbeck).

MOMA/Film Stills Archive

CAIRO (METRO–GOLDWYN–MAYER) Director: Major W. S. Van Dyke II. Producer: Joseph L. Mankiewicz (uncredited). Screenplay: John McClain, from an idea by Ladislas Fodor. Photography: Ray June. Music: Herbert Stothert, George Stoll. Songs: Arthur Schwartz, Harold Arlen, E. Y. Harburg. Editor: James E. Newcom. Production: April 1–May 29, 1942. U.S. release: August 17, 1942. Running time: 101 minutes.
Cast: Jeanette MacDonald (Marcia Warren), Robert Young (Homer Smith), Ethel Waters (Cleona Jones), Reginald Owen (Philo Cobson), Grant Mitchell (O. H. P. Boggs), Lionel Atwill (Teutonic Gentleman), Edward Cianelli (Ahmed Ben Hassan), Dooley Wilson (Hector).

MOMA/Film Stills Archive

REUNION IN FRANCE (METRO–GOLDWYN–MAYER) Director: Jules Dassin. Producer: Joseph L. Mankiewicz. Screenplay: Jan Lustig, Marvin Borowsky, Marc Connelly, from the story by Ladislas Bus Fekete. Photography: Robert Planck. Editor: Elmo Vernon. Music: Franz Waxman. Production: June 29–September 4, 1942. U.S. release: December 2, 1942. Running time: 104 minutes.
Cast: Joan Crawford (Michele De La Becque), John Wayne (Pat Talbot), Phillip Dorn (Robert Cortot), Reginald Owen (Schultz), Albert Bassermann (Gen. Hugo Schroeder), John Carradine (Ulrich Windler), Ann Ayars (Juliette), J. Edward Bromberg (Durand), Moroni Olsen (Paul Grebeau), Henry Daniell (Emile Fleuron), Howard da Silva (Anton Stregel).

THE KEYS OF THE KINGDOM (TWEN-
TIETH CENTURY–FOX) Director: John M. Stahl.
Producer: Joseph L. Mankiewicz. Screenplay:
Joseph L. Mankiewicz, Nunnally Johnson, from
the novel by A. J. Cronin. Photography: Arthur
Miller. Editor: James B. Clark. Art Directors:
James Basevi, William Darling. Music: Alfred
Newman. Production: February 1–May 20,
1944. U.S. release: December 15, 1944. Run-
ning time: 137 minutes.

MOMA/Film Stills Archive

Cast: Gregory Peck (Father Francis Chisholm),
Thomas Mitchell (Dr. Willie Tulloch), Vincent
Price (Rev. Angus Mealy), Rosa Stradner
(Mother Maria-Veronica), Roddy McDowall
(Francis, as a child), Edmund Gwenn (Rev.
Hamish MacNabb), Peggy Ann Garner (Nora,
as a child), Jane Ball (Nora), James Gleason (Dr.
Wilbur Fiske), Anne Revere (Agnes Fiske),
Ruth Nelson (Lisbeth Chisholm), Benson Fong
(Joseph), Leonard Strong (Mr. Chia).

FILMS DIRECTED

DRAGONWYCK (TWENTIETH CENTURY–
FOX) Director: Joseph L. Mankiewicz. Pro-
ducer: Ernst Lubitsch (uncredited). Screenplay:
Joseph L. Mankiewicz, from the novel by Anya
Seton. Photography: Arthur Miller. Editor:
Dorothy Spencer. Music: Alfred Newman. Art
Directors: Lyle Wheeler, J. Russell Spencer.
Costumes: Rene Hubert. Assistant Director: F.
E. "Johnny" Johnston. Production: February
12–May 4, 1945. U.S. release: April 10, 1946.
Running time: 103 minutes.

Movie Star News

Cast: Gene Tierney (Miranda Wells), Walter
Huston (Ephraim Wells), Vincent Price (Nich-
olas Van Ryn), Glenn Langan (Dr. Jeff Turner),
Anne Revere (Abigail Wells), Spring Byington
(Magda), Connie Marshall (Katrina Van Ryn),
Henry Morgan (Bleecker), Vivienne Osborne
(Johanna Van Ryn), Jessica Tandy (Peggy
O'Malley).

Movie Star News

SOMEWHERE IN THE NIGHT (TWENTIETH CENTURY–FOX) Director: Joseph L. Mankiewicz. Producer: Anderson Lawler. Screenplay: Joseph L. Mankiewicz, Howard Dimsdale, from the story "The Lonely Journey" by Marvin Borowsky. Adaptation: Lee Strasberg. Photography: Norbert Brodine. Editor: James B. Clark. Music: David Buttolph, Emil Newman. Art Directors: James Basevi, Maurice Ransford. Assistant Director: F. E. "Johnny" Johnston. Production: November 21, 1945–January 24, 1946. U.S. release: June 12, 1946. Running time: 110 minutes.

Cast: John Hodiak (George Taylor), Nancy Guild (Christy), Richard Conte (Mel Phillips), Lloyd Nolan (Lt. Donald Kendall), Josephine Hutchinson (Elizabeth Conroy), Fritz Kortner (Anzelmo), Margo Woods (Phyllis), Sheldon Leonard (Sam), Lou Nova (Hubert), Henry Morgan (Bath Attendant), Whit Bissell (John, the Bartender).

MOMA/Film Stills Archive

THE LATE GEORGE APLEY (TWENTIETH CENTURY–FOX) Director: Joseph L. Mankiewicz. Producer: Fred Kohlmar. Screenplay: Philip Dunne, from the play by John P. Marquand and George S. Kaufman. Photography: Joseph LaShelle. Editor: James B. Clark. Music: Cyril Mockridge, Alfred Newman. Art Directors: James Basevi, J. Russell Spencer. Costumes: René Hubert. Assistant Director: F. E. "Johnny" Johnston. Production: June 24–August 22, 1946. U.S. release: March 20, 1947. Running time: 98 minutes.

Cast: Ronald Colman (George Apley), Peggy Cummins (Eleanor Apley), Vanessa Brown (Agnes), Richard Haydn (Horatio Willing), Edna Best (Mrs. Catherine Apley), Percy Waram (Roger Newcombe), Mildred Natwick (Amelia Newcombe), Richard Ney (John Apley), Charles Russell (Howard Boulder), Nydia Westman (Jane Willing).

THE GHOST AND MRS. MUIR (TWENTIETH CENTURY–FOX) Director: Joseph L. Mankiewicz. Producer: Fred Kohlmar. Screenplay: Philip Dunne, from the novel by R. A. Dick (Josephine A. C. Leslie). Photography: Charles Lang. Editor: Dorothy Spencer. Music: Bernard Herrmann. Art Directors: Richard Day, George

Davis. Costumes: Oleg Cassini (for Gene Tierney), Eleanor Behm, Charles Le Maire. Assistant Director: F. E. "Johnny" Johnston. Production: November 29, 1946–February 13, 1947. U.S. release: June 26, 1947. Running time: 104 minutes.
Cast: Gene Tierney (Lucy Muir), Rex Harrison (Ghost of Capt. Daniel Gregg), George Sanders (Miles Fairley), Edna Best (Martha), Vanessa Brown (Anna Muir), Anna Lee (Mrs. Miles Fairley), Robert Coote (Coombe), Natalie Wood (Anna Muir, as a child), Isobel Elson (Angelica), Victoria Horne (Eva), Whitford Kane (Sproule).

MOMA/Film Stills Archive

ESCAPE (TWENTIETH CENTURY–FOX) Director: Joseph L. Mankiewicz. Producer: William Perlberg. Screenplay: Philip Dunne, from the play by John Galsworthy. Photography: Frederick A. Young. Editor: Alan L. Jaggs. Art Director: Vetchinsky. Music: William Alwyn. Production: September 15–December 18, 1947. U.S. release: June 1948. Running time: 78 minutes.
Cast: Rex Harrison (Matt Denant), Peggy Cummins (Dora Winton), William Hartnell (Inspector Harris), Norman Wooland (Minister), Jill Esmond (Grace Winton), Cyril Cusack (Rodgers).

MOMA/Film Stills Archive

A LETTER TO THREE WIVES (TWENTIETH CENTURY–FOX) Director: Joseph L. Mankiewicz. Producer: Sol C. Siegel. Screenplay: Joseph L. Mankiewicz, from the *Cosmopolitan* story "One of Our Hearts" by John Klempner. Adaptation: Vera Caspary. Photography: Arthur Miller. Editor: J. Watson Webb. Art Directors: Lyle Wheeler, J. Russell Spencer. Music: Alfred Newman. Assistant Director: Gaston Glass. Production: June 3–August 9, 1948. U.S. release: January 20, 1949. Running time: 103 minutes.
Cast: Jeanne Crain (Deborah Bishop), Linda Darnell (Lora May Hollingsway), Ann Sothern (Rita Phipps), Kirk Douglas (George Phipps), Paul Douglas (Porter Hollingsway), Barbara Lawrence (Babe Finney), Jeffrey Lynn (Brad Bishop), Connie Gilchrist (Mrs. Finney), Thelma Ritter (Sadie), Florence Bates (Mrs. Manleigh), Hobart Cavanaugh (Mr. Manleigh), Celeste Holm (Voice of Addie Ross).

The Memory Shop

Movie Star News

HOUSE OF STRANGERS (TWENTIETH CEN-
TURY–FOX) Director: Joseph L. Mankiewicz.
Producer: Sol C. Siegel. Screenplay: Joseph L.
Mankiewicz (uncredited), Philip Yordan, from
a chapter of the novel *I'll Never Go There Any
More* by Jerome Weidman. Photography: Mil-
ton Krasner. Editor: Harmon Jones. Art Direc-
tors: Lyle Wheeler, George W. Davis. Music:
Daniele Amfitheatrof. Assistant Director: Wil-
liam Eckhardt. Production: December 21,
1948–February 22, 1949. U.S. release: July 1,
1949. Running time: 101 minutes.
Cast: Edward G. Robinson (Gino Monetti),
Richard Conte (Max Monetti), Susan Hayward
(Irene Bennett), Luther Adler (Joe Monetti),
Efrem Zimbalist, Jr. (Tony Monetti), Debra
Paget (Maria Domenico), Paul Valentine (Pietro Monetti), Hope Emerson (Helena Domenico), Esther Minciotti (Theresa Monetti).

MOMA/Film Stills Archive

NO WAY OUT (TWENTIETH CENTURY–FOX)
Director: Joseph L. Mankiewicz. Producer: Dar-
ryl F. Zanuck. Screenplay: Joseph L. Mankie-
wicz, Lesser Samuels. Photography: Milton
Krasner. Editor: Barbara McLean. Art Direc-
tors: Lyle Wheeler, George W. Davis. Music:
Alfred Newman. Assistant Director: William
Eckhardt. Production: October 28–December
20, 1949. U.S. release: August 16, 1950. Run-
ning time: 106 minutes.
Cast: Richard Widmark (Ray Biddle), Linda
Darnell (Edie Johnson), Stephen McNally (Dr.
Daniel Wharton), Sidney Poitier (Dr. Luther
Brooks), Mildred Joanne Smith (Cora Brooks),
Harry Bellaver (George Biddle), Stanley Ridges
(Dr. Moreland), Dots Johnson (Lefty), Amanda
Randolph (Gladys), Bill Walker (Mathew
Tompkins), Ruby Dee (Connie), Ossie Davis
(John).

ALL ABOUT EVE (TWENTIETH CENTURY–FOX) Director: Joseph L. Mankiewicz. Producer: Darryl F. Zanuck. Screenplay: Joseph L. Mankiewicz, from the story "The Wisdom of Eve" in *Cosmopolitan.* Photography: Milton Krasner. Editor: Barbara McLean. Music: Alfred Newman. Art Directors: Lyle Wheeler, George W. Davis. Costumes: Charles LeMaire, Edith Head (for Bette Davis). Assistant Director: Gaston Glass. Production: April 11–June 7, 1950. U.S. release: October 13, 1950. Running time: 130 minutes.

MOMA/Film Stills Archive

Cast: Bette Davis (Margo Channing), Anne Baxter (Eve Harrington), George Sanders (Addison de Witt), Celeste Holm (Karen Richards), Hugh Marlowe (Lloyd Richards), Gary Merrill (Bill Sampson), Gregory Ratoff (Max Fabian), Thelma Ritter (Birdie Coonan), Marilyn Monroe (Miss Caswell), Barbara Bates (Phoebe), Walter Hampden (Old Actor).

PEOPLE WILL TALK (TWENTIETH CENTURY–FOX) Director: Joseph L. Mankiewicz. Producer: Darryl F. Zanuck. Screenplay: Joseph L. Mankiewicz, from the play *Dr. Med. Hiob Praetorius* by Curt Goetz. Photography: Milton Krasner. Editor: Barbara McLean. Music: Alfred Newman. Art Directors: Lyle Wheeler, George W. Davis. Costumes: Charles LeMaire. Assistant Director: Hal Klein. Production: March 20–May 5, 1951. U.S. release: August 29, 1951. Running time: 110 minutes.

MOMA/Film Stills Archive

Cast: Cary Grant (Dr. Noah Praetorius), Jeanne Crain (Deborah Higgins), Finlay Currie (Shunderson), Hume Cronyn (Dr. Rodney Elwell), Walter Slezak (Professor Lionel Parker), Sidney Blackmer (Arthur Higgins), Basil Ruysdael (Dean Lyman Brockwell), Katherine Locke (Miss James), Will Wright (John Higgins), Margaret Hamilton (Miss Sarah Pickett).

MOMA/Film Stills Archive

FIVE FINGERS (TWENTIETH CENTURY–FOX) Director: Joseph L. Mankiewicz. Producer: Otto Lang. Screenplay: Michael Wilson, from the book *Operation Cicero* by L. C. Moyzisch. Dialogue: Joseph L. Mankiewicz (uncredited). Photography: Norbert Brodine. Editor: James B. Clark. Music: Bernard Herrmann. Art Directors: Lyle Wheeler, George W. Davis. Production: August 17–October 23, 1951. U.S. release: February 22, 1952. Running time: 108 minutes. Cast: James Mason (Diello, alias Cicero), Danielle Darrieux (Countess Anna Staviska), Michael Rennie (Colin Travers), Walter Hampden (Sir Frederic), Oscar Karlweis (Moyzisch), Herbert Berghof (Col. von Richter), John Wengraf (von Papen), Ben Astar (Siebert).

Cinemabilia

JULIUS CAESAR (METRO–GOLDWYN–MAYER) Director: Joseph L. Mankiewicz. Producer: John Houseman. Screenplay: Joseph L. Mankiewicz, from the play by William Shakespeare. Photography: Joseph Ruttenberg. Editor: John Dunning. Music: Miklós Rósza. Art Direction: Cedric Gibbons, Edward Carfagno, Edwin B. Willis, Hugh Hunt. Costumes: Hershel McCoy. Assistant Director: Howard W. Koch. Production: August 25–October 13, 1952. U.S. release: June 4, 1953. Running time: 121 minutes.
Cast: Marlon Brando (Mark Antony), James Mason (Brutus), John Gielgud (Cassius), Louis Calhern (Julius Caesar), Edmond O'Brien (Casca), Deborah Kerr (Portia), Greer Garson (Calpurnia), Richard Hale (Soothsayer), Alan Napier (Cicero), George Macready (Marullus), Ian Wolfe (Ligarius), Douglas Watson (Octavius), Edmond Purdom (Strato).

MOMA/Film Stills Archive

THE BAREFOOT CONTESSA (FIGARO INC. / UNITED ARTISTS) Director and Producer: Joseph L. Mankiewicz. Screenplay: Joseph L. Mankiewicz. Photography: Jack Cardiff (Technicolor). Editor: William Hornbeck. Music: Mario Nascimbene. Art Director: Arrigo Equini. Costumes: Fontana. Associate Producers: Franco Magli, Michael Waszynski. U.S. release: September 29, 1954. Running time: 128 minutes.

Cast: Humphrey Bogart (Harry Dawes), Ava
Gardner (Maria Vargas), Edmond O'Brien
(Oscar Muldoon), Marius Goring (Alberto
Bravano), Valentina Cortese (Eleonora Torlato-
Favrini), Rossano Brazzi (Vincenzo Torlato-
Favrini), Elizabeth Sellars (Gerry Dawes), War-
ren Stevens (Kirk Edwards), Mari Aldon
(Myrna).

GUYS AND DOLLS (SAMUEL GOLDWYN /
METRO–GOLDWYN–MAYER) Director: Joseph L.
Mankiewicz. Producer: Samuel Goldwyn. Choreography: Michael Kidd. Screenplay: Joseph L.
Mankiewicz, from the musical by Jo Swerling
and Abe Burrows drawn from the short stories of
Damon Runyon. Music and Lyrics: Frank
Loesser. Photography: Harry Stradling (East-
mancolor-CinemaScope). Editor: Daniel Mandel. Art Direction: Oliver Smith, Joseph Wright,
Howard Bristol. Costumes: Irene Sharaff. Assistant Director: Arthur Black. U.S. release: November 3, 1955. Running time: 150
minutes.

MOMA/Film Stills Archive

Cast: Marlon Brando (Sky Masterson), Jean
Simmons (Sarah Brown), Frank Sinatra (Na-
than Detroit), Vivian Blaine (Miss Adelaide),
Robert Keith (Lieutenant Brannigan), Stubby
Kaye (Nicely-Nicely Johnson), B. S. Pully (Big
Jule), Sheldon Leonard (Harry the Horse), Regis
Toomey (Arvid Abernathy).

THE QUIET AMERICAN (FIGARO INC. /
UNITED ARTISTS) Director and Producer: Joseph
L. Mankiewicz. Screenplay: Joseph L. Mankiewicz, from the novel by Graham Greene.
Photography: Robert Krasker. Editor: William
Hornbeck. Music: Mario Nascimbene. Art Direction: Rino Mondellini, Dario Simoni. Production Manager: Forrest E. Johnston. Associate Producers, Michael Wasynski, Vinh Noan.
U.S. release: February 8, 1958. Running time:
120 minutes.

MOMA/Film Stills Archive

Cast: Audie Murphy (the American), Michael
Redgrave (Thomas Fowler), Claude Dauphin
(Inspector Vigot), Georgia Moll (Phuong),
Kerima (Miss Hei), Bruce Cabot (Bill Granger),
Fred Sadoff (Dominguez), Richard Loo (Mr.
Heng).

Columbia Pictures

SUDDENLY, LAST SUMMER (HORIZON FILMS / COLUMBIA PICTURES) Director: Joseph L. Mankiewicz. Producer: Sam Spiegel. Screenplay: Gore Vidal, Tennessee Williams, from the play by Tennessee Williams. Photography: Jack Hildyard. Editor: William Hornbeck. Art Director: Oliver Messel. Costumes: Oliver Messel, Jean Louis (for Elizabeth Taylor), Norman Hartnell (for Katharine Hepburn). Music: Buxton Orr, Malcolm Arnold. U.S. release: December 22, 1959. Running time: 114 minutes.
Cast: Elizabeth Taylor (Catherine Holly), Montgomery Clift (Dr. Cukrowicz), Katharine Hepburn (Violet Venable), Mercedes McCambridge (Mrs. Holly), Albert Dekker (Dr. Hockstader), Gary Raymond (George Holly).

The Memory Shop

CLEOPATRA (TWENTIETH CENTURY–FOX) Director: Joseph L. Mankiewicz. Producer: Walter Wanger. Screenplay: Joseph L. Mankiewicz, Ranald MacDougall, Sidney Buchman, from the works of Plutarch, Suetonius, Appianus, and *The Life and Times of Cleopatra* by Charles Marie Franzero (London 1957). Second Unit Directors: Ray Kellogg, Andrew Marton. Photography: Leon Shamroy, (Second Unit) Claude Renoir, Pietro Portalupi (DeLuxe Color–Todd-AO). Editors: Dorothy Spencer, Elmo Williams. Production Designer: John DeCuir. Costumes: Irene Sharaff (for Elizabeth Taylor), Vittorio Nino Novarese (men), Renie (women). Music: Alex North. Choreography: Hermes Pan. Production Managers: Forrest E. Johnston, C. O. Erickson. Assistant Director: Fred R. Simpson. Production: September 28, 1961– July 28, 1962. U.S. release: June 12, 1963. Running time: 243 minutes.
Cast: Elizabeth Taylor (Cleopatra), Richard Burton (Mark Antony), Rex Harrison (Julius Caesar), Pamela Brown (High Priestess), George Cole (Flavius), Hume Cronyn (Sosigenes), Cesare Danova (Apollodorus), Kenneth

Haigh (Brutus), Andrew Keir (Agrippa), Martin Landau (Rufio), Roddy McDowall (Octavius), Richard O'Sullivan (Ptolemy), Gregoire Aslan (Pothinus), Herbert Berghof (Theodotus), Isabel Cooley (Charmian), John Doucette (Achillas), Michael Hordern (Cicero), Carroll O'Connor (Casca), Robert Stephens (Germanicus), Gwen Watford (Calpurnia), Andrew Faulds (Candidus), Jean Marsh (Octavia).

THE HONEY POT (CHARLES K. FELDMAN / FAMOUS ARTISTS PRODUCTIONS / UNITED ARTISTS) Director: Joseph L. Mankiewicz. Producers: Charles K. Feldman, Joseph L. Mankiewicz. Screenplay: Joseph L. Mankiewicz, from the play *Mr. Fox of Venice* by Frederick Knott, based on the novel *The Evil of the Day* by Thomas Sterling, inspired by Ben Jonson's *Volpone*. Photography: Gianni Di Venanzo (Technicolor). Editor: David Bretherton. Production Designer: John DeCuir. Costumes: Rolf Gérard. Music: John Addison. Production Managers: Attilio l'Onfrio, Eric Stacey. Production: September 20, 1965–February 26, 1966. U.S. release: May 22, 1967. Running time: 131 minutes. London premiere: March 21, 1967. Running time: 150 minutes.

Cinemabilia

Cast: Rex Harrison (Cecil Fox), Susan Hayward (Mrs. Lone Star Sheridan), Cliff Robertson (William McFly), Capucine (Princess Dominique), Edie Adams (Merle McGill), Maggie Smith (Sarah Watkins), Adolfo Celi (Inspector Rizzi).

Movie Star News

THERE WAS A CROOKED MAN . . . (WARNER BROTHERS) Director and Producer: Joseph L. Mankiewicz. Screenplay: David Newman, Robert Benton. Photography: Harry Stradling, Jr. (Technicolor-Panavision). Editor: Gene Milford. Production Designer: Edward Carrere. Costumes: Anna Hill Johnstone. Music: Charles Strouse. Title Song: Charles Strouse, Lee Adams. Executive Producer: C. O. Erickson. Production: March 11–July 3, 1969. U.S. release: December 25, 1970. Running time: 125 minutes.

Cast: Kirk Douglas (Paris Pitman, Jr.), Henry Fonda (Woodward Lopeman), Hume Cronyn (Dudley Whinner), Warren Oates (Floyd Moon), Burgess Meredith (Missouri Kid), Lee Grant (Mrs. Bullard), Arthur O'Connell (Mr. Lomax), Martin Gabel (Warden Le Goff), John Randolph (Cyrus McNutt), Michael Blodgett (Coy Cavendish), Claudia McNeil (Madame).

MOMA/Film Stills Archive

SLEUTH (PALOMAR PICTURES INTERNATIONAL / TWENTIETH CENTURY–FOX) Director: Joseph L. Mankiewicz. Executive Producer: Edgar J. Scherick. Producer: Morton Gottlieb. Screenplay: Anthony Shaffer, based on his play. Photography: Oswald Morris (DeLuxe Color). Editor: Richard Marden. Production Designer: Ken Adam. Costumes: John Furniss. Music: John Addison. Associate Producer: David Middlemas. Assistant Director: Kip Gowans. U.S. release: December 10, 1972. Running time: 138 minutes.

Cast: Laurence Olivier (Andrew Wyke), Michael Caine (Milo Tindle).

OPERA

LA BOHÈME BY GIACOMO PUCCINI. English adaptation by Howard Dietz, from the Italian libretto by Giuseppe Giacosa and Luigi Illica. Direction: Joseph L. Mankiewicz. Sets and costumes: Rolf Gérard. Conductor: Alberto Erede. Premiere: December 27, 1952 (matinee), at the Metropolitan Opera (New York).
Cast: Richard Tucker (Rodolfo), Robert Merrill (Marcello), Jerome Hines (Colline), Clifford Harvuot (Schaunard), Lawrence Davidson (Benoit), Nadine Conner (Mimi), Patrice Munsel (Musetta), Paul Franke (Parpignol), Alessio de Paolis (Alcindoro), Algerd Brazis (Sergeant).

Opera News

TELEVISION

CAROL FOR ANOTHER CHRISTMAS (XEROX CORPORATION / TELSUN FOUNDATION, INC., FOR THE UNITED NATIONS. AMERICAN BROADCASTING CO.) Producer and Director: Joseph L. Mankiewicz. Screenplay: Rod Serling, from the novel *A Christmas Carol* by Charles Dickens. Photography: Arthur Ornitz. Editor: Robert Lawrence. Art Director: Gene Callahan. Costumes: Anna Hill Johnstone. Music: Henry Mancini. Production Manager: C. J. DiGangi. Production Supervisor: C. O. Erickson. Executive Producer: Edgar Rosenberg. Production: October 8–October 25, 1964 (Michael Myerberg Studios, Long Island, New York). Air date: December 28, 1964. ABC-TV.
Cast: Sterling Hayden (Grudge), Peter Fonda (Morley), Ben Gazzara (Fred), Richard Harris (Ghost of Christmas Present), Steve Lawrence (Ghost of Christmas Past), Percy Rodriguez (Charles), Eva Marie Saint (Wave), Peter Sellers (King of the Individualists), James Shigeta (Japanese Doctor), Barbara Ainteer (Charles's Wife), Joseph Wiseman (Ghost of Christmas Future), Britt Ekland, Pat Hingle, Robert Shaw.

Eleanor Wolquitt

Index